Documentary History Of Education In Upper Canada, Volume 23

John George Hodgins, Ontario. Dept. Of Education

DOCUMENTARY HISTORY

OF

Education in Upper Canada,

FROM THE PASSING OF THE

CONSTITUTIONAL ACT OF 1791

TO THE

CLOSE OF THE REVEREND DOCTOR RYERSON'S ADMINISTRATION OF THE EDUCATION DEPARTMENT IN 1876

VOL. XXIII., 1871-72.

FORMING AN APPENDIX TO THE ANNUAL REPORT OF THE MINISTER OF EDUCATION.

BY

J. GEORGE HODGINS, I.S.O., M.A., LL.D.

OF OSGOODE HALL, BARRISTER-AT-LAW, EX-DEPUTY MINISTER
OF EDUCATION ; HISTORIOGRAPHER TO THE EDUCATION DEPARTMENT OF ONTARIO.

TORONTO:
PRINTED AND PUBLISHED BY L. K. CAMERON,
Printer to the King's Most Excellent Majesty
1908.

PREFATORY NOTE TO THE TWENTY-THIRD VOLUME.

This Volume furnishes a sort of aftermath to the one which preceded it. It is largely devoted to the reconstruction, on broad and comprehensive lines, of our School System as sketched out for it in the recent School Legislation of 1871.

This reconstruction involved the extension of the Course of Study for the Public Schools by the Council of Public Instruction, so as to include in it the Elements of Mechanical and Natural Science. It also necessitated an enlargement of the scope and object of the Grammar Schools, the better class of which are hereafter to be also known as High Schools and Collegiate Institutes. The Course of Study in this three-fold grade of Schools, as revised by the Council of Public Instruction, included, (1), a good elementary and preliminary Course of English; (2), a Classical and Modern Language Course; and, (3), a superior, but, purely English Course, including a knowledge of English Literature.

The standard of admission to any grade of the Grammar Schools was fixed, so as to include as a basis, a satisfactory knowledge of what was the final Course of Study in the Public Schools; this was prescribed to prevent the influx, as had formerly been the case, of ill-trained and badly prepared Pupils. The design and intention of thus keeping up the standard of admission was that, when admitted, the Parents might intelligently determine which Course of Study should be pursued by their children.

In determining the new and enlarged Course of Study, not only for the Public Schools, but also for the three-fold grade of Grammar Schools, the former lists of Text-books had to be carefully revised, so as to furnish the best aids in promoting the study of the subjects embraced in the enlarged Curriculum, as prescribed.

With a view to aid in the maintenance of the various grades of Grammar Schools, a new financial principle was adopted in regard to the apportionment to them of the Legislative Grants,—that of "payment by results"; which had been for some time in satisfactory operation in England, and which was strongly recommended by our successive Inspectors.

The adoption of this principle, upon the specific report of the Inspectors as to the work actually done in the School, had a most beneficial effect, as it embodied the true principle of payment for good work efficiently done, as certified by the Grammar School Inspectors.

As a fitting sequel to the enlarged Course of Study in our various Schools, was the issue of a Commission by the Government to collect and report full and authentic information in regard to the subject of Technical Education, chiefly in the United States. The result of this new departure was the establishment of a College of Technology in Toronto, which was afterwards enlarged in its scope and functions and re-organized as the School of Practical Science.

As the result also of a specific Report by the Chief Superintendent of Education, on the character and condition of Schools, in Europe and the United States, for the Deaf and Dumb, and also for the Blind, the Government established similar Institutions,—one at Brantford, and the other at Belleville.

With a view to increase the efficiency of the Public School Teachers, and to make the profession of Teaching more worthy of the name than it had hitherto been, the Course of Study in the Normal School, and the exercises, to that end, in the (Model) Schools of Practice, were greatly enlarged and improved; and, in addition, arrangements were made for holding Teachers' Institutes in the outlying portions of the Province by Inspectors and Teachers of experience, so that Teachers who could not readily attend the Normal School, might be stimulated to qualify themselves better for the discharge of their duties in the Schools.

In addition to this scheme for the improvement of the Teachers' profession, a greatly improved system of examination and classification of Teachers was adopted, whereby the local Boards of Examiners could, after examination, based upon a uniform system for the whole of the Province, issue Second and Third Class Certificates of Qualification,—reserving to the Council of Public Instruction the right, on the report of the Central Committee of Examiners, to alone issue First Class Certificates available in any part of the Province. In other respects the old system of granting Certificates to Teachers and Public School Inspectors was greatly enlarged and improved.

With a view to create an additional interest in the condition of the Schools, and to stimulate the zeal of Ratepayers, Municipal Councils and Trustees, in the continued success of our School System, the Chief Superintendent issued Circulars, calling their attention to the great advantages to be derived from the increased facilities which the new School Act provided for the improvement of the status and character of both Public and Grammar Schools.

It was not to be supposed that an educational movement of this enlarged and comprehensive kind would escape criticism, and even misrepresentation. Nor did it; but, in a timely and able Letter, addressed to the "Public Press" by the Chief Superintendent, he pointed out the value and importance of the recent legislation in raising the standard of Public and High Schools, in elevating the condition of the Teaching profession, and in practically providing for an advanced stage of education, which would fit the pupils in the Schools for those Commercial and Mechanical pursuits in after life, to which,—as a rule,—they all looked forward.

The subject of Schoolroom accommodation, and the condition of the School premises have, as will be seen, been fully discussed in the chief Superintendent's Annual Report, and the excellent example of other Countries, in dealing with these questions, pointed out.

The usual extended reports of the proceedings of the various Churches in University matters are fully recorded in this Volume.

The important questions, are also discussed, of the "compulsory education" of children, where Parents neglect that obvious duty; and the necessity, as well as convenience, of Township School Boards, instead of School Section Trustees, so as to facilitate the attendance of children at their nearest School, instead of one at some distance in a local School Section, for the support of which the Parent pays taxes.

In the proceedings of the Legislature it will be seen that additional School legislation was proposed by two Members, and also an elaborate scheme of University Reform by another Member; but the House of Assembly refused to give these measures its sanction, being satisfied, (in the case of the Public and High Schools,) that the comprehensive School legislation of 1871 would accomplish all that was desirable for the present time; nor was it disposed to enter again upon a season of unrest and agitation in regard to the University question.

J. GEORGE HODGINS,
Historiographer of the Education Department.

TORONTO, 12th February, 1908.

CONTENTS OF THE TWENTY-THIRD VOLUME.

CHAPTER I.

REPORT OF AN INQUIRY IN REGARD TO SCHOOLS OF TECHNICAL SCIENCE IN CERTAIN PORTIONS OF THE UNITED STATES, 1871.

NOTE. Early in 1871 the Government decided to take steps for the establishment of a School, or College, of Technology, and, as a preliminary step, to appoint a Commission to make inquiries on the subject in the United States. For this purpose the following Commission was issued to Doctor Machattie, of London, Ontario, and myself. The Commission was as follows:—

I hereby appoint and instruct the Bearers of this Letter,—J. George Hodgins, Esquire, LL.D., of Toronto, Deputy Superintendent of Education for Ontario, and A. Machattie, Esquire, M.D., F.C.S., of London, Ontario, to proceed to the United States for the purpose of inspecting and reporting upon any Technical, or Science School, or College, there established, as to their Buildings, Departments of Study and general Appliances.

I shall also esteem it a favour conferred, if the Principals, or other Authorities, of such Schools, or Colleges, will afford them the requisite facilities for the prosecution of their inquiries.

TORONTO, 12th January, 1871.   JOHN CARLING, Commissioner of Public
                                  Works for the Province of Ontario.

ACCOMPANYING LETTER FROM THE CHIEF SUPERINTENDENT OF EDUCATION FOR ONTARIO.

I have the honour to state that J. George Hodgins, Esquire, LL.D., and A. Machattie, M.D., F.C.S., the Bearer of this Letter have been requested and deputed by the Government of this Province to enquire into the nature, Management and Operations of the several Scientific Institutions of the United States, and especially those relating to Technical Education in connection with Mechanics, Manufactures and Agriculture.

I beg, therefore, to recommend them to the kind attentions of Managers and other Gentlemen connected with those Institutions in the United States.

[Seal]   EGERTON RYERSON, Chief Superintendent
TORONTO, 12th January, 1871.   of Education for the Province of Ontario.

REPORT OF DOCTORS HODGINS AND MACHATTIE ON TECHNICAL EDUCATION, OR SCHOOLS OF INDUSTRIAL SCIENCE, IN CERTAIN PORTIONS OF THE UNITED STATES.

TO THE HONOURABLE JOHN CARLING, M.P.P., COMMISSIONER OF PUBLIC WORKS AND AGRICULTURE, PROVINCE OF ONTARIO.

The Undersigned, having been deputed by your Department "to proceed to the United States, for the purpose of inspecting and reporting upon any Technical, or Science, Schools, or Colleges, there established, as to their Buildings, Departments of Study, and general Appliances," beg leave to report as follows:—

2. Owing to the limited time at our disposal, we were compelled to confine our inquiries and observations to the following Institutions devoted to Technical Educa-

1—XXIII.

tion. They are, however, among the most important ones in the United States, which give instruction in this special subject. They are as follows:—

1. THE LAWRENCE SCIENTIFIC SCHOOL.
   (*Connected with Harvard University, Cambridge, Massachusetts.*)

2. THE SHEFFIELD SCIENTIFIC SCHOOL.
   (*Connected with Yale College, New Haven, Connecticut.*)

3. THE SCHOOL OF MINES.
   (*Connected with Columbia College, New York.*)

4. THE MASSACHUSETTS INSTITUTE OF TECHNOLOGY.
   (*City of Boston, Massachusetts.*)

5. THE FREE INSTITUTE OF INDUSTRIAL SCIENCE.
   (*City of Worcester, Massachusetts.*)

6. THE COLLEGE OF CHEMISTRY, PHYSICS, MECHANIC ARTS, ETCETERA.
   (*Connected with Cornell University, Ithaca, New York.*)

7. THE RENSSELAER POLYTECHNIC INSTITUTE.
   (*City of Troy, New York.*)

8. THE COOPER UNION OF SCIENCE AND ART.
   (*City of New York.*)*

3. It is worthy of note that four of these important Institutions exist in one State, that of New York, three in the State of Massachusetts, and one in Connecticut. These States form the great manufacturing and industrial centres of the Union. The establishment, therefore, in them of these Schools indicates a wise sagacity on the part of their Founders.

4. Having been furnished by you with an Official Letter of Authority to proceed with the inquiry, we decided to pursue it in a manner which would enable us to obtain, the fullest information in regard to each Institution visited. With this view, we agreed upon the following plan:—

(1) Personally to inspect the Institution, its Lecture Rooms, Laboratories, etcetera.

(2) To take a sketch, or note, of everything of interest bearing upon our inquiries, which we might observe in each Institution, and to get information in regard to the Systems of Heating and Ventilation.

(3) To procure Plans of Buildings, and copies of the Reports of Institutions visited, or other Documents of value, on the subject of Technical Education.

(4) To obtain from the Heads of the Institutions visited, replies to a series of upwards of sixty Questions, which we had previously drawn up for this purpose. The answers to these Questions will not be given separately, but will be incorporated by us in the text of this Report.

5. We were received with great courtesy by the Heads of the Institutions visited, and by the Professors; and every facility was freely afforded to us to obtain full and satisfactory information on the subjects of our inquiry.

6. Before attempting a brief discussion of the necessity and advantage of Schools of Technology, or Industrial Science, in this Country, and pointing out the many facilities and appliances for imparting instruction in this subject in the United States, we deem it desirable as a preliminary, to condense in a brief form, several important financial items of information in regard to the Institutions visited, as follows:

* Of the 337 other Colleges and Collegiate Institutes in the United States, 50 report a "Scientific Department," with an attendance of nearly 3,000 students. There are 175 other higher Educational Institutions in the United States, videlicet: 101 Theological Colleges; 52 Medical and Dental Colleges; and 23 Law Schools.

I. *Cost of the Buildings, Fittings, and Apparatus.*

(NOTE.—The figures are in most cases approximate.)

Number.	Name of Institution.	Original Cost of Building.	Original Cost of Fittings.	Original Cost of Apparatus, etectera.
1	Lawrence Scientific School, Harvard College	$30,000 (An old building)	(uncertain)	(uncertain)
2	Sheffield Scientific School, Yale College....................	$100,000	(uncertain)	$15,000
3	Massachusetts Institution of Technology, Boston	$290,000	$10,000	$15,000
4	School of Mines, Columbia College, New York.........	$80,000 Temporary build'gs	(uncertain)	$25,000 { Minerals, $3,000 add'nl
5	Institute of Industrial Science, Worcester, Massachusetts....................	$67,000 Workshop, $30,000	$5,000	$5,000
6	Rensselaer Polytechnic Institute, Troy, New York......	$40,000	$5,000	$8,000
7	College of Chemistry, Physics, &c., Cornell University, New York...............	$300,000 A proportion only	(uncertain)	$25,000
8	Cooper Union for Science and Art, New York	$630,000	$6,000	$10,000

II. *Revenue and Expenditure.*

(1) REVENUE.

(NOTE.—The figures are, in most cases, an approximation.)

No.	NAME OF INSTITUTION.	Fees from Students.	Other Sources.	Total.
		$	$	$
1	Lawrence Scientific School, Harvard College...........	6,500	13,500	20,000
2	Sheffield Scientific School, Yale College			
3	Massachusetts Institute of Technology, Boston..	31,000	19,000	50,000
4	School of Mines, Columbia College, New York.........	12,000	68,000	80,000
5	Industrial Science Institute, Worcester, Massachusetts..	700	17,000	17,700
6	Rensselaer Polytechnic Institute, Troy, New York	23,000	None.	23,000
7	Cornell University, Ithaca, New York..................	22,500	37,500	60,000
8	Cooper Union, New York	Free.	43,000	43,000

(2) EXPENDITURE.

(NOTE.—The figures are, in most cases, approximate.)

No.	NAME OF INSTITUTION.	Salaries.	Other Expenses.	Total.
		$	$	$
1	Lawrence Scientific School, Harvard College	13,500	3,500	17,000
2	Sheffield Scientific School, Yale College................			30,000
3	Massachusetts Institute of Technology, Boston	44,500	5,500	50,000
4	School of Mines, Columbia College, New York.........	63,100	16,900	80,000
5	Industrial Science Institute, Worcester, Massachusetts..	13,400	3,600	17,000
6	Rensselaer Polytechnic Institute, Troy, New York.....	20,000	3,000	23,000
7	Cornell University, Ithaca, New York..................	50,000	10,000	60,000
8	Cooper Union, New York	6,200	33,800	40,800

III. *Professors, Students' Fees, etcetera.*

No.	NAME OF INSTITUTION.	Instructors.			Students. Min'm ages 16 and 18.	
		Professors	Instructors.	Total.	Numbers.	Fees per annum.
1	Lawrence Scientific School, Harvard College....	8	3	11	35 {	Chem. $200 Eng'eer 150
2	Sheffield Scientific School, Yale College	21	1	22	125	150
3	Massachusetts Institute of Technology, Boston..	18	14	32	240	150
4	School of Mines, Columbia College, New York..	8	12	20	150	200
5	Industrial Science School, Worcester, Massachusetts	4	2	6	80	100
6	Rensselaer Polytechnic Institute, Troy, New York	9	2	11	150	200
7	Cornell University, Ithaca, New York..........	12		12	?150 {	45 being raised.
8	Cooper Union, New York	3	21	24	1280	None.

Note.—The Professors and Instructors were, as we invariably found, paid fixed Salaries, without reference to the number of Students in attendance, or the Fees paid by them. These Salaries varied, in the case of Professors, from $2,500 to $5,000 per annum. Students were invariably required to pay for breakages, but not in all cases for Chemicals used,—the latter expense, however, is very trifling. In those Institutions receiving an Apportionment from the United States National Fund for the promotion in the several States, of Industrial and Scientific Education, a condition was imposed by the State Legislature to provide tuition free for a limited number of Students.[*] Hence, at the Worcester Institute of Industrial Science, out of the eighty Students in attendance, only seven of them paid an annual Fee of $100, the other seventy-three were admitted free, either from the State, or from the City of Worcester. In no case were Students boarded, or lodged, on the School Premises. At Cornell University, a Boarding Hall was provided near the Institution, more as a protection to Students against high charges in the Village of Ithaca. It is proposed, however, as soon as possible, to discontinue it.

IV. *Course of Study in the Various Institutions Visited.*

7. The Course of Study in each of the Institutions visited, varied according to the number of Professors and Instructors employed, and the extent of the accommodation provided. They all, however, embraced the subjects of Mathematics, Chemistry, Natural Philosophy, Drawing, Civil and Mechanical Engineering, and the Modern Languages. This latter branch of instruction was invariably provided for, as so many of the Scientific Text Books and Works, which are required to be used, or consulted, are written in French and German. In the great majority of cases, four years was the period allowed to complete the Course,—two years preliminary, and two years professional; so that Graduates of Colleges were only required to pursue the professional course of two years.

[*] This Fund was created by an Act of Congress, passed in 1862, apportioning "to each State a quantity of public Land, equal to 30,000 Acres, for each Senator and Representative in Congress, according to the census of 1860." The object of the Grant was to provide in each State of the Union, for "the Endowment, support and maintenance of at least one College, where the leading object shall be, (without excluding other Scientific and Classical studies, and including Military Tactics), to teach such branches of learning as are related to Agriculture and Mechanic Arts in such manner as the Legislatures of the States may respectively prescribe, in order to promote the liberal and practical education of the industrial classes in the several pursuits and professions of life." The Act further provides that "a sum, not exceeding ten per centum upon the amount received by any State, may be expended for the purchase of lands for sites and Experimental Farms, whenever authorized by the respective Legislatures of the States."

NOTE.—In Massachusetts, the Grant is annually divided among several Institutions: in New York, the whole of it was given to Cornell University, and in Connecticut, to Yale College, for the benefit of Sheffield Scientific School.

8. As an example of the best and most comprehensive Course of Study for a School of Industrial Science, we give in the Appendix, a copy of that adopted by the Sheffield Scientific School at Yale College, and at the Massachusetts Institute of Technology, at Boston,—the latter being one of the latest and most complete Institutions of the kind in the United States.

V. *Subjects to be Taught in the Proposed Canadian Institution.*

9. As to the subjects which should be taught in the proposed College of Technology, or School of Industrial Science for Ontario, we may state that the following are regarded as essential to the usefulness and efficiency of any Institution of the kind proposed.

(1) *Pure and Applied Mathematics.*—This department should include Mathematics proper, Natural Philosophy, Civil, Military and Mechanical Engineering and Surveying. To render the teaching in this department efficient, the Students should be required, among other things, and as part of their regular instruction, to visit with their Professor, or his Assistant, the larger Engineering, or Manufacturing Establishments. In vacation time, Mining Students should be taken, if possible, on excursions to convenient Mining Districts. The Engineering Students should be required to undertake practical Surveys of a given section of Country, for Railway, or other purposes.

(2) *Architecture and Drawing.*—This Department should embrace Free-hand, Architectural, Engineering and Topographical Drawing, with Plans, Sections, etcetera.

(3) *Pure and applied Chemistry.*—This important department, should include Organic and Inorganic chemistry; Chemistry as applied to the Industrial Arts, and to Mining and Metallurgy.

(4) *Natural Science.*—This department should include Geology, Mineralogy, Zoology and Botany, and their industrial applications.

(5) *Modern Languages.*—The only two, which are essential to be taught in this department, are the French and German languages. The Student, being already familiar with English, would require the addition of the other two, as so large a proportion of the best works on Scientific Literature is written in French and German.

10. We think it necessary to advert in connection with this matter to a possible cause of failure in an Institution of this kind, which should be avoided, namely, attempting too much at first. Whatever is undertaken should be done as thoroughly as is compatible with the means at the disposal of the Institution; but to establish at the outset a large educational staff, before any experience has been obtained of the kind of Students, or the nature of the Studies most in demand, is only calculated to weaken each individual department. We would recommend, therefore, for the sake of economy, that the number of Teachers should at first be small; and that each Teacher should instruct in all departments of his particular subject, until experience shows in what branches of Study increased assistance may most profitably be employed. Although all the subjects taught in the various Technical Schools are important, some are more important than others. Whereever the financial condition admits of it, the tendency is to increase the number of subjects taught, and the number of Teachers, or Professors, but some Institutions still suffer from having undertaken too many subjects with insufficient means.

11. The kind of instruction, and the method of giving it, should be as practical as possible. As a rule, Students of special subjects are not considered desirable; as it is believed that a Student, say of Chemistry, will make a better Chemist if he studies the

other subject as included in a Scientific Education, although in doing so he necessarily devotes less time to Chemistry. Young Institutions, however, are scarcely in a position to make these distinctions, although, in most thoroughly established Technical Schools specialists are discouraged as much as possible without being excluded. Great prominence is given to the study of Modern Languages, because of the high value of the Scientific Literature of France and Germany.

Note.—Although the building should be constructed to provide for instruction in the five departments named, it might not be deemed desirable to introduce immediately the two latter important departments, (of the Natural Sciences and Modern Languages.) The introduction of the three other departments is, however, vital to the success and usefulness of the Institution. Provision might also be made for popular Lectures and instruction in the evenings, at which Teachers, young men, Mechanics and others employed during the day might attend. This we found to be an interesting feature in some of the Institutions which we visited. At the Massachusetts Institute of Technology at Boston, Mr. Lowell, with his usual munificence, had provided at a cost to himself, of $3,000 per annum, an evening Course of Lectures, which had been attended by an average number of 500 Persons—chiefly Teachers, and persons engaged in Manufacturing Establishments.

VI. *Character and Cost of the Proposed Buildings.*

12. We have had in all our enquiries especial reference to the character, cost and convenience of the proposed Building for this Province. After a careful consideration of the whole subject,—looking at what has been done, and what has been deemed essential, elsewhere, and fully apreciating the wants and necessities of our own people, —we do not think that it would be desirable or expedient to erect a Building capable of accommodating less than from 120 to 150 Students, or providing for less than the five departments of instruction, which we have enumerated,—three of which to be established at once, and the other two subsequently.

13. Under the system which we recommend, the Professor af Mathematics should be prepared to instruct Students of Architecture and Civil, Mechanical, and Mining Engineering, in those branches of pure and applied Mathematics, and Natural Philosophy which individually they require. The Professor of Chemistry must teach the elements of Chemistry and its applications to any particular Industrial pursuit: and the Professor of Drawing should also suit his instructions to the end which Students have in view. Of the Natural Sciences, Geology, Botany and Zoology,—prominence must be given to one, or all according to circumstances, and French and German should be taught to those who wish to avail themselves of the rich Scientific Literature in these languages.

14. By such a Course of Instruction, as is sketched out above, provision is made for the Professional Education of Architects, Civil, Mechanical and Mining Engineers, Chemists, Metallurgists and Teachers of Science: and according as the want for increased teaching facilities in any one of the branches is felt, that want can be supplied.

15. An Institution of the capacity indicated,—including a main Building, and detached Laboratories, besides providing for Heating, Ventilation, Fittings, Furniture, Apparatus, Models of Machinery, Architectural and Drawing Models, Chemicals, Books for the professional Library of the Instructors, etcetera,—could, we have no doubt, be provided at a cost not exceeding $50,000.

16. For convenience we give the following approximate Statement of the proposed capacity, cost, etcetera, of the projected Institution:—

1. *The Main Building for Instruction, Designed to Accommodate from 120 to 150 Students.*

1. The Principal's Room, or Office ....⎫
2. Waiting, or Visitors' Room ....⎪
3. Entrance Hall and Coat Rooms ....⎪
4. Public, or General Lecture, Hall ....⎪
5. Model Room for Machinery ....⎪
6. Physical Laboratory for Instruction in Natural Philosophy.........⎪
7. Geological and Mineralogical Collection Room ....⎪
8. Lecture Room for Mathematics, Engineering and Surveying,—⎪
    for 60 Students ....⎪
9. Lecture Room for Architecture and Drawing,—for 60 Students.....⎬ $25,000
10. Lecture Room for Geology, Mineralogy, Zoology, and Botany,—⎪
    for 60 Students ....⎪
11. Lecture Room for Modern Languages,—for 60 Students ....⎪
12. Lecture Room for Chemistry and Metallurgy,—for 120 Students.....⎪
13 to 17. Five Ante rooms for Professors' Studies and Libraries...⎪
18, 19. Two Attic Rooms for Drawing ....⎪
20, 22. In Basement—Workshops, General Store and Heating⎪
    Apparatus ....⎭

II. *Detached Buildings for Chemical Laboratories.*

1. Quantitative Chemical Laboratory ....⎫
2. Qualitative Chemical Laboratory ....⎪
3. Assay and Metallurgy Room ....⎬ $5,000
4. Balance Room ....⎪
5. Store Room for Chemicals ....⎪
6. Private Laboratory for Professor ....⎭

    III. STEAM HEATING AND VENTILATION 5,000
    IV. FITTINGS AND FURNITURE FOR ROOMS AND LABORATORIES..... 6,000
    V. APPARATUS AND CHEMICALS 4,000
    VI. MECHANICAL MODELS 3,500
    VII. PROFESSIONAL LIBRARY FOR THREE PROFESSORS................... 1,500
                                                      $50,000

VII. *Estimated Annual Expenditure.*

This we can only estimate in general terms at from $12,000 to $15,000 per annum as follows:—

(1) Salaries of three Professors and Servants, etcetera..from $7,000 · to $8,000
(2) Apparatus, Chemicals and Models ....from 1,500 to 2,000
(3) Fire, Water and Light ....from 2,000 to 2,500
(4) Repairs and Furnishing, etcetera ....from 800 to 1,000
(5) Contingencies, Printing, etcetera ....from 800 to 1,000

                                          $12,100 to $14,500

VIII. *Construction of the Buildings of a Technical College.*

17. We have obtained Plans of the latest and best constructed of the Technical Schools which we visited, and have also taken notes of many details of construction and arrangements. These, with such verbal explanations as we shall be able from per-

some conservatories might also be provided at the expense. The Architect who may prepare the Plans of the proposed buildings, at the extreme part, will hear accordance with the signs of the several rooms building about to be erected on Victoria Square— where we understand the proposed buildings to erected. In their are a few suggestion in regard to the inside arrangement of the building which we would respectfully beg to offer, as follows:—

(1) The proposed division, as to dormitory and in the construction, care should be taken to provide accommodation sufficient in the rooms.

(2) In order to promote a thorough system of Ventilation, as many flues as possible should be inserted in the interior and external wall. The external air were be honey-combed with flues. These flues are very numerous being near leading to the top of the building and constructed as the Commons rooms precaution against Fire being taken. The great objection to every institution which we visited was its imperfect Ventilation; and to secure a through and satisfactory solution of the vexed question a thorough Ventilation are required in those Buildings which in their construction as well abundant supply with Ventilating flues with openings at the top and bottom of the rooms.

(3) Closely connected with the Ventilation are the Heating of the Buildings. The result of our inquiries in the different sources has to our an most successful plan adopted was that which combines the main features of the Hot-air and Steam Heating Systems. The principal objection to the Hot-air system that the Air is not merely heated but made very dry, in most cases considerable amount of character in reason of its contact with the highly-heated iron surfaces in the flues in the chambers of the Furnace. The main objection to Steam heating is that it never warms the Air of the room where a steam current is become and without providing for a supply of fresh Air from without. In combining these two systems the plan now in favour at present is to construct a series of near flues in a Chamber sufficient in area and which pure Air from without is constantly introduced. The Air being heated by the Coils is forced by means of Fans or other machinery and passes through Flues into the Rooms to be heated, and there having served its purpose is at becomes impure carried away by means of the Ventilating flues. To supplement this system it has been found most desirable to have a small auxiliary Steam Coil in each Room and it may be turned on or off at the pleasure of the occupants.

(4) Each of the Lecture Rooms should be connected with an ante-room to serve as a Study or retiring for the Professors and it is found a recent a small Library of reference Books being of the particular subject taught in the Lecture Room.

(5) The Rooms for Drawing should be placed in the Attic, or upper Story of the Building. Thus only the best could be made available for the Drawing Classes by placing a partition in the centre of the room, and lighting each division of the Room partly by means of a Sky-light and partly by means of a Window near the Ceiling—forming a continued line of the Sky-light at the top—the Drawing Tables being arranged so that the light falls on them from the left or at each of about 45°.

(6) Black-boards are an essential feature in a School of Technology. No Lecture Room is complete without them; but they are still more necessary in the Rooms for Drawing as the work is mostly done on large mechanical drawings. The best Black-boards which we saw were those constructed of Slate.

(7) The Laboratory working Tables for Students should be constructed on the above system between the Windows and placed at the sides of the Rooms and not in the middle.

(8) A Room for Models of Machinery and other Mechanical Contrivances, as well as for Architectural Models should be provided. This Room should be large enough to permit of easy access to the Models by the Students for the purpose of sketching and drawing them. Such a Room with a good collection of enlarged Models of Machinery would serve as a substitute for Machine Shops (without involving their expense), especially if it had also specimens of Tools, Lathes and other appliances of useful handicraft etcetera

(9) As a counterpart to this Room for Models there should be one for a collection of Mineralogical and Metallurgical specimens and Models of Crystallography. If these collections of Models and specimens could be placed on the same floors as the respective Lecture Rooms devoted to Mechanics Metallurgy, etcetera and be connected with them, the convenience and completeness of the arrangement would contribute largely to lessen the labours of the Professor, while easy access to the Models, etcetera, would promote the progress and efficiency of the Classes.

(10) At the sides of the Lecture Rooms (at the end) and behind the Platform, it would be a great convenience to construct (in most of the Lecture Rooms) Glass Cases, in which to arrange the Apparatus, and keep it from dust, when not in use. The neatness economy of such an arrangement would amply repay the Institution for the original

cost of the Cases, and would ensure the care and safety of the Apparatus, a good deal of which being fragile in its nature and delicate in its construction, would suffer greatly from exposure, or carelessness.

(11) A large public Lecture, or Examination, Hall, with suitable convenience for a Lecturer, is an essential feature in an Institution of this kind. In such a Hall popular evening Lectures on practical Scientific Subjects might be given, at which Persons engaged during the day might attend. Such a Hall would also be useful for Examinations, or for any public exercises connected with the Institution.

(12) Finally, plainness, combined with neatness and convenience, should characterise the entire Building. No unnecessary ornament, or decoration, should be used; but every part of the Building should have a practical adaption to the purposes for which it is designed. On this and other points we have obtained detailed information, which may be of service when the Plans are being prepared.

IX. *Admission to the American Institutions—Fees—Vacation.*

18. The minimum age at which Students are admitted to the several Institutions we visited was from 16 to 18 years. In all cases they were required to pass a prescribed Examination chiefly in Arithmetic, Algebra, (to Quadratic Equations), Geometry, English Grammar and Geography.

19. The Fees payable annually by each Student, (when not a State beneficiary) varied from $100 to $200. $150 we found to be the usual Fee. In Cornell University it was at first only $30; it has now been raised to $45 per annum, with a prospect of a still further rise. A first supply of Apparatus and Chemicals was usually given to each Student; subsequent supplies had to be paid for at about cost prices, while breakages were at the risk of the Student, who was required to pay for them.

20. The School Term in each of the Institutions, visited, generally extended from July, or August, to September, or October, giving to the Students a Vacation of about two months in Summer, and an interval of two weeks, or more at Christmas.

X. *Discipline in the American Institutions.*

21. In regard to the question of daily Discipline among the Students of the Institutions which we visited, the invariable reply was that it was of the simplest kind—that it involved no anxiety on the part of the Authorities, or Professors. The young men were of that age and character which required little more than an appeal to their feelings, their ambition and their honour. This, and the fact that their continuance in the Institution depended upon their daily application and their individual progress, had a sufficiently salutary effect upon them to ensure good conduct, and a desire to conform to the Rules of the Institution.

XI. *Mode of Teaching, Examinations, etcetera.*

22. In most of the Institutions visited, the mode of teaching was by conversational Lecture, combined with a daily system of questioning on the lesson of the preceding day. The Students were required to take notes of a certain class of Lectures; but, where practicable, Blackboard Exercises on the part of the whole Class was invariably the chief feature of the daily exercise, or "recitations" of Students. This was followed by a brief explanation of the Lessons for the next day. At the end of each month, (in some Institutions), and invariably at the end of each half year in all of them, the Students were subjected to a rigid Written Examination, followed, in many cases, by an Oral one, designed to test more fully the personal knowledge of the subject on the part of each individual Student. The result of the half yearly Examination determined the status as well as the continuance in the Institution of the Student, and thus a healthy stimulus was kept up throughout the whole Course.

sonal observation to give, can be placed at the disposal of the Architect, who may prepare the Plans of the proposed Building. As to its exterior, that will likely harmonize with the style of the Normal School Buildings, already erected on Victoria Square—where we understand the proposed building will be erected; but there are a few suggestions in regard to the interior arrangement of the Building which we would respectfully beg to offer, as follows:—

(1) The proposed Building should be detached; and, in its size and construction, care should be taken to provide abundance of light in all of the Rooms.

(2) In order to promote a thorough system of Ventilation, as many flues as possible should be inserted in the interior and exterior walls. They should, as it were, be honey-combed with flues. These Wall flues should terminate in main flues, leading to the top of the Building; or, if desirable, in the Chimneys, proper precautions against Fire being taken. The great defect complained of in every Institution which we visited was its imperfect Ventilation and the nearest approach to a satisfactory solution of the vexed question of thorough Ventilation was reached in those Buildings which, in their construction, had been abundantly supplied with Ventilating flues, with openings at the top and bottom of the Rooms.

(3) Closely connected with the Ventilation is the Heating of the Buildings. The result of our inquiries in this direction showed that the best and most successful plan adopted was that which combined the main features of the Hot-air and Steam Heating Systems. The principal objection to the Hot-air system is that the Air is not merely heated, but made very dry. In most cases it is considerably altered in character by reason of its contact with the highly-heated, (often red-hot), surface of the Iron in the chambers of the Furnace. The main objection to Steam heating is that it merely warms the Air in the room, (which is often impure, or becomes so,) without providing for a supply of fresh Air from without. In combining these two systems, the plan most in favour at present is, to construct a series of Steam Coils in a Chamber sufficiently large, into which pure Air from without is constantly introduced. This Air, being heated by the Coils, is forced, by means of Fans or other mechanical appliances, through Flues into the Rooms to be heated, and there, having served its purpose, is, as it becomes impure, conveyed away by means of the Ventilating flues. To supplement this system, it has been found most desirable to have a small auxiliary Steam Coil in each Room, which may be turned on or off at the pleasure of the Occupants.

(4) Each of the Lecture Rooms should be provided with an Ante-room to serve as a Study, or otherwise, for the Professors; and in it should be placed a small Library of professional Books bearing on the particular subject taught in the Lecture Room.

(5) The Rooms for Drawing should be placed in the Attic, or upper Story, of the Building. The entire flat could be made available for the Drawing Classes by running a partition down the centre of the room, and lighting each division of the Room, partly by means of a Sky-light, and partly by means of a Window near the Ceiling.—forming a continuation of the Sky-light at the top—the Drawing Tables being arranged so that the light should come from the left at an angle of about 45°.

(6) Black-boards are an essential feature in a School of Technology. No Lecture Room is complete without them; but they are not so necessary in the Rooms for Drawing, as the work is chiefly done on Drawing-boards, etcetera. The best Black-boards which we saw were those constructed of Slate.

(7) The Laboratory working Tables for Students should be constructed on the alcove system between the Windows, and placed at the sides of the Rooms, and not in the middle.

(8) A Room for Models of Machinery and other Mechanical Contrivances, as well as for Architectural Models, should be provided. This Room should be large enough to permit of easy access to the Models by the Students, for the purpose of sketching and drawing them. Such a Room, with a good collection of enlarged Models of Machinery would serve as a substitute for Machine Shops (without involving their expense), especially if it had also specimens of Tools, Lathes and other appliances of useful handicraft, etcetera.

(9) As a counterpart to this Room for Models, there should be one for a collection of Mineralogical and Metallurgical specimens and Models of Crystallography. If these collections of Models and specimens could be placed on the same floors as the respective Lecture Rooms devoted to Mechanics, Metallurgy, etcetera, and be connected with them, the convenience and completeness of the arrangement would contribute largely to lessen the labours of the Professor, while easy access to the Models, etcetera, would promote the progress and efficiency of the Classes.

(10) At the sides of the Lecture Rooms, (at the end) and behind the Platform, it would be a great convenience to construct (in most of the Lecture Rooms) Glass Cases, in which to arrange the Apparatus, and keep it from dust, when not in use. The neatness economy of such an arrangement would amply repay the Institution for the original

cost of the Cases, and would ensure the care and safety of the Apparatus, a good deal of which being fragile in its nature and delicate in its construction, would suffer greatly from exposure, or carelessness.

(11) A large public Lecture, or Examination, Hall, with suitable convenience for a Lecturer, is an essential feature in an Institution of this kind. In such a Hall popular evening Lectures on practical Scientific Subjects might be given, at which Persons engaged during the day might attend. Such a Hall would also be useful for Examinations, or for any public exercises connected with the Institution.

(12) Finally, plainness, combined with neatness and convenience, should characterise the entire Building. No unnecessary ornament, or decoration, should be used; but every part of the Building should have a practical adaption to the purposes for which it is designed. On this and other points we have obtained detailed information, which may be of service when the Plans are being prepared.

IX. *Admission to the American Institutions—Fees—Vacation.*

18. The minimum age at which Students are admitted to the several Institutions we visited was from 16 to 18 years. In all cases they were required to pass a prescribed Examination chiefly in Arithmetic, Algebra, (to Quadratic Equations), Geometry, English Grammar and Geography.

19. The Fees payable annually by each Student, (when not a State beneficiary) varied from $100 to $200. $150 we found to be the usual Fee. In Cornell University it was at first only $30; it has now been raised to $45 per annum, with a prospect of a still further rise. A first supply of Apparatus and Chemicals was usually given to each Student; subsequent supplies had to be paid for at about cost prices, while breakages were at the risk of the Student, who was required to pay for them.

20. The School Term in each of the Institutions, visited, generally extended from July, or August, to September, or October, giving to the Students a Vacation of about two months in Summer, and an interval of two weeks, or more at Christmas.

X. *Discipline in the American Institutions.*

21. In regard to the question of daily Discipline among the Students of the Institutions which we visited, the invariable reply was that it was of the simplest kind—that it involved no anxiety on the part of the Authorities, or Professors. The young men were of that age and character which required little more than an appeal to their feelings, their ambition and their honour. This, and the fact that their continuance in the Institution depended upon their daily application and their individual progress, had a sufficiently salutary effect upon them to ensure good conduct, and a desire to conform to the Rules of the Institution.

XI. *Mode of Teaching, Examinations, etcetera.*

22. In most of the Institutions visited, the mode of teaching was by conversational Lecture, combined with a daily system of questioning on the lesson of the preceding day. The Students were required to take notes of a certain class of Lectures; but, where practicable, Blackboard Exercises on the part of the whole Class was invariably the chief feature of the daily exercise, or "recitations" of Students. This was followed by a brief explanation of the Lessons for the next day. At the end of each month, (in some Institutions), and invariably at the end of each half year in all of them, the Students were subjected to a rigid Written Examination, followed, in many cases, by an Oral one, designed to test more fully the personal knowledge of the subject on the part of each individual Student. The result of the half yearly Examination determined the status as well as the continuance in the Institution of the Student, and thus a healthy stimulus was kept up throughout the whole Course.

XII. *Admission of Females to these Institutions.*

23. Although in most of the Institutions visited, no Regulations have been adopted to prevent the admission of female Students to the Classes, yet practically they do exist,—for in none of them are there any such Students. In three out of the eight Institutions visited, the Authorities refuse to admit them; in the others they successfully discourage their attendance. To the popular Evening Classes and Lectures, however, at the Massachusetts School of Technology, (Boston), the Institute of Industrial Science, (Worcester, Massachusetts), and the Cooper Union, (New York), [where numbers of females can come together] they are freely admitted. Those reported in attendance at the Massachusetts Institutions, during the time of our visit, were chiefly the School Teachers, who were fitting themselves for employment as Instructors in Drawing and Chemistry in the Public Schools of that State. These subjects, (especially Drawing), we understand, having been recently prescribed by the Legislative for introduction into these Schools.

XIII. *Management and Government of the Proposed College.*

24. Having given at some length, the statistical and other details of the various Schools and Colleges visited by us, it now remains to make some general observations founded on the information during our inspection of these Institutions.

25. We are naturally led to consider, in the first place, whether, or not, Technical Schools in the United States have been an assured success. To this question we can give an almost unqualified answer in the affirmative; for although there are cases in which the result has been a partial, or complete, failure, this is invariably attributed by those who possess experience on the subject, to the organization and government of the School, and not to the character of the education given in it. We have had the strongest testimony as to the necessity of keeping Institutions for Technical Education entirely apart from, and independent of, any other Literary, or Scientific, Schools, or Colleges; and to this point we would most particularly draw attention, for we consider it one of the chief essentials to success.

26. On no point, we repeat, was the testimony at the Institutions we visited more clear, distinct and uniform than that the proposed School of Technology, should, in its teaching and management and government, be kept entirely distinct from any other Institution. To attach it as an Appendage to any School, or College for teaching purposes, would be to ensure its ultimate failure. The more efficient the Institution to which it might be attached for these purposes, (paradoxical as it may appear,) the more certain and speedy would be the failure of the School. Even at the two distinguished American Universities of Harvard and Yale, where scientific Schools exist, their efficiency and success is just in proportion to their entire practical separation for teaching and other purposes from the other parts of the University.[*]

27. At Columbia College, too, the scientific part of that University, (the School of Mines), is situated at quite a different part of the City from the rest of the College; and it is chiefly taught and managed by a different set of Professors, etcetera, from those connected with the College proper. The plan upon which Cornell University appears to have been projected may seem to conflict with the experience of the older Universities on this point. But, while it is admitted that the conception and design of Cornell University were noble and munificent in themselves, yet it is regarded by sagacious men as an experiment at present,—the success of which time alone can de-

---

[*] A pamphlet issued at Yale, on the relations of the Colleges to the University, states that "The Classical, or Academic, and the Scientific departments (ordinarily called Yale College, and the Sheffield School of Science) are distinct Colleges for the Undergraduate Students of the University—distinct in Teachers, Scholars, Buildings, Apparatus, and special working Libraries.   .   .   The ranges of Studies in the two Colleges, the Academic and Scientific, are so diverse in character, that the interests of the Students and of Education are better subserved by two distinct Faculties working separately, than by one single combined Faculty." Another pamphlet says:—
"The Instructors of the Sheffield School are appointed by the Yale College Corporation, but they constitute a Body as distinct from the Academic Faculty as the Faculties of Law, Medicine and Theology."

monstrate. Even in Cornell the separation in the teaching and management was more marked than we expected to find it; but until a larger teaching staff is provided, the union of professorships in different departments of the University must be regarded as a serious defect in its organization.

28. There are one or two facts connected with this subject which we think worthy of your consideration, and which will tend to illustrate our meaning more clearly:—

(1) Schools of Technology are *sui generis*. Their chief specialty is, in the highest sense, "Object Teaching,"—or teaching by illustration and practice. They require much Mental, but still more of Manual effort and Physical Labour on the part of the Students. The Classes, and even the individual Students, require more constant teaching oversight and professorial supervision than in Colleges, or Universities. This being the case, it must be obvious that the Professor of a College, or of any other purely Literary Institution, is not so well adapted, (either by his daily habits of professorial routine, or by the character and mode of his instruction—its literary purpose and objects—), for taking charge of Classes in another Institution of a totally different character, as a person specially qualified for the work. Of course we speak generally; for no doubt a person may be found now and then who combines in himself, even in an eminent degree, the double qualification of which we speak.

(2) Again: a divided interest in two Institutions is fatal to success in either, or both. It is contrary to the nature of things that it should be otherwise. Personal associations, leanings, preferences, and interest, singly, or combined, tend to sway the individual more or less strongly towards one or other Institution with which he may be connected. The result must, in the end, be, (as we have stated,) fatal to success in either, or both. Besides, in the joint management of Institutions partaking somewhat of the same character, and yet dissimilar in their objects, interests clash and points of difference arise, often unpleasant in themselves, which must invariably prove fatal to the efficiency of one, or other. Although, as we understand, it is the intention of the Government to erect the School of Technology in Victoria Square, (on the Normal School plot), yet we would strongly recommend that it be not associated, or connected with that Institution in any way, but left entirely under the care, management and control of the Government itself.

29. Such being the purport of our inquiries and observations on this subject, we beg respectfully to submit the results of them to your consideration, with a view to their practical application.

XIV. *Question as to the Advisability of Machine Shops.*

30. The only Institution which we visited to which a Machine Shop was attached was that at Worcester, Massachusetts. In one, or two, others a small Work Shop, with Lathes, Tools, etcetera,) was provided. The general feeling on the subject is, that they are expensive and of doubtful utility, and that, if introduced at all, it should be to a very limited extent, and not for the purpose of training skilled Mechanics. At Worcester, where a good Machine Shop exists, it is to some extent made available for the younger Students, who are treated as Apprentices. But, even there the Shop is deemed an experiment. As the work done in the Shop is thorough and of a saleable description, it competes in the open market, and brings its full value. The labour being cheaper than in other Machine Shops, it would appear that such a Shop might not only be self-supporting, but profitable. There is, however, one serious drawback to this, that the experienced Workmen are compelled to devote much time to Novices and Apprentices; but as the primary object of the Machine Shop is, not to make money, but to teach—the want of profit can scarcely be regarded in the light of a failure.

31. As a substitute for Machine Shops in the other Institutions, Tools, Models, and Drawings are freely provided. The Students are also required, as a regular part

of their Class training, (and with a view to familiarize them with the actual details of work), to make regular visits of inspection in the neighbourhood to Machine Shops, Engines, Mills, Furnaces, Chemical Works, etcetera. And when practical, (especially during the holidays), facilities, or encouragements, are given to the Students to visit with a Professor, Mining districts, large Engineering constructions, important Buildings, etcetera.

NOTE.—Students in the Engineering and Surveying Departments are statedly assigned given Sections of Country, in which they are required to "locate" a line of Railway, or to make a Topographical Survey of it, as the case may be.

XV. *Necessity for Models of Machinery, Lathes, Collections of Tools, etcetera.*

32. As already intimated, a substitute for a Machine Shops, (in connection with the Students' visits of inspection to Manufactories, Mills, etcetera), a collection of enlarged Models of Engines, and Machinery of various kinds, is absolutely necessary. These Models should be of sufficient size and construction to enable the Student easily to understand the details of their Mechanism, to take them apart and reconstruct them, to make sketches, Isometric, Perspective and Working Drawings of them, with the necessary details of Plans and Sections, etcetera.

33. In addition to these enlarged Models, small Models, Charts, Diagrams, and Photographs of Works and Machinery, etcetera, should be procured. Whenever practical, original Working Plans and Drawings, with the Estimate, (or copies), and Specifications of Engineering Works, or Machinery, which have been actually constructed, should also be obtained. The latter, in the hands of Students, give a reality to their theoretical instruction, which is invaluable to them in the progress of their Studies. After a study of such Plans and Drawings, a visit of inspection to the Work, or Machinery itself will more deeply impress on the Student's mind the minutiæ of its details, and familiarize him more with the intricacy, and yet simplicity, of its parts, than a week's laborious study of the theory of the construction of the same piece of Machinery, or Work.

XVI. *Laboratories for Students—Metallurgy.*

34. We have before briefly referred to the subject of Students' Laboratories, and the necessity of a Mineralogical and Metallurgical collection of Models and Specimens. We cannot too strongly press upon your notice the necessity of providing amply for this department of Instruction in the proposed Institution. The Students should have every facility for pursuing their practical studies in Chemistry and Metallurgy, in the Laboratories which we have already named. In a Country like ours, whose Mining interests are yet in their infancy, and which must every year increase in magnitude, we should seek to train skilled men, who, by their knowledge and ability, can so materially aid in the development of this most important department of national wealth and industry.

XVII. *Persons to be benefitted by the College of Technology.*

35. To these suggestions on the Appliances of Technical Education, it may be well to add some of the advantages which, in our opinion, are likely to result from founding a Technical School, or College, in Ontario. We should anticipate, from what we have seen elsewhere, and from the character of the rapidly increasing industries of Canada, great benefits, both to the Students themselves and to the Country generally. Graduates and Students of a well conducted and efficient Technical School necessarily share in its reputation; and a Diploma, or Certificate, from a good School is usually a passport to remunerative employment. A glance at the record of the after

history of the Graduates of some of the Technical Schools in the United States is amply sufficient to establish this statement. At one which we visited, we were informed that the Principal was quite unable to supply the constant demand for Students to fill professional situations of a high and lucrative character. That the Students themselves are sensible of the value of the training, is almost always shown by after Donations to the Museum, or Scientific Collections, and in some cases, where they have obtained pecuniary assistance in their Studies, by afterwards contributing in money the amount of the Fees which they had, while Students, been unable to pay.

36. To the general community a School of Industrial Science is of great value as a central source of information to Manufacturers and others on all new discoveries pertaining to their pursuits. From the Professors in such a School, advice and opinions on Scientific questions can be had, and in well trained Students is to be obtained the Scientific and practical assistance required in most Manufacturing Establishments. The Students themselves become Teachers of Science; and both they and their Professors extend the limits of Science by original investigation. Every civilized Country is devoting increased attention to this kind of education, as the best means of keeping their Industries abreast of the general and rapid progress in all the Industrial Arts and Manufactures; and we, therefore, believe for this, and for the other reasons given above, that a Technical College for the Province of Ontario is not only likely to prove beneficial and successful, but is an obvious and growing necessity.

37. It may, nevertheless, be asked: what particular classes of our population are likely to be benefitted by the projected School of Technology? We have in part anticipated a reply to this question in what we have already stated. It may, however, be desirable briefly to enumerate the various professions and callings which it is designed practically to benefit by the proposed Institution. They may, (following the classification at the Yale Scientific School,) be grouped together as follows:—

(1) *Civil Engineers.*—Those who have to do with the construction of Roads and Bridges, Railways, Acqueducts, Reservoirs, Drainage Systems and public works in general.

(2) *Mechanical Engineers.*—With reference to the superintendence of Manufactories, Workshops, Machine Shops, Railways, the invention and construction of Machinery, the applications of Steam, etcetera.

(3) *Mining Engineers.*—With reference to the development of the Mineral wealth of the Country, the superintendence of Mines.

(4) *Metallurgists and Assayers.*—Those who have to do with the analysis of Iron, Lead, Copper, Gold and Silver Ores.

(5) *Chemists.*—With reference to Agriculture, Manufactures, Pharmacy and various commercial pursuits.

(6) *Physicians and Sanitary Advisers.*—In certain preparatory studies in Physics, Chemistry, Botany, etcetera.

(7) *Men of Science.*—Either as Professors, Teachers, Explorers, Investigators, etcetera.

XVIII. *Value of Such Schools Elsewhere.*

38. Quoting from a later Writer on this subject he says:—With the development of the Natural Sciences and the growth of the constructive Arts, Natural Science long ago gained a place in the Curricula of the great Universities of Europe; and afterwards special Schools were founded for teaching the applications of Science to the Arts. In France the Ecole des Ponts et Chaussées, originally started in 1747, as a Drawing School, was organized in 1760 for the training of Engineers. In the States of Germany, a number of similar Schools were organized early in the present century. In America the Renselaer Polytechnic Institute, the pioneer in technical Education, was founded in 1824, and was the only School devoted to applied Science until the

forties, when Joseph Sheffield and Abbot Lawrence established the Schools of Science that bear their names, in connection, respectively, with Yale and Harvard Universities. With the development of Railroads, which dates from the thirties, and of manufacturing, which began in the United States but a few years earlier, urgent need was felt for Schools which should fit younger men to grapple with the problems which the new industries offered.*

It is not necessary in this Report to refer except briefly to the invaluable results which have flowed in Europe from the establishment of such Schools. In England, (without referring to the newer departments of Science in the National Universities, and other valuable Science Education agencies), the Department of Science and Art, and its latest development, (as a great School of Observation), of the South Kensington Museum, have given an immense impetus to Industrial Education and Instruction in practical Science in all the large Cities and Towns of the three Kingdoms. In Prussia, Switzerland and other parts of the Continent of Europe, the progress in this direction has been of late years greater than in the Mother Country. But the recent work by Mr. Scott Russell, shewing the present unsatisfactory state of Technical Science and Instruction in Great Britain, (as compared with its higher development in other parts of Europe), has stimulated scientific men in Britain; and there is no doubt that the next few years will witness a vast improvement in this respect.†

39. During our recent visit to the United States we made particular inquiries into the value and results to the community of the establishment of Technical Schools in that Country. The replies received from the Authorities of those Institutions which had been long enough in existence to render any appreciable service were most gratifying. They furnished us in most cases with details showing where and how their Students and Graduates were employed after they had left the Institution concerned. Numbers of them were Professors, Assistant Professors and Instructors elsewhere; many were employed by the Federal and State Governments on Explorations in the distant Territories and in Surveys elsewhere; numbers more were employed on Railways, in Manufactories, in Mining, Assaying and in Public Works requiring the highest Engineering skill. On this latter part, one fact was mentioned which practically illustrated

* In an Act passed by the Legislature of Nova Scotia in 1907, a Section provides that · "There shall be established in Halifax, an Institution for the purpose of affording facilities for Scientific Research and Instruction and professional training in Civil, Mining, Mechanical, Chemical, Metallurgical and Electrical Engineering or any other departments which may from time to time be added."

Mr. F. H. Sexton, the Director of Technical Education in Nova Scotia, referring to this Act says that while the benefits to the Province that will accrue from the Nova Scotia Technical College will be great and lasting, the benefits to the individual will be probably much more, from the Secondary Technical Schools which have been established under the " Act Relating to Technical Education. ' It is the aim of these Schools to bring Scientific Education of a practical nature directly to the Workingman and his children because they are usually unable to leave their homes to secure instruction which will increase their knowledge and help to secure them promotion in their chosen calling. This year there are in the Province three classes of such Schools namely :—Coal Mining Schools, Engineering Schools, and Local Technical Schools. All the classes are now held in the evening, and are especially adapted to the needs of men working in the daytime, and to the industrial needs of the locality in which they exist. The Government of Nova Scotia has thus started a system of Technical Education on broad, comprehensive, simple lines, and is prepared to follow it up as far as reasonably warranted by the increasing need of the people for it.—F. H. SEXTON.

† Since this Report was written, I have had occasion to refer to the subject of the promotion of Scientific and Technical Education in this Province. In a letter on the subject, written to the Toronto papers in 1901, I thus referred to the great advance which Germany has made in this direction. I said :—It was not until the return of English Scientific Experts from a semi-professional visit to various Cities in Germany in 1896 that the movement in favor of a more diffused system of higher Scientific Training took form in England. So strongly impressed were these men of Science, (Sir Philip Magnus and his Colleagues), with the result of their enquiries, that they embodied their observations on the subject in the form of a Report to the Duke of Devonshire, Lord President of the Council, and head of the English Education Department.

The Scientific Experts, to whom I have referred, state in their Report that, as far back as fifty years ago, Germany began to prepare herself for the coming industrial struggle in Europe of to-day. It was her belief in the future application of Chemistry to industrial purposes, that led to the creation and equipment at a great cost, of Chemical Laboratories, as the dependence of her industries on the researches of chemical experts in the factories and works was universally recognized. In one of these works alone, one hundred scientifically trained Chemists, and thirty Engineers are employed.

The Report goes on to state that the brilliant achievements of Germany in the field of Chemical industries have encouraged her to establish well-equipped Electrical Laboratories. Sir Philip Magnus and his Associates declare that there are no Laboratories in England which can compare in detail and completeness of equipment with those of Darmstadt and Stuttgart; and no facilities exist in that Country for original and independent research, in physical subjects, to be compared with those afforded in the Imperial Physical Institute at Charlottenberg. In addition to a new building at Nusenberg, a range of Laboratories and Class-rooms for lectures, devoted to chemical technology, has also been erected at a cost of $250,000; at Stuttgart a similar erection, in connection with its Museum, has cost $1,000,000; and lately, a new group of Buildings has been erected there, for the practical study of pure Chemistry, and training in Electro-technology, at a further cost—with additions to the Building—of $875,000. At Darmstadt, a reconstructed Building, for similar purposes, has cost $600,000, while the Technical High School of Charlottenberg, at Berlin, will cost, when completed, $2,250,000.

the great value of such Schools. The planning and construction of the great Suspension Bridge, which it is designed to throw across the East River, at New York, to connect that City with Brooklyn, have been confided solely to the Engineering skill of the Graduates of the Rensselaer Polytechnic Institute, at Troy, New York. The Chief Engineer of that extensive work, (Mr. W. A. Roebling), and all his Assistants are from that one Institution; and they have, we understand, fully and satisfactorily solved the problem of the practicability of that great work. Of the other Graduates of that and other Schools, we learned that they were employed in all the National undertakings requiring Engineering skill. They are also employed as State Geologists, Surveyors-General of States, Engineers of Railways, Superintendents of Iron Works, Manufactories, etcetera. The development of American talent and ingenuity may be gathered from the fact that the number of Patents for Inventions issued by the Department at Washington each year is about 10,000!

XIX. *Necessity for a School of Technology for Ontario.*

40. No one who has attentively studied the educational progress which we have made during the last ten years, or carefully watched the development of the material resources and manufacturing industries of this Province, but must have been painfully struck with the fact that, while we have liberally provided for the merely intellectual wants of our people, we have almost entirely neglected making any provision for training, and then turning to practical account that superior scientific and industrial skill among ourselves, which in other Countries contribute so largely and effectively to develop their Physical and Industrial resources. We have hitherto been content to receive our supply of such skilled Assistance from abroad; and we have left to European and American Institutions the duty of the development of Canadian talent and ability of such of our youths as have enterprise and means enough to go abroad to acquire that practical knowledge of the Industrial Arts, which we deny to them in their native land.

41. In this respect our American neighbours furnish a favourable contrast, and display their usual national sagacity. In their great industrial and manufacturing centres, they have established Institutions devoted to Industrial Science and Education. Nor have they been content with a meagre provision in this respect. In the small State of Massachusetts, (with a population in 1870 of 1,457,000), they have already established three such Institutions as the Government now propose to establish in this Province. In the neighbouring State of New York, they have no less than four Schools of Technology, (more or less extensive), one of which was established nearly fifty years ago. The result has been that in all of their great Civil, Military, Engineering and Industrial and Mining projects, they have always been able to command the best skill and talent among themselves; and that talent always receives a sufficient encouragement by being constantly employed, either in the service of the State, or in the great Railway, Mining, or Industrial, enterprises which are so largely developed and encouraged in the United States.

42. As to our own Country, some may doubtingly ask: what need is there that we, (a young Country), should provide for instruction in the Industrial and Mechanical Arts? To this we reply, that the almost unconscious development among ourselves of the Manufacturing interests of the Country has reached a magnitude and importance that it would be suicidal to those interests, (in these days of keen competition with our American neighbours), and injurious to their proper development, not to provide without delay for the production among ourselves of a class of skilled Machinists, Manufacturers, Engineers, Chemists and others. No one can visit any of the industrial centres which have sprung up in different parts of the Country and in our larger Towns, without being struck with their value and importance, and the number and variety of the skilled Labourers employed. Inquiry into the source of supply of this Industrial class reveals the fact, that, from the youngest Employé up to the Foreman

of the Works, they are almost entirely indebted to the British Isles, to the United States and other Countries for that supply.

43. If you pursue your inquiries further, and ask what provision is made in the Schools of the Town, or other establishments in the County for instructing young Lads in the elements of Mechanics, Chemistry and Natural Philosophy, and thus preparing them in some degree for supplying the natural demand created in these Establishments? you will find that there has been little done of a practical nature in this direction; and that these subjects have been allowed to occupy a subordinate place in the Course of Study in the Public Schools. There are exceptions, of course, in some Schools, but not to any great extent.* We are glad to find that this will be no longer the case; but that, influenced by a knowledge of the facts which we have stated, provision has been made in the New School Bill, for giving due prominence to these important subjects in all of our High Schools.

44. As a fitting sequel to this provision in the High Schools, for developing the taste and stimulating the desire of our youths to prepare themselves for industrial pursuits, is the proposal to establish a School of Technology. Such an Institution will supply a great desideratum; and, with the elementary training now proposed in our High Schools, will enable us to provide within ourselves for the supply which the Manufacturing Establishments that have grown up in the Country, so imperatively demand. A Boy, who in his School career shows a Mechanical turn, or Scientific taste, will no longer have to seek its higher development outside of our own Country, or, from want of means, leave it ungratified. He will now have provided, almost at his own door, an Institution which will be admirably fitted to give the freest scope to his talent and genius in this particular direction.

45. Rising up above this mere local view of the question, other broader and more comprehensive ones force themselves upon our attention. Are we not conscious of the extraordinary Scientific and Industrial progress of the present day? Do we not hope for, and predict under God's providence, a great future for this Country? Have we not in the assertion of our incipient nationality, entered the lists of industrial competition with the United States, and even with England and other Countries? And do we not, therefore, require to make, without delay some provision for training that class of our young men, who must in the future take the leading part in that competition? The wonderful progress of the Mechanic Arts, is within the memory of most of us. The marvellous revolution, caused by the practical application of Steam and Telegraphy, (those golden links of Science), to Locomotion, Commerce, Industry, and intercommunication, has so stimulated the inventive genius of man, that we now cease to be astonished at any new discovery; and only await each successive development of Science still more wonderful than the last, to calmly discuss its merits and advantages. In this active race of competition, our Province, (the leading one in the Dominion), cannot stand still. With all of our inventions, we have not yet been able to discover a royal road to learning; and our youth cannot, Minerva-like, spring fully armed into the arena of competitive Science and Skill. We must, therefore, provide liberally for their patient and practical instruction in every grade and department of knowledge, so that, with God's blessing, we shall not fall behind in the great race of national intelligence and progress.

XX. *Recent Important Movements in Great Britain and Ireland in the Direction of Technical Education.*

46. We have, we trust, satisfactorily shown what is being done in the United States to promote Technical Education, and have sought to demonstrate the necessity for our own movement in this direction. We will now endeavour to show what steps

---

* From the last Report of the Chief Superintendent of Education for Ontario, we find that out of 6,500 Pupils in the Grammar Schools, 1,681 were reported in classes of Physical Science, only 885 in Drawing, and 429 in the elements of Mensuration and Surveying.

have recently been taken in Britain the more efficiently to promote Science education in the Mother Country.   From a recent Report of a Committee of the House of Commons, (appointed after the results of the Paris Exhibition of 1867 had demonstrated the comparatively inferior position of England in certain developments of industry), "to inquire into the Provisions for giving Instruction in Theoretical and Applied Science to the Industrial Classes," dated 1868, we find that this whole subject was fully discussed.   8,276 questions were proposed to and answered by Representatives from the Government Departments of Education and Science, the Universities and Colleges, Mechanics' Institutes, Science Schools, and Manufacturing centres of England and Scotland.   (A separate Commission was issued for Ireland, to which we shall presently refer.)   From the Report itself, founded upon this mass of evidence, we make a few extracts to which we would especially invite your attention.   These extracts go to prove most conclusively that it is not from want of "practical experience and manipulative skill," which "are possessed in a pre-eminent degree" by British Artisans, that comparative failure is owing, but to the absence of "scientific training" and thoroughness "elementary education" which latter is so universal among the working populations of Germany and Switzerland.

47. Speaking of the "Relation of Industrial Education to Industrial Progress," the Committee remark:

"The industrial system of the present age is based on the substitution of mechanical for manual power. . . .   The acquisition of Scientific knowledge has been shown by the Witnesses to be only one of the elements of an Industrial education and of Industrial progress. . . .   The other indispensable element of Industrial success is the acquisition of practical experience and manipulative skill.   The evidence given before your Committee places beyond all doubt the fact that these latter acquirements are possessed in a pre-eminent degree by our manufacturing population of every grade, according to their several necessities.   They are obtained in our Factories, our Forges, our Workshops, our Shipyards and our Mines, which in their organization and appliances are the Models which, with a few special exceptions, other Nations have hitherto imitated and followed, but not surpassed."

48. In endeavouring, therefore, to account for the fact that the English Manufacturers and Artisans are surpassed by their Continental rivals, the Report goes on to discuss the whole question in the following striking language:—

"Although the pressure of foreign competition, where it exists, is considered by some Witnesses to be partly owing to the superior scientific attainments of foreign Manufacturers, yet the general result of the evidence proves that it is to be attributed mainly to their artistic taste, to fashion, to lower wages, and to the absence of trade disputes abroad, and to the greater readiness with which Handicraftsmen abroad, in some Trades adapt themselves to new requirements. . . . .   Only two Witnesses from Birmingham, the one. an eminent Merchant, the other a manufacturing Jeweller, and Mr. Gill, a Woollen Manufacturer, of Innerleithen, in Scotland, attribute the loss of certain trades to the superior skill, appliances and education of the German, Belgian and American Manufacturers; and the great steel works of Krupp, in Westphalia, have been named as the only instance of a Factory which is said to possess an organization superior to that of any Establishment in the same branch of industry in this Country."

At the same time, nearly every Witness speaks of the extraordinary rapid progress of Continental Nations in Manufactures, and attributes that rapidity, not to the Model Workshops which are met with in some foreign Countries, and are but an indifferent substitute for our own great Factories, and for those which are rising up in every part of the Continent of Europe; but, besides other causes, to the scientific training of the Proprietors and Managers in France, Switzerland, Belgium and Germany, and to the elementary instruction which is universal amongst the working population of Germany and Switzerland.   There can be no doubt, from the evidence of Mr. Mundella, of Professor Fleeming Jenkin, Mr. Kitson, and others, and from the numerous reports of competent observers, that the facilities for acquiring a knowledge of theoretical and applied Science are incomparably greater on the continent of Europe than in this Country, and that such knowledge is based on an advanced state of secondary education.

All the Witnesses concur in desiring similar advantages of education for this Country, and are satisfied that nothing more is required, and that nothing less will suffice, in order that we may retain the position which we now hold in the van of all Industrial Nations.   All are of opinion that it is of incalculable importance economically that our

Manufacturers and Managers of Industrial Establishments should be thoroughly instructed in the principles of their Arts.

They are convinced that a knowledge of the principles of Science on the part of those who occupy the higher Industrial ranks, and the possession of elementary instruction by those who hold subordinate positions, would tend to promote Industrial progress by stimulating improvement, preventing costly and unphilosophical attempts at impossible inventions, diminishing waste, and obviating, in a great measure, ignorant opposition to salutary changes.

Whilst all the Witnesses concurred in believing that the economical necessity for general and Scientific Education is not yet fully realized by the Country, some of them consider it essential that the Government should interfere much more actively than it has done hitherto, to promote the establishment of Scientific Schools and Colleges in our great Industrial centres."

49. As to the "conclusions" at which the members of the Committee arrived, we give them in their own words, as follows:—

The evidence which has been given before your Committee, and in part summarized in the preceding pages, together with the information which is accessible to them in common with other members of the community, has convinced them:

(1) That with the view to enable the working class to benefit by Scientific Instruction, it is of the utmost importance that efficient elementary instruction should be within the reach of every child.

(2) That unless regular attendance of the children for a sufficient period can be obtained, little can be done in the way of their Scientific Instruction.

(3) That elementary instruction in Drawing, in Physical Geography, and in the Phenomena of Nature, should be given in elementary Schools.

(4) That adult Science Classes, although of great use to Artizans, to Foremen, and to the smaller Manufacturers, cannot provide all the Scientific Instruction which those should possess who are responsible for the conduct of important Industrial undertakings. That all whose necessities do not oblige them to leave School before the age of 14, should receive instruction in the elements of Science as part of their general education.

(5) That the re-organization of secondary instruction, and the introduction of a larger amount of Scientific teaching into secondary schools, are urgently required, and ought to receive the immediate consideration of Parliament and the Country.

(6) That it is desirable that certain Endowed Schools should be selected in favourable situations, for the purpose of being reconstituted as Science Schools.

(7) That superior Colleges of Science, and Schoos for special Scientific Instruction requiring costly Buildings and Laboratories, cannot be supported by Fees alone, without aid from one or more of the following sources, namely, the State, the localities, and endowments or other benefactions.

(8) That such Colleges and Special Schools are most likely to be successful if established in centres of Industry, because the choice of such centres tends to promote the combination of Science with practice on the part both of the Professors and of the Pupils.

(9) That the Provinces of England, especially the Agricultural Districts, have not received a sufficient proportion of the State grants for Scientific Education.

(10) (Local.)

(11) That some slight addition to the emoluments of Science Teachers would probably tend materially to promote the establishment and permanence of elementary Science Classes.

(12) (Local.)

(13) That the Managers of Training Colleges for the Teachers of elementary Schools should give special attention to the instruction of those Teachers in theoretical and applied Science, where such instruction does not exist already.

(14) That Teachers in elementary Day Schools should be paid on results for teaching Science to the older Scholars, in the same way as payment is now made for Drawing in such Schools. That the education of higher Science Teachers should be encouraged, by the granting of Degrees in Science at Oxford and Cambridge, as at other Universities, and by the opening of a greater number of Fellowships to distinction in Natural Science, as well as in Literature, and Mathematical and Moral Science."

50. From the same Report, and from the evidence of Doctor Lyon Playfair, contained in that Report, we learn that "in Scotland, where the superior Primary Instruction of the Artizans removes one of the obstacles to their acquiring Scientific

Instruction, the Watt Institution of Edinburgh, and the Andersonian University of Glasgow, have rendered good service, the former during nearly half a century, the latter for more than 20 years; they can boast amongst their Scholars such names as those of Nasmyth, James Young, and many others."

51. Doctor Playfair says:—

"The four Scotch Universities for very many years have given much more Science Instruction than the Universities in England, and the effect of that has been that they have got a great hold of the population; there are more University Students in proportion to the population in Scotland than there are in any other part of the world; there is one University Student for every 866 of the Scotch population, while there is only one University Student for every 5,445 of the population in England; and one University Student to every 2,894 of the population in Ireland, so that it will be seen that we have got in Scotland much more hold of the people on account, I believe, mainly of our teaching subjects which relate to their future vocations in life. We have lately in Edinburgh established a Professorship of Engineering, and one also of Agriculture. We had an old foundation of Agriculture, and we have now put it on an efficient footing. For the first time I believe, in the history of British Colleges we have established Degrees in Technical Science equal in rank to that of Masters of Arts, or Doctor of Medicine, or Bachelor of Law; our new Degrees being applicable to Agriculture, Engineering and Veterinary Surgery.

52. From the "Report of a Commission on Science and Art in Ireland," dated in 1869, we learn that in that Country a "College of Science" had been recently established. The object of this College is to afford "a complete and thorough course of instruction in those branches of Science which are more immediately connected with and applied to all descriptions of Industry, including Agriculture, Mining and Manufactures; that it should in this way supplement the elementary Scientific Instruction already provided for by the Science Schools of the Department; and that it should assist in the training of Teachers for these Schools."

53. From the same Report we condense the following summary of the latest Regulations (1869) of the Science and Art Department for the promotion of education in those subjects in the United Kingdom:—

The action of the Science and Art Department is to aid instruction in Science in the following subjects:—1, practical, plane and solid Geometry; 2, Machine construction and Drawing; (3), Building construction, or Naval Architecture and Drawing; 4, elementary Mathematics; 5, higher Mathematics; 6, theoretical Mechanics; 7, applied Mechanics; 8, Acoustics, Light and Heat; 9, Magnetism and Electricity; 10, Inorganic Chemistry: 11 Organic Chemistry; 12, Geology; 13. Mineralogy; 14, Animal Physiology; 15, Zoology; 16, Vegetable Physiology and Economic Botany; 17, Systematic Botany; 18, Mining; 19, Metallurgy; 20, Navigation; 21, Nautical Astronomy; 22, Steam; 23, Physical Geography. And in Art in:—(1) elementary Drawing as an education of the power of observation, and (2) Drawing, Painting, Modelling, and designing for Manufacture and Decoration.

As respects Science, the aid consists of—

(a) Public examinations, in which Queen's Medals and Queen's Prizes are awarded, are held at all places complying with certain conditions.

(b) Payments on results to Teachers, as tested by Examination.

(c) Scholarships and Exhibitions.

(d) Building Grants.

(e) Grants towards the purchase of Apparatus, etcetera.

The Examinations are held in May by the local Committees. The Examination Papers are prepared by the professional Examiners in London, and are sent to the local Secretary; one evening is set apart for each subject, so that the Examination in each subject is simultaneous.

Payments are made to the Teachers on the results of the May examination. Any Person may qualify to earn payments on results—

(a) By obtaining a First, or Second, Class in the advanced grade of the Class Examination; or,

(b) By taking Honours.

	1867.				1868.			
	England	Ireland	Scotland	Total.	England	Ireland	Scotland	Total.
Number of Science Schools...	150	53	9	212	210	76	15	301
Number of persons under instruction	6,441	2,125	1,664	10,230	9,480	2,870	2,611	14,961
Number of persons examined.	3,288	1,409	223	4,920	5,077	1,714	360	7,161
Number of papers worked....	5,933	1,895	385	8,213	9,843	2,813	457	13,113
Amount paid to Teachers*....	£5,513	£2,017	£446	£7,976	£8,455	£3,269	£381	£12,105
Number of Teachers qualified to earn payments engaged..	138	50	12	200	206	75	12	293

There are two forms of Scholarship in connection with Elementary Schools.

1st. In the *Elementary School Scholarship*, £5 are granted to the Managers of any Elementary School for the support of a deserving Pupil, selected by competition, if they undertake to support him for a year and subscribe £5 for that purpose. The payment of £5 by the Science and Art Department is conditional on the Scholar passing in some branch of Science at the May examination.

2nd. *The Science and Art Scholarship* is of a more advanced character, and does not depend on any corresponding contribution on the part of the locality. A Grant of £10 is made towards the maintenance, for one year, of the most deserving Pupil, or Pupils, in Elementary Schools who have passed certain examinations in Science and in Drawing.

In both of these cases the Scholar must be from twelve to sixteen years of age, and one Scholarship is allowed per 100 Pupils in the School.

The Exhibitions are:—

1st. *Local Exhibitions*, for advanced Scientific Instruction, to enable Students to complete their education at some College, or School, where Scientific Instruction of an advanced character may be obtained. Grants of £25 per annum for one, or two, or three, years are made for this purpose, when the locality raises a like sum by voluntary subscriptions. And if the Student attend a State School, such as the Royal School of Mines in London, the Royal College of Chemistry in London, or Royal College of Science in Ireland, the fees are remitted. The Exhibition must be awarded in competition.

2nd. *Royal Exhibitions* of the value of £50 per annum, tenable for three years, to the Royal School of Mines, London, and the Royal College of Science, Dublin, are given in competition at the May examinations. Six are awarded each year—three to each Institution. Free admissions are also given to all Gold Medallists.

Besides these the *Whitworth Scholarships*, of the value of £100 per annum, tenable for two or three years, are also given in competition at the May Examinations.

A Grant in aid of a new Building, or for the adaption of an existing Building, for a School of Science may be made at a rate not exceeding 2s. 6d. per square foot of internal area, up to a maximum of £500 for any one School, provided that the School—

(a) Be built under the Public Libraries Act;

(b) Be built in connection with a School of Art, aided by a Department Building grant;

And certain other conditions.

A Grant towards the purchase of Apparatus, Diagrams, etcetera, of 50 per cent. of the cost of them, is made to Science Schools.

As respects Art the aid is:—

Firstly. Towards the teaching of elementary Drawing in Schools for the poor This aid consists of payments to the Managers of Schools instructed by Teachers certificated for Drawing (a), of 1s., 2s. or 3s., on account of children who pass a very elementary, or "first grade," Examination; (b), of 5s. or 10s. for children, or Pupil Teachers, who pass the more advanced, or "second grade," Examination; and (c), of Prizes to successful children and Pupil Teachers.

The "first grade" consists of free hand Drawing in Outline from Flat Examples, Drawing from regular Solids, or objects of simple form, and of easy problems in practical Geometry.

* This is the amount up to the present time, all the claims not having yet been paid.

The second grade Examination is of a higher standard than that of the first grade, but in the same subjects, with the addition of Perspective and Mechanical Drawing. Examinations are held in May, in any Elementary School, taught by a Master, holding a Certificate for Drawing, or who has passed a second grade Examination in any of the above three subjects of Drawing.

Secondly,—Towards Art Instruction in night classes for Artisans, held in Elementary Schools, in Literary, Mechanics' or similar, Institutions. This aid consists of payments to the Managers of £10 or £15 on account of Artisans, or their children, above twelve years of age, taught Drawing of the second or third grades, by Certificated Teachers; of Prizes to successful Students; and of payments towards the local expenses of Examination.

The "third grade" is represented by works embracing the whole course of instruction in night Classes, or Schools of Art, such as Drawing from Examples, from Casts, or Models, from Nature, the Antique, or the Life; Painting, Flowers, Landscape, or from Life; Designing, or Drawing for Decorative purposes.

Thirdly,—to Schools of Art being held in a Room entirely devoted to Art Instruction. This aid consists of similar payments to the Managers to those awarded to night Classes, and of the following additional payments:—

20s. on account of every Artisan satisfactorily instructed in Art.

£15, or £30 on account of Art Pupil-Teachers.

£5, or £10 on account of Students trained for Art Teachers, or national Art-scholars.

£3, on account of free Studentships to Artisans, submitting advanced works.

£10, on account of expenses of annual Report and Examination.

Prizes are given to successful Students, and the advanced Studies of the Schools of Art are brought together in a national competition, when gold, silver and bronze Medals, and other Prizes, are awarded. All payments are contingent on the employment of Certificated Teachers.

Elementary Schools, Night Classes, and Schools of Art, are aided to the extent of 75 per cent. in the purchase of examples.

Grants are made in aid of building Schools of Art.

Fourthly,—By the maintenance of the National Art Training School, at South Kensington, in which highly qualified Students from local Schools of Art, are admitted and trained as Masters for Schools of Art, or as Designers, or Art-workmen. Such Students receive an allowance for their support of from 15s. to 40s. weekly.

Fifthly,—Through the National Museum of Decorative Art and at the National Art Library, which are made as far as possible, circulating collections for the benefit of local Schools of Art.

Number of Schools to which Grants were made in—

	England.	Ireland.	Scotland.
Schools of Art....................................	80	5	9
Night Classes...................................	59	2	2
Elementary Schools..............................	500	29	59

Payments on the Results of Art Examinations, 1867.

	England.			Ireland.			Scotland.		
	£	s.	d.	£	s.	d.	£	s.	d.
Schools of Art....................................	4,701	11	7	235	6	1	875	9	1½
Night Classes...................................	658	12	10¾	53	5	0	35	6	9½
Elementary Schools..............................	2,650	18	0	136	10	0	293	14	0

54. Such are the encouragements, in the Mother Country, to Scientific Education. We forbear to enter into further details in regard to the condition and progress of Industrial Science in other parts of Europe. Germany, supreme in the art and appli-

ances of War, is fast becoming the Workshop of Europe. Even in these other Countries, where the physical labour is abundant, Science in its application to the Mechanic Arts, is felt to be not so much a labour-saving as a labour-multiplying power. It is, therefore, to a new Country, a substitution in part for immigration of a most valuable and substantial kind, and one which should be stimulated in every possible way. It is estimated that in the United States alone, Steam and Water applied to Machinery, is equivalent to the power of one hundred millions of men! The results of labour, under such circumstances, becomes less dependent upon physical effort, than on the skill and ability of the Workman in the use of Tools and Mechanical contrivances. The question of Technical Education, is therefore not an open and debatable one. It is a national necessity.

55. We trust that the information which we have collected and embodied in this Report, will put the Goverment in possession of all the facts which they desire to obain in regard to Schools of Technology in the United States.

TORONTO, January, 1871.   J. GEORGE HODGINS,
                                  ALEXANDER T. MACHATTIE, } Commissioners.

I. COURSE OF STUDY IN THE MASSACHUSETTS INSTITUTE OF TECHNOLOGY, BOSTON, 1870-71.

The Massachusetts Institute of Technology was chartered in 1861, and was first opened to Students in 1865. Its claims to recognition as a leader in the development of Technical Education may perhaps be summarized as follows:—It was the first School in the world to institute laboratory instruction in Physics and Chemistry to Students in large classes as a part of the regular Course of each Candidate for a Degree; the first to equip a Mining and Metallurgical Laboratory for the instruction of Students by actual treatment, of ores in large quantities; the first to establish a Laboratory for testing the strength of materials of construction in commercial sizes; and the first in America to establish a department of Architecture. Later still it was the first School in America to establish distinct and Specialized Courses of Study in Electrical Engineering, in Chemical Engineering and in Naval Architecture.

It is a College of general Technology, embracing almost every branch of study which finds application in the Arts. There are thirteen distinct Courses of Study:— Civil and Topographical Engineering, Mechanical Engineering, Mining Engineering and Metallurgy, Architecture, Chemistry, Electrical Engineering, Biology, Physics, General Studies, Chemical Engineering, Sanitary Engineering, Geology and Naval Architecture.

Thus, at the Boston Institute of Technology there are not only Professors of Civil Engineering and of Mechanical Engineering, but Professors of Mechanism, Steam Engineering, Railroad Engineering, Highway Engineering, Hydraulic Engineering, Topographical Engineering, etcetera. Again, the chemical staff of twenty-four Persons is distributed over General Chemistry, Analytical Chemistry, Organic Chemistry, Industrial Chemistry, and Sanitary Chemistry. There are separate Laboratories for Water Analysis, for Food Analysis, for Gas Analysis, for Dyeing, Bleaching, etcetera.

The second characteristic of the Institute is the predominance of Laboratory, Shop, and Field Practice, Experiment and Research. These are used wherever it is found practicable to supplement, illustrate, or emphasize, the work of the Recitation, or Lecture Room.

It is now generally recognized that a complete system of Industrial Education should consist of three parts:—First, Manual Training Schools, for developing the eye and hand, not with the object of producing Artizans, but for training alone; Second, Trade Schools for special training in the technique of the different Trades; Third, higher Technical Schools for the fundamental principles of the Sciences, and fitting men in the broadest way to become leaders in the application of the Sciences to the Arts.

The Massachusetts Institute of Technology at Boston, provides a four years' Course of Scientific and Literary Studies and practical Exercises, embracing pure and applied Mathematics, the Physical and Natural Sciences with their applications, Drawing, the English Language, Mental and Political Science, French and German. The Course is so selected and arranged as to offer a liberal and practical education in preparation for active pursuits, as well as a thorough training for the professions of the Civil and Mechanical Engineer, Chemist, Metallurgist, Engineer of Mines, Architect, and Teacher of Science. All the Studies and exercises of the first and second years are pursued by the whole School. At the beginning of the third year, each Student selects one of the following special Courses of Study: —

1. A COURSE IN MECHANICAL ENGINEERING.
2. A COURSE IN CIVIL AND TOPOGRAPHICAL ENGINEERING.
3. A COURSE IN CHEMISTRY.
4. A COURSE IN GEOLOGY AND MINING ENGINEERING.
5. A COURSE IN BUILDING AND ARCHITECTURE.
6. A COURSE IN SCIENCE AND LITERATURE.

CONDITIONS OF THE ADMISSION OF STUDENTS.

To be admitted to the first year's class the student must have attained the age of sixteen years, and must pass a satisfactory examination in arithmetic, so much of algebra as precedes equations of the second degree, plane geometry, English grammar and geography. In general, the training given at the best High Schools, Academies, and Classical Schools, will be a suitable preparation for the studies of this School.

In order to enter the second year's class, the student must be at least seventeen years of age, and must pass a satisfactory examination upon the first year's studies, besides passing the examination for admission to the first year's class; and a like rule applies to the case of students seeking admission into the classes of the succeeding years.

Graduates of Colleges will, in general, be presumed to have the requisite attainments for entering the third year as regular students, and may do so on satisfying the department they purpose to enter that they are prepared to pursue their studies to advantage.

A knowledge of the Latin language is not required for admission; but the study of Latin is strongly recommended to persons who propose to enter this School.

ELEMENTARY COURSE OF INSTRUCTION.—FIRST YEAR.

Mathematics.—Algebra, beginning with Quadratic Equations and including Logarithms. Solid Geometry. Mensuration. Plane Trigonometry. Applications of Trigonometry to Navigation.

Physics.—Sound. Heat.

Chemistry.—Experimental study of General Inorganic Chemistry.

English.—Composition. History and Structure of the Language.

French.—Grammar and Translation.

German.—Grammar and Translation.

Descriptive Geometry.—Problems of position relative to the Point, the Right Line and the Plane.

Mechanical Drawing.—Use of Instruments, Water-colors and India-ink. Graphical construction of problems in Geometry, Trigonometry and Descriptive Geometry.

Free-hand Drawing.—With Chalk and Crayons. Machinery. Ornamentation.

ELEMENTARY COURSE OF INSTRUCTION.—SECOND YEAR.

Mathematics.—Spherical Trigonometry. Analytic Geómetry of two and three dimensions. First Principles of the Differential and Integral Calculus.

Descriptive Astronomy.—The Earth. The Sun. Time. Gravitation. The Moon. Planets. Comets. Nebulæ Constellations.

Surveying.—Field Work. Plotting Surveys. Computing Areas. Plans.

Physics.—Light. Magnetism. Electricity.

Chemistry.—Qualitative Analysis. Organic Chemistry.

English.—Composition. Reading. History of the Language.

French.—Grammar and Translation.

German.—Grammar and Translation.

Descriptive Geometry.—Projections, Perspective, Shades and Shadows.

Mechanical Drawing.—Goemtric, Perspective, and Isometric Drawing.

Free-hand Drawing.—Machinery. Ornamentation. Landscape.

1.—COURSE IN MECHANICAL ENGINEERING.

Machinery.—Cinematics. Principles of Mechanism. Measurement of the Dynamic Effect of Machines. Regulating Apparatus, as Brakes, Fly-Wheels, Governors, etcetera. Friction and Rigidity. Materials, Construction, and Srength of Machinery. Action of Cutting Tools.

Mathematics.—Differential and Integral Calculus. Analytic Mechanics.

Applied Mechanics.—Dynamics of Solids. Hydrostatics and Hydrodynamics. Thermodynamics.

Descriptive Geometry.—Applications to Masonry, Carpentry, and Machinery.

Metallurgy.—Metallurgical Processes, Constructions and Implements.

Drawing.—Machinery.

Physics.—Laboratory Practice.

Geology.—Physiographic Geology. Lithology. Outline of Geographical History. Dynamical Geology.

English.—Logic. Rhetoric. History of English Literature.

Constitutional History.—England and the United States.

French.—(Spanish may be substituted.) Grammar and Translation.

German.—Grammar and Translation.

II.—COURSE IN CIVIL AND TOPOGRAPHICAL ENGINEERING.

Engineering.—Survey, Location, and Construction of Roads, Railways, and Canals. Measurement and Computation of Earthwork and Masonry. Supply and Distribution of Water. Drainage. Hpdrographical Surveying. River and Harbor Improvements. Field Practice.

Topography.—As practised by the United States. Coast Survey.

Mathematics.—Differential and Integral Calculus. Analytic Mechanics.

Applied Mechanics.—Stress. Stability, Strength, and Stiffness.

Spherical Astronomy.—Higher Goedesy. Latitude and Longtitude.

Descriptive Geometry.—Applications to Masonry and Carpentry.

Drawing.—Plans, Profiles, Elevations, Sections, etcetera.

Physics.—Laboratory Practice.

Geology.—Physiographic Geology. Lithology. Outline of Geological History. Dynamical Geology.

English.—Logic. Rhetoric. History of English Literature.

Constitutional History.—England and the United States.

French.—(Spanish may be substituted.) Grammar and Translation.

German.—Grammar and Translation.

III.—COURSE IN CHEMISTRY.

Industrial Chemistry.—Study of Chemical Manufactures. Glass, Pottery, Soda-ash. Acids, Soap, Gas, etcetera. The Arts of Dyeing, Calico Printing, Tanning, Brewing, Distilling, etcetera.

Metallurgy.—Metallurgical Processes, Constructions, and Implements.

Assaying.—Wet and Dry Ways.

Descriptive and Determinative Mineralogy.—Use of the Blowpipe.

Note. The foregoing Studies are elective. Each Student must select one, or more, of them. The following Studies are required :—

Quantitative Chemical Analysis.—Laboratory Practice.

Drawing.—Chemical or Metallurgical Apparatus. Plans of Works.

Physics.—Laboratory Practice.

Geology.—Physiographic Geology. Lithology. Outline of Geological History. Dynamical Geology.

English.—Logic. Rhetoric. History of English Literature.

Constitutional History.—England and the United States.

French.—(Spanish may be substituted.) Grammar and Translation.

German.—Grammar and Translation.

IV.—COURSE IN MINING ENGINEERING.

Engineering.—Survey and Construction of Roads and Railways, Measurement of Earthwork and Masonry. Hydraulics. Draining. Field Practice.

Descriptive and Determinative Mineralogy.—Use of the Blowpipe.

Assaying.—Wet and Dry Ways.

Quantitative Chemical Analysis.—Laboratory Practice.

Metallurgy.—Metallurgical Processes, Constructions, and Implements. Furnaces, Crucibles, Blowing Machines, Fuels, and Fluxes.

Mathematics.—Differential and Integral Calculus. Analytic Mechanics.

Applied Mechanics.—Stress. Stability, Strength, and Stiffness.

Drawing.—Sections and Maps. Mines. Metallurgical Apparatus.

Physics.—Laboratory Practice.

Geology.—Physiographic Geology. Lithology. Outline of Geological History. Dynamical Geology.

English.—Logic. Rhetoric. History of English Literature.

English.—Logic. Rhetoric. History of English Literature.

Constitutional History.—England and the United States.

French.—(Spanish may be substituted.) Grammar and Translation.

German.—Grammar and Translation.

V.—COURSE IN BUILDING AND ARCHITECTURE.

Architectural Design.—The Elements of Design. The Principles of Composition. Exercises. The Study of Executed Works.

Construction.—Building Materials and Processes. The Study of Works in Progress.

Drawing.—Plans, Elevations, Sections, and Details. Ornament. Sketching from Buildings.

Mathematics.—Differential and Integral Calculus. Analytic Mechanics.

Applied Mechanics.—Stress, Stability, Strength, and Stiffness.

Descriptive Geometry.—Applications to Masonry and Carpentry.

Geology.—Physiographic Geology. Lithology. Outline of Geological History.

English.—Logic. Rhetoric. History of English Literature.

Constitutional History.—England and the United States.

French.—(Spanish may be substituted.) Grammar and Translation.

German.—Grammar and Translation.

VI.—Course in Science and Literature.

Mathematics.—Differential and Integral Calculus. Analytic Mechanics.

Chemistry.—Quantitative Analysis. Pure and Applied Chemistry.

Physics.—Physical Research.

Architectural Design.—The Elements of Design. The Principles of Composition. Exercises. The Study of Executed Works.

Note. The foregoing Studies are elective. Each Student must select one, or more, of them. He may in addition choose any of the special subjects of the other Professional Courses, such as Descriptive Geometry, Engineering, Spherical Astronomy, Metallurgy, or Mineralogy. The following Studies are required:—

History.—Guizot—Histoire Generale de la Civilisation en Europe.

Drawing.—Subjects determined by each Student's choice of Studies.

Physics.—Laboratory Practice.

Geology.—Physiographic Geology. Lithology. Outline of Geological History. Dynamical Geology.

English.—Logic. Rhetoric. History of English Literature.

Constitutional History.—England and the United States.

French.—(Spanish may be substituted.) Grammar and Translation.

German.—Grammar and Translation.

I.—Fourth Year Course in Mechanical Engineering.

Machines.—Strength and Proportions of the Parts of a Machine. Hand Machinery,—Cranes, Derricks, Pumps, Turn-tables, etcetera.

Motors.—Hydraulic Motors. Water-Wheels. Water-Pressure Engines. Power and and Strength of Boilers. Steam Engines,—Stationary, Locomotive, Marine. Air and Gas Engines.

Building Materials.—Stones, Bricks, Mortars and Cements.

Descriptive Geometry.—Applications to Masonry, Carpentry, and Machinery. Modelling.

Drawing.—Machines. Working Plans and Projects of Machinery, Mills, etcetera.

Political Economy.

Natural History.—Zoölogy, Physiology.

French.—(Italian may be substituted.) Grammar and Translation.

German.—Grammar and Translation.

II.—Fourth Year Course in Civil and Topographical Engineering.

Engineering.—Structures of Wood,—Framing Trusses, Girders, Arches, Roofs, Bridges. Structures of Stone,—Foundations, Retaining Walls, Arches, Bridges. Structures of Iron,—Foundations, Beams, Girders, Columns, Roofs, Bridges. Field Practice.

Physical Hydrography.—As practised by the United States. Coast Survey.

Machinery and Motors.—Hand Machinery. Water-Wheels. Boilers. Steam Engines.

Building Materials.—Stones, Bricks, Mortars, and Cements.

Descriptive Geometry.—Applications to Masonry and Carpentry.

Drawing.—Plans, Profiles, Elevations, Sections, etcetera.

Political Economy.

Natural History.—Zoölogy, Physiology.

French.—(Italian may be substituted.) Grammar and Translation.

German.—Grammar and Translation.

III.—Fourth Year Course in Chemistry.

Chemistry.—Pure and Applied. Quantitative Analysis. Preparation of Chemical Products. Special Researches.

Building Materials.—Stones, Bricks, Mortars, and Cements.
Drawing.—Apparatus. Machinery and Plans of Works.
Political Economy.
Natural History.—Zoölogy and Physiology.
French.—(Italian may be substituted.) Grammar and Translation.
German.—Grammar and Translation.

IV.—Fourth Year Course in Mining Engineering.

Mining.—The Useful Minerals. Modes of Occurrence. Prospecting. Boring, Blasting. Sinking Shafts,—Timbering, Walling, and Tubbing. Driving Levels. Methods of Mining. Ventilation. Lighting. Winding Machinery. Ladders and Man-Engines. Underground Transportation. Pumps. Dressing and Concentration of Ores.—Crushers, Stamps, Washers, Amalgamators, etcetera. Details of American Mining.
Machinery and Motors.—Hand Machinery. Water-wheels. Boilers. Steam-engines.
Engineering.—Structures of Wood, Stone, and Iron. Foundations, Walls, Arches, Domes, Beams, Trusses, Girders, Roofs.
Chemistry.—Quantitative Analysis. Laboratory Practice.
Geology.—Historical Geology. Palæontology. Detailed study of American Geology.
Building Materials.—Stones, Bricks, Mortars, and Cements.
Drawing.—Geological Mamps and Sections. Plans and Sections of Mines, Quarries and other open Workings. Mining Machinery and Implements.
Political Economy.
Natural History.—Zoölogy and Physiology.
French.—(Italian may be substituted.) Grammar and Translation.
German.—Grammar and Translation.

V.—Fourth Year Course in Building and Architecture.

Archiectural Design.—Exercises in Composition. History of Archiecture. The other Arts of Design.
Professional Practice.—Specifications. Contracts. Estimating and Measuring Superintendence.
Drawing.—Architecture, Landscape, and the Human Figure. Lithography and Etching. Modelling. Drawing from Memory.
Engineering.—Structures of Wood, Stone, and Iron. Foundations, Walls, Arches, Domes, Beams, Trusses, Girders, Roofs.
Descriptive Geometry.—Applications. to Masonry and Carpentry.
Warming, Lighting, Ventilating, Acoustics.—Lectures.
Building Materials.—Stones, Bricks, Mortars and Cements.
Political Economy.
Natural History.—Zoölogy and Physiology.
French.—(Italian may be substituted.) Grammar and Translation.
German.—Grammar and Translation.

VI.—Fourth Year Course in Science and Literature.

The Higher Mathematics.
Chemistry.—Special Researches.
Physics.—Special Researches.
Architectural Design.—Exercises in Composition. History of Architecture. The other Arts of Design.

Note. The foregoing Studies are elective. Each Student must select one, or more, of them. He may in addition choose any of the special subjects of the other Professional Courses, such as Machinery and Motors, Descriptive Geometry, Engineering, Mining, or Geology. The following Studies are required:—

Mental Science.
Building Materials.—Stones, Bricks, Mortars, and Cements.
Drawing.—Subjects determined by each student's choice of studies.
Political Economy.
Natural History.—Zoölogy and Physiology.
French.—(Italian may be substituted.) Grammar and Translation.
German.—Grammar and Translation.

II. COURSE OF STUDY IN THE SHEFFIELD SCIENTIFIC SCHOOL OF YALE COLLEGE, NEW HAVEN, CONNECTICUT, 1870-71.

Candidates must be not less than sixteen years of age, and must bring satisfacto·y testimonials of moral character from their former Instructors or other responsible Persons.

For admission the Student must pass a thorough examination in Davies's Bourdon's *Algebra* as far as the General Theory of Equations, or in its equivalent; in *Geometry*, in the nine books of Davies's Legendre, or their equivalent: and in *Plane Trigonometry*, Analytical Trigonometry inclusive; and also in *Arithmetic*, including the "Metric System," *Geography, United States History,* and *English Grammar,* including Spelling. An acquaintance with the *Latin* Language is also required, sufficient to read and construe some Classical Author, and Allen's Latin Grammar is commended as exhibiting the amount of grammatical study deemed important. Practice in *Drawing,* if it can be obtained before entrance, will be of great advantage.

Candidates for advanced standing in the three regular Classes are examined, in addition to the preparatory Studies, in those already pursued by the Class they propose to enter. No one can be admitted as a Candidate for a Degree after the commencement of the Senior year.

The arrangement of the Studies is indicated in the annexed scheme.

Freshman Year—Introductory to all the Courses.

FIRST TERM.—*German*—Whitney's Grammar and Reader. *English*—Marsh's English Language; Exercises in Composition. *Mathematics*—Davies's Anaytical Geometry, and Spherical Trigonometry. *Physics*—Atkinson's Ganot, with experimental Lectures. *Chemistry*—Eliot and Store's Manual; Laboratory practice. *Elementary Drawing*—practical lessons in the Art School. *Laws of Health*—Lectures by Professor F. Bacon.

SECOND TERM.—*Language, Physics, Chemistry, and Drawing*—as stated above. *Mathematics*—Church's Descriptive Geometry.

THIRD TERM.—*Mathematics*—Surveying and Plotting. *Botany*—Gray's Manual. Other studies continued.

In Chemistry and Metallurgy.—Junior Year.

FIRST TERM.—*Chemical Analysis*—Fresenius: Recitations and Lectures. Use of the Blowpipe. *Laboratory Practice*—Qualitative Analysis. *English. German. French.*
SECOND TERM.—*Chemical Philosophy*—Wurtz: Recitations and Lectures. *Laboratory Practice*—Qualitative Analysis, continued. Examination for poisons. Quantitative Analysis, begun. *Zoology.*—Lectures. *English. German. French.*
THIRD TERM.—*Mineralogy*—Dana. Lectures and Practical exercises. *Organic Chemistry*—Lectures. *Zoology*—Lectures and Excursions. *Laboratory Practice*—*Quantative Analysis,* continued. *English and French*—continued

In Chemistry and Metallurgy.—Senior Year.

FIRST TERM.—*Metallurgy*—Percy. Lectures. *Agricultural Chemistry*—Recitation and Lectures. *Geology*—Dana. Lectures and recitations. *Zoology*—Lectures. *Laboratory Practice*—Volumetric and Organic Analysis. *Determinative Mineralogy, English and French*—continued.

SECOND AND THIRD TERMS.—*Metallurgy*—Lectures. *Agricultural Chemistry*—Lectures. *Geology*—Dana. *Anatomy Physiology*—Academical Lectures. *Laboratory Practice*—Mineral Analysis and Assaying. *Determinative Mineralogy.*—*English* and *French*—continued.

In Civil Engineering.—Junior Year.

FIRST TERM.—*Mathematics*—Church's Descriptive Geometry, with applications. Analytical Geometry of Three Dimensions. *Surveying*—Higher Surveying. *English, French and German.*

SECOND TERM.—*Mathematics*—Davies's Shades, Shadows, and Linear Perspective. Church's Differential Calculus. *Astronomy*—Norton's Astronomy, with practical problems. *English, French and German.*

THIRD TERM.—*Mathematics*—Isometrical Projection. Differential and Integral Calculus. Topographical Surveying. *Drawing*—Topographical. *English and French.*

In Civil Engineering.—Senior Year.

FIRST TERM.—*Field Engineering*—Henck's Field Book for Rail Road Engineers. Location of Roads. *Mechanics*—Peck's Elements. Thermo-dynamics. *Military Science*—Lectures. *Geology*—Dana. *Drawing*—Architectural. *Stone Cutting*, with graphical problems. *English and French.*

SECOND TERM.—*Mechanics*—Peck's Elements, continued. Application of Calculus to Mechanics. Principles of Mechanism. Theory of Steam Engine. *Civil Engineering*—Strength of Materials. Bridge Construction. Stability of Arches and Walls. *Military Science*—Lectures. *Geology*—Dana, continued. *Drawing*—Mechanical. *English and French.*

THIRD TERM.—*Mechanics*—Mechanics applied to Engineering. *Hydraulics*—Theory of Turbines and other Water Wheels. *Civil Engineering*—Building Materials (Lectures). Mahan's Civil Engineering. *Mathematics*—Geodetic Surveying. *Drawing*—Structural.

Note. Students who pursue a higher course in Engineering, for one year after graduating as Bachelors, may receive the Degree of Civil Engineer.

In Mechanical Engineering.—Junior Year.

Pure Mathematics—Descriptive Geometry, with applications. Analytical Geometry of three dimensions. Differential and Integral Calculus. *Mechanics*—Analytical Mechanics. Principles of Mechanism. *Drawing*—Shades, Shadows, and Linear Perspective. Elements of Mechanical Drawing and Principles of Construction. Shading and tinting, and drawing from patterns. *Metallurgy. English, French, and German.*

In Mechanical Engineering.—Senior Year.

Applied Mechanics—Strength of Materials. Thermo-dynamics. Theory and construction of the Steam Engine and other prime movers. Theory of Machines. Mill work. Examination of Machinery. Mechanical Construction. Use of Tools. *Drawing*—Drawing from actual Machines. Designs of Machines. *English, French, and German.*

In Natural History.—Junior Year.

Either Geology, Mineralogy, Zoology, or Botany may be made the principal study some attention in each case being directed to the other three branches of Natural History.

FIRST TERM.—*Zoology*—Daily laboratory instruction; Zoological Excursions. *Botany*—Gray's Text Book; Use of the Microscope. *Chemistry*—Academical Lectures. *French*—begun. *German*—continued.

SECOND TERM.—*Zoology and Palæontology*—Laboratory Practice. Lectures. *Botany*—Lectures; Gray's Text Book. *Physical Geography*—Lectures and Recitations. *Chemistry*—Laboratory Practice. *French and German*—continued.

THIRD TERM.—*Zoology and Palæontology*—Laboratory Practice. Lectures. Excursions (Land and Marine). *Botany*—Excursions. Practical Exercises. Gray's Manual. *Mineralogy*—Dana. Lectures. Practical Exercises. *French*—continued. *Drawing*—Free Hand Practice.

In Natural History.—Senior Year.

FIRST TERM.—*Language*—Whitney's Language and the Study of Language. *French* —Selections. *Zoology and Palæontology*—Laboratory Practice. Lectures. Excursions. *Botany*—Excursions. Herbarium Studies. *Geology*—Dana's Manual. Excursions.

SECOND TERM.—*Zoology and Palæontology*—continued. *Botany*—Herbarium—Studies. Botanical Literature. Essays in Descriptive Botany. *Geology*—Dana. Lectures. *Anatomy and Physiology*—Academical Lectures. *French*—Selections. *Whitney on Language*—continued.

THIRD TERM.—*Zoology, Botany, and Palæontology*—continued, with Excursions. *Photography*—Practical instruction.

Note. Besides the regular Courses of Lectures on structural and systematic Zoology and Botany, and on special subjects, Students are taught to prepare, arrange, and identify Collections, to make Dissections, to pursue original investigations, and to describe Genera and Species in the language of Science. For these purposes large collections in Zoology and Palæontology belonging to the College are available, as are also the private Botanical collections of Professor Eaton.

In Preparation for Medical Studies.

Note. During one year the work of this Course will be chiefly under the direction of the Instructors in Chemistry; during the second year under that of the Instructors in Zoology and Botany. In Chemistry especial attention will be given to the examination of Urine and the testing of Drugs and Poisons. Zoology to comparative Anatomy, Reproduction, Embryology, the laws of hereditary descent and human parasites; and in Botany to a general knowledge of structural and physiological Botany, and to Medicinal, food-producing and poisonous Plants. The Studies of the Select Course in Physical Geography, History, English Literature, etcetera, are followed by these Students.

In Studies Preparatory to Mining, and in Select Studies Preparatory to other Higher Pursuits, to Business, etcetera.—Junior Year.

Young men desiring to become Mining Engineers, can pursue the regular Course in Civil, or Mechanical, Engineering, and at its close can spend a fourth year in the study of Metallurgy, Mineralogy, etcetera. Should there be a sufficient number of Students desiring it, a Course of Lectures on the subject of Mining will also be provided.

FIRST TERM.—*Mechanics*—Peck's Elements. *History*—Modern History of Europe, Recitations *and* Lectures. *English* Literature. *German*—Selections. *French*—Fasquelle's Course, and Reader.

SECOND TERM.—*Astronomy*—Norton's Astronomy, with practical problems. *Agricultural Chemistry*—Lectures. *Physical Geography*—Lectures and Recitations. *Zoology* —Lectures. *Botany*—Lectures; Gray's Text Book. *History*—continued. *German*—Selections. *French*—Selections from Classic Authors.

THIRD TERM.—*Botany*—Gray's Text Book. Excursions and practical instruction. Gray's Manual. *Zoology*—Excursions and Lectures. *Mineralogy*—Dana. *Literature* —Study of Classical English Authors. *Drawing*—Free Hand, and Architectural. *French*—Selections.

In Select Studies.—Senior Year.

LANGUAGE.—Whitney's Language and the Study of Language. Hadley's Brief History of the English Language. *French*—continued. Compositions.

NATURAL SCIENCE.—*Botany and Zoology*, continued. *Agricultural*—Lectures. *Agricultural Chemistry and Physiology*—Lectures. *Geology*—Recitations and Lectures. *Human Anatomy and Physiology.*—Lectures. *Astronomy*—Lectures.

PHILOSOPHY AND HISTORY.—Lectures and Recitations in *Military Science, History, Political Philosophy, International Law, Political Economy,* etcetera.

III. NECESSITY FOR INSTRUCTION IN SCIENTIFIC AND TECHNICAL SUBJECTS IN ONTARIO— ILLUSTRATIVE EXAMPLES OF THAT NECESSITY.

At a Meeting of the Canadian Institute of Toronto in February, 1871, Doctor Hodgins briefly showed the necessity of the establishment of the proposed Technological School projected by the Government, and also the advisability of conducting the School entirely apart from any other general, or special Education Establishment for the diffusion of knowledge, and quoted the experience of United States authorities on that Subject.

He said that during a trip through the manufacturing towns and Cities of this Province he had ascertained from the leading Manufacturers, that all their most skilled Artizans had to be imported from Great Britain, that very large wages had to be paid to them, and that these Artizans were generally unwilling to impart their mechanical knowledge to others, for the reason that having found that their personal knowledge and skill so lucrative, they declined to impart it to others, and thus to divide and lessen the profits to themselves at present derivable therefrom.

These facts demonstrated the want of some School, such as that projected by the Ontario Government, where those of the youth of the Province desiring to acquire a practical knowledge of Mechanical Engineering and kindred subjects, could be enabled to do so.

He and a gentleman, residing in London, had recently made a trip through the United States, for the purpose of visiting and inspecting the Technological Schools there established, and they had found that these Establishments, where they were connected, or affiliated in any way, with Universities, or Schools for general learning, did not exhibit any very gratifying success. It was already contemplated at Yale and Harvard to disconnect their Technological branches from the Universities and to make them separate Institutions, in short, the facts ascertained during this trip in search of information, led them to the conclusion that Technological Schools flourished most when conducted independently of any other Scholastic Institution. And even, without any information concerning the experience of those who have had the conducting of these Schools, it seems reasonable to suppose that an Institution devoted to the teaching of hard, dry, operative subjects ought to have nothing in common with a University, where the literary branch of that Institution, with its more attractive subjects of Study might, and would, divert the minds of many from the purely practical teaching of technical Science, the pursuit of which in Canada would tend immensely to the growth and material wealth of the Country, and not less to the profit and success of the student himself. He and his Colleague had prepared a Report of their trip for the Government, and had embodied these views in it; and he was glad to see that the Cabinet had obtained the necessary appropriation of money, and intended getting the Institution started as soon as possible. . . . He was convinced that their scheme had wisdom and experience to recommend it.

From the remarks of the Honourable Attorney General in the House, he thought that the plan of teaching to be adopted was that of a similar and very successful Institution, conducted on the isolation principle at Boston, Massachusetts, videlicet, that of Object Teaching by Models, Diagrams, Pictorial Illustrations, etcetera, on a large and practical Scale.

IV. CIRCULAR ISSUED BY THE GOVERNMENT ON THE ESTABLISHMENT OF A COLLEGE OF TECHNOLOGY TO THE MANUFACTURERS OF ONTARIO.

In March, 1871, the Government issued a Circular, addressed to "the Manufacturers of Ontario," pointing out, that, in order to provide a system of Technical Education for Ontario, (as recommended by the Commissioners), the Legislature, during its late Session, had voted the sum of $50,000 for the purpose of erecting suitable Buildings, and providing necessary Apparatus, for a Technical, (or Industrial Science), School, or College, for Ontario.

The Circular stated "that the object of the proposed School of Industrial Science," was,—

"To provide, in a two-fold form, for the education of Mining and Civil and Mechanical Engineers; of Manipulation in Metals; of Workers in Wood, Leather, Woollen and Flax Fibres; of Designers, Modellers and Carvers in the Decorative and Industrial Arts; and of persons desirous of studying Chemistry, as applied to our various Manufactures."

The Government Circular then asked the Manufacturers to reply to a series of questions proposed to them, and to state their views as to the actual requirements of the profession, or business, in which "the party replying was engaged." To this Circular replies were received from eighty-nine persons engaged in engineering, manufactures, etcetera.

CHAPTER II.

PROCEEDINGS OF THE SENATE OF UNIVERSITY OF TORONTO, 1871.

January 16th, 1871. Read a Letter from the Provincial Secretary, returning approved by the Visitor the Statutes authorizing a further Expenditure upon the Boiler and Engine House of the University Building.

The Committee on the Observatory, (through Professor Cherriman,) presented their Report for the year ending 30th June, 1871.

Moved by Professor Cherriman, seconded by Doctor Daniel Wilson, That the Report be received and adopted, and duly forwarded to the Secretary of State for the Dominion. (Carried).

Professor Cherriman presented the Report of the Committee appointed to prepare the Memorial, relative to the Scheme for Superannuation of Professors and Masters, submitting a Draft Memorial to the Government on the subject.

Moved by the Vice Chancellor, seconded by the Reverend Doctor McCaul, That the Report just read be adopted. (Carried).

April 25th, 1871. There not being a quorum present the Senate adjourned.

May 1st, 1871. The following were appointed on the Committee of Upper Canada College for ensuing year, videlicet: Doctor L. W. Smith, the Reverend Doctor John Jennings, and Mr. J. H. Morris, in addition to the *ex officio* Members.

Read the Regulations respecting Higher Degrees, drafted by the Committee in that behalf as follows:

"The Candidate, on giving notice of application for the Degree, shall specify the Department, or Branch of Study, in which the subject of his Thesis is to assigned to him,—and he shall thereupon compose the required Thesis in the Examination Hall, at the period of the Annual Examinations in the particular Faculty, under the supervision of one, or more, of the Examiners in such special Department, or Branch of Study, without reference to Books, or to other aids; and the Examiners shall specially certify as to the fitness of the Candidate for the proposed Degree. For the Degree of Doctor of Law the Candidate is also required to compose an additional Thesis in a further and distinct Department, or Branch of Study, in the Faculty of Law."

Moved by the Vice Chancellor, seconded by the Reverend Doctor McCaul, That the Regulations be adopted, but that their operation, with respect to the Faculty of Arts, be suspended until further notice. (Carried).

Read an application from Messieurs D. A. O'Sullivan, D. J. Goggin, J. C. Glashan, U. M. Sutherland, and William Smith for leave to present themselves for Examination without having attended the Lectures of any affiliated College.

Moved by the Vice Chancellor, seconded by the Reverend Doctor McCaul, That the Petitions just read be acceded to. (Carried).

May 16th, 1871. The Vice Chancellor presented the Report of the Examinations in the Faculty of Medicine, which is as follows:—

For the Degree of M.B., 18 Candidates presented themselves,—all of whom passed satisfactory Examinations, with the exception of Mr. Donaldson, whose case is submitted for the consideration of the Senate.

The Medals are recommended to be awarded as follows: Gold, (University,) Mr. Forest; Silver, (University,) 1, Mr. Moore; 2, Mr. Henning; 3, Mr. De La Matter; Starr Gold Medal, Mr. Moore; Silver (1), Mr. Henning; (2) Mr. Forest;

The above is subject to proper proof being submitted to the Registrar by the Candidate of having, in all other respects, fulfilled the requirements of the Statutes relating to the Degree of M.B.

The following recommendations are made for Scholarships: 3rd Year, Mr. Zimmerman; 2nd Year, Mr. Close; 1st Year, Mr. Beeman.

For the Primary Examination, Messieurs Metcalfe, Moran, McClellan, Paterson, and Peterson presented themselves, and all passed satisfactorily.

Moved by the Vice Chancellor, seconded by the Reverend Doctor McCaul, That the Report be received and adopted, and that Mr. Donaldson's examination be allowed him. (Carried).

June 5th, 1871. The Vice Chancellor's Report upon the Examinations in the Faculties of Law and Arts, and in the School of Agriculture was presented and read, as follows,—

In the Faculty of Law, two Candidates presented themselves in the second year—Mr. C. A. Brough is recommended for the Scholarship, and, in view of the fact that no other Scholarship has been awarded in this Faculty, it is recommended that a Scholarship be given to Mr. R. E. Kingford, who also obtained a First Class standing.

In the third year, Messieurs E. H. Smythe, A. J. Wilkes, and S. Alward presented themselves. All of these passed satisfactorily.

In the Faculty of Arts, all the Candidates for the Degree of B.A. passed.

The following recommendations are made for Medals and Prizes: Classics, Gold Medal, Mr. W. Dale; Silver Medal, (1st), Mr. J. Henderson, (2nd), Mr. M. Kerr; Mathematics, Gold Medal, Mr. W. H. Ballard; Silver Medal, Mr. J. R. Teefy; Modern Languages, Gold Medal, Mr. H. Fletcher; Silver Medal, Mr. J. G. Robinson; Natural Sciences, Gold Medal, Mr. T. F. Fotheringham; Silver Medal, (1st Mr. H. Fletcher, (2nd), Mr. H. Archibald, (3rd), Mr. J. S. Ledgard; Metaphysics and Ethics, Gold Medal, Mr. J. R. Wightman; Silver Medal, Mr. W. H. Kingston.

Prizes—English Essay, Mr. W. Houston; Meteorology, Mr. T. F. Fotheringham.

The Prince's Prize has been awarded to Mr. H. Fletcher.

In the Third Year the Scholarships have been awarded as follows: Classics, (1st), Mr. J. Fletcher, (treble), (2nd), Mr. J. White; Mathematics, Mr. A. Killan; Natural Sciences, Mr. J. Gibson; Metaphysics and Ethics, Mr. H. J. Scott; General Proficiency, (1st), Mr. Fletcher, (2nd), Mr. Killan; Oriental Languages Prize, Mr. S. J. McKee.

In the Second Year the following are recommended as Scholars and Prizemen: Classics, (1st), Mr. T. H. Wallace, (treble), (2nd), Mr. J. C. Yule.

Mathematics, Mr. W. F. King, (double,) Mr. H. P. Milligan; Natural Sciences, Mr. J. B. Hanneton; Modern Languages and History, Mr. F. H. Wallace; Logic,

3—XXIII.

Metaphysics and Ethics, Mr. W. J. Robertson, (double); General Proficiency, (1st), Mr. F. H. Wallace, (2nd), Mr. W. J. Robertson, (3rd), Mr. W. F. King, (4th), Mr. G. E. Shaw. General Proficiency in subjects other than Classics and Mathematics, Mr. J. H. Long. Oriental Languages Prize, Mr. R. Touaner.

In the First year the recommendations are:

Classics. (1st), Mr. T. T. Macbeth, (2nd), Mr. J. Bruce; Mathematics, (1st), Mr. F. F. Manley, (2nd), Mr. J. C. Glashan, (double); Modern Languages and Natural Sciences, Mr. T. T. Macbeth; General Proficiency. (1st), Mr. T. T. Macbeth, (2nd), Mr. A. Dawson, (3rd), Mr. A. B. Aylsworth, (4th), Mr. J. C. Glashan, (5th), Mr. A. W. Marling, (6th), Mr. G. W. Thompson; Oriental Languages Prize, Mr. Barr, Mr. C. D. McDonald.

In Agriculture, two Candidates presented themselves in the First Year and passed satisfactory Examinations.

In the Faculty of Law, the Thesis of Mr. William Boys, LL.B., was reported upon as not displaying sufficient merit to entitle him to the Degree of LL.D.

In Medicine, Mr. S. P. Ford, M.B., having fulfilled the requirements of the new Regulations in that behalf, is recommended for the Degree of M.D.

In Arts the following Bachelors, having composed Thesis approved by the different Examiners, are entitled to the Master's Degree; Messieurs Armstrong, G. Baptie, G. Brunel, A. F. Campbell, E. B. Edwards, F. E. Evans, J. Fisher, W. Fitzgerald, R. D. Fraser, G. Gibson, R. Harcourt, J. S. Johnston, W. Kay, R. E. Kingsford, T. Kirkland, T. Langton, J. L. McDougall, W. Mulock, A. E. Richards, G. H. Robinson, H. H. Ross, J. Scnnyn, A. Sinclair, T. W. Wright.

Moved by the Reverend Doctor McCaul, seconded by Mr. G. R. R. Cockburn, That the Report just read be adopted. (Carried).

Read the application of Mr. Thomas B. Browning, Master of Arts of Glasgow University for admission *ad eundem gradum.*

Moved by the Reverend Doctor McCaul, seconded by Mr. G. R. R. Cockburn, That Mr. Browning be admitted *ad eundem* upon the Vice Chancellor being satisfied as to his position. (Carried).

June 8th, 1871. The Vice Chancellor presented the Report of the Upper Canada College Committee.

The Vice Chancellor reported to the Senate that they had provisionally arranged with the Agricultural and Arts Association of Ontario, as to the valuation of the Building erected on the grounds formerly occupied as an Experimental Farm, and which has been agreed to at Two thousand dollars.

The Senate then proceeded to the Convocation Hall, when Degrees were conferred and other proceedings had, as appears of record in the Book of Convocation.

June 12th, 1871. Moved by the Vice Chancellor, seconded by the Reverend Doctor McCaul, That the Examiners for the year 1871 be appointed, which was done.

The following Statutes were read a first time:

(1) Statute respecting Upper Canada College.

(2) Statute respecting the Agricultural and Arts Association, and the Building on the Experimental Farm.

June 13th, 1871. The Senate adjourned for want of a quorum

June 14th, 1871. It was moved by the Vice Chancellor, seconded by Mr. Principal G. R. R. Cockburn, That the Statute respecting an additional Mastership at Upper Canada College be read a second time and passed. (Carried). And that the Reverend Arthur Sweatman, M.A., of St. John's College, Cambridge, be recommended for the appointment to the Mastership thereby established.

Moved by the Vice Chancellor, seconded by the Reverend Doctor McCaul, That the Statute respecting the Building erected by the Agricultural and Arts Association be now read a second time and passed. (Carried).

Moved by the Vice Chancellor, seconded by the Reverend Doctor McCaul, That the attention of His Excellency the Lieutenant-Governor-in-Council be respectfully invited to the Communication of the Corporation of the City of Toronto, with respect to the construction by the City of a Main Drain, or Sewer, on Beverley Street, and that His Excellency may be pleased to pass an Order-in-Council, authorizing the Bursar to pay the sum of Two thousand dollars in full for the perpetual right to use the Drain, or Sewer, for the University Building, and all other erections on the University Grounds, whether occupied by a Tenant of the University, or other Persons, with the consent of the Senate of the University. Provided, that such Sewer be constructed to the limit of the University Grounds on College Street. (Carried).

Moved by the Vice Chancellor, seconded by the Reverend Doctor McCaul, That a Scholarship of Ten pounds be awarded to Mr. J. R. Wightman for General Proficiency at the Examinations for the year 1870,—it appearing that he was entitled to credit for a further Paper of Answers which had been mislaid by one of the Examiners. (Carried).

September 29th, 1871. The Vice Chancellor's Report of the recent Examinations for Matriculation in the various Faculties and Schools was read as follows:—

In the Faculty of Law, one Candidate, Mr. D. M. Christie, presented himself and passed satisfactorily.

In Medicine seven Candidates presented themselves, all of whom passed with the exception of Mr. Sylvester. Their names are,—Messieurs J. H. Cameron, J. R. Gordon, H. Macdonald, J. A. McGillivray, J. McLean, E. Sandison, and G. P. Sylvester.

There were three Candidates for Senior Matriculation in Arts, videlicet, Messieurs L. E. Embree, C. Clarkson, and T. Carscadden, all of whom passed.

In Junior Matriculation there was thirty-seven Candidates. They all passed satisfactory examinations with the exception of one who was rejected.

In Civil Engineering two Candidates came up, Mr. J. A. Wilson was the one who passed.

In Agriculture, Messieurs Fotheringham and Glade presented themselves, and both passed.

Several Students passed Supplementary Examinations.

Moved by Professor Croft, seconded by Professor Cherriman, That the Report just read be adopted. (Carried).

October 3rd, 1871. The following Petitions were read and assented to: From Mr. A. W. Dickey, of Windsor, Nova Scotia, Mr. E. D. Armour, of Trinity College, Toronto, and Mr. Angus Crawford, of Queen's College, Kingston, praying to be admitted *ad eundem statum.*

October 5th, 1871. There not being a quorum present the Senate adjourned.

October 25th, 1871. The Vice Chancellor submitted a Communication from the Chairman of the Walks and Grounds Committee of the City Council, desiring a meeting with a Committee of the Senate, on the subject of the Park and Grounds.

Moved by the Vice Chancellor, seconded by the Reverend Doctor McCaul, That a Committee, consisting of the Vice Chancellor, Doctor McCaul, Doctor Croft, and Doctor Jennings, be appointed to confer with said Committee. (Carried).

Moved by the Vice Chancellor, seconded by the Reverend Doctor Jennings, That the Library Committee for 1871-2 consist of Professor Cherriman, Doctor Wilson, Doctor Jennings, and the Reverend John Davison, in addition to the *ex officio* Members.

The Grounds Committee:—Professor Croft and Mr. J. H. Morris in addition to the *ex officio* Members.

The Observatory Committee:—Doctor L. W. Smith and Professor Cherriman in addition to the *ex officio* Members.

The Communications received from Messieurs Kingston, McIntyre, and Nichol, were referred to a Committee, consisting of the Vice Chancellor, Doctor McCaul, and Professor Cherriman.

The Reverend Doctor R. A. Fyfe introduced the following Resolutions:—

1st, That in accepting of Students from affiliated Colleges, having University powers, *ad eunden statum,* and refusing to receive, in the same manner, Students from affiliated Schools, which have not University powers, act as a temptation to weak Schools to seek University powers, which is not in the interests of good learning, and is contrary to the spirit of the University Act of 1853.

2nd, That the present system of conducting the appointed Examinations in the University,—that is, conducting them chiefly through the Professors of University College,—practically consigns, for all time, the affiliated Colleges to the status of Grammar Schools.

Moved by the Reverend Doctor R. A. Fyfe, seconded by the Reverend Doctor McCaul, That the proposition respecting affiliated Institutions be referred to a special Committee consisting of the Vice Chancellor, Doctor W. T. Aikins, Mr. G. R. R. Cockburn, and the Mover and Seconder, with instruction to report as soon as practicable. (Carried).

CHAPTER III.

PROCEEDINGS OF THE CHURCHES ON UNIVERSITY MATTERS, 1871.

THE METHODIST CHURCH, REPRESENTING VICTORIA UNIVERSITY.

PROCEEDINGS OF THE BOARD OF VICTORIA COLLEGE, 1871.

May 9th, 1871. The Treasurers of Victoria College presented their Annual Financial Statement. The Clerical Treasurer presented a general Financial Report, which was referred, for modification, to a Committee, consisting of the President of the College, the Treasurers and Messieurs W. H. Beatty and W. W. Dean.

The Reverend Doctor Anson Green presented a Report of the Endowment Fund.

Doctor Canniff and Doctor Berryman were admitted to an interview with the Board, relative to matters affecting the Medical Faculty, and requiring consideration. After hearing the statement of these Gentlemen, the following Resolutions were adopted by the Board:—

I. That, in view of recent Legislation, in relation to Medical Education in Ontario, the Graduation Fee for the Toronto Medical School of this University be reduced to $20, to be divided equally between the University and the Medical Faculty, and that this agreement shall apply to the year just closed.

II. That the Members of the Medical Board in Toronto, assisted by the Dean and the Secretary of the Medical Faculty, be a Committee to ascertain the selling value of the Yorkville Medical Property, and also the probable expense of a suitable new Building, near the Hospital, and that the Committee report to the Midsummer Meeting of the Board.

Some further conversation took place, during which the Members of the Board generally expressed their opinion of the necessity of employing in the Medical Faculty as Professors and Lecturers only Persons of approved moral and religious principles.

The Reverend Thomas S. Keough presented his Report as Agent. A Report from each of the Sub-agents was also read. These Reports were adopted.

Resolved, That the allowance to each of the Sub-agents for the year be $500 and Travelling Expenses.

The Treasurer's Report has read by Mr. William Kerr in the Morning Session and adopted. The Committee, to whom was referred the General Report, read by the Clerical Treasurer, reported that they had made such modifications as seemed to be in accordance with the expressed wishes of the Board, and the Report, as thus amended, was adopted.

The Report of the Reverend Doctor Anson Green and Mr. John Macdonald, as to the state of the Endowment Fund, was adopted.

The words, "at Cobourg," were ordered by the Board to be inserted in the Sentence stamped upon the College Debentures.

A discussion having taken place, as to the use of the interest accumulating on Endowment Monies now being invested, the matter was deferred.

Moved by the Reverend Doctor L. Taylor, seconded by Mr. B. M. Britton and,—

Resolved, That the following words in the Resolution of the 10th of May, 1870, be struck out, videlicet:—"But that no Investments be made without the written consent of the four Treasurers," and that the Reverend Doctor Anson Green, the Reverend Doctor Enoch Wood, Mr. John Macdonald and Mr. A. W. Lauder, be a Committee of Management for investing the Endowment Fund, in accordance with the Resolution above referred to.

The Board recommended to the Annual Conference Meeting of the Board, the re-appointment, for the next year, of the three Agents now in office.

The Reverend T. S. Keough's plan for giving greater success to the Insurance Scheme was referred to a Committee, consisting of the President of the College, the Treasurers and Mr. Keough.

The Alumni Association, having recommended the restoration of a Room in the body of the College Building, similar to the old Chapel, and to be called the "Alumni Hall," the matter was referred for consideration and final decision to the Members of the Board residing in Cobourg, and such other Persons as may, at the time, compose the Committee on Finance and Repairs. The expense of such alterations and improvements to be borne by the Alumni Association, according to their generous proposal.

A Petition from the Professors of the Faculty of Arts was read by the Secretary of the Board, asking for an increase of Salaries. After some general consideration, in which it was universally admitted that the Salaries were too low, and ought to be increased as soon as the Funds of the College would allow, the subject was postponed for kind and careful consideration at the next Meeting of the Board.

A Note was read by one of the Board, containing proposals from Professor Kingston for a modification in the Terms of Settlement with himself, as to his annuity and mortgage, and, after remarks from several Members of the Board, on the subject, the following Resolution was adopted videlicet:—That when Professor Kingston pays up his Mortgage, principal and interest, credit be given to him upon the same, for such portion of his retiring allowance as may, at the time, remain unpaid, and in full discharge of such retiring allowance.

Mr. William Beatty, LL.B., President of the Alumni Association, having informed the Board that, at a Meeting of the Association, held this day, the Alumni had agreed to procure, and give their Alma Mater, the Boulton Property, situated in the Town of Cobourg, and consisting of the residence of the late Honourable George Boulton and about forty acres of land, as a more eligible location for the University, it was moved by the Reverend Lachlan Taylor, D.D., seconded by John Beatty, M.D., and,—

Resolved, That the Board receives with deep admiration and gratitude the proposal of the Alumni to purchase, and present to the University, this valuable Property, and will be delighted to witness such a consummation of the Scheme, as will allow the opening of the University on the new and improved Site.

June 10th, 1871. An informal Meeting of the College Board took place at Belleville during the sitting of Conference there on the 10th of June.

The Meeting agreed to ask the Conference to make an additional Collection in support of the College, the Reverend H. Christopherson was spoken of as a suitable Person to act as Agent in the place of the Reverend W. W. Leach, and although, at a subsequent Meeting, another name was mentioned, it was finally agreed with the Stationing Committee to select Mr. Christopherson. The nomination was approved by the Conference.

The Conference Annual Meeting of Victoria College assembled at Belleville on the 7th of June, 1871.

The following Members of the Meeting were appointed a Committee to consider the Memorial from the Picton Quarterly Meeting and to Report to the Annual Meeting at its next sitting, videlicet:—the Reverends Ephraim Evans, D.D., John Borland, George Douglas, LL.D., J. A. Williams, E. H. Dewart, James Gray, Charles Lavell, N. R. Willoughby, and A. Sutherland.

June 12th, 1871. The Treasurers of the College presented their Reports, and addressed the Conference, in relation to the financial condition and wants of the Institution. The Agent of College also presented an account of the labours of himself and the assistant Agents during the past year. These several Reports were adopted.

It was moved by the Reverend G. R. Sanderson, seconded by the Reverend S. S. Nelles and,—

Resolved, That the cordial thanks of this Annual Meeting be presented Mr. William Kerr, Lay-Treasurer of the University of Victoria College, for the valuable and unrequitted services cheerfully performed by him in his official relation to the University, and for his great zeal and personal effort in furthering all the interests of the Institution,—a zeal which has often and largely brought under contribution his professional abilities, his time, his credit and his pecuniary resources.

Moved by the Reverend Doctor Ephraim Evans, seconded by the Reverend James Elliot, and,—

Resolved, That the thanks of the Meeting are due, and are hereby tendered, to the Reverend R. Jones, Clerical Treasurer of the College, for the zeal and diligence with which he has applied himself to the duties of his office during the past year.

The Reverend Doctor Anson Green presented the Report of the Treasurers of the Endowment Fund. The Report was accepted, and the cordial thanks of the Meeting were tendered to Doctor Green and Mr. John Macdonald for their valuable services in the management of this Fund.

The Committee on the Picton Memorial presented their Report, recommending the Annual Meeting to grant the prayer of the Memorialists. . The Report was adopted.

The following is the Report of Committee on Picton Memorial June, 1871:—

The Committee, to whom was referred the Picton Memorial on College matters, met on Friday Morning at 6. a.m.

The Reverend Doctor Ephraim Evans in the Chair. The Reverend Charles Lavell was appointed Secretary. Present: The Reverends John Borland, E. H. Dewart, A. Sutherland, Doctor Douglas, James Gray, J. A. Williams, N. R. Willoughby and C. Lavell, when it was,—

Resolved, That a full and complete Balance Sheet of the Assets and Liabilities of Victoria College be prepared and published in some cheap and convenient form for distribution, under the supervision of competent Auditors, (appointed by the Conference Annual Meeting), who have not been connected with the financial management of Institution, and which Balance Sheet shall embrace the following particulars, videlicet:—

1st. The total amount subscribed towards the $30,000 to liquidate the old debt on Victoria College.

2nd. The total amount paid on account of said subscriptions.

3rd. How the subscriptions were disposed of.

4th. The cost of procuring and collecting said subscriptions, the name of each Party, (or Agent) employed, the amount of work performed, and the remuneration given.

5th. The amount of the present liabilities on the above named amount of $30,000 principal and interest, separately, and the rate of interest.

6th. The total amount subscribed toward the Endowment Fund.

7th. The total amount paid on account of said subcriptions.

8th. How invested, and where, with the name of the Company, or individuals in detail, at what rate of interest, and how payable, yearly, half-yearly, or otherwise.

9th. What amount of interest is now due on arrears.

10th. The cost of procuring the collecting the said subscriptions and monies, with the name of each party employed, the kind of service performed, with the remuneration given.

11th. The cost of investing the aforesaid monies, how paid, percentage, or otherwise, and to whom paid.

12th. The present indebtedness of the Institution.

The following Resolutions, of which previous notice had been given, by Doctor J. B. Aylesworth were taken up.

1. That the Board of Victoria College shall hereafter cause a printed Report to be prepared, sent, or presented, to every Member of the Conference Annual Meeting, on, or before, the day upon which, in each year, the Conference Annual Meeting may be appointed to be held.

II. That such Report shall contain a full account of the proceedings, Acts and Resolutions of each Meeting of the Board of Trustees and Visitors: also the ayes and nays upon all votes of importance, such as the appropriations of money,—appointments to, or displacements from, office, the passing of By-laws, and the adoption of Reports.

III. That the Accounts in detail be included in such Reports, showing all the Income and Expenditure for the past year, and the exact state of each Fund, and how invested.

IV. That Estimates shall be presented, or a By-law, showing in detail the proposed Expenditures for the succeeding year: the Income and the sources from which it is expected; with the deficiency, if any, and the proposed provision for meeting such deficiency.

These Resolutions were adopted, with the exception of the Second, instead of which it was agreed, that the Minutes of the Board for the preceding year should be read at the Annual Meeting.

It was moved by the Reverend Samuel Rose, seconded by the Reverend A. Sutherland, and,—

Resolved, That the Conference Annual Meeting of Victoria College, recommends the Conference to provide for the taking up of a temporary Collection in all our Congregations for the reduction and ultimate extinction of the debt of Victoria College, amounting to $11,000 and interest, which has accumulated since the withdrawal of the Legislative Grant.

After considerable discussion, in which the Treasurers, Mr. W. W. Dean and others, addressed the Meeting, the Resolution was referred to the Conference for further consideration.

A Resolution from the Perth District Meeting, respecting investments of the Endowment Fund was referred to the College Board.

The following Members of the Annual Meeting were appointed Auditors videlicet: the Reverend William Hall, Mr. T. A. Ferguson, and the Reverend William Briggs. The thanks of the Meeting were presented to the Auditors of the preceding year.

The President of the Conference was authorized to fill any vacancy that may arise among the Auditors appointed under the Report on the Picton Memorial.

June 13th, 1871. The question of taking up an additional Collection in aid of Victoria College was again considered and the following Resolutions were adopted by a large majority, videlicet:—

I. That each Minister and Preacher of the Conference shall contribute, or obtain, for the above objects during the ensuing year, a sum equal to the following percentage on his income, videlicet: on all incomes under Five hundred dollars, one-half per cent.; on all incomes of Five hundred dollars and upwards, but less than one thousand dollars, one per cent.; and all incomes of One thousand dollars and upwards, one and a half per cent.

July 18th, 1871. The Reverend Thomas S. Keough was appointed Agent, and was instructed to give special attention to matters of Insurance.

The Reverend Jacob Freshman and Reverend H. Christopherson were appointed assistant Agents. The Salaries of Messieurs Keough and Freshman were fixed at the amounts given last year. The Salary of the Reverend Mr. Christopherson was fixed at $700, and Travelling and moving Expenses.

The Members of the Board in Cobourg with the Reverends William Briggs I. B. Howard, and D. H. Minaker, were appointed a Committee on Finance and Repairs.

The Secretary of the Conference Annual Meeting presented a Resolution, passed by the Perth District Meeting, and referred to the Board for consideration, relating to the investment of the Endowment Fund. In view of the absence of the Trustees of that Fund, the Resolution was referred to the next Meeting of the Board.

It was moved by the President of the College, seconded by Doctor W. H. Brouse, and,—

Resolved, That, as it is desirable to give fuller effect to various Resolutions adopted at different times by the Conference, and by this Board, in relation to the training of Candidates for the Christian Ministry, it is necessary to appoint a Tutor to render assistance in the Department of Natural Science and Classics, with the view of permitting the Professors of those Departments to conduct some additional Classes, more especially adapted to the case of Theological Students.

Moved by the President of the College, seconded by Mr. William Kerr, and,—

Resolved,—That the Reverend Richard Wilson, B.A., be appointed to the above Tutorship, and that his Salary be $400 per annum.

The Petition of the Professors in the Faculty of Arts asking for an increase of Salaries, which was presented at the May Meeting and referred to the next Meeting of the Board, was brought forward for consideration, and, after due deliberation, the following Resolution was unanimously adopted:—

That, while the Members of the Board present do not feel justified in voting at this Meeting an increase to the Salaries of the Professors, they nevertheless recognise the necessity of doing so at an early day, and hope the Board may be in a position to make a small additional allowance to each Professor at the close of the present year.

The plan proposed by the Reverend T. S. Keough, to give further encouragement to our people to insure in Queen's Insurance Company was adopted. Mr. Keough was also authorized to make an arrangement with the Company, by which he could act as an Agent in taking risks.

During the Session of the Board, Doctor Canniff, Dean of the Faculty of Medicine, and Doctor Berryman, were admitted to an interview with the Board, in reference to the affairs of the School of Medicine at Toronto. Some conversation took place in relation to the transfer of the School to some Building in close proximity to the Hospital, and the matter was referred again to a Committee consisting of the Members of the Board in Toronto with Doctor Canniff and Doctor Berryman, Doctor Canniff to be Convener of the Committee, and the Committee to report to the Board before final action is taken.

The following names were submitted by the Dean to compose the Staff of Professors and Lecturers for the ensuing Session, videlicet: Professors:—Doctor Canniff, Doctor Berryman, Doctor Reid, Doctor Barrick. Lecturers:—Doctor Agnew, Doctor Cassidy. Doctor May, Doctor Rosebrugh, Doctor Warren, and Doctor Kennedy.

December 8th, 1871. The Reverend Anson Green, D.D., and Mr. John Macdonald were appointed Trustees of the Endowment Fund, on behalf of the Treasurers,—this appointment not having been made at the previous Meeting.

The Board then proceeded to consider some matters connected with the Yorkville Medical School. Doctor Canniff, the Dean, and Mr. J. E. Rose were requested to be present to furnish information. After a lengthy conversation respecting the removal of the School to some more convenient Site near the Hospital it was,—

Resolved, That Members of the Board in Toronto, with the President of the College, the Dean of the Faculty of Medicine and Doctor Berryman, be appointed a Committee to inquire further into the advisability of selling the Yorkville property, and that the Committee be authorised to accept the offer now made of $1,200 for the same, provided the Committee find that, with this sum of $1,200, they can effect a loan on the new Property sufficient to pay for a Lot and to erect a suitable Building near the Hospital, and provided, further and always, that the Trustees of Victoria College be not involved in any financial responsibility connected with the contemplated change.

In the absence of the President of Conference the Secretary of Conference, the Reverend A. Sutherland was directed to act as Convener of the Committee.

II THE PRESBYTERIAN CHURCH (OF SCOTLAND), REPRESENTING QUEEN'S UNIVERSITY, 1871.

PROCEEDINGS OF THE BOARD OF QUEEN'S COLLEGE.

April 25th, 1871. That Treasurer reported the receipt by him of $400, (Four hundred dollars,) from Mr. Alexander Ross, an Executor of the Estate of the late Mr. E. H. Hardy, being the amount of a Bequest by that Gentleman to the College for General purposes.

The Board takes this opportunity of recording its thanks to the Executors for the payment of this Bequest, and its deep sense of the warm interest taken in the College by the late Mr. Hardy, as shown by his Annual Contributions for Scholarships, as well as by the Bequest herein acknowledged.

The Secretary was instructed to send an extract of the above Minute to Mr. Alexander Ross and Mrs. Hardy.

The draft of the Annual Report to the Colonial Committee of the General Assembly of the Church of Scotland was read and approved.

The Report of the Finance and Estate Committee and Estimates for 1872-73 were read and approved.

The Report of Messieurs John Creighton and John Kerr, Auditors, was read and received. The Board records its thanks to the Auditors for their valuable services, and agreed to request these Gentlemen to favour the Board with their services in the same capacity for the current year.

Fnancial Statements submitted by the Treasurer numbered one to five inclusive, and certified by the Auditors as correct, were read, approved and ordered to be printed, as required by the Statute, for distribution among the Members of the Synod.

The Annual Report of the Trustees of Queen's College to the Synod was read and approved.

The Report from the Curators of the Library was read and received.

The Annual Report from the Curator of the Museum was read and received.

The Principal informed the Board of the formation of a Reading Club in the City of Kingston, under the name of the University Reading Club, and stated that he had assumed the responsibility of allowing the Members of the Club to borrow Books from the College Library, subject to the By-law conditions, that the Books of the Club, purchased to the value of five dollars per Member, should be transferred to the Library and become the Property of the College, after being in use by the Members of the Club for one year. The Board approved of the action in this matter taken by the Principal.

It was moved by Mr. Barker, seconded by Mr. George H. Kinghorn that the Salary of Mr. Dupuis by $1,400, (Fourteen hundred dollars,) per annum, beginning on the first of October next. It was unanimously agreed to recommend the adoption of this Resolution to the next Meeting of the Board.

The Treasurer having reported that an Annual Contribution of $400 for the last three has been received from Mr. John Watkins of Kingston, the Board resolved to record its most cordial thanks to Mr. Watkins for his laberality, and its sense of the great importance of these Annual Contributions towards the maintenance of the College, in the midst of trying difficulties, to which the discontinuance of Government aid subjected it.

A few unimportant changes in the Calendar recommended by the Senate were approved and sanctioned.

April 26th, 1871. No report having been received from the Committee appointed to report verbal improvements in the College statutes, it was agreed to adjourn the Meeting.

April 27th, 1871. On motion of the Principal, seconded by the Reverend K. Maclennan, the following Resolution was passed unanimously,—

The death of the Reverend Hugh Urquhart, D.D., Minister of St. John's Church, Cornwall, having occurred since the last Meeting of the Board, the Trustees of Queen's College take this opportunity of recording their deep regret at his removal from the scene of his earthly labours. He was a warm and devoted Friend of this Institution. For ten successive Sessions, from 1847 to 1857, he lectured in the College on Ecclesiastical History. He was elected a Trustee in 1845, and continued in this office until this date. The Members of the Board have a high appreciation of his fidelity in the discharge of his duties in connection with this trust,—of his attainments as a Scholar and of his whole bearing as a Christian Gentleman.

The Secretary was instructed to send an extract of this Minute to Mrs. Urquhart.

The Secretary reported that the Annual Report from the Trustees to the Colonial Committee of the General Assembly of the Church of Scotland had been prepared and transmitted. The Draft of the Report was submitted and approved.

The Secretary submitted the Annual Report from the Finance and Estate Committee, which having been read, It was moved by the Reverend K. Maclennan, seconded by Mr. George T. Kinghorn, and unanimously,—

Resolved, That the Report of the Finance and Estate Committee now read be adopted, that the Board specially sanction the investment of $2,500 at 6% discount in Debentures of the Township of Brock, and $2,500 at 4% discount in Debentures of the Township of Eldon.

The Principal submitted the Annual Report of the College to the Synod which was read and approved.

The Treasurer submitted Financial Statements for the year ending 10th April, 1871, number one to four inclusive, and an abstract Statement of the Endowment Fund Account Number Five. Also the Auditors' Report thereon,—which having been read. It was moved by the Reverend Doctor Jenkins, seconded by Doctor Boulter, and,—

Resolved, That the Accounts of the Treasurer now read, Numbers one to five inclusive, for the financial year ending on the 10th of April, 1871, be printed in the usual way, along with the Report of the Trustees to the Synod, and that the grateful acknowledgment of the Board of the valuable service of Messieurs John Creighton and John Kerr, in auditing the Treasurer's Books and Accounts, be tendered to these Gentlemen, with the request that they act as Auditors for the current year.

The Annual Report of the Curators of the College Library was read and received.

The Annual Report of the Curator of the Museum was also read and received.

The Principal submitted some proposed changes in the Calendar, which were approved and sanctioned by the Board.

April 28th, 1871. The proposed alterations in the College Statutes were then submitted by the Principal, and, after due, consideration, it was moved by the Principal, seconded by the Reverend Doctor John Jenkins, and unanimously,—

Resolved, That the amendments on the Statutes therein specified be adopted.

April 29th, 1871. The Principal having intimated to the Board that Mr. William Maxwell Inglis, a Trustee of Queen's College, has been deposed from the Ministry by the Presbytery of Kingston,—It was moved by the Reverend Doctor John Jenkins, seconded by the Reverend William Bain, and,—

Resolved, That the Reverend Gavin Lang, Minister of St. Andrew's Church, Montreal, be, and is hereby appointed to fill the vacancy caused by said deposition.

June 7th, 1871. The Principal having stated that the Treasurer has received from the Church of Scotland, through its Colonial Committee, a donation of £200 Sterling, towards the current expenses of the College, in addition to the ·Committee's Annual Grant of £350 Sterling, the Board agree to record, and hereby do record, their heartfelt gratitude to the Church of Scotland for this munificent and seasonable contribution, affording as it does, a new proof of the warm interest felt by the Parent Church in the welfare of the College.

June 12th, 1871. No business was transacted and the Board adjourned.

November 21st, 1871. The following Resolutions were submitted to the Meeting.

1st. That inasmuch as the Canada Presbyterian Church has resolved to raise two hundred and fifty thousand dollars for the endowment of its Theological Institutions, it be recommended to the Synod of the Presbyterian Church in Canada, in connection with the Church of Scotland, to provide such further Endowment to the Faculty of Arts in Queen's College as to it may appear necessary, or desirable.

2nd. That tutorial work, in relation to the literary and scientific studies of Students for the Ministry, be not carried on in connection with the Theological Institutions of the United Church in Ontario and Quebec, but that provision be made by the United Church for such work in Queen's College, Kingston, and in Morrin College, Quebec.

3rd. That the Theological Department of Queen's College, and of Morrin College, and the Presbyterian College, Montreal, shall be united into one College situated in Montreal.

4th. That the Theological College, thus founded at Montreal, shall be governed in general accordance with the provisions of the Charter of the Presbyterian College, Montreal.

5th. That the Theological College of the United Church, videlicet, at Halifax, Montreal and Toronto shall be affiliated with Queen's College, so as to be represented in the University Senate.

(1) For conferring Degrees in Divinity.

(2) For taking such share in the government of the University as may be proper, in relation to the preparatory training of Students for the Ministry.

6th. That the present Principal of Morrin College shall be invited by the General Assembly of the United Church to be the first Principal of the Theological College at Montreal, that another Theological Professor shall be so invited from Queen's College, and, in the event of his declining the invitation, such Professor shall be nominated by the Presbyterian Church of Canada in connection with the Church of Scotland.

7th. That the legislation necessary to effect the foregoing changes shall be sought, and that application be made to Parliament for such legislation, in conformity with the said changes, as will bring Queen's University and College, Knox College, the presbyterian College, Montreal, Morrin College and the Theological Hall at Halifax into relations to the United Church similar to those which they now hold in their respective Churches, and to preserve their corporate existence, government, and function, on terms and conditions like to those under which they now exist.

A Report, dated the 30th of June, 1871, was read from Professors Mowat and Dupuis, Examiners of Competitors for the Watkins and Campbell Scholarships.

After some general conversation and expression of opinion relative to the Resolutions submitted to the Board for consideration,—the Meeting adjourned.

November 22nd, 1871. It was moved by the Reverend Mr. Lang, seconded by Mr. Barker, That inasmuch as the General Assembly of the Canada Presbyterian Church has adopted a Resolution different from the Resolutions which the Board was requested to consider and sent it down to Presbyteries, Sessions and Congregations, this Board does not think it desirable to pronounce opinion upon the Resolutions before it.

Moved in amendment by the Reverend D. J. Macdonnell, seconded by the Reverend Doctor John Jenkins—That the Resolutions of the Committee be considered in connection with the decision of the Canada Presbyterian Assembly. The amendment was carried.

The Trustees having fully considered the Resolutions of the Committee, in connection with the decision of the Canada Presbyterian Assembly,—It was moved by the Reverend Mr. Lang, seconded by the Honourable Donald McDonald and unanimously.—

Resolved, That the Board, feeling that whether practicable, or not, the proposals contained in these Resolutions have not received the sanction of the Canada Presbyterian Church, decline, in the meantime, and in view of the action which may be taken by the next Meeting of Synod, to pronounce any judgment upon them.

PROCEEDINGS OF THE SYNOD OF THE PRESBYTERIAN CHURCH, SCOTLAND, 1871

June 14th, 1871. Report of Queen's University. Principal Snodgrass presented and read the Annual Report of the Trustees of the University of Queen's College, and, in connection therewith, a Report from the Executive Committee appointed to provide a supplementary Endowment for that Institution. Whereupon it was moved by the Reverend D. M. Gordon, seconded by the Reverend D. J. Macdonnell, and passed unanimously:—That the Reports, with accompanying Financial Statements be received; that the Synod anew express their confidence in the judicious and careful management of the affairs of the College; record their great gratification at the re-remarkable progress of the Scheme for the Endowment of the College; and greatly acknowledge their obligations to the Very Reverend Principal Snodgrass and to the Reverend Professor MacKerras for their indefatigable exertions in connection with that Endowment, and to the Venerable the General Assembly of the Church of Scotland for authorizing their Colonial Committee to make a special donation of Two hundred pounds, sterling (£200 sterling) towards the current expenses of the College.

Report of the Trustees of Queen's College to the Synod:—

The Financial position of the College is fully and clearly shown in the Statement of the Treasurer herewith submitted, for the year ending on the 10th of April. From the Endowment Scheme, since the commencement of it in January, 1869, there has been realized $72,777.45, exclusive of Subscriptions and other Receipts on account of Revenue ($3,720.85,) and Disbursements in connection with the Scheme, ($710.92). The result of effort, together with the rigid economy observed in the ordinary Expenditure of the College, are beginning to tell very satisfactorily on the decrease of Income, caused by the suspension of the Commercial Bank and the discontinuance of the Legislative Grant. The amount of the decrease was $6,280 per annum. The actual deficiency in Revenue reported to the Synod in 1869, was $3,200.19, in 1870, $3,084.76; this year it is only $1,522.95. The total deficiency is $7,807.90. Of this sum only $1,635.36 is shown in statement Number Five to have been borrowed from the Endowment Fund, but the whole of it, although for temporary use it has been obtained from other sources, must be regarded as a loan from the Fund, to be restored to the Capital as soon as the Revenue from the Endowment shall admit of repayment. Being a debt, it is in the meantime, an unavoidable cause of delay in completing the realization of the proposed minimum Endowment of $10,000. It is hoped, however, that the practical effect of reporting it, on the present occasion, will be to stimulate to renewed exertions in behalf of the Scheme.

One of the Investments reported in Statement Number Five, is an Expenditure of $5,747.85 on the College Buildings, the Wings of which have been converted into very commodious and comfortable Dwelling Houses, now occupied by two of the Professors, and the centre part of which is the Principal's House. The annual return upon the outlay will be $450. The Investment is considered to be a good one, while the changes effected, by means of it, have given the Buildings a greatly improved appearance.

In Statement Number One is shown an expenditure of $507.76 upon repairs in the College, that is, the new Building formerly leased to the Royal College of Physicians and Surgeons. The repairs consist chiefly of alterations deemed necessary for the accommodation of the Classes, Library and Museum. The Trustees believe that the Institution has now as fine a suite of Class Rooms for College purposes as there is in the Country. The increase of convenience and comfort enjoyed during the past

Session has been much appreciated, and fully justifies the removal from the old Building to the new. Deducting the extra charge, the Expenditure for general purposes is the very moderate sum of $741.04.

The highly competent Gentlemen serving the Board as Auditors, after faithfully discharging their duties for the year, report that the Treasurer's Books are kept in an admirable manner, that the Funds of the College are most carefully and properly handled, and that the Investments on account of the Endowment Fund have been safely and advantageously made.

The full and careful records kept by the Senate for University Examinations, and by the several Professors for monthly written Examinations and ordinary daily Class work, show that the Students as a body make very satisfactory progress from year to year. But there are other means of the testing of the education given at the College, as to its character and results, more deserving of notice, because of their strictly independent application. Occasionally an Alumnus finds his way to a British University, and entering into competition with the ablest Students, both gains distinction for himself and brings honour to his Alma Mater. Going back but three years, at Edinburgh University, Mr. Robert Jardine, who, in January last was appointed President of the Church of Scotland's College at Calcutta, carried, along with the highest commendation, the Degree of Doctor of Science, by the excellence of his examinations in Mental Philosophy. Last Session, at the same seat of learning, Mr. Robert Campbell, after a severe contest, won the "Bruce of Grangehill and Falkland Prize" for Logic and Metaphysics, his strongest Fellow-competitor being a First-Class Honour Graduate of the University of London, and the second Prize for Political Economy, a Master of Arts gaining the first by a majority of only 9 marks. In this Country too, when opportunity offers competitions appear to lose none of their interests, by a representation from Queen's. At recent Law Examinations in Toronto, for example, among Candidates from all quarters, our Graduates have taken highly creditable places. In 1869, Mr. Duncan Morrison, in passing as a Barrister, stood second in the order of merit, and was exempted from oral examination. In the same year Mr. Francis H. Crysler competed for the third year Scholarship, and although he gained considerably more than the requisite number of marks, he lost the Scholarship by a difference of 18 between him and the successful Competitor. In November last he competed for the fourth year Scholarship and gained it. At his first intermediate Examination he was fourth in the order of merit. At the last Barristers and Attorneys' Examinations, Messieurs James Muir and John F. Bain were the only candidates from Queen's. The latter stood fourth among 13 as Barrister and fifth as Attorney, passing without an oral Examination. The former was first among 25 Attorneys, passing without an oral, and coming within a very few marks of the maximum. At their intermediate Examinations Mr. Muir was first and Mr. Bain third of 23 Candidates. To pass without an oral Examination it is necessary to obtain three-fourths of the maximum. Leaving these facts to speak for themselves, the Trustees deem it proper to observe that, with the efficient staff of Professors, the best accommodation, and the varied appliances of which the College is possessed, much more work can be done, without any increase of expense, than is at present performed. It is greatly to be desired that the young Men of the Country, more especially of the Presbyterian Church, would come forward in large numbers to take advantage of the benefits which are placed within their reach. All the Trustees can do, apart from the exercise of their influence as individuals, is to make known the position and capabilities of the Institution. The Members of the Corporation have much in their power, and their assistance is earnestly solicited.

The attendance at College and the Institutions in affiliation, during the past Session, was as follows:—in Arts and Theology 29, of whom 15 have the Ministry in view; in Medicine, (Royal College of Physicians and Surgeons), 35; in the Grammar School, 81; in the Ladies' Classes, 23; making a total of 168 Persons receiving instruction in connection with the University. While the Trustees have pleasure in reporting that those who are preparing for the Ministry are all diligent and promising Students, they cannot but renew the regrets expressed on former occasions at the number being so far short of the Church's wants. The hope of the increase is reviving, but it becomes the Members of Synod to consider seriously the existing disappropriation between the supply and demand.

The Classes for Ladies were superintended by three of the Professors, and the subjects taught were English Literature, Logic, Mental Philosophy, and Chemistry. Encouraging results attended the arrangement.

The course of weekly Evening Lectures on Literary and Scientific subjects, ıeferred to in last Report, wɛs followed, during the past Session, by a more exteaded Course. The assemblies which almost always filled the Convocation Hall afforded a gratifying proof of appreciation on the part of the Public. The proceeds derived from the sale of Tickets were devoted to a somewhat expensive undertaking,—the introduction of Gas into the Convocation Hall. It has been a pleasing duty to the Trustees to express their gratitude to their Professors fɔr their liberality and the very valuable improvement effected by means of it.

Since the last Report, two liberal benefactions have been received for the benefit of Students for the Ministry, the one, $500 from Mrs. Glass, of Sarnia, to form the foundation of a Scholarship in memory of her deceased Husband, Mr. Henry Glass; the other, $400 from a Gentleman in New Brunswick, with this interesting stipulation on the part of the Donor, that Candidates may belong to any Presbyterian Church in the Dominion.

To all friends who in any way forwarded the Endowment Scheme, or made donations to the Museum, Library, Scholarship and Prize Funds, during the past year, the Trustees take this opportunity of offering their grateful acknowledgment.

KINGSTON, 27th April, 1871.   JOHN HAMILTON, Chairman.

STATEMENT OF ORDINARY REVENUE AND EXPENDITURE OF QUEEN'S COLLEGE AT KINGSTON, FOR THE YEAR ENDING ON THE 10TH OF APRIL, 1871.

Revenue.

	$ cts.
Grant from Coloⁿial Committee of the Church of Scotland.	1,460 00
From the Temporalities Board	2,000 00
Dividend on Bank Stock	2,080 00
Interest on Mortgages, Government Securities, Debentures and Bank Deposits	3,837 55
Fees—Class and Graduation	156 00
Rent of the Class Room	30 00
Contribution from the College Senate towards the expenses of the removal of the Library	50 00
Kingston Observatory,—Balance	413 30

Subscriptions—		
In Canada	$680 00	
In Scotland	100 00	
Interest on Subscriptions to the Endowment Fund	159 00	
		949 00
		$10,975 85
Balance (Deficiency)		1,522 95
		$12,498 80

	$ cts.
Expenditure.	
Salaries	11,250 00
Insurance, Repairs of the College	1,248 80 ·
KINGSTON, 21st April, 1871.	$12,498 80

Certified as correct, as per separate Report.   W. IRELAND, Secretary-Treasurer.
JOHN CREIGHTON,   }   Auditors.
JOHN KERR,   }

KINGSTON, 21st April, 1871.

BALANCE SHEET, SHOWING THE ASSETS AND LIABILITIES OF QUEEN'S COLLEGE, AT KINGSTON, ON THE 10TH OF APRIL, 1971.

Debtor.		$ cts.
Royal Charter, cost of		3,107 37
Class Apparatus		3,633 92
Library,—Expenditure on the		3,399 68
Furniture Account		1,429 09
College Premises		41,740 61
Bank Stock		26,700 00
Messieurs Campbell, Mowat and Macdonnell		450 00
Young Men's Christian Association of St. Andrew's Church		54 00
Freehold Building Society, Toronto		2,798 30
Canada Dominion Stock		12,900 00
Montreal Public Property Stock		10,010 00
Debentures		18,500 00
Bills receivable		600 00
Mr. A. Livingston		133 00
Lands		600 00
Mortgages on Real Estate		15,826 55
Toronto Scholarship Stock, three shares M.B. Stock $300 00		
Kingston Scholarship Stock, three shares M.B.		
Stock	300 00	
		600 00
Merchants' Bank Endowment Fund Account		12,034 49
		$154,517 01

Credit.	$ cts.
Endowment of the New Chair in Theology	1,163 22
James Michie Bequest	2,000 00
Henry Glass Memorial Scholarship Endowment	500 00
The Reverend Alexander Lewis	432 00
Funds for Investment	2,496 96
Bursary Endowments	2,309 75
Students in Arts for Ministry (Class Fees)	180 00
Leitch Memorial Funds	2,462 03
Scholarships	1,451 65
Water Works Company	50 00
Endowment Fund Account	72,777 45
Profit and Loss Account	68,693 95
	$154,517 01

KINGSTON, 21st April, 1871.

Certified as correct, as per separate Report,   W. IRELAND, Secretary-Treasurer.
JOHN CREIGHTON,   }   Auditors.
JOHN KERR,   }

KINGSTON, 21st April, 1871.

REPORT OF THE GENERAL COMMITTEE ON THE ENDOWMENT OF QUEEN'S COLLEGE.

In the course of last Summer a number of Charges were visited, in Upper and Lower Canada. In their intercourse with the Members and adherents of these Congregations the Deputation kept steadily in view the main object of their Mission, without losing sight of those other important purposes to which reference was made in former Reports, and experienced, (your Committee rejoice to say), a renewal of that hearty welcome and earnest co-operation which, from the first, have been so serviceable in lightening the labours connected with the prosecution of the Endowment Scheme, and in rendering these labours successful. Taking into account such circumstances as are entitled to consideration, the various Charges visited have done their part. In the case of most of them the liberality exercised exceeded expectations. The aggregate of the subscriptions obtained in them is $7,052.04.

By way of reviewing the progress of this Endowment Scheme since its commencement in January, 1869, the following Statistics are submitted. Seventy-three Charges have been visited. At the dates, in the order of succession, of the Reports to the Synod, of which the present one is the third, the total amounts subscribed were various. Those collected were $25,000, $61,341, and $83,495.40,—the number of Scholarships paid, 20, 33, 45. The number of nominations was 46, 122, 190, representing respectively $4,600, $12,200 and $19,000, the value of each nomination being $100. The sum of the collection, namely, $82,495.40 includes $4,296.85, contributed to revenue, and therefore spent, and $714.68 disbursed on account of expenses incurred in conducting the Scheme, leaving $77,483.87 at the credit of permanent Endowment. Of this capital $70,197.60 has been placed in First Class Securities, which yield $4,717.79 per annum for the use of the College, being within a very small fraction of an average rate of seven per cent.

The decrease of Income caused by the suspension of the Commercial Bank, and the stoppage of the Government Grant, for which it is the first and principal object of the Scheme to provide was $6,280 per annum. To this should be added $250, the annual rent received from the Medical College until last year, and say $500 for Class Fees, this portion of the Revenue having ceased, in consequence of the granting of the nomination privileges in connection with subscriptions to Endowment, making a total decrease of $7,030. To the Income from investment now reported, and to the Capital an addition is, therefore, required, in order to meet the whole deficiency, without making any provision for certain improvements, dependent upon enlarged pecuniary resources, which it is very desirable to make as soon as possible. It is necessary to remark that the work of simply restoring the Revenue to the position in which it was prior to the suspension of the Commercial Bank will be unavoidably delayed by the annual shortcomings of the past three years. The total deficiency for that period amounts to $7,807.90. This is included in the sum therein reported as having been collected for permanent Capital, and must, therefore, be regarded as a loan from Capital, to be gradually repaid after Income and Expenditure have been equalized. Another cause of delay lies in the fact that of the $107,000 reported as having been subscribed, it is believed that, owing to the death of Subscribers and other reasons about $3,000 cannot be collected. Notwithstanding these causes of delay in the completion of the Endowment Scheme, your Committee believe that there is abundant reason why the Synod should indulge in sentiments of gratitude and confidence. Immediately after this Meeting of Synod the Deputation from the College will proceed with the work intrusted to them, full of hope that the Congregations to be visited during the present Summer will respond as cheerfully and liberally to their appeal as those which have been already canvassed.

Before the preparation of this Report was completed, your Committee had the extreme gratification of learning that the College Treasurer had received a donation of £200 Sterling, ($981.08), from the Colonial Committee of the Church of Scotland, with the special sanction of the General Assembly, to this appropriation from their

Funds, and to its application to the current expenses of the College. The value of this seasonable contribution may be appreciated when it is stated that the effect of it will be to prevent the recurrence of a deficiency in the Revenue of the College.

TORONTO, 8th June, 1871.   W. SNODGRASS, Convener.

REPORT OF THE COMMITTEE ON SCHOLARSHIP AND BURSARY SCHEME.

Your Committee regret to state, that, as appears from the accompanying Report of the Treasurer. the financial condition of this two-fold Scheme during the past year has been by no means such as it ought to be, or even as it has been in former years. In 1867, the number of Congregations contributing was 32, and the amount contributed was $343.95. In 1868, the number of contributing Congregations was 34, and the receipts $410.51. In 1869 $441.10 were received from 30, and in 1870 $444.34 were received from 31 Congregations. Up to the period of the last Report, therefore, while the number of Congregations contributing during the four preceding years had remained nearly the same, the Annual Receipts exhibited a small but gradual increase. During last year, however, only 26 Congregations have made the collection, and the amount received has only been $252.39. The consequence has been an excess of Expenditure over Revenue of $164.11.

It is deeply to be regretted that this should be the case. The reasons for the liberal support of the Scheme, which have been fully stated in former Reports, still exist, and, if possible, in still greater force. The importance of the object for which it was instituted, and which it seeks, as far as the Funds placed at its disposal will allow, to promote, namely, the encouragement and aid of those who desire to study for the Ministry, and are likely to be faithful and useful labourers in the work of the Lord, can scarcely be overestimated. No less than nine removals of Ministers from the Roll of the Synod have taken place by death and otherwise, since its last Meeting. How are their places even, and the places of others in coming years, to be supplied? And how are the extension of the Church, and the spiritual wants of an ever growing population in preaching Stations, and the remoter parts of the Dominion, to be provided for? It is impossible, if we have scarcely a third part of the number of Probationers required from year to year, to fill our vacancies. If even the present number of our Ministers is to be maintained, if it is, as it ought to be, to be annually increased, Presbyteries and Congregations ought to consider it one of their first duties to look out for suitable Students for the Ministry, and lend them a helping hand, when necessary, as in most cases it will be, particularly in the beginning of their studies.

The temporal provision for the support of a Minister and his Family is in general small, and moreover, before he can be settled, eight years must lapse, during which his expenses at College, and for preparatory training, at an annual average of $140, amount to at least $1,120. It is different with Students in Law and Medicine. In the one case five years, and in the other four years only of preparatory study are required, while their Parents are of a more wealthy, although not of a more worthy class, than those whose Sons are found willing to devote themselves to the work of the Ministry. During the long period of training for the Pastoral Office, and especially in its early portions, the Student can do very little for his own maintenance, while, if he were employed regularly on the Farm, or in the Store, for which the Education of the Grammar School might suffice, he would, from the first, be more, or less, able to maintain himself, instead of needing continued support. Hence it is that, not to speak of those of less means, Farmers, even in ordinary circumstances are for the most part, however willing, not able to pay annually $140 for a series of years for the education of their Sons for the Ministry. Young men of piety and talent, who give promise of future usefulness, must, therefore, be sought out and taken by the hand by the Church, as they are by the Canada Presbyterian Church. More liberal contributions must be made to the Scholarship and Bursary Scheme, in order that there may be a Fund to which Presbyteries and Congregations can at once point them as ready to provide what is needed to supplement what their Parents can afford. Without this, the number of our Ministers must continually decrease instead of increasing. So necessary are such means for the support and encouragement of Students for the Ministry found to be in the Canada Presbyterian Church, that in Knox's College nine Scholarships are announced for the ensuing year for the best Examinations and Essays in Theology, besides eight others for Undergraduates in Arts, and, in the Theological College in Montreal, there are no less than sixteen Scholarships, besides the liberal Exhibitions open to the competition of Students in Arts in McGill University, to which it is affiliated. Again, in the Presbyterian Church of the United States, any Student with proper credentials has no difficulty in obtaining $150 a year from the Board of Education for his support at Princeton, or any of the other Theological Colleges connected with the Church, besides the privilege of board and lodging in the College Buildings at a very moderate rate.

What then do both the reason of the case, and the experience of our own and other Churches, show us to be the urgent duty of all our Congregations and Members in this matter? Evidently that every means to be taken to seek out suitable young men who may be willing to dedicate themselves to the work of the Ministry, and, as there are comparatively few who do not need some assistance, that due provision be made for that assistance being given to those who shall, after examination, be approved of by the Presbytery and College Senate. Increased collections from every Congregation, according to its means, are necessary, so that the Scholarships awarded shall be of such an amount as not to leave as they now do, even at their highest value, from $60 to $80 a year to be defrayed by the relatives of the Students, not unfrequently a burden heavier than, with the other claims on them, they can bear. A collection of $8 on an average from each of 100 Congregations would enable your Committee to award eight Scholarships of $100, and we cannot safely aim at less. In order, however, that this may be effected, there must be a united effort. Every Congregation would require to give something, however small the amount, if it were only five dollars, and your Committee would respectfully suggest, that, in view of the great importance of the object of the Scheme to the interests and prosperity of the whole Church, Presbyteries be enjoined to see that each of the Ministers within their bounds shall duly make the collection appointed on its behalf, and remit the amount to the Treasurer, so that the Scholarships which may be awarded after the Examinations at the commencement of the ensuing College Session may be provided for.

Your Committee further trust that the Synod will again recommend this important Scheme to the sympathy and support of the Church, and will renew its recommendation that, on the day appointed for the collection, Prayer be offered up for our Colleges in all its Congregations, and the attention of their Members be directed to the claims of the Gospel Ministry upon young Men of piety and talent.

TORONTO, 7th June, 1871.   JAMES WILLIAMSON, Convener.

THE UNION OF THE PRESBYTERIAN CHURCHES AND ITS EFFECT ON THE COLLEGES CONNECTED THEREWITH.

In the course of his Address at the opening of the Session of Queen's University, in 1871, Principal Snodgrass spoke as follows in regard to the proposed Union of the Presbyterian Churches and its relation t their Colleges. He said:—

At the second Conference of Committees of the Supreme Courts of the Presbyterian Churches, negotiating for Union, held at Montreal, the matter of the Collegiate Institutions formed a prominent subject of discussion and arrangement, and there was passed a Resolution, founded upon the deliverances of the General Assembly of the Canada Presbyterian Church, and of the Synod of the Church in connection with the Church of Scotland, providing generally that the Institutions of the negotiating Churches should stand to the proposed United Church in relations like to those which they have hitherto held to the several Churches with which they are connected. Upon a motion for reconsideration, the subject was again taken up, and occupied the attention of the Conference. Proposals were submitted, which, after consideration and amendment, came to be of this effect:—That Queen's University at Kingston, bear the same relation to the United Church as it now stands in to the Church with which it is connected, and should have affiliated to it, for the conferring of Degrees in Divinity, and for the preparatory training of Students for the Ministry, the two Theological Colleges at present situated in Halifax and Toronto, and also the Theological College at Montreal, with the Theological Departments of Queen's and Morrin Colleges united to it; that Tutorial work in relation to Literary and Scientific Studies should not be carried on in connection with the Theological Institutions of the United Church, but that provision should be made by the United Church for this kind of work in connection with Queen's College, Kingston, and Morrin College, Quebec, and it was recommended that, inasmuch as the Canada Presbyterian Church has resolved to endow their Theological Colleges at Toronto and Montreal, the Church in connection with the Church of Scotland shall fully endow the Arts Faculty in Queen's College. It was further proposed that the present Principal of Morrin College should be invited to become the Principal of the Theological College at Montreal, and that failing to obtain a Professor from Queen's College, the Church in connection with the Church of Scotland shall nominate a Theological Professor for that College. The formation of opinions with respect to this scheme will depend very much upon the particular point of view from which it is regarded, upon the bearing which it is seen to have on the various interests affected by it, and upon the extent to which permanency and utility are associated with the scheme considered as a whole and with the several parts of which it consists. The final acceptance or rejection of it rests with the authorities of the several Colleges referred to, and with the Supreme Court of the Churches with which they are connected. It is expected that the decisions of these bodies shall shortly be arrived at and made known. I have deemed it my duty to take the earliest public opportunity to make this statement. And, in concluding, I think it right to say that I have declined to commit myself to it until I am satisfied of the practicability of carrying out the recommendation which has been made by obtaining a much larger Endowment and fuller equipment of this Institution than it has at present, and also of its noninterference with the honourable fulfilment of pledges given and responsibilities resumed in connection with the scheme for Endowment which was begun in January, 1869, and which has been attended with such gratifying success.

PRESBYTERIAN UNION AND THE COLLEGE QUESTION, BY ALUMNUS OF QUEEN'S COLLEGE.

As the exact nature of the relation between the Church and College has been apparently misconceived, let us distinctly ascertain what this relation is.

The Queen's University and College is governed by a Board of twenty-seven Trustees. These gentlemen appoint the Professors and control the Institution. The Board is composed of the Prinicpal, eleven other Clergymen and fifteen laymen. The Clerical element is elected directly by the Synod. The Lay Members are chosen in the following maner:—Each Congregation in the Church has the privilege of nominating triennially out of its own Membership, or the Membership of the Church generally, a representative, to be one of a list out of whom are chosen the requisite number. If any Congregation fails to elect a Representative, the list from which the Lay Trustees are selected is so much curtailed. Sometimes it happens that the same Person is nominated by two, or more, Congregations. Through this machinery a Board is formed, partly through the Synod and chiefly through the Congregations, composed of Persons in whose character, judgment and orthodoxy the whole Church has confidence, and who, (it is assured), will, on the whole, rightly discharge the trust reposed in them. That during the last thirty years they have discharged their trust in a highly conscientious way, none can gainsay. Denominational the Institution may have been, sectarian it has not been. More than one-half of the Students, who have attended its Classes, were connected with other Denominations; yet, while assiduous care over their moral and religious welfare has been evinced, not a single charge has ever been even insinuated that it was used as an engine for proselytizing purposes. Such is the extent of the connection between the College and the Church. Even if it were only a Theological Hall, a Board of Trustees, or Governors, would be required, elected in some way as the above. Its functions would be different only in this respect, that, instead of having the appointment of seven, or eight, Professors, this patronage would be exercised in the case of only two, or three.

We can see many strong reasons wherefore it would be advantageous to the United Church to have associated with it the University of Queen's College as it is: no weighty reason why the Church should not desire to have it, applying as it does to be received not in *pauperis forma*, but possessed of a valuable endowment.

This important question cannot be rightly understood unless he draws sharply and clearly the distinction between a University and a College.

What is a University?

A University is simply a Board technically termed a Senate. This Board prescribes a Curriculum, lays down a Programme of Studies, fixes upon a standard to be reached by successful Candidates for academic distinction, and appoints Examiners. It exists not for instruction, (that is the work of a College), but examination; not for imparting an educational training, or communicating information on Literary, or Scientific subjects, but for testing the results of this training. The Examiners, whom it appoints examine such Students as may be sent up by the College, or Colleges, affiliated to it; and to such Candidates as have reached the prescribed standard, and have thus been found qualified, the University awards a Certificate of Qualificationfi, in the form of a Degree.

A University may have affiliated to it one College, or several Colleges. These may exist in one locality, or in places widely remote. The University of Oxford has twenty affiliated Colleges, all within the Town of Oxford. The University of London has affiliated Colleges scattered throughout England, and some of the Colonies. While the University of Edinburgh, (prescribed in the Royal Charter of Queen's as its model), has only one College. Practically the last named form exists in Ontario. The University of Toronto has University College; Victoria University has Victoria College; Queen's University has Queen's College.

The writer is an advocate for more than one University in the Province.

Who will say that England has not been the better of possessing Cambridge, as well as Oxford? And they were founded centuries ago, when the population was sparse. Look at Germany, where higher learning flourishes more vigorously than in any other Country. She has many Universities, and we have yet to learn that injurious results have accrued from the multiplicity and variety of them,—that any agitation has ever been set on foot for the concentration of them. Would any one venture to propose to destroy the University of Edinburgh, or Glasgow, or Aberdeen, or St. Andrew's, and these were all in full vigour when the population of Scotland was not larger than that of Ontario in the present day. To propose such a thing would be deemed a retrograde step.

We believe that the educational interests of the Country can best be advanced by having a variety of Collegiate Institutions, each characterized by some distinctive feature. Thus Oxford is regarded as the special home, as the chief patron of the Classics and Philosophy; Cambridge of Mathematics; London of the Natural Sciences. Life and uniformity are very far from being synomymous.

Hear Professor Seeley, the accomplished Professor of Latin, in University College, London, one of the foremost Educationists of the day, (*vide* his Essays on a Liberal Education):—"Education in fact in England is what the Universities choose to make it." This seems to me too great a power to be possessed by two corporations, however venerable and illustrious, especially since we know them to have grown up under very peculiar circumstances, and to be fortified by Endowments against modern influences, good or bad. I wish we had several more Universities; I mean teaching, as well as examining Universities. I hope that the scheme, which was announced some time ago, of creating a University for Manchester will not be allowed to sleep. I should like to see similar schemes started in three, or four, more centres of population and industry. Is there anything more undeniable than that our material progress has outrun our intellectual,—that we want more cultivation, more of the higher Education, more ideas?"

III. THE CHURCH OF ENGLAND, REPRESENTING TRINITY COLLEGE.

PROCEEDINGS OF THE COUNCIL OF TRINITY COLLEGE, 1871.

February 9th, 1871. A Resolution was passed at the last Meeting of the Corporation, to confer with certain other Gentlemen, respecting the establishment of a School of Medicine in connection with Trinity College; and a Resolution was moved by the Chancellor, seconded by Professor Ambery, That it is deemed expedient that the Statutes be amended so as to allow of the exercise of a dispensing power as to the exaction of Tests from Students in Arts, Law and Medicine, prior to graduation. And that the said Statutes be amended also, so as to allow of the exercise of the said dispensing power as to said Tests respecting Professors, in Arts, Law and Medicine on their appointments.

February 15th, 1871. The Bishop of Toronto put in a Letter from Professor Bovell, dated the 11th September, 1870, resigning his Professorship.

Resolved, That notice be given at the Meeting to be called for the second Wednesday in March next for the Meeting of the Corporation in May next, that the Committee on Statutes will submit a Statute to amend the Statute respecting "Tests" for the Students and Professors in Arts, Law and Medicine.

March 8th, 1871. Resolved, That referring to the Resolution passed at the Meetings of the 9th and 15th of February last; be it,—

Resolved, That the same be read as not applying to Professors in Arts and Law, the reterence to them being made part of said Resolution, by inadvertence, and contrary to the intentions of the Corporation.

Resolved, That Doctors Hodder, Beaumont, Bethune, and Hallowell be appointed to certain named Professorships in the Medical School of Trinity College. And that Doctor Geikie and Doctor Fulton be appointed Examiners in the School of Medicine, with a view to their appointment to Professorships.

Resolved, That all Students be required to return to College, after the several Vacations, on the day prescribed by the Provost and Professors, under penalty of the loss of the Term. And that the Fees for the Term be paid to the Bursar at the College on a day, of which notice shall be given.

May 10th, 1871. The Bishop of Toronto named Doctor Hodder as Member of the Corporation, and Doctor Hodder, having subscribed the necessary declarations, took his seat.

Resolved, That the thanks of the Corporation of Trinity College are hereby given to the Mayor and Corporation of the City of Toronto for a handsomely bound copy of the By-laws of the City of Toronto, and for a record of the Members of the Municipal Council and Civil Officials of the City of Toronto; and that the Bursar be instructed to communicate this resolution to the Mayor.

Resolved, That the Provost and Professor Ambery be instructed to draw up a Testimonial for Mr. Gilbert, on his resigning the post of Art Lecturer; and that Mr. Hock be appointed to the same, and on the same conditions.

The Land and Finance Committee made a Report, containing several financial recommendations, as follows:—

The Committee beg to submit the Bursar's Annual Statement to the first of January last, with an Estimate of the Receipts and Expenditure for 1871, and supplementary Statements. Also the Books, showing the Capital Account and Receipts and Expenditure Account. The Committee beg also to submit the Audit of the Bursar's Accounts for the year ending on the 1st of April, 1871.

With the view of increasing the Capital, the Committee recommend the sale of certain Debentures, and that the proceeds be invested in the purchase of First Class Township Debentures, amounting in all to $51,300.00.

Resolved, That the Report be adopted.

Resolved, That the Statutes of the University and of the College be amended as follows:—

Chapter III. Heading, Degrees in Arts. "Bachelor of Arts", add to paragraph five, the words; "The Chancellor, or Vice Chancellor, are, however, empowered to dispense with the making and signing of the above Declaration, when such dispensation is sought for, on the ground that the Candidate is not a Member of the United Church of England and Ireland."

"Master of Arts" add to paragraph four the words; "except in cases provided for in the instance of Candidates for the Degree of Bachelor of Arts".

Proceedings in Medicine; and to paragraph nine the words; "except in the cases provided for in the instance of Candidates for the Degree of Bachelor of Arts".

Statutes of Trinity College Chapter II Section five and the words, "except the Corporation shall see good cause, in respect to any Professor, or Professors, of the Faculties of Medicine, to dispense with the above mentioned qualifications and subscriptions".

Resolved, That Doctor Geikie be appointed Professor of the Principles and Practice of Medicine, and Doctor Fulton Professor of Physiology and the Institutes of Medicine in the Medical School of Trinity College.

Resolved, That Doctor Bovell's resignation of his Professorship of Natural Theology be hereby accepted, and, in doing so, the Corporation wish to express their grateful recognition of the continued interest shown by Doctor Bovell in the welfare of the College from its foundation.

Resolved, That a guarantee of £300 per annum be granted to the Medical School for a period of three years from the present time.

Resolved, That the following Members of the Council be a Committee to arrange for the erection of a Building for the Medical School on the Lot owned by this Corporation near the General Hospital, at an expense not in any case to exceed $5,000, to be provided for by the sale of Municipal Debentures held by this Corporation, as may be recommended by the Finance Committee. Interest at the rate of 8% per annum on the whole sum expended, together with insurance on the Building, to form a portion of the guarantee of £300 voted by this Council to the Medical School. Provided, that, if the Committee deem it more expedient to erect the Building by mortgaging the said Lot to a Building Society, they are hereby authorized to do so. The Committee, videlicet:—Doctor Hodder, Mr. G. W. Allan, Mr. Lewis Moffatt, Mr. S. B. Harman, and Mr. W. Ince.

In view of the important change made in the Statutes of Trinity College, whereby the Chancellor and the Vice Chancellor are invested with the power of dispensing, under certain conditions, with the declaration of membership in the Church of England, in the case of Candidates for Degrees in Arts, Law and Medicine; and whereby, also, the qualification of Membership in the Church of England may be dispensed with by the Corporation, at their descretion, in respect of Professors belonging to the Faculty of Medicine; the Corporation hold it their duty to declare that the change above mentioned has been made in the interests of the Church of England, and for the purpose of increasing the influence of the College, as a Church of England Institution, and that they will not consent to make it the basis of, or the pretext for, further changes, which may, in any degree, affect the character of the College, as defined in its Royal Charter; or frustrate the intention of its original promoters and benefactors, whether such changes would touch the studies or the discipline of the College.

Therefore, the Corporation hereby declare their resolution not to make any changes in the religious teaching of the College for the purpose of accommodating that teaching to the opinions of those who are not Members of the Church of England; but still to provide that all Students in Arts be lectured on the Catechism and the Articles of the Church of England, and examined in these subjects, either in the previous, or the final Examination for the Degree of Bachelor of Arts.

The Corporation also declare that it is their purpose to maintain the existing discipline of the College, by acquiring attendance at the College Chapel, Morning and Evening, both on Sundays and on the other days of the week, from Students resident in the College, (subject only to such relaxations of the rule, as have hitherto been allowed oy the College Regulations); and of Students non-resident attendance at Chapel on Sundays, and on the Mornings of Saint Days, and on all days on which they attend Lectures in the College; except such non-resident Students as shall be living with their Parents, or Guardians, or in some private Family, with the consent of their Parents, or Guardians, and permission shall have been granted by the Corporation that they may attend Divine Service on Sundays, with their own Families, or with the Persons with whom they live.

The Corporation further declare that, regarding it as being of great moment to the College, as a Church of England Institution, that its Professors should be Members of the Church of England, it is their purpose and desire that in the appointment of Medical Professors the preference should always be given *cæteris paribus* to Members of the Church of England.

November 15th, 1871. The Bursar laid on the Table the "Capital" and the "General" Account Books,—and also the half-yearly Financial Statement up to the 1st of July last.

Resolved, That the Salary of the Steward be increased to $400 a year from the commencement of his second year of service.

Resolved, That this Council recognize the equitable claim of Sir J. L. Robinson to have a mistake corrected, as to the transfer of Lots Numbers 16 and 17 on the Garrison Common, and that the College Seal be affixed to such legal Instruments as may be requisite to carry this Resolution into effect, under the orders of the Land Committee.

Resolved, That this Corporation unanimously recommend that the Honorary Degree of D.C.L. be conferred on the Right Reverend the Bishop of Huron; and on the Venerable the Archdeacon of Assiniboia.

Report of the Committee of the Corporation of Trinity College appointed to arrange for the erection of the Building for the use of the Medical School.

On assuming their duties, your Committee found that Plans and Specifications of the proposed Building had already been prepared by the Architects, Messieurs Smith and Gunwall, and approved by the Medical Board. They were thus enabled to proceed immediately to advertise for Tenders for the work; from those the lowest was selected, which, adding his Architect fees, amounted to $5,235.00.

Provided the Corporation adopts the recommendations of the Committee, the expenditure will be as follows:

Original Contract	$4,985 00
Extra Allowance to two Contractors	250 00
Architects' Fees	250 00
Plaster of Paris	30 00
Gas Pipes	38 00
	$5,553 00

or $553 in excess of the Grant for the purpose. To meet this, and some other small items of necessary expenditure, such as heating apparatus, etcetera, your Committee recommend that an additional sum of $1,000 should be placed at their disposal.

Resolved, That the Report of the Medical School Committee be adopted; and, to enable them to carry out the recommendations mentioned therein, the sum of $1,000, in addition to the previous grant of $5,000 be placed at their disposal, interest at the rate of 8% per annum on the Grant given by the Corporation in aid of the Medical School.

The Medical Faculty of Trinity College respectfully desire to request the Council to direct a Communication to be sent at the earliest possible date to the Royal College of Surgeons of England, and the Royal College of Physicians of London, and the Royal College of Surgeons of Edinburgh, informing these Bodies of the re-establishment of the Medical Faculty, and asking that the School be regularly recognised, and that an announcement of the School and University Calendar to be sent at the same time to each of these Bodies.

December 13th, 1871. With respect to the Assessment Act, the Provost read a Memorial to the Legislature of Ontario on the subject of exempting the College and Grounds from taxation, when it was,—

Resolved, That the Memorial prepared for presentation to the Legislative Assembly be adopted; subject to the modification of the two last paragraphs, as the reference to the practice in the United States is found to be correct, or otherwise,—That the Bursar be instructed to have it engrossed and the College Seal affixed to it; and that Mr. Cumberland be requested to take charge of it.

The Committee appointed at the last Meeting to consider the papers handed in by the Medical Faculty, made a Report, when it was,—

Resolved, That the Report of the Committee, to whom the Memorial of the Medical Faculty, presented at the last Meeting, was referred, was adopted. That Doctor Hodder and the Provost be a Committee to prepare a Communication to the Trustees of the Toronto Hospital, to which the Seal of the Corporation shall be attached. That the Bursar be instructed to forward a Communication, in the form furnished by the ·Medical Faculty, to the several Bodies in Great Britain mentioned by the Faculty, signed by the Bishop on behalf of the Corporation.

IV. THE (FREE) PRESBYTERIAN CHURCH OF CANADA, REPRESENTING KNOX COLLEGE.

PROCEEDINGS OF THE SYNOD OF THE (FREE) PRESBYTERIAN CHURCH OF CANADA, 1871.

June 8th, 1871. The Assembly called for the Report of the Board of Management of Knox College. The Report was handed in and read by the Reverend Doctor Topp, Chairman of the Board. Doctor Topp read also the Report of the College Senate. The Report of the Board of Examiners was read by the Reverend J. M. King.

There was handed in further, in connection with the foregoing Reports, the Report of the Committee on the Reverend Doctor Robert Burns Memorial Fund, which Report was read for the Convener, by the Reverend J. Laing.

On motion, the Report of the Board of Management of Knox College was received, and it was agreed to refer the Reports, both of Montreal College and Knox College, to a Committee to prepare a deliverance for the adoption of the Assembly.

June 9th, 1871. It was moved by the Reverend W. Cochrane, seconded by the Reverend J. W. Smith, of Grafton, and agreed to, That the Assembly do now proceed to the election of a Professor for Knox College.

It was moved by the Reverend Doctor Waters, seconded by the Reverend W. T. McMullen, of Woodstock, That the Reverend David Inglis, of McNab Street Church, Hamilton, be appointed Professor of Systematic Theology in Knox College.

It was moved in amendment by the Reverend Andrew Wilson of Kingston, seconded by the Reverend John Ross, That the Reverend William Gregg, of Cooke Church, Toronto, be elected to fill the vacant chair of Theology in Knox College.

After a long and earnest discussion, it was agreed that, before taking the vote, the Assembly should ask Divine Guidance at the Throne of grace. The Reverend John McTavish, at the request of the Moderator, led the Assembly in prayer.

The Assembly then proceeded to take a vote, which, at the request of several Members, was done by calling the Roll. The Roll being gone through and votes marked, it was found that fifty-eight had voted for Mr. Inglis, and fifty for Mr. Gregg.

The Yeas and Nays being taken on the motion carried, the election of Mr. Inglis was made unanimous.

The Reverend David Inglis, of McNab Street Church, Hamilton, was then declared duly elected to the office of Professor of Systematic Theology in Knox College, Toronto.

June 12th, 1871. The Reverend W. Cochrane, seconded by the Reverend Doctor Waters, submitted Resolutions for the adoption of the Assembly, in regard to the Report of the Committee appointed to confer with the Reverend Doctor David Inglis as to his acceptance of the Professorship in Knox College. The third of these Resolutions were in terms following:—"That the Senate of Knox College be instructed to induct Mr. Inglis into the Professorship of Systematic Theology at the opening of the first Session of Knox College."

It was moved by the Reverend W. Cochrane, seconded by the Reverend Doctor Waters, that the Resolutions be adopted as a whole.

It was moved in amendment by the Reverend Doctor A. Topp, seconded by the Reverend J. W. Smith, That the third Resolution be amended by substituting the "Presbytery of Toronto" for the "Senate of Knox College," in said Resolution.

A vote being taken, the amendment of Doctor Topp was carried, and the Resolution was amended accordingly.

June 13th, 1871. The Assembly called for the Report of the Committee to whom was referred the Reports of the Boards of Knox College and of the Presbyterian College, Montreal, to frame a Deliverance.

The Report was handed in and read by the Reverend W. McLaren, the Convener. On motion, the Report was received, and it was agreed to consider the several clauses thereof seriatim.

1. In reference to Knox College.

The first clause was read and adopted.

The second clause was read, relating to a Lecturer on Apologetics.

It was moved by the Reverend William Gregg, and seconded, That for the word "Apologetics," the words "Homiletics and Church History" be inserted.

Before taking a vote on Mr. Gregg's motion, it was moved by the Reverend Doctor Topp, and agreed to, that the Report be sent back to the Committee to make such amendments as they may deem necessary.

June 14th, 1871. It was moved by the Reverend W. McLaren, duly seconded and agreed to, That the Resolution, adopting the first Clause of the Deliverance then submitted, agreeing to appoint a Lecturer in Knox College, be re-considered.

On a second Motion, duly seconded, the said Resolution was rescinded, and it was agreed that no Lecturer be appointed.

The second, third and fourth Clauses of the Deliverance were read and adopted.

It was moved by the Reverend J. M. King, seconded by the Reverend Doctor Macvicar, and agreed to, as follows:—That the recommendation, that a general effort be made to raise $250,000 as an Endowment for Knox College, Toronto, and for Montreal College, be adopted, and that the Assembly appoint a Committee to mature a plan, and carry the same into effect for bringing this matter before the whole Church.

June 15th, 1871. It was agreed,—1. That there be no Lecturer appointed for this year, and that the hearing of Discourses by the Students, and the teaching of Church History be left to the Senate, to be by them arranged as they may see fit.

2. That the Salaries of the Professors be two thousand dollars, ($2,000), each.

3. That the Boarding House be continued, and that it be remitted to the Board of Management to make necessary arrangements, with instructions to give prompt attention to this matter.

4. That the Assembly record its regret that the recommendation of last Assembly, as to the endowment of the Reverend Doctor Robert Burns' Memorial Chair has been disregarded by certain Presbyteries, and that the effort has thus failed; but that the thanks of the Assembly be given to the Committee, and particularly to the Convener. and Secretaries, for their valuable services and earnest, and so far successful, efforts to carry out the recommendation of the Assembly.

In reference to both Colleges, it was agreed,—

1. That the Boards of the two Colleges be a Joint Committee and be instructed to take steps towards amending the Charters of Knox College and Montreal College, so as to give the Senates of these Institutions the power of, unitedly, conferring Degrees in Divinity, under such Regulations as the Assembly may, from time to time, enact, and to report to the Assembly at Toronto, in November; the Chairman of the Board of Knox College to be the Convener of this Committee.

2. That the Sabbath immediately preceding the opening of the Colleges be observed as a day of Prayer on behalf of those Institutions.

3. That the Assembly commend to the liberality of the Church the Scheme of Scholarships for Students attending University and McGill Colleges.

REPORT OF THE BOARD OF MANAGEMENT OF KNOX COLLEGE, 1871.

The Board of Management of Knox College, in presenting their Annual Report to the General Assembly, have to state that the work of the College during the past Session has been carried on with its accustomed order and regularity. Provision having been made by the Assembly for the superintendence of the various departments of Study. in consequence of the circumstances in which the College was placed by the retirement of the Reverend Principal Willis, the instructions of the Assembly were followed out, and consequently there has been no interruption in the prescribed Course of Study for the different Classes.

It was remitted to the Board by last Assembly, to make such arrangements as might be deemed best for the continuance of the Boarding House in the College. Having had under their consideration an application from Mrs. Willing, expressing her desire to be allowed to carry it on (as had been done by her late husband, it was resolved to comply with her application for the period of a year. The result has been in every respect satisfactory. Mrs. Willing, however, has intimated her intention not to continue longer in the position which she occupies, and accordingly it will be for the Assembly to give further instructions in the matter.

It will be observed from the Report of the Senate herewith transmitted, that the number of Students in the Theological department has been thirty-three, and in the Preparatory department, thirty-six. In addition to these, not a few are taking a full course at the University, with the view of entering upon the study of Theology in Knox College. The Board have thus to report, as they do with much gratification and thankfulness, that there are about one hundred in various stages of progress in their studies, looking forward to the work of the Ministry.

The amount received during the year, through the ordinary channel for the support of the College, has been, including $350 of interest from the Endowment Fund, $6,928.14. The Expenditure has been $6,846.25. On the 1st May, 1870, the debt was $831.03. Now it is $613.13, having been reduced by $217.90.

For Bursaries there had been received from interest of the Bursary Fund and from private benefactions, the sum of $1,151. The gift of Mrs. Doctor Burns of $500 for the Bonar Scholarship, has been invested, so that the whole Bursary Fund now invested is $4,600.

The Endowment Fund, including $52.10 collected by the Reverend John Laing, of Cobourg, is $5,092.10. And the debt on the Building is $2,163.62.

In regard to the matter of the legacy of the late Mr. Alexander of Barrie, the Board have not thought it advisable to appeal against the decision of the Vice Chancellor, inasmuch as there would be no likelihood of procuring an alteration of that decision.

The Assembly, in pronouncing a deliverance on the College Report last year, expressed its approval of the contemplated movement for the Endowment of a Chair in Knox College, in connection with the memory of the late Reverend Doctor Robert Burns, and recommended that such movement receive the cordial co-operation of all the Ministers and other Office-bearers of the Church. The Board have to report, that owing to circumstances, over which they have no control, this movement, after having been hopefully commenced, has not been prosecuted further.

Several Members of the Board, having expressed their opinion that it would be desirable for Knox College to have the power of granting Degrees in Divinity, it was resolved to suggest to the Assembly the propriety of appointing a Committee to consider the subject, and to ascertain whether the Act of Incorporation could be amended for that purpose.

The Board conclude their Report by respectfully requesting the Assembly to appoint a day for special Prayer for our Theological Institutions.

TORONTO, June, 1871.   ALEXANDER TOPP, Chairman.

REPORT OF THE SENATE OF KNOX COLLEGE, SESSION 1870-1871.

The number of Students in the Theological Classes of Knox College during the Session which has now closed was thirty-three. Of these, two were of the Third year, seven of the Second, and sixteen of the First. The Class which has now completed its attendance at the College, it will be observed with gratitude, is rather larger than the average number prepared for license for some years past; and it is earnestly hoped that, by the Divine blessing, its Members may prove a valuable accession to the Church labourers in preaching the Word.

One of the Students of the first year was not regularly enrolled, but was sent up by the Presbytery of London to take advantage, by permission of the Senate, of such Classes as he might be found prepared to enter. His case has been reported to that Presbytery.

The Classes in Exegetical Theology, and in Biblical Criticism, were conducted by Professor Caven; in Systematic Theology, Apologetics and Church History, by the Reverend William Gregg, during the first Term of the Session, and by the Reverend David Inglis during the second. In accordance with the arrangement sanctioned by the College Board, that Homiletics and Pastoral Theology, with Church Government, should be taught during alternate Sessions, the Reverend J. J. A. Proudfoot lectured, for three months, on the former subject.

The details of the work done will be found in the several Class Reports. The Senate has pleasure in bearing testimony to the good results of the action taken by the General Assembly in forbidding Students to combine the University Course with that of this College. The improved attendance on the Classes during last Session shows the wisdom of this enactment.

The Preparatory Department, as during the two previous Sessions, was conducted by the Reverend Professor Young. The Students in the three years of this Department numbered thirty-six. Of this number, however, one Student, Mr. McKeracher, at the earnest request of the Home Mission Committee, was allowed to remain in a very necessitous part of the Mission Field; it being understood that he should be examined on subjects prescribed to him when he returned to Toronto.

With the approval of the Senate, the Reverend Professor Young, finding the Students of the First year generally qualified to do the work of the Second, soon after the beginning of the Session, combined the First and Second years, so that, for the greater part of the Session, there were but two Classes in the Preparatory Course.

It is proper to mention that the Students of the College, in their Literary and Metaphysical Society, gave a good deal of attention to the composition of Essays, and to Elocution; and that the amount which, in the Session previous, had been divided between this Society and the payment of a Teacher of Elocution, was appropriated last Session wholly in aid of the Society, the sum thus given to the Students being supplemented by Funds of their own, and distributed as Prizes in the Society.

The closing Examinations were conducted by the Senate in conjunction with the Board of Examiners, as appointed by the General Assembly. These Examinations, it is believed have been conducted with much care, and the attention of 'Students called to any points on which they may have proved deficient, even when the Examination, on its general merits, has been sustained. The Examiners report good satisfaction, on the whole, with the Papers given in.

As formerly, the Students were employed in occasional missionary work during the Winter. The Senate has faithfully endeavoured to limit the missionary service rendered by Students, in accordance with the Church's rule respecting this matter.

The Senate is gratified to report that the attendance of Students at the Monthly Missionary Prayer Meeting has been very good; few Students who had it in their power to attend, being absent on any occasion.

A number of Scholarships was awarded in the Theological Department during the Session; and is exclusive of those competed for by Students in the University Curriculum, who purpose studying for the Ministry.

It will be observed that several of these Scholarships were awarded in connection with the regular College Examination. The Senate is so entirely satisfied to connect all the Scholarships except two, (which will be awarded for "Essays,") with the ordinary Examinations of the College.

TORONTO, April 5th, 1871.   WILLIAM CAVAN, Chairman of Senate.

The Board of Examiners begs to report that, in accordance with the Regulations adopted, *ad interim*, at last Assembly, it examined, in the beginning of October last, the Students entering the Preparatory and the Theological Departments, respectively, of Knox College.

Those Students were found to be Members, in full communion, of the Church, and, with one exception, to have appeared before a Presbytery of the Church, and to have been, by it, recommended to prosecute their Studies for the Ministry. While all appearing for the first time, they evinced very different degrees of acquaintance with the prescribed subjects. The Examination of all was sustained, but it was agreed to delay assigning them their place in the Curriculum until the Examinations at the close of the Session. The Report of the Senate, by which these closing Examinations were conducted, will show the standing definitely assigned to each.

Fifteen Students presented themselves for examination, with a view to entrance in the Theological Classes. The Board agreed, in accordance with the power conferred on it by the Assembly, to exempt Graduates from the Examination. Only two took advantage of the exemption offered. The Examinations brought out results, on the whole, satisfactory as to the attainments of the Students submitting to them. In a few cases, in which a Student was found defective in some branches, a second Examination in these branches was appointed, and took place at Christmas. Of the Scholarships offered in connection with the examination of entrants on Theology, that for eminence in Hebrew was taken by Mr. D. L. McKechnie, and that for general proficiency by Mr. John Scringer, B.A.

The Board again conducted examinations for the purpose of awarding Scholarships to Students attending University College, and looking forward to the Ministry in the Canada Presbyterian Church. Of Congregations formerly contributing for this Fund, Cooke's Church, and Gould Street Church, Toronto; McNab Street, Hamilton; St. Andrew's Church, London; and Knox Church, Scarboro; have contributed various amounts this year also; while Knox Church, Elora, and Widder Street, St. Mary's, made their first contribution to the Scheme of $60 each.

The Board, more than ever satisfied of the beneficial operation of this Scheme, has given notice that eight Scholarships will be awarded to successful competitors next October. It is hoped that a large number of Congregations will contribute for its support.

With regard to Examinations, at the close of the Session, of Students of the Second and Third years, exempted by the Regulation of last Assembly from Examination at the beginning of it, these were conducted by the Senate. As the Regulation referred to does not make it quite plain by whom the Assembly designed that these closing Examinations should be conducted, it is hoped that the amended Regulations to be submitted to this Assembly will definitely settle this point.

TORONTO, June 6th, 1871.   JOHN M. KING, Chairman of Board of Examiners.

RECEIPTS AND EXPENDITURE, 1870-71.

Receipts.

Received from all sources, including $350 balance from the Endowment Fund $6,928 14

Expenditure.

	$ cts.	
Amount due at beginning of year		$167 76
Paid for Salaries, Doctor Willis, up to 1st August	906 94	
Paid for Salaries to Professors Caven	1,600 00	
and Young, from the 1st of July	1,200 00	
Paid Salaries of Three Lecturers, at $500 each	1,500 00	
		$5,206 94
Paid on account, Doctor Willis' retiring allowance		562 41
Paid Mrs. Willing,—light, fuel, etcetera		250 00
Paid Accounts for repairs		50 88
Paid for Library		75 65
Paid for Printing and Advertising		8 00
Paid Insurance		103 20
Paid Interest on Mortgage		151 41
Paid Interest for Advances		80 00
Paid Proportion of Charges common to all the Schemes...		190 00
Balance		81 89
		$6,928 14

TORONTO, 1st May, 1871.

BURSARY FUND.

Receipts.

	$ cts.	
Balance in hand at the beginning of year	428 14	
Received from all sources, including interest	1,151 00	
		$1,579 14

Expenditure.

	$ cts.
Bursaries, Scholarships, and Prizes paid	1,068 50
Invested, (Bonar Scholarship)	500 00
Printing, Stationery, etcetera	25 00
Balance	33 64
	$1,579 14

The amount invested for the Scholarships and Bursary Fund is ... $4,600 00

ENDOWMENT FUND.

Receipts.

	$ cts.
Balance in hand at the beginning of year	5,040 00
Balance in cash, per Reverend J. Laing	52 10
Interest received	350 00
	$5,442 10

Expenditure.

	$ cts.
Paid to Knox College Ordinary Fund	350 00
Balance now in hand	5,092 10
	$5,442 10

KNOX COLLEGE BUILDING FUND.

The amount due on Mortgage on Building is $2,163 02

TORONTO, 1st May, 1871.   WILLIAM REID.

The above Accounts have been audited and certified by

$$\left.\begin{array}{l}\text{J. McMURRICH,}\\ \text{J. L. BLAIKIE,}\end{array}\right\} \quad \text{Auditors.}$$

REPORT OF THE COMMITTEE ON THE UNION OF THE PRESBYTERIAN CHURCHES.

The Assembly called for the Report of the Committee on Union, appointed at the Meeting at Quebec in June last. The Report, consisting of the Minutes of the Meetings of the Joint Committee of the Presbyterian Churches in the Provinces of British North America, on the subject of the Union, held in St. Paul's Church, Montreal, in September and October, of the current year, inclusive, and embodying certain Resolutions and certain articles proposed as a Basis of Union, was read by the Reverend Doctor Topp, the Convener of the Committee.

November 8th, 1871. The Assembly took up for consideration the Report of the Union Committee on the subject of Collegiate Education.

It was moved and seconded that, for the consideration of this subject, the Assembly resolve itself into a Committee of the Whole House. This Motion being put to vote was lost, and it was agreed to proceed in open Assembly as at present constituted.

The first finding of the Joint Union Committee on the subject of Collegiate Education, as also the Resolutions afterwards adopted by the said Committee, were read.

It was moved by the Reverend Doctor Proudfoot, seconded by the Reverend W. McLaren, That the negotiating Churches shall enter into Union with the Theological and Literary Institutions which they now have; and that application be made to Parliament for such legislation as will bring Queen's University and College, Knox's College, the Presbyterian College, Montreal, Morrin College, and the Theological Hall, at Halifax, into relations to the United Church, similar to those which they now hold to their respective Churches, and to preserve their Corporate existence, government and functions, on terms and conditions like those under which they now exist.

That inasmuch as the Canada Presbyterian Church has resolved to make an effort to raise the sum of Two hundred and fifty thousand dollars, ($250,000), for the Endowment of its Theological Institutions, within three years, it is expected that the Synod of the Presbyterian Church in connection with the Church of Scotland will complete, during the same period, the Endowment of Queen's College, so that neither it, nor the Theological Intsitutions referred to, may be a burden to the United Church, or interfere with the prosecution of its Home and Foreign Missions.

Further, it is understood, that all other matters pertaining to the Colleges be left for adjustment to the United Church.

November 9th, 1871. The Assembly resumed consideration of the subject of the Union and Collegiate Education, as presented in the Report of the Union Committee. The Reverend Doctor Proudfoot asked and obtained leave to prefix to the Resolution offered by him, certain words necessary to connect the said Resolution with the Report then under consideration, as follows:—That the recommendations of the Joint Committee on Union be not adopted, but that [the Reverend Doctor Proudfoot's Resolution] be substituted for them.

It was moved in amendment to Doctor Proudfoot's motion, by Professor Young, seconded by Doctor Waters, as follows:—The Assembly disapprove of the Resolutions on Collegiate Education agreed to by the Joint Committee on Union, particularly in so far as these provided for the reception of certain Literary and Scientific Colleges into the same relation to the United Church as they now hold to the Presbyterian Church of Canada in connection with the Church of Scotland.

It was moved, in further amendment, by Professor Inglis, seconded by the Reverend W. Cochrane,—That in view of the proposed efforts to endow various Colleges connected with two of the negotiating Churches, and of the impossibility of completing the Union satisfactorily, until the results of these efforts are ascertained, it is not expedient to come to any decision in reference to Collegiate arrangements at the present stage of the negotiations; nevertheless, this Assembly desire to declare that, inasmuch as a large number of the Office-bearers and Members of this Church are opposed, in the present circumstances of the Country, to undertaking any general Classical, or Philosophical, teaching, as a part of the Church's work, it would, therefore, be greatly preferable that the Faculties in Arts of Queen's College and Morrin College should be placed on such a basis as, while preserving them in all their efficiency, would, at the same time, remove them from under the direct control of the Church, without its being implied that noncompliance with this suggestion will be a positive bar to Union.

It was moved in further amendment by the Reverend J. Laing, seconded by the Reverend W. Burns, That the following be added to the Resolution of Doctor Proudfoot:—In the opinion of this Assembly, it is indispensable to harmony in the United Church, if not to union altogether, that a change be made in the Constitution and direction of Queen's College, which will relieve the Church Courts of all responsibility as regards that Institution, and prevent unnecessary interference with the non-sectarian character of National Education now happily established amongst us.

Doctor Proudfoot asked leave to alter the Resolution offered by him on this subject, by making certain additions thereto, which proposed additions were read, as follows:—And further, the Assembly reappoint their Committee on Union, and instruct them, in bringing this Resolution under the notice of the Committee of the other negotiating Churches, and seeking their approval thereof, to inform them that this Church still adheres to its repeatedly expressed opposition to State Grants to Denominational Colleges in these Provinces; and further, instruct their Committee to ascertain whether there is a definite prospect of harmonious action in the United Church in this matter.

It was then moved, in further amendment, by the Reverend W. Gregg, seconded by the Reverend Thomas McPherson, That the Assembly adopt as their decision on this subject, the first finding of the Joint Committee on Union, in terms following:—That the negotiating Churches shall enter into Union with the Theological and Literary

Institutions which they now have, and that applications be made to Parliament for such legislation as will bring Queen's University and College, Knox College, the Presbyterian College, Montreal, Morrin College, and the Theological Hall at Halifax, into relation to the United Church, similar to those which they now hold to their respective Churches, and to preserve their Corporate existence, government and functions, on terms and conditions like to those under which they now exist.

The discussions on the several motions before the House being closed, the Assembly proceeded to a decision,

The Motion of Doctor Proudfoot was declared to be carried, and the Assembly decided in terms thereof as following:—

That the recommendations of the Joint Committee on Union be not adopted, but that the following Resolution be sustained for them, namely:—That the negotiating Churches shall enter into Union with the Theological and Literary Institutions which they now have; and that application be made to Parliament for such legislation as will bring Queen's University and College, Knox College, the Presbyterian College, Montreal, Morrin College, and the Theological Hall at Halifax, into relations to the United Church similar to those which they now hold to their respective Churches, and to preserve their corporate existence, government and functions, on terms and conditions like those under which they now exist.

That, inasmuch as the Canada Presbyterian Church has resolved to make an effort to raise Two hundred and fifty thousand dollars, ($250,000), for the Endowment of its Theological Institutions, within three years, it is expected that the Synod of the Presbyterian Church of Canada in connection with the Church of Scotland, will complete during the same period the Endowment of Queen's College, so that neither it, nor the Theological Institutions referred to, may be a burden to the United Church, or interfere with the prosecution of its Home and Foreign Missions.

Further, it is understood that all other matters pertaining to the Colleges, be left for the adjustment of the United Church.

And further, the Assembly reappoint their Committee on Union and instruct them, in bringing this Resolution under the notice of the Committee of the other negotiating Churches, and seeking their approval thereof, to inform them that this Church still adheres to its repeatedly expressed opposition to State Grants for Denominational Colleges in these Provinces; and further instruct their Committee to ascertain whether there is a definite prospect of harmonious action in the United Church in this matter

November 10th, 1871. The Assembly took up the Report of the Committee appointed at the Meeting of the Assembly at Quebec on the endowment of Knox College, and the Presbyterian College at Montreal. The Report was read.

The Honourable John McMurrich having declined to act as one of the Sub-Committees mentioned in the Report, it was moved and seconded, and agreed to, That the name of Mr. W. B. McMurrich be inserted in the Report, instead of that of the Honourable John McMurrich.

On motion of the Reverend Doctor Topp, duly seconded, the Assembly received and adopted the Report in terms following:—

The Assembly's Endowment Committee report the following recommendations bearing on the work intrusted to it, for adoption by the Assembly at this Meeting:—

I. The Committee having read the Resolution of the General Assembly, relating to the effort to be made to raise $250,000, and understanding that it is contemplated that the amounts already received and invested towards the Endowment of the two Colleges should be thrown into the General Endowment Fund in connection with the effort to raise the amount specified, and with a view to its equal division between the two Colleges, is of opinion that the movement in its present form to endow the Colleges, can only be successful by adhering to and acting on this understanding, and recommend it to be prosecuted on this distinct principle.

II. The Committee is of opinion that there should be, at the very earliest period, in each College not less than four Professorships, for the following subjects, videlicet:— Systematic Theology, Exegetical Theology, and Biblical Criticism, Apologetics, Church History, Homiletics, Pastoral Theology, and Church Government.

III. The Committee recommend that the subscriptions should be made payable in three equal annual instalments, or six semi-annual instalments, and that no payment shall be called for until $200,000, including the amounts on hand, be subscribed.

IV. (a) The Committee is further of opinion that it would contribute to the success of the movement if a special trust was constituted by the General Assembly for the purpose of holding and investing the Endowment Fund, and of distributing the proceeds to the Boards of Management of Knox College, Toronto, and of the Presbyterian College, Montreal, in such proportions that, including in the estimate the proceeds of the moneys already invested by the Boards of the respective Colleges for ordinary College purposes, the Colleges shall be possessed of the same Revenue from these sources; and would recommend that the General Assembly should take action at the appropriate period, with a view to the creation of such a Trust.

(b) The Committee recommend that the Trust should consist of five persons, elected by the General Assembly, two of whom should retire each year and be ineligible for re-election for a year thereafter.

(c) The Committee recommend that the money should be invested in unquestionable Securities, such as Government and County Debentures, more with a view to absolute security than to a high rate of interest.

(d) The Committee further recommend, that a professional Accountant should be appointed to audit the Accounts, and report to the General Assembly from year to year.

V. The Committee is of the opinion that it should be an understanding that the Capital Fund for the Endowment should not be infringed upon for any purpose, and that no part of the Annual Income therefrom be applied to any other purpose than the payment of the Salaries of the Professors and Officers of the Colleges at Toronto and Montreal, or the increase of the Capital Fund, and that the General Assembly should enact accordingly.

VI. The Committee has invited the Reverend John Laing, of Cobourg, to act as Superintendent and General Secretary of the Endowment movement, at a salary of $1,600 per annum, with travelling expenses, and now asks the General Assembly to give its sanction to this step, and to instruct the Presbytery of Cobourg to release Mr. Laing from his charge.

VII. The Committee recommend that the following sub-Committees should be constituted in Montreal and Toronto, to carry on, along with Mr. Laing, and in co-operation with the Presbyteries of the Church and with Members of the General Committee, in their respective localities, the work of forming plans and raising money.

The sub-Committee for Toronto—The Reverend Doctor Topp, Convener, the Reverend Professor Inglis, the Reverend J. M. King, Ministers; the Honourable George Brown, and Messieurs James Brown, W. B. McMurrich, William Kerr.

VIII. The Committee requests the sanction of the General Assembly to the addition of several names to the General Committee.

In terms of the Report, the Moderator announced to the Reverend. J. Laing, of Cobourg, his appointment as the Agent of the Church, for the purpose of promoting the Scheme of Endowment, at a salary of One thousand six hundred dollars, a year, with travelling expenses.

HISTORICAL SKETCH OF KNOX COLLEGE, BY THE REVEREND DOCTOR WILLIS.

Knox's Theological College dates from the year 1844, although its Charter of Incorporation, under the Seal of the Province, is only dated in 1858. It was then the only Theological School of the Presbyterian Church of Canada, as it now is of the "Canadian Presbyterian Church." Its professorial Staff consists of three,—one of these being Principal, as well as Professor of Divinity. To the other two Professors are assigned the departments of Church History, with the Evidences of Christianity; and Exegetical Theology, and with the oversight of the Philosophical Studies of the Students.

The latter part of the arrangement was only provided for in what was intended as a purely Theological College, to meet the case of a large class of Students, when the arrangements of the University College were not found to be so adapted to its needs as was desirable.

For a like reason Classes in the department of the Languages and Mathematics were also, for a time, taught in Knox College. But the desire of the Founders of the Institution being, as far as possible, to affiliate their College with the public

5—XXIII.

Universities, they did not contemplate,—nor does the Canadian Presbyterian Synod contemplate,—a permanent provision, at the expense of one Church, of the means of preparatory Education already provided for at the expense of the Country in common.

The College has enjoyed a very creditable course of success. The average number of the Students since its commencement has scarcely fallen below forty or forty-five; if preparatory Students, announcing themselves as prospective Students of Divinity, be included, the number attending this year, (1871), is considerably above fifty, with every prospect of exceeding this number annually, now that the union of the two Presbyterian Churches both increases the sources of supply of Pupils, and the range of the ecclesiastical and missionary field depending on it for future pastors.

Knox College is supported by funds contributed annually by the Congregations of the Church. The liberality of several individuals, or Congregations, has secured to it a few Bursaries, or Scholarships: among these some bear the names of Isaac Buchanan, one of the earliest friends of the College, and of the Reverend Henry Esson, the earliest Literary Professor of the Institution,—one of the last being "The Prince of Wales' Prize," of which His Royal Highness was the Donor shortly after his visit, with which, at the invitation of the Reverend Principal Willis, he honoured the Institution in 1860.

The Building, known as Knox College, is Elmsley House, the residence a few years ago, of the Governor of the Province, Lord Elgin. The property was purchased by the Church soon after it ceased to be used for its former purpose, and is, by the continued and creditable exertion of the Congregations, free of debt.

The Governing bodies of the College are, for the purpose of internal discipline, and daily government, the Senate, the Professors, with a few Assessors, appointed by the Synod, and a larger body called the College Board, which is for the conduct of its secular and general affairs. Both report to the Synod of the Church, to which ultimately belongs the choice of the Teachers, the arrangement of the Curriculum and the care of its whole interests.

The present Curriculum extends to six years, the latest three of these being given to Theological studies proper. Students are permitted to join at any stage of the Course, on producing satisfactory proofs of attendance elsewhere, and of proficiency. The admission to the College is through the Presbyteries, with whom lies the right of examination in order to enter.

A Boarding House in charge of a Steward is connected with the College, and residence within its walls is optional.

The College possesses a Library and Museum, the former consisting already of four, or five, thousand Volumes, the foundation of the collection being largely due to the efforts of the Reverend Doctor Robert Burns; it has since been increased by the labour of the Reverend Doctor Willis, and the gifts of many friends in Canada and Britain.

Number of Professors, three, of which one is the Reverend Principal Willis, Professor of Systematic Theology.

Text Books:—Hill's Institutes of Theology, Extracts from Calvin, Doctor Willis' Latin Biblical Criticism, Evidences of Christianity, Butler, Paley, Exegetical Theology, Elliott and Eadie on the Epistles, Alford's Greek Text, Moore on the Minor Prophets, Mental Philosophy, Moral Philosophy, Reid, with Notes by Sir W. Hamilton, the Reverend Doctor Wayland, etcetera.

CHAPTER IV.

APPORTIONMENT OF THE LEGISLATIVE SCHOOL GRANT TO PUBLIC SCHOOLS IN ONTARIO, FOR 1871.

CIRCULAR TO THE CLERK OF EACH MUNICIPALITY IN THE PROVINCE OF ONTARIO.

I have the honour to transmit herewith, a certified copy of the Apportionment for the current year, of the Legislative School Grant to each City, Town, Village and Township in Ontario.

The basis of Apportionment to the several Municipalities for this year is the School population as reported by the Local Superintendents for 1869 and as revised on comparison with previous Returns. The total amount available for apportionment is $5,000 more than last year, and in addition to the increased amount available on the basis of population, those Townships in which there are feeble Schools and a sparse population have been specially considered in the Apportionment.

Where Roman Catholic Separate Schools exist, the sum apportioned to the Municipality has been divided between the Public and Separate Schools therein, according to the average attendance of Pupils at both classes of Schools during last year, as reported and certified by the Trustees.

The Grants will be paid by the Honourable the Provincial Treasurer on the Certificate of the Chief Superintendent of Education. These Certificates will be issued on, or about the 30th of June, in favour of those Municipalities which have sent in duly audited School Accounts and Local Superintendents' Reports to this Office.

I trust that the liberality of your Council will be increased, in proportion to the growing necessity and importance of providing for the sound and thorough education of all the youth of the land.

TORONTO, 30th May, 1871.   EGERTON RYERSON.

APPORTIONMENT TO CITIES, TOWNS AND VILLAGES FOR 1871.

Cities.	Public Schools.	Separate Schools.	Total.
	$ cts.	$ cts.	$ cts.
Hamilton...............................	1,636 00	413 00	2,049 00
Kingston	1,002 00	353 00	1,355 00
London.................................	1,320 00	221 00	1,541 00
Ottawa	811 00	783 00	1,594 00
Toronto	2,988 00	1,595 00	4,583 00
	$7,757 00	$3,365 00	$11,122 00

Towns.			
	$ cts.	$ cts.	$ cts.
Amherstburgh.............................	128 00	105 00	233 00
Barrie	168 00	65 00	233 00
Belleville..............................	510 00	175 00	685 00
Berlin.................................	251 00	34 00	285 00
Bothwell	133 00	....	133 00
Bowmanville	276 00	....	276 00
Brantford	661 00	80 00	741 00
Brockville.............................	304 00	101 00	405 00
Chatham...............................	257 00	....	257 00

APPORTIONMENT TO CITIES, TOWNS AND VILLAGES FOR 1871.—*Cont'nued.*

Towns.	Public Schools.	Separate Schools.	Total.
	$ cts.	$ cts.	$ cts.
Clifton	100 00	47 00	147 00
Cobourg	345 00	97 00	442 00
Collingwood	201 00		201 00
Cornwall	298 00		298 00
Dundas	209 00	89 00	298 00
Galt	369 00		369 00
Goderich	359 00		359 00
Guelph	429 00	162 00	591 00
Ingersoll	270 00	70 00	340 00
Lindsay	185 00	130 00	315 00
Milton	100 00		100 00
Napanee	203 00	26 00	229 00
Niagara	125 00	58 00	183 00
Oakville	109 00	63 00	172 00
Owen Sound	315 00		315 00
Paris	211 00	61 00	272 00
Perth	184 00	63 00	247 00
Peterborough	300 00	127 00	427 00
Picton	173 00	53 00	226 00
Port Hope	412 00		412 00
Prescott	129 00	107 00	236 00
Sandwich	147 00		147 00
Sarnia	240 00		240 00
St. Catharines	468 00	303 00	771 00
St. Mary's	286 00	63 00	349 00
St. Thomas	183 00		183 00
Simcoe	173 00		173 00
Stratford	277 00	72 00	349 00
Whitby	238 00	63 00	301 00
Windsor	359 00		359 00
Woodstock	401 00		401 00
	$10,486 00	$2,214 00	$12,700 00

Villages.	$ cts.	$ cts.	$ cts.
Arnprior	143 00		143 00
Ashburnham	123 00		123 00
Aurora	132 00		132 00
Bath	60 00		60 00
Bradford	123 00		123 00
Brampton	179 00		179 00
Brighton	125 00		125 00
Caledonia	111 00		111 00
Cayuga	86 00		86 00
Chippawa	136 00		136 00
Clinton	179 00		179 00
Colborne	86 00		86 00
Dunnville	163 00		163 00
Elora	177 00	23 00	200 00
Embro	68 00		68 00
Fergus	148 00	13 00	161 00
Fort Erie	97 00		97 00
Gananoque	173 00		173 00
Garden Island	60 00		60 00
Georgetown	165 00		165 00
Hawkesbury	118 00		118 00
Hespeler	125 00		125 00
Holland Landing	75 00		75 00
Iroquois	72 00		72 00
Kemptville	129 00		129 00

APPORTIONMENT TO CITIES, TOWNS AND VILLAGES FOR 1871.—*Concluded.*

Villages.	Public Schools.	Separate Schools.	Total.
	$ cts.	$ cts.	$ cts.
Kincardine	183 00		183 00
Lanark	82 00		82 00
Listowel	129 00		129 00
Merrickville	107 00		107 00
Mitchell	193 00		193 00
Morrisburgh	125 00		125 00
Mount Forest	132 00	15 00	147 00
Newburgh	95 00		95 00
Newcastle	80 00		80 00
New Edinburgh	50 00		50 00
New Hamburg	118 00		118 00
Newmarket	128 00	40 00	168 00
Oil Springs	132 00		132 00
Orangeville	90 00		90 00
Orillia	136 00		136 00
Oshawa	202 00	79 00	281 00
Pembroke	45 00	45 00	90 00
Petrolia	154 00		154 00
Portsmouth	85 00	40 00	125 00
Port Colborne	62 00	38 00	100 00
Port Dalhousie	125 00		125 00
Preston	119 00	24 00	143 00
Renfrew	61 00		61 00
Richmond	54 00		54 00
Seaforth	143 00		143 00
Smith's Falls	86 00	27 00	113 00
Southampton	97 00		97 00
Stirling	82 00		82 00
Strathroy	183 00		183 00
Streetsville	72 00		72 00
Thorold	146 00	61 00	207 00
Trenton	124 00	90 00	214 00
Vienna	86 00		86 00
Wardsville	72 00		72 00
Waterloo	171 00		171 00
Welland	114 00		114 00
Wellington	54 00		54 00
Yorkville	183 00		183 00
	$7,353 00	$495 00	$7,848 00

SUMMARY OF APPORTIONMENT TO COUNTIES, 1871.

Counties.	Public Schools.	Separate Schools.	Total.
	$ cts.	$ cts.	$ cts.
1. Glengarry	2,074 00	229 00	2,303 00
2. Stormont	1,925 00		1,925 00
3. Dundas	2,148 00		2,148 00
4. Prescott	1,497 00	146 00	1,643 00
5. Russell	909 00		909 00
6. Carleton	3,477 00	148 00	3,625 00
7. Grenville	2,157 00	50 00	2,207 00
8. Leeds	3,518 00	37 00	3,555 00

SUMMARY OF APPORTIONMENT TO COUNTIES.—*Concluded.*

Counties.	Public Schools.	Separate Schools.	Total.
	$ cts.	$ cts.	$ cts.
9. Lanark	3,302 00	11 00	3,313 00
10. Renfrew	2,929 00	74 00	3,003 00
11. Frontenac	2,931 00	149 00	3,080 00
12. Addington	1,810 00	81 00	1,891 00
13. Lennox	874 00	....	874 00
14. Prince Edward	1,918 00	....	1,918 00
15. Hastings	4,222 00	25 00	4,247 00
16. Northumberland	3,992 00	92 00	4,084 00
17. Durham	3,507 00	....	3,507 00
18. Peterborough	3,106 00	62 00	3,168 00
19. Victoria	3,569 00	....	3,569 00
20. Ontario	4,593 00	23 00	4,616 00
21. York	6,014 00	173 00	6,187 00
22. Peel	2,662 00	13 00	2,675 00
23. Simcoe	6,309 00	40 00	6,349 00
24. Halton	2,049 00	....	2,049 00
25. Wentworth	3,105 00	33 00	3,138 00
26. Brant	2,185 00	....	2,185 00
27. Lincoln	2,038 00	35 00	2,073 00
28. Welland	1,942 00	23 00	1,965 00
29. Haldimand	2,444 00	36 00	2,480 00
30. Norfolk	3,301 00	27 00	3,328 00
31. Oxford	4,679 00	....	4,679 00
32. Waterloo	3,281 00	164 00	3,445 00
33. Wellington	5,667 00	343 00	6,010 00
34. Grey	6,336 00	239 00	6,575 00
35. Perth	4,225 00	98 00	4,323 00
36. Huron	6,958 00	90 00	7,048 00
37. Bruce	5,034 00	36 00	5,070 00
38. Middlesex	6,972 00	113 00	7,085 00
39. Elgin	3,356 00	....	3,356 00
40. Kent	3,203 00	137 00	3,340 00
41. Lambton	3,308 00	47 00	3,355 00
42. Essex	2,450 00	27 00	2,477 00
District of Algoma	300 00	....	300 00
	$142,276 00	$2,801 00	$145,077 00

GRAND TOTALS OF APPORTIONMENTS.

	$ cts.	$ cts.	$ cts.
Counties and Districts	142,276 00	2,801 00	145,077 00
Cities	7,757 00	3,365 00	11,122 00
Towns	10,486 00	2,214 00	12,700 00
Villages	7,353 00	495 00	7,848 00
	$167,872 00	$8,875 00	$176,747 00

CHAPTER V.

OFFICIAL CIRCULARS OF THE CHIEF SUPERINTENDENT ON THE NEW SCHOOL LAW OF ONTARIO, 1871.

I. To THE WARDEN AND MEMBERS OF THE COUNTY COUNCILS IN THE PROVINCE OF ONTARIO.

I address through you, the County Council over which you preside, this Circular on the subject of the new School law. We have jointly and harmoniously laboured together during more than a quarter of a century for the education of the youth of our common Country. Closely approaching my three score years and ten, I have been anxious, before leaving the Administration of the School System to other hands, to remedy, as far as I could, such defects in the School law as my own long experience had suggested, and as have been felt by local school Authorities; to supply wants unprovided for, or created by the progress of the School System, and to adapt it as completely as possible to the present state of society and of our Municipal Institutions. To do this I have taken special pains and incurred much labour. I have made a fourth Tour of Inquiry and Examination into the School Systems of foreign educating Countries, both in Europe and America, and reported to the Government the results, with recommendations for the improvement of our own School System.* These recommendations were submitted to a very large Select Committee of our Legislative Assembly, (a Committee selected without reference to party). The Bill which the Committee reported as the result of its lengthened and minute deliberations, was afterwards submitted by me, for consultation, to County School Conventions held in the various Counties of the Province. In the final Draft of Bill, I embodied those provisions only which received general approval after so much consultation; and expected it would meet with the equally general approval of the Legislative Assembly, if not pass without a division, as did the Grammar School Improvement Bill which I submitted to the Legislature of United Canada in 1865. But, to my surprise and regret, it met with a degree of opposition, and since an amount of misrepresentation, such as no previous School Bill has ever encountered. I am, however, thankful to be able to say that the Bill has passed the Legislative Assembly, not only unimpaired, but greatly improved in its provisions in respect to High Schools and other details.

1. The establishment of Free Schools by law has been long and almost unanimously desired by the Country; and the corresponding provision to secure to each child in the land Public School instruction during four months of each year from the age of seven to twelve years inclusive, and providing means to enable Trustees to enforce this provision in any case of wilful delinquency.

2. County Councils have complained of the expensiveness of County Boards of Examiners, consisting, as they have done, of all Trustees of Grammar Schools and Local Superintendents; and Teachers have complained of being examined for Certificates of qualifications, and their Schools being inspected, by persons who had never been school Teachers. Both of these grounds of complaint have been removed by the new School Act. Under the authority of the 11th Section of the new School Act, (of which I have sent herewith two or three copies), each County Council appoints a Board of Examiners consisting of from three to five Members, whose Qualifications are to be prescribed by the Council of Public Instruction. The Council of Public Instruction has already prescribed the Qualifications of Examiners as follows:—

"All Head Masters of Grammar, or High Schools, and all Graduates who have proceeded regularly to their Degrees in any University in the British Dominions, and have taught in a College, or School, not less than three years; and all Teachers of Common, or Public, Schools who have obtained a First-class Provincial Certificate of Qualifications, or who may obtain such Certificate under the provisions of the present law, shall be

---

* See Chapter IV. of the Twenty-First Volume of this Documentary History.

considered legally qualified to be appointed Members of a County, or City, Board of Examiners without further examination, on their obtaining from the Education Depart-. ment, for the satisfaction of the County Council, or City Board, a Certificate of their having complied with this Regulation, and being eligible under its provisions."

3. Your Council will select from these three classes of legally qualified persons a County Board of Examiners, of whom a County Inspector must be one; and the Council will, of course, before appointing any Person as Examiner, satisfy itself that such Person possesses the Certificate above specified, since, in case a County Council should appoint any Persons on the Board of Examiners who do not possess the legal qualification, it would vitiate the constitution and acts of such Board.

4. But the Act requires that each Board of Examiners shall include a County Inspector, and also provides, in the Third Section, that "The qualifications of County, City, or Town, Inspectors shall, from time to time, be prescribed by the Council of Public Instruction, which shall determine the time and manner of examination of Candidates for Certificates of Qualification, and grant Certificates of Qualification; and no one not holding such Certificate of Qualification shall be eligible to be appointed an Inspector."

According to the requirements of the Statute, the Council of Public Instruction has prescribed the qualifications of County Inspectors as follows:—

"All County and City Superintendents of Common, or Public, Schools who have held that office consecutively for three years; all Teachers of Public Schools who have obtained, or who shall obtain First-class Provincial Certificates of Qualifications of the highest grade (A); all Head Masters of Grammar, or High, Schools, who have taught the same School three years, and who shall prepare and transmit to the Education Department a satisfactory Thesis on the Organization and Discipline of Public Schools; and all Graduates who have proceeded regularly to their Degrees in any University in the British Dominions, and who have taught in a College, or School, not less than three years, and who shall prepare and transmit to the Education Department a satisfactory Thesis on the Organization and Discipline of Public Schools, shall be considered legally qualified for the office of County Inspector of Public Schools, without any further examination, on their obtaining, in each case, from the Education Department, the Certificate required by law."

5. But for any one of the above four classes of persons specified as possessing the legal qualifications for the office of County Inspector, to be eligible for appointment to that office, it will be necessary for him to procure from the Education Department, and present to the County Council, the Certificate of his qualification required by the Statute.

6. It has been my intention, in recommending these provisions of the new School Act, and it is my wish, that the office of County Inspector should, as far as possible, be filled by meritorious Common School Teachers, who, by their labour, skill and acquirements, have, or shall have, obtained the first rank in their profession. But at present the only class of Common School Teachers who possess first-class Provincial Certificates of qualification are those who have attended the Normal School. I think, therefore, that no permanent appointment of County Inspectors should be made before the Public School Teachers at large shall have had an opportunity, by examination, of obtaining a First-class, grade A, Provincial Certificate of Qualification. This can be done by the County Councils at their June Meeting appointing Inspectors from the three classes of persons, now legally qualified for six months only—say from the 1st of July to the 31st of December, 1871; and then at their next January Meetings the County Councils can, from the lists of qualified persons to be furnished them by the Education Department, make their selections and appointments of County Inspectors with a view to permanency. In this way due consideration will be given to the profession of Public School Teachers; the new School Act, with the new Programmes of School Classification and Discipline, will be brought into full operation immediately after the July Vacation; and the Councils will have time to obtain all needful information to enable them, at the beginning of next year, to make the best selection of County Inspectors to give effect to the School System in the new organization of the Public Schools.

7. It is important that each County Clerk, (as provided in the Fifty-fifth Section of the Consolidated School Act) should inform me, immediately after the Meeting of the

County Council, of the name and address of each County Inspector appointed, that I may know to whom to address the Examination Papers of Teachers, as the first Examination should take place not later than July.

8. The Sixteenth Section of the new School Act invests the County Council with important powers, by the appointment of a careful and impartial Committee, for the settlement of the many questions of complaint and dispute arising out of the formation of School Sections—questions for the investigation and settlement of which the Law has heretofore made no provision.

9. The mode of appointing Trustees of Grammar, or High, Schools by County, Town and Village Municipal Councils is unchanged by the new School Act; but the powers of the Boards of High School Trustees are made the same in respect to supporting High Schools as are the other Boards of Trustees in respect to the support of Public Schools; so that the chief reason for the union of High and Public School Boards in past years no longer exists. A more equitable and comprehensive mode of providing for the support of High Schools is also made by the new School Act, apart from the High School Building, which must be wholly provided by the Town, Village, or School, division within which the High School is situated; and the Fortieth Section of the Act makes it the duty of the County Council to prescribe the limits of each existing High School District. Under the new organization, High Schools will have much more important work to do in respect to higher English education than the Grammar Schools have ever performed.

10. I confidently trust the important powers and duties which the new School Act confers and enjoins upon County Councils will be exercised and discharged with the same intelligence, impartiality and patriotism which have characterized their proceedings during the last twenty years.

TORONTO, March, 1871.   EGERTON RYERSON.

II. TO TRUSTEES OF RURAL SCHOOLS THROUGHOUT THE PROVINCE OF ONTARIO.

The new School Act, which provides that "all Common Schools shall hereafter be designated and known as Public Schools," confers upon Trustees of School Sections great additional powers and facilities for the discharge of their important and often difficult duties.

1. By law all your Schools are made Free Schools, and as such supported entirely by Rates on taxable property. The great object desired so frequently and with so much unanimity by County School Conventions, and by the friends of educational progress generally, is thus accomplished, and the agitations which have taken place on the subject during the last twenty years, will now cease, although they have prepared the way for this grand consummation of a Free School law.

2. While the Law thus makes every man in proportion to his property, which is protected and increased in value by the labour of all, liable for the education of every child in the land, it also provides that every child shall have the right of at least four months' School instruction each year from seven to twelve years of age—that is six years; and invests Trustees with power to see that no Parent, or Guardian, shall wilfully, without penalty, violate this beneficent provision of the Law, and of which every Ratepayer has a right to claim the execution.

3. Then follows the corresponding necessary provision, that "each School Corporation shall provide adequate School Accommodations for all children of school age in their School division, or Municipality." These "adequate Accommodations" include two things:—First. protection of the Pupils from snow and cold in Winter, and from rain in Spring, Summer and Autumn. Secondly, sufficient Room, Seats, Desks, and necessary outside Conveniences for the Pupils. In default of this, the payment of the School Apportionment may be withheld, and the defaulting Trustees made personally responsible for the loss of the amount thus forfeited and lost to the School Section through their neglect; and any Parent may sue the Trustees for damages in not providing "Adequate Accommodations" for the due reception and teaching of his child.

4. Then follows also the obligation of Trustees to employ a competent Teacher. If the property of every man is taxed in proportion to its value to support a Public School, every man has a just right to claim the teaching of his children all the subjects of the Public School education. The First clause of the Eighty-first Section of the Consolidated School Act explicitly requires that, "It shall be the duty of every Teacher of a Common School to teach diligently and faithfully all the subjects required to be taught in the School;" and, therefore, a Teacher must be employed competent to teach those subjects, as far as the children of each Ratepayer may require. It would be a monstrous injustice to tax a man to defray all the expenses of a School, and then that his children could not be taught in such School the prescribed Public School subjects, on account of a Teacher being employed less advanced than some of his own children. The object of the Free School Law is not to save the pockets of certain parties, but to make the School as fit to teach in, as it is free, to all classes of children of school age, by making the property of all liable for its support, and empowering Trustees to command its resources. It is, therefore, as much the duty of Trustees to employ a Teacher as competent to teach more advanced Public School Pupils in their Section as to teach the beginners; and the best economy is to employ the best Teacher that can be obtained, as it is to employ the best Physician, or Lawyer, or Mechanic.

5. The Thirteenth Section of the Act contains a most important provision for introducing into the Schools "the teaching of the elements of Natural History, of Agricultural Chemistry, of Mechanics, and of Agriculture," and makes it the duty of the Council of Public Instruction to train Teachers, prepare a Programme of Studies, and select Text-books for that purpose,—thus giving the Public Schools a practical character in connection with various industrial pursuits of the Country that they have never yet possessed, but which has recently been largely provided for by the Legislature.

6. The Fifteenth Section of the new School Act also provides against injuriously small School divisions; and the Sixteenth Section of the Act provides for a majority of the Trustees, or any five Ratepayers, a competent and impartial tribunal of appeal against an unjust, or hurtful, formation, or alteration, of the boundaries of their School Section.

7. The Seventeenth Section of the Act provides facilities for procuring suitable School Sites, such as have often been applied for by Trustees and others, but which have not heretofore been provided by law.

8. By the Twenty-seventh Section of the School Act, the Division Court is substituted for the often tedious and uncertain mode of arbitration for the settlement of pecuniary disputes between Trustees and Teachers.

9. By the Second Sub-section of the Thirtieth Section of the Act, more extensive and defined powers are given to the Collector appointed by Trustees; and by the Third Sub-section of the same Section, the restriction heretofore imposed upon Trustees in employing a Teacher for the ensuing year between the first of October and the second Wednesday in January, is repealed.

10. By these provisions of the new School Act, and others to which I need not refer, great additional facilities are provided to enable Trustees to fulfil the important and responsible trust committed to them by their fellow-citizens for the sound Public School education of all the youth of the land—a trust which I doubt not you will fulfil in a manner worthy of your office, and commensurate with the best interests of our beloved Country.

TORONTO, March, 1871.   EGERTON RYERSON.

III. TO TEACHERS OF THE PUBLIC SCHOOLS OF ONTARIO.

The new School Act, contains more provisions to advance the profession and position of Teachers of Public Schools than any School Act, which has been passed by our Legislature since 1850.

It makes all the Schools Free by Law, and thus relieves Teachers of all labour and frequent difficulties and losses arising out of the Rate-bills on Pupils.

2. It makes permanent, during good behaviour, all Certificates granted by County Boards according to the Terms, giving no power to such Boards, or to any other Board, or Council, or individual whatever, to cancel such Certificates, except for misconduct, until they expire according to the terms of them.

3. It provides for the examination of Candidates for Teachers' Certificates of Qualification by Boards of Examiners consisting of none but those who have had experience in teaching.

4. It authorizes Regulations by which none but holders of First-class Provincial Certificates of the highest grade, or University Diplomas, with testimonials of experience in teaching equivalent to the higher grade of First-class Provincial Certificates of Teachers, shall be Inspectors of Public Schools.

5. It repeals the Section of the Consolidated School Act which prevented the employment of Teachers, except under certain circumstances, for an ensuing year between the first of October and the second Wednesday in January.

6. While the provisions of the Consolidated School Act relative to the prompt payment of Teachers' Salaries remain unchanged, the new Act provides a more certain and expeditious mode of settling pecuniary disputes between Trustees and Teachers, by the decision of a Court, than by the old method of Arbitration.

7. The highest class County Board Certificates hereafter to be awarded, (equal to second-class Provincial Certificates), will be for life, or during good behaviour, and valid in every County of the Province, instead of being liable, as heretofore, to be cancelled at the pleasure of the County Board granting them, and limited to one County.

8. The Regulations and Programmes of Studies for the Discipline of the Schools and the Classification of Pupils, will as much improve the position of Teachers and facilitate the performance of their duties, as the provisions of the Act above referred to.

9. But while provision is thus made to improve the position and protect the interests of the Teachers,—provisions such as do not exist in any other Country, or State, in America,—equal care must be taken to maintain and elevate the standard of the Teacher's qualifications; so that, while, on the one hand, the Teacher is secured in what belongs to the dignity and efficiency of his profession, the public shall be guaranteed against unqualified and incompetent Teachers. If the position of the Teacher is improved, the standard of his qualifications should be proportionably advanced; and this will tend still further to improve his position and interests and, at the same time, increase the efficiency and value of his teaching,—thus effecting a saving in the time of the Pupils, and promoting the development of their faculties, and their acquisition of knowledge.

10. It is with this view that the new School Act has provided for the more uniform and effective Examination of Candidates for the Teaching Profession, and their classification, according to qualification and merits. The *Ontario Association of Teachers* have themselves requested that the Council of Public Instruction should prepare Papers for the Examination and Classification of Teachers throughout the Province, and direct the manner of such Examination. This is provided for by the new Act. There have heretofore been four classes of Teachers' Certificates, namely, Provincial Certificates to Graduates of the Normal School, and three Classes of Certificates by County Boards. There will hereafter be but three Classes of Certificates, namely, Provincial Certificates by the Council of Public Instruction, and two classes of Certificates by County Boards. The third Class Certificates heretofore given by County Boards will hereafter cease to be given. The Examination Papers for the three Classes of Certificates to be given, will all be prepared under the direction of the Council of Public Instruction, as also the estimated value of each question, and will thus be the same in every County of the Province.

11. Each Class of Examination Papers thus prepared will be sent to the County Inspectors under seal, not to be broken except on the day and place of Examination of Candidates, and in their presence. The Examination will take place on the same day and at the same hour, at the place of Municipal Council Meetings in all the Counties and Cities of the Province, and the same time allowed, and the same mode adopted in the Examinations by every County and City Board of Examiners. The Questions and Answers by Candidates for First-class Provincial Certificates will be forthwith sealed up in the presence of the Candidates, and transmitted to the Education Department at Toronto; the value of the Answers to the Questions for the other two Classes of Certificates will be decided upon by the County Boards of Examiners, who will grant the Certificates accordingly—of which the blanks will be prepared and furnished by the Education Department.

12. The lowest Class Certificates issued by the County Board will be valid for three years, but not renewable, unless under very special circumstances, which will be provided for. Teachers of ordinary capacity and diligence, who obtain the lowest Class County Board Certificates, can, in three years, qualify themselves to obtain the highest Class County Board Certificates. If they do not possess such capacity, or will not employ such diligence for improvement in their profession, they ought to leave it, and their places will be more than filled by new Candidates; and the profession will thus be gradually purged of non-improving and incompetent Teachers, and Parents and Pupils will be relieved of their incumbency.

13. To be eligible for Examination for the highest Class County Board Certificate, (or Second-class Provincial Certificate), the Candidate must have successfully taught three years; and the Certificate obtained by him, or her, will be valid during life, or good behaviour, and will be available in all the Municipalities of the Province.

14. To be eligible for Examination for a First-class Provincial Certificate, the Candidate must have successfully taught five years, (as suggested by the *Ontario Teachers' Association*); or two years, if during that period he has held a Second-class Certificate granted under the new Regulations, and his Certificate will not only be valid during life, or during good behaviour, and available in all the Municipalities of the Province, but will, if of the first grade, (A), render him eligible for the office of County Inspector of Public Schools.

15. It is important to add, that the standard of qualifications of these different Classes of Teachers, will be the same for all Teachers, whether trained in the Normal School or not, just as the same standard of qualifications is prescribed for all Candidates for admission to the Bar as Barristers, whether they have studied in a Law Office or not; and just as the same Examination is required of all Candidates for the Degree of Bachelor of Arts in the University, whether they have attended Lectures in University College, or whether they have studied at home, with, or without, the aid of a private Tutor. There can no more be two standards for First and Second-class Provincial Certificates of Teachers, than two standards for Degrees in the Toronto University, or for admission to the Bar as Barristers-at-Law.

16. There is immense advantage in Candidates for First-class Provincial Certificates attending the Lectures, Examinations and actual teaching in the Model Schools, in connection with the Normal School, as there are immense advantages in Candidates for the Degree of Bachelor of Arts attending Lectures, Examinations and Studies in a College; and the greater is the merit of being able to obtain such a Degree, or such a Certificate, without the aid of the College, or the Normal School, as the labour and difficulty of obtaining it is so much the greater. But the standard of qualification cannot be varied to suit the varying circumstances of Candidates in the one case, any more than in the other. The Normal School, with its Model Schools, is the University for the training of Teachers for Public Schools, the same as University and other Colleges are the Training Schools for the learned Professions and for Head Masterships of the High Schools.

17. Nor must Teachers holding even the higher County Board Certificates suppose that it is an easy thing to obtain a First-class Provincial Certificate. This has never been accomplished, nor can it be accomplished, without long and severe application. In the State of Ohio, (with a population much larger than that of Ontario), and in the absence of a Normal School, during the first two years after the Law had provided for issuing State Certificates of Qualification by a Board of three, who had obtained State Certificates, only thirteen State Certificates of Qualification were granted on examination,—twelve to male Teachers, one to a female Teacher. During the third year, (the last year for which I have examined the State Superintendent's Report), eighteen State Certificates of Qualification were granted—fifteen to male Teachers and three to female Teachers. As examples, I have caused the Register of our Normal School for the last four years to be examined, with the following results: During the years 1867, 1868, 1869, 1870, (with an average attendance of about 150, each of the half-yearly Sessions), there have been granted only thirteen Provincial Certificates of the First Grade A,—that is, a fraction over three in each year, or at the rate of one and a half each Session. Of the thirteen Students who obtained A Certificates, eight entered the Normal School with First-class County Board Certificates, and two with Second-class County Board Certificates. During the same period of four years, thirty-four First-class Provincial Certificates of the Second grade B were granted to Students, fifteen of whom had obtained First-class, and nine Second-class County Board Certificates before entering the Normal School. During the same four years fifty-nine First-class Certificates of the third grade C were granted to Students, twenty-four of whom possessed First-class, and ten Second-class County Board Certificates on entering the Normal School. The total therefore, of First-class Certificates, of these grades, during four years, is 106 Students, forty-seven of whom entered the Normal School with First-class and twenty-one with Second-class County Board Certificates.

18. The question arises, how long had these Students to attend the Normal School, with its severe course of lectures, studies, exercises and practice of teaching in the Model Schools, before obtaining their First-class Provincial Certificates, and on what examination do they obtain them? I answer in the following words of my Official Report for 1869 on the subject:—

"The time required to take a Certificate depends, of course, upon the attainments and ability of the Student, and the grade and class to which he aspires. To obtain a first-class grade A the average time taken is between three and four Sessions. A few have taken such Certificates in one Session, but the majority require four, five and even six Sessions. The average time required to take a second-class certificate, grade A, is about two Sessions.

"Very few spend only one Session at the Normal School. In most cases, Students return for a second, and, in many cases, a third and fourth Session. The Certificates are awarded at the close of the Session by a Committee of Examiners, of which the Head Master and Second Master of the Normal School are members. The examination lasts for six days, during each of which the Students write for six hours. The Papers are subsequently carefully read by the Examiners, and a value, varying from one—the highest—to six—the lowest—is assigned to each. These marks, or values, are entered in appropriate columns in a Book. called the "Certificate Record," which is kept for that purpose, and which serves not only to give a condensed view of the results of the examination in each individual case, but also for subsequent reference when any question arises as to the standing of a Teacher in any particular branch, when he was in attendance at the Normal School. The grade and class of the Certificate awarded depends partly on the standing attained at this final examination (chief importance being attached to the marks awarded for Education, Aptitude to Teach, Arithmetic, Reading and Spelling, Grammar and Composition), and partly on the character the individual has earned for himself as to quickness and general ability as a Teacher."

19. It is thus seen that a Teacher, with the higher County Board Certificate, coming to the Normal School, has to incur the expense, time and labour of from one to two years, terminated by an examination of 36 hours in order to obtain the highest Provincial Certificate. The Course of Studies in the Normal School was last revised in 1858, and may be found [on pages 68, 69 of Volume XXII of this History], together with the

methods of instruction, and the General Regulations and Programme of Lectures. Such is the standard of qualifications for all Teachers in order to entitle them to First-class Provincial Certificates; and just in proportion as they approach that standard will they be qualified thoroughly to manage and teach the Public Schools, as well as to inspect them; and just as the Public Schools approach the standard of the Model Schools, (the Normal School system of Common School Organization, Discipline and Teaching in practice), will be their increased value in the knowledge they impart the faculties they develop, the habits and character they aid to form in the youth of our Country. Every Teacher should aim to occupy as high a place as possible in his profession, in his character, his example, his habits, his success, his usefulness.

TORONTO, March, 1871.   EGERTON RYERSON.

PROGRAMME FOR THE EXAMINATION AND CLASSIFICATION OF TEACHERS OF THE PUBLIC SCHOOLS IN THE PROVINCE OF ONTARIO.

Prescribed by the Council of Public Instruction for Ontario, 28th March, 1871, as authorized by the Ontario School Act of 1871.

CONDITIONS REQUIRED OF CANDIDATES FOR CERTIFICATES OF QUALIFICATION AS TEACHERS.

1. To be eligible for examination for a Third Class (County) Certificate, the Candidate, if a female, must be 16 years of age; if a male, must be 18 years of age; and must furnish satisfactory proof of temperate habits and good moral character.

2. Candidates for Second Class (Provincial) Certificates must furnish satisfactory proof of temperate habits and good moral character, and of having successfully taught in a school three years, except in the special cases hereinafter provided.

3. Candidates for First Class (Provincial) Certificates must furnish satisfactory proof of temperate habits and good moral character, and of having successfully taught in a School five years, or two years, if during that period he has held a Second Class Certificate granted under these Regulations.

3. Candidates for First Class (Provincial) Certificates must furnish satisfactory proof of temperate habits and good moral character, and of having successfully taught in a school five years, or two years if during that period he has held a Second Class Certificate granted under these Regulations.

VALUE AND DURATION OF CERTIFICATES.

1. First and Second Class Certificates are valid during good behaviour and throughout the Province of Ontario; and a First Class Certificate of the highest grade (A), renders the holder eligible for the office of County Inspector.

2. Third Class Certificates are valid only in the County where given, and for three years, and not renewable except on the recommendation of the County Inspector; but a Teacher, holding a Third Class Certificate, may be eligible in less than three years, for examination for a Second Class Certificate, on the special recommendation of his County Inspector.

EXPLANATORY NOTE.

1. Attendance at the Normal School for Ontario, with the required practice in the Model Schools, and passing the requisite examinations for a First Class Certificate, shall be considered equivalent to teaching five years in a public or private School. So also, attendance at the Normal School, with the required practice in the Model Schools, and passing the requisite examinations for a Second Class Certificate, shall be considered equivalent to teaching three years in a public or private School.

2. In regard to teachers in French or German settlements, a knowledge of the French or German Grammar, respectively, may be substituted for a knowledge of the English Grammar, and the Certificates to the Teachers expressly limited accordingly.

MINIMUM QUALIFICATIONS REQUIRED FOR THIRD CLASS CERTIFICATES OF TEACHERS IN THE PUBLIC SCHOOLS.

Reading.—To be able to read any passage selected from the Authorized Reading Books intelligently, expressively and with correct pronunciation.

Spelling.—To be able to write correctly any passage that may be dictated from the Reading Books.

Etymology.—To know the prefixes and affixes, (Authorized Spelling Book, pages 154-169).

Grammar.—To be well acquainted with the elements of English Grammar, and to be able to analyze and parse, with application of the rules of syntax, any ordinary prose sentence, (Authorized Grammars).

CHAPTER VI.

CIRCULAR TO THE WARDEN AND MEMBERS OF THE COUNTY COUNCILS IN ONTARIO, IN REGARD TO THE APPOINTMENT OF COUNTY SUPERINTENDENTS, OR INSPECTORS, OF SCHOOLS AND OTHER INFORMATION.

In March last, I addressed, through you, to the County Council over which you preside, a Circular Letter on the subject of the New School Law. In that Circular, I explained some of the provisions of the Law, and the duties and powers of County Councils created by it.

In the Sixth paragraph of that Circular I referred to the appointment of County Inspectors of Public Schools, and suggested under the circumstances stated, the advisableness of a temporary appointment of such Inspector; but, it having been represented to me that some of the best qualified Persons for the office would not like to give up their positions and prospects for the temporary and uncertain appointment to the office of County Inspector for six months, and others having complained that it would be unjust to have any appointment to office made without their having an opportunity to become legally eligible to be appointed to it, I brought the matter before the Council of Public Instruction, which directed a special Examination to be held, to commence the 18th of this month, for all Candidates for the office of Public School Inspector. Due notice was given of such Examination, and all Candidates, who felt themselves able to become legally qualified for the office, presented themselves, and underwent an examination of six hours per day, during five days. A list of the names of all those who have become legally qualified for the office of Public School Inspector in any County of Ontario, including yours, is herewith appended. A few, (by special understanding entered into when the School Act was under the consideration of the Legislature), have received Certificates of Qualification upon the ground of their having been County Superintendents during the last three consecutive years; but their names are not included in the printed list as eligible for the office in other Counties, but are sent to the Councils of the Counties to which alone their Certificates of Qualifications are respectively confined. It is, however, not obligatory on a County Council to appoint one of these locally qualified Superintendents as County Inspector, if it believes any other Candidate, whether resident, or non-resident, for the office is better qualified, and will do more to promote the efficiency of the Public Schools.

I need not here repeat any of the suggestions I have made in my Circular of March last, except to remind the Council of the necessity of the immediate appointment of the County Inspector, or Inspectors, and of the Board of Examiners; of which I beg to be informed as soon as possible. In all cases these appointments should take effect the first of next July.

As in the revised Programme of Studies for the Public Schools, soon to be published, provision will be made for the thorough teaching of the three primary subjects of all good Education—Reading, Writing, and Arithmetic—and for the teaching of other subjects directly connected with the social progress and practical pursuits of the people at large, and for the classification of the Pupils, and the time of teaching each subject, per week, I am sure your County Council will feel with me how important it is to have an Inspector of Schools, practically acquainted with School organization, and thoroughly competent to examine and teach every class and every Pupil in the School, and to see that the Pupils are duly classified, and that every subject of the Programme is thoroughly taught, and that the School is in all respects what it ought to be, and what it can be made. Heretofore the inspection of the Schools has, as a general rule, been merely nominal, because the Inspectors were, for the most part, not practical Teachers, and not wholly devoted to the duties of their office. The New School Act is intended to remedy this evil, and give to our School System the right arm of strength, by requiring that the Inspectors be practical men, and wholly devoted to the duties of their office; and I trust that your Council will see that these important provisions of the Act are carried into full effect, by not appointing any but a thoroughly qualified Inspector, who shall wholly devote, at least, five days in the week to his work, as does every School Teacher.

The office of Inspector is the highest prize held out in the School System for the meritorious Teacher, and ought not to be snatched from him by any outsider, of whatever pretensions, more especially as no Teacher of a Public School can be legally qualified for the office except one who has obtained the highest grade of the highest Class Certificate of Qualifications in his profession.

TORONTO, 30th May, 1871.   EGERTON RYERSON.

NOTE. The list of qualified Persons for the office of County Inspectors is too long to be inserted here, but it can be seen in the *Journal of Education* for July, 1871.

The following additional information was also sent to the Wardens:—

I. WHEN THE NEW SCHOOL ACT OF 1871 WENT IN FORCE.

The general provisions of the new School Act went into force on the day on which the Act itself received the Royal Assent. Certain portions of the new Law cannot, however, go into operation until the Regulations designed to give them effect shall have been prepared and approved by His Excellency the Lieutenant-Governor-in-Council. They will, when ready, be published.

II. QUALIFICATIONS OF PUBLIC SCHOOL INSPECTORS AND COUNTY EXAMINERS.

Prescribed by the Council of Public Instruction for Ontario, under the Authority of Sections Seven and Eleven of the School Act of 1871.

1. Qualifications of County Inspectors.

All County and City Superintendents of Common, or Public, Schools who have held that office consecutively for three years; all Teachers of Public Schools who have obtained, or who shall obtain, First-class Provincial Certificates of Qualifications; all Head Masters of Grammar, or High, Schools, who have taught the same School three years, and who shall prepare and transmit to the Education Department a satisfactory Thesis on the Organization and Discipline of Public Schools; and all Graduates who have proceeded regularly to their Degrees in any University in the British Dominions, and who have taught in a College, or School, not less than three years, and who shall prepare and transmit to the Education Department a satisfactory Thesis on the Organization and Discipline of Public Schools, shall be considered legally qualified for the office of County Inspector of Public Schools, without any further examination, on their obtaining, in each case, from the Education Department, the Certificates required by Law.

III. QUALIFICATIONS OF COUNTY EXAMINERS.

All Head Masters of Grammar, or High, Schools, and all Graduates who have proceeded regularly to their Degrees in any University in the British Dominions, who have taught in a College, or School, not less than three years; and all Teachers of Common, or Public, Schools who have obtained a First Class Provincial Certificate of Qualifications, or who may obtain such Certificate under the provisions of the present School Law, shall be considered as legally qualified to be appointed Members of a County or City Board of Examiners, without further examination, on their obtaining from the Education Department the Certificates required by Law.

I. *Regulations for giving effect to the foregoing.*

I. Candidates eligible to act as County, or City, Examiners will, on application, be furnished with the requisite Certificate from the Education Department.

II. A Candidate for the office of County, or City, Inspector of Public Schools, must, in order to be eligible for that appointment, obtain from the Education Department a Certificate of his qualification for the office. This will be transmitted to him on his furnishing satisfactory proof that he possesses the legal qualifications. In the case of University Graduates and Head Masters of High Schools, a satisfactory Thesis is required on the Organization and Discipline of Public Schools, etcetera.

III. The Thesis to be prepared ought not to exceed twenty-five or thirty pages of foolscap, written on one side only, and should embrace the following topics, or subjects, chaptered as numbered, videlicet: —

1. Organization of Schools; Classification of Pupils; the System of Monitor Teachers —its use and abuse; School Buildings and In and Out-door arrangements; School Furniture and Apparatus, etcetera.

2. School Management; Time Tables and Limit Tables of Study; School Rules; School Register; Roll-book; Visitor's Book.

3. General principles of Education; Art of Teaching, with examples of the mode of treating various subjects; characteristics of the successful Teacher; how to secure attention; how to interest the Class.

4. Characteristics of good style of questioning; correction of errors; recapitulations, etcetera.

5. Principles of Mental, Moral and Physical Culture of Childhood; Gymnastics and Calisthenics.

6. School Discipline; Rewards and Punishments; Prizes; authorized system of Merit Cards.

7. School Libraries; how best to make them available; School Museums, or local collections, their value, and how to promote their formation and use.

8. Principles of the School Law relating to Public School Trustees, Teachers and Inspectors of Schools.

IV. EXAMINATION OF COMMON SCHOOL TEACHERS.

In regard to the examination of Teachers it is proposed that the same Examination Papers will be used on the same day in every County of the Province. In these Examinations special prominence will be given to School Organization and Discipline, as well as to School House Accommodation, Internal Arrangements, Construction, etcetera.

V. CONSOLIDATED SCHOOL ACTS, (1850-1871).

The entire text of the School Acts of 1850, 1860 and 1870-1 will be incorporated in one Act, so that Local Superintendents, Trustees, Teachers and other interested parties will be able to see at a glance what modifications in our present School Laws have been made by the new Act.

VI. NEW SCHOOL REGISTERS.

A new edition of Public School Registers, (including the modifications in the Courses of Study required by the new School Act of 1871), will be shortly prepared and published. They will be sent to the County Clerks, for distribution, through the Local Superintendents, or Inspectors, but none will be sent out direct to individual Schools from the Education Department.

VII. ANNUAL SCHOOL REPORTS.

Local Superintendents of Counties and Townships, and Boards of School Trustees in Cities, Towns and Villages, will please lose no time in transmitting their Annual School Reports (now due) to the Education Department, together with such general remarks on the state of the Schools in their various localities as they may desire to make.

VIII. FOUR KINDS OF LIBRARIES WHICH MAY BE ESTABLISHED UNDER THE DEPARTMENTAL REGULATIONS.

"The Public School Libraries are becoming the crown and glory of the Institution of the Province."—*Lord Elgin.*

"Had I the power I would scatter Libraries over the whole land, as the sower sows his seed."—*Horace Mann.*

Under the Regulations of the Education Department, each County Council can establish four classes of Libraries in their Municipality, as follows:—City, Town, Village and Township Councils can establish the first three classes, and School Trustees either of the first and third classes.

1. An ordinary Common School Library in each School House for the use of the Ratepayers and children.

2. A General Public Lending Library, available to all the Ratepayers of the Municipality.

3. A Professional Library of Books on Teaching, School Organization, Language and kindred subjects, available to Local Superintendents and Teachers alone.

4. A Library in any Public Institution, under the control of the Municipality, for the use of the Inmates, or in the County Jail, for the use of the Prisoners.

It cannot be too strongly urged upon School Trustees, the importance and even the necessity of providing, (especially during the Autumn and Winter months), suitable reading Books for the Pupils in their School, either as Prizes, or in Libraries. Having given the Pupils a taste for reading and general knowledge, they should provide some agreeable and practical means of gratifying it.

Text Books must be paid for at the full Catalogue price. Colleges and Private Schools will be supplied with any of the Articles mentioned in the Catalogue at the prices stated. Local Superintendents and Teachers will also be supplied, on the same terms, with such Educational Works as relate to the duties of their Profession.

IX. INTER-COMMUNICATIONS IN THE JOURNAL OF EDUCATION.

A department is already reserved in the *Journal of Education* for Letters and Inter-communications between Local Superintendents, School Trustees and Teachers, on any subject of general interest relating to Education in the Province. As no personal or party, discussions have, ever since the establishment of the *Journal*, appeared in its columns, no Letter, or Communication partaking of either character, can be admitted to its pages; but, within this salutary restriction, the utmost freedom is allowed. Terse and pointed Communications of moderate length on School Management, Discipline, Progress, Teaching, or other subjects of general interest are always acceptable, and may be made highly useful in promoting the great objects for which the *Journal* was established.

6a—XXIII

CHAPTER VII.

I. PROGRAMME OF COURSE OF STUDY FOR PUBLIC SCHOOLS, 1871.

Prescribed by the Council of Public Instruction for Ontario, under the authority of the School Laws of Ontario.

BASIS OF INSTRUCTION.—EXPLANATORY MEMORANDUM ON THE FOLLOWING PROGRAMME.

1. The great object of this Programme is to secure such an education of youth as to fit them for the ordinary employments and duties of life. This includes:—

2. *First.* Reading, Writing, Arithmetic, and the use of the English language. Every youth, whether in Town, or Country, should be able so to read that reading will be a pleasure and not a labour, otherwise his little knowledge of reading will be seldom, if ever, used to acquire information; he should be able to write readily and well; he should know Arithmetic so as to perform readily and properly any financial business transactions, and be able to keep Accounts correctly; he should be able to speak and write with correctness the language of the Country. These subjects are the first essentials of education for every youth, and in which he should be primarily and thoroughly taught.

3. *Secondly.* An acquaintance with the properties and growth of the Plants we cultivate and use, and the Soils in which they grow; the Instruments and Machinery we employ, and the principle of their construction and use; our own Bodies and Minds, and the laws of their healthy development and preservation. Large experience shows not only the importance of a knowledge of these subjects of Natural Science and Experimental Physics, but that they can be taught easily for all ordinary practical purposes to Pupils from six to twelve years of age.

4. *Thirdly.* Some knowledge of Geography and History, of the Civil Government and Institutions of our own Country, and, in all cases, of the first principles of Christian Morals, so essential to every honest man and good citizen.

5. These are the subjects which should be embraced in a Common School Curriculum, and which have been and can be easily learned by Pupils under twelve years of age. Those who aspire to a higher and more accomplished English education, can obtain it in the High Schools.

6. The length of time during which a Pupil shall continue in any Class must depend upon his, or her, progress. The promotion of a Pupil from a lower to a higher Class is at the discretion of the Master, or Mistress, of the School, and, if any difference arise on this subject between the Master, or Mistress, of a School and the Trustees, or any Parent of a Pupil, the Inspector of the School must decide; but no Pupil is to be promoted to a higher Class without being thoroughly acquainted with all the subjects taught in the lower Classes. A Pupil, on being admitted into a School, must be examined by the Master, or Mistress, and placed in the Class into which such Pupil is qualified to enter. In all cases the order of subjects in the Programme must be followed, and the time prescribed for teaching each subject per week must be observed, nor must any subject of the Course be omitted. Where a Class is too large for all the Pupils to be taught together, or where there is an obvious inequality in the ability and progress of the Pupils,—such Class may be divided into two divisions,—First and Second.

7. When the Pupils in a School amount to more than Fifty, and less than One hundred, the Trustees must employ an additional Teacher as an Assistant.

N.B. The work assigned for home preparation varies with the Class in which the Pupil is placed. In the first and second Classes, the lessons are designed to occupy half-an-hour every evening; in the third and fourth, from an hour to an hour-and-a-half; and in the fifth and sixth, from an hour-and-a-half to two hours. Parents are expected to see that their children attend to their work at home

SUBJECT	FIRST CLASS.	SECOND CLASS.	THIRD CLASS.	FOURTH CLASS.	FIFTH CLASS.	SIXTH CLASS.
READING	First and Second Reading Books.	Third Reading Book, to Page 164.	Third Reading Book.	Fourth Reading Book to page 244.	Fourth Reading Book	Fifth Reading Book.
SPELLING	First and Second Reading Books.	Third Reading Book to page 164 additional, and Spelling Book.	Third Reading Book, additional, and Spelling Book.	Fourth Reading Book to page 244 additional, and Spelling Book.	Fourth Reading Book additional, and Spelling Book.	Reading and Spelling Books.
WRITING	Letters of Alphabet and Simple Words.	Simple Words.	Capitals and words neatly and legibly.	Neatly and legibly.	Neatly and legibly, and with fair rapidity.	Neatly, legibly and rapidly.
ARITHMETIC	Arabic Notation to 1,000. Addition and Subtraction. Simple questions in Mental Arithmetic.	Arabic Notation to 1,000,000, and Roman Notation to M. Arithmetical Tables. Simple Rules and Reduction. Simple questions in Mental Arithmetic.	Arabic and Roman Notation to four periods. Compound Rules, Least Common Multiple and Great Com. Measure and Vulgar Fractions to Reduction, inclusive. Mental Arithmetic.	Principles Arabic and Roman Notation. Vulgar Fractions, Decimal Fractions, Simple Proportion, with reasons of rules. Mental Arithmetic.	Proportion, Practice, Percentage, Stocks, theory of said rules. Mental Arithmetic.	General Review. Involution and Evolution, Compound Interest. Mental Arithmetic.
GRAMMAR		Pointing out the Nouns, Verbs, Adjectives, Adverbs, Pronouns and Prepositions on any page of a Second Reader.	Parts of speech. Gender, person and number of Nouns, and comparison of adjectives. Separating simple sentences into their two essential parts.	Principal grammatical forms and definitions. Analysis of simple sentences. Parsing simple sentences.	Analysis of prose sentences contained in a Reading Book. Parsing, with application of Rules of Syntax.	Analysis of verse sentences in a Reading Book. Parsing, with application of Rules of Syntax.
OBJECT LESSONS	Lessons on common Objects and things (a). On Natural History (b), and on Moral Duties (c).	Lessons on common Objects and things. Lessons on Natural History. Lessons on Moral Duties.				

COMPOSITION	....	Simple sentences, orally and in writing. Short descriptions of simple Objects.	Simple sentences of any kind, orally, or in writing. Short descriptions of simple Objects.	Simple and complex sentences, orally, or in writing. Grammatical changes of construction. Short narrative or description. Familiar letters.	Simple and complex sentences of any kind. Grammatical changes of construction. Narrative and description. Familiar and Business Letters.	Composition on any assigned subject. Paraphrase of any assigned passage.
GEOGRAPHY	Cardinal points of the Compass, Map definitions and Map notations.	Definitions. Map of World generally. Maps of America and Ontario.	Map of Canada generally.	Maps of Europe, Asia and Africa. Maps of Canada and Ontario.	Political Geography, products, etcetera, of principal countries of the World.	Physical Geography of the Continents generally. Use of the globes.
HISTORY	....	....	....	Elements of Canadian and English History.	Canadian and English History continued.	Elements of Ancient and Modern History.
CHRISTIAN MORALS AND CIVIL GOVERNMENT.	....	....	....	Christian Morals (c).	Elements of Civil Government.	
HUMAN PHYSIOLOGY AND NATURAL HISTORY	....	....	....	General view of the animal kingdom.	Human Physiology.	
NATURAL PHILOSOPHY	....	....	....	....	....	Nature and use of the Mechanical Powers.
AGRICULTURAL CHEMISTRY AND BOTANY.	....	....	....	Elements of Chemistry and Botany in First Lessons in Agriculture, on pages 9-76.	Remainder of First Lessons in Agriculture, but Pupils in Cities and Towns may omit Lessons 30, 31, 32, 34 and 37.	Review previous subjects.

SUBJECT.	FIRST CLASS.	SECOND CLASS.	THIRD CLASS.	FOURTH CLASS.	FIFTH CLASS.	SIXTH CLASS.
ALGEBRA					Definitions and first seventeen exercises of authorized Text Book.	Authorized Text Book, Quadratic Equations.
GEOMETRY					Definitions, postulates and Axioms. First thirty propositions of B. I.	Books I. and II.
MENSURATION					Definitions. Mensuration of Surfaces.	Definitions. Mensuration of Surfaces and Solids.
BOOK-KEEPING					Single and double entry.	Single and double entry. Commercial forms and usages.
DOMESTIC ECONOMY (Girls only).					In First Ryerson's Lessons of Agriculture, Lesson 38.	
LINEAR DRAWING	On Slates.	On Slates.	On Slates and Blackboard,	Outlines of Maps, common Objects on Paper.	Outline of Maps and common Objects on Paper and Blackboard.	Outline and perspective sketches of common Objects on Paper and the Blackboard.
VOCAL MUSIC	Simple Songs.	Simple Songs.	Simple Songs.	Simple Songs.	Simple Songs.	Simple Songs.

(a) EXAMPLES OF GALLERY LESSONS.

COMMON THINGS.—(*To be illustrated by specimens of the articles named.*)

	Geometrical Forms.	
India Rubber.	Pens.	Currants.
Colors.	Pins.	Spices.
Whalebone.	Needles.	Silk.
Glass.	Fruits.	Buttons.
Leather.	Flowers.	Metals.
Fur.	Nuts.	Coral.
Cotton.	Vegetables·	Clocks.
Linen.	Cork.	Slate.
Hemp.	Oil.	Candle.
Water.	Salt.	Glue.
Fire.	Sugar.	Chalk.
Wool.	Starch.	Sponge.
Paper.	Cheese.	Bread.
Milk.	Butter.	Crockery.
Coffee.	Raisins.	Ivory.
Tea.		Camphor.

(b) EXAMPLES OF GALLERY LESSONS.

ANIMALS, ETC.

(*Illustrated by the Object Lesson Pictures of the Animal, etcetera, named.*)

Cow.	Tiger.
Horse.	Leopard.
Dog.	Elephant.
Sheep.	Rhinoceros.
Cat.	Hippopotamus.
Chickens.	Deer.
Pig.	Camel.
Turkey.	Whale.
Geese.	Shark.
Ducks.	Herring.
Goat.	Porpoise.
Song Birds.	Turtles.
Birds of Prey.	Serpents.
Parrots.	Lizards.
Lion.	Etcetera.

(c) EXAMPLES OF GALLERY LESSONS.

FAMILIAR TALKS WITH PUPILS ON MORAL DUTIES (ONE PER WEEK, ON FRIDAY AFTERNOONS.)

I. Love and hatred.
II. Obedience, willing and forced.
III. Truth and Falsehood, Dissimulation.
IV. Selfishness and Self-denial.
V. Gentleness and cruelty—in word and action.
VI. Cleanliness and Tidiness.
VII. Loyalty and love of Country.
VIII. Generosity and covetousness.
IX. Order and Punctuality.
X. Perseverance.
XI. Patience.
XII. Justice.
XIII. Self-control.
XIV. Contentment.
XV. Industry and Indolence.
XVI. Self-conceit.
XVII. Destructiveness.
XVIII. Tale-telling—when right and when wrong.
XIX. Forbearance and sympathy—due to misfortune and deformity.
XX. Tendency of one fault to give rise to another, etcetera.

II. GENERAL LIMIT TABLE OF STUDIES IN THE PUBLIC SCHOOLS OF ONTARIO.

NOTE. Where a Class may be very small, or where the Pupils of a Class may be well up in one or more subjects of the Programme, and deficient in others, the Teacher, with the sanction of the Inspector, may allow variations from the prescribed time. In any other unforeseen case of inconvenience or difficulty in giving effect to this Limit Table, the Inspector will communicate with the Chief Superintendent of Education.

Subject.	Class.	Time Per Week	Limit Table in each Subject for Promotion from a Lower Class to a Higher One.
READING	First	6½ hours.	EACH PUPIL ON PROMOTION IS— To be able to read with ease and fluency any passage in the First, or Second, Books of Reading Lessons; also to be able to enunciate clearly the elementary sounds of the Language.
SPELLING	First	1½ hours.	To be able to spell any word in the First and Second Books, and to give its meaning in familiar terms.
WRITING	First	2½ hours.	To be able to form correctly and legibly on Paper, all the letters of the Alphabet, and to combine them into short words.
ARITHMETIC	First	4½ hours.	I. To be able to read and write any Arabic numeral up to 1,000. II. To add and subtract ordinary numbers readily and accurately. III. To solve with ease, simple examples in such Rules.
OBJECT LESSONS	First	2 hours.	Same as for Second Class.
GEOGRAPHY	First	2½ hours.	To know: I. The Cardinal points of the Compass. II. Generally the Geography of the locality and surrounding Country. III. The meaning of Geographical terms, the definitions, etcetra, Map notation. IV. To be able to point out on a Map of the World, each Continent and Ocean, and to know which part of the Map is North, South, East or West.
LINEAR DRAWING	First	1 hour.	On Slates.
VOCAL MUSIC	First	1 hour.	Simple Songs.
READING	Second	6½ hours.	To be able to read fluently and well, any passage in the Third Book, as far as page 164.
SPELLING	Second	1½ hours.	To be able to spell any word in the Second Book, or in the first 164 pages of the Third Book, and to be able to write to dictation correctly, any passage selected therefrom, to give in familiar terms the meaning of any word therein, and to know the Saxon Prefixes and Affixes, and Spelling Book.
WRITING	Second	2½ hours.	To be able to write the words in the Copy Book, Number 2, with neatness and legibleness; also, to write legibly on paper from dictation with modern rapidity.
ARITHMETIC	Second	4½ hours.	I. To be able to read and write any Arabic number up to 1,000,000. II. Roman Notation up to M. III. To be thoroughly and practically acquainted with the Addition, Subtraction, Multiplication and Division Tables, and the Tables of Money, Weights and Measures. IV. To be able to work readily and with accuracy ordinary questions in the four simple Rules and Reduction. V. To be able to apply the simple Rules to Decimal Currency. VI. To be able to solve simple questions in Mental Arithmetic.

II. GENERAL LIMIT TABLE OF STUDIES.—*Continued.*

Subject.	Class.	Time Per Week	Limit Table in each Subject for Promoting from a Lower Class to a Higher One.
GRAMMAR...........	Second ...	2½ hours.	To be able to point out readily and accurately the Nouns, Pronouns, Adjectives, Verbs, Adverbs, and Prepositions, contained in any page of the Second Book of Reading Lessons.
GEOGRAPHY.........	Second ...	2½ hours.	I. To thoroughly review part assigned the Junior Section. II. To know a Map of the World, so as to give relative positions, boundaries of Continents and Oceans, and the Position of a few of the principal Islands, Seas, Gulfs, Bays, etcetera. III. To know the Map of America, so as to give the boundaries of the Continent, and to describe the position from recollection, or to point out on the Map, Countries and their Capitals, and the Capes, Bays, Islands, Mountains, Lakes, Rivers, etcetera. IV. To know the Map of Ontario generally.
COMPOSITION	Second ...	½ hour.	I. To be able to form simple sentences orally and in writing. II. To be able to write a short description of any common Object.
OBJECT LESSONS......	Second ...	2 hours.	I. To have gone through the course of lessons on Common things, as is, or may be, prescribed. II. To have gone through those on Natural History, as may be prescribed. III. To have through those on Moral Duties, etcetera, as may be prescribed.
LINEAR DRAWING....	Second ...	1 hour.	On Slates.
VOCAL MUSIC........	Second ...	1 hour.	Simple Songs.
READING.............	Third	5 hours.	To be able to read fluently and well any passage in the Third Book.
SPELLING	Third	2 hours.	To be able to spell correctly any word in the Second, or Third Book, and to write to dictation correctly as to spelling, any passage from said Lessons, to give the meaning of any Word in these Lessons, and Spelling Book.
WRITING............	Third	2½ hours.	To be able to form Capitals well, and to write from dictation legibly and neatly on paper,—Copy Book Number three, to be kept clean and neat. and the writing in it to be of regular size and slope.
ARITHMETIC.........	Third	5 hours.	I. To revise carefully former Limit Table. II. To be able to read and write with facility in Arabic notation, any number of not more than four periods to the left of the Decimal point. III. Roman Notation up to the expression of the present year. IV. Principals of Arabic and Roman Notation. V. To be thoroughly and practically acquainted with the Simple and Compound Rules, with Reduction ; Great Common Multiple ; Least Common Multiple ; and fractions as far as reduction of compound fractions. VI. To be able to solve problems in these rules with accuracy, neatness and dispatch. VII. To be able to solve simple Problems in Mental Arithmetic in these Rules, with facility.

II. GENERAL LIMIT TABLE OF STUDIES.—*Continued.*

Subject.	Class.	Time Per Week	Limit Table in each Subject for Promoting from a Lower Class to a Higher One.
GRAMMAR	Third	2½ hours	I. To know the different parts of Speech. and to be able to point out the Words belonging to each in any page of the Reading Book. II. To know the Number, Gender and Person of Nouns, and the comparis n of Adjective-, an: the relation between Adjectives and Nouns. III. To be able to separate each simple sentence into Noun-part and V. rb-part. IV. To be able to form simple Sentences, both orally and in writing.
COMPOSITION	Third	½ hours	I. To be able to form Sentences of any specific kind, either orally, or in writing, such as simple, compound, interrogatory, etcetera. II. To be able to write short descriptions of simple objects c rrectly, as to spelling, grammatical forms, etcetera.
GEOGRAPHY	Third	2½ hours	I. To review thoroughly portion as-igned to the Second Division. II. To know the names and uses of the principal lines drawn on the Map of the World, such as Meridians, Equator, Parallels of Latitude, Tropics, Arctic and Antarctic Circles. III. To know the Map of Canada generally.
LINEAR DRAWING	Third	1 hour	On Slates and Blackboard.
VOCAL MUSIC	Third	1 hour	Simple Songs.
READING	Fourth	5 hours	To be able to read fluently and well any passage contained in the first 244 pages of the Fourth Book.
SPELLING	Fourth	2 hours	To be able to spell or define any Word in the Second, or Third, Books, or in the first 244 pages of the Fourth Book, and to write to dictation correctly, as to spelling and Capitals, any passage contained in said Lessons, and Spelling Book.
WRITING	Fourth	2½ hours	T be able to write neatly, legibly and rapidly on paper from dictation.. Copy Books to be kept scrupulously clean and free from blots. Writing therein to be of proper slope, even in iorm, and the Capital carefully made.
ARITHMETIC	Fourth	5 hours	I. T. thoroughly r-view former Limit Tables. II. To be able to write with ease all Numbers in Arabic N tation, n t incl ding more than six places to the right of the decimal point. III. To be acquainted with the principles of Arabic and Roman Notation. IV. To be thoroughly and practically acqainte l with Vulgar Fractions, Addition, Subtraction, Multipl cation and Division of Decimal finite and infinite; Reduction of Vulgar Fractions to Decimals, and mixed Repetend- to Vulgar Fractions; to be well acquainted with Simple Proportion; to understand the reason of the processes. V. To be able to solve ordinary problems in Mental Arithmetic with ease and accuracy.
GRAMMAR	Fourth	2½ hours	I. T. be thor ughly and familiarly acquainted with the principal Grammatical Forms and Defini ions.

II. GENERAL LIMIT TABLE OF STUDIES.—*Continued.*

Subject.	Class.	Time Per Week	Limit Table in each Subject for Promoting from a Lower to a Higher One.
GRAMMAR.—*Con.*	Fourth ...	2½ hours.	II. To be able to separate any easy Sentence, into classes, and to distinguish between Subject and Predicate. III. To be able to parse the words of any easy Sentence, giving the relation of the words, but not the rules of Syntax.
COMPOSITION	Fourth ...	½ hours.	I. To be able to form complex Sentences, either orally, or in writing. II. To be able to make grammatical changes of construction. III. To write a short narrative or description, or a familiar letter, correctly as to Spelling, Grammatical and Mechanical forms.
GEOGRAPHY	Fourth ...	2½ hours.	I. To be thoroughly acquainted with the subject, as far as it is assigned to former sections. II. To know the maps of Europe, Asia and Africa in the same manner as they are required to know maps of Europe and America. III. To know the Maps of Canada and Ontario.
HISTORY	Fourth ...	2½ hours.	Elements of Canadian and English History.
NATURAL HISTORY ...	Fourth ...	1½ hours.	General view of the Animal Kingdom.
CHRISTIAN MORALS ..	Fourth ...	1 hour.	Christian Morals.
CHEMISTRY AND BOTANY	Fourth ...	1½ hour.	Elements of Chemistry and Botany in First Lessons in Agriculture, pp. 9-76.
LINEAR DRAWING	Fourth ...	1 hour.	Outlines of Maps, common objects on paper.
VOCAL MUSIC........	Fourth ...	1 hour.	Simple Songs.
READING	Fifth	2½ hours.	To be able to read fluently and with expression, any passage in the Third, or Fourth, Books.
SPELLING	Fifth	1 hour.	To be able to spell and define any word in the Second, Third, or Fourth Books, and to write to dictation correctly, as to Spelling, Capitals and Punctuation, any passage contained therein, and Spelling Books.
WRITING	Fifth	2½ hours.	To be able to write neatly, legibly and rapidly on Paper from dictation. Copy Books to be kept as in Second Division, writing therein to be carefully executed, regular as to size and shape, letters carefully joined and well-formed. Capitals well formed.
ARITHMETIC	Fifth	3 hours.	I. To review thoroughly the subjects as far as assigned in previous Limit Tables. II. To be familiarly and practically acquainted with Arabic and Roman Notation. III. To be practically acquainted with Compound and Conjoined Proportion, and with Commercial Arithmetic, including Practice, Percentage, Insurance, Commission, Brokerage, Purchase and Sale of Stock, Custom House Business, Assessment of Taxes and Interest. IV. To be able to work Problems in these Rules, and to know the reason for the various processes. Mental Arithmetic. To be able to solve ordinary problems in these Rules with Accuracy.
GRAMMAR	Fifth	2 hours.	I. To be thoroughly and familiarly acquainted with all the Grammatical forms and definitions.

II. GENERAL LIMIT TABLE OF STUDIES.—*Continued.*

Service.	Class.	Time Per Week	Limit Table in each Subject for Promoting from a Lower to a Higher One.
GRAMMAR.—*Con*	Fifth	2 hours.	II. To be able to analyze and parse any Sentence contained in their Reading Books, distinguishing between principal and subordinate clauses. Kinds of subordinate clauses. Grammatical and logical subjects and Predicates. III. To be able to parse the words of any ordinary Prose Sentence contained in their Reading Books, giving relation, Rules of Syntax, etcetera.
COMPOSITION	Fifth	1 hour.	I. To be able to form complex, compound, or simple Sentences of any specific kind, either orally, or in writing. II. To make readily the different Grammatical changes of construction. III. To be able to write a familiar or Business Letter on any subject, with proper attention to Grammatical structure, Mechanical form, etcetera.
GEOGRAPHY	Fifth	2 hours.	I. To be thoroughly acquainted with the subject as far as is assigned to the other division. II. To know more minutely the Political Geography, Products, etcetera, of the principal Countries in the World. III. To have an idea of the physical Geography of all the Continents.
HISTORY	Fifth	2 hours.	I. To review thoroughly the parts assigned to Fourth Class. II. The History of Canada and England continued.
HUMAN PHYSIOLOGY	Fifth	1 hour.	Human Physiology.
NAT. PHILOSOPHY	Fifth	1½ hours.	I. Mechanical Power, etcetera. Part I. to page fifty-three., omitting paragraphs 47 to 53, inclusive.
CHEMISTRY AND BOTANY	Fifth	1½ hours.	Remainder of First Lessons in Agriculture. Pupils in Cities and Towns may omit Lessons 30, 31, 32, 34 and 37.
ALGEBRA	Fifth	2 hours.	I. To know the definitions. II. To be able to work the examples in exercises, from I. to X., XIII. to XVII.
GEOMETRY	Fifth	1½ hours.	Definitions, Postulates and Axioms. First 30 Propositions of Book One.
MENSURATION	Fifth	1½ hours.	I. To be able to solve Problems concerning Rectangles, Triangles and Circles.
READING	Sixth	2½ hours.	To be able to read fluently and with expression, any passage in the Fourth, or Fifth, Books.
SPELLING	Sixth	1 hour.	To be able to spell and define any word in the Reading Books, and to write to dictation correctly, as to Spelling, Capitals and Punctuation, any passage selected from these Books, and Spelling Book.
WRITING	Sixth	2½ hours.	To be able to write in a good business style of penmanship. Copy Books to be kept as indicated above in 2nd Division.
ARITHMETIC	Sixth	3 hours.	I. To revise former Limit Tables thoroughly. II. To finish Commercial Arithmetic and be thoroughly acquainted with Involution and Evolution.

II. GENERAL LIMIT TABLE OF STUDIES.—*Continued.*

Service.	Class.	Time Per Week	Limit Table in each Subject for Promoting from a Lower to a Higher One.
ARITHMETIC.—*Con*...	Sixth	3 hours.	III. Compound Interest and Annuities. IV. To be familiar with the theory as well as practice of these Rules, and to be able to work ordinary problems in them with accuracy, neatness and dispatch. V. Mental Arithmetic as in former sections.
GRAMMAR	Sixth	2 hours.	I. To give evidence that they know all the Grammatical Forms and Definitions. II. To analyze prose, or verse contained in Readers, distinguishing between principal and subordinate clauses—kinds of subordinate clauses. Analyze subject and predicate, give relation of Words, Grammatical and logical subject and predicate. III. To be able to parse the words contained in their Readers, or Grammars, with application of rules of Syntax, etcetera.
COMPOSITION	Sixth	1 hours.	I. To be able to do all in former Limit Tables. II. To be able to write a Composition on any simple subject, and to spell and punctuate it properly. III. To be able to paraphrase any assigned poetical passage.
GEOGRAPHY	Sixth	2 hours.	I. To know thoroughly the former Limit Tables. II. Physical Geography of the Continents. III. The use of the Globes.
HISTORY	Sixth	2 hours.	Elements of Ancient and Modern History.
CHEMISTRY AND BOTANY...........	Sixth	2 hours.	To understand the elements of Chemistry, as taught in the first part of Doctor Ryerson's First Lessons on Agriculture, pages 9-70. Structure of Plants, e cetera, pp. 70-76 of Doctor Ryerson's First Lessons on Agriculture. Lessons II. III. and XXII.
ALGEBRA...........	Sixth	2 hours.	Thoroughly review part assigned to the Juniors, and complete Quadratic Equations.
GEOMETRY	Sixth	1½ hours.	I. To know the Definitions, Postulates, and Axioms, and to be able to demonstrate the first 30 Propositions of First Book. II. To thoroughly review part assigned the Juniors, and finish the First Book. III. To be familiar with the meaning of the different terms used in the First and Second Books, and to go through the first two Books.
MENSURATION........	Fifth and Sixth.	1 hour.	Review the work gone over while in the Junior section. Mensuration of Solids. NOTE.—Girls take easy lessons on Reasoning instead of Geometry. Parts I. II.
BOOK-KEEPING.......	Fifth and Sixth.	1 hour.	I. To know the definition of the various Books used. To understand the relation between Debtor and Creditor, and the difference between Single and Double Entry. II. To know how to make original entries in the Books used for this purpose, such as Invoice Book, Sales Book, Cash Book and Day Book. III. To be able to Journalize any ordinary Business transaction, and to be familiar with the nature of the various Accounts in the Ledger, and with the mode of conducting and closing them.

II. GENERAL LIMIT TABLE OF STUDIES.—*Continued.*

Service.	Class.	Time Per Week	Limit Table in each Subject for Promoting from a Lower to a Higher One.
Book-keeping.—*Con.*	Fifth and Sixth.	1 hour.	IV. To be familiar with the forms of ordinary Commercial Paper, such as Promissory Notes, Drafts, Receipts for the payment of money, etcetera.
Nat. Philosophy....	Fifth and Sixth.	1½ hours.	Nature and use of Mechanical Powers.
Civil Government...	Fifth and Sixth.	1 hour.	Elements of Civil Government.
Drawing	Fourth and Fifth	1 hour.	To evince facility in marking sketches of Maps and common objects on Blackboard.
Singing	Whole School.	1 hour.	To know the present principles of Vocal Music (provision to be made by the Trustees for the practice of Vocal Music).
Gymnastics........	Boys	1 hour.	(Provision to be made at the discretion of the Trustees for Gymnastics and Calisthenics.)
Needle Work	Girls ..... Second and Third	1 hour.	Note.—To be taught only in lower divisions of Girls Schools, or Classes.
Domestic Economy..	Girls ..... First and Second.	1½ hours.	In place of Euclid, where there is a female Teacher. To have a general knowledge of the subject as taught in pages 171-188, (Lesson 38) of Doctor Ryerson's First Lessons on Agriculture.

III. LIST OF AUTHORIZED TEXT BOOKS FOR USE IN THE PUBLIC SCHOOLS OF ONTARIO, 1871.

(Sanctioned by the Council of Public Instruction).

Note. In the following list, some Books are prescribed, and others are recommended. The use of the Books recommended is discretionary with the respective Public School Boards.

I. *English.*

Text Books Prescribed:—

The Canadian National Series of Reading Books. (Authorized edition).

The Spelling Book, a Companion to the Readers. (Authorized edition).

Miller's Analytical and Practical English Grammar. (Authorized edition).

An English Grammar for Junior Classes. By the Reverend H. W. Davies, D.D. (Authorized edition).

A History of English Literature, in a Series of Biographical Sketches. By William Francis Collier, LL.D.

II. *Arithmetic and Mathematics.*

Text Books Prescribed:—

Advanced Arithmetic for Canadian Schools. By Bernard Smith, M.A., and Archibald McMurchy, M.A.

Elementary Arithmetic for Canadian Schools. By the Reverend Barnard Smith, M.A., and Archibald McMurchy, M.A.

Elements of Algebra. Todhunter's, or Sangster's.

Euclid's Elements of Geometry. Pott's, or Todhunter's.

III. *Geography and History.*

Text Books Prescribed:—

Lovell's General Geography. (Authorized edition). By J. George Hodgins, LL.D., Barrister-at-Law.

Easy Lessons in General Geography. By J. George Hodgins, LL.D. (Authorized edition).

A School History of the British Empire. By William Francis Collier, LL.D.

A History of Canada and of the other British Provinces of North America. By J. George Hodgins, LL.D., Barrister-at-Law.

Outlines of General History. By William Francis Collier, LL.D.

Text Book Recommended:—

The Great Events of History. By William Francis Collier, LL.D.

IV. *Physical Science.*

Text Books Prescribed (see Prefixed Note):—

Rudimentary Mechanics. By Charles Tomlinson. Portions relative to the Mechanical Powers.

The Animal Kingdom. By Ellis A. Davidson.

How Plants Grow; a Simple Introduction to Botany, with Popular Flora. By Asa Gray, M.D.

V. *Miscellaneous.*

Text Books Prescribed:—

First Lessons in Agriculture. By Reverend Doctor Ryerson.

Our Bodies.* By Ellis A. Davidson.

Easy Lessons on Reasoning. By Archbishop Whately.

Text Books Recommended (see Prefixed Note).

A Comprehensive System of Book-keeping, by Single and Double Entry. By Thomas R. Johnson. A work on Book-keeping is to be sanctioned.

Field Exercise and Evolutions of Infantry. Published by Authority. Pocket edition, (for Squad and Company Drill).

The Modern Gymnast. By Charles Spencer.

A Manual of Vocal Music. By John Hullah.

Three Part Songs. By H. F. Sefton. (Authorized edition).

National Mensuration.

Scripture Lessons,—Old and New Testaments. (National).

Lessons on the Truth of Christianity. (National).

Right Lines in their Right Places. By Ellis A. Davidson.

Teacher's Guide, and Bartholomew's Primary School Drawing Cards. By Miss J. H. Stickney.

The Drawing Book for the Dominion of Canada, in Progressive Studies; seven numbers.

William Hermes' Drawing Instructor. For advanced Students.

Writing Copy Books, used in the Normal and Model Schools for Ontario. In Five Parts.

VI. *French and German Schools.*

The following Books, approved by the Combined Committee of the Council of Public Instruction for Quebec, are also sanctioned for use by French Pupils, in Public

---

* The following Works are also highly recommended for perusal both by Teachers and Pupils, videlicet:— "The House I live in," by T. C. Girtin, Surgeon (Longmans), and "Our Earthly House and its Builder," (Religious Tract Society). Cutter's "First Book on Anatomy, Physiology and Hygiene, for Grammar Schools and Families," is the prescribed book for High Schools, and may be used in the Public Schools if desired.

Schools of this Province in which there are both Protestant and Roman Catholic Pupils:—

Cours d'Arithmétique Commerciale. (Senécal, Montreal).

Abrégé de la Geographie Moderne. (Société d'Education de Quebec).

La Geographie Moderne, de M. Holmes, M.A.

Grammaire pratique de la langue Anglaise. (Par P. Saddler, Paris).

Traité Elementaire d'Arithmetique. (Par F. X. Toussaint).

Le Premier Livre de l'Enfance. (de Poitevin).

Cours de Versions Anglaises. (Par P. Saddler, Paris).

Grammaire Française Elementaire. (Par F. P. B.)

For German Schools, Klotz's German Grammar is sanctioned.

NOTE. Inspectors, Trustees and Teachers will please see that these Books alone are used in the Schools so that uniformity may be observed in them.

CHAPTER VIII.

THE LAWS RELATING TO GRAMMAR AND HIGH SCHOOLS IN ONTARIO, 1871.

THE CONSOLIDATED HIGH SCHOOL ACT, WITH WHICH IS INCORPORATED THE HIGH SCHOOL IMPROVEMENT ACTS OF 1865 AND 1871.

AN ACT RESPECTING HIGH SCHOOLS IN ONTARIO, BEING CHAPTER LXIII OF THE CONSOLIDATED STATUTES OF ONTARIO.

Her Majesty, by and with the advice and consent of the Legislative Council and Assembly of Canada, enacts as follows:—

Name of each County High School.

1. There shall be one, or more, High Schools in each County and Union of Counties in Ontario, to be distinguished by prefixing to the term "County," the name of the City, Town, or Village, within the limits of which it may be situate.

[NOTE. The legal distinction, authorized by the Second Section of this Consolidated Act, between Senior and Junior County High Schools has been done away with by the Grammar School Improvement Act of 1865.]

Where other County High Schools shall be Situated.

3. All other High Schools established, on or before the First day of January, one thousand eight hundred and fifty-four, shall be continued at the places where they are respectively held; but the High School Board of each of the said Schools may change the place of holding such School, by a Resolution to be passed for that purpose and approved of by the Governor-in-Council: and the place of holding any High School established since the First of January, one thousand eight hundred and fifty-four, may be changed by the County Council of the County within which it is established.

Investment of Income from High School Lands, etcetera.

4. All Moneys arising from the sale of Lands at any time set apart for the encouragement of High Schools in Ontario, and not specially granted to, or vested in, or for the benefit of any particular College, High School, or other Seminary, or place of Education, or otherwise departed with by the Crown, and all Annual Grants which have been, or may, after this Act takes effect, be made by Parliament, or which may be otherwise available from any other sources for that purpose, shall form a Fund to be

called The Ontario High School Fund, and shall be invested in Government, or other Securities by the direction of the Governor-in-Council.

(NOTE. The Fifth Section of the Consolidated Act is repealed).

Basis of Apportionment to the High Schools.

6. . . . . The Chief Superintendent of Education shall annually apportion [. . . such Annual Income . . . in the manner provided by the Seventh Section of the High School Improvement Act of 1865], as follows: 7. The Apportionment payable half yearly to the High Schools shall be made to each School conducted according to law, upon the basis [the length of time each such High School is kept open]— of the daily average attendance at such High School of Pupils, (and their proficiency in the various branches of study named) in the Programme of Studies prescribed according to law for High Schools; such attendance shall be certified by the Head Master and Trustees and verified by the Inspector of High Schools.]

(Note. The Seventh Section of of Consolidated Act is repealed)

High School Apportionment Payable Half-yearly.

8. The sums of Money annually apportioned . . . as aforesaid, shall be payable to the Treasurer of the County entitled to receive it, [one-half at the end of each six months, and on receipt at the Education Department of the half-yearly Return and Annual Report, duly certified], which sums shall be payable in such manner as may be determined by the Governor.

To be Expended in the payment of Teachers' Salaries alone.

And such Moneys [together with the "sums provided from local sources,"]* shall be expended in the payment of the Salaries of Teachers, and for no other purpose.

Apportionment to Each High School.

9. The sums of Money apportioned out of the High School Fund [and "sums provided from local sources,"] . . . shall be distributed amongst the several High Schools . . . within the restrictions imposed by this Act [and the High School Improvement Act], and under such Rules and Regulations as may, from time to time, be made by the Council of Public Instruction for Ontario, and approved by the Governor-in-Council.†

$20,000 annually Granted for Superior Education.

10. In addition to the sums applicable in aid of High Schools as aforesaid, or under the One hundred and twentieth Section of the Act respecting Public Schools in Ontario the sum of twenty thousand dollars shall be yearly appropriated out of the Consolidated Revenue Fund of this Province, for the encouragement of Superior Education in Ontario.

This Grant to be Distributed to Colleges by Parliament.

And shall be distributed . . . as may be designated by an annual vote of the Provincial Parliament.

Council of Public Instruction to appoint Inspector.

11. The Council of Public Instruction shall appoint Inspectors of High Schools, prescribe duties‡ and fix their remuneration.

---

* See the Sixth Section of the High School Improvement Act of 1865.

† These Rules and Regulations, in connection with the Seventh Section of the High School Improvement Act of 1865, are appended.

‡ The duties of the Inspector of High Schools will be given further on.

High Schools to prepare Pupils for College.—Programme.

12. In each County High School provision shall be made for giving, by a Teacher, or Teachers of competent ability and good morals instruction in all the higher branches of a practical English and Commercial Education,† including the [Natural Sciences, with special reference to Agricutlure,] the elements of Natural Philosophy and Mechanics, and also in the Latin, Greek, French and German Languages (to those Pupils whose Parents, or Guardians may desire it), and Mathematics, so far as to prepare Students for University College, or any College affiliated to the University of Toronto—according to a Programme of Studies and General Rules and Regulations, [which shall be prescribed, from time to time,] by the Council of Public Instruction for Ontario, with the approval of the Lieutenant Governor-in-Council; and the Council of Public Instruction shall have power to exempt any High School, (which shall not have sufficient funds to provide the necessary qualified Teachers), from the obligation to teach the German and French languages.]

Penalty for not Observing the Official Regulations.

And no High School shall be entitled to receive any part of the High School Fund, which is not conducted according to such Programme, Rules and Regulations. [The Thirty-seventh Section of the School Law Improvement Act of 1871 also declares that "no Public, or High, School shall be entitled to share in the fund applicable to it, unless it is conducted according to the Regulations provided by law."]

Condition of Sharing in High School Fund.

[The Sixth Section of the High School Improvement Act of 1865, further enacts: 6. No High Schoool shall be entitled to share in the High School Fund, unless a sum shall be provided, from local sources, exclusive of Fees, equal at least to one-half the sum apportioned to such School, and expended for the same purpose as the said fund.]

Local Assessment for High Schools in Cities, Towns and Villages.

12¼. The School Law Improvement Act of 1871 provides that, 36. The Grammar, or High, School Grant shall be exclusively applied in aid of High Schools; and of the sums of money required to be raised from local sources for the support of a High School a sum equal to one-half of the amount paid by the Government to any High School in a City or Town withdrawn from the jurisdiction of the County, together with such other sum as may be required for the accommodation and support of such School, shall be provided by the Municipal Council of such City, or Town, upon the application of the High School Board. In the case of a High School in Towns, incorporated Villages, or Townships, one-half of the amount paid by the Government shall be paid by the Municipal Council of the County in which such High School is situated, upon the application of the High School Board; and such other sums as may be required for the maintenance and School Accommodation of the said High School, shall be raised by the Council of the Municipality in which the High School is situated, upon the application of the High School Board; or, in the event of the County Council forming the whole or parts of a County into one, or more, High School District, then such other sums as may be required for the maintenance of the said High School shall be provided by the High School District, upon the application of the High School Board, in the manner hereinafter provided:

(1) The Council of any Municipality, or the Councils of the respective Municipalities, out of which the whole, or part, of such High School District is formed, shall, upon the application of the High School Board, raise the proportion required to be paid by such Municipality, or part of the Municipality, from the whole, or part of the Municipality, as the case may be.

† Under the new Regulations, provision is not only made for Book-keeping but for a knowledge of Commercial Transactions and Telegraphy.

7a—XXIII.

Condition of Receiving Public or High School Grant.

37. . . . Each High School, conducted according to law, shall be entitled to an Apportionment at the rate of not less than Four hundred dollars per annum, according to the average attendance of Pupils, their proficiency in the various branches of Study, and the length of time each such High School is kept open, as compared with other High Schools.

Head Masters to be University Graduates.

13. [The Thirteenth Section is repealed by the Eleventh Section of the High School Act of 1865, as follows: 11. After the passing of this Act, no Person shall be deemed to be legally qualified to be appointed Head Master of a High School, unless he be a Graduate of some University within the British Dominions; but any Person legally qualified and appointed to be a Head Master in any High School during the year next* before the passing of this Act shall be deemed qualified notwithstanding this Section.]

Heads of Colleges to be Members of the Council of Public Instruction.

14. The President of University College and the President, or other Head, of each of the Colleges in Ontario, affiliated to the University of Toronto, shall, for the purposes of this Act, be Members of the Council of Public Instruction.

Council of Public Instruction to Prescribe Text Books, etcetera.

15. Such Council shall prepare and prescribe a list of Text Books, Programme of Studies and General Rules and Regulations for the organization and government of the County High Schools, to be approved by the Governor-in-Council, and shall also appoint Inspectors of High Schools, prescribe their duties, and fix their remuneration.

Allowance for Elementary Military Instruction.

[The Twelfth Section of the High School Act of 1865, also provides that 12. It shall be lawful for the Governor-in-Council to prescribe a Course of Elementary Military Instruction for High School pupils, and to appropriate out of any Money granted for the purpose, a sum not exceeding Fifty dollars per Annum to any School, the Head Master of which shall have passed a prescribed Examination in the subjects of the Military Course, and in which School a Class of not less than five Pupils has been taught for a period of at least six months; such Classes and instruction to be subject to such inspection and oversight as the Governor-in-Council may direct.†]

DUTIES OF MUNICIPAL COUNCILS TO HIGH SCHOOLS.

Cities to be Counties for High School Purposes.

[The First Section of the High School Act of 1865, enacts that 1. Each City shall, for all High School purposes, be a County; and its Municipal Council shall be invested with all the High School powers now possessed by County Councils; but when, and so long as, the only High School of the County is situated within a City, the Council of such County shall appoint one-half of the Trustees of such High School.]

[*Note.* The first part of the Sixteenth Section of this Act has been superseded by the Thirty-sixth Section of the School Law Improvement Act of 1871. See Section 124.]

---

* *i. e.* From the 20th of September, 1864, to 20th of September, 1865.

† This Twelfth Section introduces a new feature into the instruction to be given in our High Schools, and will enable them to become feeders to some Canadian Sandhurst, or West Point Military Academy, yet to be established. It does not relate to Military drill in the School, but to a preliminary Course of elementary Military Studies, such as Military History, Drawing, etcetera. No Regulations have yet been prepared on the subject.

Municipal Assessment, to whom payable and when.

16. And all sums collected by the Municipal Council shall be paid over to the Treasurer of the County High School, for which the Assessment is made. And the sums raised by local assessment or subscriptions for the support of High Schools shall be payable each year on, or before, the Fourteenth day of December.

Audit of High School Treasurer's Accounts.

The Forty-fifth Section of the School Law Improvement Act of 1871 also declares that: 45. The Treasurer of every High School Board shall submit his Accounts to the County Auditors to be audited by them, in the same manner as the County Treasurer's Accounts are audited, and it shall be the duty of the County Auditors to audit such Accounts.

Condition of Establishing a New High School.

17. The Seventeenth Section of this Act has been altered by the Eighth Section of the High School Act of 1865, and by the Thirty-fifth Section of the School Law Improvement Act of 1871, as follows: 8. No additional High School shall be established in any County unless the High School Fund shall be sufficient to allow of an Apportionment at the rate of not less than Four hundred dollars per annum to be made to such additional School, without diminishing the Fund which may have been available for High Schools during the then next preceding year. 35. . . . And, as far as the Fund will permit, it shall be lawful for the Lieutenant-Governor-in-Council to authorize the establishment of additional High Schools upon the conditions prescribed by the Grammar School Act and this Act.*

[The Municipal Institutions Act, chapter fifty-four of the Consolidated Statutes for Upper Canada, also contains the following enactments: 286. The Council of every County, City and Town separated, may pass By-laws for the following purposes:

Lands for Grammar Schools.

[1. For obtaining in such part of the County, or of any City, or Town separated within the County, as the wants of the people may most require, the real property requisite for erecting County Grammar School Houses thereon, and for other Grammar School purposes, and for preserving, improving and repairing such School Houses, and for disposing of such property when no longer required.

Aiding Grammar Schools.

[2. For making [any additional] provision in aid of such Grammar Schools, as may be deemed expedient.†

Pupils Competing for University Prizes.

[3. For making a permanent provision for defraying the expenses of the attendance at the University of Toronto, and at the Upper Canada College and Royal Grammar School there, of such of the Pupils of the Public Grammar Schools of the County as are unable to incur the expenses, but are desirous of, and, in the opinion of the respective Masters of such Grammar Schools, possess competent attainments for, com-

---

* This Eighth Section raises the minimum Apportionment to be made to a new Grammar School from $200 to $300. This Section, in connection with the Sixth on page 160, will have the effect ot providing for each new School at least $450, exclusive of Fees, instead of the former pittance of $200 and fees.

† This optional aid must be in addition to the sums required to be raised "from local sources," by the Sixth Section of the Act of 1865.

peting for any Scholarship, Exhibition, or other similar Prize, offered by such University or College.

[4. For making similar provisions for the attendance at any County Grammar School, for like purposes, of Pupils of the Common Schools of the County.

Endowing Fellowships, Scholarships and Exhibitions.

[5. For endowing such Fellowships, Scholarships, or Exhibitions, and other similar Prizes, in the University of Toronto, and in the Upper Canada College and Royal Grammar School there, for competition among the Pupils of the Public Grammar Schools of the County, as the Council deems expedient for the encouragement of learning the youth thereof.]

THE CHIEF SUPERINTENDENT OF EDUCATION.

18. The Chief Superintendent of Education for Ontario shall . . . notify each County Council, through the Clerk of the Council, of the . . . Apportionment of High School moneys to such County, and shall certify the same for payment to the Provincial Treasurer.

The Chief Superintendent to report Annually on High Schools.

19. The Chief Superintendent of Education shall make annually to the Governor, on or before the first day of July, a report of the actual state of the High Schools throughout Ontario, showing the amount of moneys expended in connection with each, and from what sources derived, with such suggestions for their improvement as he deems useful and expedient.

The Chief Superintendent to Administer the Grammar School Law.

He shall see that the County High School Fund apportioned by him is, in all cases, applied to the purposes hereinbefore prescribed, and that each County High School is conducted according to the Rules and Regulations legally established.*

To furnish Trustees with Acts, Forms and Regulations.

And he shall prepare suitable Forms, and give such instructions as he judges necessary and proper for making all Reports and conducting all proceedings under this Act, and shall cause the same, with a sufficient number of copies of this Act, and, so far as the same relate to High Schools, copies of the General Rules and Regulations established and approved of as aforesaid, to be printed in a convenient form, and transmitted to the parties required to execute the provisions of this Act.†

HIGH SCHOOL TRUSTEES.

Appointment by the Municipal Council of High School Trustees.

20. In each County, [or City,] in which one, or more, High Schools are established, there shall be a Board of Trustees, consisting of not less than six, nor more than eight, fit and proper Persons [for each School], appointed by the Municipal Council in the manner hereinafter provided.

(NOTE.—In Cities, the Members of the Board of High School Trustees may number eight, as provided by this Twentieth Section of the Act; but in Towns and Incorpor-

---

* All Communications with the Government relating to Schools in Ontario, conducted under the authority of any Act of the Legislature, should be enclosed to the Education Department, Toronto: otherwise they will be referred back to that Department, to be brought before His Excellency through the proper Officer.

† A copy of the Act, and its Rules, Regulations, and Programme, is supplied gratuitously to the Chairman and Secretary of each Board of High School Trustees for the use of the Board. Extra copies can be obtained from the Depository, at 35 cents per copy, including postage, which is required, by the Post Office Department, to be paid in advance.

ated Villages, they can only number six, who shall be appointed by the Council f the County and of the Town, or Village, concerned.)

Quorum of the High School Board.

Of which Board three shall be a quorum for the transaction of business. [In a united Board of High and Public School Trustees, the quorum is fixed at seven.]

Order of the Retirement of Trustees.

21. . . . Annually on the 31st day of January in each year, two of the Members of each Board of Trustees for the time being shall retire from the said Board in rotation, according to seniority in office. [The latter part of the Twenty-third Section of this Act provides that] any retiring Trustee may (with his own consent) be re-appointed, and all Trustees for the time shall hold office until their Successors are appointed as herein provided.

Appointment of Trustees by County and Local Municipalities.

[The Twenty-second and the first part of the Twenty-third Sections of this Act are repealed by the latter part of the Second Section of the High School Act of 1865, as follows: 2. Each County Council, at its first Session to be held after the First day of January next, shall select and appoint as Trustees of each High School situated in a Town, or incorporated Village, and within its jurisdiction, three fit and proper Persons as Trustees of such High School; and the corporation of the Town, or incorporated Village municipality, within the limits of which such High School is, or may be, situated, shall also, at its first Session in January next, appoint three fit and proper Persons as Trustees of such High School, one of whom, in the order of their appointment, in each case, shall annually retire from office on the thirty-first day of January in each year (but may be re-appointed);

Villages hereafter Incorporated.

[And, on the incorporation hereafter of any Village, in which a High School is established, the County and Village Councils shall at their first Meeting in January next thereafter, appoint Trustees in like manner as aforesaid, for the High School in such incorporated Village;

Mode of Filling Vacancies.

[And the vacancy occasioned by the annual retirement of Trustees, as also any occasional vacancy in their number, arising from death, resignation, removal from the Municipality, or otherwise, shall be filled up by such County, Town, or Village, Council, as the case may be; provided that the Person appointed to fill such occasional vacancy shall hold office only for the unexpired part of the term for which the Person whose place shall have become vacant was appointed to serve;

Trustees to be a Corporation: Powers.

[The Third Section of the same Act also provides that: 3. The Trustees appointed as aforesaid, shall be a Corporation, and shall succeed to all the right, names, powers, and obligations conferred or imposed upon Trustees of Grammar Schools, by Chapter Sixty-three of the Consolidated Statutes for Upper Canada, and by this Act].

High School Districts to be defined.—Trustees.

The Fortieth Section of the School Law Improvement Act of 1871 also declares that 40. Every County shall determine the limits of each High School District for each

Grammar School now existing within the County; and may form the whole, or part, of one, or more Townships, Towns and Villages within its jurisdiction into a [new] High School District; and the High School Board of such District shall possess all the powers within the said District, for the support and management of their High School, and in respect to the County Council, as are possessed under the Grammar School Acts and this Act by High School Boards in respect to the support and management of the Schools under their care; and such County Council may appoint and determine the continuance and succession in office of six duly qualified Persons as Members of such [new] High School Board. Provided, however, that existing Grammar School divisions already established shall be called High School Districts, and continue as such till otherwise altered by By-law of such County Council.

High School Trustees to be a Corporation.

24. The Board of Trustees of each County High School shall be a Corporation, by the name of "The Trustees of the ———— County High School," prefixing to the term "County," the name of the City, Town, or Village, within which such High School is situated.

Powers of the Trustee Corporation.

And shall have and possess all the powers usually enjoyed by Corporations, so far, as the same are necessary for carrying out the purposes of this Act;* and they shall meet at, or near, the place where each such School is held, on the first Wednesday in February in each year. The Thirty-fourth Section of the School Law Improvement Act of 1871, declares that, (34), Boards of Grammar School Trustees shall be designated High School Boards; and the Grammar Schools shall be designated and known as High Schools.

Duties of the Board of High School Trustees.

25. It shall be the duty of such Trustees:

To appoint Officers of the Board, etcetera.

(1) To appoint annually, or oftener, from amongst themselves, a Chairman, Secretary and Treasurer, and subject to the provisions hereinbefore contained, to fix the times and places of the Board Meetings, the mode of calling and conducting such Meetings, and of keeping a full and correct account of the proceedings of such Meetings.

To take Charge of County High School.

(2) To take charge of the County High School, for which they are appointed Trustees, and the Buildings and Lands appertaining to it.

High School Property Vested in Trustees.

[The Fourth Section of the High School Act of 1865, also provides that: 4. All property heretofore given, or required, in any Municipality, and vested in any Person, or Persons, or Corporation, for High School purposes, or which may hereafter be so given, or acquired, shall vest absolutely in the Corporation of High School Trustees having the care of the same, subject to such trusts as may be declared in the Deed, or Instrument, under which such property is held. See also the Twenty-eighth and following Sections of the Act.]

To appoint and Remove Masters, Teachers, Officers, etcetera.

(3) To remove, if they see fit, and in case of vacancies, appoint the Master and other Teachers in such School, and to fix their Salaries and prescribe their duties.

* By the Provincial Statutes' Interpretation Act, Chapter Five of the Consolidated Statutes for Canada. Section Six, Sub section Twenty-four, Corporations are required to have a Common Seal, which should be attached to all formal or legal Documents emanating from the Board, all Agreements, Contracts, etcetera.
The Seal is required as authenticating the concurrence of the whole body corporate. *Marshall* v. *School Trustees*, No. 4, Kitley, 4, Common Pleas Report (U. C.) 375.

Differences between Trustees and Masters.—How Settled.

[The Twenty-seventh Section of the School Law of Improvement Act of 1871, de clares that: 27. All matters of difference between Trustees and Teachers . . . authorised by the Ninth Section of the High School Act of 1865. . . . . . to be settled by arbitration, shall hereafter be brought and decided in the Division Court by the Judge of the County Court, in each County . . . provided that the decision of any County Judge in all such cases may be appealed from, as provided for.]

(4) To appoint such other Officers and Servants in such School as they may judge expedient, and fix their remuneration.

To Erect, Repair, and Furnish Schools, etcetera.

(5) To do whatever they deem expedient with regard to erecting, repairing, wa:m ing, furnishing, and keeping in order the Buildings of such School, and its Append ages, Lands and Enclosures belonging thereto, and to apply for the requisite sums to be raised by Municipal authority for any such purpose;*

To impose, and Sue for Rate Bill, on Parents.

(6) To settle the amount to be paid by Parents and Guardians for each Pupil attending such School, and to fix the times of payment, and apply the moneys received therefor as they may judge expedient towards making up the Salaries of Teachers, providing the proper Apparatus, Maps, Text Books and Registers, and defraying any other necessary expenses of such School; and they may sue for and recover such amounts, and, when collected, the same shall be paid over to the Treasurer of the said High School Board:

To unite with the Public School Board on certain conditions.—Their Joint Powers.

(7) To employ, in concurrence with the Trustees of the School Section, or the Board of Public School Trustees, in the Township, Village, Town, or City, in which such High School may be situate, such means as they may judge expedient for unit ing one, or more, of the Public Schools of such Township, Village, Town, or City, or departments of them, with such High School; but no such union shall take place with out ample provision being made for giving instruction to the Pupils in the elementary English branches, by duly qualified English Teachers;

And the Schools, thus united, shall be under the management of a Joint Board of High and Public School Trustees, who shall consist of and have the powers of the Trustees of both the Public and High Schools.

[The Fifth Section of the High School Act of 1865 also provides that: 5. In all cases of the union of High and Public School Trustee Corporations, all the Members of both Corporations shall constitute the joint Board, seven of whom shall form a quorum.]

[But such union may be dissolved at the end of any year by a Resolution of a majority present at any lawful Meeting of the joint Board called for that purpose.]

[On the dissolution of such between any High and Public School, or department thereof, the School property held, or possessed, by the joint Board shall be divided, or applied to School purposes, as may be agreed upon by a majority of the Members of each Trustee Corporation; or if they fail to agree within the space of six months after such dissolution, then, by the Municipal Council of the City, Town, or incorporated Village within the limits of which such Schools are situated, and, in the case of unin corporated Villages, by the County Council.]

To supply Text Books and hold Public Examinations.

(8) To see that the Pupils of such High Schools are supplied with proper Text Books; that public half-yearly Examinations of the Pupils are held, and due notice

---

* This clause of the Twenty-fifth Section should be taken in connection with the Thirty-sixth Section of the Act of 1871.

given of them; and that such School is conducted in accordance with the legally established Regulations. [See latter part of the Twelfth Section of this Act].

To give orders on Treasurer for Salaries and Expenses.

(9) To give the necessary Orders upon the County Treasurer for the amount of public Money to which such School is entitled, and upon their own Treasurer for any Moneys in his hands, for the payment of the Salaries of the Officers of such School, and of any necessary expenses.

To make an Annual Report to Chief Superintendent of Education.

(10) To prepare and transmit, before the Fifteenth day of January, to the Chief Superintendent of Education, an Annual Report, in accordance with a form of report, which shall be provided by him for that purpose, and which Report shall contain a full and accurate amount of all matters appertaining to such School.

[The School Law Improvement Act of 1871, has the following additional provisions applicable to High Schools:—

Grammar School Act to apply to High Schools.

[35. All the provisions of the Grammar School Act shall, as far as is consistent with the provisions of this Act, apply to High Schools, their Trustees, Head Masters and other Officers, as fully as they apply to Grammar Schools and their Officers, etcetera.

Admission of Pupils to High Schools.

[38. The County, City, or Town Inspector of Schools, the Chairman of the High School Board, and the Head Master of the High School, shall constitute a Board of Examiners for the admission of Pupils to the High School, according to the Regulations and Programme of Examination provided according to Law; and it shall be the duty of the Inspector of High Schools to see that such Regulations are duly observed in the admission of Pupils to the High Schools; Provided, nevertheless, that the Pupils already admitted as Grammar School Pupils according to law, shall be held eligible, without further examination for admission as Pupils of the High Schools; And provided, furthermore, that Pupils from any part of the County, in which a High School is, or may be, established, shall be admitted to such School on the same terms as pupils within the Town, or Village, of such School.

Inspectors of High Schools.

[39. The Inspector, or Inspectors, of Grammar Schools now authorized by law shall be known as the Inspector or Inspectors of High Schools.

Vacation from 1st July to the 15th August in High Schools.

[44. The Summer Vacation in the High Schools throughout the Province shall be from the First day of July until the Fifteenth day of August, inclusive.

Inconsistent Provisions of other Acts Repealed.

[48. All the provisions of the Grammar and Common School Acts which are inconsistent with this Act are hereby repealed.

Masters of certain High Schools shall make Meteorological Observations.

26. The Master of every [authorized] County High School [Station, in connection with the Education Department,] shall make the requisite Observations for keeping, and shall keep, a Meteorological Journal, embracing such Observations, and kept according to such form as may, from time to time, be directed by the Council of Public Instruction; and all such Journals, or abstracts of them, shall be presented annually, by the Chief Superintendent of Education, to the Governor, with his Annual Report, and, if not already done, every [authorized] County High School [Station] shall be provided, at the expense of the County, with the following Instruments:—

List of Meteorological Instruments therefor.

One Barometer; one ~~Thermometer~~ for the temperature of the Air; one Daniel's Hygrometer, or other Instrument for showing the Dew-Point; one Rain-Gauge and Measure; one Wind-Vane.

Abstracts of Observations to be transmitted to the Chief Superintendent.

And the Chief Superintendent of Education shall procure these Instruments at the request and expense of the Municipal Council of any County, and shall furnish the Master of the [authorized] County High School [Station] with a Book for registering Observations, and with Forms for abstracts thereof, and such Master shall transmit the same to the Chief Superintendent, and shall certify that the Observations required have been made with due care and regularity.

Allowance for making Meteorological Reports.

[The Eleventh Section of the High School Act of 1865, further provides that: 10. Each of the High School Meteorological Stations, at which the daily Observations are made, as required by Law, shall be entitled to an additional Apportionment out of the High School Fund, at a rate not exceeding Fifteen dollars per month for each consecutive month during which such duty is performed and satisfactory monthly abstracts thereof are furnished to the Chief Superintendent, according to the Form and Regulations provided by the Department of Public Instruction.

Number and Locality of such Meteorological Stations fixed.

[But the number and locality of such Meteorological Stations shall be designated by the Council of Public Instruction, with the approval of the Governor-in-Council.

SPECIAL GRANTS OF GRAMMAR SCHOOL SITES.

[The Twenty-seventh Section, being obsolete, has been repealed.]

Conveyance of Property for Grammar Sites to Trustees.

28. In case any Persons residing in Ontario, interested in any School established in any City, Town, Village, or Township therein, whether as Parents of children frequenting such Schools, or as contributors to the same, or both, have occasion, or are desirous to take a Conveyance of Real Property for the use of such Schools, such Persons may elect from among themselves, and appoint any number of Trustees, not exceeding seven nor less than five, to whom, and to whose Successors, to be appointed in the manner specified in the Deed of Conveyance, the Real Property requisite for such School may be conveyed.

Powers of Trustees of Grammar School Sites.

And such Trustees, and their Successors in perpetual succession, by the name expressed in such Deed, may take, hold and possess such Real Property, and commence and maintain any action at Law, or in Equity, for the protection thereof, and of their right thereto; but there shall not be held in trust, as aforesaid, more than Ten Acres of Land at any one time for any one School; and this Section shall not extend to Public Schools.

Grammar School Deed to be Registered.

29. The Trustees shall, within twelve months after the execution of any such Deed, cause the same to be registered in the Office of the Registrar of the County in which the Land lies.

Certain cases provided for, if Site be not suitable.

30. In case any Lands in Ontario have been, or, after the passing of this Act, be surrendered, granted, devised, or otherwise, conveyed to the Crown, or to the Trustees of any County High School, or to any other Trustees, in trust for the purposes of, or as a Site for any such High School, or for any other Educational Institution established in any County, or place therein, for the benefit of the inhabitants thereof generally, and, in case such Lands be found not to afford the most advantageous Site for

such School, or Institution, or there be no School, or Institution bearing the precise designation mentioned in the Deed of Surrender, Grant, Devise, or other Conveyance, or, in case it may be for the benefit of such School, or Institution, that such Lands should be disposed of, and others acquired in their stead for the same purpose, or the proceeds of the sale applied thereto.

Such Lands may be surrendered to the Crown.

The Trustees, in whom any such Lands are vested in trust, as aforesaid, may, (with the consent of the Municipal Council expressed at a legal Meeting and certified under the hand of the Head and the Corporate Seal of the Municipality in which such School, or Institution, has been, or is to be, established), surrender and convey such lands to the Crown unconditionally, and such Conveyance shall vest the Lands absolutely in the Crown, without formal acceptance, by the Crown, the Governor, or any other Officer, or person, for the Crown.

Such Land to be Sold for the benefit of such School, etcetera.

31. Any Lands surrendered, granted, devised or otherwise conveyed to the Crown for any such purpose as aforesaid, may be sold by order of the Governor-in-Council, and the proceeds applied to the purchase of other Lands to be vested in the Crown for the purposes of the same Shcool, or Institution, or, in the case of there being no School bearing the precise designation intended, as aforesaid, by the Person who granted, or devised, the Lands to be Trustees, from, or through whom the Lands so sold came to the Crown, then, for the purposes of the High School or other Public Educational Institution established for the benefit of the inhabitants of the Municipality generally, which, in the opinion of the Governor-in-Council, comes nearest in its purposes and designs to that intended by such Person as aforesaid.

Lands may be Purchased with Proceeds.

32. If such proceeds be applied to the purchase of Lands for Grammar School purposes, the Title to such Lands may be vested in the Board of Trustees for any High School, by their corporate name; and if there be any surplus of such proceeds after such purchase, or if it be found that no lands are required as a Site for, or for other purposes of such School, or Institution, then such surplus, or proceeds, (as the case may be), may be invested, or applied, for the purposes of such School, or Institution, in such manner as the Governor-in-Council deems most for the advantage thereof.

33. No purchaser of Land from the Crown under this Act shall be in any way bound to see to the application of the purchase money.

34. Nothing in this Act shall impair the rights of any private party in, or upon, any lands, in so far as such rights would have existed and could be exercised without this Act.

Crown may grant such Lands, etcetera.

35. The Crown may grant to the Trustees of any High School, or of any other Public Educational Institution, established for the benefit of the inhabitants of the Municipality generally, any Lands which have been, or may, after the passing of this Act, be surrendered, granted, devised, or otherwise conveyed to the Crown as aforesaid.

CHAPTER IX.

I. CIRCULAR TO THE BOARD OF TRUSTEES OF HIGH SCHOOLS IN ONTARIO, WITH ACT AND REGULATIONS.

I herewith transmit the Programmes of Studies under the new School Act. Most of the Regulations, in respect to the duties of Masters and Pupils, and for all purposes of Discipline, are the same in the High Schools as in the Public Schools; the few particulars in which they differ are noted and provided for in the Regulations, which I trust will remove many causes of past misunderstandings and facilitate the management of the Schools on the part of both Trustees and Teachers.

2. What were heretofore known as Common Schools are now called Public Schools, and what were formerly called Grammar Schools are now termed High Schools. The Programmes of Studies for both these classes of Schools were vague and indefinite, and no sufficient agencies existed to give them effect, imperfect and general as they were: but, under the new Schools Act, (providing as it does for the efficient Inspection of Schools and means to enable Trustees of High Schools, as heretofore of Public Schools, to provide and pay a sufficient staff of qualified Teachers), the Schools are not only classified, but also the subjects taught in them. Hitherto the Grammar Schools have been considered as almost exclusively Classical Schools, and the Programme of Studies for them was chiefly formed with that view; but, under the new Schools Act, it is especially provided that they shall be High English Schools as well as Elementary Classical Schools, and for Girls as well as for Boys. When it is provided in the Act that in each High School, "provision shall be made for teaching to both male and female Pupils the higher branches of an English and Commercial Education, including the Natural Sciences, with special reference to Agriculture," it was clearly intended that the lower, or elementary, branches of an English Education should not be taught in the High Schools, but in the Public Schools. It was also intended that all Pupils to be eligible for admission to the High Schools for the study of Classics, as well as for higher English, must first be grounded in the elements of a sound education in their own native language, as strongly urged by the latest Royal and Parliamentary Commissions on Education in England, but strangely overlooked hitherto, as little Boys, six and seven years of age, have been put to the study of ancient and foreign languages, and left to grow up to manhood without ever having been formally taught their native tongue, or the essential elements of a practical English education. This anomaly is provided against by the new Act in the future education of Canadian youth, at least so far as the Public High Schools are concerned. Accordingly the 38th Section of the new Act, which became law on the 15th of last February, provides as follows:—

ADMISSION OF PUPILS TO HIGH SCHOOLS.

38. The County, City, or Town, Inspector of Schools, the Chairman of the High School Board and the Head Master of the High School shall constitute a Board of Examiners for the admission of Pupils to the High School, according to the Regulations and Programme of Examination provided according to Law; and it shall be the duty of the Inspector of High Schools to see that such Regulations are duly observed in the admission of Pupils to the High Schools; Provided, nevertheless, that the Pupils already admitted as Grammar School Pupils according to Law, shall be held eligible without further examination for admission as Pupils of the High Schools; And provided, furthermore, that Pupils from any part of the County in which a High School is, or may be, established shall be admitted to such School on the same terms as Pupils within the Town, or Village, of such School.

4. In accordance with this provision of the Act, the Council of Public Instruction has prescribed, that "the subjects of examination for admission to the High Schools shall be the same as those prescribed for the first four classes of the Public Schools." It will be seen from the explanatory remarks preceding the Programme that some subjects of the Fourth Class of the Public School Programme are omitted in regard to Pupil Candidates for the Classical Course of the High School. The examinations for admission to the High School must be on Paper, and the Examination Papers, with the Answers, are to be preserved for the examination of the High School Inspector, that he may not depend wholly on the individual examination of Pupils, as to whether the Regulations have been duly observed in the examination and admission of Pupils.

5. It is to be observed also, that although Pupils are eligible for promotion from the Public, to the High School, after passing a satisfactory examination in the subjects of the first Four Classes of the former, it is quite at the option of the Parents, or Guardians, of Pupils, whether they shall enter the High School, or not, before they complete the whole Programme of Studies in the Public Schools, when they can then enter an advanced Class in the High School.

6. The prescribed Programme of Studies for the High Schools is not intended to be obligatory before the commencement of 1872, except in as far as Boards of Trustees and Head Masters may think proper to introduce it this current half-year, and ex----- - - far as it relates to admission to the High Schools—the conditions of ad-

mission of new Pupils taking effect immediately. I may also remark, that as the Senate of the Toronto University contemplate, (as is understood,) some change in the Matriculation Curriculum, it is probable some modifications of the Classical Course of the High Schools may be required and made before the commencement of 1872.

7. While the 34th Section of the new Act provides that each Board of High School Trustees shall make provision for teaching "the Latin, Greek, French and German languages to those Pupils whose Parents, or Guardians desire it;" the same Section also provides, that "the Council of Public Instruction shall have power to exempt any High School, which shall not have sufficient Funds to provide the necessary qualified Teachers, from the obligation to teach the German and French languages."

8. As to Collegiate Institutes, provided for by the 41st Section of the new Act, I shall not be in a position to submit to the Lieutenant-Governor-in-Council the recognition and payment of any High School as a Collegiate Institute, until I receive the Inspector's Report, in connection with the application and statement of the Board of Trustees, as to whether the conditions of the Act are fulfilled in regard to the number of "Masters teaching the subjects of the prescribed Curriculum, and the average number of male Pupils studying the Latin, or Greek, language." But, in each case of satisfactory report and application, I shall recommend that the recognition of the High School as a Collegiate Institute take effect from the First of July.

9. The Legislature, at its last Session, added $20,000 to the High School Grant, exclusive of the Collegiate Institutes; and with the greatly increased powers of High School Boards of Trustees, and the improved Regulations and Programme, I trust the efficiency and usefulness of High Schools will be immensely promoted. I therefore conclude this Circular by reminding you again of the province of High Schools as a part of our System of Public Instruction; and to refer you to the words employed by the Council of Public Instruction, in the explanatory Memoranda, prefatory to the Programme of the Course of Studies for the High Schools.

TORONTO, 13th August, 1871.   EGERTON RYERSON.

II. PROGRAMMES OF COURSE OF STUDY FOR THE HIGH SCHOOLS.

Prescribed by the Council of Public Instruction for Ontario, under the authority of the School Laws of Ontario.

NOTE.—This Programme is published for the information of the Trustees and Head Masters of High Schools, but will not be obligatory until January, 1872. In consequence of changes being contemplated in the Curriculum of the University of Toronto, modifications may be made in the Classical Programme before it comes into force.

EXPLANATORY MEMORANDA.

The fundamental principle of our System of Public Instruction is, that every youth, before proceeding to the subjects of a higher English, or of a Classical Education, shall first be grounded in the elementary subjects of a Public School Education. No Candidates are, therefore, eligible for admission to the High Schools except those who have manifested proficiency, by passing a satisfactory examination in the subjects of the first Four Classes of the Public School Programme.

The objects and duties of the High Schools are two-fold:—

First, commencing with Pupils who, (whether educated in either a Public, or Private School), are qualified as above, the High Schools are intended to complete a good English education, by educating Pupils not only for Commercial, Manufacturing and Agricultural pursuits, but for fulfilling with efficiency, honour and usefulness the duties of Municipal Councillors, Legislators, and various Public Offices in the service of the Country.

The *Second* object and duty of the High Schools, (commencing also with Pupils qualified as above, is to teach the languages of Greece and Rome, of Germany and France, the Mathematics, etcetera, so far as to prepare youth for certain Professions, and especially for the Universities, where will be completed the education of men for the learned Professions, and for Professorships in the Colleges, and Masterships in the Collegiate Institutes and High Schools.

I.—THE ENGLISH COURSE FOR HIGH SCHOOLS.

SUBJECT.	FIRST FORM.	SECOND FORM.	THIRD FORM.	FOURTH FORM.
ENGLISH GRAMMAR AND LITERATURE.	English Grammar, including Etymology, Advanced, or Sixth, Reader, and Collier's History of English Literature.	Collier's History of English Literature, including English Grammar, including Etymology.	English Classics (critically and analytically read), Selection Number one.	English Classics (critically and analytically read), Selection Number two.
COMPOSITION	Practice in writing familiar and Business Letters.	Practice in Composition.	Practice in Composition.	Practice in Composition.
READING, DICTATION AND ELOCUTION	Practice in reading and writing to dictation from first four Reading Books.	Practice in writing to dictation.	Same as Form II., with Elocution.	Elocution.
PENMANSHIP	Practice in Penmanship.	Practice in Penmanship.		
LINEAR DRAWING	Free hand and Map Drawing, Outlines of Plain and Solid Figures.	For Boys, Mathematical Drawing, and for Girls, Shading and Landscape.	Drawing of Animals, Human Form, Mathematical Projection, Shading and Colouring.	
BOOK-KEEPING, ET CETERA.	Single and Double Entry.	Single and Double Entry, Commercial Forms and usages.	Banking, Custom House, General Business Transactions.	Subject of Form III., with Telegraphy.
ARITHMETIC	Practice, Proportion, Interest, Simple and Compound.	Discount, Stocks, Exchange, Involution and Evolution, Scales of Notation.		General Review.
ALGEBRA	Definitions and first seventeen Exercises of authorized Text-book.	To end of Quadratic Equations.	Authorized Text-book, to end of Section XIV.	To end of authorized Text-book.
GEOMETRY	Euclid, Book I.*	Euclid, Books II. and III.†	Book IV., with principles of Book V.	Book VI., with review of whole subject.

LOGIC	....	....	Easy lessons in Reasoning, Part I. to page 71.	Easy Lessons in Reasoning, completed.
TRIGONOMETRY	....	....	Plane Trigonometry, to Solution of Triangles (inclusive).	Application of Plane Trigonometry.
MENSURATION	Definitions, Mensuration of Surfaces.	Definitions, Mensuration of Surfaces and Solids.		
HISTORY	Outlines of English and Canadian History.	Elements of Ancient and Modern History. English and Canadian History, continued.	Outlines of History of Greece and Rome.	Outlines of Modern History.
GEOGRAPHY AND ASTRONOMY.	Political geography, products, etcetera, of principal Countries of the World. Modern (Mathematical, Physical and Political).	Physical Geography of the Continents generally. Ancient Geography (Pillow's).	General review of subject. Use of Terrestrial Globes.	Outlines of Astronomy—Celestial Globe.
NATURAL PHILOSOPHY	Nature and use of the Mechanical Powers.	Composition and Resolution of Forces; Centre of Gravity; Moments of Force; Principle of Virtual Velocities and Hydrostatics, (Tomlinson).	Pneumatics and Dynamics.	Elements of Electricity and Magnetism. ‡
CHEMISTRY AND AGRICULTURE.	Ryerson's Agriculture, Part 1.	Agriculture (Ryerson) completed.	Elements of Chemistry.	Elements of Chemistry.
NATURAL HISTORY.	"How Plants Grow," (Gray).	Animal Kingdom.	General review.	
PHYSIOLOGY.	....	Human Physiology, (Cutter's).		
CHRISTIAN MORALS.	Christian Morals.			
ELEMENTS OF CIVIL GOVERNMENT.	....	....		"Elements of Civil Government."

* Girls not in Geometry will take in Form I., Easy Lessons in Reasoning, Part I.
† Girls not in Geometry will take in Form II., Easy Lessons in Reasoning, Part II.
‡ The subjects of Electricity and Magnetism may be taken up earlier in the Course, at the discretion of the Head Master.

II.—THE CLASSICAL COURSE, FOR HIGH SCHOOLS, AND COLLEGIATE INSTITUTES, WITH FRENCH AND GERMAN.

Prescribed by the Council of Public Instruction for Ontario, under the authority of the Consolidated School Laws of Ontario.

SUBJECT.	FIRST FORM.	SECOND FORM.	THIRD FORM.	FOURTH FORM.
ENGLISH GRAMMAR AND LITERATURE	English Grammar, including Etymology. Advanced or Sixth Reader.	Collier's History of English Literature.	English Classics (critically and analytically read). Selection Number I.	English Classics (critically and analytically read). Section Number 2.
COMPOSITION	Practice in writing familiar and business letters.	Practice in Composition.	Practice in Composition.	Practice in Composition.
PENMANSHIP	Practice in Penmanship.	Practice in Penmanship.		
LINEAR DRAWING	Map and free hand Drawing. Outlines of Plain and Solid Figures.	For Boys, Mathematical Drawing, and for girls, Shading and Landscape.	Drawing of Animals, Human Form, Mathematical Projection, Shading and Colouring.	
ARITHMETIC	Practice, Proportion, Interest, Simple and Compound.	Discount, Stock, Exchange, Involution and Evolution, Scales of Notation.		
ALGEBRA	Definitions and first Seventeen Exercises of authorized Text-book.	To end of Quadratic Equations.	Authorized Text-book, to end of Section XIV.	To end of authorized Text-book.
GEOMETRY	Euclid, Book I.*	Euclid, Books II and III. †	Book IV, with principles of Book V.	Book VI, with review of the whole subject.
TRIGONOMETRY			Plane Trigonometry, to Solution of Triangles (inclusive).	Application of Plane Trigonometry.
HISTORY	Outlines of English and Canadian History.	Elements of Ancient and Modern History.	Outlines of History of Greece and Rome.	Outlines of History of Greece and Rome, continued.

* Girls not in Geometry will take in Form I, Easy Lessons in Reasoning, Part I.
† Girls not in Geometry will take in Form II, Easy Lessons in Reasoning, Part II.

GEOGRAPHY AND ASTRONOMY	Political Geography, products, etceters, of principal countries in the World. Modern (Mathematical, Physical, and Political).	Outlines of Ancient Geography (Pillans).	Ancient Geography, continued.	
NATURAL HISTORY	"How plants grow," (Gray).	Animal Kingdom.	General Review.	
CHRISTIAN MORALS	Christian Morals.			
ELEMENTS OF CIVIL GOVERNMENT				"Elements of Civil Government."
FRENCH*	Pujol, Part I; or De Fivas' Grammas, with Exercises.	Pujol, Part II, with selections from Part IV, or De Fivas' Grammar and Exercises, with Collot's Conversations, and De Fivas' Elementary Reader.	Pujol, Part III, with selections from Part IV, or De Fivas' Grammar and Exercises, with conversations. Voltaire, Hist. de Charles XII, Chapters VI, VII, VIII. Corneille, Horace, Acts I, II.	
GERMAN*	Grammar (Ahn).	Grammar (Ahn), Adler's Reader	Goethe, Hermann, and Dorothea, Canto II.	
LATIN	Latin Grammar commenced. Harknees' Introductory Book, or Smith's Principia Latina, Part I.	Latin Grammar (continued). Arnold's 2nd Latin Book, Smith's Principia Latina. Harknes' Latin Reader.	Cæsar, Virgil, Æneid, Book II commenced. Latin Prose Composition. Prosody commenced.	Cicero (for the Manilian Law). Horace, Odes Book I. Latin Prose Composition. Prosody continued.
GREEK		Greek Grammar commenced. Harkness' 1st Greek Book, or Smith's Initia Græca.	Greek Grammar continued. Harkness or Smith continued. Lucian, Charon.	Lucian, Life. Homer, Iliad, Book I.

8—XXIII.

* The German and French Languages are optional.
NOTE.—Provision is not made in the Programme for the Honour work in the Universities, as Pupils intended for the Honour work in the Universities will require special arrangement.

REGULATIONS FOR THE ADMISSION OF PUPILS TO HIGH SCHOOLS AND COLLEGIATE INSTITUTES.

1. *Admission of Pupils.*—The School Law of 1871, Section 38, provides that "The County, City, or Town, Inspector of Schools, the Chairman of the High School Board and the Head Master of the High School shall constitute a Board of Examiners for the admission of Pupils to the High School according to the Regulations and Programme of Examination provided according to Law; and it shall be the duty of the Inspector of High Schools to see that such Regulations are duly observed in the admission of Pupils to the High Schools; Provided, nevertheless, that the Pupils already admitted as Grammar School Pupils according to Law, shall be held eligible without further examination for admission as Pupils of the High Schools; And provided furthermore, that Pupils from any part of the County in which a High School is, or may be established, shall be admitted to such School on the same terms as Pupils within the Town, or Village, of such School.

2. *Duties of Inspectors.*—The Inspectors shall receive and be responsible for the safe keeping, unopened, of the Examination Papers, until the day of Examination. He shall also, at the close of the Examination of Candidates for admission, submit the Answers of Candidates to the Board for examination and report; but, under no circumstances, shall a Certificate of admission be awarded to any Candidate until the Report on his Answers shall have been considered and approved by a majority of the Board, including the Inspector.

3. *Viva voce and Special Examinations in Reading.*—The Board of Examiners shall subject the Candidates to *viva voce* examination in Reading, of the result of which a record shall be made.

4. Each Examiner, by his acceptance of office, binds himself in honour to give no information to Candidates, directly or indirectly, by which the examination of that Candidate might be affected

5. *Time and place of each Examination.*—The Examination of Candidates for admission to the High School, or Collegiate Institute, shall be held in such place as may be agreed upon by the Examiners.

6. *Proceedings at each Examination.*—The Inspector shall preside at the opening of the Examination; and, at nine o'clock on the morning of the first day, in the presence of such of his Colleagues as may be there, and of the Candidates, he shall break the Seal of the Package of Examination Papers received for that Examination, from the Education Department. He shall also break open the Seal of each additional Packet of Examination Papers as required, in the presence of a Co-examiner and of the Candidates. He shall further see that at least one Examiner is present during the whole time of the Examination, in each Room occupied by the Candidates. He shall, if desirable, appoint one or more of his Co-examiners (1) to preside at the Examination in any of the subjects named in the Programme: (2) to read and report upon the Answers as they are received.

7. The Examination, except in Reading, shall be conducted wholly on Paper.

8. The Candidate, in preparing their Answers, will write only on one page of each sheet. They will also write their names on each sheet, and, having arranged their papers in the order of the Questions, will fold them once across and write on the outside sheet their names. After the Papers are once handed in, the Examiners will not allow any alteration thereof, and the presiding Inspector is responsible for the subsequent safe-keeping of the same, until he has handed them to the High School Inspector.

9. The presiding Inspector, or Examiner, must be punctual to the moment in distributing the Papers, and in directing the Candidates to sign their Papers at the close of the allotted time. No writing, other than the Signature, should be permitted after the order to sign the name is given. The Candidates are required to be in their allotted places in the Room before the hour appointed for the commencement of the Examination. If a Candidate be not present till after the commencement of the Examinations, he cannot be allowed any addition time on account of such absence.

8a—XXIII

10. In examining the Answers of Candidates, it is desirable that at least two Examiners should look over each Paper.

11. The Department will, on the margin of the Questions, assign numerical values to each Question, or part of a Question, according to their judgment of its relative importance. The local Examiners will give marks for the Answers to any Question in correspondence with the number assigned to the Question, and the completeness and accuracy of the Answers.

12. In order that a Candidate may obtain admission to the High School, or Collegiate Institute, the sum of his marks must amount to at least seventy-five per cent, of the assigned value of the Answers given in the margin of the Examination Questions.

13. The names of successful Candidates shall be arranged alphabetically.

14. In the event of a Candidate copying from another, or allowing another to copy from him, or taking into the Room any Book, Notes, or anything from which he might derive assistance in the Examination, it shall be the duty of the presiding Examiner, if he obtain clear evidence of the fact at the time of its occurrence, to cause such Candidate at once to leave the Room; neither shall such Candidate be permitted to enter during the remaining part of the Examination, and his name shall be struck off the list. If, however, the evidence of such case be not clear at the time, or be obtained after the conclusion of the Examination, the Examiners shall report the case at a general Meeting of the Examiners, who shall reject the Candidate if they deem the evidence conclusive.

15. The subjects of examination for admission to the High Schools, or Collegiate Institutes, shall be the same as those prescribed for the first four Classes of the Public Schools, but for Pupils intended for the Classical Course, the entrance test in Arithmetic is the standard prescribed for the Third Class in the Public Schools, and omitting from the subjects of the fourth Class Christian Morals, Animal Kingdom and the elements of Chemistry and Botany. The Examination Papers on those subjects shall be prepared by the High School Inspectors. The Examinations for admission to the High School must be on Paper, and the Examination Papers with the Answers are to be preserved for the examination of the High School Inspector, that he may not depend wholly on the individual examination of Pupils as to whether the Regulations have been duly observed in the Examination and admission of Pupils.

16. Although Pupils are eligible for promotion from the Public to the High Schools, after passing a satisfactory Examination in the subjects of the first four Classes of the former, it is quite at the option of the Parents, or Guardians, of Pupils, whether they shall enter the High School, or not, before they complete the whole Programme of Studies in the Public Schools, when they can then enter an advanced Class in the High School.

17. All Candidates passing a satisfactory examination before the local Board, shall receive from it a Certificate of eligibly for admission, and shall be temporarily admitted by the Head Master. But their attendance will not be credited to the School should the Inspector of High Schools disapprove of their admission.

18. The High School Board will provide the stationery required for conducting the Examinations.

Pupils entering the High Schools, must take either the English, or the Classical Course of Studies.

20. Pupils shall be arranged in Classes corresponding to their respective degrees of proficiency. There may be two or more divisions in each Class, and each Pupil shall be advanced from one division, or Class, to another, with reference to attainments, without regard to time, according to the judgment of the Head Master; and, if any difference takes place between the Parent, or Guardian, of a Pupil and the Head Master, in regard to the advancement of such Pupil, the Inspector of the High School shall decide.

21. No departure from the prescribed Programme is allowable. Where options are authorized the permission must not be given to any Pupil without the recommendation of the Head Master and the sanction of the Board of Trustees.

22. Pupils who have been admitted to the High Schools under the previous Regulations, must be taught those subjects of the first four Classes of the Public School Programme with which they are not acquainted.

REGULATIONS FOR GRAMMAR AND HIGH SCHOOLS, PRESCRIBED BY THE COUNCIL OF PUBLIC INSTRUCTION.

POWERS AND DUTIES OF THE HEAD MASTER, TEACHERS AND PUPILS.

The Regulations published for Public School Masters are extended to High School Masters, and the following additional Regulations are also prescribed:—

Examinations for Scholarships, Exhibitions and Prizes, which may have been instituted, shall be conducted by the Head Master, but the High School Board may, if they shall think proper, associate other Persons with the Head Master in the Examinations for such Scholarships, Exhibitions, or Prizes.

A Report of the progress and conduct of each Pupil shall be furnished to his Parent, or Guardian, monthly, by the Head Master.

The Regulations published for Public School Pupils are extended to High School Pupils, except that Number 11 shall read as follows:

The Fees, whether monthly, or quarterly, shall be payable in advance, and no Pupil shall have the right to enter, or continue in, the School until he shall have paid the appointed Fee. Regulation Number 7, under the same head, is inapplicable to High Schools.

GRAMMAR AND HIGH SCHOOL ACCOMMODATIONS.

No Grammar or High School shall be entitled to receive any Grant unless suitable Accommodations shall be provided for it.

The School should have,—

(1) A Site of an Acre, in extent, but not less than half an Acre.

(2) A School House, (with separate Rooms where the number of Pupils exceeds Fifty), the Walls of which shall not be less than ten feet high in the clear, and which shall not contain less than nine square feet on the floor for each child in attendance, so as to allow an area in each Room, for at least one hundred cubic feet of Air for each child. It shall also be sufficiently Warmed, and Ventilated, and the premises properly Drained.

(3) A sufficient Fence, or Paling, round the School Premises.

(4) A Play Ground, or other satisfactory provision for Physical Exercise, within the Fences, and off the Road.

(5) A Well, or other means of procuring Water for the School.

(6) Proper and separate Offices for both sexes, at some little distance back from the School House, and suitably enclosed.

(7) Suitable School Furniture and Apparatus, videlicet: Desks, Seats, Blackboards, Maps, Library, Presses and Books, etcetera, necessary for the efficient conduct of the School. (See also Note to (a) of Regulation 4, of the "Duties of Inspector.")

LIST OF AUTHORIZED TEXT BOOKS FOR THE HIGH SCHOOLS IN ONTARIO.

(Sanctioned by the Council of Public Instruction.)

NOTE.—In the following list some Text Books are prescribed under the authority of the Fifteenth Section of the Consolidated High School Act, and others are recommended. The use of the Books recommended is discretionary with the respective High

School Boards. The Council has decided that the Text Books on English subjects authorized for High Schools may also be used in the Public Schools.

I. *Latin Text Books Prescribed.*

Harkness's New Series, videlicet:—
1. An Introductory Latin Book. By Albert Harkness, Ph.D.
2. A Latin Reader, intended as a Companion to the Author's Latin Grammar. By Albert Harkness, Ph.D.
3. A Latin Grammar for Schools and Colleges. By Albert Harkness, Ph.D.

If preferred, the following may be used instead of the above series:

Arnold's First and Second Latin Books and Practical Grammar, revised and corrected. By J. A. Spencer, D.D. *or,*
Doctor Smith's Principia Latina. Part I. Revised by H. Drisler, LL.D.
A Smaller Grammar of the Latin Language. By William Smith, LL.D.

Latin Dictionary Recommended: (See note above.)

A Latin-English and English-Latin Dictionary. By Charles Anthon, LL.D., *or,*
The Young Scholar's Latin-English and English-Latin Dictionary. By Joseph Esmond Riddle, M.A.

II. *Greek Text Books Prescribed.*

A First Greek Book, comprising an outline of Grammar and an Introductory Reader. By Albert Harkness, Ph.D., *or,*
Doctor Smith's Initia Græca.
A smaller Grammar of the Greek Language, abridged from the larger Grammar of Doctor George Curtins.

Greek Lexicon Recommended: (See note above.) Liddell and Scott's Greek-English Lexicon.

III. *Ancient History, Classical Geography, and Antiquities. Text Books Prescribed.*

A Manual of Ancient History. By Doctor Leonhard Schmits.
First Steps in Classical Geography. B. Professor James Pillans.

Classical Dictionaries, etcetera, Recommended: (See note above).
A Classical Dictionary of Biography, Mythology and Geography. By Wm. Smith, LL.D.
A Dictionary of Greek and Roman Antiquities. By Wm. Smith, LL.D., *or,*
A Classical Dictionary. By Charles Anthon, LL.D.
A Manual of Roman Antiquities. By Charles Anthon, LL.D.
A Manual of Greek Antiquities. By Charles Anthon, LL.D.

IV. *French and German Text Books Prescribed.*

Text Books in French and German will be prescribed.
History of Charles XII. of Sweden. By Voltaire.
Horace: A tragedy. By Corneille.
A Complete Dictionary of the French and English Languages. By Gabriel Surenne. Spiers' New Abridged Edition.

V. *English Text Books Prescribed.*

The Canadian National Series of Reading Books. (Authorized edition.)
The Spelling Book, A Companion to the Readers. (Authorized edition.)

Miller's Analytical and Practical English Grammar. (Autorized edition.)

A History of English Literature, in a Series of Biographical Sketches. By William Francis Collier, LL.D.

VI. *Arithmetic and Mathematics. Text Books Prescribed.*

Advanced Arithmetic for Canadian Schools. By Barnard Smith, M.A., and Archibald McMurchy, M.A.

Elementary Arithmetic for Canadian Schools. By the Reverend Barnard Smith, M.A., and Archibald McMurchy, M.A.

Elements of Algebra. Todhunter's, or Sangster's.

Euclid's Elements of Geometry. Potts', or Todhunter's.

VII. *Modern Geography and History. Text Books Prescribed.*

Lovell's General Geography. (Authorized edition.) By J. George Hodgins, LL.D., Barrister-at-Law.

A School History of the British Empire. By William Francis Collier, LL.D.

A History of Canada, and of the other British Provinces of North America. By J. George Hodgins, LL.D., Barrister-at-Law.

Outlines of General History. By William Francis Collier, LL.D.

Text Books recommended:—

The Great Events of History. By William Francis Collier, LL.D.

VIII. *Physical Science. Text Books Prescribed:* (See note above.)

Rudimentary Mechanics, by Charles Tomlinson, with Cassell's Hand-Book of Natural and Experimental Philosophy, *or,*

Manual of Mechanics, by the Reverend Samuel Haughton, M.A., F.R.S., with Introductory Course of Natural Philosophy. Edited from Ganot's Popular Physics, by W. G. Peck, M.A.

The Animal Kingdom, by Ellis A. Davidson.

How Plants Grow; A Simple Introduction to Botany, with Popular Flora. By Asa Gray, M.D.

Lessons in Elementary Chemistry. By Henry E. Roscoe, B.A., L.R.S.

IX. *Miscellaneous. Text Books Prescribed.*

First Lessons in Agriculture, by Reverend Doctor Ryerson.

First Book on Anatomy, Physiology and Hygiene, for Private Schools and Families, by Calvin Cutter, M.D., *or* (for Public Schools).* Our Bodies, by Ellis A. Donaldson.*

Easy Lessons on Reasoning, by Archbishop Whately.

Text Books recommended: (See note above.)

A Comprehensive System of Book-keeping, by Single and Double Entry. By Thomas R. Johnson. A work on Book-keeping is to be sanctioned.

Field Exercise and Evolutions of Infantry. Published by Authority. Pocket edition, for Squad and Company Drill).

The Modern Gymnast. By Charles Spencer.

A Manual of Vocal Music. By John Hullah.

Three-Part Songs. By H. F. Sefton. (Authorized edition.)

National Mensuration.

Scripture Lessons—Old and New Testaments. (National.)

*The following Works are also highly recommended for perusal, both by Teachers and Pupils, videlicet:—" The House I live in," by T. C. Girtin, Surgeon, and "Our Earthly House and its Builder" (Religious Tract Society.) "Our Bodies," by Ellis A. Davidson, is the prescribed Book for Public Schools, and may be used in the High Schools if desired.

Lessons on the Truth of Christianity. (National.)

Right Lines in their Right Places, by Ellis A. Davidson.

Linear Drawing, by Ellis A. Davidson.

Teacher's Guide, and Bartholemew's Primary School Drawing Cards, by Miss J. H. Stickney.

The Drawing Book for the Dominion of Canada, in progressive Studies, seven numbers.

William Hermes' Drawing Instructor. For advanced Students.

Writing Copy Books, used in the Normal and Model Schools for Ontario. In Five Parts.

NOTE. As it was intended to take up the subject of the revision of the Programme for Public School (in connection with that of again considering the High School Programme), I took occasion in the absence of the Chief Superintendent at his Island home to consult with the Masters of the Normal School, and with Mr. Marling on the subject. In a private note to Doctor Ryerson, I said : —

I. I have had a meeting every day with Sangster, Davis, Carlyle and Marling to confer on the new Public School Programme. We have made some modifications in Sangster's programme, and have considerably reduced it for the Rural Schools. I will get it set up for the consideration of the Members of the Council of Public Instruction, and will send you an early copy.

TORONTO, 6th April, 1871.   J. GEORGE HODGINS.

II. I also wrote to the Chief Superintendent on another subject as follows : —

The Public Works Architect has prepared the plan of the Model School alterations. I got him to go over the Building and Grounds with Sangster and myself, and we suggested several modifications on the original draft he had prepared. I was anxious, before getting a tracing of the Plans made to send out for your approval, to get Doctor Carlyle and Mrs. Cullen, (of the Girls' Model School) to go over them with Sangster and me, so as to get the best plan we could, and the advice and experience of the heads of the Normal and Model Schools, which I think of importance. They have been teaching there for years, and many suggestions and improvements would naturally suggest themselves to them, which the going over with Sangster, Marling and myself would enable us to embody, if desirable, in the new plans.

TORONTO, 6th April, 1871.   J. GEORGE HODGINS.

III. FROM DOCTOR RYERSON TO J. GEORGE HODGINS.

It was intended that the Committee of Examiners should examine the Normal School Students at the close of each Session, the same as other Candidates for Certificates.

Doctor Sangster has frequently expressed a wish that the Students of the Normal School should be examined by an independent Committee, and he and Doctor Davis have complained of the burden and responsibility of it. I have thought it would exempt the Normal School from a repetition of attacks upon it, and, leaving the Teachers generally no ground of complaint that partiality was shown to Students of the Normal School in the matter.

LONG-POINT COTTAGE, April 7th, 1871.   EGERTON RYERSON.

IV. J. GEORGE HODGINS TO DOCTOR RYERSON.

Quite a number of Students of the Normal School were with me this afternoon to know if they would be examined under the *new* programme, or on the Course of Study which they have been pursuing all the Winter.

They say that in several subjects, (such as Botany and Chemistry,) the Second Division have received no instruction whatever. It would, therefore, be manifestly unjust to apply the new Programme to them.

The more I think of it the more I am convinced that we should retain our own Normal School examinations, and have the Normal School Masters Co-examiners with the Committee now appointed.

There would be nothing to indicate in what respects the Normal School differs from, or is superior to, self training, if there are not separate examinations, so as to give the Normal School imprimatur to a Certificate of its Students. The training in the Normal School can never practically have an equivalent substitute.

TORONTO, April 19th, 1871.   J. GEORGE HODGINS.

CHAPTER X.

PROCEEDINGS OF THE COUNCIL OF PUBLIC INSTRUCTION.

February 24th, 1871. Several Communications were laid before the Council.

Ordered, That the Letters of Mr. Zoeger and Mr. Schmidt be referred to the Committee on Text Books, for their Report.

Ordered, That permission be given to Mr. Warwick to publish the "Spelling Book," provided he furnishes the proper securities, and makes any emendations that may be required.

The Provisions of the School Act of 1871, respecting the inspection of Public Schools, and the formation of Board of Examiners were considered, and it was,—

Ordered, I. Qualifications of Inspectors.—All County and City Superintendents of Common, or Public, Schools, who have held that office consecutively for three years; all Teachers of Public Schools who have obtained, or who shall obtain, First-class Provincial Certificates of Qualifications; all Head Masters of Grammar, or High, Schools, who have taught the same School for three years, and who shall prepare and transmit to the Education Department a satisfactory Thesis on the Organization and Discipline of Public Schools; and all Graduates who have proceeded regularly to their Degrees in any University in the British Dominions, and who have taught in a College, or School, not less than three years, and who shall prepare and transmit to the Education Department a satisfactory Thesis on the Organization and Discipline of Public Schools, shall be considered legally qualified for the Office of County, or City, Inspector of Public Schools, without any further examination, on their obtaining, in each case, from the Education Department, the Certificate required by Law.

II. *Qualifications of Examiners.*—All Head Masters of Grammar, or High, Schools, and all Graduates who have proceeded regularly to their Degrees in any University in the British Dominions, who have taught in a College, or School, not less than three years; and all Teachers of Common, or Public, Schools, who have obtained a First Class Provincial Certificate of Qualification, or who may obtain such Certificate under the provisions of the present Law, shall be considered as legally qualified to be appointed Members of a County, or City, Board of Examiners without further examination, on their obtaining from the Education Department the Certificate required by Law.

March 17th, 1871. Several Communications were laid before the Council.

Ordered, That a special Certificate of Qualification as Inspector of French Public Schools, in the County of Essex, be granted to Mr. Girardot.

Ordered, That Mr. Boyle be regarded as qualified for a County, or City, Inspectorship under the Minute already adopted.

Ordered, That the Qualifications of Inspectors and Examiners adopted at the previous Meeting of the Council be amended as follows:—

I. In the Qualifications of Inspectors, after the words, "Provincial Certificate of Qualification," insert the words: "of the highest grade (A)."

II. In the Qualifications of Examiners, Strike out the words at the end, videlicet: "the Certificate required by Law," and insert the words: "for the satisfaction of the County Council, or City, Boards a Certificate of their having complied with these Regulations and being eligible under their provisions."

The Chief Superintendent of Education made a general verbal statement of his views as to the Examination and Classification of Teachers under the new School Law. The subject was deferred.

March 21st, 1871. The following Report of the Committee on Text Books was received and adopted:—

The Committee on Text Books beg leave to report that they have received a Report from Doctor Sangster and Mr. Alexander Marling, relative to Text Books on Book-keeping and Writing, which they submit herewith. They now recommend to the Council the authorization of a revised edition of "The Dominion Accountant," and of the Writing Copy Books prepared by the Department. They further recommend that the Regulations of the Council relative to copyright shall be carried out, previously to the authorization of these Books.

Ordered, That Mr. Girardot, if appointed an Inspector by the County Council of Essex, as allowed by a previous Minute, be authorized to inspect any English Public Schools there may be in the French Settlement of that County.

The Council then proceeded with the revision of the Programme for the Examination and Classification of Teachers of the Public Schools, and it was ordered to be reprinted, as amended.

March 28th, 1871. Several Communications were laid before the Council.

Ordered, That a Certificate of Qualification as a Town Inspector be granted to the Reverend Robert Torrance.

Ordered, That, as authorized by the Twelfth Section of the School Act of 1871, the Reverend George Paxton Young, M.A., the Reverend J. D. G. MacKenzie, M.A., Inspector of High Schools, and Mr. James A. McLellan, M.A., be appointed a Committee to prepare Papers for the Examinations, (to be held under the authority of the Eleventh and Twelfth Sections of said Act), of Candidates for Certificates as Public School Teachers, also to examine the Answers of Candidates for First Class Certificates, and to report the results of such Examination.

Ordered, That the Reverend George Paxton Young, M.A., be appointed a Member of the Committee on Text Books, in place of the Reverend William Ormiston, D.D.

Ordered, That, with respect to the Qualifications of Inspectors and Examiners, the word Graduates shall be held to mean Graduates in Arts, and that the necessary words be added, when those requirements are published.

Ordered, That an advertisement be published, stating that the Council are desirous of appointing an additional Inspector of High Schools, and that applications of Candidates can be sent in at any time before the first day of May next.

The Departmental Regulations for giving effect to the Minutes, as to Inspectors and Examiners, were considered and revised, the Council expressing the desire to limit the required Thesis to twenty-five, or thirty, pages, and to reduce the number of Topics originally proposed to be treated therein.

The Examination Programme for Public School Teachers, having been printed, as amended at the previous Meeting, was further revised and finally adopted, as follows. videlicet:—

(NOTE. This Programme is printed in Chapter V of this Volume).

April 25th, 1871. Ordered, That, in compliance with the wishes of many Candidates for the office of Inspector of Public Schools, and to remove any possible ground of complaint of restrictive partiality, the Council of Public Instruction hereby authorizes a special Examination of Candidates for First Class Teachers' Certificates of the Grade A. The Examination will commence precisely at nine o'clock A.M., on Thursday, the Eighteenth of May next, in the Theatre of the Normal School, at Toronto. Candidates must transmit their names, with the requisite testimonials, to the Chief Superintendent of Education, at Toronto, on or before the Fifteenth day of May.

April 28th, 1871. Several Communications were laid before the Council.

Ordered, That, with respect to the Letter of the Reverend A. McColl ,of Chatham, it was not the intention of the Council to make a difference between City and Town Inspectors of Public Schools, as to qualifications for office. The term "Town" should have been inserted with the terms "County" and "City" in the Minute of the Council specifying the qualifications of Public School Inspectors.

With respect to the Letter of Mr. James Cormton, of Charlotteville, and the Memorial in his behalf, signed by the principal gentlemen in the County of Norfolk, the Council of Public Instruction orders the following Minute :—

"That the Council does not feel itself justified in departing from the declared intentions of the Government and Legislature in providing for the more practical qualifications and more liberal support of Public School Inspectors, namely, that with the particular exceptions agreed to, when the Bill was passing through the Legislature, they should be practical Teachers, able to take charge of any Public School, and show how it should be organized and managed, and how any subject of its Programme should be taught; and be professionally and wholly devoted to their work, as much as any Teacher of a School. However respectable and literary a Gentleman may be, if he has not the technical knowledge and practical experience of a First Class Teacher of a Public School, he cannot be considered legally qualified for the special work of a County Inspector of Public Schools, according to the avowed intention of the new School Act to make the inspection an agency of improving both the Teachers and the Schools.

Ordered, That the Council, having taken into consideration the service of Mr. J. C. Patterson as a Teacher in Grammar and Common Schools, and the fact of his appointment as Town Inspector, consent to accept his qualifications for the office of Inspector for the Town of Windsor as equivalent to those required in the First Section of the Official Regulations.

Ordered, That, as the standing of M. J. Kelly, M.D., to whom was awarded a First Class ungraded Certificate, would have entitled him to grade A, if the Certificates had then been graded, a Certificate of eligibility as Inspector be granted to him, and that such Certificates be also awarded to Messieurs John Livingstone and William Carlyle on similar grounds.

Ordered, That the applications of Messieurs J. B. Gray and S. Rathwell be not allowed, their standing being not regarded as equivalent to Grade A.

May 1st, 1871. Several Communications were laid before the Council, but no business of public importance was transacted.

May 8th, 1871. Several Communications were laid before the Council.

Ordered, That the usual Examination of the Normal School Students be held at the close of the present Session, upon the Programme in force at the opening of the Session, and that, to conduct such Examination, the Masters of the Normal School be, on this occasion, associated with the Committee appointed by the Minute of 28th of March.

Ordered, That, if it appears from the records that the standing of Mr. James B. Gray was equal to that afterwards required of Students of the Grade A, a Certificate of eligibility as Inspector be awarded to him.

Ordered, That in view of the peculiar circumstances of the County of Essex, and the proposed appointment of Mr. Girardot as Inspector for the French Schools, to whom a Certificate of eligibility has already been awarded, Mr. Bell be regarded as eligible for an Inspector's Certificate limited to that County.

Ordered, That Mr. James McLellan, M.A., be appointed as an additional Inspector of High Schools, at a Salary of $2,000 per annum. The appointment to take effect on 1st July. Mr. McLellan's appointment having been decided upon, it was resolved that it be made unanimous.

Ordered, That with respect to the Qualifications of Examiners the first part of that Minute be amended, to read as follows:—

"All Head Masters of Grammar or High Schools, and those Graduates in Arts, who have proceeded regularly to their Degrees in any University in the British Dominions, and have taught in a College, or School, not less than three years; all Candidates for Degrees in Arts in the Universities of the United Kingdom, who previously to the year 1864, possessed all the statutable requirements of their respective Universities for admission to such Degrees, and have taught in a College, or School, not less than three years," and so on, as already adopted.

May 26th, 1871. Several Communications were laid before the Council, including the Examiners' Report.

Ordered, That Certificates of the First Class, Grade A, and Certificates of eligibility as Inspector be granted to the Gentlemen named in the Examiners' Report.

Ordered, That Certificates of eligibility as Examiners be granted to all those Chairmen and Secretaries of County Boards of Public Instruction who have held either of those offices during five consecutive years.

May 29th, 1871. Several Communications were laid before the Council.

Ordered, Upon an Examination of the case of the Reverend E. H. Jenkins, the Council regard him as equitably entitled to the Certificate applied for.

May 31st, 1871. The Council made further progress in the Examination of the proposed Programmes of Study for Public and High Schools.

June 2nd, 1871. The Council made further progress in the Examination of the proposed Programmes of Study for Public and High Schools, which were ordered to be finally revised for adoption by the Council at a future Meeting.

June 6th, 1871. *Ordered*, That the next Examinations of Candidates for Certificates of Qualification as Public School Teachers shall be held as follows:—

The Examination for Second and Third Class Certificates will commence at nine o'clock a.m., on Tuesday the Twenty-fifth of July, 1871.

The Examination for First Class Certificates will commence at nine o'clock a.m., on the following Tuesday, the First of August.

On the recommendation of the Chief Superintendent of Education, and after consultation with other Members of the Council, now absent, it was,—

Ordered, That Doctor James Carlyle be appointed an additional Master in the Normal School, with the view of his taking the Mathematical subjects and in order that the services of the Head Master may be secured for teaching the Natural Sciences. The Salary of Doctor Carlyle to be Fifteen hundred dollars per annum, to commence the first of July.

June 19th, 1871. Several Communications were laid before the Council.

The revised Programme and Regulations for Public and High Schools were further considered, but their adoption was deferred.

July 4th, 1871. The resignation of Doctor Sangster, the Head Master of the Normal School having been under consideration, it was,—

Ordered, That the resignation of Doctor Sangster be accepted, to take effect the 31st July.

That in accepting Doctor Sangster's resignation, the Council desires to record its deep sense of the faithfulness, ability and success with which he has discharged his duties, first as Second Master, and then as Head Master of the Normal School during several years, and the improvements which have taken place in both the Normal and Model Schools under his administration which he now voluntarily resigns. The Council hopes that Doctor Sangster may be as successful in the future, as he has been in the past, both as a Student and as a Teacher, and wishes him all possible happiness in whatever situation he may occupy.

The revised Regulations and Programme of Course of Study for Public Schools, as corrected, were adopted. (See Chapter VII of this Volume).

July 8th, 1871. Ordered, That the Reverend H. W. Davies, D.D. be appointed Head Master of the Normal School, with the title of Principal, the appointment to take effect on the 1st of August, and his Salary to be at the rate of $2,000 per annum.

Ordered, That Mr. Thomas Kirkland, M.A., Head Master of the Whitby High School, be appointed the Natural Science Master in the Normal School, with the Salary at the rate of $1,500 per annum, the appointment to take effect the 1st of August.

Ordered, That Mr. James L. Hughes be appointed the Master in the Boys' Model School, with a Salary at $850 per annum. Appointment to take effect on the 1st of July.

Ordered, That Mr. William Scott be appointed First Assistant in the Boys' Model School, with a Salary at $700 per annum. Appointment to take effect on the 1st of July.

Ordered, That Mr. Alexander McPhedran be appointed Second Assistant in the Boys' Model School, with a Salary at $550 per annum. The appointment to take effect on the 1st of August.

August 9th, 1871. Several Communications were laid before the Council.

Ordered, That the Reverend Frederick Burt of Minden, be granted a Certificate of eligibility as Inspector.

Ordered, That the Examination of Candidates for Public School Teachers' Certificates be changed by the omission of the requirement of the Third Book of Euclid, for Class II.

Ordered, That public notice be given that, in consequence of the alterations in the Model School Building, the re-opening of the Model School will be deferred till the first Monday (4th) of September.

Ordered, That, with reference to the previous Minute respecting Mr. Orr's Book on Book-keeping, the Book be authorized only on compliance with the additional condition of the price being reduced to not more than Fifty cents.

The Programme and Regulations for the High School were adopted. (See Chapter VIII of this Volume).

September 12th, 1871. Several Communications were laid before the Council.

In accordance with the Report of the Committee of Examiners; First Class Provincial Certificates were granted to several Candidates.

The following Report of the Committee on Text Books was read and adopted:—

The Committee on Text Books beg leave to recommend to the Council that 500 Copies be taken of Mr. Sefton's Elements of Vocal Music, and that it be authorized for use in the Normal and Model Schools. They recommend that the following Books also be prescribed:—

For Public Schools:—"Rudimentary Mechanics." (portions relative to the Mechanical Powers), by Charles Tomlinson. "Our Bodies," by Ellis A. Davidson.

For High Schools:—First Book on Anatomy, Physiology and Hygiene, by Calvin Cutter, M.D., (may also be used in Public Schools).

For High Schools and Public Schools:—The Animal Kingdom, by Ellis A. Davidson.

For High Schools and the Normal School:—Rudimentary Mechanics, by Charles Tomlinson, with Cassell's Hand Book of Natural and Experimental Philosophy, or Manual of Mechanics, by Reverend Samuel Haughton, M.A., F.R.S., with Introductory Course of Natural Philosophy, edited, from Ganot's Popular Physics, by William G. Peck, LL.D.

The Committee also recommend the use of the following Works:—The Drawing Book of the Dominion of Canada, in seven parts. Teachers' Guide by Miss J. H. Stickney, with Bartholomew Primary School Drawing Cards and Slates. Right Lines in Right Places, by Ellis A. Davidson. Linear Drawing by Ellis A. Davidson. William Horne's Drawing Instructor, for advanced Students.

Ordered, That Mr. Warwick's Edition of the First Book be approved, but that he be informed that the plates are too faintly brought out, in some instances, and, further, that the Publishers of Books, of which the copyright is under the control of the Council. are not permitted to advertise on those Books the names of any works not sanctioned by the Council.

Mr. Warwick was also to be desired to state how soon he would be prepared to issue the rest of the series.

October 10th, 1871. Several Communications were laid before the Council.

Ordered, That Miss Louisa H. Jones be appointed First Assistant in the Girls' Model School, in place of Miss McCausland, resigned, and that Miss Anna Adams be appointed Second Assistant, in place of Miss Jones promoted. The appointments to take effect on the 1st of October.

Ordered, That the Council having considered the application of Mr Nicholas Wilson, do not see any reasons for departing from the rules as applied to others, who have passed through the Normal School and who desire to qualify themselves as Inspectors.

Ordered, That the Note to the Regulations, respecting the mode of reckoning the number of Schools under the control of each Inspector, be amended so as to read as follows:—

NOTE. Each Public, or Separate, School House in use for a School. in a legally established, (or duly recognized), School Section, or Division, within the jurisdiction of the Inspector, shall be counted as one School, (whether such School be in actual operation, or temporarily closed, for not longer than six months). And each department of a School, with a Register of its own, and taught in a separate Room, or flat. of a Building, so as to involve the additional oversight and examination of an ordinary School, on the part of an Inspector at his official visits, shall also be counted as one School; but a School with one, or more, departments, when closed shall only be regarded as one School, for the time limited above,—beyond which time no School which is closed shall be counted.

November 6th, 1871. Two Communications were laid before the Council.

Ordered, That the Letter of the Inspector of South Grey be referred to the Committee on Text Books.

Ordered, That a Communication be sent to Mr. John Murphy, asking if he has any reply to make to the charges, on which he was suspended, and that the further consideration of the matter be deferred, the suspension being in the meantime continued.

The application from Mr. Charles Rolleston Ashbury, for a pension as a superannuated, or worn out, Public School Teacher, was approved for eighteen years' service in this Province.

The subject of the superannuation of Public School Teachers having been submitted by the Chief Superintendent of Education for the consideration of the Council, it was,—

Ordered, That it be referred to a Committee consisting of the Very Reverend Dean Grasett, the Reverend Doctor Jennings, and the Honourable William MacMaster, with the request that they will report on the same at the next Meeting.

Ordered, That the Winter Examination of Candidates for Certificates of Qualification as Teachers be commenced, for Second and Third Class Certificates, on Monday the 18th of December, and for First Class Certificates on Tuesday, the 26th of December.

Ordered, That the Regulations of the Superannuated, or Worn Out, Teachers' Fund be amended, and be as follows:—

1. Teachers who became superannuated, or worn out, on, or before the first day of January, 1854, and who produce the proofs required by Law of character and services as such, may share in this Fund according to the number of years they have respectively taught a Public School in Ontario, by depositing with the Chief Superintendent of Education the preliminary Subscriptions to the Fund required by Law.

2. Every Teacher engaged in teaching since 1854, in order to be entitled, when he shall have become Superannuated, or worn out, to share in this Fund, must contribute to it a sum of Five dollars for each year from the time when he began to teach up to the time of his first Annual Subscription, and Four dollars, (as required by the Statute), for each subsequent year during which he was engaged in teaching. No Subscriptions can be received either for arrears, or otherwise, from those who have ceased to teach.

3. No Teacher shall be eligible to receive a Pension from this Fund, who shall not have become disabled for further survice while teaching a Public School, or who shall not have been worn out in the work of a Public School Teacher.

4. All applications must be made according to the prescribed form, and be accompanied with the requisite Certificates and proofs of service, in order to entitle the applicant to share in this Fund.

5. In case the Fund shall, at any time, not be sufficient to pay the several claimants the highest sum permitted by Law, the Fund shall be equitably divided among the several Claimants according to their respective periods of service.

6. Communications and subscriptions in connection with this Fund must be sent to the Chief Superintendent of Education.

7. No Certificate in favour of an Applicant shall be signed by any Teacher already admitted as a Pensioner on the Fund.

NOTE. With respect to the arrears of Subscription, it is to be observed that they can be paid at any time while the Teacher is still engaged in that capacity, not after he has ceased to teach. No payment is required for any year during which the Teacher was not employed, or for any year prior to 1854, even if the Teacher was teaching before that time.

It is further to be remembered that payment of the arrears is not obligatory, but is to the interest of the Teacher, as the years, (from 1854), for which there has been no Subscription, will not be reckoned in making up the time of service for the Pension.

In no case are Subscriptions required except for the years of teaching for which a Pension will be claimed.

The School Law of 1871 provides, that,—

On the decease of any Teacher, his Wife, or other legal Representative, shall be entitled to receive back the full amount paid in by such Teacher, with interest at the rate of seven per centum per annum.

Any Teacher retiring from the profession shall be entitled to receive back from the Chief Superintendent of Education one-half of any sums paid in by him to the Fund.

NOTE. In regard to this Meeting of the Council, of the 6th of November, I wrote the following Note to Doctor Ryerson still at his Island Home:

A Council Meeting was held to-day. The Reverend Doctor McCaul, the Reverend G. P. Young and Dean Grasett were present. The Reverend Doctor Jennings called to say that he could not come, but he would concur in whatever was done. Doctor McCaul was not in favour of signing a personal recommendation of your Book on Christian Morals. He thought the recommendation of the Council was quite sufficient, and that the precedent might not be a good one. The Reverend Mr. Young spoke very heartily of the Book, and so did Dean Grasett, but wished to let the Committee report on it at a fuller Meeting.

Thinking it was desirable to reprint the Regulations on the Superannuated Teachers' Fund. I got the Council to consent to a revision of the Regulations, relating to that Fund, the alterations were chiefly verbal, and designed to adapt them to the new state of things, and to our present practice. I should not have brought them before the Council until your return; but I thought it well to reprint the Regulations, with additions, and send them to the Inspectors, so as to allay the agitation, as the less of a disturbing element among Teachers which we have the better, during the next Session of the House. I think it would be well, (as it is your intention,) that the Normal School and other examinations should be held on the same days, and, from the same Examination Papers,—as for the County Examination. There is one matter about the Normal School Examinations which it would be well to provide for. There is a large number of Students who have never obtained a Second Class Certificate, and who, (so the Reverend Doctor Davies tells me,) will not be able to get one. These Students should be encouraged to go up at the various County Boards, and get Third Class Certificates, so as to increase the number of available Teachers. The more there are, the better, and just now the dearth of Teachers is a matter of complaint.

TORONTO, November 6th, 1871.   J. GEORGE HODGINS.

November 13th, 1871. Several Communications were laid before the Council.

The Chairman reported that the special Committee had considered the Book on Christian Morals, by the Reverend Doctor Ryerson, and recommend it for the sanction of the Council, subject to the conditions imposed by the Statute with respect to Religious Instruction.

Ordered, That the Council having examined the First Lessons in Christian Morals ior Canadian Families and Schools by the Reverend Egerton Ryerson, D.D., LL.D., recommend it for use, as designed, "in Canadian Families and Schools," with the proviso, in the case of Schools, (as contained in the Consolidated School Act, Section 129), that "No person shall require any Pupil in any School to read, or study, in, or from, any Religious Book, or to join in any exercise of devotion, or Religion, objected to by his, or her, Parents, or Guardians, but, within this limitation, Pupils shall be allowed to receive such Religious Instruction as their Parents and Guardians desire, according to any General Regulations provided for the government of Common Schools.

Ordered, That the Chief Superintendent be authorized to make such provision for the examination of those Candidates for Certificates, who speak the German Language, as he may deem expedient.

December 14th, 1871. Several Communications were laid before the Council.

Ordered, That the Reverend Mr. Dewar's application be referred to the Grammar School Inspectors, Messieurs Mackenzie and McLellan.

Ordered, That the principles recommended by the Head Master for adoption in framing the new Curriculum for the Public Schools be approved. and that the Prospectus be printed.

On the recommendation of the Chief Superintendent, the use of the Normal School Rooms was granted to the Board of Examiners for the County of York, for the Examinations in December, 1871.

The Chief Superintendent reported that, with respect to the correspondence from Mr. John Murphy, he had arranged that he be transferred to the Model School, and not continued as a Resident in the Building.

Mr. Vere Foster's Communication and Writing Books were referred to the Committee on Text Books.

CHAPTER XI.

REMARKS OF THE CHIEF SUPERINTENDENT ON THE INTRODUCTORY OPERATIONS OF THE NEW SCHOOL ACT—RECENT EXAMINATIONS OF TEACHERS—EXPLANATIONS—OBJECTIONS ANSWERED.

The new School Act is now brought into general operation. The Programmes for the Classification and Examination of Public School Teachers have been devised, published, and acted upon; the Regulations for the improved Organization and Discipline of both the Public and High Schools, in relation to all their Officers and every part of their operations, have been compiled, adopted and published; the Programmes of Studies for both classes of Schools and for the classifications of Pupils, have been arranged, considered and prescribed. A special Examination for Candidates for County Inspectorships of Public Schools, with all the needful Examination Papers, has been granted, provided for and completed; the Papers for Examination of Students in the Normal School, and granting First and Second Class Certificates to those entitled to them. have been prepared and Examinations conducted under the direction of the same Committee, as have the Papers for the Examination of Teachers throughout the Province been prepared by the same Committee; and all the instructions necessary for the information and guidance of County Councils, County Inspectors, County Boards of Examiners, Boards of Trustees of both High and Public Schools, and for Teachers, have been drawn up and transmitted to the Bodies, or parties to whom they appertain. The first Examinations of Teachers throughout the Province have taken place under the new system, and the results have been reported. Even a number of High and Public School Teachers and County Inspectors have met in their Conventions, and, during the labours of a four days' Session, have delivered their opinions on the new state of things.

2. At this epoch, and under these circumstances, it becomes my duty to make some remarks on what has transpired and been said in connection with those preliminary proceedings for giving effect to the provisions of the new School Act; and, in doing so, I address these special Remarks, in this case, to those Conductors of the Public Press who may please to insert the observations I have to offer.

3. It is known under what a storm of misconception, misrepresentation and hostility the new Act was passed, and became Law on the 15th of last February. The provisions of the Act are as practical as they are clear and explicit, and are comprehensive as they are brief, touching upon every part of our School System, and contemplating its complete re-organization. All the preliminaries of that re-organization have been gone through with; and the principal Bodies empowered to act under the new Law have performed their first duties. In changes so great, and in a work so complex and comprehensive, it might naturally be expected that serious obstacles and much opposition would be encountered; but not one of the more than forty County Councils, in exercising their first functions under the new Law, has expressed the slightest dissatisfaction with any of its provisions; not one of the County Boards of Examiners has expressed other than strong approval of the new System of Examinations as a vast improvement upon the old System; nor have I heard from a single Board of School Trustees, whether of High Schools, or Public Schools, in Town, or Country, other than a feeling of satisfaction with the additional facilities with which the new Law provides them for the discharge of their duties; and I believe all parties agree that it contains the mainspring of an immense elevation in the position and usefulness of the Teacher's Profession. Even in a recent Annual Association of Teachers, the most restless and faultfinding of the number present could not otherwise than express satisfaction with the general provisions of the new Act, and protested against one Section only, the

most benevolent Section of the whole Act,—the Section which requires each licensed male Teacher to pay for the License, (or monopoly of teaching which such license gives to him against any unlicensed Teacher), at the rate of two dollars each half year towards the support of Superannuated, or worn-out, Members of his own Profession.

4. It is to me, therefore, a source of inexpressible satisfaction to know that while "clouds and darkness" of the unprecedented opposition surround me, while promoting this my last act of School Legislation, an almost cloudless sky of general approval attends its introduction throughout the land; and I am persuaded that approval will strengthen into high satisfaction with the Law, and a strong determination to maintain it, as soon as its advantages shall have been more fully experienced.

Various Objections, Chiefly to the High Standards of the Act of 1871, Answered.

5. But it is proper for me to notice objections which have been made to certain steps which have been taken to give effect to the new School Act. These objections relate almost entirely to the high standard which is alleged to have been fixed for giving Certificates to Teachers, and the expressed belief that many Schools will have to be closed for want of legally qualified Teachers. When I state, as I shall presently explain, that I have provided that not a single School throughout the land shall be closed for want of a legally qualified Teacher, and yet without lowering the standard of regular Certificates, it will be seen at once how imaginary are the forebodings of certain Newspapers and their sympathizing Correspondents.

6. Let us now look at the facts of the whole case. It is admitted on all hands, and it was so admitted in the Legislature when the new School Act was a Bill under consideration, that the standard of Public School Teachers' qualifications was too low; that the Examinations of Teachers by the "County Boards of Public Instruction" were inefficient and unsatisfactory; some called them "shams" and "farces," with very few exceptions; all admitted that whatever good these County Boards, as then constituted, had done in the infancy of our School System, they had, in the majority of instances, long outlived their usefulness, either in elevating the qualifications of Teachers, or in promoting the efficiency or permanence of the Teacher's Profession, and that some change was necessary.

7. It was, furthermore, alleged, that undue partiality had been shown in granting Provincial Certificates to Students of the Normal School, who were no better qualified than many First Class County Board Teachers, and that these were quite as worthy of a Provincial Certificate as First Class Normal School Teachers. Although I knew the imputation and statement to be utterly unfounded, I concurred in the principle involved in it: namely, that all those Teachers throughout the land who are equally well qualified with Normal School Teachers who have received First and Second Class Provincial Certificates, are entitled to Certificates of the same Class, and should have the earliest, and all possible, facilities to obtain them. Accordingly I recommended to the Council of Public Instruction the appointment of a Committee of Examiners, composed of most able and experienced Teachers, and wholly unconnected with the Normal School. I first proposed that one and the same set of Examination Papers for First and Second Class Certificates for Normal School Teachers and other Teachers throughout the Province, with the same values of Answers to Questions; but it was objected, that, as the sessional Examination of Normal School Teachers would take place several weeks earlier than the Examination of Teachers in the various Counties, the Papers would become known. My answer was, that I thought this could be prevented by proper precautions, but that if, in some instances, any of the Questions should become known to the Candidates, it would be to the comparative disadvantage of the Normal School Candidates, and to the corresponding advantage of non-Normal School Candidates for Certificates. But my recommendation was overruled, when I suggested to the Examiners that they would make the Papers for the Examination of

9—XXIII

Teachers in the Counties somewhat easier than those which had been used in the Examination of Normal School Teachers. This, I have been assured, has been done, and that no Questions have been given the Answers to which are not contained in the Text Books prescribed for teaching in the Public Schools; and it may be shown by comparing the Normal School Examination Papers, published in my last Annual School Report, with the Examination Papers recently used in the County Board Examinations, and which are being prepared in sets for distribution, and which will be published in the *Journal of Education* and in my forthcoming Annual School Report, for as general information as possible.

8. Now, what is the result? The result is, that but fourteen Candidates have presented themselves in all the Counties of the Province for Examination for First Class Certificates, and a surprisingly small number of Candidates for Second Class Certificates, more than half of whom have failed in the Examinations. A majority of more than three-fourths of the Candidates have presented themselves for Third Class Certificates. Of these, a large number had held First Class County Board Certificates, but many of them are reported to have failed in their Examinations for Third Class Certificates. These facts not only authorize the statement, but furnish the most complete demonstration of the injustice of the attacks upon the Normal School System, and of the utter defectiveness of the former County Board Examinations of Teachers.

9. It now happens that the very parties who have heretofore been most vociferous as to the equal qualifications of First Class County Board Teachers with First Class Normal School Teachers, now complain that the standard of Examinations for Certificates has been suddenly raised too high, in consequence of which many worthy Teachers will be disqualified, and many Schools must be closed for want of legally qualified Teachers. My answer is, that the standard for Provincial Certificates has not been raised at all, but is the same, (with some mitigation), as that which has been required in giving Provincial Certificates to Normal School Teachers; and the standard of Examinations for Third Class County Certificates is the same as that required merely for admission to the Normal School. The simple fact is, that these Examinations are now made realities, and not what the Brockville *Recorder* and others have called the old County Board Examinations,—"shams" and "farces." I am sure that no intelligent man, after examining the Programmes for the Examinations for even the First and Second Class Provincial Certificates, will say that they are in any respect too high for Life Certificates of Teachers of Schools, for the support of which all classes of the community are taxed, and on which they are chiefly depending for the education of their children; and I am persuaded that in less than three years, a sufficient number of Teachers will become regularly qualified, under these Programmes, to supply all the Public Schools of the Country, without requiring temporary Certificates at all, except in a few and rare instances.

10. But it is said, "You are, in the meantime, shutting up many Schools for want of Teachers." I answer, not so; for, although a County Inspector has not authority to give temporary Certificates to rejected Candidates, nor have I authority to authorize him to do so, yet he can do so on the recommendation, or with the consent of a majority of his fellow-Examiners of the County Board, as, in such cases, although the Candidates have failed in their recent Examinations, they may not be considered as having been absolutely rejected, when the Examiners recommend temporary Certificates to be granted to them. But, in addition, the County Inspector can give temporary Certificates to other Applicants whom he may find qualified to teach particular Schools that might not otherwise be supplied. In this way, not a single School need be closed for want of a legally qualified Teacher; and the regular standard of qualifications can be maintained, until Teachers become qualified according to it in sufficient numbers to supply all the Schools. It is also to be remarked, that the Certificates heretofore given by County Boards are perpetuated according to the terms of them, and are not affected by any failures of the holders of them at the recent Examinations,—not even those

9a—XXIII.

Certificates given during the pleasure of the Board, as no Board has been authorized to cancel any such Certificates. But it is manifest that a Third Class Certificate under the new system signifies more, and is of more value that a First Class old County Board Certificate.

11. It is, however, objected again, "It is hard for old Teachers to be set aside, because they cannot qualify under the new system." I answer, as Government exists not for Office-holders, but for the people, so the Schools exist not for the Teachers, but for the youth and future generations of the land; and if Teachers have been too slothful not to keep pace with the progressive wants and demands of the Country, they must, as should all incompetent and indolent public Officers, and all lazy and unenterprising citizens, give place to the more industrious, intelligent, progressive and enterprising. The sound education of a generation of children is not to be sacrificed for the sake of an incompetent although antiquated Teacher.

12. But, under the new Act additional provision is made which will more than double the fund for the assistance of disabled, or worn-out, Teachers of Public Schools. Among the Clergy of different Religious Persuasions, funds are established by required subscriptions for their relief or partial support in old age. In the Wesleyan Church, for example, every one of the (now six hundred) Ministers is required to pay five dollars per annum towards the support of superannuated Ministers and their Widows,—a Regulation which has been in force more than a quarter of a century. In the Civil Service in England, from two to five per cent. is deducted from the Annual Salary of each Officer, or Clerk in the employment of the Government towards the support of such Officers and Clerks in old age. The same principle is embodied in the School Act, by requiring each licensed male public Teacher to pay Four dollars per annum into a Fund for the support of Superannuated Teachers. In case a Teacher dies, the whole amount of his Subscription, with interest at the rate of seven per cent., is paid back to his Widow, or legal Representative. If a Teacher becomes superannuated, he receives · a Pension in proportion to the amount of the Fund, according to the number of years he has taught; if he leaves the Profession, he is entitled to receive back one-half of the sum which he has paid in towards the support of the worn-out Members of it, which is even more than a Wesleyan Minister could obtain who should abandon his work. The objectors to such an arrangement are those Teachers who do not intend to make teaching the profession of their life, but who make teaching, for the time being, a stepping-stone to some other pursuit or profession. They wish to avail themselves of its license to make what money they can out of it, without paying anything in return, even in behalf of those who spend their vigour of life in the work. The subscriptions to this Fund are paid through the County Inspectors and Chief Superintendent, and are deposited forthwith in the Bank to the credit of the Treasurer of the Province, as are all the Fees of the Model Schools, and the Moneys received at the Apparatus and Library and Prize Book Depositories, and paid out by the Provincial Treasurer.

I believe that the new School Act, in the various applications and operations of its provisions, will prove the greatest legislative boon for the educational advancement of the Country which has been conferred upon it since 1850.

TORONTO, August, 1871.   EGERTON RYERSON.

P.S.—Since penning the foregoing remarks, I learn that no less than 195 Candidates, (mostly Teachers heretofore), have applied for admission to the Normal School, of whom 180 have been admitted. This is a much larger number than ever before applied for admission at the commencement of any Session; and never before did the Candidates come, as a whole, so well qualified for admission. An additional Master has been employed to give the instruction necessary for training Teachers "to provide for teaching in the Public Schools the elements of Natural History, of Agricultural Chemistry, of Mechanics, and of Agriculture," as required by the 13th Section of the new Act.

I have also just received the Report of the Committee appointed to prepare the Examination Papers, and to examine and report upon the Answers to the questions for First Class Certificates. Of fourteen Candidates, nine have been successful.

The following are the names of the successful Candidates, arranged alphabetically:—

First Class A.

John Cameron, (eminently good) .... County of Grey.
Andrew Hay, (eminently good) .... County of Perth.
A. W. Ross, (see Letter below) .... County of Middlesex.
W. H. Ross .... County of Middlesex.

First Class C.

P. Mactavish .... County of Waterloo.
A. M. Rae .... County of York.
J. C. Thompson .... County of Middlesex.
A. Tod .... County of Middlesex.
T. B. Woodhull .... County of Middlesex.

The Report of the Committee of Examiners is as follows:—

We beg to report that, as the result of the recent examinations for First Class Certificates, we find that four gentlemen are entitled to receive First Class Certificates of the highest grade, and five to receive First Class Certificates of the Third grade.

We would call special attention to the very great excellence of the papers given by Mr. John Cameron and Mr. Andrew Hay.

The Examiners have placed Mr. A. W. Ross in the First Class in consideration of the surpassing excellence of his paper in English Literature and Composition, and the excellence of his papers in Natural Philosophy, History and Etymology.

TORONTO, August, 1871.   ·   GEORGE PAXTON YOUNG,
J. G. D. MACKENZIE,   } Examiners.
J. A. McLELLAN,

THE RECENT EXAMINATION PAPERS FOR PUBLIC SCHOOL TEACHERS.

LETTER FROM THE REVEREND GEORGE PAXTON YOUNG ON THESE PAPERS.

I notice a statement which was published in one of the City Papers, to the effect that all the difficult theoretical Questions in Algebra, in the Examination for Second Class Certificates, were taken from Sangster, and none from Todhunter, although Todhunter's Algebra for beginners, equally with Sangster's Algebra, is authorized for use in the Public Schools. A few words on the subject may be of service.

The complaint is that all the difficult theoretical questions in the Second Class papers in Algebra were taken from Sangster, and none from Todhunter. People would naturally suppose, from such a statement, that the Paper contained a large number of theoretical Questions. The fact is, that there were only four theoretical Questions in it altogether. Of these, one, the last in the Paper, was not taken into account in fixing the total number of marks on which the average prescribed by the Council of Public Instruction, in order that a Candidate may receive a Certificate of a certain grade, was calculated. This Question, therefore, could be an injury to no Candidate, although it might be a benefit to some. Of the remaining three theoretical Questions, one was taken neither from Sangster, nor from Todhunter; and the other two are found in Todhunter, as well as in Sangster. And, to crown all, although Todhunter is authorized as a Text Book to be used in Schools, Sangster's Algebra is the only Text

Book specified by the Council of Public Instruction in their Programme for the Examination of Teachers. In the revised Programme for the Examination and Classification of Teachers, prescribed on the 28th of March, 1871, under the heading, "Minimum Qualifications for Second Class Provincial Certificates," will be found the following:—
"Algebra: To be acquainted with the subject as far as the end of Section 153 of the authorized Text Book, (Sangster)."

I have not named the Gentleman on whose Letter I have been commenting, because I wish, as far as possible, to avoid personal controversy. My object is simply to prevent statements, which are unfounded, from being received throughout the Country.

TORONTO, 7th September, 1871.   GEORGE PAXTON YOUNG.

EXAMINATION FOR FIRST CLASS PROVINCIAL CERTIFICATES OF QUALIFICATION AS PUBLIC SCHOOL TEACHERS, COMMENCING 1ST AUGUST, 1871.

The Paper on Algebra.

Note 1.—The Question 2 (c) is the first in the Paper that presents any difficulty. It was correctly solved by Mr. W. H. Ross, although his solution was wanting in simplicity and elegance.

Note 2.—Question 4, although by no means difficult, was solved by very few of the Candidates. A correct solution was given by Mr. T. B. Woodhull.

Note 3.—The question 5 (c) was solved by only one gentleman, Mr. James C. Thompson.

Note 4.—A greater number of solutions than I expected were given of the Questions 8 (a) and 8 (b).

The Paper on Natural Philosophy.

Note 5.—The Question 3 (b) presented difficulty to some of the Candidates, because there is no rule given in the Text Book by which it can be directly solved. I intentionally set the question, in the August Examination, in the form in which it appears in order that Candidates might be taught to emancipate themselves from the bondage of Rules committed to memory, and might be thrown back on principles. Solutions were given by Mr. John Cameron and Mr. Andrew Hay respectively.

Note 6.—I have found that a large number of Candidates for First Class Certificates have most indefinite conceptions as to how the velocity of a body, which is moving with a variable velocity, is, at any instant, to be estimated. The answer to Question 6 (a) was given by Mr. James C. Thompson, in which the only defect is, that the pronoun "it," in the expression "if it were constant," is, perhaps, somewhat vague. Mr. Thompson means the velocity acquired.

Note 7.—Question 8 was attempted by a number of Candidates, but not successfully solved by any.

SPIRIT OF SOME TEACHERS IN REGARD TO THE RECENT EXAMINATIONS.

As an indication of the admirable spirit in which some of the Teachers of the Province look upon the recent effort to elevate the character of their Profession by the recent Examinations, even although the result was adverse to themselves, we give an extract from a Letter, among many, received by the Education Department on the subject   The Writer says:—
I may take this opportunity of expressing my thanks to Doctor Ryerson and his Colleagues. for the many blessings conferred upon us (Teachers) as a class, by the new School Act; and although many of my Fellow-Teachers strongly condemn the stringent measures adopted by the new Boards of Examiners, I consider it the only effectual way of raising the standard of Education, and also the position of the Teachers, throughout the Country

Another Teacher in a Letter says:—

As my friends in my native County have requested me to accept the office of Public School Inspector for that County, and trusting that I might prove to be more useful in that capacity there, than 'as Teacher here, it would have afforded me much pleasure to have acceded to their wishes, had I possessed the necessary legal qualifications.

As a practical Teacher, who has not lost a single day for twenty years, although excluded from this office myself, I beg most heartily to congratulate you upon the success of your unremitting exertions in elevating the position of the Teacher, as well as the wisdom displayed in limiting this office as a reward for those only who are talented and worthy.

EXAMINATION PAPERS FOR SECOND PROVINCIAL AND THIRD CLASS CERTIFICATES OF QUALIFICATION AS PUBLIC SCHOOL TEACHERS.

NOTE. I only select the Examination Papers which relate to the work and duties of Public School Teachers, as such:—

Education.—Second Class.

1. Discuss briefly the question, What is Education?

2. What basis of classification would you adopt in an ordinary School? What elements besides mere proficiency would you consider?

3 State briefly the utility of Botany as a subject of study in Public Schools.

4. What means would you adopt to secure the interests of your Pupils in the work of the School?

5. Give the principal arguments in favour of Prizes in Schools, and state what means you would adopt to reduce to a minimum the disadvantages of the Prize System.

6. Name some of the uses and abuses of the Monitorial System. What plan would you adopt in employing Monitors in a Public School?

7. Describe how you would teach (1) Dictation; (2) English Grammar to a class of beginners; (3) Algebra.

8. State the Law (a) as to the proceedings to be taken on the formation of a new School Section; (b) the principal duties of Trustees in Rural Sections.

Education.—Third Class

1. What is meant by School Organization?

2. You take charge of a Rural School of 50 Pupils, shew how you would proceed to classify.

3. Construct a Time Table for such a School.

4. Describe how you would proceed with a Class beginning the study of Arithmetic.

5. What measures would you take to create an interest in the School throughout the Section.

6. State the leading points of the Law in regard to Public School Teachers and their duties.

7. Describe how you would teach (1) Dictation; (2) English Grammar to a class of beginners.

Then follow papers on Arithmetic, Mensuration, Book-keeping, Algebra, Euclid, Natural Philosophy, Chemistry, Botany, Physiology and the Algebraic Proof of the Binomial Theorem.

CHAPTER XII.

CIRCULAR FROM THE CHIEF SUPERINTENDENT TO THE IN-SPECTORS OF PUBLIC SCHOOLS IN ONTARIO, 1871.

The School Act of 1871 has laid the foundation of a new era in the Public School Education of our Country. This Act has remedied the most serious defects which experience has found in preceding School Acts; it has made the teaching of Children and youth a Profession, and confided to the highest class of Public School Teachers the oversight of the Schools. It has made the Schools entirely Free in all the Townships of the Land; and it requires suitable School accommodation to be provided for all Children of School age, (that is, from five to twenty-one years), and secures ·to every Child the right of, at least, four months' School instruction per annum, from seven to twelve years of age, inclusive. It enables County Councils to discharge their important duties much more efficiently and conveniently than heretofore, and gives a value and permanence to Teachers' Certificates of Qualifications which they never before possessed. It provides for a uniform and adequate standard of Teachers' qualifications throughout the Land, and requires the teaching of those subjects which are a requisite preparation for the Agricultural, Mechanical and Manufacturing pursuits of the Country. It provides for the accomplishment of these objects by an agency which we have never yet had except in solitary instances, but without which, no system of Education can be made efficient; namely competent Inspectors of Schools, duly compensated.

2. Efforts have hitherto been directed to organize the machinery of the School System, and to provide the apparatus necessary to render it effective; and most nobly have the people of the Country co-operated and done their part in bringing the whole School System into efficient operation. But, as long as the inspection of the Schools was in the hands of men who were not paid, or expected to devote their studies and time to the duties of their office, and who, for the most part, were not practical Teachers, and who formed their standard of good Schools and good teaching from what existed twenty, or thirty, years ago, and not from what the best Schools have been made, and the improved methods of School Organization, Teaching and Discipline, which have been introduced during the present age, we could not expect any considerable improvement to the internal state and character of the Schools, except from the improved character of the Teachers, and in instances where regularly trained Teachers, or Teachers who have kept pace with the progress of the times, have been employed; and even they have been able to do little in comparison of what they might have done, had their hands been strengthened and their hearts encouraged by the example, counsel and influence of thoroughly competent Inspectors.

3. It is but just and right, not to say patriotic, that the people should receive full value, in the practical character and efficiency of the Public Schools, in return for their sacrifices in establishing and maintaining the Schools. I cannot, therefore, impress upon you too strongly the importance of your office, and the reasonable expectations of the Country as to its usefulness. The Law has prescribed your general duties; but the Law has imposed upon me the duty of giving Instructions as to the manner in which you should discharge your duties, and has enjoined upon each Inspector the observance of those Instructions.

4. Your first duty will naturally be to make yourself familiar, not only·with the provisions of the School Law, but with the Programme of Studies and the Regulations, which the Council of Public Instruction have, after long and careful consideration, adopted to give effect to the new School Act.

5. In the Programme of Studies, the subjects essential to a good Public School Education are prescribed and classified, as also the number of hours per week of teaching each subject; but the mode, or modes, of teaching and illustrating the several

subjects specified in order, is left to the independent exercise of the genius and talents of each Teacher. In preparing this Programme, the Reports of the latest Royal Commissioners in England on Popular Education, and the opinions of the most experienced Educationists, have been consulted. It will be seen from the number and order of the subjects, and the time prescribed per week for teaching each of them, that the first years of Common School Studies are almost entirely devoted to teaching the three primary and fundamental subjects of a good education,—Reading, Writing and Arithmetic, including only such other subjects, and to such a degree, as to relieve the Pupils from the tedium of the more severe and least attractive Studies, and develop their faculties of observation and taste for knowledge as suggested by the largest experience of the most advanced Educators. The subjects of the Programme are limited, in both number and range, to what is considered essential, and to what experience has proved can be thoroughly mastered by Pupils of ordinary capacity and diligence within thirteen years of age. The thorough teaching of a few subjects, within practical limits, will do more for intellectual development, and for the purposes of practical life, than the skimming over a wide range of topics. The subjects of Natural Science required by the Thirteenth Section of the new School Act to be taught in Schools, and provided for in the Programme, are such, and are prescribed to such an extent only, as is absolutely necessary for the advancement of the Country,—in Agriculture, in the Mechanical Arts, and Manufactures, apart from Science and Literature. And when the cheap and excellent Text Books prescribed are examined, in connection with the subjects specified, it will be found that nothing has been introduced which is impracticable, or for mere show, but everything for practical use, and that which admits of easy accomplishment.

6. The Regulations specify not merely the duties of Trustees, Parents, Teachers, and Pupils in respect to the Schools, but also the mode of visiting and inspecting them, which, I doubt not, will receive your careful and practical attention.

7. Your immediate duty, on entering into office, will be to receive the copies of Official Correspondence and all other official Papers from your Predecessor, or Predecessors, in office, as the Eleventh Clause of the Ninety-first Section of the Consolidated School Act requires each Local Superintendent, "on retiring from office to deliver over copies of his Official Correspondence, and all such Papers in his custody, to the order of the County Council." As the Apportionments can not be made before the 1st July, it will be your duty to make them, and to make them according to average attendance, authenticated by the Returns which may be placed in your hands, and according to the directions to Local Superintendents which are printed on the back of those Returns. There may be delay in some instances, arising from change of Inspectors of the Schools; but the inconvenience of such delay cannot occur again, and cannot extend over two, or three, weeks.

8. Your second, but most important, duty will be the Examination of Teachers for Certificates of Qualification. Hitherto, each County Board has consisted of a considerable number of Members, most of whom, and, in some instances, all of whom, have had no experience as Teachers; each Board has appointed the time, as well as the place, of its own Meeting, has prepared its own Examination Papers for three classes of Teachers, and has then given Certificates according to its discretion, both as to Class and duration. Under the new Act, each Board of Examiners consists of not more than five Members, who have had experience in Teaching, and is under the direction of the County Inspector, who must be a First Class Teacher of the highest grade; and the Meeting of such Board is appointed to be held the same Day in every County and City in the Province. The Examination Papers for three Classes of Teachers are all prepared, and the value of each Question, and the time allowed for Examinations in each subject, determined by a Committee of practical Teachers, under the sanction of the Council of Public Instruction,—that Committee consisting, at present, of Professor Young, (late Grammar School Inspector), and the two Inspectors of High Schools. The Examination Papers for each County will be sent under the Seal of the Department, to the County Inspector, which Seal is not to be broken except in the presence of the

Candidates for Examination on the day, and at the hour, appointed. The merit of the Answers to the Questions for Second and Third Class Certificates will be decided upon by each County Board of Examiners, but the Answers to the Questions for First Class Certificates will be transmitted to the Education Department at Toronto, to be decided upon by the Council of Public Instruction, on the Report of its Committee of Examiners. Special instructions will accompany the Examination Papers; but I may here remark that what have heretofore been termed "Third Class County Board Certificates," are not permitted, by the provisions of the new Act, and what are called, and provided for under the new Act as Third Class Certificates, are quite equal, if not above what have heretofore been called Second Class County Board Certificates. They are available for three years and throughout the County in which they are granted. No new Candidate for teaching can receive a higher than a Third Class Certificate at his first Examination, or before the expiration of three years from that time, unless on the special recommendation of the Inspector for his attainments, ability, and skill in teaching. No Teacher is eligible to become a Candidate for a Second Class Certificate, who does not produce testimonials of having taught successfully for three years; but he may be eligible at a shorter period, after having received his Third Class Certificate, on the special recommendation of the County Inspector.

9. Second Class Certificates, under the new Act, it should be observed, are of much more value, and should be of a higher character, than First Class Board Certificates under former Acts, as the latter was limited to a County, and could be cancelled at the pleasure of the Board that granted it; but the former is a Life License, (during good behaviour), and is available to every part of the Province. Each County Inspector, and the other Members of each County Board of Examiners must, therefore, be impressed with the duty of not granting a Second Class Certificate to any Candidate without satisfactory proof that he, or she, is a successful Teacher of three years' standing, (except in the case above specified), and a clear conviction, in their own minds, that such Candidate is qualified to teach all the subjects of the Public School Programme. This is required, not only by the patriotic spirit of the Law, and conformity to the objects and principles of the School System, but as an act of common justice to every Ratepayer in the Province. The Schools are made Free by Law; and every man in the Country is taxed according to his property to support the Public Schools; and every Taxpayer has a corresponding right to have his Children educated in the Public Schools in all the subjects of the Public School Programme of Studies; and he is deprived of this right if a Teacher is employed who cannot teach his Children these subjects as required. Whether, therefore, you grant many, or few, Second Class Provincial Certificates I trust you and your Co-examiners will give no such Certificate as a personal favour, but simply upon the ground of ability to render the public educational service to the Country which the Law contemplates, and which every Ratepayer has a right to demand.

10. Should the question arise as to a possible scarcity of Public School Teachers under the new Law, I answer, as experience has shown in this, and other analagous cases, that, however high your standard of qualifications may be, a sufficient number of Candidates will work up to it,—when the value and dignity of the employment are proportionably raised. But two other answers may be given to the question. First,— Each County Inspector can grant a temporary Certificate, (as each Local Superintendent has heretofore done), in any case of necessity, but he should not grant such Certificate except in case of necessity, and upon examination, nor unless he is satisfied that the Applicant can teach all the subjects required in the School Section for which, (and for which alone), such Certificate is granted. Secondly,—That existing Certificates of Qualification held by Teachers are valid according to their terms, and will, therefore, still be available to their Holders should they fail to obtain Certificates of Qualification under the new Law. And should a Candidate for a Second Class Provincial Certificate fail to obtain one at the first examination, he will be eligible, (as he has successfully

taught a Public School three years), to "try again" at the next ensuing half-yearly Examination.

11. The Examination of Candidates for Second and Third Class Certificates is also to be attended by Candidates for First Class Certificates, and will require about five days,—six hours each day, from nine until twelve o'clock and from two until five. As soon as the Answers of Candidates to the Examination Papers on the first subject shall have been collected, the Inspector can appoint a Sub-committee of his Colleagues to examine them, while the Candidate under another Sub-committee of Examiners, are preparing their Answers to the Papers on the other subjects, and so on throughout the days of Examination; so that, (as in the recent Examination of Candidates in Toronto, for Certificates of Qualification for County Inspectorships by a Committee of the Council of Public Instruction), the County Board of Examiners may finish their work of examining the Answers of Candidates, and awarding Certificates, within a short time after the Candidates shall have finished their Answers. It is, perhaps, hardly necessary to remark that no Candidate should be allowed more than the prescribed time before returning the Examination Papers with such Answers as he may have been able to prepare. And should a Candidate for a Second Class Certificate fail to obtain one, he may be awarded a Third Class Certificate, if deserving of it, or fall back upon his old County Board unexpired Certificate, if a possessor of one.

12. In regard to the additional Examination of Candidates for First Class Certificates, (which will commence on the 1st of August), it will not be necessary for the other Members of the County Board to remain for that, as you only have to preside, and unseal and distribute the Examination Papers, and collect them, with the Answers of Candidates, at the appointed times, and then transmit the whole of them to the Education Department at Toronto. But the Regulations, as to the eligibility of Candidates, you must carefully observe. You will remember that no Teacher is eligible to be a Candidate for a First Class Provincial Certificate, who has not obtained a Second Class Provincial Certificate. For this Regulation, there are two reasons. First,— The new Act does not authorize, or permit, the Council of Public Instruction to grant any other than First Class Certificates. The Twelfth Section of the Act says, "First Class Certificates of Qualification shall be awarded by the Council of Public Instruction only, and Second and Third Class Certificates by County and City Boards of Examiners only." If a Candidate for a First Class Provincial Certificate should fail to receive such a Certificate, it must be preceded by Examination for, and the obtaining of, a Second Class Provincial Certificate. Secondly,—The Examination for a Second Class Certificate assumes that a Candidate has passed the Examination for a Second Class Certificate, the same as admission into the Military School, and the Examination for a First Class Certificate, must be preceded by Examination for, and the obtaining of, a Second Class Certificate.

13. It is also requisite that a Candidate should furnish satisfactory proof of having successfully taught School for five years, in order to be eligible for examination for a First Class Certificate,—a preliminary condition first recommended by the Ontario Teachers' Association. It would be unjust to Trustees, Parents and Youths, that any man should be sent forth with the authority and prestige of a public License for Life, as a First Class Teacher, without his having given full proof, not only of his Knowledge of all the subjects of the Programme required to be taught in Public Schools, but of his ability and skill to teach them. The County Board of Examiners have, of course, no means of ascertaining the Candidate's aptitude and skill as a Teacher, except from the testimony of his having taught successfully during five years. An an equivalent for this, in the case of Normal School Candidates, there is their course of training under the instruction of able Masters in all the subjects of their Examination,—including a Course of Lectures on School Organization and Teaching, observing and practising teaching in the Model School,—on an average from two to five Sessions. The severe and protracted course of exercises and practice in regard to School teaching alone, apart from those on other subjects, must impress every thinking person with the

immense advantage, as well as great expenditure of time and labour in a Normal School training for the profession of teaching, such as is required for the profession of Law, or Medicine, or the apprenticeship required to become an Architect, or Carpenter.

14. But I no not think there will be many Candidates for First Class Certificates at the first Examination. I think that, as the Programme for First Class Certificates cannot be mastered without much application and study, and is, in some respects new, most of the Candidates for First Class Certificates will come up for Second Class Certificates, at this July Examination, and prepare themselves for the Examination for First Class Certificate the first part of next January.

15. *Inspection of Schools.*—After completing the Examinations of Candidates for Teachers' Certificates, (of which blank Forms will be sent to you to fill up and sign), your next work will be to visit and inspect the Schools. I have not, (as authorized by Law), prepared and issued needful instructions on this and other duties of County Inspectors. I have preferred the adoption of the accompanying Regulations on the subject by the Council of Public Instruction; and I need do little more than direct your attention to these comprehensive and minute Regulations. There are, however, two, or three, matters connected with your inspection of the Schools on which I think it advisable to remark. You will probably find more, or less, of the Schools very imperfectly, or not at all, organized for the advantage of either Teachers, or Pupils. A newly appointed Inspector,—a First Class Teacher,—one who had been trained at the Normal School, told me the other day, that the last School he taught, and which he ceased teaching on the day before he conversed with me, was in such a state, when he took charge of it, that he requested the Trustees to be present on the first day of his assuming charge of the School, and to witness the Examination of the Pupils with a view to their classification. It was found that some Pupils had read as far as the Fifth Reader, and yet could not do a question in simple Subtraction, and knew little of the Books they had read. It, therefore, became necessary to put Pupils back from the Fifth to the Third Reader, and to make other changes in their relative positions,—changes which were at first displeasing to some Parents and Pupils, but, in making which, he was sustained by the Trustees. The result was that, in the course of three months, all parties gratefully acknowledged the surprising improvement in the School, and now deeply regretted his retirement from it. I dare say you will find the necessity of a similar re-organization of some, if not many, of the Schools under your inspection; and your first work will be to see that all the Pupils are classified according to the Programme of Studies, which divides them into six Classes, the time per week of each subject is prescribed in the Time and Limit Table, which accompanies the Programme of Studies. It will be seen by this Programme, I repeat, that, in the first three Classes, or years, of Study, the attention and time of the Pupils will be chiefly occupied with the three fundamental subjects of Reading, Writing and Arithmetic, and that the other elementary subjects of these three Classes, or years, are intended to develop the faculties of observation, to improve the Mechanical skill in the use of Pen and Pencil, to relieve attention from drier and harder Studies and thus facilitate the progress of the Pupils in the primary and essential subjects of Public School Education.

16. Much time and labour will be required in this your first inspection of the Schools. It might be well, on your first visit, to devote one whole day to the inspection of each School, and. where practicable, to be at the School House five, or ten, minutes before the opening of the School to see how the Teachers bring in and seat their Pupils. You could devote the forenoon to observing the manner in which the Teacher proceeds in teaching and managing the School; during which time you could form a tolerable idea of the ability, skill and merits of the Teacher, and the condition of his School. You could then devote the afternoon to examining and teaching the School yourself; to the classification of the Pupils, is necessary, and then privately give such advice. and make such suggestions to the Teacher as you might deem expedient. I think this

course of proceeding may be advantageously pursued by Inspectors generally; and, in this way, the Inspector may, to a certain extent, where necessary, become a normal Instructor and Helper of Teachers, as well as Overseer and Organizer of the Schools,—rendering them vastly more valuable to the Country than they have ever been.

17. The Regulations are sufficiently explicit as to the matters of attention and inquiry in your inspection of the Schools, and I hope, as therein directed, you will not omit to note in a Book, to be kept for the purpose, a brief statement of the condition in which you find the School, the proceedings and qualifications of the Teacher, the modes of teaching, classification, and government of the Schools, School Premises and Accommodation, etcetera, and transmit the same, or a copy of it, to the Education Department, on your completing the visitation of the Schools. This has been done, not only by every Inspector in England, but by the Inspectors of our Grammar Schools from the beginning. This Report is not for publication, but to enable the Education Department to know precisely the condition, defects and wants of the Schools, and to suggest and adopt, as far as possible, the requisite means for their improvement. It is also desirable to know the real condition and character of the Schools at the commencement of the new System of inspection, and of the Free School Law, so that their future progress may be duly noted and appreciated.

18. The Provisions of the School Law, in regard to your duties in investigating and deciding on matters of complaint and many other things, are too plain to require any particular explanations from me. This Department will always answer any inquiries you may have to make, and aid you in every possible way in the performance of the duties of your responsible office.

19. Having finished my Life's work in respect of School Legislation, I may not have occasion to address you another Circular on the subject of the School Law; but I shall watch with the deepest interest the operations and results of these recent and important improvements in our School System.

TORONTO, 26th June, 1871.   EGERTON RYERSON.

CHAPTER XIII.

PROCEEDINGS OF THE ONTARIO TEACHERS' ASSOCIATION, 1871.

The Eleventh Annual Convention of the Ontario Teachers' Association commenced its sessions in the Theatre of the Normal School Buildings on the 8th ultimo. There was a fair representation of Teachers from the various parts of the Province. The President, Reverend Professor Young, presided. Mr. Hodgson read a portion of Scripture, and the President offered up Prayer. The President desired to thank the Association, as this was the first opportunity he had to do so, for the honour they had conferred upon him in electing him President; but at the same time to state that he thought it undesirable that a Member of the Council of Public Instruction should continue in the Chair, as matters concerning that Body might come up for discussion. Therefore, after delivering his inaugural Address this evening, he would beg leave to resign. Several gentlemen expressed their regret at the decision of the President, and pressed him to reconsider the matter, and continue in office. The President asked to allow the matter to remain in abeyance until the evening, which was agreed to. In the evening, Reverend Mr. Inglis opened the proceedings with devotional exercises.

Professor Young then delivered the following Address:—

I have chosen as the subject of my Address, the Act recently passed regarding Public and High Schools, with the Regulations made, under the Act, by the Council of Public Instruction.

County Inspectors of Public Schools

The Fifth Section of the Act provides that "in each County, or union of Counties, there shall be one or more School Officers, to be called County Inspectors, who shall have charge of not more than One hundred and twenty, nor less than Fifty Schools each." Under the School Law, as it formerly stood, it was competent for County Councils to appoint County Inspectors; but only in a few cases was the power to make such appointments exercised; and the consequence was, that the inspection bestowed on the Common Schools was less satisfactory than might have been desired. Of the Local Superintendents, who are henceforth to be known in our Schools no more, it is not at all necessary to speak harshly. A considerable number of them performed their duties with ability and zeal; and, as a class, they were serviceable to the cause of Education; but, as King Arthur said, when he lay bleeding of his mortal wound, "I have done my work"—they have done their work. The impression throughout the Country was universal, that it was time for the old order to change, and to give place to something more adapted to the stage of educational development at which we have arrived; and hence the Section of the Act, which abolishes the system of inspection by Local Superintendents, and renders the appointment of County Inspectors imperative, has met with no serious opposition from any quarter.

The duty of prescribing the qualifications of County Inspectors is laid on the Council of Public Instruction. The Council has resolved to grant Certificates of Qualification to Graduates of a British, or Colonial, University, who have taught in a School for three years, and to First Class Public School Teachers of the highest grade. I do not mention, as a separate class, High School Masters who have taught in a School for three years, because a Degree is henceforth to be made the qualification for the Mastership of a High School.

Each Graduate, before receiving a Certificate, must write a Thesis on School Organization, to be submitted to the Examining Committee of the Council. It appears from the public papers, that the dignity of some Graduates has been hurt by this Regulation; but I do not feel that there is the shadow of a ground for the offence that has been taken. For, in the first place, an ordinary University Degree is not the most satisfactory guarantee possible that the holder possesses even the literary and scientific attainments necessary for the office of Public School Inspector. A Graduate, as such,— a mere pass Graduate, it may be, of an inferior University,—is not entitled to carry himself loftily, as though all further enquiry into his fitness for so important an office as that of County Inspector were something like an insult. And, in the second place, a Graduate, were it certain that his acquirements are ever so high, is not necessarily, even although he may have taught in a School for three years, well acquainted with the organization of Public Schools, and with the methods of teaching, which should be followed there. The Examination, which he passed before receiving a Degree, did not extend to these points, while First Class Public School Teachers have been examined on them more than once. Where is the hardship, then, of his being asked to write a Thesis, showing that he has, at least, had his attention called to the subject?

I cannot doubt that the Resolution of the Council to grant Certificates of Qualification to those Public School Teachers only, who are in the highest grade of the First Class, will meet with the approval of all who are in a position to give an impartial opinion. Apart from the unseemliness of having a School inspected by a gentleman whose Certificate might be of an inferior grade to that held by the Teacher of the School, the effect of throwing the office of Inspector open to any Public School Teachers, except those who are at the head of their profession, would be to lower the general character of the office, and so to hinder the attainment of the ends for which County Inspectorships were instituted. We look for great things from the Inspectors. We expect them to be the means of reviving the Public Schools, and advancing them to the highest possible state of efficiency. That they may be able to render such a service, they must be men whom Teachers and Trustees and Ratepayers everywhere will look up to with respect, whose counsel will be sought with confidence, whose approbation will be valued, and for whose name reverence will be felt; but it would be foolish to expect County Inspectors as a body to answer this description, if Persons were admitted to the Inspectorships who were not competent to take a First Class Certificate of the highest grade.

The Examination of Public School Teachers.

Next in importance to the Sections of the School Act establishing County Inspectorships, are those which relate to the Examination of Teachers.

Scarcely anything has in time past been felt to be a more serious evil, by those who have interested themselves in the working of our Educational System, than the want of uniformity in the Examination and Classification of Teachers. When I was Inspector of Grammar Schools, I heard the complaint frequently made, that a Candidate, who found it difficult to obtain a Third Class Certificate from one Board, might without difficulty get a Second, or First Class Certificate from another. This disparity in the standards set up by different Boards, besides giving rise to numerous cases of individual dissatisfaction, tended to bring down the general standard of qualification, and threw suspicion on the value of the Certificates held even by First and Second Class Teachers who had fairly won the position that had been assigned to them. The provisions which the new Act makes, with the view of remedying the evil referred to, are as follows:— First Class Certificates are henceforth to be given only by the Council of Public Instruction; and Second and Third Class Certificates only by County Boards of Examiners. The Papers for Second and Third Class Certificates, as well as for First, are to be prepared by the Council of Public Instruction, through a Committee of their appointment, or otherwise; so that Candidates for Second and Third Class Certificates, though presenting themselves before different Boards, shall still have the same Papers to answer. Moreover, by a Regulation of the Council of Public Instruction, the value of the several Questions in the Examination Papers must be fixed by the Committee of Council; correct Answers to the Questions in the Examination Papers, must receive the same the effect of which is, that all Candidates for Certificates of a particular Class, who give number of marks for the Answers, by whatever Board they may be examined.

It is perhaps not possible, in the meantime, to go further than this, in the way of securing uniformity in the Examination and classification of Public School Teachers. Of course, even where Examination Papers are the same, and the values affixed to the several Questions are also the same, there may still be a serious want of uniformity in the Examinations, in consequence of the different estimates which different Examiners make of imperfect Answers. In estimating imperfect Answers, some of the County Boards, which have to decide the fate of Applicants for Second and Third Class Certificates, will be much more severe than others, and thus the ideal of absolute uniformity in the Examination and Classification of Teachers will not by any means be attained. I was at one time disposed to think that County Boards of Examiners might be dispensed with, and Certificates of all Classes, First, Second and Third, granted by one Examining Body. This would secure uniformity as far as such a theory is possible; it would probably not involve much more expense than is entailed by the present system; and it would be objected to on the ground of centralization by those only who allow their ears to be filled with a popular cry, and do not consider that centralization, which separates Examiners from local partialities and suggestions, is, in such a matter, the very thing to be desired. But, after what I have learned of the number of Applicants likely to come forward from year to year for Second and Third Class Certificates, I do not see how a single small Committee could overtake the work of reading all the Papers that would be given in. I acquiesce, therefore, in the method of examining and classifying Teachers now prescribed by Law, as perhaps the best attainable in present circumstances.

The Examining Committee, appointed by the Council of Public Instruction, consists of a Member of the Council, who is chairman of the Committee, and of the two

High School Inspectors. Besides a special Examination for Certificates of Qualification for the office of Public School Inspector, the Committee has recently had to conduct, with the assistance of the Normal School Masters, the Examination of both divisions of the Normal School, and it is at present engaged with the general Examination of Candidates for First Class Certificates throughout the Province. In this general Examination the Normal School Masters take no port. Although, as a Member of the Council, I accepted these arrangements as suitable to the transition year through which the School System is passing, I think that in future it would be better if the Normal School Masters had nothing whatever to do with the Examination of Candidates for Teachers' Certificates. There are undoubtedly some advantages in Teachers having a share in the Examination of their Pupils, but these, in the present instance, are far more than outweighed by the imperative necessity which exists that no one set of Applicants for a Certificate of a particular Class should be subjected to a different ordeal from another, and also that no possible whisper of partiality on the part of a Teacher to his own Pupils should go abroad. This necessity is now more imperative than ever, inasmuch as both Second and Third Class Certificates have a greater value than formerly; Second Class Certificates having been made permanent during the good behaviour of the Holders, and valid in all the Municipalities of the Province; and a First Class Certificate of the highest grade rendering the Holder eligible for the office of Public School Inspector. My opinion, therefore, is clear, that Normal School Masters should not have a place in the future on the Examining Committee; and not only so, but also, that, if possible, there should be but one Examination for the Pupils of the Normal School, and for other Applicants for Teachers' Certificates.

In fact, the way seems to have been paved for this, however unintentionally, by the recent School Act. The Section of the Act, which provides that Second Class Certificates shall be granted only by County Boards, applies, I presume, to Normal School Students as well as to other Persons; and hence those Normal School Students, forming the majority of the whole, who do not aspire to more than Second Class Certificates, must appear before County Boards for Examination, along with other Applicants for Certificates. It is true that an understanding might be come to with County Boards to issue Certificates to Normal School Students on the ground of Examinations conducted by the Committee of the Council of Public Instruction; this, I suppose, would be consistent with the Statute; but is scarcely what the Statute contemplated, and I am convinced that the Council of Public Instruction will not think of such an arrangement. If the larger division of Normal School Pupils must thus necessarily attend the County Board Examinations, why may not the other and smaller division attend the same Examinations? It would be for their own advantage to do so; for, should a Normal School Student be examined merely by a Committee of the Council of Public Instruction, and fail to obtain a First Class Certificate, he could not receive a Second Class Certificate; the Council having no power to issue such a document; but, by presenting himself before a County Board, he might, in the event of his failing to obtain a First Class Certificate from the Council, receive a Second Class one from the Board.

Inspection of the High Schools—Classification of the High Schools—Apportionment of the High School Grant.

I now pass on to the subject of High School Inspection.

Increased provision for the inspection of the High Schools is undoubtedly required to be made. The task of visiting, twice a year, more than a hundred Schools scattered over the Province, is too heavy to be laid on the shoulders of any one man; and, (what is of more consequence), the Council of Public Instruction was unable, so long as there was but one Inspector, to frame suitable Regulations for the Apportionment of the High School Fund among the different Schools. In the last two Reports which I had the honour, as Grammar School Inspector, of giving in to the Chief Superintendent of Education, I showed that the effect of apportioning the Government Grant, according to attendance merely, was to empty into the Grammar Schools all the upper Classes of the Common Schools. This was the case particularly in Union Schools. Of course, nobody used any undue influence to bring such a result about; nevertheless, somehow, it came about. The Common Schools were degraded by having almost all their Pupils, male and female, drained off as soon as the children were able to parse an easy English Sentence; and the Grammar Schools were crowded with Boys and Girls for whom a Grammar School Course of Study was not adapted. For these evils, the only remedy possible, as far as I can see, is to make the amount of the Government Grants to the different High School dependant not on Numbers alone, but on results likewise. To speak mathematically, what each School shall receive out of the Public Treasury should be a function of the two variable quantities, the number of Pupils in attendance, and the character of the instruction imparted; but, in order that results might be taken into account, more than one Inspector was indispensable.

Each of the two Inspectors, whose services are now available, will be required to visit all the High Schools once a year. Having to visit the Schools only once a year, and not twice, as was the case in my day, the Inspectors will be able to devote to each School a much larger portion of time than was formerly allowed. In fact, as new consequences are to be made to hand on the Reports of the Inspectors, the Inspection of the Schools must receive a somewhat new character. The Inspectors will make a very detailed enquiry into the work done in the several Schools, and examine all the departments of that work, from the highest to the lowest; and, it is believed, that, as the result of such minute investigation,—much more minute than has been either possible, or necessary, hitherto,—they will be able to arrange the High Schools into Classes, according to the educational results which the several Schools exhibit. These Classes might be three in number,—first, second and third. It is not proposed that the Inspectors shall be asked to arrange the Schools in the several classes in the order of merit; this would be too much for them to attempt; but there does not seem to be any insuperable difficulty in the way of their agreeing on a Report to the Chief Superintendent, to the effect that such a School is, in their judgment, entitled to rank in the first, or highest, Class; such another School in the second; and such another School in the third. The Inspectors will not make their rounds together, but at different times, so that a School, which may have been visited by one of the Inspectors at a somewhat unfavourable season, may have the advantage of being visited at a more favourable season by the other. Of course, in carrying out these arrangements, a great responsibility will lie on the Inspectors, and High School Masters, who find their Schools in the Third Class, will be prone to fancy that they have suffered injustice; but, where both Inspectors concur in placing a School in a particular Class, the Country will not easily be convinced that the judgment is erroneous. In the event of the Inspectors differing regarding a particular School, a balance will have to be struck between their judgments. It is presumed that the Inspectors will always be men in whose capacity and integrity the utmost confidence can be placed.

Suppose the High Schools to have been so arranged, in the manner I have described, according to educational results; what then? All the Schools, which are placed in the Third Class, should, in my opinion, receive a certain fixed sum for each Pupil; those in the Second Class, a certain larger sum for each Pupil; and those in the First Class, a certain still larger sum for each Pupil. To encourage good teaching, the Grant for each Pupil in the Second Class Schools should be very decidedly in advance of that paid for each in the Third Class Schools; and a similar principle should be followed in determining the allowance to First Class Schools. Where a School is so bad as to be deemed by the Inspectors unworthy of being placed in any of the three Classes, it should receive no Grant.

If a scheme such as this be found practicable, and be adopted by the Council of Public Instruction, it cannot fail, I think, to be productive of the best consequences. It will not only be a heavy blow and great discouragement to the practice of herding Boys and Girls out of the Public Schools into the High School without reference to their fitness for a High School Course of Study, but it will also stimulate High School Masters to put forth all their strength to raise their respective Schools to the highest rank. It will at the same time teach Trustees a lesson which some of them need to learn. With Trustees the question often is not,—"Where can we get the best Teacher?" but,—"At how low a rate can we 'hire' a Teacher?" A very accomplished and successful Grammar School Master once complained to me of the injustice the Trustees were doing him, in withholding a considerable portion of the Government Grant to which he was entitled, and using it partly as a reserve fund, and partly to pay an undue proportion of the Salary of a Common School Teacher who did some work in the Grammar School; and, in the course of the conversation which I had with him, he stated that one of the Trustees had expressed himself to the effect that the Grammar School Master was too well paid; he, (the Trustee in question), thought that a six-hundred-dollar Teacher would be good enough. Now, with such Trustees, unintelligent and narrow-minded, it is of no use to urge rational considerations of the higher order. As Schiller says, "Against stupidity the Gods contend in vain." But there is one consideration to which even the most stupid Trustee is not likely to be insensible, namely, that, when the Apportionment to a particular School is made to depend a good deal on the educational rank which the School takes, six-hundred-dollar Teachers will no longer be as profitable as they may formerly have been. If by engaging a thousand-dollar, or a twelve-hundred dollar Teacher you might have made your School a First Class School, while by leaving it in the hands of a six-hundred-dollar Teacher you keep it in the Third Class, it may turn out that in choosing the six-hundred-dollar man you saved money in one direction, to lose as much, perhaps more, in another.

The scheme of Apportionment, which I have sketched proceeds on the idea, not that the total Grant is a definite amount, but that a definite amount is to be paid for each Pupil in a School according to the class in which the School is placed. Permit me to ask attention to this. At present, as you are aware, a definite total sum lies at the disposal of the Chief Superintendent for distribution among the High Schools. The effect of this is that what one School gains another must lose. A stationary Government Grant is, besides, a check on progress; for, should any considerable number of the Schools make such advancement as to render it necessary to engage additional Masters, a great increase of the total Expenditure for Salaries would be requisite, which increase, however, with a stationary Grant, there are no means of meeting. But, if the views which I have ventured to suggest were adopted, and a definite amount paid for each Pupil in a School according to the educational rank of the School, there would, in consequence of the Grant expanding in the same proportion in which the Schools become more numerously attended and better conducted, be no check on progress; nor would the gain of one School be the loss of another; each would be rewarded on a consideration simply of its own doings,—which surely is the right principle.

It may perhaps be urged as an objection to the scheme which I have submitted, that it would involve the Expenditure of a considerably larger sum of money than is at present allowed by the Legislature for High School purposes. I suppose that this would be the case: but I am persuaded, that, if the scheme were found practicable, its advantages would be so marked that the Country would not grudge the money that might be needed to carry it out. Last year, in the Parliamentary Committee on the Upper Canada College question, certain views, expressed by one of the Witnesses, seemed to be assented to by a Member of the Government, who was on the Committee; but he remarked, turning to some Members of the Opposition, who were present:— "If we were to propose any such thing there would be an outcry about the expense." On this, one of the parties more immediately addressed, replied:—"If the Government bring down any proposal, which can be shown to be for the advancement of the true interests of education we will heartily concur in it, whatever the expense may be. There is nothing we will not pay to have our children well educated." I refer to this little passage of arms because it brings out what I believe is the truth, that all parties in Parliament, those in power and those who expect to get into power, will agree to grant whatever funds can be shown to be necessary for the working of the Educational System. Indeed, an eminent Member of the House said to me in a conversation which I had with him some time ago:—"Expense in a matter of this kind is not to be considered."

Course of Study to be Pursued in the Public and High Schools.

Let me now advert to those Sections of the Act, which bear on the Course of Study to be pursued in the Public and High Schools.

As regards the Public School Programme, the chief thing to be noticed, is the introduction into it of a new Scientific element. By the Thirteenth Section of the Act, the Council of Public Instruction is required to make provision "for teaching in the Public Schools the elements of Natural History, of Agricultural Chemistry, of Mechanics, and of Agriculture." It must not be thought that it is intended, by the introduction of these branches of Study into the Public Schools that less attention than formerly is to be given to our old and valued friends, the three R's. Reading, Writing and Arithmetic must ever continue to be the main strands in the cord of elementary knowledge,— the sides of the triangular base of the pyramid of education. If there were the least danger that the admission of Science into the Public Schools would lead to the neglect of Reading, Writing and Arithmetic, I for one would say:—Keep Science at the outside of the door. I trust, however, that it may be found possible, without detriment to the just claims of the R's, to do something in the way of bringing the children in our Public Schools to an acquaintance with the elements of Science. This is eminently the age of Science. The most wonderful discoveries are being daily made; while at the same time a Scientific Literature at once popular and exact, is bringing the results of philosophical research within the reach of the general public. In these circumstances, a School System, which should fail to furnish the elementary education, that would give every child in the Province the means of fitting himself to look with intelligence, when he grows up, on the great Scientific movement going on around him, and to take part, if qualified, in the work of original Scientific Investigation would be seriously defective. The only question, it seems to me, which can here be raised, is whether the teaching of the elements of Science should be confined to the High Schools, or made part of the work of the Public Schools also,—the Legislature has taken the latter view. I observe that it is fortified in this by the opinion of the British Royal Commission on Education; for, in reporting on the most suitable Course of Study for a class of Schools similar to our Public Schools, the Commissioners recommend the introduction of elementary Scientific subjects. It may also be remarked that a large number of Boys and Girls will probably complete their education in the Public Schools; so that if they do not obtain an acquaintance with the elements of Science in these Institutions, they will get it nowhere else. Some persons, when they see the Programme of Study which the Council of Public Instruction has drawn up for the Public Schools, may very possibly scoff at the extremely elementary character of the lessons to be given in Natural History and Agricultural Chemistry, and Mechanics, and may say:—What is the use of learning anything where so little is learned? But, if the little be only well taught, it will be invaluable. It will create a taste for more. It will be an instrument for the acquisition of more. It will introduce into the mind new conceptions,—seed-thoughts, which may germinate, and bring forth, in due time, who can tell what fruits?

In the High Schools the study of Latin and Greek is henceforth to be optional. A thorough elementary Classical Education is still to be provided for Boys, (and Girls, if you please), who may purpose to enter a University; but Boys and Girls, who have no such intention, are not to be debarred from receiving a superior High School education adapted to their wants. In order to give effect to the views of the Legislature, the Council of Public Instruction has addressed itself to the task of framing two Programmes for High Schools, one Classical, and the other Non-classical. In the Non-classical Course prominence is given to various branches of Science, the Curriculum being, in this respect, a continuation of what was prepared for the Public Schools; and an attempt is made

10a—XXIII

to exhibit, in definite outline, a scheme of advanced Study in the English Language. I have elsewhere stated at length, and with all the earnestness in my power, my opinion in regard to the value of the English language, as an instrument of education; and I will now merely say, that in order to vindicate for English a far higher place than it has yet received in our provincial Schools, it is not necessary to institute a comparison between it and the ancient Classical Languages, or the modern German and French; for it is perfectly certain that the great mass of the Boys and Girls in our Schools must receive almost their entire culture, so far as dependent on the Study of Language, neither from the ancient Classics nor from French and German, but from their own Language. In illustration of the fact that the study of the English Language and Literature may be rendered not only fascinating, but extremely useful even for the accomplishment of many of the results for which it has hitherto been the habit to look almost exclusively to Latin and Greek, let me quote a passage from a Lecture of Professor Tyndall, one of the best writers, as well as ablest philosophers of the present day:—

"If I except discussions on the comparative merits of Popery and Protestantism, English Grammar was the most important discipline of my boyhood. The piercing through the involved and inverted sentences of Paradise Lost; the linking of the verb to its often distant nominative, of the relative to its distant antecedent, of the agent to the object of the transitive verb, of the preposition to the noun, or pronoun, which it governed,—the study of variations in mood and tense, the transformations often necessary to bring out the true grammatical structure of a sentence,—all this was to my young mind a discipline of the highest value, and, indeed, a source of unflagging delight. How I rejoiced when I found a great Author tripping, and was fairly able to pin him to a corner from which there was no escaping. I speak thus of English, because it was of real value to me. I do not speak of other Languages, because their educational value for me was almost insensible. But," he adds,—and the words merit attention, as showing how the appreciation of one means of culture does not necessarily lessen, with a broad minded man, the appreciation of another,—"knowing the value of English so well, I should be the last to deny, or even to doubt, the high discipline involved in the proper study of Latin and Greek."

The single difficulty which I foresee in the way of carrying out to the most happy results the Programmes with which the Council of Public Instruction has been engaged, is the lack of competent English and Scientific Teachers. To teach the higher branches of English well, demands a somewhat rare faculty. And, as regards Science, I am satisfied from recent examinations in which I have taken part, that many of the Public School Masters need to have their notions about Science entirely reconstructed. I make no apology, Gentlemen, for speaking frankly. An idea seems to be entertained that Scientific knowledge consists in being acquainted with rules for working Problems. I was amused with a Note which a Gentleman, who came up at the recent Normal School Examination, appended to his Answers to a Paper in Natural Philosophy, which bore my name at its head:—"Mr. Young," said he, "if you had given me Problems in Steam I would have shown you how to work them." Now, as it is possible that I may have something to do again in the examination of Teachers, although I fervently hope not, I give notice to all whom it may concern, that I attach not the slightest importance to the working of Problems in Steam, or in anything else. What I value is, facts apprehended as bound together by a principle, or what is the same thing, principles as summary expressions for classes of clearly apprehended facts. The knowledge of Rules without an acquaintance with the principles lying at the bottom of them may have a little, a very little, technical use; but educationally it is worthless. It might be dangerous, perhaps, to hint that even the High School Masters may not all possess the requisite Scientific accomplishment to qualify them for the duties which are now to devolve upon them. Are they not, most of them, Graduates of a University?

The Establishment of Collegiate Institutes.

The last point to which I shall ask your attention is the authority given to the Lieutenant-Governor-in-Council to establish Collegiate Intstitutes.

The effect of that part of the School Act which makes the Study of Latin and Greek in the High School optional, will probably be to banish Classics almost entirely from the majority of the High Schools, and in a great measure to concentrate the Study of Latin and Greek in a few localities. If this should happen, it would not be a misfortune. It may reasonably be expected that as large a number of good Classical Pupils will be produced in the few Schools which will become the foci of Classical Instruction, as are now sent forth from the whole body of the High Schools; while, at the same time, the mass of the Schools, at least after the High School System fairly gets under weigh, and the Teachers have grown familiar with their new duties, will be doing a genuine and important work, which they were not doing previously. In order, however, that Classical Study may be properly maintained in the Schools where it is likely henceforth to be mainly prosecuted, these Schools must receive special pecuniary aid; and for furnishing such aid under what are considered proper conditions the 41st Section of the Act makes provision. "Whereas," the Section runs, "it is desirable to encourage the establishment of superior Classical Schools, it shall be lawful for the Lieutenant-Governor-in-Council to confer upon any High School, in which not less than four Masters are fully engaged in teaching the subjects of the prescribed Curriculum, and in which the daily average of male Pupils studying the Latin, or Greek, Language shall not be less than sixty, the name Collegiate Institute, and towards the support of such Collegiate Institute it shall be lawful for the Lieutenant-Governor-in-Council to authorize the payment of an additional sum, at the rate of, and not exceeding, Seven hundred and fifty dollars per annum, out of the Superior Education Fund; provided that, if in any year, the average of Pupils above described shall fall below sixty, or the number of Masters be less than four, the additional Grant shall cease for that year; and if the said average shall continue to be less than sixty, or the number of Masters less than four, for two successive years, the Institution shall forfeit the name and privileges of a Collegiate Institute, until restored by the Lieutenant-Governor-in-Council, under the conditions provided by this Section."

I go heartily along with the framer of the Act in desiring the establishment of superior Classical Schools. A few Schools of the type of Upper Canada College might, with great propriety, be planted in different parts of the Province, not perhaps immediately, but with a wise regard to circumstances. I cannot say, however, that I look with favour of the proposed Collegiate Institutes. A year ago, on the invitation of the Grammar School Masters' Association, I stated to that Association my objections to the Institutes; I stated the same objections when called to give evidence before a Committee of the Provincial Parliament; and, as my views remain unchanged. I will now state them to you. Whether I am right, or wrong, no harm can arise from having the subject ventilated. In the first place, then, I dislike the proposed Collegiate Institutes because of the character of instability which must necessarily attach to them. The Act provides, as we have seen, that, if in any year the average of male Pupils fall below sixty, or the number of Masters be less than four, the additional Grant shall cease for that year; and if the said average shall continue to be less than sixty, or the number of Masters less than four, for two successive years, the Institution shall forfeit the name and privileges of a Collegiate Institute. Thus, a School may this year be a Collegiate Institute, with the pecuniary advantages, such as they are, which that dignity brings along with it; but next year it may lose all special pecuniary advantage, and, the year following, the extinguisher may descend upon it, and out it goes,—as a Collegiate Institute. I cannot persuade myself that it is desirable that the Institutions intended to be the great centres, where Boys preparing for a University are to be fitted for matriculation, should be established under such conditions of uncertainty. In the second place, the Collegiate Institutes are to be developed out of the ordinary High

Schools; and this, I believe, is considered by some persons whose judgment is entitled to great respect, a recommendation of the System; but I look upon it as an objection, because it entails the consequence that the Institutes may be established in any locality where a High School exists. I cannot help thinking it would be better to have these Institutions fixed in the leading Cities of the Province. In the third place, the funds provided by the 41st Section of the School Act for the support of the Institutes are inadequate. I have already said that my conception of the Collegiate Institutes is, that they are to be somewhat of the type of the Upper Canada College, although on a less extensive scale. Now, it is simply idle to talk of setting up Institutions of this character, unless you are prepared to give the Masters Salaries on which Persons with the tastes of educated gentlemen can live. The Salary of the Head Master of a Collegiate Institute should not be less than $1,600 a year; and if you have two other Masters with $1,200 each, and a fourth with $800, this makes in all $4,800. But what provision does the Act make for the support of Collegiate Institutes? A Collegiate Institute will have its share of the Government Grant, one-half as much more from local sources, and a bonus of $750. The Government Grant will probably not amount to much more than $1,000. Some very intelligent High School Masters, who have spoken to me on the subject, are afraid that this estimate is too high; but, if we say $1,000, this will make the Anual Income of a Collegiate Institute, independently of Fees, only about $2,250. It may be supposed that the Fees will amount to a large sum. This is the case at present in some Schools, as, for instance, in Galt and Kingston; but, throughout the Province, the current is strongly flowing in the direction of Free Education, in the High Schools as well as in the Public Schools. The effect of this tendency will be to lower the Fees in all the High Schools, except a few which happen to be placed in peculiar circumstances; so that the Income which may be looked for from this source will be, in most cases precarious, and is likely more and more so every year. The 36th Section of the Act may, perhaps, be thought sufficient to meet the difficulty; for it gives High School Boards the power to levy, not only a sum equal to one-half the Government Grant, but such other sums as may be required for the maintenance of the High Schools; but the Masters of Collegiate Institutes would not, I suspect, care very much to have their Salaries from year to year dependent on the generosity of High School Boards. For these reasons, I should have been better pleased with the School Act, had the 41st Section been omitted. It is a cumbrous, and I fear, it will prove a not very manageable, appendage to an otherwise complete and harmonious School System.

Would you give no special encouragement, then, it may be said, to superior Classical Education? Certainly, I would. In the first place, if the principle were adopted, which I have advocated in this Address, of paying Schools for results as well as for attendance, and if such payments were made, not by the division of a definite total sum among the Schools, but by the allotment to each School of a fixed amount for each Pupil, according to the educational rank taken by the School, such a scheme, the rate of payment to first-class Schools being made, (as I think it should be), greatly in excess of that paid to the lower Schools, would provide for Schools of the first-class, whether Classical, or Non-classical, as liberal pecuniary encouragement, at least, as the 41st Section of the Act proposes to allow to the Collegiate Institutes. And, in the second place, I would be prepared, as I before intimated, to found, when the proper time should seem to have arrived, in the more important localities, such as Ottawa, Kingston, Hamilton, and London, Schools somewhat of the character of Upper Canada College, only on a reduced scale. Of course, if those who hold the strings of the public purse will not give money to carry out such plans, nothing more can be said; there is an end of the matter. But we are bound to proceed upon the assumption that the Legislature will not grudge a moderate expenditure,—for after all, it would be moderate,—demanded by the best interests of the Country. Our Legislators surely all understand that there are higher feats of statesmanship than saving money.

The Address was listened to with marked attention, and a vote of thanks was passed to the Lecturer.

Some Causes of Failure by Teachers in Teaching.

Mr. H. I. Strang, B.A., of Owen Sound, conceived the first of the causes of failure in teaching to be poor education in the Teacher, but he thought that this evil would soon be remedied under the new Law. Another cause of failure appeared to him to be that Persons undertook to teach without having received professional training. He might be told that such Persons should attend the Normal School, but he held that that Institution was not adequate to train all the Teachers the Country required. A good deal might be done, however, by the Teachers themselves, in reading Educational Works and Papers and in attending the Meetings of this Association. He thought that Teachers failed, also, from lack of judgment. A great many Teachers did not consider sufficiently the differences of intellectual ability in their Pupils and laid down too many Rules. But perhaps the most serious cause of the failure was the entering of Teachers into the profession and continuing in it without any taste for their work. This fault was readily noticed by the Pupils. If a Teacher showed himself enthusiastic in his work, Pupils would be the more likely to be earnest in their Studies. Mr. McAllister, of Toronto, thought the chief cause of failure among Teachers was lack of interest in their work. He would recommend Teachers to make few Rules, but to enforce those they did make. In reference to a remark by one of the gentlemen present, the Speaker said that as a general rule, he thought that Teachers should confess their ignorance when Pupils asked them a question on some subject on which they might not be posted, or have only a partial knowledge of it. Mr. Scarlett, of Northumberland, thought that to pursue such a course might do very well in Cities where Trustees did not expect a Teacher to know everything; but to acknowledge ignorance in some of the rural Sections would, he thought, injure the reputation of the Teacher seriously. He thought that it would be better for the Teacher in case of a difficult question to allow it to remain in abeyance while he prepared himself to answer it. He agreed with Mr. Strang that two of the principal causes of failure were lack of interest and lack of judgment on the part of the Teachers. Mr. Tilley, County of Durham, held that Teachers trained in the Normal School were much superior to Teachers who obtained their Certificates from County Boards. He had no doubt that when the standard of Teachers is raised they will be better remunerated than at present. Then, too, the causes of failure would be fewer than they are now. Mr. S. Woods, M.A., of Kingston, thought that Teachers were not nearly as well remunerated as they should be, and he held that they themselves were to blame for it. Some of them thought the life an easy one, and, therefore, accepted small Salaries for their work. Were Teachers but to stand upon the dignity of their profession they would be more respected and be better remunerated than at present; the standard of the Teachers of the Province would be raised, and they would feel an increased interest in their work. He thought that Teachers should always endeavour to be cheerful in their Schools. Some Members of the profession habitually looked as though their tomb-stones were continually standing before them, with their names, ages, and all other particulars engraved on them. As a general thing the Teacher had not sufficient enthusiasm in his work. He suggested that if a Boy asked a Teacher a question concerning some subject with which he, (the Teacher), was not well acquainted, he should, instead of displaying his ignorance, direct the inquirer to some work in which he could find the information he desired. There might, however, be isolated instances in which it would be no disgrace for a Teacher to confess his ignorance. Mr. Tamblyn, of Newcastle, held it to be of great importance that the School House should be well Ventilated and Lighted, and that the Seats should be comfortable. He thought also that attention should be given to the Physical Training of Pupils, and that the Master should endeavour to be on the Playground during the hours of recreation to direct the amusement of the Scholars. He thought that one of the causes of failure in teaching was the changing of Rules too frequently. Mr. J. C. Glashan held that a Teacher should make his Pupils feel that he was taking part in their work, and that instead of conducting himself in a domineering manner toward them, he should request them to do what he might require of them. Mr. Fraser, of Woodstock, thought that a cause of failure among Teachers was their not coming together with sufficient frequency to confer on matters affecting their profession. Hitherto the Teachers had been examined for Certificates by Medical Men, Lawyers and Clergymen, but now he was happy to say they were examined by Members of their own profession. He held that the success or failure of Teachers depended greatly on the circumstances under which they taught; let the Trustees and others surrounding the Teacher manifest an interest in him and he would work with all the more enthusiasm. Professor Macoun, of Belleville, remarked that inefficient Teachers had hitherto been permitted to take charge of Schools, and the result of their teaching had been that their Successors had been employed for months in undoing their work. This evil, he thought, would now be remedied under the operation of the new School Act.

Review of the Practical Work of the Teachers' Association.

Mr. Anderson said:—This Association having reached the tenth year of its existence, we may very properly take a retrospect of its history. In the month of December, 1861, the Teachers and friends of Education in Toronto and the County of York assembled at the Court House in this City for the purpose of organizing a Teachers' Association for Upper Canada. The undertaking was not unattended with considerable difficulty. After the Upper Canada Teachers' Association had been established, and the attraction of novelty had worn off, a variety of obstacles presented themselves, which .it was very difficult to remove. Among Teachers, as among other classes, there are many who look almost exclusively at the direct personal benefits to be derived from any movement in which they take part. The Provincial Association was neither in the nature of a Trades Union to keep up prices, or a benefit society, to provide against sickness, or old age. Teachers generally receive very scanty remuneration. A man obliged to support a family on Four hundred dollars a year could scarcely be expected to travel one or two hundred miles at the cost of nearly half a month's Salary to attend Meetings resulting apparently in so little profit. There existed another serious obstacle which, by the recent Act of Parliament had happily been almost entirely removed. Two classes of Teachers existed throughout the Country, one holding Provincial and the other County Board Certificates of Qualification. No Teacher, however well qualified, was permitted to compete for a Provincial Certificate without previous attendance at the Normal School. County Board Teachers considered this provision of the Law a great injustice. Hence arose a feeling of jealousy, which began to appear in a very marked manner, immediately after the Association was formed. But as Teachers met in Convention, and became better acquainted with one another, they discovered that no class held control,—that the members were willing to throw aside local prejudices and forget the petty distinctions arising from the difference of locality in which their knowledge or experience had been acquired. But perhaps the most formidable difficulty in the way of securing combined action among us was, and is still, the want of permanence in the profession. Teaching has long been used as a means of reaching other professions. A young man proposes to study Divinity. Law, or Medicine, but his finances being insufficient to enable him to complete his course, he becomes a Teacher for a year or two, for the purpose of earning money. His leisure is entirely taken up in pursuing a special course of study entirely unconnected with teaching. Having put in his time and drawn his Salary, he troubles himself no further about either teaching, or Teachers, and, of course, gives himself no concern whatever about Teachers' Associations. It is difficult to ascertain the entire number of Teachers that enter other employments, every year. Turning to the Annual Report of the Chief Superintendent for 1867, we find that up to that year 2,544 Provincial Certificates had been granted to Students of the Normal School. Of these 964 had expired, or had been superceded by others, leaving 1,580 valid at that date; but only 601 Persons holding such Certificates were then engaged in teaching. These were among the difficulties to be met by those who ten years ago inaugurated this movement. They had but slight inducements to offer to their fellow labourers to come forward and take part in the work. The obstacles were numerous, the attractions but few. But they felt that they had a duty to perform, that they must make some sacrifice, and that ultimately success was certain; and they have not been disappointed. The fact that this Association has been in successful operation for nearly ten years, has been attended by hundreds of leading Teachers from all parts of the Province, affords ample proof that we are capable at least of working together for a common object. But more than this has been accomplished. Until recently the opinions of Teachers on educational matters have been practically disregarded. Not so when Legislation was invoked on matter affecting other classes. When a new Insolvency Bill was introduced into Parliament, leading Merchants were consulted in regard to its provisions. If a Medical Bill were brought before the House, representatives from the different Medical Schools were examined before a special Committee. If a measure affecting the legal profession was under consideration, the Members of the Bar and the Bench were respectfully requested to express their opinions. When Bank Charters required amendment, Cashiers and Presidents were forthwith summoned to the Capital. But when School Legislation occupied the attention of the people's Representatives, nobody thought of asking Teachers what they thought about matters which they above all others were most likely to understand. How are we to account for this strange inconsistency? It will not suffice to say that educational questions are of less importance than those relating to Trade, Law, or Medicine. Ask the people, with the services of which of the classes just named they could most easily dispense; and the answer will certainly not be, "With those of the Teachers." It is unnecessary to stop to enquire where the fault lies,—probably with Teachers themselves,[*] —but we may congratulate ourselves on the fact that this state of things is rapidly passing away. Important changes have just been made in the School Law by the Act of the present year; and it is highly creditable to the judgment of the respected Head of the Education Department that the new features introduced are not the result of mere theory, but are based in the matured experience of practical Teachers and Superintendents, as expressed by the deliberate decisions of this Body. At the Meeting in Hamilton in 1862, a motion was introduced affirming the desirability of establishing a Central Board of Examiners to issue Provincial Certificates of Qualification in lieu of the recently-abolished system of issuing County Board Certificates. The mover of the Resolution recommended the plan adopted in the Examinations of the London University, that is, that the Questions should be prepared by this Central Board, transmitted under Seal to the County Boards, opened in presence of the Candidates, and the Answers returned to the Central Board for adjudication. This motion was lost by a small majority; but at several subsequent Meetings was carried unanimously. At the Teachers' Convention of 1865 an additional clause was proposed, and strongly urged by several speakers, to the effect that all Candidates for Certificates of Qualification, wherever educated, or trained, should be examined by this Board, which should include no individual whose Pupils were required to undergo its examination. By the late School Act and the Regulations of the Council of Public Instruction precisely this plan of licensing Teachers has been adopted, and is now in operation throughout the Province. With regard to certain matters of detail there will no doubt be much difference of opinion; but as a whole this may be regarded as one of the most important features of the new Law. It removes one of the main causes of ill-feeling among Teachers, establishes merit as the sole standard of graduation, and, judging from the experience of past years, will have the effect of retaining in our ranks many of our best Teachers, who, under the old Law, would be induced to enter other employments. Had we done nothing more than to bring this matter prominently before the proper Authorities and help to effect the change that has just been made, our organization would not have existed in vain. A thorough System of School Inspection is of vital importance to the efficiency of our Schools. Until the present year two serious evils existed. Incompetent persons were frequently appointed to the office of Superintendent, and many who were

---

[*] True: for at all the County School Conventions, held by the Chief Superintendent, he has invariably asked Teachers to be present.

competent, not being sufficiently remunerated to spend their whole time in the work, made the duties of the office subordinate to their other avocations. In addition to the injury sustained by the Schools themselves, how humiliating and vexatious to the competent Teacher to be compelled to listen to criticisms on his system of imparting instruction from officials entirely ignorant of School organization, or of the best method of teaching. How galling to the man of education to be examined by a Superintendent far inferior to himself in attainments and whose stock of knowledge would be considerably increased by attending one of said Teacher's junior Classes. In the case of that Class usually termed professional men who held this office the fault was not so much a lack of education as a want of interest,—although the knowledge of a profession does not necessarily include a knowledge of teaching, and not always a thorough acquaintance with the subjects taught. As might naturally be expected, so much time, only, as could be spared from professional duties would be devoted to School visiting. Hence the more successful and popular as a professional man the less efficient and useful as a Local Superintendent. Let it not be supposed that all Persons holding this position were inefficient. There have been many worthy exceptions,—men thoroughly competent, conscientious, and devoted to their work; and it is gratifying to know that special provision has been made in the School Law to render these eligible for appointment to the office of Inspector without further examination. In order to supply a remedy, this Association, on more occasions than one, recommended that all such Superintendents should possess, at least, the qualification of First Class Teachers, combined with practical experience in teaching, and that appointments should be made for Counties instead of Townships. By the late School Act and the Regulations based on it, these recommendations have been fully carried out. School Inspectors are now to be selected from among the highest grade of practical Teachers only. It is unnecessary further to enumerate the provisions of the recent Statute. Nearly all the important changes introduced have been recommended by Teachers themselves. The utmost readiness has been shown by the Legislature, the Chief Superintendent of Education, and the Council of Public Instruction, to listen to the suggestions of the Ontario Teachers' Association. If the results should prove unsatisfactory we have ourselves to blame. Altogether the result of our labours has been highly satisfactory. Let us not suppose, however, that our mission is accomplished. This Association has now a definite part to perform in the great work of education, which can be done by it alone. A few years ago its utility was considered doubtful and its success uncertain; now its existence has become almost a necessity. But let not the good that has already been accomplished induce us to relax our efforts; let it rather encourage us to put forth renewed exertions. Every man owes something to his profession besides a certain amount of labour for which he receives pay. There may be callings more honoured, but there are none more honourable than that of the Teacher. The foreign foe that invades our shores is not more to be dreaded than the ignorance that lurks in our midst; and the military hero that defends us from the one deserves not better from his Country than he who rids us of the other. The faithful, devoted Teacher is a true patriot. It is not by whining and complaining about want of respect that Teachers can hope to secure their proper position. They must be true to themselves. Let them but respect their calling and it will command the respect of others. The man makes the position respectable, and not the position the man. Now more than ever a feeling of harmony and good will exists among our Members. A disposition to unite more closely together is everywhere apparent. Our past history affords ground for satisfaction and thankfulness. Let us hope that a career of still greater usefulness is before us. A vote of thanks was passed to Mr. Anderson, for his practical remarks.

The Examination Papers Criticized.

Mr. S. Woods, of Kingston, complained of the Papers sent out by the Board of Examiners. After some remarks, in which he severely criticized The Reverend Doctor Davies' Grammar, he moved that the Central Board of Examiners shall, in future, be composed of a Committee of Public School Inspectors. The motion was seconded by Mr. McCallum. After some further conversation, Mr. Buchan moved an amendment to the effect that, while approving of many of the Examination Papers sent out by the Central Committee, the Association would wish to ask that, in future, that useless technicalities of particular Text Books be omitted; and that, in future, the Papers bear the names of the individual Examiners preparing them. Mr. Seath seconded the amendment. Mr. Husband moved in amendment to the Amendment, that the Executive Committee of the Teachers' Association be appointed for the purpose of preparing Examination Papers, and that it be composed exclusively of those who have been Teachers in Public Schools, and that such a Board be composed of three Persons. Mr. Wood closed the debate, after which, the motion was withdrawn, and so were the Amendments it called forth. Mr. Anderson then moved that the Association highly approve of the general plan of Examinations of the Public School Teahcers now in operation throughout the Province, being in accordance with the views frequently expressed by this Association. He would suggest that, in the future, each Paper bear the name of the Public Examiner preparing it.—Carried.

The Best Mode of Teaching Spelling and English Grammar.

Mr. Hodgson read an introductory paper on these two important subjects. Amongst other practical suggestions, the Paper recommended that the practice of Spelling with syllables should be followed; and that, in Grammar, the analytical method should be tried. Mr. R. Lewis, of Toronto, held that, as Spelling was for the purpose of enabling a Person to write correctly, instead of to speak, it should not be taught so much orally, as by Writing a portion of each Reading Lesson. He had adopted this plan in his School, and had found the results to be highly satisfactory. With regard to Grammar, he was of opinion that it should be taught as little as possible from the Book, and very much by practice in Writing, Composition, etcetera. Mr. H. I. Strang said that it was his custom to give to his Scholars Sentences to write from dictation. He then marked the Words they mispelled, and made lists of them. These lists he gave to the Scholars, and required them to study the words of which they were composed more particularly than the other Words in the Sentence he had dictated. Mr. Archibald McCallum, of Hamilton, approved of the plan of requiring Words to be spelled in syllables. He was of opinion that the study of Grammar might advantageously be left off until the reasoning powers should be pretty well developed; but he held with Mr. Lewis, that Pupils should be required to commence the writing of Composition at an early period of their School career. Mr. Scarlett agreed with Mr. Lewis, that the Pupils should be required to learn to Spell from Writing. Mr. Lewis remarked that this was the Prussian System, and it had proved very satisfactory. Mr. Scarlett would give Pupils in the First Book short lessons, and require them to write down every word; and in the more advanced Books he would require the Pupils to write down the more difficult of the Words in their lessons. He thought that Pupils should be required to commence the study of Grammar orally very young, and he considered it a good plan to cause Students in Grammar to write something on some object shown them by the Teacher, and then submit it to him for correction.

Union of the Grammar School Masters' Association with the Teachers' Association.

The Convention took up the Report of the Committee on Union, which recommended: 1st. That the Societies known under the names of the Ontario Teachers' Association and the Ontario Grammar Schoolmasters' Association, be united under the name of the Ontario Teachers' Association. 2nd. That the Association have three different sections, representing respectively, 1st, Teachers in High Schools; 2ndly, Inspectors; 3rdly, Public School Teachers. 3rd. That in all subjects pertaining to Education generally, the Association shall act unitedly, both in discussing and deciding upon such subjects. 4th. That subjects pertaining specially to any one, or two, of the sections mentioned in the second clause, shall be discussed by the Members of all the sections, but that the decision of the subject shall rest alone with the section, or sections, particularly interested. 5th. That, in the event of any dispute regarding the class in which any specified subjects may be included, the decision be made by a majority of the Board of Directors present, and that such decision be final. The Report, after a full discussion, was adopted.

Professor Goldwin Smith's Lecture.

The Speaker said that the character of Cowper was summed up in these few words, "England, I love thee well." He said that poetry was as potent to reform as the laws, and Cowper was one of those who added materially to its reformation. Cowper's Father was an indulgent man, and his son, therefore, was denied nothing that could be procured; but his Mother died when the poet was only six years of age, and Cowper afterwards wrote one of the most beautiful and affecting Poems that he ever composed respecting the death of his maternal Parent. After his Mother died he was left with a Guardian until he was of a responsible age, when he was sent to Westminster School, where he became an adept in the use of Latin phrases among other qualifications. Cowper's Religion was not only of good works, but it produced good works. He was active among the poor, both in his religious demonstrations and in works of charity. After the lecture a vote of thanks was rendered to the Lecturer.

Report on Public School Legislation.

Mr. John Cambpell submitted the Report of the Committee on this subject:—1. That the thanks of the Association are due to the Chief Superintendent of Education and to Members of the Legislature for their efforts in introducing many advantageous amend·nents into the Consolidated Public School Act, which are calculated to elevate the position of Teachers, and render more effectual the Schools of this Province. The Committee desire, however, to submit to the consideration of the Convention certain features of the Bill, which they regard as objectionable, or open to alteration and improvement.

Provision in the Bill in Regard to the Superannuation Fund.

Mr. Johnston, (Cobourg), objected to the Superannuation Fund. If it was good for the Public School Teachers, it was equally good for the Grammar School Teachers; but the Legislature did not impose it upon the latter class. He thought the provision illegal, as the Inspector had no legal right to withhold a portion of the Government Grant from the Teacher for this purpose. He moved,—"That, while approving of the majority of the changes introduced into our Educational System by the School Act of 1871, they entirely disagree with the Section relating to the Superannuated Teachers' Fund; and that the Executive Committee be authorized to have Petitions printed and circulated throughout the Province, for the signatures of Teachers, asking the Legislature to repeal this Section. Mr. Macintosh seconded the Motion. He thought the Teachers were quite competent to take care of their own future. If Teachers volunteered to contribute a sum yearly to a general fund, they, of course, had a right to do so, but he objected to being compelled to contribute. He would advise Teachers not to give the order for the Government Grant, and thus effectually resist the payment of any contribution to this Fund. It was equally objectionable in the interests of the Inspectors, because they were made to perform the service of bailiffs, and collect this money from the Teachers. Mr. Harrison observed, with regard to the question of legality, that the Inspector was authorized by the Act to deduct the amount of the contribution. Mr. Fraser, (Woodstock), maintained that Teachers who spent the best part of their lives in the work should receive pensions, if any at all, from the Public Treasury, just as men did who served their Country in the army. Mr. Buchan, (of Hamilton), said that the argument had been advanced that the Fund would tend to make secure a better class of Teachers, but he was of opinion that it would have a decidedly opposite effect, for he thought it would be a poor inducement to School Teachers when they knew that they were to spend the better portion of their days in teaching, and in old age be thrown upon the mercy of the Fund, and receive, perhaps, a hundred dollars a year. Mr. Lewis was opposed to all pensions. Teachers should be paid well enough to enable themselves to provide for old age. If the principle of pensions was good, it should be carried out something after the manner of Life Insurances. As it was, Teachers had no certainty of a fixed sum if they became incapacitated for work. Mr. Reasin thought the Section had been too sharply condemned. Teachers might be glad to receive even a small amount in their old age. Mr. Fraser, (York Township), protested against the clause as most unjust. Mr. McCallum moved an amendment that this Association recommend that all male Teachers in the Province be included in this Superannuation Regulation, provided that the management of this Fund be entrusted to this Association, on its obtaining an Act of Incorporation. Mr. Wood, (of Kingston), said that if there was to be anything of the kind at all, he thought that a voluntary association would be much better. He had been speaking with a Minister of the Methodist Body, who had informed him of a certain Fund that they had among them as a Superannuation Fund for worn out Ministers, and he was much more favourable to such a scheme than to the one they were compelled by the by-law to sustain. Mr. Watson, (of York), thought that the majority of Teachers in the Country were in favour of a Superannuation Fund, properly managed and under their own control. He had known several men who had paid a few dollars to the Fund, and now they were receiving large benefits from it. Mr. McCallum had interviewed the Chief Superintendent as to the manner of application, and had been informed that every obstacle had now been removed. He was, therefore, favourable to the principle of the Fund, and he thought some of the Members present would be glad some day to join the scheme. Mr. Hunter asked if this Association should take upon it, in addition to its other duties, the duties of an Insurance Company? Mr. McCallum believed they could do it. The vote was then taken on the motion, which was carried unanimously.

A Uniform System of Granting Teachers' Certificates.

Mr. McCallum moved that this Convention cordially approve of the President's suggestion in his Address, that the time of Examination of the Normal School Teachers and County Teachers be the same, that there be one set of Papers for said Examinations, and that the Masters of that School should not form part of the Examining Committee. Some discussion followed on this motion, in which Mr. Yeomans, Mr. Macintosh, Mr. Lewis, Mr. Strang, Mr. Currie, Mr. Johnston, Mr. John Campbell, and others, took part, the general opinion being expressed in the motion. Mr. Macintosh moved in amendment that the last part of the motion, namely, "that the Masters of the Normal School should not form part of the Examining Committee," be struck out. The vote was taken, and the original motion was carried unanimously.

Undue Haste in Education.

Mr. G. D. Platt, Public School Inspector of the County of Prince Edward, delivered an Address on undue haste in Education, which he considered a growing evil, and to remedy which he thought Teachers should, among other things, endeavour to inculcate into the minds of their Pupils a taste for Education, and to impart instruction as far as possible without the use of Text Books. He thought very many Teachers were guilty of the charge of proceeding too rapidly in the education of the young. Not that a good Education could be obtained any too soon, but that haste in this matter was something calculated to prevent the attainment of the end in view. Education had a resemblance to vegetation. The seed required time for growth and development, and would not allow of much hurry without injury. A forced growth almost always resulted injuriously. The process of digestion was another illustration. Undue stuffing of physical food and an overloading of the organs of digestion were prejudicial to physical health and muscular activity. Many Teachers were constantly stuffing the memories of children without reference to its baneful effects. What we wanted was more training and less stuffing,—more discipline and less attention to storing the memory. Farmers believe in deep ploughing,—in turning up the sub-soil to the influence of the sun and atmosphere. Teachers ought to practice deep teaching, instead of skimming over the minds of children, and imparting a superficial Knowledge of things. At the conclusion of the Address Mr. Platt was tendered a hearty vote of thanks.

Examinations for Teachers' Certificates.

Moved by Mr. E. B. Harrison, seconded by Mr. J. J. Tilley:—"That in the opinion of this Convention, it is desirable that all Candidates for Teachers' Certificates shall be examined at such times as to afford them an opportunity of receiving Certificates of Qualification previous to the time of opening the Schools, and that the day of the week be taken instead of the day of the month; and that the Council of Public Instruction be requested to make the necessary changes." (Carried).

Report on the Text Books in the Schools.

The Committee on Text Books reported as follows:—1. While strongly approving of uniformity in Text Books, the Committee in respect to the works below mentioned, recommend that, until such time as more suitable Text Books are provided, it be permissable to employ in our Schools standard British or Canadian publications,—"Lovell's General Geography," "Davies' English Grammar." 2. Algebra.—The Committee recommend that for elementary instruction in Algebra, Todhunter's smaller treatise be employed, while for the use of advanced Students, Sangster's treatise be retained. 3. Arithmetic.—The Committee regret exceedingly that while changes have been made in Text Books on Arithmetic without any sufficient cause, or agitation, on the other hand Text Books against which the Association has long and earnestly protested are retained.

Finally, with regard to every future educational Text Book submitted for approval to the Council of Public Instruction, the Committee recommend that such treatise, previously to such approval, be submitted to a Committee nominated by the Ontario Teachers' Association. The clause with regard to Arithmetic was withdrawn. The rest of the Report was adopted without amendment.

Moved by Mr. Kirkland, seconded by Mr. Glashan,—"That this Association highly approve of the new Text Books in Arithmetic, (a few typographical errors excepted), but would request the Author in the next Edition to add the Miscellaneous Examples from the English Edition." (Carried).

The Necessity for Teachers' Institutes.

The Committee that was appointed to prepare a Report on Teachers' Institutes submitted the following:—That under the present system of Examination it is essentially necessary to have some connecting link between our Schools and Examining Boards to provide professional training for such Teachers as do not feel disposed to attend the Normal School; and believing that Teachers' Institutes properly conducted would partially remedy the existing state of affairs, and that they would tend to systematize the whole work of our Public Schools throughout the Province, the Committee would therefore strongly urge the formation of County Institutes to be held immediately before the Summer Examinations, attendance at such Meetings to be noticed by Examiners in awarding Certificates, and to carry out the idea would recommend that the Chief Superintendent be respectfully requested to take immediate steps to put the present Law in force for this purpose.

Expenses of Representatives attending the Council of Public Instruction.

Moved by Mr. Hunter, seconded by Mr. McCallum,—"That in the event of the Legislature conceding the request of the Association for representation in the Council of Public Instruction, and furthermore, in the event of the Legislature declining to assume the expenses incurred by the attendance on the Council of such representatives as are not resident in Toronto, such expenses be defrayed by the Association." (Carried).

CHAPTER XIV.

INSPECTION OF SEPARATE SCHOOLS OBJECTED TO IN 1865 AND 1871.

Although the Separate School Act of 1863 specifically provided for the inspection of Separate Schools, by directions of the Chief Superintendent, yet it was objected to in Kingston in 1865 and in Toronto in 1871. That Law authorized the Chief Superintendent of Education to provide for this inspection of Separate Schools, and also of the Registers of those Schools. He therefore authorized the Inspectors of Grammar Schools to inspect such of these Schools as were within the limits of that part of Upper Canada assigned to them for inspection purposes.

In October, 1865, the Inspector appointed to the eastern part of Upper Canada was refused permission to inspect the Roman Catholic Separate School in Kingston. This refusal having been reported to the Chief Superintendent, he wrote to the Chairman of the Roman Catholic Separate School Board in Kingston on the subject. In his Letter he said:—

As the Law requires me to make and pay the Apportionment of the Legislative Grant to Separate Schools, it is my duty and right to see whether the data on which I make and pay such Apportionment are properly prepared and are reliable. This can only be done by having the Registers of Separate Schools examined by a duly appointed Officer.

The 26th Section of the Separate School Act of 1863 expressly provides that "the Roman Catholic Separate Schools, with their Registers shall be subject to such inspection as may be directed, from time to time, by the Chief Superintendent of Education. . ."

The same objection was made by Archbishop Lynch in Toronto in 1871, and he addressed the following Letter on the subject to the Chief Superintendent of Education:—

To our great amazement we find that our Separate Schools are visited by the Inspectors of the Common Schools. We take this occasion to protest against this intrusion, as it is contrary to the spirit of the Law establishing Separate Schools; and we will be obliged to give notice to the Trustees not to receive those visits; not that we are afraid of them, but we do not want their interference.

In his reply to the Archbishop, Doctor Ryerson said:—

I beg to observe that the protest you make, and the intention you avow, are in direct opposition to the Separate School Act, the 26th Section of which expressly provides [for such inspection]. (See this Section quoted above).

I have construed the Separate School Act, to authorize Trustees of Separate Schools in Cities, Towns and Incorporated Villages, to appoint . . . . the Local Superintendent of their Schools, but that does not preclude this Department from directing an inspection of the Register and condition of any Separate School. . . . .

Doctor Ryerson then referred to the General Regulations under which the Grammar School Inspectors were directed to inspect Separate Schools in the Neighbourhood of Grammar Schools. He then said:—

I believe these visits were very acceptable to the Managers and Teachers of the Separate Schools, and the Inspector's Report respecting them was most favourable. . . . . But in one, (Kingston), he was refused admittance . . . by the Head Teacher of the principal Separate School. . . . . .

A few days after I had written [to Kingston on the subject], I received a Letter from the Roman Catholic Bishop of Kingston, (Doctor Horan), apologizing for the conduct of the Head Teacher of the Separate School, who had mistaken his duty, and assuring me that the Inspector would be courteously received at any time he might think proper to visit the School. . . . .

I can adduce indubitable proof that I have sought to administer the Law, as much for the benefit of Separate Schools, as of Public Schools, and have given the Separate Schools the advantage of every doubt, and of any discretionary power I might have, to assert them. . . . . .

But while I have thus sought to aid Separate Schools to the utmost extent of my power, and to give the most liberal construction of the School Law in their behalf, I must say that I think your Grace's protest and intimated course of proceedings, are directly contrary to the express provisions of the Separate School Act,—the inspection of which class of Schools, under the authority of this Department, is not, as a matter of suffrage, at the discretion of the Trustees of Separate Schools, but a matter of right, provided for by Law, and which every Government ought to possess, and exercise to inspect, at its discretion, the doing of every School, or Institution, aided out of the public revenues of the Country.

NOTE. Archbishop Lynch at once courteously assented to such inspection of the Separate Schools in his Diocese, as might be directed by the Chief Superintendent of Education.

FRENCH AND GERMAN SEPARATE SCHOOLS.

There was one class of Separate Schools which gave the Chief Superintendent very little trouble. These were the French and German Schools,—chiefly Roman Catholic—which were scattered here and there throughout Upper Canada. All that had to be done in their case was to give them such teaching facilities, as enabled them to go into operation under Teachers who could speak the Language of the Ratepayers concerned, and that language only.

Happily that facility could be given under the general,—not the Separate,—School Law, and that with the sanction of the Chief Superintendent.

There were two principles which Doctor Ryerson laid down at an early period in his administration of the Education Department.

The first was,—that whenever he could meet special cases by a liberal and often, (with the sanction of the Government,) a generous interpretation of his powers under the School Acts, and in terms of his Commission as Chief Superintendent of Education, it was his duty to give that interpretation, in cases not specifically provided for,—except by analogy,—in the School Law.

The second principle which Doctor Ryerson laid down, and, which he generally adhered to, was not to propose too frequent changes in legislation, with a view to meet special cases; but only to seek such legislation at intervals of from five to ten years.

Fortunately I was familiar with Doctor Ryerson's views, as expressed in the first of the foregoing principles, which he had laid down for his guidance, when the first application was made in 1851 to grant a Certificate of Qualification to a French Teacher in the County of Essex,—which had been largely settled by French-Canadians. When this application reached me from the Board of Public Instruction for the County of Essex, Doctor Ryerson was absent. I, therefore, as Acting Chief Superintendent, submitted the application, which had been received, to the Council of Public Instruction for Upper Canada with the recommendation that it be granted. This was concurred in by the Council of Public Instruction; and I was, therefore, enabled to inform the Essex County Board that:—

The Council of Public Instruction for Upper Canada has sanctioned a liberal construction of the Programme to which you refer, making the term "English" convertible into the term "French" where it occurs, and when applied to French Candidates for Examination before the County Board of Public Instruction. The Certificate should, of course, be expressly limited to teaching in the French language.

A copy of this intimation was also sent to the then Local Superintendent of Education at Sandwich, with the following addition:—

The School Act expressly authorizes Trustees to employ any qualified Teacher they please; should, therefore, the one to whom you refer, obtain a Certificate from the County Board, the Trustees can engage his services, and no Board, or School Officer, can prevent them, as has been assumed in a Memorial transmitted to me by the Secretary of the County Board of Public Instruction, from certain inhabitants of School Section Number Six, Sandwich.

In 1858, a partial extension of the principle here laid down, was applied to German Teachers; and, to meet the case, a knowledge of the German Grammar was, by the Council of Public Instruction, substituted in the Programme of Examination, for a knowledge of the English Grammar.

In 1871, a further difficulty arose, owing to a delay of the Council of Public Instruction to provide fully for the examination and licensing of German Teachers in the German settlements of Upper Canada. To meet a special case, which occurred in the County of Waterloo, I told the Local Superintendent, who had called upon me, in Doctor Ryerson's absence:

To grant six months' Certificates to such German Candidates as would present themselves for examination in July; (and I said that), by giving the Department early notice of the real requirements in the case, attention would be given to the matter by the Council of Public Instruction, and every provision made for the examination of such Candidates, at all future Examinations.

This was confirmed by Doctor Ryerson on his return and he informed the Local Superintendent of the County, that Examination Papers in German Reading, Spelling, Etymology and Grammar might be prepared by Members of the County Board, and that the other ordinary Examination Papers could be used in the case of the Teachers who could read English.

Similar applications, made subsequently, were dealt with in the same spirit; and, in this way, every facility was given by the Education Department for the successful operation of French and German Separate Schools in the French and German Settlements in Upper Canada.

STATEMENT OF MAPS, APPARATUS AND PRIZE BOOKS SENT OUT TO THE SEPARATE SCHOOLS DURING THE YEARS 1867-1871.

1867.

Name of Place.	Roman Catholic Separate Schools		
	Maps and apparatus.	Prizes.	Libraries.
	$ c.	$ c.	
Toronto...	29 33	68 28	None.
Hamilton .	159 09	22 00	None.
Ottawa....	None.	60 00	None.
Lindsay...	None.	None.	None.

1868.

	$ c.	$ c.	
Toronto...	131 58	252 50	None.
Hamilton .	None.	20 00	None.
Ottawa ...	10 00	110 00	None.
Lindsay...	170 26	15 08	None.

1869.

	$ c.	$ c.	
Toronto...	83 00	344 11	None.
Hamilton .	50 75	60 00	None.
Ottawa . ..	None.	92 50	None.
Lindsay...	None.	35 82	None.

1870.

Name of Place.	Roman Catholic Separate Schools		
	Maps and apparatus.	Prizes.	Libraries.
	$ c.	$ c.	$ c.
Toronto...	74 75	613 46	None.
Hamilton .	None.	50 00	None.
Ottawa ...	None.	115 00	None.
Lindsay...	None.	24 00	200 00

1871.

	$ c.	$ c.	$ c.
Toronto...	111 05	433 18	None.
Hamilton .	None.	60 00	None.
Ottawa ...	30 00	75 00	None.
Lindsay...	None.	None.	20 72

NOTE. It was owing to the active efforts of the Reverend M. Stafford, Roman Catholic Priest at Lindsay, that an excellent Library was established in that Town in 1870. It was replenished in the following year.

CHAPTER XV.

REPORT AND SUGGESTIONS WITH RESPECT TO THE HIGH SCHOOLS AND COLLEGIATE INSTITUTES OF ONTARIO, FOR THE YEAR 1871.

BY THE REVEREND J. G. D. MACKENZIE, M.A., AND JAMES A. MCLELLAN, M.A., LL. B., INSPECTORS OF HIGH SCHOOLS.

Having sent in to the Department our Semi-annual Reports, more, or less, in detail, of the results of our inspection of the High Schools and Collegiate Institutes during the past year. we have the honour to submit the usual Annual summary of our Remarks and Suggestions.

Classics and English Classes in the Grammar and High Schools.

The heavy yoke of compulsory Latin having been taken from the necks of our youthful population, on the memorable 15th of February, 1871, there was, of course, a numerous exodus from the region of "qualifying" Classics, the Girls, especially, effecting a speedy migration into the more congenial English sphere. Yet the abandonment of Classical Study has been by no means so general as might have been anticipated, under more or less of violent reaction after unnatural constraint. Perhaps the greater difficulties of the English Course, with its much larger quantum of Science, have saved some copies of the Introductory Book and Reader from being consigned to dust and oblivion; but we may hope that those who have taken the Classical Course, when free to do otherwise, mean work, and will, many of them, do work which shall help to redeem the ancient Classics in this Province from any unmerited prejudice, that may still exist against them. A powerful stimulus is about to be applied in every department,—the stimulus of merit recognised and rewarded; of inefficiency and failure visited with pecuniary loss. Of the Classics, as on every other subject, this must exert a quickening influence. Masters will be inspired with an honourable emulation; and even Pupils may be brought to feel that upon their personal exertions depend, in large measure, the prestige and the very resources of their Schools. Classes will be kept more on the *qui vive;* the blunders they make will have a special gravity, and call for special vigilance on the Master's part. Even in rural parts we may hope that no toleration will be extended,—as we know unhappily that toleration has been extended,—to such specimens of Virgilian Astronomy as "Jupiter fastening the stars over the kingdoms of Lybia,"— *"Lybiæ defixit lumina regnis;"* and even, if in rural parts Latin should die out, we shall not be greatly afflicted if we can only get the Mother Tongue to thrive. Already there has been improvement in quarters where laxity was the order of the day,—more of thoroughness and accuracy; more of accidence, less of Anthon. Still there are weak points. We should be glad to see Grammar, for example, more systematically studied as an independent subject, not limited to what is suggested by the Text that is being read. We are not of those who consider versifying as one of the highest exercises of the human intellect, and have no desire to perpetuate here the undue attention which, under the old training, was usually given to it; but we cannot refrain from expressing our great regret that the faculty of writing Latin Prose is possessed in so small a degree by the Pupils of our High Schools. As a general rule, even Arnold's Book is by no means mastered; but little, for the most part, is done in it, and that little not well done; whilst the attempt to deal with a translated extract from Cicero,—the translation being extremely literal,—has proved, with very few exceptions, a failure.

In the study of the Mother Tongue progress has unquestionably been made. There is more of dexterity, not perhaps in quoting, but in applying the rules of Grammar; there is more of accuracy in Spelling. The Inspector, amongst some four, or five, distinct exercises in English, exacts a Letter to be written, quite impromptu, in the School, and in his presence. Not a few of these Compositions are most creditable,— easy, graceful, and natural,—the Girls usually taking the lead.

Inferior Place of Reading in the Grammar and High Schools.

Whilst in some of the Schools great attention is paid to the most important subject of Reading, and the scientific method of teaching it is successfully pursued, in many others a lamentable deficiency must be reported. In not a few Schools it is almost entirely neglected, no place being assigned to it in the Programme of weekly exercises. In many others it occupies altogether a subordinate position, and forms only incidentally a part of the School work; as, for example, when a class in History, or English Literature, is to recite, its members are permitted, before recitation, to "go over" the Lesson as an exercise in Reading; and in only a few Schools is it taught with a true regard to scientific principles, and with a full appreciation of its worth as a means of culture. It

11a—XXIII.

seems to be taken for granted that it is essentially a Public School subject, and that it is so well taught as to relieve the High Schools of all responsibility in the matter, especially when there are so many other departments in the prescribed Course which seem to be practically of higher importance. This is certainly a grave mistake. Even if the Public Schools were to do their work as efficiently as possible, it is the function of the High Schools to complete what the humbler Institutions may have well begun. Many children leave the Public Schools at so early an age, that they cannot have become good Readers in the true sense of the word; and, therefore, to perfect them in this rare and valuable accomplishment is a duty as commanding as any that pertains to the High Schools. And, if it is the business of the latter to improve upon what is excellent in the teaching of the former, they certainly cannot escape the obligation to remedy what is defective. Now, Reading, as well as some other branches, has not been generally taught with a high degree of efficiency. Its value as a means of cultivation of the vocal organs, and as a discipline of the intellect and heart, has not been generally recognized. And while Arithmetic and some other subjects have had their enthusiastic Teachers and admirers, Reading has been considered as comparatively unimportant; at least few have been so thoughtful as to "do it reverence." The cultivation of the vocal organs ought to begin when the child begins to speak; it certainly should be kept constantly in view when the child begins to read. At quite an early age a thorough mastery of the different sounds of the language, and the habit of distinct enunciation, are to be acquired, as well as flexibility of voice and facility of utterance. To this end thorough teaching is required. A Student may become tolerably proficient in Arithmetic and Algebra, with but little instruction; but in order to become a good Reader the aid of a capable and thorough Teacher is indispensable. The Pupil must hear a correct enunciation of the consonant and vowel sounds, to be able by practice to acquire it for himself; he must hear the Teacher give these sounds in a clear, full and melodious tone of voice, in order to become completely master of a similar clearness, and fulness, and melody of tone; he must hear these sounds given again and again with an endless variety of pitch, and force, and inflection, in order to make thoroughly his own like habits of distinct enunciation and readiness of utterance.

That these things are heard in the generality of Public Schools none will be found to affirm. On the contrary, the monotone of the primary School Rooms, where most careful attention and exquisite skill are essential to the right cultivation of the plastic organs of speech, and their accessories,—the hard, metallic tone, the imperfect enunciation, the utter inflexibility of voice, have become proverbial.

It seems to be considered that, since the easy sentences of the primary Reading Books are not the vehicles of what is brilliant in thought, or touching in pathos, there is little, or nothing, to be done but to make the child familiar with the forms of words and approximately familiar with their sounds. But even such sentences as,—"Ben and Fan are at tea,—Ned has a new bow, it is made of yew, he ran off to-day to try and get a few nuts," have their meaning; they can be read with some degree of naturalness; they may be made subservient, since they are in general arranged with special reference to this important end,—to that invaluable cultivation of the vocal organs to which reference has been made. In consequence of inattention to this most important matter in the Primary Schools, habits of imperfect speech are formed, which are almost ineradicable, which assuredly can be eradicated only by the most painstaking and persevering efforts in the more advanced classes of the Public Schools, and in the High Schools. Speaking generally, such efforts have not been made, partly because the Masters, especially in the High Schools, have had too much work to do, but chiefly, it is thought, because the importance of this interesting branch of Education has not been fully appreciated. The exercise of Reading, instead of being made,—what it might easily be made,—interesting, profitable, and attractive, is too often a dry routine, as irksome to the Teacher as it is profitless to the Pupils; the aim of all concerned seems to be to dispose of the repulsive task as quickly as possible. The "Teacher" may, indeed, call attention to a mispronunciation, or a neglected pause; or may mildly suggest that the Reading is too rapid and indistinct, or not sufficiently expressive; he may even formally state some of the characteristics of good Reading, but after all, little real effort is made to improve the style of Reading.

It is not enough that the Teacher should speak of faulty enunciation; he must show his Pupils what correct enunciation is, and drill them into its attainment. It is not enough to censure in general terms rapid Reading; he must show them the effect of a better style and make them strive to secure it. He may occupy half an hour urging the necessity of "Reading with intelligence and expression;" but five minutes spent in showing them by example what such Reading really is, would be much more interesting, and infinitely more profitable to the Pupils. For the way to good reading, like that to virtue, and many other things, is "long by precept, but short by example." But it is not enough that the exercise of reading should be made a means for the cultivation of the vocal organs; it should be made an instrument for the discipline of the intellect and the emotions. Hence care should be taken that the lesson is thoroughly comprehended,—instead of which it is too frequently the inelegant and mechanical utterance of unmeaning sounds. If the subject of the lesson be argumentative, let the Pupils fully perceive the cogency of the argument and comprehend the value of the truth it establishes. If it is poetic, let them be made to appreciate its moral as well as its artistic beauties If it involves the pathetic, let it be so read that it cannot fail to have an influence on the affections. And thus truth for the intellect, beauty for the imagination, and pathos for the heart, shall combine their influence in the formation of a character at once of beauty and of power. It has been said that the Americans are, as a nation, deficient in melody of speech,—"that music of the phrase, that clear, flowing, and decided sound of the whole sentence, which embraces both tone and accent, and which is only to be learned from the precept and example of an accomplished Teacher." The deficiency here mentioned may become a national characteristic of ourselves, unless Reading attain a higher place in the estimation of our Teachers, and in the work of the School Room. But let the subject be carefully taught in all the Classes of the Public Schools; and let the work thus well begun be heartily carried on by earnest and capable Teachers in the High Schools, and we shall, perhaps, avoid the squeaking voice, the nasal twang, the soulless expression of beautiful thoughts, the certain legacy of bad teaching, and acquire perfect enunciation, an ease of utterance, a general melody of speech, that will make our language which the cynic poet terms "harsh, whistling, grunting, gutural,"—scarcely less musical than the soft bastard Latin, "whose syllables breathe of the sweet South."

The Study of French and German in the High Schools.

German is taught in a few of our High Schools; French, in all, with one, or two, exceptions. By far the greater proportion of those Pupils who have taken up French, are Girls. It is gratifying to observe this growing taste amongst our Girls for a graceful and elegant language, so peculiarly a woman's study and accomplishment as French is. It is to be hoped that such works as the "History of Charles XII," and Corneille's Tragedy, "Horace," will come to the aid of a high and pure English literature, in fortifying the minds of our young women against the many publications of the day, that are calculated to turn the minds of young people, and to destroy the charities and joys of the Christian Home. We do not doubt that the French which is acquired at our High Schools by the more advanced Pupils, will be turned to good account, although we cannot refrain from adding, that it would be none the worse for greater attention to purity of accent.

We hope to be able to report, after the next inspection, a large increase in the numbers studying German.

Failure in Teaching Mathematics in the High Schools.

We regret to have to state that, with a few gratifying exceptions, the standing of the Schools in this Department is rather low. In some cases, perhaps, the Mathematical

Teachers, having passed through their University Course, and graduated with a minimum of mathematical knowledge, do not possess that thorough mastery of the subject which is essential to successful teaching. In others, again, there seems to be no just appreciation of its value, both as a means of intellectual discipline and as a necessary element in material progress. But the deficiency referred to may, doubtless, be accounted for chiefly by two causes,—the low attainments of the Pupils when admitted to the High Schools, and the unreasonable amount of work thrown upon the Masters. The latter, indeed, may to some extent, be a consequence of the former; but we are of the opinion that, even if the standard for admission were strictly maintained, it would still be impossible for one Master to perform, efficiently, all the work required at his hand, and raise his School to that state of excellence which alone can justly entitle it to the name of High School Much less can it be expected that so desirable a result can be attained to under the system which has hitherto prevailed, of crowding Pupils into the High Schools who should have remained years longer in the Public Schools.

We regard, therefore, the appointment of an Assistant Teacher in each of the Schools in which but one Master has been employed, as absolutely necessary, if the High Schools are to accomplish the purpose for which they have been instituted.

With this additional assistance, we can venture to predict a rapid increase in the efficiency of the Schools,—a more thorough and satisfactory training in all the Departments of the prescribed Course, including Mathematics. We should like, however, to see somewhat more enthusiasm among our Teachers of Mathematical Science,—a living consciousness of its worth as an instrument of Education. There was a time when far too much was claimed for it by its worshippers,—when it alone was deemed an all-sufficient means for the harmonious evolution of the intellectual powers. This over-zealous assertion of its exclusive merits provoked a reaction,—a "counter-exaggeration," —the influence of which has not yet passed away. Without adopting the extreme opinions of the Mathematical enthusiast, it might easily be shown that, when properly taught, Mathematics cultivate and develop, to a high degree, the powers of memory, abstraction, and generalization,—that they familiarize the mind with the forms of strict logical inference, and impart habits of accuracy in the use of language, caution in the admission of premises, ingenuity in analysis and comparison, and power of continuity of thought,—and are, therefore, entitled to a prominent place in every system of liberal Education. Their value as a logical exercise of mind is very great. They make the mind familiar with the characteristics of sound reasoning, and arm it with sagacity to discover the fallacies most likely to ensnare it. However valuable logic itself may be as the science of the necessary laws of thought, its full utility is realised only in the practical application of its prinicples. The mere mastery of the formal laws of thought is not sufficient; there must be exercise, or practice, in the processes which the mind must follow in all correct reasoning. Logic may unfold the characteristics of the laws of thought, and thence deduce the necessary conditions of cogency in reasoning; but the mind can become familiar with these conditions, and habituated to their observance, only by practice in their application.

For this purpose Mathematics stand pre-eminent, affording as they do constant exercise in the practical application of logical principles, and, therefore, educating the mind to a sagacity in detecting error, that the mere study of the formal laws of thought cannot impart. Yet it has been said that this Science can only educate to a minimum of thought, because its principles and every step in its processes are self-evident. Such an assertion could have only emanated from an uncandid critic, or a novice, in the Science. If by self-evident prinicples are meant such as are passively received,—as the assertion in question implies,—then Mathematical principles are not self-evident; still less are the propositions whch are deduced from its principles, and which themselves become principles in the endless chain of argument by which the Science is developed. The fundamental principles of pure Mathematics strike the mind with a conviction of their truth as soon as they are understood; and the successive steps in Mathematical demonstration are "equally self-evident," as soon as their relation is clearly comprehended; this is the true meaning of self-evident truths in Mathematical Science.

But a vigorous exercise of mental power is necessary to comprehend the relations between abstract propositions so comprehensive, and to perceive their self-evident nature in their necessity and universality. This is true of pure Mathematics, and still more of applied Mathematics, in which, to the difficult abstractions of pure science, are added new conceptions of physical laws, which increase the complexity of the data, the abstruseness of the connecting propositions, and the consequent laboriousness of the train of reasoning. Is there no energy of thought required to comprehend the successive steps in the sublime Geometry of Newton? The eleventh Section of his Principia "is characterized by a spirit of far-reaching thought, which distinguishes it beyond any other producton of the human intellect." Does it require only a minimum of thought to follow his reasonings, and to fully grasp the fruitfulness of his results? By the application of analysis, the complicated dynamics of the Planetary System are brought within reach of the human intellect,—do the investigations determine thought to "its feeblest development?" We are, however, extending to too great a length our "plea for Mathematics." The value of Mathematics, and, in fact, of every other branch, as a means of mental discipline, depends on the mode in which they are taught; and, in this respect, the Mathematical teaching in the High Schools is not all that it should be. Too much is made of rule and formula, and too little of principles.

Let us particularize somewhat. Trigonometry is taught in so few of the Schools that it requires no special remark at present. Greater attention is given to Euclid. In the few first-class Schools it is taught with an intelligent appreciation of its value in discipline, and of the mode in which it should be taught, in order that this value may be fully realized. But, in many of the Schools, the lesson in Geometry is a mere routine,—the Pupil having no clear ideas of the premises from which he reasons, of the conclusion to be established, and of the true logical processes of the demonstration. The "two invaluable lessons," which Mill says "we learn from our first studies in Geometry," are, therefore, certainly not learned. The Pupils are not taught to "lay down, in express and clear terms, all the premises from which they intend to reason; and to keep every step in the reasoning distinct and separate from all the other steps," making "each step safe before proceeding to another step, and expressly stating, at every point of the reasoning, what new premises are introduced," so that logical habits of mind may be formed, and so acute a perception of the form and essence of sound reasoning, that the mind is enabled, instinctively, as it were, to detect the presence of even the most subtle fallacies. Something more should be done than mere book-work, even if the propositions are "gone over" with some degree of thoroughness. The knowledge acquired should be applied to the solution of independent problems,—a course which but few of the Schools follow. "Deductions" form no place in too many Schools; and in many others the opinion is held and acted upon, that "four Books" should be thoroughly mastered before any attention is given to independent propositions. This is a mistake. Just so soon as a Pupil has fairly mastered any of the Propositions, he can certainly be taught to exercise his ingenuity upon others, whose solutions depend solely on the application of the principles he had already acquired. By such a course, the Propositions themselves would be better understood,—by such a course only can the benefits to be derived from Geometry, as an instrument of Education, be completely realized. In Arithmetic, we find the Pupils, too generally, slaves of rule and formula,—not capable of interpreting the formula, (which ought to be banished from Arithmetic), and perfectly in the dark as to the reasons of the rule. They are quite oblivious of the fact that it has a principle, or, granting that it has, they have not the slightest idea that it concerns them to know it. The rule is memorized; it is applied to the solution of questions to which it is supposed to be applicable, from the fact that they are "set under it," and whose phraseology goes far to verify the supposition. And all this is too often not only countenanced, but encouraged, by the Teacher, who is sometimes heard to declare that "it is useless to spend time in teaching principles,—what our Pupils want is, to become practical Arithmeticians!" Precisely so. We wish to make them practical Arithmeticians, but the slave of rules can never be truly practical. He only can be truly practical, whose knowledge is founded on principles which he comprehends, and who has been so trained to habits of analysis, that he is independent of all formal rules. We have found that the rule-taught "practical" Boys are not very practical in the solution of a practical question unless they are told what "rule" applies. They apply the rule to the examples under it; they work mechanically; they are mere machines, except as to accuracy; they "manufacture" figures, and the practice may be of some little use as an exercise of the muscles of the fingers; but is absolutely useless as an exercise of mind. Let us give a few examples illustrative of the "practical" teaching. In some of the Schools this question was proposed:—"If I give to five Boys four dollars each, how much do I give away in all?" Without dwelling on the fact that very few Pupils in any of the Schools could work the question in accordance with the principle which it was intended to illustrate, we may state that not a few solved the question "by the Rule of Three." They gave the answer, $20. "How did you get is?" "I said, as one Boy is to five Boys, so is four dollars to the answer!" "But why did you follow that roundabout way of doing it?" "Because 'tis a question in simple proportion." In fact, the phraseology suggested the rule. In a very good School, in which the Pupils were quite expert in the application of the rule when the knew what rule to apply, the following question was given:—"Bought 5,225 lbs. of coal at $7.25 per ton of 2,000 lbs., what was the cost?" None of the class could "find the cost." The Teacher, somewhat chagrined at their failure, said, "If you'll allow me to state the question, I think they'll do it." Assent was, of course, given, and he stated the question thus:—"If 2,000 lbs of coal cost $7.25, what will 5,225 lbs. cost." And the question was soon worked out by several of the Class; they had recognized the familiar language of the "Rule of Three," which was thus made to usurp the place of the simple Rules. In all the Schools the following questions, among others, were proposed:—"My purse and money together are worth $48.60; the money is eleven times the value of the purse: what is the purse worth?" "An army lost one-tenth of its number in its first battle, a tenth of its remainder in its second battle, and then had 16,200 men left; how many men formed the army at first?" It will, perhaps, hardly be believed that more than ninety-five per cent. of the Pupils in the High Schools failed in the first question, and a much larger percentage failed in the second! Here are some of the records. In a School of 21 Pupils neither question solved; in one of 25, neither question; in one of 23, neither; in one of 32, one solved the first question; in one of 19, neither question solved; in one of 60, neither solved; in one of 25, neither solved; in one of 92, one solved both; in one of 43, one solved both; in one of 84, one solved the first; in one of 120 (present), ten solved the first, and three the second; in one of 72, five solved the first, and one the second; in one of about 120, twenty-nine solved the first, and one the second.

These questions are certainly not difficult; the first is very easy; but the Pupils could not assign it a place under any of the Rules they had learned, and it was therefore to them a very enigma. Yet but few of them had difficulty in following the analysis:— "There is the purse itself?" Yes,—"There is the money which is worth eleven purses." Yes,—"Both are therefore worth twelve purses." Yes,—"Thence 12 times purse's worth, is equal to $48.60, and the purse is worth one-twelfth of that sum, that is $4.05." Yes, they could all see that; and all wondered that they "had not thought of that before." The solutions to the second question were few and far between. One Master objected to the question as being beyond the province of Arithmetic,—as being too Algebraic,— and declared that he "would never bring his Pupils face to face with such questions!" Yet, the question is not difficult, even for children. At all events, quite a number of very "little fellows" who had barely "got through Fractions," were able to fully understand the solution:—"One-tenth of the army having been destroyed in the first battle, there were nine-tenths left." Yes. "One-tenth of that is how much?" Nine hundredths. "Then taking nine-hundredths from nine-tenths, which is ninety-hundredths, what is left?" Eighty-one hundredths. "And if eighty-one hundredths of the army are equal to 16,200, what is one hundredth equal to?" Two hundred, that is the whole army, is equal to what?" To 100 times 200, or 20,000 men, and they were greatly mortified that a question so easy had proved too much for them. In a few Schools the examination in Arithmetic was excellent, the Pupils well trained to think out questions, independently of formal rules, and they, therefore, answered well questions on principles, and readily solved far more difficult problems than those given above. What has been said concerning Arithmetic, may be applied to Algebra. It is not generally taught as a Science; there are rules committed to memory; and there is the mechanical application of the rules,—this, but nothing more. Let it not be supposed, that we consider the Masters wholly to blame for this state of things. They have had more work than they could possibly do, and do it well; but if assistance be given them,—and this is indispensable,— we have no doubt that our next inspection will show a marked and gratifying improvement.

The Teaching of Natural Science Important.

The value of Natural Science as a part of a School Curriculum, can hardly be over-estimated. The way to truth by reasoning has long been known and followed by not a few; but the way to truth by observation and experiment is a comparatively recent discovery. Indeed this discovery has hardly yet been turned to account; we are disinclined to leave the beaten path,—the stereotyped course of Study,—but we can no longer resist the tendencies of the age, and Experimental Science must now have a place in every Curriculum. Our Schools will be greatly benefited by the change. The introduction of a new Study, possessing in itself a rare quickening power, will be found not to task the children beyond their strength, but to give increased power in mastering the branches of the old routine. "There is no intellectual discipline more important than that which these Sciences afford; the study, on the one hand of Mathematics and its applications, on the other of Experimental Science, prepares us for the principal business of the intellect." As these subjects had been but just introduced at the time the Schools were visited, they call for but few remarks. We may, however, be permitted to express a hope, that Teachers will bear in mind that these Sciences are experimental. that habits of observation cannot be cultivated by merely memorizing the facts and principles and classifications given in Text Books,—that by such a course, these interesting subjects, instead of being in an eminent degree attractive, will become utterly repulsive and lose all their quickening power,—that they can be best taught without Text Books; and that if they are not well taught, they should not be taught at all.

The Undesirable Establishment of New High Schools.

Many Schools have been established in localities where they were indisputably not needed, and where there is no probability of their being required to do *bona fide* High School work. This premature action is possibly due partly to the existence of an aristocratic feeling on the part of locally prominent men, through which the Public School is looked upon as something "low,"—suitable only for the *ignobile vulgus;* partly to a spirit of rivalry, which leads to the demand for a "High School," because a certain Town, or Village of not greater progressive tendencies has one; partly because, from the mode of distributing the Grammar Shcool Fund under the old Law, "it paid" to have a High School to do Public School work,—and partly because there exists a deplorable ignorance of the noble work that can be accomplished by an efficient Public School. Whatever may be the causes, the effects upon national education are simply disastrous. If the School is established through the influence of the few, it has to contend with the perpetual indifference,—and sometimes antagonism,—of the many. If it is opened in conformity with the popular voice, the Public School is almost destroyed, in the attempt to keep up a High School, which, in spite of such attempts, remains what it was at its beginning,—a mere abortion. It is not too much to say that High Schools have been opened in places which cannot, or at all events which do not, maintain a decent Public School. The result is that the Public School is bad, and the so-called High School considered even as a Public School, is worse; we say considered as a Public School; in fact, it can be said without exaggeration, that only by a very liberal exercise of the imagination, can such Schools be regarded as even fair Public Schools. From what we have seen, we know that High Schools have been established ever since the new School Act came into operation, in localities which had not, and have not now, made due provision for the wants of their Public Schools, and which are in fact violating the Public School Law, through an inability or an unwillingness to provide the requisite number of Teachers to do the Public School work. In one of the places referred to,—which had paved the way for the establishment of a "High School," by dismissing one of its Public School Teachers,—we found 100, 90, and 75 Pupils respectively, in the three divisions of the Public School! Imagine a Girl of seventeen years of age, in charge of 100 Pupils in the "Infant" Class! And yet this Village "felt it must have a High School," and it has one! Since this tendency to establish High Schools is rife among us, we would respectfully suggest that no such School should be permitted in any place that has not a thoroughly efficient Public School. No man in his senses will say that a High School ought to be opened where there is not such a Public School. Let a thorough inspection of the Public Schools of every place that asks for a High School be specially made by the High School Inspectors, or by other authorities, and let the request be not complied with, whenever it is found that a good Public School is not maintained; for assuredly, any locality that is too mean-spirited to establish and maintain a good Public School cannot be expected to equip and maintain an efficient High School.

More than Literary Qualifications of High School Teachers Required.

We had intended to make a few remarks on this topic, but must be content with a bare reference to it. It is the opinion of not a few, that, as a University Degree is no indication as to a man's ability as a Teacher, some additional qualification should be demanded,—some evidence that, in addition to scholarship, there is a knowledge of School Organization, Methods of Discipline, Government, Modes of Teaching, etcetera. Something of this kind seems to be necessary. The stripling fresh from his College Halls is placed on a level with the experienced Teacher, too often thinking that, having taken Honours in Languages, or Science, he consequently knows all about the work of the arduous profession upon which he has entered. Could not lectures on "Pedagogy" be delivered in the Universities for the benefit of those intending to teach? Or could not provision be made for giving such instruction in the Normal Schools?

Admission of Pupils to the High Schools.

The Examination and admission of Pupils is elementary work, but it is very important work. It virtually decides whether the Public School has done its part, and in what condition the High School ought to receive those who are to be the recipients of the higher instruction it has to communicate. The experience of years has taught on this head lessons of great value, which our Educational Authorities have not failed to turn to good account; and so distinct and positive has this teaching been, that there is perhaps no feature of our School System in which we are more directly led to safe and sound conclusions. The utter inefficiency of the old Grammar School arrangements in this respect, with their low standard of attainment, and their very imperfect mode of Examination, was so notorious, and the mischief done to both classes of Schools so great, that every one was brought at last to feel that the evil was one that was eating the very life out of our Schools. It was felt that the starting point had been fixed so deplorably low, that no goal of high attainment would be reached; and that nothing short of a radical change in conducting the Examinations for admission would save the education of the Country. Professor Young's strong sketches left no doubt as to the real state of things, and very suggestive were they of the sort of educational chaos into which the Country was being brought. "Boys and Girls alike, with the merest smattering of English Grammar,—every child supposed to have any change of wriggling through the meshes of the Inspector's examining net,—driven like sheep into the Grammar School, and put into Latin in order to swell the roll of Grammar School Pupils, and to entitle the School to a larger share of the Grammar School Fund." It is well that we should keep that picture before us, with all its associations of unworthy manœuvring to combine the maximum of money with the minimum of Education, both that we may the better appreciate our deliverance from such a state of real degradation, (for it was nothing else), and be led to watch the more anxiously any efforts, if haply such should be made, to check and turn back the upward movement which the new School Law has so happily initiated. In connection with this low standard,—parsing a simple sentence in English being practically the only test,—we may mention one fact that shows, amongst many others, how terribly in the day of which we are speaking, things were unhinged and out of course. As soon as the new School Act became Law, the Inspector received instructions from the Department to apply with greater strictness the old method and standard, until they should be superseded by the new. Just one change was made, but that was found all-sufficient : the parsing, instead of being given orally, was exacted in writing. The effect was most remarkable. About one-half of the Candidates presented to the Inspector as fit subjects for High School tuition were found, to a lamentable extent, incapable of spelling correctly in writing,—whatever they may have been able to do orally,—words certainly not amongst the most difficult in the language, more particularly those very terms of Grammar which were almost every day in their mouths. Much harm, unfortunately, had already been done, but how much more would have been done but for the salutary interposition of the Inspector between the High School, with its coveted Legislative Grant, and the pushing tendency of the local Authorities! At last came the system under which we have been working for a twelvemonth,—the Board of Examiners attached to each School, whose admissions are made final on approval by the Inspector, who is "to see that the Regulations and Programme of Examination provided according to Law are duly observed," and, therefore, not vitiated by the admission of Pupils who do not come up to the prescribed standard. It is plain enough that this is a vast improvement on the old plan, yet far from perfection; for one thing it wants, and without that it will never command public confidence,—uniformity. It is felt that, though it protects the High School from many an unfit Pupil that would have crept in under the "simple parsing" system, it nevertheless works unequally, and with all the care the Inspector can exercise, it must work unequally, so great is the disparity between the different sets of questions, as put by different Examining Boards. There is, it is true, the expedient of exacting a higher percentage where the questions are easier, and this has been resorted to in some cases, but the proceeding is viewed with so much disfavour, and is so much regarded as an arbitrary act of the Inspector, that we have no high opinion of it as a remedy. There is but one course which can be considered fair to all, and that is, providing the same Examination for all, subject always, of course, to that indispensable safeguard, revision by the Inspectors . That course, we are glad to see, has been adopted by the Department, under whose instructions questions for the Entrance Examinations have been prepared by the High School Inspectors, to be submitted to all the Schools. This will excite general satisfaction, as a most commendable move in the direction of uniformity, and, we may hope, will quite dispel that feeling of uneasiness to which the absence of uniformity has given birth.

In a few, a very few, instances, the local Examining Boards have objected to the revision, by the High School Inspector, of their reports of the Entrance Examination results. They seemed to think the exercise of such a power of revision by the Inspector a reflection upon their honour as men, and their ability as Examiners, and signified their intention of "trying to have repealed the obnoxious Section of the Act which confers such powers." We cannot sympathize with this feeling. No one can deny the right, nay the duty, of the Government to exact such conditions for the admission of Pupils as shall secure that degree of qualification at entrance, without which it is impossible for the Schools to accomplish the work for which they were designed, and for which they annually draw a liberal allowance from the Public Treasury. Is the constitution of the Local Boards such as to guarantee that these conditions shall be satisfied?

With the highest respect for the gentlemen composing these Boards, we venture to think not. The work of examination is practically in the hands of the High School Master and the Chairman of the Board of Trustees; these constitute a majority of the Examiners, and are questionless a unit upon all the questions concerning the admission of Pupils. Now we have a high opinion of the honour, integrity, and ability of the Chairmen of our Boards of Trustees, and in all these points we believe our High School Masters will compare favourably with any Teachers in the world; but as it is the ambition,—laudable enough we are sure,—of these gentlemen to have as many Pupils as possible in their School, in order that it may compare faovurably with others, and secure a fair proportion of the High School Fund; their inclination may, therefore, warp their judgment, and render them unwittingly less strict than they ought to be in fulfilling the requirements of the School Law. But there is no need of theorising,—of any speculative arguments upon this point. Granting all that can possibly be desired by the most sensitive spirit,—granting that the Examining Boards are composed of men of unimpeachable integrity and unquestionable ability, there still remains the stubborn fact,—that, both under the old Law and under the new, Pupils have been hurried into the High Schools who were utterly unqualified. If it be asked why the Inspectors did not exercise the veto power which had been given them, we reply, because, as there were upwards of a hundred different Examining Boards and, therefore, as many different standards of admission, there was no uniform and certain test which they could apply to the different cases. All the Examining Boards had adopted fifty per cent. of the total marks assigned to the Examination Questions, as the standard for the admission of Candidates; and there would have been no difficulty in applying this test of a successful Examination, had the questions been the same for all the Schools. But here there was great diversity; fifty per cent. on the Examination Papers used in a few of the Schools, constituted a higher standard than sixty, or seventy, or eighty, or even a hundred per cent. would have been in other cases. But if we attempted to exact a higher percentage upon these inferior Papers, when it was known that fifty per cent. had been adopted throughout the Country as the minimum for entrance, we were immediately taxed with the exercise of arbitrary power.

"You passed Pupils in the K. School on a minimum of fifty per cent. and why do you exact a higher standard from us?" was the remonstrance not unfrequently heard. It was useless to urge that the K. School had set most excellent Papers, and that its fifty per cent. was in reality higher than seventy per cent. on proportionally easier Papers. Hence, acting upon their own convictions, and in accord with the expressed opinion of the ablest and most experienced Masters, the Inspectors made the recommendation above referred to,—that Examination Papers should be prepared under the authority of the Department, so as to make the Entrance Examination and the test for admission the same for all the Schools. If this be carried out, the Inspectors can have no difficulty in exercising the veto power in cases which call for the discharge of so unpleasant a duty,—certainly, when the standard is fixed and uniform, they cannot be charged with having exercised their power in an arbitrary manner. The gentlemen whose views we are discussing, admitted that, upon the removal of all restraint, the "tendency" would be to crowd the High Schools with unprepared Pupils, and thus lessen their efficiency,— or rather prevent their attaining to that degree of efficiency which alone can render them worthy of the name. But they thought that this evil could be remedied by the classification of the Schools, and the application of the principle of "payment by results." We cannot admit this.

Average attendance must always be an element in determining the distribution of the High School Fund; and as many Schools can have no expectation of ranking high, these will be tempted to compensate by numbers what they lose in grade.

Moreover, when Schools have attained to a high grade, they cannot easily be degraded; the "tendency" above stated would prevail; many unqualified Pupils would be admitted; and, although the efficiency of the School would in reality be impaired, any attempt to degrade it would be at once designated as an "act of arbitrary power."

Many of the Schools are now quite low enough; but remove all check to the admission of Pupils, and there is yet a lower depth to which they may sink,—a depth of utter uselessness—a depth in which they must be an unmeasured injury to the highest interests of Education.

The objection that the veto power is a reflection upon the uprightness of the Members of the Board, is without weight; at least, it has no greater weight than if urged against the inspection of the Schools themselves. For the High School Master, to all intents and purposes, is the Examining Board, the Chairman of the Board of Trustees leaving,—at least in a great many cases,—the business of the Examination entirely in his hands.

If, therefore, the inspection of the Examination Papers and the results of the Examination, is a "reflection" upon the honour of the Examiners, much more is the inspection of the Schools, which subjects all the classes of the most able and accomplished Teacher to the test of Examination by a disinterested and independent Examiner.

Payments by Results very Desirable.

In applying this principle of "payment for results," there are two great points to be settled.

First.—The mode of ascertaining the status of the School.

Secondly.—The principle, based on the ascertained status of the School, according to which each School is to receive its due proportion of the Legislatuve Grant.

In estimating the status of the School, we propose to adopt the following mode of procedure:—We commence with assigning to each subject of Study, in the authorized Programme, a maximum valuation, in marks, arranging the subjects in five groups, —four of which we regard as equivalent,—fixing the relative value of the remaining one according to the best of our judgment.

(1) English Branches; (2) Classics; (3) Mathematics; (4) Natural Science; each valued at 120. (5) Modern languages, 80. After adequate inspection of each subject, we propose to indicate the standing of the School in each by a graduated system of marking similar to that which has been adopted in grantng Teachers' Certificates, adopting four classes however; with a determinate percentage for each. We think it would be desirable that the standing of the Schools, as determined by the Inspectors, should be published in the *Journal of Education*, at what might be deemed a convenient time, in Tabular form, of which the following will serve as a specimen:—

	English	Classics	Mathematics	Natural Science	Modern Languages
School at A.	I.	II.	I.	I.	II.
School at B.	II.	I.	II.	II.	I.
School at C.	III.	IV.	IV.	II.	IV.

We use the expression "adequate inspection," not intending thereby the Examination of all the classes in each subject, which our experience under the new system convinces us is impossible within the time at our command, but such inspection as shall enable the Inspector to form, on fair and reasonable grounds, an honest, and, as far as may be, accurate judgment of the ability and success with which each subject has been taught. In some of the subjects the Inspector may find it necessary to examine all the Classes before he can arrive at such a decision as will satisfy him, and with judicious management it will be quite possible to do this in these particular instances; but to attempt it in all cases is out of the question, and, happily, is not indispensable. We desire to have it distinctly understood that, in expressing by a definite valuation our estimate of the "proficiency of the Pupils," we shall take largely into account the degree of ability, fidelity and sound judgment displayed by the Master, in the instruction and government of his Pupils. Where the general discipline of the School is unsatisfactory, a lower condition as to attainment will usually result, and will bring its due penalty with it; but, in some instances, it might be deemed advisable to make a deduction from the Appropriation in proportion to the gravity of the case.

A Tabular Statement similar to the one which has been given above, in which the status of each School in each of the departments of Study should be exhibited, having been prepared, one of the four following modes of procedure might be adopted for the purpose of determining the Appropriation.

1. The average performance of the School might be taken, and the School placed with reference to its average, in one, or other, of the four Classes it is proposed to form. Certain Rates, varying of course, in amount, would be attached to the Pupils, according to the class in which each School should be placed. This is substantially the plan recommended by Professor Young in his Address to the Teachers' Association.

2. A system of deductions for shortcomings might be applied.

3. A certain amount might be appropriated to each of the four departments of Study, and distributed in varying rates per pupil, according to the standing of the School in each department.

4. Some method might be adopted for combining, in another way, the new element of proficiency with the mode at present pursued, which takes into account average attendance only.

Plan 1 is extremely simple, but is open to this objection, that under it the good work in one department would counterbalance the bad, and thus,—the status of the School having been once fixed, poor work, if confined to a single department, would escape all penalty, unless the work were so poor as to justify the extreme penalty of degrading the School.

2. The difficulty referred to as connected with plan Number 1, may be met, without degrading a School to a lower class, by making a deduction for (marked) inefficiency in any department, according to the following plan. It will be observed that the same number of marks has been assigned to each of the departments of Classics, Mathematics, Natural Science, and English, whilst two-thirds of that unmber has been assigned to Modern Languages. What we would call a perfect School,—that is, first class in every department,—would, therefore, be represented by the number $4\frac{2}{3}$ (Classics 1 $+$ Mathematics 1 $+$ Natural Science 1 $+$ English 1 $+$ Modern Languages $\frac{2}{3}$). Now, let every School that obtains the required percentage, (say 75), of the aggregate of marks be placed in the First Class; but, if a School has failed to obtain this percentage in any department by a certain number of marks, let the fraction, or percentage, which this number of marks is of the whole percentage, (75), be deducted from the number representing a perfect School. For example,—suppose that one of the First Slass Schools has obtained the requisite First Class percentage in Modern Languages, Natural Science, English, but only two-thirds of it in Mathematics, and one-third in Classics; then its standing will be,—Modern Language 1 $+$ Natural Science 1 $+$ English 1 $+$ Mathematics $\frac{2}{3}$ $+$ Classics $\frac{1}{3}$,—that is, 4; but a perfect School should be $4\frac{2}{3}$, therefore, the School in question will be only $\frac{4}{4\frac{2}{3}} = \frac{6}{7}$ of a perfect School; and thus will lose one-seventh of what it would be entitled to as a perfect School. This method of procedure would remedy the defect alluded to.

3. Another plan may be suggested, inferior in point of simplicity to plan Number 1, but free from its defect. Let the standing of the Schools in each department be determined as before; let the total average attendance in each Class of the several departments be ascertained from the half-yearly Returns and the Reports of the Inspectors; let the Grant be distributed among the different departments in proportion to the marks allotted to each, as given above; let the amount apportioned to each department be divided in given ratios among the number of 1st, 2nd, 3rd and 4th class Pupils in that department, so as to ascertain the amount per Pupil to be given to each class, and so for all the departments; then the amount per Pupil to be given to each School, according to its rank, or classification, in the several departments, is readily determined. This scheme will probably be made plain by illustration. Suppose the returns give a total average attendance of one thousand Pupils, and that $14,000 is the amount of the Grant; we

wish to find how much per Pupil is to be given to each School. The distribution of this amount according to the value assigned to each department will be as follows:—

English branches .... 120 marks = $3,000
Classics .... 120 marks = 3,000
Mathematics ....: 120 marks = 3,000
Natural Science .... 120 marks = 3,000
Modern Languages .... 80 marks = 2,000

Now we find from the Inspectors' Reports the one thousand Pupils classified as follows,—

Class.	I.	II.	III.	IV.
English	250	350	220	180
Classics	200	250	250	300
Mathematics	150	350	250	250
Natural Science	200	275	250	150
Modern Languages	120	140	240	300

We now divide the $3,000 apportioned to the English Department amongst Two hundred and fifty first class Pupils, three hundred and fifty, Second, two hundred and twenty, Third, and one hundred and eighty, Fourth, in given ratios, say four, three, two, one, determining the amount for each Pupil in the different Classes, and proceed in the same manner with the other departments. Making the calculation according to the above suppositions, we should have for each Pupil in,—

Class.	I.	II.	III.	IV.
English	$4 50	$3 37	$2 29	$1 12
Classics	5 12	3 84	2 50	1 27
Mathematics	5 00	3 75	2 50	1 25
Natural Science	5 00	3 75	2 50	1 25
Modern Languages	5 72	4 29	2 86	1 43

Hence, if a School of forty, (average), be first class in all the departments, the portion will be $25.34 × 40; if it had been ranked first class in Classics and Mathematics, second class in English and Natural Science, and third class in Modern Languages, the several amounts per Pupil will be, English, $3.37; Classics, $5.12; Mathematics, $5.00; Natural Science, $3,75; Modern Languages, $1.43; Total per Pupil, $18.67. The total Apportionment in this case will be $18.67 x 40.

4. If we start with the assumption that a Pupil in Class I, and, therefore, receiving an education, the best that is given in our High Schools, may be regarded, with a view to the appropriation, as equivalent to a larger number in an inferior class, we have suggested to us the idea of a set of multipliers to be combined with the statement of average attendance, as it is made at present. Let these multipliers be in the first four departments of study, 4, 3, 2, 1; and in Modern Languages, 2.7, 2, 1.4, .7. Let us apply this method in the case of some particular School,—one for example, of the following numbers, (average attendance), and standing:—

High School at B——, average attendance in English Course, forty-five; in Classical Course, fifteen; in Mathematics, sixty; (= sum of E. and C.) in Natural Science, fifty; and in Modern Languages, twenty. These last two averages, it will be seen would be required in the half-yearly Return, but it would give but little additional trouble to introduce them. We suppose the status of the Schools to be as follows:—Classics, I; Mathematics, II; English, I; Natural Science, III; Modern Languages, II; its claim upon the Grant would then be ascertained in the following manner:—

		$
English, Class	I. 45 by 4—	200
Mathematics	II. 60 by 3—	180
Classics	I. 15 by 4—	60
Natural Science	III. 50 by 2—	100
Modern Languages	II. 20 by 2—	40
	Total	$580

Each School having been treated in this way, the maximum required to calculate the rate would be of course the sum of the totals thus obtained; let us assume this maximum to be 90,000, and that the Legislative Grant amounts to $20,000: the appropriation to this particular Schools is easily arrived at by means of the proportion,—90,000 : 580 : $20,000 : $129, nearly. This is, in short, as compared with the mode in use at present,—an application of the principle of Compound Fellowship instead of Simple. Of course, in actual calculation, the several totals which would be inconveniently large, could be reduced in any convenient proportion.

The Proposed Classification of Schools.

At the present moment it would be impossible to apply either the third, or the fourth, scheme, as the half-yearly Returns,—which, as we have said, would require to be slightly altered in form for either of those plans,—do not furnish the requisite information; but it may serve a good purpose to classify the Schools on the basis of Plan I; and we have, therefore, the honour to submit the following list, which we ask your permission to make public in this way, under the impression that it will both prepare Masters and Trustees for the application of the principle of "payment for results," and give a definite conception of its probable effects There will be, of course, a revision of the list at the close of the next inspection, when we fully expect that we shall have the satisfaction of removing to a higher grade several of the Schools which, in consequence of their staff of Masters being incomplete, unwise haste in admitting Pupils, so as to crowd the lower classes, or other unfavourable circumstances, do not at present occupy the status which they will, doubtless, eventually reach.

Class I.—Galt, Hamilton, Kingston, Ottawa.—4.

Class II.—Barrie, Brampton, Clinton, Cobourg, Colborne, Dundas, Gananoque, Napanee, Oshawa, Paris, Perth, Peterborough, Port Hope, St. Catharines, St. Marys, Stratford, Toronto, Welland, Whitby.—19.

Class III.—Beamsville, Belleville, Berlin, Bowmanville, Brantford, Brockville, Cayuga, Chatham, Elora, Farmersville, Fergus, Fonthill, Goderich, Grimsby, Guelph, Ingersoll, Lindsay, London, Markham, Morrisburgh, Newcastle, Newmarket, Omemee, Owen Sound, Picton, Prescott, Sarnia, Simcoe, Smith's Falls, Smithville, St. Thomas, Uxbridge, Windsor, Woodstock, Weston.—35.

Class IV.—Alexandria, Almonte, Arnprior, Bradford, Brighton, Caledonia, Carleton Place, Collingwood, Cornwall, Dunnville, Iroquois, Kemptville, Kincardine, L'Orignal, Manilla, Metcalfe, Milton, Mount Pleasant, Niagara, Newburgh, Norwood, Oakville, Oakwood, Orangeville, Osborne, Pakenham, Pembroke, Port Dover, Port Perry, Port Rowan, Renfrew, Richmond Hill, Scotland, Stirling, Strathroy, Streetsville, Thorold, Trenton, Vankleek Hill, Vienna, Walkerton, Wardsville, Waterdown, Williamstown.—45.

It will be seen that four Shcools only have been placed in the first class; those, therefore, which stand in the second class must be regarded as possessing a high rank, although not the highest. It is unnecessary to point out that, as to the amount apportioned from the Legislative Grant, their position will be a very good one indeed, as there are so few Schools above them.

We deem it right to draw attention specially to the fact, that in some cases where undue anxiety has been manifested to swell the number of "Entrance Pupils," what has been gained in numbers has been lost in status, there being in such cases but a small number of advanced Pupils as compared with the total number enrolled.

In relation to Class IV, we agree in considering the following Schools as not only at present far below the standard of High Schools, but as likely to remain so for years to come, since the Villages in which they are situated have not as yet Public Schools in a sufficiently effective condition to furnish material for the support of anything worthy of the name of High School, videlicet, Richmond, Pakenham, Osborne, Alexandria, Metcalfe, Manilla, Oakwood, Stirling, Scotland and Wardsville. Walkerton has been placed in Class IV. because it is a new School, and has been visited by only one of the Inspectors. It has its position to win.

As the pecuniary interests of the Schools are directly involved in their status, as determined by the Inspectors, it will not take us by surprise if our arangements be sharply criticized; and very probably some of the Masters and Trustees will feel disappointed at seeing their Schools in a lower position than they have been expecting to occupy. We need not say that our judgment has been exercised with careful deliberation and strict impartiality, and we place this list before the public with a full conviction that substantial justice has been done to all. The subjoined Statement, for which we are indebted to Mr. Marling, of the Education Office, exhibits conclusively the superiority of the new system to the old, enabling us, as it does, to compare the Apportionment, as it was for the half year immediately preceding the period at which we write, with the Apportionment as it would have been if the new system had been in force, and if the rate attached to each class, (which is given here simply for the purpose of illustration), had been fixed by the proper authority.

Statement Respecting the High School Apportionment for the First Half of 1872.

The Apportionment for the first half of 1872 was based upon average attendance, without taking into account the minimum rate of $400 per annum for each School, the intention being to make up the Grant, at the distribution to take place at the end of the year, to the minimum sum of $400, to those Schools which would not have gained that sum during the year on the basis of attendance simply.

But to illustrate, partially at least, the effect of "paying by results," the Apportionment actually made for the first half of 1872 is exhibited in the subjoined Statement, column 3, (at the rate of $9 per Pupil), and in column 4, the Apportionment is given as it would have been had each smaller School received at least the minimum of $200 for the half-year, the rate being reduced to $8.55; while, in column 5, is shown a supposed Apportionment with the same amount to be distributed, and the same attendance, but with rates of grant differing according to the classes in which the Schools have been respectively placed by the Inspectors, while the minimum Grant of $200 is secured to each School.

The rates thus adopted, by way of example, are $10.50 for Class I, $9.50 for Class II, $7.70 for Class III, and $5 for Class IV. Should this mode of distribution be adopted, the rate to be assigned to each class will be considered and determined by the proper authority.

NAMES OF HIGH SCHOOLS.	Average Attendance First Half, 1872.	Apportionment on basis of Attendance at $9 per Pupil, (as paid.)	Apportionment on basis of Attendance, at $8.55 per Pupil, reserving a Minimum of $200 for each.	Apportionment on basis of Attendance, at the following rates: Class I ...$10.50 Class II... 9.50 Class III.. 7.70 Class IV.. 5.00
CLASS I.		$	$	$
Galt..................	121	1,089	1,034	1.271
Hamilton.............	130	1,170	1,111	1,365
Kingston.............	71	639	607	745
Ottawa..............., ..	77	693	658	808
Total 1st Class.......	399	$3,591	$3,410	$4,189
CLASS II.		$	$	$
Barrie	41	369	350	390
Brampton.............	61	549	522	580
Clinton..............	31	279	265	295
Cobourg	103	927	881	979

Statement respecting the High School Apportionment, First Half of 1872.—*Continued.*

High Schools.	Average Attendance: First Half, 1872.	Apportionment on basis of Attendance, at $9 per Pupil, (as paid).	Apportionment on basis of Attendance, at $8.55 per Pupil, reserving a Minimum of $200 for each.	Apportionment on basis of Attendance, at the following rates: Class I....$10.50 Class II... 9.50 Class III... 7.70 Class IV.. 5.00
CLASS II.		$	$	$
Colborne......................	38	342	325	361
Dundas........................	64	576	547	608
Gananoque....................	39	351	333	371
Napanee......................	114	1,026	975	1,083
Oshawa.......................	67	603	573	636
Paris..........................	37	333	316	352
Perth..........................	49	441	419	466
Peterborough.................	112	1,008	958	1,064
Port Hope....................	62	558	530	589
St. Catharines...............	134	1,206	1,146	1,273
St. Mary's....................	36	324	308	342
Stratford.....................	58	522	496	551
Toronto.......................	111	999	949	1,045
Welland.......................	40	360	342	380
Whitby........................	93	837	795	884
Total 2nd Class......	1,290	$11,610	$11,030	$12,249
CLASS III.		$	$	$
Beamsville....................	29	261	248	223
Belleville.....................	61	549	522	470
Berlin.........................	18	162	200	200
Bowmanville..................	45	405	385	346
Brantford.....................	61	549	522	470
Brockville....................	60	540	513	462
Cayuga	30	270	256	231
Chatham......................	45	405	385	346
Elora.........................	20	180	200	200
Farmersville	30	270	256	231
Fergus........................	25	225	214	200
Fonthill	20	180	200	200
Goderich	31	279	265	238
Grimsby......................	38	342	325	293
Guelph........................	30	270	256	231
Ingersoll......................	41	369	351	316
Lindsay	30	270	256	231
London.......................	162	1,458	1,385	1,247
Markham......................	25	225	214	200
Morrisburgh..................	31	279	265	238
Newcastle.....................	29	261	248	223
Newmarket....................	34	306	291	262
Omemee.......................	41	369	350	315
Owen Sound..................	67	603	573	516
Picton........................	63	567	539	485
Prescott	28	252	239	200
Sarnia........................	33	297	282	254
Simcoe	51	459	436	392
Smith's Falls.................	40	360	342	308
Smithville	27	243	231	208
St. Thomas...................	53	477	453	408
Uxbridge.....................	22	198	200	200
Weston........................	32	288	274	246
Windsor.......................	19	171	200	200
Woodstock....................	42	378	359	323
Total 3rd Class......	1,413	$12,717	$12,235	$11,113

Statement respecting the High School Apportionment, First Half of 1872—*continued.*

High Schools.	Average Attendance, First Half, 1872.	Apportionment on basis of Attendance, at $9 per Pupil, (as paid.)	Apportionment on basis of Attendance, at $8.55 per Pupil, reserving a Minimum of $200 for each.	Apportionment on basis of attendance, at the following rates: Class I....$10.50 Class II... 9.50 Class III.. 7.70 Class IV.. 5.00
CLASS IV.		$	$	$
Alexandria	16	144	200	200
Almonte	10	90	200	200
Arnprior	16	144	200	200
Bradford	20	180	200	200
Brighton	14	126	200	200
Caledonia	28	252	239	200
Carleton Place	11	99	200	200
Collingwood	18	162	200	200
Cornwall	13	117	200	200
Dunnville	28	252	239	200
Iroquois	64	576	547	320
Kemptville	20	180	200	200
Kincardine	26	234	222	200
L'Orignal	16	144	200	200
Manilla	24	216	205	200
Metcalfe	14	126	200	200
Milton	20	180	200	200
Mount Pleasant	23	207	200	200
Niagara	14	126	200	200
Newburgh	40	360	342	200
Norwood	26	234	222	200
Oakville	21	189	200	200
Oakwood	12	108	200	200
Orangeville	15	135	200	200
Osborne	15	135	200	200
Pakenham	17	153	200	200
Pembroke	10	90	200	200
Po t Dover	22	198	200	200
Port Perry	19	171	200	200
Port Rowan	19	171	200	200
Renfrew	17	153	200	200
Richmond Hill	23	207	200	200
Scotland	24	216	205	200
Stirling	15	135	200	200
Strathroy	27	243	231	200
Streetsville	13	117	200	200
Thorold	37	$333	$316	$200
Trenton	22	198	200	200
Vankleekhill	16	144	200	200
Vienna	32	288	273	200
Wardsville	28	252	239	200
Waterdown	25	225	214	200
Williamstown	32	288	274	200
Total 4th Class	922	$8,308	$9,558	$8,720

Summary.

4 Schools Class I	399	$3,591	$3,410	$4,189
19 Schools Class II	1,290	11,610	11,030	12,249
35 Schools Class III	1,413	12,717	12,235	11.113
43 Schools Class IV	922	8,308	9,558	8,720
	4,024	$36,226	$36,235	$36,271

Note.—It will be observed that the system of payment set forth in column 4, secures an increased rate for Schools placed in the first or second class, while Schools of the third and fourth classes receive less: but the provisions for a larger minimum Grant than formerly protects them in the enjoyment of at least $400 from Government per annum, and prevents the superior schools from receiving very large Grants. Richmond and Walkerton received no Grants for the first half of 1872.

12a XXIII.

The preceding Statement tells its own story. It is quite manifest that great injustice has been done to our good Schools by allowing the poor Schools,—some of them worse than useless, as checking the improvement of the Public School,—to absorb public money which ought to have gone to encourage and strengthen the Schools that are doing true High School work in a creditable way, so as to confer a real benefit on the Country. It is true much, under the new system, has to be left to the judgment of the Inspectors, and Inspectors are but men, and may err; but certainly no errors made by Inspectors, in the honest and impartial exercise of their judgment, are likely to inflict on our deserving men and our best Schools, anything like the discouragement and the injury which must result where numbers only are taken into account.

J. G. D. MACKENZIE,
J. A. McLELLAN, } Inspectors.

TORONTO, 187—.

LETTER FROM DOCTOR TASSIE, HEAD MASTER OF THE COLLEGIATE INSTITUTE AT GALT, TO THE CHIEF SUPERINTENDENT OF EDUCATION ON THE HIGH SCHOOL COURSE OF STUDY.

The course of study for the High School I have seen of course, and think well of it, except that the standard for entrance, as regards the English Branches and Common Arithmetic is too high, while that for Mathematics is too low. However, the Schools as now constituted are calculated to be an inestimable benefit to the Country at large, and I congratulate you that, towards the close of your public career, you have accomplished completely, conjointly with the establishment of a College, or School, of Technology, the Educational Structure in Ontario.

We have attending our School at present about 160 pupils, all Boys and Men, of course, and for the tuition of those we have a Staff of four Masters, Heads of Departments; and three assistants, this apart from Collateral Branches, Drawing, Music and Drill, with Fencing and Gymnastics, for each of which there is a separate Master. About 120 of these Pupils are the sons of the wealthy educated classes. not in Ontario only, but also in Quebec and the Southern States.

You will easily perceive that the School has so completely outgrown the other Schools that in some respects, indeed in many, its circumstances are altogether different, so that Rules and Regulations, admirable as they may be, as applied to them, would be fatal to our existence, I hope then you will accord to us considerable liberty of action, or if the Law lately passed will not allow of this, you will not oppose our going to the Legislature to get a Separate Act suited to our circumstances.

The needs of our School are precisely those of Upper Canada College, Helmuth College, Lennoxville School, etcetera. The chief exemption we would ask, as essential to the existence of the School, is to have the privilege of taking in the Pupils of the same age and state of advancement that the foregoing Schools do. We do not in the least seek exemption from inspection and control, but merely such relaxation from the general system as may be necessary for not our well being only, but for the actual existence of our School in its present shape.

GALT, September 25th, 1871.   WILLIAM TASSIE.

REPLY TO THE FOREGOING LETTER BY THE CHIEF SUPERINTENDENT OF EDUCATION.

I have the hour to state in reply to your letter of the 25th ultimo, that in regard to the High School Programme, the Classical part is necessarily provisional; and in revising that, after the action of the Senate of the University of Toronto, in regard to the Matriculation Examination, the Council of Public Instruction may amend anything in the details of other parts of the Programme which the experience of the half-year may suggest, as reported by the Inspectors, and suggested by such experienced Masters as yourself.

In respect to the Programme for Collegiate Institutes the only material variation from the High School Programme can be its extension, so as to include the Honour Subjects of Matriculation into the University. But I think your wishes may be met by authorising a preparatory class, or Department, in connection with the Collegiate Institutes, but for the pupils in which an apportionment from the High School Fund cannot be made, as that Fund must be apportioned to all Collegiate Institutes and High Schools upon the same conditions. If this will meet your case, 1 will be happy to submit to the Council of Public Instruction a regulation to give it effect.

TORONTO, 3rd October, 1871.   EGERTON RYERSON.

(NOTE. Except it may have been verbally, but there does not appear to have been any written reply received from Doctor Tassie to this Letter).

CHAPTER XVI.

ANNUAL REPORT OF THE NORMAL, MODEL, HIGH AND PUBLIC SCHOOLS IN ONTARIO, FOR THE YEAR 1871.

TO HIS EXCELLENCY THE HONOURABLE WILLIAM PEARCE HOWLAND, C.B., LIEUTENANT-GOVERNOR OF THE PROVINCE OF ONTARIO:

May it Please Your Excellency,—

I herewith present my Report to your Excellency on the condition of the Normal, Model, High and Public Schools of the Province of Ontario, for the year 1871, and for the Twenty-eighth year of my incumbency.

It is gratifying to be able to state that, although the large increase of the School Fund* by local effort, in 1870, over that of 1869, was $116,938, yet the increase of that Fund for 1871 by the same local efforts over that of 1870 amounts to the unprecedently large sum of $179,594. Thus the "School Fund," for 1871, was $671,456, and for 1870, $564,536,—the County assessment, for 1870, being $385,284, and for 1871, $492,481. The whole number of Pupils in the Schools is now 446,326,—an increase of 3,808 over last year.

I will now proceed to give a summary view of the condition of the High and Public Schools of Ontario, condensed from the Tables accompanying this Report:—

I.—*Table A.—Receipts and Expenditure of Public School Moneys.*

1. The amount apportioned from the Legislative Grant in 1871 was $178,975. The amount apportioned for the purchase of Maps, Apparatus, Prize and Library Books was $15,195,—increase, $789.

2. The amount from County Municipal Assessment was $492,481, showing a remarkable increase of $107,196, or an increase eight times greater than the increase of 1869 over that of 1870.

3. The amount available from Trustees' School Assessment was $1,027,184, (now over a million of dollars), increase $76,085.

4. The amount from Clergy Reserves Moneys and from other sources, applied to School purposes in 1871, was $410,633,—increase, $3,688.

5. The Total Receipts for all Public School purposes for the year 1871 amounted to $2,124,471, or considerably over two millions of dollars, showing an increase of $180,106 over the total Receipts of the preceding year, being the greatest and most gratifying increase ever reported since the establishment of our Public School System. Considering

---

* The legal definition of the term "School Fund" is that the School Fund is made up of the Legislative Grant and the County Assessment. and does not include the School Trustees Assessments. or receipts from other ources. The term "School Moneys" includes the "School Fund" as well as other moneys.

that this was the first year of the operations of the new School Act of 1871, this result is most encouraging, and speaks well for the educational prosperity of the Country.

6. As an evidence of the continued financial prosperity of our Public Schools, I insert the following interesting Table, showing the progressive increases in the amounts levied by the Municipal and School Trustee Corporations, and also the yearly increase in the total Receipts since 1860,—the year in which the School Law Amendment Act was passed. These facts strongly illustrate the growing interest felt in the prosperity of our Schools by the local School Authorities. The Table is as follows:—

—	1860.	1861.	1862.	1863.	1864.	1865.
County Municipal Assessment	$278,693	$278,085	$274,471	$287,768	$304,382	$308,092
Trustees' School Assessment	556,682	587,297	620,268	631,755	659,380	711,197
Total receipts	1,324,272	1,381,279	1,396,123	1,432,885	1,484,187	1,545,000
Increase in total receipts	14,452	57,006	14,843	36,762	51,301	60,813

—	1866.	1867.	1868.	1869.	1870.	1871.
County Municipal Assessment	$319,154	$351,873	$362,375	$372,743	$385,284	$492,481
Trustees' School Assessment	760,366	799,708	855,538	890,834	951,099	1,027,184
Total receipts	1,607,971	1,670,335	1,789,332	1,827,426	1,944,364	2,124,471
Increase in total receipts	62,970	62,364	118,997	38,098	116,938	180,106

1. The amount paid by Trustees for Salaries of Teachers in 1871 was $1,191,476. This, of course, does not represent the total Salaries of Teachers, but simply the amount which has been paid to Teachers up to the date of the Trustees' Report; these Reports, under the new system of inspection, were more promptly prepared than on any previous occasion. The balances due the Teachers were included in the unusually large balance reported in the Trustees' hands,—being $88,872, as against only $29,774 of the previous year.

2. For Maps, Globes, Prize Books and Libraries $33,083,—decrease, $808. The Legislative aid given to Trustees for these objects was $15,195.

3. For Sites and Building of School Houses, $261,833,—increase, $54,233. This unprecedentedly large increase is without parallel, and is no doubt due to that most salutary provision of the new School Law, which requires the Trustees to provide suitable Accommodation for all the Pupils in their School divisions. Even this great increase, (of $54,363), in the Trustees' Expenditure for Sites and School Houses does not, (for the reasons stated in the first paragraph of this Section), represent the total Expenditure under this head for 1871, owing to the unusual balance in the hands of Trustees at the end of the year. The increased Expenditure must, therefore, be estimated as nearly $75,000 more than in 1870. The increased Expenditure under these heads, in 1870, was but $16,129, and, in 1869, only about $5,000. This Expenditure of upwards of One quarter of a million dollars for Sites and School Houses in 1871 is a permanent increase in the value of Public School property, and indicates much additional material prosperity in the several neighbourhoods which were benefited by the Expenditure.

4. For Rents and Repairs of School Houses, $63,152,—increase, $1,292.

5. For School Books, Stationery, Fuel and other expenses, $253,748,—increase, $67,620. The "other expenses" are, doubtless, for fuel and other contingencies not formerly reported by the Trustees.

6. Total Expenditure for all Public School purposes, $1,803,294,—increase, $91,233. The total increase in Expenditure for Public School purposes, (even during the shorter period in 1871, as explained above), was nearly $100,000 over that of 1870,—not including the large balance, $88,872, reported in the Trustees' hands at the date of their Reports.

7. Balances of School Moneys not paid at the end of the year when the Returns were made, $321,176,—increase, $88,872; a large proportion of which is due for Sites and School Houses and to Teachers, as already explained.

II.—*Table B.—School Population, Ages of Pupils, Pupils attending Public Schools, Average Attendance.*

The Statute requires that the Trustees' Returns of School population shall include the number of children between the ages of five and sixteen, resident in their School Division; but it confers the equal right of attending the Schools upon all residents in such division between the ages of five and twenty-one years.

1. The School population reported by Trustees, (including only children between the ages of fiive and sixteen years), was 489,615,—increase, 5,649.

2. The number of Pupils between the ages of five and sixteen years attending the Schools was 423,033,—increase, 2,545. Number of Pupils of other ages attending the Schools, 23,293,—increase, 1,263. Total number of Pupils attending the Schools, 446,326, —increase, 3,808.

3. The number of Boys attending the Schools, 235,066,—increase, 1,685. The number of Girls attending the Schools, 211,260,—increase, 2,123.

4. The ages of Pupils are this year reported for the first time. There are 2,291 under five years of age; 197,293 between five and ten; 198,168 between ten and sixteen; 22,491 between sixteen and twenty-one, and 26,083 whose ages are not reported.

5. The number reported as not attending any School is 38,535,—increase, 7,270; of these 38,535, 12,018 were between the ages of seven and twelve years, which are the ages fixed by the new Law, during which all the children of a School Division should receive instruction in some School. The attention of Trustees, Parents, and Inspectors is called to this fact, in the hope that this ominous and humiliating item will soon be greatly lessened, or disappear, through the Christian and patriotic exertions of the people at large, aided by the new amendments in the School Law on the subject of Compulsory Education.

III.—*Table C.—Number of Pupils in the Different Branches of Instruction.*

1. This Table has been rendered necessary in consequence of the system of classification of Pupils which the new Programme has introduced into the Public Schools. It presents a most striking fact, and shows that the number of Pupils which have been put back from the higher classes of the old system to the first and second classes under the new system are 31,164, or 22.751 of the first class, and 8.413 of the second. It also shows how faithful have been the County Inspectors in the discharge of this most unpleasant part of their duties, in carefully examining and classifying, according to their attainments, the Pupils in the various Schools.

2. Another gratifying fact is shown by this Table in the large number of Pupils who are reported as studying the additional subjects required to be taught by the new Public School Act.

3. The Table is referred to for further information in regard to the number of Pupils in each of the several subjects taught in the Schools,—indicating, as noted, a gratifying increase in the numbers engaged in studying the higher branches of the Programme.

IV.—Table D.—Religious Denominations, Certificates, Annual Salaries of Teachers.

1. *Number of Teachers, Male and Female.*—In the 4,598 Schools reported, 5,306 Teachers have been employed,—increase, 141; of whom 2,641 are male Teachers,—decrease, 112; and 2,665 are female Teachers,—increase, 253. It will thus be seen that the number of female Teachers is year by year increasing, and that of males decreasing.

2. *Religious Persuasions of Teachers.*—Under this head there is little variation. The Teachers are reported to be of the following persuasions:—Church of England, 911,—increase, 42; Church of Rome, 623,—increase, 31; Presbyterians, (of different classes), 1,583,—decrease, 6; Methodists, (of different classes), 1,662,—increase, 153; Baptists, (of different classes), 298,—decrease, 16; Congregationalists, 66,—decrease, 10; Lutherans, 15,—decrease, 6; Quakers, 19,—increase, 5; Christians and Disciples, 34,—decrease, 13; reported as Protestants, 44,—decrease, 73; Unitarians, 14,—increase, 10; other persuasions, 37.

N.B.—Of the 623 Teachers of the Church of Rome, 374 are employed in the Public Schools and 249 are Teachers of Roman Catholic Separate Schools.

3. *Teachers' Certificates.*—Total number of certificated, or licensed, Teachers reported is 5,306,—increase, 245; Provincial Certificates, 1st Class, 327,—increase, 8; 2nd Class, 517,—increase, 168; County Board Certificates of the old Standard, 1st Class, 1,512,—decrease, 449; 2nd Class, 1,503,—decrease, 599; 3rd Class, 400,—increase, 70; New County Board Certificates, 657; Interim Certificates, 390.

4. Number of Schools in which the Teacher was changed during the year, 900,—increase, 233. I cannot but regret this growing tendency in the part of Trustees to change their Teachers. Such a change cannot, as a general rule, be beneficial to the Pupils. It has the effect of rendering the instruction desultory, and without any continuity, and weakens the tie which should exist between Pupil and Teacher.

5. Number of Schools which have more than one Teacher, 328,—increase, 6. Under the new Law, this increase must be much greater next year.

6. *Annual Salaries of Teachers.*—The highest Salary paid to a male Teacher in a County, $825,—the lowest, $100 (!); in a City, the highest, $1,000,—the lowest, $400; in a Town, the highest, $1,000,—the lowest, $260; in an Incorporated Village, the highest, $600,—the lowest, $240. The average Salary of male Teachers in Counties was $254,—of female Teachers, $182; in Cities, of male Teachers, $629; of female Teachers, $236; in Towns of male Teachers, $483; of female Teachers, $225; in Incorporated Villages, of male Teachers, $419; of female Teachers, $186. While the increase in the number of Schools reported is 14, and the increase in the number of Teachers employed is 141, the increase in the number of Pupils is 2,545, there is no increase in the largest Salaries paid Teachers, except in Cities, Towns, or Villages. Amongst the worst enemies to the efficiency and progress of Public School education, are those Trustees and Parents whose aim is to get what they mis-call a "cheap Teacher," and who seek to haggle down the Teacher's remuneration to as near starvation point as possible, although in reality, they are intellectually starving their own children and wasting their time by employing an inferior Teacher. Business men find it to their interest to employ good Clerks, as one good Clerk is worth two poor ones; and in order to obtain and retain good Clerks they pay them good Salaries. Experience has long shown the soundness of this business rule and practice in the employment of Teachers; yet how many Trustees and Parents, in School matters, abandon a rule on which not only the Merchant, but the sensible Farmer acts in employing Labourers, preferring to give high wages for good Labourers, than to give lower wages to poor Labourers. Good Teachers cannot be got for inferior Salaries.

V.—Table E.—School Sections, School Houses and Titles, School Visits, School Lectures, School Examinations and Recitations, Prizes, Time of Keeping Open the Schools, Prayers, Sunday Schools, etcetera.

1. The whole number of School Sections reported, 4,653,—increase, 14, chiefly in new Townships. The number of Schools reported as kept open is 4,598,—increase, 32, these also mostly in new Townships.

2. *Free Schools.*—I rejoice to be able to state that after twenty years had elapsed since the question of Free Schools was first left as a subject of discussion and voting at the Annual School Meetings, the voice of the Country, which had been so fully and so repeatedly expressed on it, has at length had an utterance in the Legislature; and that, from the year 1871, the Public Schools of the Province of Ontario have been declared Free to all residents between the ages of five and twenty-one years.

3. The number of School Houses built during the year in Counties was 202, of which 78 were of Brick, 15 of Stone, 84 Frame, and 25 Log. Three School Houses in Cities are reported as having been built during the year; 11 in Towns, and 6 in Incorporated Villages. Those built, I am happy to state, have been mostly of Brick.

4. The whole number of School Houses reported is 4,676, of which 98 are Brick. 425 Stone, 1,928 Frame, 1,425 Log. I shall refer to this subject in a subsequent part of this Report.

5. *Titles to School Sites.*—Freehold, 4,212,—increase, 62; Leased and Rented, 464,—increase, 22.

6. *School Visits.*—By Inspectors, 10,934,—increase, 486; by Clergymen, 7,617.—increase, 893; by Municipal Councillors and Magistrates, 3,241,—decrease, 95; by Judges and Members of Parliament, 395,—decrease, 122; by Trustees, 1,905,—increase, 330; by other Persons, 3,068,—decrease, 1,490. Total School visits, 75,809,—increase, 2. This does not indicate any diminution of zeal and interest in Public School education on the part of those whose duty, and interest, and privilege it is to elevate and strengthen public opinion in this first work of civilization, and by personal presence and counsel to prompt and encourage the most indifferent Parents to educate their children.

7. *School Lectures.*—By Inspectors, 2,278,—decrease, 486; by other persons, 365,—increase, 75. Whole number of School Lectures, 2,643,—decrease, 411. The Lectures. delivered by other than Inspectors are, of course, voluntary; but the Law requires that every Inspector shall deliver, during the year, at least one Lecture on education in each School Section under his charge; and the number of School Sections reported, with Schools open in them, is 4,598. There are, therefore, 2,320 School Sections, with Schools open, in which the requirement of the Law, in regard to delivering an educational Lecture, has not been observed. The large reduction in the number of Township Superintendents has, of course, to do with the falling off in the number of Lectures delivered. Many of the County Inspectors have informed me that during this, their first year of office, they preferred to give the time to the examination and classification, and, in many cases, to the actual organization of Schools. Next year will, no doubt, witness a revival of this most useful and appropriate means of stimulating local zeal in educational matters. It would be singular, indeed, if one Lecture a year in each School Section, on some subject of educational requirement, or progress, could not be made instructive and popular. It is, however, gratifying to observe that the number of visits to Schools by the Inspectors was equal to the requirements of the Law. Their effect has already been most salutary upon the Schools.

8. *Time of Keeping the Schools Open.*—The average time of keeping the Schools open, including the Holidays, was eleven months and six days, in 1871. This is nearly twice the average time of keeping open the Public Schools in the State of Pennsylvania and Ohio, and about three months more than the average time of keeping them open in the States of New York and Massachusetts,—arising chiefly from our making the Apportionment of the School Fund to School Sections not according to population, but according to the average attendance and the time of keeping open such Schools,—that is, according to the number of Pupils instructed in the Schools.

9. *Public School Examinations.*—The whole number of Public School Examinations was 7,284,—increase, 187; though less than two for each School. The Law requires that there should be in each School a public quarterly examination, of which the Teacher should give notice to Trustees and Parents of Pupils, and to the School Visitors, (Clergymen, Magistrates, etcetera), resident in the School Sections. I think the time has now arrived, (under the new and improved system inaugurated by the School Law and

Regulations of 1871), to make it my duty hereafter to withhold the Apportionment of the School Fund from the Schools in which this provision of the Law is violated. Good Teachers do not shrink from, or are indifferent to, public Examinations of their Schools. They seek occasions to exhibit the results of their skill and industry; but incompetent and indolent Teachers shrink from the publicity and labour attendant on public Examinations of their Schools. The stimulus to progress caused by such Examinations, together with tests of efficiency on the part of Teachers, and of progress on the part of Pupils, cannot fail to produce beneficial effects on Parents, Pupils and Teachers, as well as on the interests of general and thorough Public School Education; and such Examinations will doubtless, under the new and improved Programme of Studies, command a large attendance of Parents, Trustees, and friends of the Pupils of the School.

10. *The Number of Schools holding Public Recitations* of prose, or poetry, by the Pupils was 2,639,—increase, 73. This exercise should be practised in every School, (and I am glad its use is increasing, as it tends to promote habits of accurate learning by heart, improvement in reading and spelling, and is an agreeable and often amusing diversion for all parties concerned. The little episodes of such exercises in the ordinary routine of School duties exert a salutary influence upon the minds of Pupils and are happy interludes in the exercises on days of public Examinations; and the more agreeable and attractive such exercises, as well as School Examinations, can be made, the more rapid and successful will School progress become.

11. *School Prizes and Merit Cards.*—The number of Schools in which Prizes are reported as having been distributed to reward and encourage meritorious Pupils, is 1,376,—increase, 31,—there has also been an increase in the aggregate amount of Prize Books applied for and sent out to the Schools. As noted in my former Report, I may remark that in every instance, as far as I can learn, where the distribution of Prizes has not proved both satisfactory and beneficial, the failure may be traced to the want of intelligence, or fairness, or both, in the awarding of them. In some cases it may be ascribed to the same causes which caused the violation of the Law in not holding public Examinations of Schools,—the want of competence and industry in Teachers,—their not attending to and recording the individual conduct and progress of each Pupil, and, therefore, the absence of data essential to an impartial and intelligent judgment as to the merits of Pupils. In other cases, there has been a desire to give something to every Pupil without reference to either conduct, or progress, in order that none may complain, thus defeating the very object of Prizes, and rejecting the principle on which the true system of Prizes is established, and on which the Divine Government itself is based, namely, rewarding every one according to his works. I may also here repeat again what I have already remarked on this subject, that the hackneyed objection as to the distribution of Prizes exciting feelings of dissatisfaction, envy and hatred in the minds of those who do not obtain them, is an objection against all competition, and is, therefore, contrary to every-day practice in all the relations of life. If the distribution of Prizes is decided fairly according to merit, there can be no just ground for dissatisfaction; and facilities are now provided and their employment prescribed, with a view to determine the merit of punctuality, of good conduct, of diligence, of proficiency on the part of each Pupil during each term of the year,—a four-fold motive to exertion and emulation in everything that constitutes a good Pupil and a good School. But the indifferent and flagging Teacher does not wish such a pressure to be brought to bear upon his every-day teaching and attention to everything essential to an efficient School; nor does he desire the test of a periodical examination of his Pupils by an Examining Committee to be applied to his teaching and management of the School. The objection that the distribution of Prizes to deserving Pupils excites the envy and hatred of the undeserving is a convenient pretext to protect and permit incompetence and indifference on the part of the Teacher. The use of the Merit Cards removes many objections.

But the existence of such alleged dissatisfaction is no reason for refusing rewards to punctuality, to good conduct, to diligence, to proficiency on the part of Pupils.

There is often great dissatisfaction on the part of unsuccessful Candidates and their friends in the results of Municipal and Parliamentary elections, and the distribution of Prizes by Agricultural and Horticultural Associations; but this is no argument against the value of free and elective institutions; or does it prevent the people generally from honouring with their suffrages those on whose merits they place most value, even although they may sometimes err in their judgment. Nor do the managers of Agricultural and Horticultural Societies withhold Prizes from the most successful Cultivators of Grains and Vegetables, and Fruits and Flowers, because of dissatisfaction among the envious of the less diligent and less skilful Farmers and Gardeners.

It is the very order of Providence, and a maxim of Revelation, that the hand of the diligent maketh rich, while idleness tendeth to poverty; that to him that hath, (that is, improves what he hath), shall be given, and the neglector shall be sent empty away. Providence does not reverse its order, or administration, because some Persons are discontented and envious at the success of the faithful diligence and skill of others; or does Providence appeal alone to the transcendental motives of duty, gratitude, immortality, but presents also the motives of the life that now is, as well as of that which is to come.

I prefer the order of Providence, and the principles on which our civil institutions and all our associations for public and social improvements are conducted, to the dead-level notions of stationary Teachers, and the envious murmurings of negligent and unsuccessful Pupils and their too partial friends. Were the true principles, non-personal competition, as laid down in our system of Merit Cards, carried out by Teachers, very little objection would ever be heard against the plan of awarding Prizes in Schools.

An explanation of this feature of our School System will. be its best justification, and evince its great importance   I, therefore, present it again as follows:—

A comprehensive Catalogue of carefully selected and beautiful Prize Books has been prepared and furnished by the Department to Trustees and Municipalities applying for them; and, besides furnishing the Books at the reduced price, the Department adds one hundred per cent. to whatever amounts may be provided by Trustees and Municipal Councils to procure these Prize Books for the encouragement of children in their Schools. A series of Merit Cards, with appropriate Illustrations and Mottoes, has been prepared by the Department, and is supplied to Trustees and Teachers at a very small charge,—half the cost,—and these Merit Cards are to be awarded daily, or more generally weekly, to Pupils meriting them. One class of Cards is for punctuality; another for good conduct; a third for diligence; a fourth for perfect recitations. There are generally three, or four, Prizes under each of these heads; and the Pupil, or Pupils who get the largest number of Merit Cards under each head, will, at the end of the quarter or half-year, be entitled to the Prize Books awarded. Thus an influence is exerted upon every part of the Pupil's conduct, and during every day of his School career. If he cannot learn as fast an another Pupil, that he can be as punctual, as diligent and maintain as good conduct, and so acquire distinction and an entertaining and beautiful Book, for punctuality, diligence, good conduct, or perfect recitations or exercises, must be a just ground of satisfaction, not only to the Pupil but also to his or her Parents and friends. There are two peculiarities of this system of merit cards worthy of special notice. The one is, that it does not rest upon the comparative success of single examinations at the end of the Term, or half-year, or year, but on the daily conduct and diligence of each Pupil during the whole period, and irrespective of what may be done or not done by any other Pupil. The ill-feeling by rivalship at a single examination is avoided, and each Pupil is judged and rewarded according to his merits, as exhibited in his every-day School life. The second peculiarity is, that the standard of merit is founded on the Holy Scriptures, as the Mottoes on each Card are all taken from the Sacred Volume, and the illustrations on each Card consist of a portrait of a character illustrative of the principle of the Motto, and as worthy of imitation. The Prize Book System, and especially in connection with that of Merit Cards, has a most salutary influence upon the School discipline, upon both Teachers and Pupils, besides diffusing a large amount of entertaining and useful reading.

12. *Prayers and Ten Commandments.*—Of the 4,598 Schools reported, the daily Exercises were opened and closed with Prayers in 3,366 of them,—increase, 120; and the Ten Commandments were taught in 1,928. The Law wisely provides that "no child can be compelled to be present at Religious Instruction, Reading, or Exercise, against the wish of his Parents, or Guardians, expressed in writing." The Religious

Instruction, Reading and Exercises, are, like Religion itself, a voluntary matter with Trustees, Teachers, Parents and Guardians. The Council of Public Instruction provides facilities, even forms of Prayer, and makes recommendations on the subject, but does not assume authority to enforce or compel compliance with those provisions and recommendations. In some instances the Reading and Prayers may be according to the forms of the Roman Catholic Church; but, generally, those Exercises are Protestant The fact that in 3,366 Schools, out of 4,598, Religious Exercises of some kind are voluntarily practised, indicates the prevalent Religious principles and feelings of the people; although the absence of such Religious Exercises in a School does not by any means indicate the absence of Religious principles, or feelings, in the neighbourhood of such School. There are many Religious Persons who think the Day School, like the Farm Fields, the place of secular work, the Religious Exercises of the workers being performed, in the one case as in the other, in the Household, and not in the field of labour. But as Christian Principles and Morals are the foundation of all that is most noble in man, and the great fulcrum and lever of public freedom and prosperity in a Country, it is gratifying to see general and avowed recognition of them in the Public Schools. It is delightful to think that, (although in some few instances, this duty may be unworthily performed, yet,) from so many humble shrines of learning the Prayer for Divine Wisdom and Guidance goes up with faith to Him who has promised to give "liberally" to them that ask Him and to upbraid them not.

13. *Text Books.*—In a previous Annual Report I explained fully the steps which had been taken and the measures adopted, not only to secure a uniform series of Text Books for the Schools, but a uniform series of excellent Canadian Text Books, and the complete success of those measures. These Text Books are now universally used. As, however, it was frequently stated that the Text Books of Schools were so often changed, I append to this Report a Memorandum on the subject, showing that no changes have been made, but once, or twice, (in Arithmetic and Grammar), in twenty-five years.

14. *Maps, Globes, and other Apparatus.*—The Maps and Globes, and most of the other Apparatus used in the Schools, are now manufactured in Ontario, forming a most interesting branch of Canadian manufacture. Blackboards are used in 4,568, (or nearly all), of the Schools,—increase, 64; Globes are used in 1,344 Schools,—increase, 18; Maps are used in 3,789 Schools,—increase, 94. Total Maps used in the Schools, 29,351,—increase, 1,202.

15. The number of Sunday Schools of all denominations reported is 3,526; of Sunday School Pupils in them, 203,222; of Sunday School Teachers, 23,835. The increased prosperity of these voluntary and invaluable adjuncts to our System of Public Instruction is a matter of congratulation to all parties concerned. The specific teaching of Religious truth given in these Schools by common consent is felt to supersede, to a great extent, a necessity of taking advantage of the hour set apart for giving Religious Instruction in the Public Schools.

VI.—*Table F.—Roman Catholic Separate Schools.*

1. The number of Roman Catholic Separate Schools is 160,—decrease during the year, 3.

2. *Receipts.*—The amount apportioned and paid by the Chief Superintendent from the Legislative Grant to Separate Schools, according to average attendance of Pupils, as compared with that at the Public Schools in the same Municipalities, was $9,081,—increase, $174. The amount apportioned and paid for the purchase of Maps, Prize Books and Libraries, upon the usual condition of an equal sum being provided from local sources, was $574,—decrease, $108. The amount of School Rates from the Supporters of Separate Schools, was $34,815,—increase, $2,962. The amount subscribed by Supporters of Separate Schools, and from other sources, was $25,347, increase, $8,282. Total amount received from all sources was $69,818,—increase, $11,317.

3. *Expenditures.*—For payment of Teachers, $42,393,—increase, $654; for Maps, Prize Books and Libraries, $1,256,—decrease, $510; for other School purposes, $26,168, —increase, $11,173.

4. *Pupils.*—The number of Pupils reported as attending the Separate Schools, was 21,206,—increase, 548. Average attendance, 10,371,—increase, 336.

5. The whole number of Teachers employed in the Separate Schools was 249,— increase, 13; male Teachers, 84,—decrease, 12; female Teachers, 155,—increase, 15. Teachers of Religious Orders, male, 26,—increase, 1; female, 44,—decrease, 14.

6. The same Table shows the branches taught in the Separate Schools, and the number of Pupils in each branch; also the number of Schools using Maps, Apparatus and Blackboards.

General Remarks.—1. It is proper for me again to repeat the remark, that the Public Schools of Ontario are Non-denominational. Equal protection is secured to and enjoyed by every Religious Persuasion. No child is compelled to receive Religious Instruction, or attend any Religious Exercise, or Reading, against the wishes of his Parents, or Guardians, expressed in writing. I have known of no instance of prose-lytism in the Public Schools, nor have I received, during the year, a single complaint of interference with Religious Rights, so fully secured by Law.

2. According to the returns of the Religious Denominations of Teachers, as given in Table D, as noted above, the number of Roman Catholic Teachers of the Public Schools is 623, of whom 249 only are Teachers in Separate Schools. There were, there-fore, 374, (increase during the year, 18), Roman Catholic Teachers employed in the Non-denominational Public Schools,—an illustrative proof of the absence of exclusive-ness in the local, as well as executive, administration of the School System. I may also observe, that according to the Inspectors' Returns, for 1871, there were 489,615 children in Ontario between the ages of five and sixteen years. Of these, according to the proportion of Roman Catholic population, at least 75,000 must be assumed to be the children of Roman Catholic Parents. Of these 75,000 Roman Catholic children, only 21,200, (not one-third of the Roman Catholic School population), attend the Public Schols, in which no less than 374 Roman Catholic Teachers are employed; and yet not a complaint has been made of even attempt at proselytism, or interference with religious rights guaranteed by Law.

3. It is gratifying to be able to state that several of these Separate Schools are admirably managed, and are doing good service in their localities. The Law has been fairly and equitably administered to them, and I hear of no complaint from them.

VII.—*Table G.—High Schools, Receipts and Expenditures, Pupils' Fees.*

Receipts.—The balances reported from the preceding year, (that is, of moneys not paid out by the 31st of December, 1870), was $8,041,—decrease, $3,549. The amount received by the High School Boards from Legislative Grant for the Salaries of Teachers, was $65,536,—increase, $10,841. The amount of Legislative Grant apportioned for Maps, Prize Books, etcetera, was $1,268,—decrease, $80. The amount of Municipal Grants in support of High Schools, was $50,674,—increase, $7,076. The amount received for Pupils' Fees, was $18,985,—decrease, $390. Balances of the preceding year and other sources, $19,074,—increase, $4,074. Total receipts, $163,579,—increase, $17,972.

Expenditures.—For Salaries of Masters and Teachers, $113,861,—increase, $8,708; for Building, Rents and Repairs, $24,164,—increase, $3,774; for Fuel, Books, and Contingencies, $12,427,—increase, $3,779; for Maps, Prize Books, Apparatus, and Libraries, $2,426,—decrease, $948. Total Expenditure for the year 1871, $152,880,— increase, $15,314. Balances of moneys not paid out at the end of the year, $10,699,— increase, $2,658.

Number of Pupils, 7,490,—increase, 39. *Number of Schools,* 102.

VIII.—*Table H.—Number of Pupils in the Various Branches,—and Miscellaneous Information.*

Table H shows both the subjects taught and the number of Pupils in such subjects in each of the High Schools, the names, University Degree, (or Certificate), of the Head Masters, and the numbers of Masters employed in each School, etcetera.

Number of Pupils in English Grammar and Literature, 7,392; in Composition, 6,277; in Reading, Dictation and Elocution, 7,467; in Penmanship, 6,957; in Linear Drawing, 2,092; in Book-keeping, 2,184; in Arithmetic, 7,499; in Algebra, 4,325; in Geometry, 2,677; in Christian Morals, 2,108; in Logic, 39; in Trigonometry, 213; in Mensuration, 1,695; in History, 6,656; in Geography, 7,306; in Natural Philosophy, 2,029; in Chemistry, 1,522; in Natural History, 1,516; in Physiology, 1,142; in Elements of Civil Government, 216; in French, 2,585; in German, 232; in Latin, 5,059; in Greek, 1,007; in Gymnastics and Drill, 372.

Of the School Houses, 49 were of Brick, 21 Stone and 28 Frame; 15 were rented, or leased, the remainder freehold. Galt has the finest Play Ground of any of the High Schools; it consists of seven acres. The other Play Grounds vary in size, the smallest being one one-quarter of an acre,—or one-half of the minimum size required of the smallest Public School. The estimated value of each School House and Site varies from $30,000, (Peterborough), down to $300! (Kemptville).

60 High Schools were under Union High and Public School Boards; Kingston is the oldest High School in Ontario, dating from 1791; Cornwall, 1806; Brockville, 1818; Niagara and Williamstown, from 1828; St. Catharines, 1829. 1,628 Maps were used in the 102 High Schools; 56 Schools used the Bible; in 87 there were daily Prayers; 78 Pupils matriculated at some University during 1871; 567 Pupils entered Mercantile life; 388 adopted Agriculture as a pursuit; 222 joined the learned Professions; 532 went to other occupations. The number of Masters engaged was only 174,—the great majority of the Schools being content with the services of but one Master. This great defect the Department will endeavour to have remedied without delay. Up to the date of this Report, most of the High Schools, which had but one Master in 1871, have employed a second one, so that by the close of the year, nearly every High School will be in a position to do more justice than formerly to the Pupils who attend them.

High School Boards cannot now reasonably complain of want of means to carry out this much needed reform, (of employing a second Master). They not only receive from the Legislative Grant nearly twenty times as much per Pupil as is paid from the same source to the Public School Trustees for each Pupil in their Schools, but they can now call upon the Municipal Councils of their District for the entire balance required to support their School efficiently. I shall revert to the subject of High Schools in a subsequent part of this Report. In the meantime, I would refer to the admirable Report to me of the able Inspectors, Messieurs Mackenzie and McLellan, [given in Chapter XV of this Volume].

In regard to the establishment of new High Schools the Department has not encouraged their multiplication, unless it could be shown that their existence in the locality desiring them was a necessity, and that their proper standing and character could be maintained. With this view, the following conditions were laid down by the Department for establishing both High Schools and Collegiate Institutes:—

The new School Law of 1871 provides for the establishment and maintenance of three classes of superior English, or Classical, Schools, videlicet:—

I. High Schools for teaching Classical and English subjects,—in which Boys and Girls may be instructed together, or separately.

II. High Schools in which Boys and Girls may be instructed in English subjects alone.

III. Collegiate Institutes, for giving instruction in Classical and English subjects, in which there shall be four Masters and an average daily attendance of at least sixty Boys in Greek and Latin.

Conditions for Establishing High Schools.

Parties wishing to have a High School of either class in their locality, authorized by His Excellency the Lieutenant-Governor-in-Council, are requested to furnish the Education Department with the following information:—
1. The distance of the proposed High School from the nearest adjoining High Schools.
2. The population of the Town, or Village Municipality, in which it is proposed to place the High School.
3. The boundaries of the proposed new High School District as fixed by the County Council, (with copy of the proceedings of Council in the case).
4. The amount of taxable property in such High School District.
5. The description of the proposed High School building, as regards,—
(a) Its situation; the extent of its Site; size of Playground; and extent of outward conveniences, etcetera.
(b) Size, Site and description of the proposed Building; number of Class-rooms devoted to teaching; Room for Teacher; Hat, Cloak, Map and Book Presses, etcetera.
6. Written guarantee must be given to the Department by responsible parties, (1) that a suitable Building distinct from the Public School House, (or if in the Public School Building, on a separate flat, or in a separate wing), will be provided; (2) that at least two competent Teachers shall be employed in the proposed High School.

Conditions for Establishing Collegiate Institutes.

Trustees of High Schools who desire to have the title of Collegiate Institute conferred upon their School by the Lieutenant-Governor, are requested to furnish the Education Department with the following information.
1. The name and designation of each Master employed in the School, and the number of his teaching hours per day.
2. The name and designation of each Assistant Teacher, (if any), and the number of his teaching hours per day.
3. The aggregate attendance of Boys studying Latin, or Greek, during the whole of the previous civil year, and during the two Terms of the School preceding the application.
4. The daily average attendance of Boys in Latin and Greek during the periods named.
5. The Income from all local sources during the preceding civil year.
6. The description of the proposed Collegiate Institute Building, as regards,—
(a) Its situation and extent of its Site; description and size of the Building; and its state of repair.
(b) The number of Rooms devoted to teaching purposes in it; and their sizes.
(c) Description of Apparatus for illustrating Natural Philosophy and Chemistry; number and description of Maps; number of Volumes in Library, (if any).
(d) Size of Play Ground and extent of outside Conveniences, etcetera.
7. A written guarantee must be given by the Trustees that the requirements of the Act and Regulations of 1871, in regard to Collegiate Institutes, will be fully complied with.

These Regulations have been found to work admirably, and up to the date of this Report the following High Schools and Collegiate Institutes were, on the recommendation of the Department, authorized by the Lieutenant-Governor-in-Council, and notice thereof given as follows:—

Collegiate Institutes and High Schools Authorized by the Governor.

His Excellency the Lieutenant-Governor has been pleased to confer upon the undermentioned High Schools the name and privileges of Collegiate Institutes, in accordance with the provisions of the School Law of Ontario, videlicet:—
1. Galt High School, 12 Masters, and an average attendance of 120 Boys, in Classics.
2. Hamilton High School, 4 Masters and an average attendance of 74 Boys, in Classics.
3. Peterborough High School; 4 Masters, and an average attendance of 73 Boys in Classics.
4. Cobourg High School; 4 Masters, and an average attendance of 65 Boys, in Classics.
5. Kingston High School; 4 Masters, and an average attendance of 63 Boys, in Classics.

6. St. Catharines High School; 4 Masters, and an average attendance of 62 Boys, in Classics.

7. Ottawa High School; 4 Masters, and an average attendance of 63 Boys, in Classics.

His Excellency has been pleased to authorize the establishment of the following new High Schools,—suitable accommodation and the employment of two Masters having been guaranteed, videlicet: —

1. Parkhill, in the County of Middlesex.
2. Campbellford, in the County of Northumberland.
3. Mitchell, in the County of Perth.
4. Walkerton, in the County of Bruce.
5. Sydenham, in the County of Frontenac.
6. Hawkesbury, in the County of Prescott.

IX.—Table I.—Meteorological Stations and Observations.

Of late years the practical value of the science of Meteorology, as I intimated last year, has been recognized by all civilized Governments, and systems of simultaneous Observations have been widely established, the results of which must tend to elucidate the laws which control Atmospheric Phenomena. The recent establishment of the Storm Signal Office at Washington, and the extension of the system to this Dominion, will, no doubt, exhibit fresh evidence of the practical value of Meteorological Observations. The daily Weather Reports and the "Probabilities" founded on the Observations, have been most valuable, instructive and interesting. The system of "Drum Signals" established on the English Coast by the late Admiral Fitzroy, (although not appreciated at first, has become a necessity, and, under the good Providence of God, has been the means of averting great destruction of life and property. The Admiral, when head of the Meteorological Office in England, thus referred to the importance of returns of Temperature, and the especial need of Observations in British America: —

Tables of the Mean Temperature of the Air in the year, and in the different months and seasons of the year, at above one thousand Stations on the Globe, have recently been computed by Professor Dové, and published under the auspices of the Royal Academy of Sciences at Berlin. This work which is a true model of the method in which a great body of Meteorological facts, collected by different Observers and at different times, should be brought together and co-ordinated, has conduced, as is well known, to conclusions of very considerable importance in their bearing on Climatology, and on the general laws of the distribution of Heat on the surface of the Globe. In regard to Land Stations, Professor Dové's Tables have shown that "data are still pressingly required from the British North American Possessions intermediate between the Stations of the Arctic Expeditions and those of the United States; and that the deficiency extends across the whole North American Continent, in those latitudes from the Atlantic to the Pacific."

A recent Return published, (in 1872), under the authority of the Parliament of Canada evinces the gradual progress being made in the establishment of a complete Meteorological System for the Dominion, which cannot fail to be of great service to the cause of Science and to the great Agricultural as well as the Maritime interests of the Country.

The High School System of Ontario secures the continuous residence of a class of men, at different points, who are well qualified by education to perform the work of Observation. and the Law authorizes the establishment and maintenance of a limited number of Stations, selected by the Council of Public Instruction, with the approval of His Excellency, the Lieutenant-Governor, at which daily Observations are taken of Barometric Pressure, Temperature of the Air, Tension of Vapour, Humidity of the Air, direction and velocity of the Wind, amount of Cloudiness, Rain, Snow, Auroras, and other Meteoric Phenomena. The Observations are taken at 7 a.m., 1 p.m., and 9 p.m. The Instruments used have been subjected to the proper tests. Full abstracts of the daily records are sent to the Education Office monthly, in addition to a weekly Report of certain Observations, which is prepared for publication in any local newspaper the Observer may select. Abstracts of the results for each month are regularly published in the *Journal of Education*, and the Observers' Reports, after strict examination, are arranged and preserved for further investigations.

In my Report of 1867, the results of most of the Observations were presented in the form of synchronous curves, but as the expense proved an objection, a synopsis is now given in figures. For the same reason the important notes of the observers are omitted.

I have pleasure in adding that the Observers are, upon the whole, discharging their duties with fidelity, and that through their exertions the materials for investigating the Climatology of the Province are rapidly accumulating.

X.—*Table K.—Normal and Model Schools.*

The County Examinations held throughout the Province, in 1871 and 1872, have demonstrated the great value and usefulness of the Normal School. Every one of its Students who was examined has acquitted himself well, and of the seven who obtained First Class Certificates in July, 1872, five were Normal School Students. The great practical value of the instruction given to the Students of that Institution by the Reverend Doctor Davies, the new Principal, Doctor Carlyle and Mr. Kirkland fully sustain the high reputation which the Institution has acquired throughout the Country. The whole System has been of late years brought to a degree of thoroughness and practical efficiency, even in its minutest details, that I have not witnessed in any other Establishment of the kind. The standard of admission to the Normal School has been raised much above that of former years, and, therefore, the Entrance Examination, (which is always in writing), has been made increasingly severe. 138 of those admitted have been Teachers. The establishment of the third Mastership, with a view to give greater prominence to the subject of Natural Science, has had a most beneficial and salutary effect upon the introduction and teaching of those subjects in our Public Schools, as required by the new School Act. The newly enlarged Buildings for the Model Schools will add greatly to the practical character and efficiency of these Schools of practice in the Normal School Course.

Last year I felt so impressed with the importance of increased facilities for Normal School training, that I suggested to the late Attorney-General Macdonald the advisability of establishing two additional Normal Schools,—one in the Eastern and one in the Western part of the Province, and the subject was referred to in Your Excellency's Speech at the opening of the Session in December last. I am glad that the subject has not been lost sight of, but that my suggestions will likely be carried out this year, and possibly three additional Normal Schools established. To this matter, as well as that of Teachers' Institutes, I shall refer in a subsequent part of this Report.

Table K contains three abstracts, the first of which gives the gross number of applications, the number that had been Teachers before entering the Normal School, attendance of Teachers-in-training, Certificates, and other particulars respecting them during the twenty-three years' existence of the Normal School; the second abstract gives the Counties whence the Students have come; and the third gives the Religious persuasions of these Students.

Table K shows that of the 6,418 admitted to the Normal School, (out of 7,104 applications), 3,130 of them had been Teachers; and of those admitted, 3,280 were males, and 3,138 were females. Of the 3,280 male Candidates admitted, 2,179 of them had been Teachers; of the 3,138 female Candidates admitted, 951 of them had been Teachers. The number admitted the first Session of 1871 was 166, the second Session, 183,—total, 349. Of the whole number admitted, 151 were males, and 198 females. Of the male Students admitted, 91 had been Teachers; of the female Students admitted, 47 had been Teachers.

XI.—*Table L.—Other Educational Institutions in Ontario.*

The Public and High Schools are only a part of our educational agencies, the Private Schools, Academies and Colleges must therefore be referred to in order to form an approximate idea of the state and progress of Education throughout the Province. Table L contains an abstract of the information collected respecting these Institutions. As the information is obtained and given voluntarily, it can only be regarded as an approximation to accuracy, and, of course, very much below the real facts. According to the information obtained, there are 16 Colleges, (some of them possessing University powers), with 1,930 Students; 285 Academies and Private Schools,—increase, 1,—with 6,511 Pupils,—decrease, 51; which were kept open 11 months, and employed 392 Teachers,—increase, 19. Total Students and Pupils, 8,441,—decrease, 51.

XII.—*Table M.—Free Public Libraries in Ontario.*

1. This Table contains three Statements:—First, the names of the Municipalities which have been supplied with Libraries, (or additions), during the year, and the value and number of Volumes sent out to each; Second, the Counties to which Libraries have been supplied during the past and former years, and the value and number of Volumes in them, and also of other Public Libraries; Third, the number and subjects of Volumes which have been furnished, as Libraries and Prize Books, to the several Counties each year since the commencement, in 1853, of this branch of the School system.

2. *(Statement No. 1).* The amount expended in Library Books during 1871 is ** ₀₀₀ of which one-half has been provided from local sources. The number of Volumes supplied is 4,825.

3. *(Statement No. 2).* The value of Public Free Libraries furnished to the end of 1871 was $138,825,—increase, $3,300. The number of Libraries, exclusive of sub-divisions, 1,175,—increase, 29. The number of Volumes in these Libraries was 243,887, —increase, 4,825.

Sunday School Libraries reported, 2,845,—increase, 412. The number of Volumes in these Libraries was 375,128,—increase, 29,273.

Other Public Libraries reported, 389. The number of Volumes in these Libraries was 174,471,—increase, 30.

The total number of Public Libraries in Ontario is 4,409,—increase, 441. The total of the number of Volumes in these Libraries is 793,486,—increase during the year, 34,128 Volumes.

4. *(Statement Number 3).* This important Statement contains the number and classification of Public Libraries and Prize Books which have been sent out from the Depository of the Department from 1853 to 1871 inclusive. The total number of Volumes for Public Free Libraries sent out, 247,497. The classification of these Books is as follows:—History, 43,023; Zoology and Physiology, 15,427; Botany, 2,823; Phenomena, 6.154; Physical Science, 4,813; Geology, 2,112; Natural Philosophy and Manufactures, 13,297; Chemistry, 1,558; Agricultural Chemistry, 795; Practical Agriculture, 9,741; Literature, 23,638; Voyages, 21,570; Biography, 28,501; Tales and Sketches, Practical Life, 69,744; Fiction, 1,312; Teachers' Library, 2,989. Total number of Prize Books sent out, 563,869. Grand Total of Library and Prize Books. (including, but not included in the above, 16,867 Volumes sent to Mechanics' Institutes and Sunday Schools, paid for wholly from local sources), 827,617.

5. In regard to the Free Public Libraries, it may be proper to repeat the explanation that these Libraries are managed by Local Municipal Councils and School Trustees, (chiefly by the latter), under Regulations prepared according to Law by the Council of Public Instruction. The Books are procured by the Education Department, from Publishers both in Europe and America, at as low prices for cash as possible; and a carefully-prepared classified Catalogue of about 4,000 Works, (which have been approved by the Council of Public Instruction), is printed, and sent to the Trustees of each School Section, and the Council of each Municipality. From this select and comprehensive Catalogue the local Municipal and School Authorities desirous of establishing and increasing a Library select such Works as they think proper, or request the Department to do so for them, and receive from the Department not only the Books at prices about from twenty-five to thirty per cent. cheaper than the ordinary retail prices, but an Apportionment in Books of 100 per cent. upon the amount which they provide for the purchase of such Books. None of these Works are disposed of to any private parties, except Teachers and School Inspectors, for their professional use; and the rule is not

to keep a large supply of any one Work on hand, so as to prevent the accumulation of Stock, and to add to the Catalogue yearly new and useful Books which are constantly issuing from the European and American Press. There is also kept in the Department a record of every Public Library, and of the Books which have been furnished for it, so that additions can be made to such Libraries without liability to send second copies of the same Books.

XIII.—*Table N.—Summary of the Maps, Apparatus, and Prize Books Supplied to the Counties, Cities, Towns and Villages During the Year.*

1. The amount expended in supplying Maps, Apparatus, and Prize Books for the Schools, was $30,076,—increase, $1,265. The one-half of this sum was provided voluntarily from local sources; in all cases the Books, or articles are applied for and fifty per cent. of the value paid for by the parties concerned before being sent out. The number of Maps of the World sent out was 184; of Europe, 276; of Asia, 239; of Africa, 207; of America, 232; of British North America and Canada, 323; of Great Britain and Ireland, 181; of Single Hemispheres, 216; of Scriptural and Classical, 144; of other Charts and Maps, 447; of Globes, 123; of sets of Apparatus, 43; of other pieces of School Apparatus, 466; of Historical and other Lessons, in sheets, 13,055. Number of Volumes of Prize Books, 60,420.

2. It may be proper to repeat that the Map, Apparatus, and Prize Book branch of the School System was not established till 1855. From that time to the end of 1871 the amount expended for Maps, Apparatus, and Prize Books, (not including Public Libraries), was $323,119, one-half of which has been provided from local sources, from which all applications have been made. The number of Maps of the World furnished is 2,635; of Europe, 4,098; of Asia, 3,325; of Africa, 3,058; of America, 3,463; of British North America and Canada, 3,916; of Great Britain and Ireland, 3,869; of Single Hemispheres, 2,764; of Classical and Scriptural Maps, 2,772; other Maps and Charts, 5,891; Globes, 2,065; sets of Apparatus, 444; single articles of School Apparatus, 15,081; Historical and other Lessons in sheets, 167,267; Volumes of Prize Books, 563,869.

3. I also repeat the following explanation of this branch of the Department:—

The Maps, Globes, and various articles of School Apparatus sent out by the Department, apportioning one hundred per cent. upon whatever sum, or sums, are provided from local sources, are nearly all manufactured in Ontario, and at lower prices than imported articles of the same kind have been heretofore obtained. The Globes and Maps manufactured, (even the material), in Ontario contain the latest discoveries of Voyagers and Travellers, and are executed in the best manner, as are Tellurians, Mechanical Powers, Numeral Frames, Geometrical Powers, etcetera. All this has been done by employing competitive private skill and enterprise. The Department has furnished the Manufacturers with copies and Models, purchasing certain quantities of the articles, when manufactured, at stipulated prices, then permitting and encouraging them to manufacture and dispose of these articles themselves to any private parties desiring them, as the Department supplies them only to Municipal and School Authorities. In this way new domestic manufactures are introduced, and mechanical and artistical skill and enterprise are encouraged, and many aids to School and Domestic Instruction, heretofore unknown amongst us, or only attainable in particular cases with difficulty, and at great expense, are now easily and cheaply accessible to private families, as well as to Municipal and School Authorities all over the Country. It is also worthy of remark, that this important branch of the Education Department is self-supporting. All the expenses of it are reckoned in the cost of the Articles and Books procured, so that it does not cost either the Public Revenue or School Fund a penny beyond what is apportioned to the Municipalities and School Sections providing a like sum, or sums, for the purchase of Books, Maps, Globes, and various Articles of School Apparatus. I know of no other instance, in either the United States, or in Europe, of a branch of a Public Department of this kind conferring so great a benefit upon the public, and without adding to public expense.

Explanatory Remarks on the Working of the Depository.

As certain parties have objected to the Depositories for the supply of High and Public Schools with Maps, Charts, Apparatus, Prize and Library Books, as an inter-

13a—XXIII.

ference with private trade, I reply that just as well might they object to the interference of Government in many other matters which come directly in contact with the interests of private Trade and Manufacture, as I shall further illustrate. In doing so I shall briefly refer to the objects for which our Department of Education exists, and explain the prinicples on which the Depository has been established.

The General Question Practically Discussed.

In every Country the interests of Education, at least in its elementary organization, is committed to the care and oversight of some department of Government. Experience proves the necessity of doing so. But, it may be asked:—"What is expected of such a Department in its administration of the system?" "Is it the merely perfunctory duty of keeping a certain statutory machinery in motion, receiving formal Reports, and making the same in Return, which is expected? Or is it the dealing with the great interest of Popular Education as if it were the nation's life blood, every pulsation of which indicated·a healthy, vigorous growth of intellectual and moral life, or the torpidity of bare existence, maintained at large cost, but producing little fruit and no satisfactory returns? The prevention of this latter, and the promotion of the former are, we think, the true objects for which popular Education is especially entrusted to the care and oversight of a responsible Public Department. If it be so, the question then is,—"How can this be best accomplished, and in what light should the Schools be regarded and treated, so as to bring about the best possible results;" whether as the joint property of the State and people, their interests should be paramount to private interests, or should they be treated merely as Institutions which should be made to subserve the interests of the Trades and Professions, whether it be of Book-sellers or of Private Schools, or Private Institutions for the training of School Masters.

Example of Alleged Interference Acquiesced in pro Bono Publico.

Normal Schools were at first derided as an interference with proprietary rights in special Schools, select Academies, local "Colleges," and other Institutions made available for preparing Teachers. At length, after various discussions, now and then revived, this point was conceded, and Normal Schols are now regarded, on this Continent, at least, as the exclusive property of the State, and not of private individuals, or corporations. Thus, the right of the State to prepare and fit the primary agents of Education for their important work, was admitted by all except by interested parties. Then arose the other question, as to who should not only provide those trained agents, but, (regarding each School as one of a number claiming equal privileges and facilities for promoting instruction), should also supply them with the requisites for imparting that instruction. The right to prepare the agents themselves was conceded, but the right to procure and place in their hands such tools, or means and instruments of performing their work, as were considered most desirable and suitable, was resisted, ostensibly on public, but in reality on private, grounds.

A Few Pertinent and Practical Questions Discussed and Answered.

Again, it was said, (speaking on behalf of those interested), "you have, at length, successfully interfered with the private interests of the higher Teachers' profession, and taken the work of instructing and training Teachers out of private hands, and now you wish to interfere with the business and private interests of the Book-seller and Map maker, for the benefit of the Public Schools." Is this so, however, we ask as a matter of fact; is not every Book furnished to the Public Schools, and every Map constructed for them, purchased from some Book-seller and Geographical Publisher? "Certainly; (it is replied), we know that your Schools are supplied from some Book-seller and Publisher, but you do not purchase from us,—we make no profits out of your transactions,—and, therefore, your interference with our private gain in the promotion of purely public interests, is unwarrantable, and should not be sanctioned by the Legislature. You have no right, as against private interests to regard the interests of Public Schools, in the aggregate, or as a unit; nor have you a right to establish one Grand Central Depot, out of which, at equal cost, and with equal freeness and facility), to supply the near as well as the distant Public Schools, in the new and poor Townships, which should have the same facility to obtain its supply of approved Library Books, Maps and other Appliances at a reduced cost, as the most prosperous Schools in the older Townships. You authorize and recommend a Book and Stationery Depository as a central source of supply for Schools by Boards of Trustees in individual Cities and Towns, and we approve of it, as it subserves our local interest, but we decidedly object to a Book and Map Depository on a Provincial footing, because we cannot use it in the same way with equal advantage. The Board of Trustees in every City and Town can lawfully purchase by wholesale, and keep a depot for the supply of all its Schools with Books, etcetera, and is authorized by the School Act of 1871, to collect a monthly Fee to support such a local Depository, and the plan is commendable on the principles of prudence, economy, and proper oversight, but to allow you to do the same thing under Legislative sanction, for the Schools of the whole Province is an interference with "trade." Nay more, the Departments in England, Canada, and even Ontario, establish and maintain, by a Parliamentary vote, a Stationery Office for the exclusive supply of the various branches of Government, with Paper, and all kinds of Stationery without purchasing from local dealers; but we cannot allow you to apply the same central, economic principle, to the supply of the various departments of Schools under your control."

Examples of Government Interference with Private Trade.

And yet, with these patent violations of trade monopoly palpable to every observer, the Education Department of Ontario has been singled out for attack; while the further facts are ignored, that every Government in Europe has its depot for making and supplying Army Clothing, its dockyards for making Ships, its exclusive Printing Office under contract for all its Departments; its own Architects and Engineers for all its Public Buildings; its absorption in England, Canada and elsewhere, of the exclusive right of carrying private Letters;—that a gigantic monopoly in England of the whole Telegraph System of Britain has been lately established, and that in Canada and the Eastern Provinces Railways have been constructed, aided, and even run, for public traffic; and that in Ireland, if not in England, they are even now considering the expediency of taking out of private hands, the vast net-work of Railways in those Kingdoms.

These facts, and their suggestive teachings, are ignored, by certain interested parties, where the facts stated are little known, or thought of, because their discussion would be inconvenient, and their application would be fatal to the plans of those opposed to our Depository.

Of course, if the Depository were broken up, one of two things must be done, either to transfer its operations to individual Booksellers, for their benefit, or introduce an irresponsible system of Book supply.

Practice and Opinions of American Educationists in Regard to a Depository. [*]

XIV.—*Table O.—Superannuated and Worn-out Teachers of Public Schools.* [†]

It apears from the Table that 257 have been admitted to receive aid, of whom 133 have died, have not been heard from, or have resumed teaching, or have withdrawn from the Fund before or during the year 1871, the amount of their subscriptions having been returned to them. . . . .

[*] This information and that contained in the next two sections of this Report, have already been given in a former Chapter of this Volume, so that it is not repeated here.
[†] The first of this division of the Report is omitted, as it has already been given in previous Reports.

Official Regulations in Regard to the Superannuation Fund.

5. The Regulations for the administration of the Superannuated Teachers' Fund, adopted by the Council of Public Instruction, are as follows:—

(1) Teachers who became superannuated, or worn-out, on or before the first day of January, 1854, and who produce the proofs required by Law, of character and service as such, may share in this Fund according to the number of years they have respectively taught a Public School in Ontario by depositing with the Chief Superintendent of Education the preliminary subscriptions to the Fund required by Law.

(2) Every Teacher engaged in teaching since 1854, in order to be entitled, when he shall have become superannuated, or worn-out, to share in this Fund, must have contributed to it at the rate of Five dollars per annum for each year from the time when he began to teach, up to the time of his first annual subscription of four dollars, (as required by the Statute), for each subsequent year during which he was engaged in teaching. No subscription, either for arrears, or otherwise, can be received from those who have ceased to teach, [and in all cases the annual payment, unless made within the year for which it is due, will be at the rate of five dollars].*

(3) No Teacher shall be eligible to receive a pension from this Fund, who shall not have become disabled for further service, while teaching a Public School, or who shall not have been worn out in the work of a Public School Teacher.

(4) All applications must be accompanied with the requisite Certificates and proofs according to the prescribed forms and instructions. No Certificate in favour of an applicant should be signed by any Teacher already admitted as a pensioner on the Fund.

(5) In case the Fund shall at any time not be sufficient to pay the several claimants, the highest sum permitted by Law, the income shall be equitably divided among them, according to their respective periods of service.

NOTE. The following are Extracts from the School Law of 1871.

(6) . . . . On the decease of any Teacher, his wife, or other legal Representatives, shall be entitled to receive back the full amount paid in by such Teacher, with interest at the rate of seven per cent. per annum.

(7) . . . . . . Any Teacher retiring from the profession shall be entitled to receive back from the Chief Superintendent one-half of any sums thus paid in by him to the Fund.

. XV.—*Table P.—Educational Summary for 1871.*

This Table exhibits, in a single page, the number of Educational Institutions of every kind, as far as I have been able to obtain Returns, the number of Students and Pupils attending them, and the amount expended in their support. The whole number of these Institutions in 1871, was 5,004,—increase, 34; the whole number of Students and Pupils attending them was 463,057,—increase, 3,896; the total amount expended for all educational purposes was $2,297,694,—increase, $123,952; total amount available for educational purposes, $2,629,570,—increase, $215,513.

XVI.—*Table Q.—General Statistical Abstract of the Progress of Education in Ontario, from 1842 to 1871, Inclusive.*

This most important Table is highly suggestive, it is only by comparing the number and character of Educational Institutions at different periods, the number of Pupils attending them, and the sums of money provided and expended for their support, that we can form a correct idea of the educational progress of a Country. The statistics for such comparisons should be kept constantly before the public mind to prevent erroneous and injurious impressions, and to animate to efforts of further and higher advancement.

Congratulations have often been expressed at the great improvements which have been made in all of our Institutions of Education, in regard both to the subjects and methods of teaching, as in the accommodations and facilities of instruction; also in the number of our Educational Institutions, in attendance upon them; and in the pro-

---

* With respect to the arrears of subscription, it is to be observed that they can be paid at any time while the Teacher is still engaged in that capacity, not after he has ceased. No payment is required for any year during which the Teacher was not employed, or for any year prior to 1854, even if the Teacher was teaching before that time.

It is further to be remembered that payment of the arrears is not obligatory, but is to the interest of the Teacher, as the years (from 1854) for which there has been no subscription, will not be reckoned in making up the time of service for the pension.

In no case are subscriptions required except for the years of teaching, for which a pension will be claimed.

vision for their support. But it is only by analysing and comparing the statistics contained in Table Q, that a correct and full impression can be formed of what has been accomplished educationally in Ontario during the last twenty years. Take a few items, as example. In 1842, the number of Public Schools was only 1,721. In 1851, this had increased to 3,001; and in 1871, to 4,598, and the number of Pupils attending them from 168,159 in 1851, to 425,126 in 1871. The amount paid for the support of Public Schools has been increased from $468,644 in 1851, to $1,191,476 in 1871, (not including balances not paid at the date of the local Reports), besides the amount paid for the purchase, erection, repairs of School Houses, etcetera, of which there are no reports earlier than 1850, but which at that time amounted to only $56,756, and $77,336 in 1851, but which in 1871 amounted to $611,818,—making the aggregate actually paid for Public School purposes in 1871, $1,802,294, or, with the balances available and not paid out at the date of the local reports, $2,124,471. These facts will be more clearly seen from the following Table, in addition to which may be added the Normal and Model Schools, the system of uniform Text Books, Maps, Globes, Apparatus, (of domestic manufacture), Prize Books and Public Libraries :—

REPORT FOR THE YEAR.	1850.	1851.	1860.	1861.	1865.	1866.	1867.	1868.	1869.	1870.	1871.
Number of Public Schools reported.............	3,059	3,001	3,969	4,019	4,303	4,379	4,422	4,480	4,524	4,565	4,598
Amount paid for Public School Teachers' salaries	$ 353,756	$ 391,308	$ 895,591	$ 918,113	$ 1,041,052	$ 1,066,880	$ 1,093,616	$ 1,144,543	$ 1,175,166	$ 1,222,681	$ 1,191,476
Amount paid for erection, repairs of School-houses,&c..	56,756	77,336	264,183	273,305	314,827	320,353	379,672	441,891	449,730	489,380	611,819
Balance forward each year....	24,016	16,893	164,498	189,861	139,121	220,738	197,147	200,898	202,530	232,303	321,176
Total amount available each year.................	434,488	485,537	1,324,272	1,381,279	1,545,000	1,607,971	1,670,335	1,789,332	1,827,426	1,944,364	2,124,47

XVII. *Objects of Art in the Educational Museum.**

This fourth branch of the Education Department is probably the most attractive as it is both suggestive and instructive. The other three branches are:—(1) The Department proper for the Administration of the Laws relative to the Public and High Schools. (2) The Normal School for the training of skilled Teachers. (3) The Depository for the supply of Maps, Apparatus and Prize and School Books. (4) The Educational Museum.

The more recent additions to the Museum may be referred to under the following heads :—

1.—*Assyrian and Egyptian Sculpture in the Museum.*

Of the exceedingly valuable collection of Sculptures with which Mr. Layard's Explorations at Nineveh have enriched the British Museum, we have several of the most interesting casts authorized by that Museum. This selection includes:—I. A colossal, human headed, winged Bull; II. A four winged Figure with Mace; III. Slabs representing (1) Sardanapalus I., with winged human Figure and Offerings; (2) the Eagle headed Deity, (Nisroch), with mystic Offerings, besides the Sacred Tree; (3) an Attendant, (Eunuch), with Bow and Arrows, etcetera; (4) Sardanapalus and Army besieging a City; (5) a Royal Lion Hunt; (6) Sardanapalus II, at an Altar pouring a Libation over dead Lions; (7) Sardanapalus III, and his Queen feasting after the Lion Hunt; (8) a very striking slab representing a wounded Lioness; (9-11 Horses, Lions, male and female Figures; IV. Black Obelisk from the great Mound, set up by Shalmaneser, (King of Assyria), about 850 years B.C.; V. Two most interesting Stones,

*A good deal of the information, in regard to the Museum, not given in this Report is similar to that contained in the year's Report. It is therefore omitted here.

(recently added to the British Museum collection), containing records in Cuniform Character, etcetera, of the sale of Land, about 1120 B.C.; VI. Large Statue of Memnon; VII. Lid of large Carcophagus; VIII. Side of an Obelisk from Temple of Thoth, (from Cairo); IX. Rosetta Stone, with inscription in honour of Ptolemy.

2.—Casts of Gems, Medals, etcetera.

(1) A beautiful Set of (470) Casts of celebrated Poniatowski Gems. (A similar collection is in the Ashmolean Museum, at Oxford). (2) A Set (of 170) Medals, illustrative of Roman History, the Emperors, etcetera; (3) a collection of Medals of the Popes; (4) a Set of the Great Seals of England; (5) 38 Medals of the Kings of England; (6) 80 of the Kings, etcetera, France; (7) 24 of Russian Emperors, etcetera; (8) 250 modern celebrated men; (9) besides numerous casts of Medallions, Tazza, pieces of Armour, etcetera; (10) a beautiful collection of casts of Leaves, Fruit, etcetera; (11) about 60 Busts, life size, of noted modern characters, etcetera.

3.—Ivory Carvings, Chromo-Lithographs, Photographs.

From the collection of the Arundel Society, published in connection with the South Kensington Museum, have been procured, (1) a full set of 150 specimens Ivory Carvings, of various periods from the Second to the Sixteenth century, in Fictile Ivory; (2) 60 Chromo-lithographs, beautifully coloured, illustrating Italian art; (3) 573 Photographs of National Portraits, illustrative of English History, including the Tudor period; (4) 400 miscellaneous Photographs of Objects of Art, Scenes, etcetera; (5) 170 Engravings of Modern Sculpture.

4.—Electrotypes of Art Treasures.

Of the rich and beautiful collection of Elkington and Franchi's Electrotypes of Art Treasures in the South Kensington collection, we have a small selection owing to the expense of the copies for sale.

5.—Samples of Food Analysis.

From the authorities of the South Kensington Museum we have a full set of the printed Labels of the numerous samples of Food Analysis exhibited in the Museum. We have specimens of the Analysis boxes with glass covers, so as to enable us to form a similar collection on a smaller scale, for our own Museum. This collection, when made, will form a most interesting and instructive study for the farmer and food consumer.

6.—India Rubber Manufactures.

Through the kindness of Messieurs Macintosh and Company, the eminent India Rubber Manufacturers of Manchester, we obtained several interesting specimens of Rubber-work, illustrative of the various uses to which India Rubber is applied. Some of these specimens are highly artistic in design.

7.—Naval Models.

Beautiful Models of War and Merchant Ships, Yachts, and Boats, including a line of Battle ship, Steam Ram, and Steam Vessels.

8.—Miscellaneous Objects of Art.

Greek, Roman and English Coins, with a few Curiosities and specimens of Natural History, etcetera.

Some striking Photographs of Objects and places in India, from the Indian Office in London, and Models from the National Life-Boat Association.

The South Kensington Museum is unrivalled in the beauty and extent of its internal fittings and arrangements, no less than in the extent and value of its collections of Objects of Art. and of industrial and practical value, as well as of articles of *vertu* of great historical interest. It is itself the parent Institution of many of the admirable collections and local Museums and Schools of Art throughout the three Kingdoms. The travelling collections of Objects of Art, which it sends to the local Exhibition of these Schools of Art is most varied and interesting. This, it may well be said, is "Object teaching" on a grand scale, and in a most attractive form, for the adult masses of England, Ireland and Scotland. and so it emphatically is. This is clearly the policy of the Educational Authorities in England, as it has been for years to some extent on the Continent of Europe. Looking over these large and attractive popular Museums, it is gratifying that we had thus far been enabled, by the liberality of our own Legislature, to keep pace in a humble degree with the great efforts which are now being systematically made in England to popularize Science and Art. These efforts are not only designed to promote this object, but at the same time they tend to interest and instruct the masses not only by cultivating the taste, but by gratifying and delighting the eye by means of well appointed Educational Museums and popular Exhibitions.

XVIII.—*Report of the Inspectors of Grammar and High Schools.*

In connection with recent discussions on the condition of our High Schools; I desire to direct special attention to the practical and excellent Report of the two Inspectors of High Schools, [which will be found in Chapter —— of this Volume]. The Reports of these Inspectors, (the Reverend J. G. D. Mackensie, M.A., and J. A. McLellan, M.A.), this year are alike kind and faithful, and are replete with practical remarks and suggestions; they point out most forcibly the defects of many, both High and Public Schools, and show clearly in the interests of higher English, as well as of sound Classical Education, the necessity of a thorough reform in the present system, as contemplated by the principal provisions of the High School provisions of the Act which were adopted last year by the Legislative Assembly. I am glad that, under the new Act, the principle of apportioning the High School Fund, according to results of teaching, and not merely according to the numbers of Pupils in the Schools, will be carried out. This feature of the proposed change in the mode of distributing the High School Grant, I shall discuss more fully in a subsequent part of this Report, in connection with the valuable and instructive joint report of the High School Inspectors, to which I have referred.

XIX. *Extracts from the Reports of Inspectors of Public Schools.*[*]

In commencing a new era of School progress, I have felt it to be indispensable, with the aid of the newly-appointed and efficient County Inspectors, to give a summary account of the present condition of the Schools,—especially in their internal,—or, as we might regard it, in their social aspects. This has been felt to be the more important at this period of our Educational history, in order to ascertain exactly where we are, and thus to fix a starting point of renewed progress and efficiency under the new School Act of 1871.

One of the Inspectors, in referring to the operation of the new School Act, says:— The state of the educational interests of this County may be judged by the fact, that in the last year of its existence. the old Board granted upwards of forty First Class Certificates, for terms varying from one to three years. There were also First Class Certificates, (few in number), that had been granted to endure during the pleasure of

Under this heading, the Chief Superintendent repeats the remarks on these Reports which he made on them in the preceding year ; they are, therefore, in part, not repeated here

the Board. Several of those holding such First Class Certificates, appeared at the first and second meeting of the New Board, and a considerable number of them did not attain a Third Class standing, and were evidently disqualified for the office which they had held.

At our July examination no one applied for a First Class Certificate, and only two for a Second. Of these last only one was successful; while no less than thirteen of the thirty-seven Candidates for Third Class Certificates failed to reach the minimum standard of excellence and were rejected.

There were evidences of improvement to be seen at the December examination. Out of twenty-eight Candidates eight were rejected.

They establish two general and suggestive facts,—one of warning, and one of encouragement:—

1. The first fact is that the internal condition of the Schools generally has not materially improved for years; that the character of the School Accommodation, the constant change of Teachers, and the paramount desire in many places to obtain their services, if at all, at a "cheap" rate, have told fearfully upon the *morale* of the Schools, and have discouraged all hope of real progress and advancement. Both Schools and Pupils have, under such a system, been brought into a chronic state of change, and experiment,—alike forbidding even a quiet respectability of standing, and utterly precluding anything like real progress and efficiency.

2. The second fact established by the Inspectors in their Reports,—and it is a most encouraging one,—is that the people generally, when approached in the right spirit, are most anxious to better, at least, the material condition of their Schools. They see that in most cases the School House and School Premises are far below even the passable state in which they should be found,—that their condition, in some wealthy neighbourhoods, is wretched,—even deplorable,—that the health of child and Teacher are alike endangered by the often unthinking parsimony of the Ratepayers. To have these things pointed out and a remedy suggested have been all that in very many cases has been required. In the majority of other cases a gentle pressure has sufficed to bring about a better state of things.

XX.—*General Remarks on the Subjects of Instruction and Condition of the Schools, and the Operation of the School Law Improvement Act of 1871.*

There is, however, another and more serious obstacle to the improvement in our Schools, which I regret to find it more difficult to remove than it is to induce Trustees to improve the condition of the School House and Premises. I refer to the objections to go beyond the merest rudiments of Education, or to employ an additional Teacher where one is manifestly inadequate to perform the duties required to make the School efficient, or to maintain proper discipline in it.

In my Report for last year I sought to explain and illustrate the necessity of some improvement in this respect. I showed that the normal condition of all systems of Education was to be content to reach a state of "passable respectability" and there remain.

Statistical Growth of the Schools in Advance of their Prosperity.

Now I appeal to Trustees and Teachers alike to aid the Inspectors and this Department in the effort made to effect the removal of this state of apathy and to awaken a desire to see that some substantial progress is made in the amount and quality of the Education to be provided in our Public Schools. The statistical results of the growth of our School System are fast growing upon us. They are indeed marvellous. A few years ago the number of our Schools did not much exceed 2,000, nor did the number of the Pupils in them reach 100,000, while the Expenditure for all purposes did not, even in 1851, equal $500,000. Now, while the number of the Schools has more than doubled, the increase in the number of Pupils and in the gross expenditure of the Schools is over four hundred per cent! No one, not even the most ardent admirer and defender of our School System, will, for a moment, maintain that in efficiency the Schools have at all kept pace with, or even approached this natural and yet most gratifying increase in the number and expenditures of our Schools. It is to a thoughtful consideration of these facts, and to a united effort to improve the internal condition of our Schools, that I would invite the attention of the friends of our Educational System.

Interesting Educational Statistical Facts.

The population of this Province, according to the recent census is 1,620,842. The number of children of School age is on an average a little over one-fourth of the whole. The number of Elementary Schools is not much below 5,000, and are maintained at an annual cost of above $2,000,000, or over one dollar per head of the population. Such being the magnitude to which our Educational System has grown, every man will feel how imperative it is upon us to see that that system is as thorough and complete in all of its details as possible; and that in no respect should it be allowed to fall below the average standard now reached by other educating countries. For convenience I give the gratifying statistics of our educational progress in this place.

REPORT FOR THE YEAR.	1860.	1861.	1862.	1863.	1864.	1865.	1866.	1867.	1868.	1869	1870	1871
	$	$	$	$	$	$	$	$	$	$	$	$
County Municipal Assessment..........	278,693	278,085	274,471	287,768	304,382	308,092	319,154	351,873	362,375	372,743	385,284	492,481
Trustees' School Assessment..........	556,682	587,297	620,268	631,755	659,380	711,197	760,966	799,708	855,558	890,834	951,099	1,027,184
Total Receipts........	1,324,272	1,381,279	1,396,123	1,432,885	1,481,187	1,545,000	1,607,971	1,670,335	1,789,332	1,827,426	1,944,364	2,124,471
Increase in Total Receipts.............	14,452	57,006	14,843	36,762	51,301	60,813	62,970	62,364	118,997	38,093	116,938	180,106

Putting these facts in another form, (with some additional ones), we can see at a glance the nature and extent of educational progress which we have made during the last twenty-one years:—

REPORT FOR THE YEAR.	1850.	1851.	1860.	1861.	1865.	1866.	1867.	1868.	1869.	1870.	1871.
Number of Public Schools reported...................	3,059	3,001	3,969	4,019	4,303	4,379	4,422	4,480	4,524	4,566	4,598
	$	$	$	$	$	$	$	$	$	$	$
Amount paid for Public School Teachers' Salaries .	353,716	391,308	895,591	914,113	1,041,052	1,066,880	1,093,516	1,146,543	1,175,166	1,222,681	1,191,476
Amount paid for erection, repairs of School-houses, etcetera......................	56,756	77,336	264,183	273,305	314,827	320,353	379,672	441,891	449,730	489,380	611,819
Balance forward each year....	24,016	16,893	164,498	189,861	189,121	220,738	197,147	200,898	202,530	232,303	321,176
Total amount available each year......................	$434,488	485,537	1,324,272	1,381,279	1,545,000	1,607,971	1,670,335	1,789,332	1,827,426	1,944,364	2,124,471

Two Current Objections Considered.

I desire first to refer to the objection made to the increase in the number of practical subjects required to be taught in our Public Schools, and then to the minor objection to employ two Teachers in the larger Schools.

And first, I may remark, that had the new "Programme of Subjects for Study in the Public Schools" been partially omitted, or had it been given a subordinate place to the essential elementary subjects of Reading, Writing and Arithmetic, then the first objection might have had force; and secondly, that no system of education has any pretensions to completeness, or even to what is of more consequence, a thorough practicalness of character, unless it had provided for teaching those additional subjects which the necessities of the Country and the pursuits and occupations of the people require.

By reference to the Programme of Studies, it will be seen from the number and order of the subjects in it, and the time prescribed per week for teaching each of them, that the first years of Public School Studies are almost entirely devoted to teaching the three primary, or fundamental, subjects of a good Education,—Reading, Writing and Arithmetic, including only such other subjects and to such a degree, as to relieve the Pupils from the tedium of the more severe and less attractive Studies, and to develop their faculties of observation and taste for knowledge, as suggested by the largest experience of the most advanced Educators. The subjects of the Programme are limited in both number and range to what is considered essential, and to what experience has proved can be thoroughly mastered by Pupils of ordinary capacity and diligence within thirteen years of age. The thorough teaching of a few subjects, within practical limits, will do more for intellectual development, and for the purposes of practical life, than the skimming over a wide range of topics. The subjects of Natural Science required by the Thirteenth Section of the new School Act to be taught in the Schools, and provided for in the Programme, are such, (and are prescribed to such an extent only), as is absolutely necessary for the advancement of the Country,—in Agriculture, the Mechanical Arts, and Manufactures, apart from Science and Literature, and are even less than are required by Law to be taught in some of the Western States of the Union.* And when the cheap and excellent Text Books prescribed are examined, in connection with the subjects specified, it will be found that nothing has been introduced which is impracticable, or for mere show, but everything for practical use, and that which admits of easy accomplishment.

Education Directed Towards the Pursuits and Occupations of a People.

On this subject Doctor Playfair gives the following striking illustration:—

The great advantage of directing education towards the pursuits and occupations of the people is that, while it elevates the individual, it at the same time gives security for the future prosperity of the Nation. There are instances of Nations rich in natural resources of industry, yet poor from the want of knowledge how to apply them; and there are opposite examples of Nations utterly devoid of Industrial advantages, but constituted of an educated people who use their Science as a compensation for their lack of raw material. Spain is an example of the first class, and Holland of the second. Spain, indeed, is wonderfully instructive, and her story is well told by Buckle, for you see her rise in glory or fall in shame, just as there are conditions of intellectual activity or torpor among her inhabitants. . . . This Nation has everything in the richest profusion to make it great and prosperous. Washed both by the Atlantic and Mediterranean, with noble Harbours, she might command an extensive commerce both with Europe and America. Few Countries have such riches in the natural resources of industry. A rich soil and almost tropical luxuriance of vegetation might make her a great food-exporting Nation. Iron and Coal, Copper, Quicksilver and Lead abound in profusion, but these do not create industries unless the people possess knowledge to apply them. When that knowledge prevailed, Spain was indeed among the most advanced of industrial Nations. Not only her metallurgic industries, but her Cotton, Woollen and Silk manufactures were unequalled; her Shipbuilding also was the admiration of other Nations. But all have decayed because Science withers among an uneducated people, and without Science Nations cannot thrive. Turn to Holland, once a mere province of Spain. She has nothing but a maritime position to give her any natural advantage. Not so bad, indeed, as Voltaire's statement, that she is a land formed from the sand brought up on the sounding-leads of English sailors, although she is actually created from the debris of Swiss and German Mountains brought down by the Rhine. Hence within her lands are no sources of mineral wealth; but she has compensated for its absence by an admirable education of her people. For my own Country, I have no ambition higher than to get Schools approaching in excellence to those of Holland. And so this mud-produced Country, fenced round by Dykes to prevent the Ocean from sweeping it away, is thriving, prosperous and happy, while

---

* Thus in the state of Illinois no Teacher is entitled to receive a Certificate of Qualification unless he is able to teach the elements of the Natural Science, Physiology, and the Laws of Health.

Arithmetic.—Arabic and Roman Notation to four periods; Simple and Compound Rules; Least Common Multiple; Greatest Common Measure; Reduction of Fractions; and Mental Arithmetic.

Grammar.—Principal grammatical forms and definitions; analysis and parsing of simple sentences.

Geography.—Definitions, Map notation and a knowledge of the Maps of the World, the Four Quarters, Ontario, and the Dominion.

Composition.—So far as to be able to write short narratives, or descriptions of objects, and familiar Letters.

Elements of Linear Drawing.—Outline of Maps, and common Objects on Paper.

History.—Elementary parts of Canadian and English History.

This, we see, is the whole Course required of Pupils before their entrance into the High Schools. A more simple Course of elementary study, elaborated as it is in the Limit Table, could not be devised, so as to possess any practical value at all; and no one will pretend to say that it is beyond the capacity of the Pupils for whom it is designed. I shall, therefore, not discuss it further, but simply glance at the remainder of the subjects prescribed for Pupils who complete their elementary education in the Public Schools. Even here we shall find that the Course of Instruction is practically narrowed down to a completion of the remainder of the subjects in the Fourth Class, and to the subjects in the Fifth Class,—for the Sixth Class, with the exception of small additional work in a few subjects, involves practically nothing more than a simple review of the previous Course.

The Additional Subjects in the Course of Study for Public Schools.

As to the additional subjects which have been introduced into the Course of Study in the Public Schools, I may state that they are the elements of Mechanics, (including Drawing), Commercial instruction, the elements of practical Science, Agriculture and Natural History. It is only in regard to two, or three, of these additional subjects that any discussion has arisen.

This branch of our subject opens up a wide field of practical discussion, and, to my mind, involves the whole question of a complete and comprehensive System of Public Instruction. It also introduces the second essential point in our System of Public Instruction, (which I have above indicated), videlicet:—"That the Course of Study prescribed should be sufficiently comprehensive to be adapted, not only to the pursuits and occupations of the people, but also to individual groups or classes of Pupils."

First Objection:—That the New Subjects are Premature.

Several objections on various grounds have been urged against the introduction of the new subjects into our Public Schools, but they may all be classified under two general heads:—

1. That their introduction is premature, (and that even if not premature),
2. They are unnecessary.

To my mind, the first objection involves a painful admission, and one humiliating to our boasted educational progress.

Thirty years have now elapsed since the first foundations of our Educational System were traced out, and twenty-five years at least, (now a quarter of a century), since our present structure was reared. No one will pretend to say that the founders of that System burthened it with a superfluous array of topics, or embarrassed the young learner with a multiplicity of subjects of study.

Our Present System Sketched in 1846.—We can Remain no longer in a State of Educational Probation and Tutelage.

In laying the foundations of our present System of Education, in 1846, after extensive inquiry in Europe and America, I endeavoured to sketch a comprehensive

Course of Study for our. Public Schools. Additional experience has but confirmed my views on this subject. But I did no more in those early days than to provide for the teaching of the merest elements of a plain English Education. It was left to after days to fill up the outline, and to supply wants in our Educational System as they arose. That time, as I trust I shall briefly demonstrate, has fully come. After twenty-five years of educational infancy it is high time that we should take a step, or two, in advance, if we do not desire to remain laggards in the great race of national progress and enlightenment. That we are not prepared to do so, and that our period of probation, or tutelage, is not felt to be sufficiently protracted, I am not prepared to admit. I at once, therefore, join issue with those who say that the introduction of the new elementary subjects into our Public School Course is premature. I feel that such a declaration involves a painful admission that our twenty-five years' progress has been illusory, and that we are not yet honestly prepared, or ready, to add the new elementary subjects to our School Course. Such an admission is, I think, contrary to fact, and is humiliating to our admitted position as one of the acknowledged educational leaders in the Provinces of our young Dominion.

Second Objection:—That Even if the New Subjects are not Premature, they are. Unnecessary.

The second objection contains a fundamental error, which should be fully met and thoroughly exposed. Unless our people entirely get rid of the idea that the new subjects of Study in the Public Schools are unnecessary, we shall never be able to build up our educational structure, with any degree of symmetry, as originally planned. And, what is more serious, if not fatal to our national growth, if we declare the new subjects to be unnecessary, we shall never, under our Educational System, attain to that national position to which the lovers of our Monarchical institutions, or the founders of our Confederation have wisely aspired.

Pressure on us to Advance.—We Cannot Remain Stationary.

Those who have occupied such a position as has enabled them to take an extensive outlook of the educational field here and elsewhere, have noticed with deep interest the restless activity which is observable everywhere. Discoveries in Science by eminent men, and their practical application to the necessities of Commercial, Profesional, and social life, have become so marked a feature of the present day, that they cease to be a wonder. Formerly such discoveries were regarded as the fond dream of the enthusiast; and every new application of Science to the practical arts was resisted by hundreds of interested opponents, who sneered at the discovery, and scorned the pretensions of the learned theorists whose knowledge of the principles of their Science, or Art, was a wonderful mystery to them, as also to the unenlightened Artisan.

Painful Results of our Present Limited Course of Instruction.

What is indicated is of common occurrence even in our day; and, painful as is the admission, it is no less true, that thousands of lads and young men are leaving our Public Schools in the rural districts every year, who are practically ignorant of even the elementary principles of Science, which they find developed in the Industrial Appliances with which they are immediately brought into contact upon leaving School. Take one in twenty of these lads, and ask him to give you anything like a correct idea of the principles of the Threshing Machine, Fanning Mill, Reaper, any of the Mechanical Powers, Railway Locomotive, or the thousand and one adaptations of Science to industry which he daily sees, and he will frankly tell you he knows little, or nothing, about them, and that in very many cases he never heard of them at School! Are we prepared to defend and perpetuate a state of things which produces such results, and be content to allow the Canadian youth of our day, with their ingenuity and varied intellect, to leave our Public Schools, (aptly called the "People's Colleges"), so unfit even to understand, much less to control and direct in the great Industrial enterprises and Mechanical inventions of the day? Every one who looks at the matter dispassionately will, I am sure, join with me in uttering an emphatic No; they will rather the more heartily join in every effort to enable our lads to take their place in the world's arena, fully equipped for the battle of life.

The Dominion, or National, Standpoint of View.

Let us look at this matter from another standpoint, as suggested by the Commissioners on Technical Education in my last Annual Report:—

.We are a young Country, placed in close proximity to a large and wonderfully progressive people. In the good providence of God, we are permitted to construct, on the broad and deep foundations of British liberty, the corner-stone of a new nationality, leaving to those who come after us to raise the stately.edifice itself. Apart from the Christianity of our people, what more lasting bond and cement of society in that new nationality, than a free and comprehensive Christian education for the youth of the land, such as we have sought to establish? Our aim should, therefore, be to make that system commensurate with the wants of our people, in harmony with the progressive spirit of the times, and comprehensive enough to embrace the various branches of human knowledge which are now continually being called into requisition in the daily life of the Farmer, the Artizan, and the Man of Business. And yet no one who has attentively studied the educational progress which we have made during the last ten years, or, (as a recent Report printed by the Legislature remarks), no one who has carefully watched the development of the material resources and Manufacturing Industris of this Province, but must have been painfully struck with the fact that, while we have liberally provided for the other wants of our people, we have almost entirely neglected making any provision for training, and then turning to practical account, that superior Scientific and Industrial skill among ourselves, which, in other Countries contribute so largely and effectively to develop their physical and industrial resources. The remarkable and almost unconscious development among ourselves of the manufacturing interest of the Country has reached a magnitude and importance that it would be suicidal to those interests, (in these days of keen competition with our American neighbours), and injurious to their proper development, not to provide without delay for the production among ourselves of a class of skilled Machinists, Manufacturers, Engineers, Chemists, and others. No one can visit any of the Industrial centres which have sprung up in different parts of the Country and in our larger Towns without being struck with their value and importance, and the number and variety of the skilled Labourers employed. Inquiry into the source of supply of this Industrial class reveals the fact, that, from the youngest Employés up to the Foreman of the works, they are almost entirely indebted to England, Ireland, Scotland, the United States, and other Coutries for that supply. . . . .

The marvellous revolution caused by the practical application of steam and telegraphy, (those golden links of Science), to locomotion, commerce, industry and intercommunication, has so stimulated the inventive genius of man, that we now cease to be astonished at any new discovery, and only await each successive development of Science still more wonderful than the last, to calmly discuss its merits and advantages. In this active race of competition our Province, (the leading one in the Dominion), cannot stand still. With all our inventions we have not yet been able to discover the royal road to learning; and our youth cannot, Minerva-like, spring fully armed into the arena of competitive science and skill. We must, therefore, provide liberally for the patient and practical instruction in every grade and department of knowledge, so that, with God's blessing, we shall not fall behind in the great race of national intelligence and progress.[*]

Shallow Education a Grievous National Wrong,—A Warning.

The Honourable Mr. Wickersham, State Superintendent of Pennsylvania, thus illustrates the great loss which the Country sustains by the mere "read, write and cipher" system which some advocate for Public Schools, especially in the absence of men of broad views and intelligent culture. He says:—

Many of our people seem to think that if they have their children taught simply to read, write, and cipher, it is enough. Others add to these branches a smattering

[*] Report of Inquiry in regard to Schools of Technical Science. By Doctors Hodgins and Machattie, page 19.

of Geography and Grammar, and call their children well educated. This superficial education is breeding among our people shallowness, rawness, conceit, instability, and a want of self-respect, honour, and dignity. It is lowering the tone of society, subjecting us to the rule of unprincipled Demagogues, filling high positions with incompetent men, and weakening public virtue. Every social interest and every Governmental concern in this Country is suffering for want of more men of broad views, ripe culture, and high sense of right. I heartily endorse the sentiment uttered by President Porter, of Yale College, in his recent inaugural Address, that, —

The lessons on History, both the earlier and more recent, are distinct and vivid: that in a Country like ours, wealthy, proud, and self-confident, there can be neither permanence, nor dignity, if the best knowledge and the highest culture do not influence its population and institutions.

II. THE NEW SUBJECTS OF MECHANICS, DRAWING, PRACTICAL SCIENCE, NATURAL HISTORY, AGRICULTURE, VOCAL MUSIC, AND COMMERCIAL INSTRUCTION DISCUSSED SEPARATELY.

1. I may remark that, with a view to meet the necessities of the case, (as indicated above), and as stated last year, "one great object of the new School Act was to make our Public Schools more directly and effectively subservient to the interests of Agriculture, Manufactures and Mechanics."

2. In my first Special Report on "A System of Public Elementary Education for Upper Canada," printed by the Legislature in 1846, I stated the institutions necessary for these purposes; and in the concluding remarks of two recent Annual Reports I have expressed strong convictions on the subject.

When we consider the network of Railroads which are intersecting, as well as extending from one end to the other of our Country, the various important Manufactures which are springing up in our Cities, Towns and Villages, and the Mines which are beginning to be worked, and which admit of indefinite development, provision should undoubtedly be made for educating our own Mechanical and Civil Engineers, and chief workers in Mechanics and Mines; but I here speak of the more elementary part of the work of practical education, which should be given in the ordinary Public Schools.

I.—*Preliminary Suggestions in Regard to the Amount of and the Way in which Instructions in Schools should be Given.*

The Superintendent of the State of Maine, in his last Report, asks and answers the following questions in regard to a Course of Study for our Public Schools:—

1. What, (he asks), shall be taught in our Common Schools?—*Answer.* Those things necessary to our children as men and women. When shall the several branches be taught?—*Answer.* As fast as their faculties of sensation, perception and reasoning develop. How shall they be taught?—*Answer.* In the order of development of the child's faculties, and with all the allurements possible to the inventive powers of the adult mind.

2. Doctor Lyon Playfair also answers the latter question in the following forcible language:—

The Pupil must be brought in face of the facts through experiment and demonstration. He should pull the Plant to pieces, and see how it is constructed. He must vex the Electric Cylinder until it yields him its sparks. He must apply with his own hand the Magnet to the Needle. He must see Water broken up into its constituent parts, and witness the violence with which its elements unite. Unless he is brought into actual contact with the facts, and taught to observe and bring them into relation with the Science evolved from them, it were better that instruction in Science should be left alone. For one of the first lessons he must learn from Science is not to trust in authority, but to demand proof for each asseveration. All this is true education, for it draws out faculties of observation, connects observed facts with the conceptions deduced from them in the course of ages, gives discipline and courage to thought, and teaches a knowledge of Scientific method which will serve a lifetime. Nor can such an education be begun too early. The whole yearnings of a child are for the Natural Phenomena around him, until they are smothered by the ignorance of the Parent. He is a young Linnæus roaming over the Fields in search of Flowers. He is a young Conchologist, or Mineralogist gathering Shells, or Pebbles on the Sea Shore. He is an Ornithologist, and goes Bird-nesting; and Ichyologist, and catches Fish. Glorious education in nature all this, if the Teacher knew how to direct and utilize it. The present system is truly ignoble, for it sends the workingman into the world in gross ignorance of everything he has to do in it. The utilitarian system is noble in so far as it treats him as an intelligent being who ought to understand the nature of his occupation, and the principles involved in it. If you bring up a Ploughman in utter ignorance of everything relating to the food of Plants, of every Mechanical principle of Farm Implements, of the Weather to which he is exposed, of the Sun that shines upon him, and makes the Plants to grow, of the rain which, while it drenches him, refreshes the Crops around, is that ignorance conducive to his functions as an intelligent being? All Nations which have in recent years revised their Educational Systems, have provided a class of Secondary Schools for the Industrial Classes, especially devoted to teach them the principles of Science and Art relating to their Industries. Holland compels every Town of 10,000 inhabitants to erect such Schools.

3. The Superintendent of the State of Kansas makes the following highly suggestive remarks on this subject:—

A practical education is by far the best. Close observation in every-day life leads to this. Inquiry and observation are encouraged by visiting with the Pupils the Telegraph Office, the Printing Office, the Book-bindery, Mills and Factories of all kinds, the Foundry and Machine Shops. Attention should be called to the points of interest, and the working of the Machinery fully explained, together with the practical utility and importance of each particular avocation, their mutual dependence upon each other, and their general influence upon society. Such visits give the Pupil a much better idea of the manner in which the various departments of business are conducted, and of the operation of the Machinery, than all the apparatus that can be found.

II.—*Reform in the Mode of Teaching in the Public Schools.*

A recent Writer, (Professor Allen, of Pennsylvania), in an Essay on "Reform in Primary Teaching," points out in graphic language the defects in the mode of dealing with "children in the School Room." He summarizes a few practical suggestions on the subject as follows. His "new departure" consists:—

1. In dividing School life into two periods, known respectively as the how, or fact period, and the why, or philosophical. Instruction during the first period consists in giving processes, familiarizing Tables, acquiring rapidity and accuracy in performing, and should be wholly, or nearly so, conversational.

2. As all Studies in the School Room may be classed under the three heads of Language, Mathematics and Natural Science, and, as the elements of all Physical and Natural Science should be taught to the youngest child that enters the School, every child should have daily one lesson in Language, one in Mathematics, and one in Science.

3. Instruction should first be given in how to properly use the senses, that they may convey to the mind accurate knowledge, properly certified to or tested. Very much attention should be given to securing greater accuracy of the perspective faculties. This embraces three studies, all that any Pupil at any time of life ought to pursue. In connection with this, Drawing, Writing and Music come in, not as studies, but as changes, which is, in the true sense of the word, rest.

4. The spoken instead of the written word should first be taught. No attention, or time, should be given during this first period to teach the letters, or figures. Words should be printed, or written, (better the latter), simply as forms, or as pictures are made. These may be taken from Wall Cards, or from lessons put upon the Board by the Teacher. As Spelling would not be used did we not write, and as we use it properly only in Writing, Spelling should not be taught until Writing is learned, and oral Spelling should never be used as a process for teaching Spelling.

As Words should be taught before Letters, the time will not be long before the Letters and figures will be known by the Pupils, and you will have been saved a vast amount of vexatious, tedious, and patience-trying work, and the Pupil will have been saved that rough, stony and thorny path over which the most of us have trodden in sorrow. They will have picked up these little waifs, or integral parts, of language the natural way.

If we desire to teach language efficiently and correctly, we must bear in mind that habits of speech are caught much more easily and readily than taught.

5. Physical Science should be taught by bringing the subjects and things of which they treat as far as possible into the presence of the child. Let his eyes see and his hands feel the subjects and things presented. In doing this every School Room becomes a miniature Museum. I should like to exhibit such an one as I now have in mind, collected entirely by the children of the School. In thus studying these subjects the child is brought in direct contact with the material with which he daily meets and has to do with in after life. His vocabulary is increased, as well as his knowledge of the meaning and spelling of words. All his exercises should be written.

14—XXIII.

6. No Primary School ought to be open for a longer period each day than four hours, and the rooms should be so arranged and such fixtures furnished as will allow the Pupil to be standing, or sitting, as he may desire. Children thus situated, it is found, seldom sit. This is nature's plan.

7. None but experienced Teachers and those of much learning and culture, ought ever to be placed in Primary Schools. Consequently the primary Teacher ought to have a higher Salary than in any other grade.

The Superintendent of the State of Maine, in an instructive paragraph of his last Report, thus gives the result of his own experience on the best mode of "keeping children employed in School." He says:—

During the last Winter I endeavoured, by visiting the Schools, and by public Lectures, to solve the question, How shall young children be kept busy in their Studies so as to render them interested and profited by them? While visiting the Schools, I noticed that from one-half to two-thirds of the children were idle a large portion of the time. To remedy this state of things, and feeling that the time of these children is as valuable as it ever will be, I devised a Course of Exercises by which the children could be employed while the Teacher might be engaged in other duties. I, therefore, introduced Script-hand Writing on the Blackboard and on their Slates. Contrary to the generally received opinion, young children will learn Script-hand more easily than the printed forms of the Letters. Little children delight in imitating the older ones, and whenever I presented the subject to the young children, they bounded to the work with the most intense pleasure. Many Teachers have pursued the course with most interesting results. It places a new power in the hands of both Teacher and Pupil, and gives the children something to do. My cardinal motto in this, as in other work, has been, that children love to do things when they know how to do them.

Other exercises in Arithmetic, Spelling, Drawing and Geography, were introduced, so that under skilful management a large proportion of the time could be employed not as a compulsory exercise, but one in which the children delighted to engage. I deem these as vital points in advancing the condition of our Schools; and I notice that, in proportion as Teachers have taken hold of these matters, have their services been in demand and higher wages obtained.

III.—*Shorter School Hours, and not Shorter Programme.*

The suggestion as to a School-teaching day of only four hours has many able advocates. The State Superintendent of Kansas has collected their opinions on the subject, and thus introduces them:—

Now, if it be true, that the voluntary attention of children under ten years of age cannot be retained, without detriment, longer than fifteen or twenty minutes at one time, on any given subject, and we believe it is, not only from our own experience, but from the observations of distinguished Educators, both in this Country and in Europe, then, the hours of study in our Schools should be shortened.

A law reducing a School-day to four hours, instead of six, as at present, would be a great blessing, not only to the children in School, but to the cause of Education in general. A session of two hours in the forenoon, and two in the afternoon, with a recess of fifteen minutes in the middle of each for all the Pupils in the School, and a recess of ten minutes in the middle of each subdivision for all the children under ten years of age, would make a judicious subdivision for study and relaxation under the four-hour system. It is sincerely believed that with the diminished time in School, and recesses as indicated, the Pupils will learn more in a given time, and retain what they do learn, better than they possibly can with longer sessions. Then why protract the School Sessions till every child is completely worn out and disgusted with everything that pertains to Books, School and Education, when his whole nature revolts at the very thought of this wicked and unwise course of action? The surroundings and appliances of the School Room, the comfort and conveniences of the Furniture, and the time for study and relaxation; in short, everything should be conducive in the highest degree to calm, quiet study.

Mr. E. Chadwick, C.B., of England, has written a very remarkable pamphlet, containing a statement of facts that ought to command the attention of the civilized world. It was published pursuant to an Address to the House of Lords. He says:—

Struck by the frightful disproportion between the powers of childish attention and the length of School hours, he had directed questions to many distinguished Teachers on the subject. For instance:—

Mr. Donaldson, Head Master of the Training College at Glasgow, states that the limits of voluntary and intelligent attention are with children of from five to seven

14a—XXIII.

years of age, about fifteen minutes; from seven to ten years of age, about twenty minutes; from ten to twelve years of age, about fifty-five minutes; from twelve to sixteen or eighteen years of age, about eighty minutes, and continues:—I have repeatedly obtained a bright voluntary attention from each of those classes five or ten or fifteen minutes more, but I observed it was at the expense of the succeeding lesson.

The Reverend J. A. Morrison, Rector of the same College, speaking on the same subject, says:—

I will undertake to teach one hundred children in three hours a day, as much as they can by possibility receive; and I hold it to be an axiom in education, that no lesson has been given, till it has been received; as soon, therefore, as the receiving power of the children is exhausted, anything given, is useless, nay injurious, inasmuch as you thereby weaken instead of strengthen the receiving power. This ought to be a first principle in Education. I think it is seldom acted on.

In Denmark children may attend School one part of the day, and work the other part. A School House in Copenhagen is furnished for a thousand children; one Session is held in the morning, a thousand attending; in the afternoon a second thousand attend, both Schools being under the same general management. This system secures a happy union of bodily and mental exercise. It is profitable whether considered in an intellectual, moral, or pecuniary, point of view, and is based on sound principles. Experience proves that a few hours of mental labour is better for the educational progress of the Student, than of a whole day of forced application to Books, as was the custom in early times.

IV.—*Results of the Short Hours System.—Example.*

The Report of the Schools in Boston furnishes the following illustrative example of the short hour system:—

There is one peculiarity in the management of the Woburn High School which, for several reasons, is worthy of special consideration. The "half-day system," which has been in operation there for several years, requires the attendance of the Pupil but one-half of each day, provided he has faithfully performd his duties. It is thought that this system has a good influence upon the character of the Pupil, as it increases his self-reliance, and cultivates a feeling of responsibility; upon his health, also, as during the time in which he is preparing his lessons he escapes the necessary restraint of the School Room and its vitiated Atmosphere; and upon his mind, as undisturbed by the distracting influences that are unavoidable in a large School, he can accomplish much more in the same time, and with much more satisfaction. It is an economical arrangement, also. Says the Superintendent:—"The present High School House was intended to accommodate ninety Pupils. With this system it will accommodate just twice that number." (One half attending in the morning and the other half in the afternoon). "Hence, it is to-day, saving an expenditure of from Twenty to Thirty thousand dollars in the erection of a new High School Building."

The results of this system are so entirely satisfactory to all parties interested, and its advantages so obvious, that I would commend it for adoption in those Towns whose citizens are not prepared to incur the expense of erecting new High School Buildings, or of enlarging existing ones, to accommodate the increasing number of Pupils prepared to enter upon the High School Course of Study.

V.—*Written Examinations as an Educational Help.*

In the opinion of most Educators, the system of written Examinations is found to be a most valuable help in the process of Education. The State Superintendent of Minnesota thus writes, and his opinions are endorsed by the Teachers of his State in the Resolution below. He says:—

There is no exercise in which Pupils can engage that will be a source of more profit to them, or of greater satisfaction to Teachers and Parents than this work. Nothing would be of more lasting benefit to all classes in our High and graded Schools than to have daily Drills in expressing their ideas on Paper, taking for a subjcet some of their regular lessons. By this means lasting benefit will accrue to the Pupil by enabling him to express his ideas clearly and readily. The Teacher in correcting the work, should do it, not only in respect to the Pupils' knowledge of the subject, but also in relation to the knowledge exhibited in the use of Capital Letters, Punctnation, Penmanship, Spelling, neatness of paper, and style of expression. This matter of written Examinations was discussed in the last Convention of County Superintendents to urge upon Teachers of all grades its great importance. No one will, I think, over-estimate the importance of this work, who knows how much difficulty the Pupils in our best Schools, find in expressing their ideas on paper, even when writing on a subject with which they are best acquainted. Any one who can do well in a written Examination can do well in an oral one. But often, those who recite well, orally, show very many errors as soon as they answer questions on paper.

Resolved,—That we heartily approve and recommend the practice of frequent written and oral Examinations in our Public Schools, and that we deem it essential to the best interests of all our Schools that such Examinations be had at least as often as once a month.

VI.—*Object Teaching as an Introduction to Practical Science in the Schools.*

As "Object Teaching" is a most valuable mode of introducing the study of prac-tical Science into the Schools, I think it well briefly to state the principles on which it is based, and to notice an interesting fact relating to our Depository in connection with its adoption in the neighbouring State of New York, taken from the Report of the State of Iowa. The Report says:—

In the History of Education no era is more distinguished than that which Pestalozzi introduced. This great Philanthropist and Educator originated the most signal reform in the training of young minds,—the most radical, far-reaching, and philosophical that has ever been undertaken by man. Like all noted characters who stand for the ruling ideas of the age in which they live, he "builded wiser than he knew." He started on the assumption that all methods of Education to be normal, should be natural, and immediately put his own hand to the work of revolutionizing the Systems of Instruction he found around him. This idea he would make supreme. The child is pre-eminently a creature of sense; it lives in the objects around it, and, therefore, those objects, and not dry abstract names and propositions, should be the material of its study.

Things and not Words, that was the motto. Give the child what it can see, and hear, and feel; and from the known properties of such objects it will ascend by the common route of all true discovery to other attributes which are yet to be known. Pestalozzi plied his Contemporaries with the question, how, in the first instance, is the area of human knowledge extended in any line of research whatever. Since the days of Bacon men were asking Nature questions, and she never had failed to respond event-ually to their inquiries. And now the theory was, that the children under the direction of a competent Teacher, should make their own discoveries in the same way.

The idea took entire possession of Pestalozzi, and henceforth his whole life was given up to the work of drawing out and elaborating his scheme. It is a significant fact that his own efforts towards realizing his plan were for the most part a series of diversified experiments with the most disheartening and unsatisfying results. Failure followed upon failure, and yet his enthusiasm and depth of conviction, only gathered fire and intensity from each successive disappointment. He organised Schools and wrote Books; indeed he sacrificed all he had and his life in the great reform.

It will suffice to say that the system he inaugurated spread itself rapidly through-out the European States, and extended itself into our own Country. It practically gave Prussia its peerless system of Public Schools which has been the pole-star of Educationists in all other parts of the civilized world. Whatever of superiority that System has, it was directly to the infusion of Pestalozzianism in it and the new moral impulse which the whole work of Popular Instruction received through that movement. Commending itself to the great minds of all Countries, it was transplanted, almost within the life-time of its founder, to Prussia, Germany, Sardinia, Greece, Denmark, England, and many of the Colonies of Great Britain, and through the munificence of William MacClure, and the labours of James Keef, a disciple of Pestalozzi, it gained a foothold in 1809 on American soil, through a systematic, although somewhat inauspicious, effort in the City of Philadelphia.

The Report thus speaks of the introduction of "Object Teaching" into New York from the Educational Depository of Ontario:—

The system was introduced and modified in adaption to the Anglo-Saxon mind and character in the best Schools of Canada, and the celebrated Normal and Model Schools of Toronto. These Schools were visited by Professor E. A. Sheldon, of Oswego, New York, who incidentally found in the Depository there the Books published by the "Home and Colonial Society" on elementary instruction; these he brought home with him, together with Pictures, and other Apparatus used in illustrating the Lessons, and such practical hints in Organization and Method as those promising Schools afforded.* There

_____
* Incidentally this is a practical tribute to the value and usefulness of our Educational Depository.

soon sprung up in Oswego, under the enterprising and persistent labours of this indefatigable Educator, an Institution, which, until the present time, has maintained the character of being the great centre of Objective Teaching in the United States. Thence, in all directions, in Schools of all sorts, Normal Schools, Schools of Applied Science, Institutes, Teachers' Associations Academies, Colleges, indeed everywhere, the system has taken more, or less, root. In the Public Schools, especially the whole System of Primary Instruction has been revolutionized by the introduction of these methods, and the higher departments of our graded School System have felt the same re-fashioning influence to an extent scarcely less perceptible.

VII.—*Necessity for Teaching Practical Science in the Schools.—Examples.*

I have already referred to the necessity, founded upon our own experience and deficiencies, for introducing the new subjects of Study into our Public Schools. I have shown that the springing up and growth of various kinds of Manufactures and Industries among us have compelled the Department to suggest means,—even at a later period in our educational history than it should have been done,—by which we should be able to produce skilled Artizans among ourselves. Judged by the experience and example of other educating States and Countries, our Legislature,—although a little behind time,—has wisely provided and required that the elements of the Natural Sciences shall be taught in our Public Schools. I shall now give a few of those illustrative examples, in order to show that other Countries, whose Educational System can boast of no higher degree of efficiency than ours, whose Industrial necessities are no greater, and the intelligence of whose people is not beyond that of ours, have even gone further in this direction than we have thought of doing.

Example of the State of Illinois.

In the much younger State of Ilinois,—whose wilds were even first explored by white men from Canada,—the Legislature has by enactment declared that:—

No Teacher shall be authorized to teach a Common School who is not qualified to teach the Elements* of the Natural Sciences, Physiology and the Laws of Health, in addition to the branches previously required.

The Superintendent of Public Instruction in that State, (The Honourable N. Bateman), in his Official Circular to County Inspectors, of May last, thus defines, with great judgment and propriety, the limits to which these subjects shall be taught in the Schools. He says:—

The 8th Section of the Act provides that, "the State Superintendent of Public Instruction shall make such Rules and Regulations as may be necessary and expedient to carry into efficient and uniform effect the provisions of this Act." The duty, therefore, of so construing the provision in respect to the Natural Sciences as to give it practical effect, devolves upon the State Superintendent, and he must perform it as best he may; and the conclusions reached by him, in the premises, must govern and be observed by all concerned throughout the State, to the end that "efficient and uniform effect" may be given to the provisions in question.

Botany.—In seeking a proper solution to this enquiry, as to which of the many departments and branches of Study included in the general term, "Natural Sciences," shall be designated and prescribed? I have given prominence to the observed facts and tendencies of the childish nature, and tried to find and follow the path thereby indicated; considering it safe and logical to have Teachers begin their preparation with those departments of Science towards which children manifest the earliest and most spontaneous inclination. Passing Physiology and Hygiene, concerning which there is no option, is not the Love of Flowers an almost instinctive and universal sentiment of childhood? Who can describe the irrepressible delight of the little ones, wandering among the Violets and Roses over the soft verdure of Lawn and Meadow, or beneath the leafy draperies of the bright green Woods? What would be thought of a child, sound in body and mind, who should not love these things? If this be a postulate of the youthful nature everywhere, does it not point unmistakably to Botany, as one of the first, if not the very first, of the Natural Sciences towards which the inquisitive, beauty-loving and knowledge-craving spirit of the child should be intelligently directed? I think it does.

---

* The State Superintendent thus defines the meaning of the term *Elements.* He says: " The ' Elements ' of a Science are its fundamental principles, its rudiments, its primary rules, laws and facts; the simplest and most essential things involved in a knowledge of it."

Natural History.—And where does the law of "natural selection" next lead the little children,—where do they love best to turn for enjoyment and curious scrutiny when weary of their treasures of Plants and Flowers,—where, but to "Pussy" and "Towser;" to "Pony" and "Brindle;" to the solft-eyed Calves and frisking Lambs; to the matronly Hens with their noisy broods, and the gay-plumaged Birds, hopping and twittering in Bush and Tree? Are we not still in the plain, beaten path of a universal truth,—a common experience? Do children tire of watching those wonderful Creatures, noting their motions, habits and ways? This, then, is another postulate of the youthful nature which it cannot be unwise to seize upon and turn to account, and it points to Zoology.

Mechanics.—Next to these two forms of life, as seen in the growth of Plants and Animals, the predilections of children are not so spontaneous and 'uniform. But the thread of observation will still guide us to one more selection. When tired, for the time, of its Plants and Flowers, and of its living Pets, the average child will turn to its Toys,—examine their parts and structure, ask how they are made, their uses and materials, meantime testing their strength and endurance in numerous unthought of ways,—taking them to pieces, or breaking them in pieces, to see what is inside, and to try their powers of reconstruction. The little experimenter goes on from one Mechanical device to another, until his strength and skill are exhausted and baffled, or rewarded with success. Long before he has even heard the names of the Six Machines of Science, he is familiar with the practical operation of nearly all of them, and ready for further instruction. The blandishments of Music, the wonder-working powers of Light and Heat, and the red bolts leaping from the dark bosom of the Storm Cloud, have all been observed with awe, or delight, while yet the words Acoustics, Optics, Caloric and Electricity were to him without sense, or meaning. The branch of Physics that shall satisfy him with its grand revelations upon all these subjects, is Natural Philosophy.

2. *Example of the State of Wisconsin.*—In the equally young State of Wisconsin the Law also provides that:—

The State Superintendent of Public Instruction shall, before each Examination held under the provisions of this Act, appoint three competent Persons, residents of this State, who shall constitute a State Board of Examiners, and who shall, under the Rules and Regulations to be prescribed by the said Superintendent, thoroughly examine all Persons desiring State Certificates in the branches of Study in which applicants are now required to be examined by County Superintendents for a First-grade Certificate, and in such other branches as the State Superintendent may prescribe. The branches of Study in Natural Science, etcetera, to which the Act refers, and in which applicants are now required to be examined, are:—

The elementary principles of Natural Philosophy, Physiology, Botany, Zoology, Chemistry, Geology, Political Economy and Mental Philosophy.

VIII.—*Importance of Teaching Elementary Science in the Public Schools.*

1. Doctor Lyon Playfair, in an Address before the Social Science Congress in England, thus deplores the absence of provision for teaching elementary Science in the Schools:—

The educational principle of Continental Nations is to link on Primary Schools to Secondary Improvement Schools. The links are always composed of higher subjects, the three R's being in all cases the basis of instruction; elementary Science, and even some of its applications, is uniformly encouraged and generally enforced. But as we have no Schools corresponding to the Secondary Improvement Schools for the working classes, we suppose we can do without, used as links. No armour plate of knowledge is given to our future Artisan, but a mere veneer of the three R's, so thin as to rub off completely in three, or four, years of the wear and tear of life.

2. In regard to the study of Natural Science in the Schools, the Royal Commissioners appointed to enquire into Systems of Schools, say:—

We think it established that the Study of Natural Science develops better than any other Studies the observing faculties, disciplines the intellect by teaching induction as well as deduction, supplies a useful balance to the Studies of Language and Mathematics, and provides much instruction of great value for the occupations of after-life

IX.—*The Study of Natural History in the Schools.*

1. On the interest which can be excited in children in the study of Natural History, I can add little to the suggestive remarks of the Superintendent of the State of Illinois. But in further illustration of the subject, I would add a few words by Professor

Agassiz, formerly a distinguished Teacher in Switzerland, latterly a more distinguished Professor in the United States. In an Address at an educational meeting in Boston, "On the desirability of introducing the study of Natural History into our Schools, and of using that instruction as a means of developing the faculties of children, and leading them to a knowledge of the Creator," Professor Agassiz observes:—

I wish to awaken a conviction that the knowledge of Nature in our day lies at the very foundation of the prosperity of States; that the study of the Phenomena cf Nature is one of the most efficient means for the development of the human faculties, and that, on these.grounds, it is highly important that this branch of Education should be introduced into our Schools as soon as possible. To satisfy you how important the Study of Nature is to the community at large, I need only allude to the manner in which, in modern times, men have learned to control the forces of nature, and to work out the material which our earth produces.

2. Thomas Carlyle wrote:—

For many years it has been one of my constant regrets, that no School Master of mine had a knowledge of Natural History, so far, at least, as to have taught the little winged and wingless neighbours that are continually meeting me with a salutation which I cannot answer, as things are. Why didn't somebody teach me the Constellations too, and make me at home in the Starry Heavens which are always overhead, and which I don't half know to this day? But there will come a day when, in all Scottish Towns and' Villages, the School Masters will be strictly required to possess such capabilities.

3. The Superintendent of Public Instruction in the State of Kansas, thus points out a practical and suggestive way of interesting children in the study of Natural History. He says:—

Excursions to the Fields and Woods, to the Hill sides and deep Valleys, afford an excellent opportunity for observing and studying Nature in her various departments. The Pupils should be encouraged to collect and preserve specimens of the different varieties of Plants. Every variety of Mineral, from the most common Clay to the Gem, specimens of Rocks and Mineralized animal and vegetable Remains. They will soon learn that an abundance of Shells, in a Fossil, or petrified state, are found in Limestone; of Vegetables in Sandstone, Slate, Clay, etcetera; and numerous Bones, and even whole Skeletons of Quadrupeds, Birds, Amphibious Animals, Fishes and also Insects, occur in Rocks of various descriptions.

The formation of Cabinets, Herbaria and Acquaria, should be encouraged in every School. An Aquarium in a School Room is a source of never-ending interest. It opens a new department in Nature hitherto but little studied. Nature always rewards her closest Students with the most signal success. The most important discoveries have been made by men whose early lives were spent in a close observance of Nature. In this extensive range of subjects the Teacher will easily discover the peculiar taste and aptitude of his Pupils. Let them be encouraged in that department in which the God of Nature has designed them to work. It is solemnly believed that ninety-nine hundredths of all the difficulties incident to the Home circle and the School Room arise from the persistent efforts of Parents and Teachers to force children to disregard Nature's teaching. It is not the province of the Educator to make mind, nor to prevent, or distort it, but to lead it out, to develop it by timely assistance. Independent individual thought, study and exertion develop that originality of mind which boldly leaves the old beaten paths of Science and fearlessly strikes out into new and unexplored fields, to reap the rich rewards in store. Mental impressions in early life are hard to obliterate. How important, then, that the susceptible mind be thoroughly imbued with the love of order, right and justice; with respect for equity, good government and rightful authority.

X.—Drawing: Its Importance and Value in our Schools.

1. So important and necessary was Drawing, (which is now prescribed in our Schools), felt to be, as a branch of learning, that in 1870, the Legislature of Massachusetts passed the following Law on the subject:—

The General Statutes are hereby amended so as to include Drawing among the branches of learning which are by said Section required to be taught in the Public Schools.

Any City or Town may, and every City and Town having more than ten thousand inhabitants shall, annually make provision for giving free instruction in Industrial, or Mechanical, Drawing, to persons over fifteen years of age, either in day, or evening Schools, under the direction of the School Committee.

2. On the operation of this enactment, the Board of Education for the State of Massachusetts remarks:—

A special Agent, (Mr. W. Smith, Art Master of Leeds, England), was appointed by the Board in July, 1871, as Director of Art Education, and is now engaged in the work of aiding in the carrying out the requirements of the Law of 1870, relating to the teaching of Drawing in the Public Schools. . . . His labours thus far, have met with gratifying success. . . . It is now admitted by all who have examined the subject, that everyone who can learn to write can learn to draw, and that Drawing is simpler in its elements and can be more easily acquired than Writing. Special Instructors are no more required for Drawing than for Writing and Arithmetic. Teachers must learn and teach elementary Drawing as they learn to teach other branches. It has been found abroad that Teachers can acquire a sufficient knowledge of Drawing without any great sacrifice of time or patience.

The Honourable Henry Barnard, so well known as a leading Educationist, in the United States, thus speaks of the ease in which children can be instructed in Drawing:—

Drawing should be taught in every grade of our Public Schools. The first instinct, or inclination, of the child is to handle the pencil, and "draw something." The sparks of what may be "that sacred fire," should not be smothered, but fanned into a flame. Drawing is the alphabet, or rather the language of Art; and when this is understood, the child is the possible Sculptor, Painter, or Architect. Instruction in these elements of Art, corrects the taste and gives the hand skill; it gives the trained, artistic eye which detects the incongruous, the ungraceful, and the ill-proportioned, and which, on the other hand, the graceful, harmonious, and symmetrical, never escape.

The instructed eye derives the same intense delight from the pleasures of sight as the instructed ear from the harmonies of sound. The introduction of this branch of Study into our Public Schools will do more than anything else to popularize Art, and give the whole people a taste for Art in its nobler as well as simpler forms.

4. The Board of Education in Lowell, Massachusetts, (a well-known manufacturing Town), thus summarizes the value and importance of Drawing in the Schools:—

The importance of Drawing, as a branch of Public Instruction, has been recognized in the Manufacturing Countries of Europe for a long time; which fact has given them great advantage in the Manual Arts. Sixty years ago, the great Napoleon caused Drawing to be made a prominent Study in the Schools of France; the success of the Artisans of that Country in decorative and ornamental productions is one of the results, bringing immense wealth to its shores from other lands, our own paying no small part.

In Germany the teaching of Drawing has been universal for generations. A Teacher who could not draw and teach Drawing, would no sooner be employed in one of her Schools than one who had not learned to read and write. This training shows itself in the superior skill and accuracy of the German Soldier, and it adds vastly to the value of the German Mechanics, enabling them, in some parts of our Country, to get from fifty cents to a dollar a day more than Workmen of equal merit in other respects.

At the World's Exhibition, in London, in 1851, with respect to Manufactures requiring artistic skill, England stood lowest but one among the Countries represented, and the United States stood lowest of all. The Educators of England, aided by the Manufacturers, immediately caused Drawing and Artistic Schools to be established in all the large Towns of the Kingdom, for the training of her Workmen and Workwomen. The result was, that, at the Paris Exhibition, sixteen years later, England advanced from next to the foot to the first place on the list. Is mortification any adequate name for the feeling with which we learn that the United States continued complacently at the foot?

A change has commenced, the Educators of the Country having been aroused in all directions. Cincinnati employs six public Drawing Teachers, at an expense of $5,700. New York, San Francisco, Philadelphia, Brooklyn and Chicago have made this branch a part of their School Instruction in all grades, and now our old Commonwealth has introduced it by Law into all her five thousand Public Schools.

We may expect results at least equal to those reached in England, and may have a reasonable hope that sixteen years hence we shall have disappeared from our accustomed place at the foot of the list. We speak of Drawing only as applied to training the hand and eye for industrial purposes, for that is, we think, its valuable feature as a branch of Public Education.

Drawing is the written language of the eye, even as words are the written language of the brain. It is especially the language of Mechanic Art. Constant difficulty is experienced for want of Workmen who can even read this language,—that is, who can work from a Drawing, or Plan, without constant explanations, which Machinists say is the cause of no small loss in dollars and cents to both Employers and Employed, and consequently to the community at large. It is, therefore, from this point of view that

Public Educators are at present called to regard the subject, leaving higher walks of Art to be considered in future years.

5. The English Commissioners in their Report thus summarize the opinions of those gentlemen examined by them in regard to the subject of Drawing. They say:—

Mr. Stanton remarks that "whether we regard it as a means of refinement, or as an education for the eye, teaching it to appreciate form, or as strengthening habits of accurate observation, or again as of direct utility for many professions and trades, it is equally admirable." Doctor Hodgson stated it as his opinion that "Drawing should be taught to every child as soon as he went to School, and added that it was already taught to all the Boys, (nearly 1,000), in the Liverpool Institute." From Mr. Samuelson's Letter to the Vice-President of the Committee of Council on Education, Drawing appears to be always regarded as a most important subject of instruction in the Technical Schools on the Continent of Europe; and the bearing of this on the excellence ascribed to the foreign Artisans and Superintendents of labour cannot be mistaken.

6. Honourable Joseph White, Secretary of the Board of Education of Massachusetts, commending the efforts made in the State to introduce Drawing, very emphatically observes:—

Let these Schools be opened in all our Manufacturing Towns, and we may expect to find,—

I. A great improvement in respect to the taste and skill exhibited in the various products of industry.

II. A rapid multiplication of valuable labour-saving Machines

III. And, better than all, an increase of the numbers and a manifest advance in the intellectual and moral condition and character of the Artisans themselves. In proportion as the intellect asserts its sway over mere force, as the cultivated brain controls the hand, labour ceases to be a drudgery, and becomes a pleasure and delight; it is no longer a badge of servility, but an instrument of power.

These recommendations, (says General Eaton, United States Commissioner of Education), are worthy of being repeated throughout the Country for the benefit of every Manufacturing Town. Indeed the efforts for the training of Mechanical Skill are so rapidly spreading in all civilised lands that only by a corresponding attention to these elements of instruction can our Manufacturers hope to compete with those in other quarters of the Globe.

7. Honourable B. G. Northrop, Secretary of the Board of Education in Connecticut, says:—

In Central Europe, Technical Education is provided for; almost every Trade has its School, and they contribute largely to the thrift of Germany and Switzerland. The universality of instruction in Drawing is a marked feature; and I urge upon all Superintendents and those in authority to have Drawing introduced alongside of Geography and Arithmetic.

8. In his valuable work "In the School Room," Professor John S. Hart thus illustrates, by a striking example, the importance of Drawing in our Public Schools:—

When it comes to skilled labour between the educated and the ignorant an intelligent Mechanic is worth twice as much as one ignorant, or stupid. Here is a case in point:—

Many years ago a very instructive fact on this point came under my own personal observation. A gentleman of my acquaintance had frequent need of the aid of a Carpenter. The work to be done was not regular carpentry, but various odd jobs, alterations and adaptations to suit special wants, and no little time and materials were wasted in the perpetual misconceptions and mistakes of the successive Workmen employed. At length a Workman was sent, who was a German, from the Kingdom of Prussia. After listening attentively to the orders given, and doing what he could to understand what his Employer wanted, Michael would whip out his pencil, and in two or three minutes, with a few lines, would present a sketch of the article, so clear that any one could recognize it at a glance. It could be seen at once, also, whether the intention of his Employer had been rightly conceived, and whether it was practicable. The consequence was that so long as Michael was employed there was no more waste of materials and time, to say nothing of the vexation of continued failures. Michael was not really more skilful as a Carpenter than the many others who had preceded him; but his knowledge of Drawing, gained in a Common School in his native Country, made his services worth from fifty cents to a dollar a day more than those of any other Workman in the Shop, and he actually received two dollars a day when others in the same shop were receiving only a dollar and a quarter. He was always in demand, and he always received extra wages, and his work, even at that rate, was considered cheap.

What was true of Michael in Carpentry would be true of any other department of Mechanical industry. In Cabinet-making, in Shoe-making, in Tailoring, in Masonry, in Upholstery, in the various contrivances of Tin and Sheet-iron with which our houses are made comfortable, in Gas-fitting and Plumbing, in the thousand and one necessities of the Farm, the Garden and the Kitchen, a Workman who is ready and expert with his Pencil, who has learned to put his own ideas or those of another rapidly on Paper, is worth fifty per cent. more than his fellows who have not this skill.

XI.—*Technical Education: Its Purpose and Object.*

The subject of Technical Education is thus defined by the Board of Education in the State of Massachusetts:—

Technical Education is instruction in the peculiar knowledge or special skill required in any business, or occupation,—the training which will render the talents of the citizen most useful to the State in that particular Craft, Trade, or Profession, in which he, or she, is engaged, whether as Mechanic, Farmer, Sailor, Engineer, Teacher, Merchant, Architect. Minister, Doctor, or Lawyer. As the education of the Common Schools fits the youth for the performance of his general duties as a citizen, of the citizen most useful to the State in that particular Craft, Trade, or Profession. which he has chosen, Divinity, Law and Medical Schools, for special, or Technical Instruction in those professions, have long been in successful operation.

A Resolve was passed by the last General Court "relating to Technical Instruction in Schools," by which the Board of Education was directed to report "a feasible plan for giving in the Common Schools of the Cities and larger Towns of this Commonwealth additional instruction, especially adapted to young persons who are acquiring practical skill in Mechanic, or Technical Arts, or are preparing for such pursuits."

It is appropriate, in connection with this part of my Report, briefly to refer to what is being done in other Countries to provide for further instruction in elementary and practical Science, but at a stage beyond that of our High Schools. The object of this instruction, taken in its most comprehensive sense, is, (as just explained), to render the talents of the citizen most useful to the Státe in that particular Craft, Trade, or Profession in which he, or she, is engaged, whether as Mechanic, Farmer, Sailor, Engineer, Teacher, Merchant, Architect, Minister, Doctor, or Lawyer. Thus the special Technical Schools already established in various Countries are:—

1. Normal Schools for Teachers.
2. Divinity Schools for Ministers.
3. Law Schools for Lawyers.
4. Medical Schools for Physicians.
5. Art Schools of Painting and Sculpture for Artists.
6. Schools for Civil Engineers and Architects.
7. Chemical Schools for Chemists.
8. Geological Schools for Geologists.
9. Schools of Mines for Metallurgists.
10. Agricultural Schools for Farmers.
11. Schools of Navigation for Sailors.
12. Commercial Schools, (or Colleges), for Merchants.
13. Schools of Technology for Artisans, etcetera.

This latter class of Schools are of quite recent origin in England, the United States, and, I am happy to say, in Ontario also. Early in 1871 the Government of Ontario sent two Commissioners, (Doctors Hodgins and Machattie), to the United States to make inquiries "in regard to Schools of Practical Science." As the result of these inquiries, a Report was made to the Government, and a "College of Technology" was established in Toronto in that year. In France, Switzerland, and in most of Germany, the education of Artisans commences when they are Boys at School. Experience has shown that this is the proper time to begin this kind of instruction, as Boys are remarkably apt in picking up knowledge of this kind, (which appeals to their senses); besides, it gives a pleasing variety to the otherwise, and to them, monotonous, routine of the School.

XII.—*Connection Between Education and Invention.*

As to the effect of this kind of instruction on the inventive ingenuity of a people, the Honourable B. G. Northrop, Secretary of the Board of Education in Connecticut, gives the following illustrations from his own State:—

It is plainly due to the former excellence of our Schools, and the universality of Education among the people, that Connecticut has always taken the lead in the number, variety, and value of its inventions. Our Manufactories are relatively more numerous and more diversified in their processes and products than those of any other State. The ingenuity and inventive talent of our people have ever been remarkable, as is shown by the statistics of the Patent Office.

The whole number of Patents granted to citizens of the United States for the year 1871 was 12,511, of which:—

To citizens of Connecticut were	667,	being one to each 806
To citizens of District Columbia	136,	being one to each 970
To citizens of Massachusetts	1,386,	being one to each 1,051
To citizens of Rhode Island	184,	being one to each 1,181
To citizens of New York	2,954,	being one to each 1,450
To citizens of New Jersey	496,	being one to each 1,827

Provision for Teaching Vocal Music in our Schools.

1. Vocal Music being now required to be taught in our Schools, we insert the following striking illustration of its value and importance as a softening and humanizing influence as a subject of instruction, from the Report of the Secretary of the Board of Education in Connecticut, for last year. It will be seen how successfully he combats the statement so often put forth that instruction in Vocal Music is of no practical use to large numbers of children, because of their inability to sing. He says:—

Music is taught in our best Schools and should be in all. In many instances it has taken its proper place as one of the regular Studies. It is the testimony of multitudes of Teachers, that Music helps instead of hindering progress in other Studies. It stimulates the mental faculties and exhilarates and recreates Pupils, when weary with Study. Some branches are pursued largely for the mental discipline which they impart. No Study that can be taken up so early, is a better discipline in rapid observation and thinking; none so early and easily develops the essential power of mental concentration. In Singing by note, a child must fix his thoughts and think quickly and accurately. The habit of fixing the attention thus early formed, will aid in all other Studies. There is abundant testimony that Scholars progress more rapidly in the common branches, where Singing is taught. Vocal Music aids in graceful Reading, by promoting better articulation, improving the voice and correcting hard and unpleasant tones. The influence in cultivating the sensibilities, improving the taste and developing the better feelings of our nature, amply compensate for the time required for this Study. Its efficacy in School Government, making work a play, giving a systematic recreation,—enjoyed the more because always in concert, and with the sympathy and stimulus of companionship, —is admitted by the most successful Teachers. Trouble in the School Room often comes from that restlessness, which proper intervals of Singing would best relieve. Singing is a healthful, physical exercise. In primary Schools, Gymnastic Exercises often accompany the singing. When children are trained to erectness of posture, and to the right use of the vocal organs, speaking, Reading and Singing are most invigorating exercises; expanding the chest, promoting deep breathing, quickening the circulation, and arousing both the physical and mental energies. Diseases of the respiratory organs are the great scourge of this climate, and occasion more than one-fifth of our mortality. It is said that in New England and New York, more than forty thousand die annually of diseases of the throat and lungs. The remarkable exemption of the German people, alike in Germany and America, from pulmonary disease, is attributed, by eminent medical authority, largely to the universal habit of singing, in which they are trained from their earliest years, both at home and at School. Thus their lungs are expanded and invigorated. The broad chest is a national characteristic. There is a common but erroneous impression that only a favoured few can learn Music. How is it then that every child in Germany is taught Singing as regularly as Reading? But facts may be found nearer home. In late Examinations of all the Schools in New Haven, "only two hundred and forty-eight children out of over six thousand were found unable to sing the scale, and one hundred and forty of these belonged to the primary grades;" that is, out of this multitude, only one hundred and eight above the primary grades could not sing. Superintendent Parish says:—"A systematic course of training the voices of the little ones in the Primary Rooms, has been commenced. Thus far the experiment has been a complete su'ccess. Children from five to eight years of age, readily sing the scale, singly and in concert, and read from the Blackboard, notes on the staff by numerals and syllables with as little hesitation as they call the letters and words of their reading lessons."

In the Hancock School of Boston, of about one thousand Girls, less than a dozen were unfitted from all causes for attaining to a fair degree of success in Singing. General Eaton, the National Commisioner of Education, and Governor English, when visiting the Schools in New Haven, expressed their surprise and gratification at hearing children in the Primary Schools, sing at sight exercises marked on the Blackboard by the Teacher.

2. The Report of the School Committee of Boston, of the present year, after explaining the system of instruction adopted, and noticing some of the happy effects of musical exercises in the Public Schools, remarks:—

"The primary School is, of all others, the place where instruction in Music, if we would ever expect it to attain anything like a satisfactory result, as a part of our Common School instruction, ought to begin. The child of five, or six years, can easily be taught the first rudiments of Music, and a few plain principles in the management of the voice, if early adopted, and carried up through the lower and intermediate classes; especially if to this were added some instruction in the art of correct vocalization, and the proper management of the registers, greater strength, a more resonant tone, purer intonation, exacter enunciation, precision, ease, fluency of delivery,—everything that is improving to the voice would finally result.

3. In an Address, delivered before the National Teachers' Association, at Cleveland, Ohio, an eminent Teacher and authority says:—

Music should enter into Common School Education, because, —
1st. It is an aid to other Studies.
2nd. It assists the Teacher in maintaining the discipline of the School.
3rd. It cultivates the æsthetic nature of the child.
4th. It is valuable as a means of Mental discipline.
5th. It lays a favourable foundation for the more advanced culture of later life.
6th. It is a positive economy.
7th. It is of the highest value as a sanitary measure.
8th. It prepares for participation in the Church Service.

And again:—
Through the medium of the Music Lesson the moral nature of the child may be powerfully cultivated.

Music meets the demands of that nature: it infuses itself into his life; it intwines itself about his heart. and becomes a law of his being. Hence, his Songs may more directly and powerfully than any other agency give tone and direction to his moral character; they may be made the means of cultivating his nationality and patriotism; they may promote a love of order. virtue, truth, temperance, and a hatred of their opposites; they may subserve his Religious advancement, implanting lessons at once salutary and eternal.

Regular Musical instruction is now incorporated with the School Studies of nearly every City and large Town in New England and the Northern and Western States, not only with the happiest musical results, but with marked good influences upon the health, general intelligence, capacity for receiving general instruction, and orderly habits of the youth so taught.

Facilities for Giving a Practical Commercial Education in the Schools.

As I intimated last year, one of the felt wants in our system of Public and High Schools, has been facilities for giving Boys instruction in matters relating to Commercial and Business transactions. That want has been supplied; and both in the High and Public School Law, provision has been made for giving Pupils instruction in subjects relating to Commercial Education. For years this subject has received attention in the Model School of Ontario, and Boys have been thoroughly prepared in Book-keeping and other kindred branches, so as to fit them at once for practical work in the Counting House and other departments of Mercantile life. The result has been that Boys trained there have been much sought after by Merchants and others. In the

Schools generally, beyond a little theoretical Book-keeping, no special attention has been hitherto paid to Commercial subjects, but in the new Programme of Study prescribed for the Schools, Pupils are required: —

1. To be practically acquainted with Compound and Conjoined Proportion, and with Commercial Arithmetic, including Practice, Percentage, Insurance, Commission, Brokerage, Purchase and Sale of Stock, Custom House Business, Assessment of Taxes and Interest.

2. To know the definition of the various Account Books used. To understand the relation between Debtor and Creditor, and the difference between Single and Double Entry.

3. To know how to make Original Entries in the Books used for this purpose, such as Invoice Books, Sales Book, Cash Book and Day Book.

4. To be able to Journalize any ordinary transaction, and to be familiar with the nature of the various Accounts in the Ledger, and with the mode of conducting and closing them.

5. To be familiar with the forms of ordinary Commercial Paper, such as Promissory Notes, Drafts, Receipts for the payment of Money, etcetera.

6. In the English Course for the High Schools, Pupils are required to be acquainted with Commercial Forms and Usages, and with practical Telegraphy.

III.—PROVIDING ADEQUATE SCHOOL ACCOMMODATION.

1. Since the date of my last Report, very much attention has been given to the question of School House Accommodation. The extracts which I have given in the Appendix from the Reports of the County Inspectors, are full of interest on this subject. They show,—

(1) The actual condition of the School Houses in the rural parts of the Country.

(2) The laudable desire on the part of most of the Trustees and Ratepayers to remedy the lamentable state of things which has been pointed out to them.

(3) The apathy, timidity, or penuriousness which influence the remainder to do nothing.

2. The operation of the provision of the new School Law on this subject, as reported to the Inspectors, show, therefore, that one of the most valuable features of the School Legislation of last year was that which provided for increased School House Accommodation. Thinking that it would not be necessary to provide for the Trustees and Ratepayers to do what was an obvious duty in this respect, no provision was made in the comprehensive School Law of 1850 for this essential part of our School economy, nor was it even embodied in the School Law Amendment Act of 1860, which was designed to remedy certain proved defects in the Law. Indeed, not until after twenty years experience had demonstrated the actual want of some general Regulation relating to School House Accommodation being made, did the necessity for a clearly-defined Regulation on the subject force itself on public attention.

3. Although some opposition was made, at first, to this most desirable reform, yet on the whole, it has been hailed as a real boon by the vast majority of the Trustees. Never was there such singular unanimity on any one subject among the intelligent friends of our improved School System as on this. It has, (when proper explanations have been given to the parties concerned), been regarded as a most enlightened step in advance. The provision of the School Law has been framed, as we think all will admit, in the interests of humanity, cleanliness, order and decency. It is true that in many cases a thoughtless apathy or inattention alone had prevented anything from being done to improve the condition of the School Premises; but, in other cases, timidity on the part of the Trustees, or the fear of taxation on the part of the Ratepayers, had paralyzed local efforts; and from year to year nothing was done to put the School House in even a reasonable state of repair. Hence the necessity for the interposition of some higher authority, in the shape of Statute Law, to arouse public

attention to the subject, and virtually to decide the question in favour of the health of the Teacher and Pupils and the advancement of the School. These were, really, the parties who had suffered so long from local apathy or selfishness, while they were power-less to effect any change for the better.

4. Were it not vouched for, in the Appendix, by the written testimony of the Public School Inspectors, who have examined and reported to the Department upon the state of the School Houses and Premises under their jurisdiction, it could scarcely be believed that Trustees and Parents would, in so many cases, have allowed their children to con-gregate, day after day, and year after year, in the miserable hovels which, up to this year, had existed as so-called School Houses in many parts of the Province. And yet so it was. Neither the ill-health of the Teacher, nor the listless faces of the children, added to the warning of Medical men, or the counsel of Local Superintendents, could, in many localities, rouse Trustees, or Ratepayers, from their apathy. "Their Fathers, or other relations, or friends, had gone to the School, and it was good enough for them." This, or some other valueless excuse, was too often their reply, and hence nothing was done, or would be attempted. Not even, in many cases, would the spirited example of their neighbours in other localities influence them; and often, in inverse ratio to the wealth of the neighbourhood, would the spirit of selfish economy prevail, and even be defended on the plea of poverty!

5. It is true that many people had no definite idea as to what was actually required to be done, in order to provide what was really necessary to put their School House and Premises in a proper and efficient state. Such people would say,—"Tell us what we should do, and we will cheerfully do it." "We know that our children and the Teachers are sufferers, and that they are not in such a School House as we should like them to be in. But we do not know the proper size to build the School House, the space for air we should leave, or the best way to ventilate the Building, or Premises. If the Law, or Regulations, would lay down some definite general Rules on the subject, we should be glad to follow them, but we do not like to spend money on a new School House, and then find that we were all wrong in our calculations on the subject." Such excuses as these were often urged, and they were reasonable in some cases. Trustees, too, would say, when pressed to do something to better the condition of the School House:—"We would gladly do so, but the Ratepayers object to the expense, and we do not like to fall out with our neighbours. If you say that we must do it, we will undertake it, for then the responsibility will be on you, and we shall do no more than our duty in complying with the School Law." Some Trustees have felt so strongly the necessity of improving the condition of their School Premises, and yet have lacked the moral, and even the legal, courage to do their duty, independently of this pressure, that they have privately intimated their desire to the Inspector that he would enforce the Law in this matter in their School Section.

6. It affords me real pleasure to say that, in carrying out the Law and Regulations on this subject, the Inspectors generally have displayed great judgment and tact. They have even taken unusual pains to enlist the sympathies and best feelings of Trustees and Ratepayers in favour of this much-needed reform. They have answered objections, smoothed difficulties, removed prejudices, met misrepresentations by full information and explanation, and have done everything in their power to introduce, as I have suggested to them, a gradual change for the better in the condition of the School House, the Out-buildings, Fences and Premises generally.

I.—*Prizes for Plans of School Sites and School Houses.*

7. With a view to encourage as well as develop a taste and talent for improved School House accommodation, and to enlist the energies and skill of the local School Authorities in this good work, I decided to issue a Circular offering Prizes for the best plans of Sites and School Houses. This I was enabled to do out of a small sum placed in the Estimates for that purpose. In this way I have sought to give a further illus-

tration of a principle which I have always held, and which has always characterized the administration of our School System from the beginning. This principle is, that the Department should seek rather to aid the People to help as well as educate themselves through themselves, than to take the matter out of their hands, or compel them to do what was obviously their duty to do.

(NOTE. The following is inserted here as bearing upon this subject).

II.—Circular from the Chief Superintendent offering Prizes for Rural School House Plans.

Although Plans of School Houses had been published in the *Journal of Education for Upper Canada* during the year 1849-1872, it was thought desirable to offer Prizes for a series of the best Plans of School Houses. The following Notice was, therefore, inserted in the *Journal of Education* for June, 1872:—

With a view to improve the School Accommodation in the various rural School Sections, and to act as an incentive to improved School Architecture, as well as to aid Trustees in the matter, the Department of Public Instruction will pay to any Inspector, Trustee, or Teacher, the following prizes for Ground Plans of School Houses, and for Block Plans of School Sites, which may be found best adapted to rural School Sections, videlicet:—

I. For the best Ground Plan of a rural School-House, (on the scale of eight feet to an inch), $10,—I. For the best First Floor, (Ground), Plan of a School House, with Porch, Cap and Cloak-room, Map and Book-presses, Teacher' accommodation, etcetera, capable of accommodating from 60 to 75 children, $15. 2. For the best Ground Plan of a rural School House with the additions and at least two School Rooms capable of accommodating from 100 to 125 children, $20. 3. For the best Ground Plan of a rural School House, with additions, and at least three Rooms capable of accommodating from 150 to 175 children, $25.

II. For the best Block Plan of a School Site, (on the scale of forty feet to an inch.—For the best Block Plan of a School site, of an acre in extent. Position of School-House Wood-Shed, Privies, Well, Fence, Play Ground for Boys and for Girls, Shade Trees, etcetera, to be marked on the plan, $20: 2. The best Block Plan of a School Site, on the same scale, of half an acre, $15.

The Plans to be neatly prepared in ink, and to be accompanied by full written explanations. They are to be marked by some word, or motto, the key to which is to be enclosed in an envelope, which will be opened after the Prizes shall have been awarded.

Plans, etcetera, to be addressed to the Reverend Doctor Ryerson, Chief Superintendent of Education.

The Prize Plans will be the property of the Education Department, and will be required for publication in the *Journal of Education.*

Thirty persons competed for these Prizes for the best interior Plans of School-Houses, of various dimensions, and for the best Block Plans, of one acre and half acre School Sites.

Of these thirty Plans, four were of superior merit, in various features, nine were of varying excellence, while seventeen either did not come up to the standard required, or had other palpable defects in them.

The motto envelopes having been opened after the Prizes were awarded, the names of the Winners of the Prizes, were found to be the following:—

Number 1,—Mr. Otto Klotz, Ex-Local School Superintendent, Preston: "Education is the Bulwark of Liberty." Two prizes $40

Number 2.—Mr. Henry De La Matter, Head Master, High School, Owen Sound: "Le jour viendra." Two prizes 25

Number 3.—Mr. S. S. Cann, Teacher, Port Hope: "Docendo Discimus (Number 1.) Two prizes 25

Number 4.—Mr. Robert Little, Inspector, County Halton: "Docendo Discimus,"
Two Prizes 20
Number 5.—Mr. James Dickie, Hamilton; "Alpha," Two prizes 15
Number 6.—Mr. James H. Ball, M.A., Inspector, County of Welland: "Epis-
copon." 15
Number 7.—Mr. George F. Payne, Teacher, East Zorra: "Iota" 15
Number 8.—Mr. John Irwin, Teacher, Belleville: "True Economy" 15
Number 9.—Mr. Francis C. Powell, Teacher, Port Elgin: "All is not gold that
glitters" 10
Number 10.—Mr. John B. Somerset, Inspector, County of Lincoln, and Mr. J.
H. Comfort, Inspector, St. Catharines: "Multum in Parvo" each. 10
Number 11.—Mr. William O'Connor, Teacher, Seaforth: "Felix" 10
Number 12.—Mr. Richard Harcourt, Inspector, County of Haldimand: [after-
wards Minister of Education] "Per Vias Rectas" 5
Number 13.—Mr. W. Laing, Hamilton: "Rural Maple Leaf." 5
Number 14.—Mr. Hugh Robertson, Teacher, Toronto: "Interests" 5
Number 15.—Mr. D. McIntyre, Teacher, Lancaster "E. L. F" 5
Number 16.—Mr. Robert S. Gould, Teacher, Canning, "Ami de Mouvement" 5
Number 17.—Mr. G. D. Platt, Inspector, Prince Edward County: "Hopeful"... 5

Total, for the seventeen approved Plans $230
Thirteen Plans, (numbers 18 to 30,) were not accepted as not coming up to the standard required.

III.—What was done Elsewhere in Regard to School Accommodation in 1871,

8. Before referring to the provisions of the Law and Regulations in force in Ontario in regard to School House Accommodation, I think it will be interesting and instructive to take a glance at what is done elsewhere in the direction of building and repairing School Houses. I take the example of some of the American States as their System of Education and modes of proceeding are similar to our own. The result discloses the painful fact that although the Expenditure in 1871 for School Sites and the Building and repairs of School Houses in Ontario was $345,000, or about $75,000 more than in 1870, yet the average expenditure per School for the same objects was very much below that of the various American States, which have reported the facts on the subject, and which I have given in the Table below. Thus:—

In Ontario, for 4,600 Schools the expenditure was $345,000
In Massachusetts, for every 4,600 Schools the expenditure was ... 1,865,700
In New Jersey, for every 4,600 Schools the expenditure was 1,840,000
In Connecticut, for every 4,600 Schools the expenditure was ... 1,538,700
In Pennsylvania, for every 4,600 Schools the expenditure was ... 993,600
In Michigan, for every 4,600 Schools the expenditure was 782,000
In New York, for every 4,600 Schools the expenditure was 736,000
In Ohio, for every 4,600 Schools the expenditure was 628,600
In Iowa, for every 4,600 Schools the expenditure was 624,000

9. Thus we see that the ordinary Expenditure of the least generous of these States for School Sites, Buildings, and repairs,—and those States much younger than our Province,—is nearly double that of the extraordinary Expenditure of last year in Ontario; while Pennsylvania spent nearly three times the amount per School that Ontario did, Connecticut nearly five times and New Jersey and Massachusetts nearly six times as much per School during 1871 as did Ontario.

IV.—Actual Expenditure for Sites, Buildings and Repairs of School Houses in Ontario.

10. Among the most eminent Educators, it has been generally held that the Public Expenditure for Education was a good national investment, and one which always paid

a high rate of interest to the State. Investment in Real Estate for School Sites and Buildings is among the most valuable which can be made. It is always available and tangible and capable of being readily converted into money. Our own Expenditure for Sites, Buildings and repairs of School Houses last year was $345,000, or upwards of $50,000 more than the sum expended for a like purpose in 1870. The Expenditure of some of the leading States in the adjoining Republic for the same objects was as follows : —

State.	Date of Report.	Expenditure.	Number of School Sections.
Pennsylvania	1871	$3,386,263	15,700
Massachusetts	1871	2,058,853	5,076
New York	1871	1,594,060	11,350
Ohio	1870	1,391,597	13,951
Illinois	1870	1,371,052	11,011
Iowa	1871	1,096,916	7,823
Michigan	1870	852,122	5,008
New Jersey	1871	597,400	1,501
Connecticut	1871	550,318	1,644
Wisconsin	1870	417,775	....
Ontario	1871	345,000	4,600

The Expenditure in the State of New York for School Sites and Houses has been nearly Ten millions of dollars, during the last five years, or nearly Two millions of dollars per year!

IV.—*Valuation of School House Property in the United States.*

11. The following statistics of the value of School Houses, etcetera, will be interesting : —

Name.	Date of Report.	Valuation of School Property.	Number of School Sections.
New York	1871	$23,468,266	11,728
Illinois	1870	16,859,300	11,011
Pennsylvania	1871	15,837,183	15,700
Massachusetts	1871	15,671,424	5,076
Ohio	1870	13,818,554	13,951
Indiana	1870	7,282,639	9,032
Iowa	1871	6,764,551	7,823
New Jersey	1871	3,677,432	1,501
Missouri	1870	3,441,411	....
Wisconsin	1870	3,295,268	....
Maine	1871	2,488,853	4,003
Minnesota	1871	1,582,507	2,625

V.—*Condition of the School Houses in some American States.*

Only in a few of the States do the Authorities report the condition of the School Houses. The following facts are, however, instructive : —

In Maine, 1,772 School Houses are reported in "bad condition."

In Pennsylvania, 1,517 School Houses are reported as "unfit for School purposes."

In Vermont, 779 School Houses are reported as "unfit for School purposes."

In New Hampshire, 385 School Houses are reported as "unfit for School purposes."

VI.—*Provision of the Ontario Law on School House Accommodation.*

1. The new School Act of 1871 very properly declares that Trustees "shall provide Adequate Accommodation for all the children of School age, [*i.e.*, between the ages of five and twenty-one years, resident] in their School Division," (*i.e*, School Section City, Town, or Village). It also provides that "no School Section shall be formed which shall contain less than fifty resident children, between the ages of five and sixteen years, unless the area of such Section shall contain more than four square miles."

15—xxiii

These "Accommodations," to be adequate, should include, (as prescribed by the special Regulations),—

(1) A Site of an Acre in extent, but not less than half an Acre.*

(2) A School House, (with separate Rooms, where the number of Pupils exceeds fifty), the Walls of which shall not be less than ten feet high in the clear, and which shall not contain less than nine square feet on the Floor for each child in attendance, so as to allow an area in each Room, for at least one hundred cubic feet of Air for each child.‡ It shall also be sufficiently Warmed and Ventilated, and the premises properly Drained.

(3) A sufficient Fence, or Paling, round the School Premises.

(4) A Play-ground, or other satisfactory provision for physical exercise, within the Fences, and off the Road.

(5) A Well, or other means of procuring Water for the School.

(6) Proper and separate Offices for both sexes, at some little distance from the School House, and suitably enclosed.

(7) Suitable School Furniture and Apparatus, videlicet:—Desks, Seats, Blackboards, Maps, Library, Presses and Books, etcetera, necessary for the efficient conduct of the School.

2. In his official visitations to the Schools, the Inspector is required to inquire into the tenure of the Property; the Materials, Dimensions, and plan of the Building; its condition; when erected; with what Funds built; how Lighted, Warmed, and Ventilated; if any Class Rooms are provided for the separate instruction of part of the children; if there is a Lobby, or Closet, for Hats, Cloaks, Bonnets, Book Presses, etcetera; how the Desks and Seats are arranged and constructed; what arrangements for the Teacher; what Play-ground is provided; what Gymnastic Apparatus, (if any); whether there be a Well, and proper conveniences for private purposes; and if the Premises are fenced, or open, on the Street, or Road; if shade Trees and any Shrubs, or Flowers, are planted.

3. In his inquiries in these matters, the Inspector is especially directed to see whether the Law and Regulations have been complied with in regard to the following matters: (should he discover remissness in any of them, he is directed to call the attention of the Trustees to it, before withholding the School Fund from the Section, with a view to its remedy before his next half-yearly visit):—

(1) *Size of Section.*—As to the size of the School Section, as prescribed by the Fifteenth Section of the School Law of 1871.

(2) *School Accommodation.*—Whether the Trustees have provided "adequate Accommodation for all children of School age, [i.e., between the ages of five and twenty-one years, resident], in their School Division," [i.e., School Section, City, Town, or Village] as required by the Section of the School Act of 1871.

(3) *Space for Air.*—Whether the required space of nine square feet for each Pupil, and the average space of one hundred cubic feet of Air for each child have been allowed in the construction of the School House and its Class Rooms.

(4) *Well; Proper Conveniences.*—Whether a Well, or other means of procuring Water is provided; also, whether there are proper conveniences for private purposes of both sexes on the Premises.

4. The Trustees having made such provision relative to the School House and its Appendages, as are required by the Fourth clause of the Twenty-seventh Section, and

---

* Size of School Grounds.—The School Grounds, wherever practicable, should, in the rural Sections, embrace an Acre in extent, and not less than half an Acre, so as to allow the School-house to be set well back from the Road, and furnish Play-grounds within the Fences. A convenient form for School Grounds will be found to be an area of ten rods front by sixteen rods deep, with the School-house set back four or six rods from the Road. The Grounds should be strongly Fenced, the Yards and Outhouses in the rear of the School-house being invariably separated by a high and tight board Fence; the front Grounds being planted with shade Trees and Shrubs. For a small School, an area of eight rods front by ten rods deep may be sufficient, the School-house being set back four rods from the front.

‡ Thus, for instance, a Room for fifty children would require space for 5,000 cubic feet of Air. This would be equal to a cube of the following dimensions in feet, videlicet: 25 x 20 x 10, which is equivalent to a Room 25 feet long by 20 wide and 10 feet high.

NOTE.—Temperature.—In Winter the Temperature during the first School hour in the forenoon, or afternoon, should not exceed 70°, or 60° during the rest of the day.

15a—XXIII.

the Seventh clause of the Seventy-ninth Section of the Consolidatd School Act, and as provided in Regulation 9 of the "Duties of Trustees," it is made by the Regulation the duty of the Master to give strict attention to the proper Ventilation and Temperature, as well as to the Cleanliness of the School House; he *shall also prescribe such Rules for the use of the Yard and Out-buildings connected with the School House, as will insure their being kept in a neat and proper condition; and he shall be held responsible for any want of Cleanliness about the Premises. He is also required to see that the Yards, Sheds, Privies, and other Out-buildings are kept in order, and that the School House and Premises are locked at all proper times; and that all deposits of sweepings, from Rooms, or Yards, are removed from the Premises.

VII.—*Characteristics of a Good School House.*

1. In a recent edition of the School Laws of Michigan, it is truly stated that,—

The essential characteristics of a good School House are, 1st, a sufficient amount of space to accommodate the School and its Classes; 2nd, a convenient distribution of room in halls and School Rooms to allow free movement of the Classes and of the entire School, without crowding, or confusion; 3rd, an arrangement of lights, such as will throw an equal and sufficient illumination throughout the Room; and 4th, adequate provisions for Warming and Ventilating the Rooms. To these may be added as desirable features, ample and pleasant School Grounds, good Walks and Out-houses.

2. A great mistake has been made in some School Houses, by seating them in such a way as to have all the Pupils in the Room face the windows. Such an arrangement cannot be otherwise than injurious to the eyes of the Pupils, as the strong light is constantly shining into them. Pupils should always be seated with their backs to the windows. There should be no wondows in front of them. The Seats should face northwards.

VIII.—*Principles of Ventilation for School Houses.*

1. The State Superintendent of Michigan remarks:—"Ventilation becomes easy as soon as it is known that it is embraced in these two essential operations, videlicet:—1st, to supply fresh Air; 2nd, to expel foul Air. It is evident that fresh Air cannot be crowded into a Room unless the foul Air is crowded out, and it will not go out unless fresh Air comes in to fill its place. It is useless to open Ventilating Flues, as I have seen in some of our School Houses, for the egress of bad Air, while there is no provision for drawing in a supply of fresh Air. If the Flues worked at all, it would be simply to empty the room of all Air,—an impossibility.*

2. The following, (taken from the United States Commissioner's Report on Education for 1871), furnishes an illustration of the nicety of observation brought by the Scientific men of Switzerland to the aid of Education. The Report says: —

Doctor Breiting, of Basle, has examined the air of the School Rooms of that City. From the result of this estimation we select one, taken in a Room measuring 251.61 cubic metres, (2.921.88 cubic feet, equal to a room twenty-four feet long, fifteen feet wide, and eight feet high), having 10.54 square metres, (115.77 square feet), of windows and doors, and containing, on the day of examination, fifty-four children.

Time.	Amount of carbonic acid gas.†
7.45 a.m., comencement of School	2,21 per cent.
8 a.m., end of first recitation	4 80 per cent.
9 a.m., after the Recess	4.07 per cent.
10.10 a.m., after the brief Recess	6.23 per cent.
11 a.m., end of School hour	8.11 per cent.
11.10 a.m., the Room being empty	7.30 per cent.
1.45 p.m., commencement of School	5.03 per cent.
2 p.m., beginning of Recess	7.66 per cent.
3 p.m., end of Recess	5.03 per cent.
4 p.m., end of Singing lesson	9.36 per cent.
4.10 p.m., the Room being empty	5.72 per cent.

* In the report of the N. Y. Teachers' Association, held at Albany, in July. 1872. the following passage occurs:—The death of at least two of these faithful Teachers leaves a lesson that ought to be heeded by every Parent and Teacher. The death of both is traced directly to improper Heating and Ventilation in Rooms in which they were called to teach. We believe this to be the most fruitful source of disease, or death, among our Teachers, and we might add, among the children and youth of our land.

† NOTE.—The pure Atmosphere contains, .0004 carbonic acid Gas, and more than 1 per cent. of carbonic acip Gas is generally considered detrimental to health.

Proceedings in other Countries in Regard to School Accommodation.

1. In England "the (Parliamentary) Grant is withheld altogether,—if the School be not in a Building certified by the Inspector, to be healthy, properly Lighted, Drained and Ventilated, supplied with Offices, and containing in the principal School Room at least eighty cubical feet of internal area per each child in average attendance."

2. In Section 29 of the New School Act for Nova Scotia, (many details of which are copied from our Acts), passed in May, 1871, the following are the provisions, in regard to School Accommodation. They are even more comprehensive and minute than ours:—

The School Accommodation to be provided by the District, (School Section), shall, as far as possible, be in accordance with the following arrangements:—

For a District having fifty Pupils, or under, a House with comfortable Sittings, with one Teacher.

For a District having from fifty to eighty Pupils, a House with comfortable Sittings and a good Class Room, with one Teacher and an Assistant.

For a District having from eighty to one hundred Pupils, a House with comfortable Sittings and two good Class Rooms, with one Teacher and two Assistants, or a House having two Apartments, one for an elementary, and one for an advanced department with two Teachers; or, if one commodious Building cannot be secured, two Houses may be provided in different parts of the District, with a Teacher in each, one being devoted to the younger children, and the other to the more advanced.

For a District having from one hundred to one hundred and fifty Pupils, a House with two adequate Apartments, one for an elementary and one for an advanced department, and a good Class Room accessible to both; with two Teachers, and, if necessary, an Assistant; or, if the District be long and narrow, three Houses may be provided, two for elementary departments, and one for an advanced department, the former being located towards the extremes of the District and the latter at, or near, the centre.

For a District having from one hundred and fifty to two hundred Pupils, a House with three Apartments, one for an elementary, one for an advanced, and one for a High School, and at least one good Class Room common to the two latter, with three Teachers, and, if necessary, an Assistant; or if necessary Schools may be provided for the different Departments in different parts of the District.

And generally, for any District having two hundred Pupils and upwards, a House, or Houses, with sufficient accommodation for different grades of elementary and advanced Schools, so that in Districts having six hundred Pupils and upwards, the ratio of Pupils in the elementary, advanced, and High School departments, shall be respectively about eight, three, and one.

3. In Nova Scotia, the Board of School Examiners appointed for each District by the Governor-in-Council is authorized by Law,—

To declare upon the Inspector's Report, or upon other reliable information, the School House, or Houses, or Buildings used as such, unfit for School purposes, and shall forward such declaration to the Trustees of the Section, and the Board shall thereafter withhold all Provincial aid from any such Section, if measures are not adopted whereby a suitable House, or Houses may be provided, according to the ability of the Section.

From the Regulations of the Nova Scotia Council of Public Instruction on this subject, we make the following extracts:—

As to the size and commodiousness of the Building, provision should be made for one-quarter of the population of the Section; and whatever that number may be, the School House should be of such capacity as to furnish to each Scholar at least 150 cubic feet of pure atmospheric Air, or seven square feet of superficial area, with ceiling running from thirteen to sixteen feet in height.

Adding two feet nine inches to the length for every additional row of Desks. Where the number of Scholars amount to upwards of fifty, there should be a Class Room attached.

Plans of School Houses have been issued by the Council of Public Instruction, and the requirements of the Act are so explicit as to be a sufficient guide to Boards of Trustees.

4. In Prince Edward Island the Law declares that,—

Every School House hereafter to be erected and used as such, within any District now, or hereafter, established under this Act, and not already contracted to be built, shall not be less in clear area than four hundred square feet, nor in the height of posts than ten feet clear between the floor and ceiling, or be built nearer to the Highway than ten yards.

5. In Victoria, (Australia), no School receives aid from the Central Board unless the following, (among other conditions), be complied with, videlicet:—

That, in the case of new Buildings the School Room contain not less than eight square feet for each child in average attendance, and that the walls be not less than ten feet in height to the eaves; that in all cases the School Room be sufficiently Warmed, Ventilated and Drained; that there be proper and separate Offices for both sexes; that there be a Play-ground attached, or other satisfactory provision made for physical exercise; and that the School be properly provided with the amount of School Furniture and Apparatus, videlicet:—Desks, Forms, Blackboards, Maps, Books, etcetera, necessary for the efficient conduct of such School.

6. In South Australia,—

Grants-in-aid are allowed towards the cost of building School Houses, to an amount not exceeding Two hundred pounds for each School. The conditions to be observed in order to obtain this assistance are, that a declaration must be made by the Trustees that the Building for which the Grant is conceded shall be used for Public School purposes, and no other, without our written assent; that the area shall not be less than 600 square feet; that the Building shall be substantially constructed, and composed of good material; and that it shall be properly furnished with the usual appliances for teaching. Approved Plans and Specifications for the Building of District School Houses are supplied by us for the guidance of the promoters; but a departure from the Plans is allowed if sufficient reasons be shown for it,

7. In Michigan, the School Law provides, (Section 48), that,—

The Director shall provide the necessary appendages for the School House, and keep the same in good condition and repair during the time School shall be taught therein. The Director is also authorized and required to procure all needful appendages and repairs, without any vote of the District in the case. It is not optional with the District to pay such expenses. When audited by the Moderator and Assessor, the Account becomes a valid claim against the District, and can be collected if the District fails to pay it.

On these provisions of the Law, the State Superintendent remarks:—

The Law has wisely empowered one Officer, and made it his duty to keep the School House in good repair. He should see to it that the Windows are properly filled with Glass; that the Stove and Pipe are in a fit condition, and suitable wood provided; that the Desks and Seats are in good repair; that the Out-houses are properly provided with Doors, and are frequently cleansed; that the Black-boards are kept painted, and everything is provided necessary for the comfort of the Pupils, and the success of the School.

8. The School Laws of the State of Connecticut, (Sections 68 and 69), declare that:—

No District shall be entitled to receive any Money from the State, or from the Town in which it lies, unless such District shall be supplied with a School House and Out-buildings pertaining thereto, which shall be satisfactory to the Board of School Visitors.

Whenever a District shall have voted to erect a new School House, the same shall be built according to a Plan approved by the Board of School Visitors, and by the Building Committee of such District.

9. In Sweden, a piece of land, from one to twelve Acres, is attached to each School for the benefit of the Teacher and the Pupils. In 1867, the number of Schools possessing such a piece of land for working was 2,016. In Norway the School Districts must, in addition to Salary, furnish the Teacher with a Dwelling House, with land enough to pasture at least two Cows, and lay out a small Garden.

IV.—COMPULSORY ATTENDANCE, THE COMPLEMENT OF FREE SCHOOLS.

1. The principle of Free Schools,—a free and open School-door to every child in the land,—having been unanimously conceded by the Legislature, it becomes a serious question, whether so great a boon shall be rendered practically valueless or not, to a considerable portion of the community from the apathy of those most interested.

In answering this question, it is necessary to understand the object which the Legislature had in view in granting the boon of Free Schools. It should be for no light reason, or for no unimportant object that the Legislature should lay down the broad, yet highly benevolent principle, that the entire property of the Country should bear the whole burthen of providing a free and liberal education for every youth in the land. Nor is it unimportant; for the very adoption of so broad a principle of taxation shows that the Legislature regarded it as one of those momentous social questions, which could only be met and solved by it successfully, by the frank and unreserved adoption of a principle, so comprehensive in its character, as that of universal taxation for education, —or Free Schools.

The Sad Lessons which Ignorance has Taught should not be Lost Sight of.

2. Society has had so many terrible lessons of gross evils, which Ignorance and its twin-sister, Crime, have entailed upon it, that it has at length learned the truly wise one, that to banish ignorance, Education must be universal, and that to prevent, or lessen, crime, Education must be Christian in every part, and be an ever present and restraining influence upon it. If, however, those least capable of appreciating so great a boon as free and Christian Education, and who, at the same time, from the growth of ignorance among them, are capable of inflicting the greatest injury upon society, refuse to accept it, it becomes a legitimate question whether society has not the right, as it has the power, to protect itself, or whether with that inherent power of protection, it will suffer ignorance and crime to triumph over it. Such a question is easily answered. The instinct of self-preservation,—of common sense,—the best interests of humanity, and of the very class which rejects the boon, all point to the one solution, the only remedy:—Compulsory enforcement of the right which every child possesses, that he shall not grow up a pest to society, but that he shall enjoy the blessings which a Christian Education can alone confer upon him.

The Compulsory Features of the Ontario School Law.

3. The provision of the School Law of Ontario of 1871 on this subject is the legitimate consequence of the adoption of the principle of Free Schools; for if every man is to be taxed, according to his property, for the Public School Education of every child in the land, every Taxpayer has a right to claim that every child shall be educated in the various branches of a good English Education; otherwise the Law is a mere pretext for raising money by taxation under false pretences.

4. And, if every man is to be taxed according to his property for the education of every child, and if every child has a right to School instruction, some provision was needful to secure both the Ratepayer and the child against the oppression and wrong which might be inflicted by an unnatural Guardian, or Parent. Society at large, no less than the parties immediately concerned, requires this protection; and the protecting provision of the Law, in this respect, is milder and more guarded than the corresponding one in other Countries where Public School Education is provided for and guaranteed to every child in the Country. According to the new Act, no Parent, or Guardian, is liable to punishment whose wrong against society and his youthful charge is not wilful and criminal. If such a protection in this mild and guarded form is found, on trial, to be insufficient for the purposes intended, a more stringent one will no doubt be enacted by the Legislature hereafter.

Compulsory Education Involves an Improvement in its Quality and Amount.

1. Doctor Lyon Playfair, in a recent Address, thus argues the logical necessity for Compulsory Education, and of its improved quality:—

An improved quality of Education is a necessity for its enforced reception by the people. The principle of compulsion, timidly and hesitatingly put forth in the recent English Education Act, is nevertheless contained in it. The logic of circumstances drove Parliament into the recognition of compulsion; and the same logic will oblige the Legislature to make it efficient. Let us look at the facts which compelled the recognition of the principle. The right of suffrage has for its corollary the duty of instruction. You cannot give political power to a people and allow them to remain ignorant. That would be a political suicide of a Nation. An uneducated people are like a Nation, one, or two, generations back in its history. They cannot grasp the ideas of the age in which they live, and are powerless to shake themselves free from the prejudices which the progress of thought has proved to be dangerous errors. They are unable to do so, as they cannot take possession of the inheritance of the intellectual wealth accumulated by their predecessors; for they do not know how to read the Books forming the testament by which it was bequeathed. An uneducated people, endowed with political power, is, therefore, an anomaly, in the highest degree dangerous to a Nation. Hence, when we bestowed on the people the right of suffrage it became necessary that they should have sufficient instruction as its corollary. Secondly, we have now established what every civilized Nation except England has long had,—education by local Rates. A civic support of Education has again for its corollary enforced instruction of the individual citizen. For if it be right that the State should compel a community to educate all its citizens, it must be right to give power to that community to extend the education to every citizen.

He says further that,—

But you cannot enforce Education unless you make it of a quality which you are certain will be useful to the person receiving it. Compulsory Education then involves an improvement in its amount and quality. Compulsion is of two kinds, direct and indirect. By the direct method every Parent is bound to keep his children at School or be punished for the neglect. The indirect compulsion means that Education shall be made the first tool with which labour can be begun, and, if that tool be not in the possession of the Candidate for employment, the Employer must not engage him. The indirect plan has the high authority of Adam Smith in its favour, but it is unnecessary to indicate a preference between the two methods, for both may be good and necessary. In the Act of last Session only the direct system is recognized, although the others form the basis of our Factory Acts. Direct compulsion is most easily applied when it is least required, that is, when public feeling is entirely in its favour, and denounces the Parent who neglects the education of his child as much a niggard as if he starved it by refusing bread. But in England you have about half a million of these niggards to deal with, and their commonness prevents an adequate public censure of the magnitude of their crime against society.

Compulsory Education in Australia and America.

2. The Commissioners appointed in Victoria, (Australia), to report upon the "operation of the system of Public Education in that Country," speaking of Compulsory Education say, in the Report of 1868:—

Whilst fully admitting the divided state of opinion in reference to this subject, as well as the serious, practical difficulties that beset it, we have resolved to submit the recommendation that a Law rendering instruction imperative should be adopted in Victoria. The existence in constitutional theory, at all events, of an equality of political rights between all classes of Her Majesty's Subjects in this Colony suggests the paramount importance of early provision being made, by means more effectual than any that have hitherto existed, for the diffusion of sound instruction amongst the rising generation of all classes.

3. In the Report of Doctor Fraser, (now Bishop of Manchester), on the "Common School Systems of the United States and Canada," he says:—

From many sections of the community, and especially from those who would be called the Educationists, the cry is rising both loud and vehement that greater stringency is required in the Law, and that compulsory attendance is the proper correlative of "Free Schools." For, it is argued, if the State taxes me, who perhaps have no children, towards the support of the Schools, "for the security of society," I have a right to claim from the State, for the security of the same society, that the Schools which I am taxed to maintain shall be attended by those for whose benefit they were designed.

Feeling in England in Regard to Compulsory Education.

4. The Honourable B. G. Northrop, (late Secretary to the Board of Education in the State of Connecticut, and now Commissioner of Education in Japan), thus refers to the state of feeling on the subject in England.

The new School Law of England permits all local School Boards to enforce attendance. Public sentiment throughout England is now changing rapidly in favour of making compulsory attendance national and universal, instead of permissive. As one of the many illustrations of this change, the Reverend Canon Kingsley, formerly favouring non-compulsion, now advocates the compulsory principle.

The Motto of the National Educational League, of which George Dixon, M.P., is President, is "Education must be Universal, Unsectarian, Compulsory." At the late General Conference of Nonconformists, held lately in Manchester, and attended by 1,885 delegates, there seemed to be great unanimity in favour of enforced attendance. This assembly was as remarkable in its character as its numbers. The argument of Mr. Jacob Bright, M.P., on this subject was received with great applause. He said that the best part of the Education Act, that which is worth all the rest put together, is the permission to compel attendance, which should be the absolute Law throughout the entire Kingdom.

The labouring classes are not opposed to such a Law. They would welcome it. In England the working classes are asking for a national Compulsory System of Education. By invitation of J. A. Mundella, M.P., I attended the National Trades-Union Congress, held lately at Nottingham, for a week That Body seemed unanimous in favour of Compulsory Attendance. One of the leading Members, an able and effective Speaker said, that in large and crowded assemblies of workingmen, he had often distinctly asked:—"Do you agree with me that we want a national Compulsory System of Education?" and not a dissenting voice had he ever heard from the Workingmen.

In a late School Report to the Government it is stated that:

By the 1st of May, By-laws for enforcing the attendance of children at School had been sanctioned by Your Majesty, in accordance with the terms of the 74th Section of the Act, on the application of the School Boards of—

1. London, with a population of 3,265,005
2. 65 Municipal Boroughs, (out of 100) 4,267,642
3. 41 Civil Parishes, (out of 279) 608,000

Total 8,140,657

Compulsory attendance at School is, therefore, now the law for upwards of one-third of the whole population of England and Wales, and for about two-thirds of the whole Borough population.

State of Feeling in Prussia and other Parts of Europe in Regard to Compulsory Education.

5. Mr. Northrop also gives the following sketch of the state of feeling in Prussia, in regard to compulsory Education. He says:—

My former objections to obligatory attendance were fully removed by observations recently made in Europe. Mingling much with plain people in Germany, and other Countries where attendance at School is compulsory, I sought in every way to learn their sentiments on this question. After the fullest enquiry in Prussia, especially among Labourers of all sorts, I nowhere heard a lisp of objection to this Law. The masses everywhere favour it. They say Education is a necessity for all. They realize that the School is their privilege. They prize it and are proud of it. Attendance is voluntary, in fact, nobody seems to think of coercion. The Law is operative, but it executes itself because it is right and beneficent, and commands universal approval. It is only the legal expression of the public will.

Universal Education, more than anything else, has fraternized the great German Nation. It has improved her social life, ennobled her Homes, promoted private virtue, comfort and thrift, and secured general prosperity in peace. It has given her unequalled prestige and power in war. "Whatever you would have appear in a Nation's life, that you must put into its Schools," was long since a Prussian motto. The School has there been the prime agent of loyalty. Love of Country is the germ it long ago planted in the heart of every child. The fruit now matured gladdens and enriches the whole land. Wherever that lesson is heeded, it will enrich the world. Devotion to Fatherland is a characteristic sentiment of the German people. Shall such a people, with such a history, complain of Compulsory Attendance? This Law itself has been a Teacher of the Nation. It has everywhere proclaimed the necessity and dignity of the Public Schools. Kings, and nobles, and Ministers of State, have combined to confirm and diffuse this sentiment, until now it pervades and assimilates all classes.

In various parts of Prussia and Saxony, I enquired of School Directors, Parents and others, "Do you have any difficulty in executing the coercive Law?" The answers were all substantially the same. "Many years ago," replied one, "there was some opposition. But the results of the Law have commended it to all, and they obey it without complaint, and almost without exception." The present generation of parents, having themselves experienced its advantages, are its advocates. Said a resident of Dresden. "A healthy child of School age can hardly be found in this city who has not attended School." Were the question of Compulsory Attendance to be decided to-morrow in Saxony by a plebiscite, it would be sustained by an almost unanimous verdict. Public opinion is now stronger even than the Law. The people would sooner increase than relax its rigour. I nowhere learned of any recent cases of punishment for infractions of it. In many places I was assured that the penalty is practically unknown.

The People in Advance of the Government on Compulsory Education.

6. The principle of obligatory instruction was advocated by the people before it was enacted by the Government. The address of Luther to the Municipal Corporations of 1554 contains the earliest defence of it within my knowledge, in which he says,— "Ah, if a State in time of War can oblige its citizens to take up the Sword and the Musket, has it not still more the power, and is it not its duty, to compel them to educate its children, since we are all engaged in a most serious warfare, waged with the spirit of evil, which rages in our midst, seeking to depopulate the State of its virtuous men? It is my desire, above all things else, that every child should go to School, or be sent there by a magistrate." *

Germ of the Principle of Compulsory Education.

7. The germ of this system in Prussia is found in a decree of Frederick II, 1763:— We will that all our Subjects, Parents, Guardians and Masters, send to School those children for whom they are responsible, Boys and Girls, from their fifth year to the age of fourteen. This Royal Order was revived in 1794, and in the Code of 1819 made more stringent, with severe penalties;—First, warnings, then small fines, doubling the fines for repeated offences, and, finally, imprisonment of Parents, Guardians and Masters.

The penalties now are:—

1. Admonition, in the form of a note of warning from the President of the Local School Commission.

2. Summons to appear before the School Commission, with a reprimand from the presiding Officer.

3. Complaint to the Magistrate, (by the Commission), who usually exacts a fine of Twenty cents, and for a second offence Forty cents, for a third Eighty cents, doubling the last fine for each repetition of the offence.

The Registers of attendance and absence are kept with scrupulous exactness by the Teacher, and delivered to the President of the School Commission. Excuses are accepted for illness, exceedingly severe weather, great distance from School, and sometimes on account of the pressure of work in harvest time.

Failure of the Old System to do its Work.—Compulsory Attendance.

8. The State Superintendent of Michigan, in his last Annual Report to the Legislature of that State, says:—

There are young men and women who were born in this State, and have been reared almost within sight of the School House that was always open to receive them, and yet to-day are unable to read and write. If there is anything which makes every lover of our free institutions sick at heart, it is to be transacting business with a young man, a fellow citizen, and when some Paper is drawn requiring his signature, to learn that he is compelled to make his mark, and this, too, notwithstanding that he has spent his whole life within reach of a School. The next question which is to engage the attention of the Legislature, that is of vital importance to the educational interests of the State is how to secure the constant and regular atendance of all the children upon the Public, or Private, Schools. The question is a grave one, but one that must be met and rightly solved. The word compulsion grates harshly upon the ears of free-men, and its meaning grates more harshly on their sensitive hearts. It may be found, however, that the system of Compulsory Education is one not to be so much dreaded as has been supposed. Those who have thought most upon the subject are looking with favour upon the system. Every thoughtful man is coming to see the danger that imperils the Nation if so large a proportion of the people are suffered to grow up in ignorance. The question is really resolving itself into this:—Shall we have education, even if it be in a certain sense compelled, and a strong and noble Country, or ignorance and anarchy?

Defect in American Systems as Compared with the European.

9. To those familiar with the best Systems of Education in Europe, our System presents one sad defect; they see that not half of the children of this Country attend School with any regularity, and that there are thousands upon thousands who never see

the School Room at all. One of the prominent Educators from Europe, in an Address at the Cooper Institute, after praising very much many things he had seen in this Country, said,—"That in general our System of Education was the best in the world, but it needed one thing to make it perfect, and that is, that Education should be made compulsory." "I should be uncandid," he further said, "if I did not frankly tell you that North Germany and Switzerland excel you in the thoroughness and universality of their Systems, and this, I believe, is entirely owing to the fact that in those Countries the Parent has not the right to deprive his child of the excellent training which the State has provided. When the Parent fails in his duty the State stands in *loco parentis;* and this is what you chiefly need to perfect your educational system." In Sweden, Education is compulsory upon all classes, whether rich or poor, or whether living near to, or distant from, School. Every child must continue his studies until he has become proficient in certain branches. The least that is required embraces Reading, Writing, the elements of Arithmetic, the Catechism, Bible History, and Singing. Many of the children live at a great distance from School. The statistical Reports show that 20,000 have to go from three to four miles, and 70,000 not less than two miles. This, of course, requires the whole day, leaving home in the morning and returning in the evening. Trivial excuses for absences are not allowed. The period of School life is not measured by years, but is determined by the progress made. There must be acquired a thorough knowledge of the required branches before any child can leave School. As a result it is almost impossible to meet with a Swede, of either sex, who is unable to read and write, or to find a single Cottage, however isolated, even buried in the very depths of the forests, that is destitute of the Bible and other valuable Books.

A recent Report of the School System of Sweden and Norway, and for which I am indebted to our American Minister at Stockholm, General C. C. Andrews, shows that ninety-seven per cent. of all children of schoolable age throughout that Kingdom were in attendance in some of her public or private Schools during the year 1869.

Discussion on the Subject of Compulsory Education in the United States.

10. The subject of Compulsory Education is one that has called forth much discussion in the educational conventions of this Country for the past two years, and many conscientious and earnest men strongly advocate the policy of requiring all children entitled to the benefits of the provision made by the State for their education, to attend some Public, or Private, School. The argument is, that granting that the stability of the Government, and the perpetuity of her institutions depend upon the intelligence of the mass of the people, that the same necessity that would justify the Government in coming into the family circle and taking the Father, Brother, or Son, and sending him into the Army to defend that Government against those who would overturn it, would equally justify the Officer of the Law in compelling the citizen of the State to educate his children so far that they may be qualified for good citizenship. If a judicious and conservative Law, compelling all Parents to send their children to School, between the ages of eight and sixteen, as long as free Schools are provided and accessible, could be enforced among our population, it would work good results towards diffusing Education among all classes.

A Sadder Aspect of the Question of Non-attendance at School.

11. In order to give the friends of Education in this Province the fullest information on some of its sadder, or graver, features, of this subject, I turn now to consider another aspect of this question.

General Eaton, the United States Commissioner of Education at Washington, in his Report to Congress for 1871, thus discusses the question of "Education and Crime." He says:—

The Teacher who would understand fully the benefit of an early and proper education of the young, must include in his observations the effect of its neglect. He must not only go to the Workshop, the Editorial Room, the Publishing House, and the University, but observe carefully the population gathered in Reformatories and Prisons. He will recall the axiom, that whatever exposes men to commit crime is a source of crime. In 1866, there were 17,000 persons reported in the Prisons of the United States. Had the Teacher questioned these as to the cause of their crime, a very large proportion would have pointed either to total ignorance, or a neglect, or perversion, of education in their youth.

Results of Investigations on this Subject in the United States.—Conclusions.

12. In New England, the statistics on this subject have, in some cases, received considerable attention. Esteeming them measurably accurate, I have secured the

preparation of an article on the relations of Education to crime in New England, from an able and scholarly Writer, and a careful Observer. In presenting his views, he gives, after a critical examination of the literature on the subject, the results of information obtained by personal visits and observations, and comes to the following conclusions:—

I. At least eighty per cent. of the crime in New England is committed by those who have no education, or none sufficient to serve them a valuable purpose in life. In 1868, twenty-eight per cent. of all the Prisoners in the Country were unable to read or write. From three to seven per cent. of the population of the United States commit thirty per cent. of all our crime, and less than one-fifth of one per cent. is committed by those who are educated.

II. As in New England, so throughout all the Country, from eighty to ninety per cent. have never learned any Trade, or mastered any skilled labour; which leads to the conclusion that "Education in labour bears the same ratio to freedom from crime as Education in Schools.*

III. Not far from seventy-five per cent. of New England crime is committed by persons of foreign extraction. Therefore, twenty per cent. of the population furnishes seventy-five per cent. of the criminals. It is noticeable, however, that the Emigrant coming hither with education, either in Schools, or labour, does not betake himself to crime.

IV. From eighty to ninety per cent. of our Criminals connect their courses of crime with intemperance.

V. In all Juvenile Reformatories ninety-five per cent. of the Offenders come from idle, ignorant, vicious homes. Almost all children are truant from School at the time of their committal; and almost all are the children of ignorant Parents. These children furnish the future inmates of our Prisons; for "Criminals are not made in some malign hour, they grow." In the face of these facts, what can be said but this:—Ignorance breeds crime, Education is the remedy for crime that imperils us.

13. The following will illustrate the extent and minuteness with which statistics are gathered in other Countries, showing the illiteracy of criminals.

COUNTRY.	READING.					WRITING.				ARITHMETIC.				GRAMMAR.			
	Well.	Tolerably well.	Poorly.	Only knew letters of the Alphabet.	Entirely ignorant.	Well.	Tolerably well.	Poorly.	Entirely ignorant.	Well.	Knew the elements well.	Knew the elements tolerably well.	Entirely ignorant.	Good.	Middling.	Poor.	Number of prisoners examined.
Saxony ..	230	768	218	39	28	173	657	381	73	183	635	443	13	161	1,005	118	1,284
Wurtemburg....	....	....	....	....	1	....	....	....	19	....	....	....	....	....	....	....	2,091

* In a letter from the experienced Director of the American Prison Association, New York, he says :—Agreeably to your request I re-state to you, in written form, what was stated in recent conversation with you.

1. Mr. Edwin Hill, of London, a candid and careful inquirer, who holds a high position in the Government, says that his investigations on the subject of criminality have satisfied him that there are born every day in Great Britain from six to eight children who, from the circumstances of their birth, and early surroundings in life, are virtually compelled to enter upon a career of crime.

2. I have lately received from Count Sollohut, of Russia, a letter giving the results of an experiment in prison discipline conducted by him in Moscow. For six years, that is from its origin, he has been Director of the House of Correction and Industry in that city. Within the period named, more than 2,000 Criminals have passed through the Establishment, and been discharged from its custody, only nine of whom—less than half of one per cent.—have been returned to it for criminal acts. You will be curious to know how so extraordinary a result has been accomplished. The Consul's Letter explains it. Not only is every Prisoner required to learn a Trade, but he is permitted to choose the Trade he will learn. So long as he continues an Apprentice, he is allowed no share in his earnings: but as soon as he has mastered his business a part of the income from what he produces, by no means inconsiderable, is his own, but is not given to him until the time of his liberation. Count Sollohut assures me that the intelligence and zeal of the Apprentices in mastering their several Trades are such that instances are not rare in which it is accomplished in six months! So potent a thing is hope, and the prospect of bettering their condition, even as Criminals. The first general result of this system is, that fully nine-tenths of the Prisoners in this Jail master a Trade so completely, that, on their discharge, they are capable of taking the position of Foreman in a Shop; and the second is, that there are scarcely any relapses; but. on the contrary, those who have been subjected to its discipline are, almost to a man, through the Trades they learned in Prison, earning and eating honest bread.

You will agree with me, that the second of the facts related above is as cheering and hopeful for fallen humanity as the first is deplorable and disheartening. If Prison Officers, by a wise application of energy, can accomplish such results as those recorded by Sollohut, surely society, by the use of a like wisdom and zeal, may so adjust its arrangements as to afford a substantial remedy to the state of things alleged by Mr. Hill to exist this moment in England.

New York, 1871.   E. C. WINES, LL.D.

Bavaria.—Curious Statistics.—Churches, Schools and Crime.

PROVINCES.	Number of Churches to every 1,000 Buildings.	Number of School-houses to every 1,000 Buildings.	One School-house to how many inhabitants	Average of Crimes to every 100,000 inhabitants.
Upper Bavaria........	14·9	5·4	502	667
Lower Bavaria........	10·1	4·5	508	870
Palatinate	3·9	10·8	230	425
Upper Palatinate......	11·1	6·2	379	690
Upper Franconia......	4.8	6·7	412	444
Middle Franconia.....	7.1	8·3	309	459
Lower Franconia......	5·1	10·4	176	384
Suabia	14·6	8·1	435	609

Necessity for More than "Fact-Knowledge."—The Moral Nature.

14. Doctor Taylor Lewis remarks with great force.—

Experience has abundantly shown that no amount of mere fact-knowledge, or of scientific knowledge, in the restricted modern sense of the term, can give security that the man possessing it may not turn out a monster of crime, and a deadly scourge to society. Of itself, we mean, or in its direct effects; for, as an aid to a higher position among men, and thus, as furnishing a worldly motive to correct outward behaviour, it might, undoubtedly, operate as a salutary check.

The same may be said of the pursuit and acquisition of wealth, or of anything else that gives rise to a worldly prudence taking the place, for a time, of moral principle. When this, however, is not the case, or such an education gives less distinction, by being more and more diffused, then, instead of a check, it may become a direct incentive to crime, by creating increased facilities for its commission.

Regular Training Schools of Crime.

15. Evidence is constantly accumulating that the processes of the Burglar, of the Incendiary, of the Counterfeiter, of the Poisoner, of the Railroad Destroyer, and of the Prison-breaker, etcetera, are actually making progress with the progress of crime. They are becoming arts, but we cannot rank them among the elegant, or useful.

There is reason to believe that before long Books may be written upon them, and that there may be such a thing as a Felon's Library.* The same may be maintained in respect to what may be called the more speculative knowledge. When wholly destitute, as it may be, of moral truth and moral intuitions, it may only wake up the dormant faculties of the soul for the discovery of evil, and make them all the more acute for its perpetuation.

As Education Advances, Crime Diminishes.

16. The State Superintendent of Kansas illustrates another fact in the following language : —

Ignorance is the fostering mother of vice. The relation of cause to effect which binds ignorance to crime is now a fact, demonstrated by the unerring figures of statistics. In proportion as Education advances in a Country, the number of Criminals diminishes.† Crime and ignorance, masked by day, go hand in hand by night, to perform deeds of wickedness and shame

* As if to show Doctor Lewis a true prophet, a Telegram of November 2nd states that the police, in breaking up an organized band of House-breakers, near Chillicothe, Ohio, found, among other articles, a number of Books for the instruction of novices in the art of Burglary.

† The interesting Report of M. Duruy upon elementary instruction in France gives conclusive figures upon this subject. Thus, in comparing the period 1828-1836 with 1838-1847, we find that the whole number of Persons under twenty-one years accused of crime had diminished but 285; while, in comparing the decade 1838-1847 with 1853-1862 the number had decreased 4,152, almost eighteen times as many. In 1847, Persons under sixteen were tried at the Court of Assizes : in 1862, there were but 44. In Germany, in Prussia, as instruction is improved and extended, crime diminishes. In the prisons of Vaud, Neufchatel, and Zurich, there are but one or two prisons : they are often empty. In Baden, where, within thirty years, much has been done to promote education : from 1854 to 1861, the number of prisoners decreased from 1,425 to 591 ; some prisons were closed.

IV. SUPERSEDING SCHOOL SECTION DIVISIONS AND ESTABLISHING TOWNSHIP BOARDS OF EDUCATION.

Since the date of my last Report, I am glad to observe that a movement has been made, in various parts of the Province, towards the abolition of School Section Divisions, and the establishment of Township Boards of Education.

Even since 1850, there has been a provision in our School Acts for the establishment of Township Boards, as contained in the Thirty-second Section of the Consolidated School Act; but, as that Section is worded, no such Board could be established unless a majority of the votes in every single School Section of the Township was in favour of it. It has happened that out of twelve School Sections in a Township, the majority of the Ratepayers in eleven of them voted for the establishment of a Township Board; but the majority in one Section voted against it, and thus defeated the wishes of eleven-twelfths of the Ratepayers. Under these circumstances, the Thirty-second Section of the School Act has remained a dead letter for twenty years, except so far as one Township, (Enniskillen), is concerned,—although a large majority of the County School Conventions, on two occasions, have voted in favour of Township Boards. The Law was, in 1871, wisely altered so as to leave the question to the decision of the Ratepayers in a majority of the School Sections of a Township. Should, therefore, the vote of a majority of the Ratepayers in a Township be favourable to a change, the Municipal Council of such Township is authorized to form the Township into one School Municipality, under one Board of Trustees, (as is the case in Cities, Towns, and Villages), doing away with the great inconvenience of separate School Section Divisions and Rates, and giving to Parents the right to send their children to the School nearest to their residences.

Success of Township Boards in Various American States.

1. After trying the School Section System for some time, Massachusetts, Pennsylvania, Ohio, Iowa, Wisconsin, and other States, have adopted the Township Board System, and pronounce it immensely superior to the School Section System. In the State of New York, a compromise System is authorized by the School Law; that is, one or more School Sections can "either severally, or jointly, resolve themselves into Union Free School Districts, with Boards of Education, having authority to grade and classify the Schools under their charge." From the Report of the Superintendent of Public Instruction for 1870, we learn that there are now 250 such united Districts in the State; of them he says:—

Having had frequent occasion to examine the provisions of this Law, i.e. the "Union Free School Act"), and being somewhat familiar with its workings, I am of the opinion that it is the best School System yet devised for all localities where the number of Scholars, as in Villages, is sufficient to admit of a thorough classification.

The Reverend Doctor, (now Bishop), Fraser, in his Report to the English Commissioners, says:—

In the State of New York. Union Schools, [or united Sections], appear to be the most popular and flourishing of all the rural Schools.

In this Province, the Township Council, if the experiment should not prove satisfactory, can, at any time, repeal its own By-law establishing such Board.

2. *Connecticut.*—The Secretary to the State Board of Education in Connecticut, thus graphically illustrates the comparative effects of the adoption of the Township over the School Section System in that State. In order to understand the facts as stated, I have found it necessary to change the words "Town" to Township, and "District" to School Section, where they occur in the following extracts.

The tendency to manage Schools Township-wise is growing. More Townships united their School Sections last year than in any former one. Once united, they stay so. At least there is no instance where a Township has taken this step, and after grading any of its Schools, gone back to the School Section plan. Let public sentiment advance as it has done for five years, and the School Section System will soon be abandoned. The people are fast learning the economy and efficiency of the Township

System. They see that it favours the wise expenditure of the public money, gains better and more permanent Teachers, longer Schools, and helps the poorer and outlying School Sections. The Township System, too, lessens the frequency of tax Assessments and Collections. Many a School House is going to decay because the funds requisite for such purposes would necessitate a Section Tax. The expense of the assessment and collection of such a Tax makes too large a share of the Tax itself. In most of the Sections, the amounts thus provided were very small. So small, that it would have been wiser and more economical for the Township to pay the bills. . . . Facts on this subject are better than theories. I have, therefore, requested one of the School Visitors of Brantford to describe the effects of the change in that Township. His published Letter shows what they did, how they did it, what they gained by it, and why they voted almost unanimously "not to go back." It will be seen that, prior to the union, there was much ill-feeling in regard to School matters, that the discipline was deplorable, average attendance low, and the Teachers changed generally every Term; under the new System, the people are better satisfied. School Committee and Teachers more permanent, Schools graded, Terms lengthened, the motion made at the last Annual Meeting to reduce the School year from forty to thirty weeks not receiving a single vote. The average attendance has improved twenty-five per cent. Scholarship wonderfully improved.—one hundred per cent. better than it was four years ago.

3. *Massachusetts.*—The late Horace Mann, so noted for his enlightened views on Education, deprecating the District or School Section Ssystem, says:—

I consider the Law authorising Townships to divide themselves into [School Sections] the most unfortunate on the subject of Common Schools ever enacted in the State [of Massachusetts]. In this opinion, ex-Governor Boutwell, the eminent Educationist of the same State, concurs, and hopes that the day will speedily be seen when every Township, in its municipal capacity, will manage its Schools, and equalize the expenses of Education.

Practical Experience of Maine, Massachusetts and Vermont.

The State Superintendent of Maine, in his recent Report, devotes a considerable space to the discussion of the Township vs. School Section System. He says:—

I submit the following argument against the Section System, and in favour of the Township plan,—an argument drawn from the experience and best thoughts of Massachusetts and Vermont. For the past three years I have urged upon the citizens of Maine, the desirability and necessity of adopting the Township System of School organization in place of the Section System, if they desired to attain higher and larger School results than at present. Lewiston, Auburn, Lisbon, Orono, and a few other Townships, in which the educational sense is lively, have abolished the Section System, and adopted the Municipal form, with the happiest results, and with especial advantage to the out-lying rural Districts. Such has been the consequence wherever the change has been made, better School Houses, superior teaching, and longer School Terms.

The Western States have never allowed the School District un-system to be engrafted upon their educational enterprises. Our eastern Educators, emigrating westward, have carefully avoided this element of inequality and disintegration in building up the "Daily Public School" for our younger sister States. Even Massachusetts, who gave us the doubtful legacy of the District System plan, abolished the same in her own School System, and although subsequently she gave the Towns the privilege of returning to the "old ways," but fourteen Towns, [Townships], in the entire Commonwealth availed themselves of the opportunity. These were remote, sparsely settled Towns, generally cut into Sections by natural barriers, forbidding an advantageous unification. We have an ardent desire, therefore, to remove all obstacles to the highest possible realization in our educational efforts.*

---

* In another part of his Report the Superintendent of Maine thus illustrates the character of this progress under the Township System : he says:

"Quite a number of the Townships, like Lewiston, Auburn, Lisbon, Durham, Greene, Turner, raised the current year more money than ever before, much more than required by law, for the support of the Schools. Lewiston has provided herself with a Superintendent at an annual salary of $2,000 and travelling expenses. She is also taking steps to make her education more practical by putting into it an Industrial element. Already her Public Schools are the best in the State. But the greatest educational achievement of the year is the abolition of the miserable District System by the Town of Lisbon, by which Act the Town became the owner of all the School-houses, the Schools of the same length, with the whole management of the Schools in the hands of the Superintending School Committee. Having voted to abolish the District System at the March meeting, the Town, believing it would be judiciously expended by the Superintending School Committee, then voted to raise fifty per cent. more money than required by law for the support of the Schools, which gives three good terms of school the present year. Old School-houses have been repaired and new ones built. Lisbon has now four new School-houses that cost $12,000 in the aggregate and while I regarded her Schools, less than three years ago, as among the very poorest in the County, they are now, thanks to her public spirited citizens and her very efficient Superintending School Committee, far ahead of all others in the County, excepting the Schools of Lewiston and Auburn, the the two other Towns in the County which have abolished the District System. I am fully satisfied that if an intelligent discussion of the subject, that a large part of the Towns in the State would at once abolish the District System, and thus double the efficiency of the Schools, with not more than one-tenth part of the present trouble in their management. And without this abolition I am also fully satisfied there can be no great and steadfast improvement of the Schools.

Life and Progress.—Teachers understand how impossible it is to secure in a small School, or in a small Class, that healthful and proper stimulus which is almost an incident to the large School or the large Class.   One who has himself ever been an entire Class, or one of two or three constituting a Class, will remember how difficult it was to create in himself any such measure of interest as would make the labour of preparation other than a dreary task, and this evil extends to the Teacher as well as to the Pupil.   He, too, needs stimulus.

The small Section fails to secure that aggregate of interest on the part of the inhabitants toward the School which is essential to make it successful.   This aggregate of interest is the sum total of individual interest.   Five families have less interest in a School than have ten, ten less than fifteen, and so on.   The Teacher thus receives less stimulus from his surroundings in small than in large Districts.   So with the Pupils.

Too many Officers.—Is not our present System defective in that it requires too many Officers?   The average number of individuals in each Township who are the School Officers of the Township, will be found to be from fifty to sixty, if we estimate three Trustees to each Section; the whole number of School Officers in the State, (Province), something more than fifteen thousand!   Such an army ought to do the work well, we say.   Yet, who does not believe that one-fifth the number would do it far better?   This gives one School Officer for every ten or fifteen children.   What an absurdity!   Who believes in this multiplicity of Officers, which almost inevitably results in no supervision at all?   Why not elect a Township Council of fifty in number?   Who would care to live in a Township thus supervised?   Is it not that six men are found better than fifty, that six are elected?   Six men competent for the School duties of the Township would be infinitely more efficient than fifty, even if it were possible to secure fifty men as competent as the six.

Unity the Rule.—The State [Province] is a unit for certain purposes.   The Township is a unit for certain other purposes.   For the purpose of Education the Section has also been regarded as a unit.   For almost every other purpose the Township has been found to be the true unit.   Indeed, in several respects, in the educational part even, the Township System prevails.   Would it not be wiser to make the Township a unit for educational purposes?

Small Schools, Small Stipends.—It is quite natural to think that a Teacher who can be secured for a small stipend will answer for a "small School," so that small Schools will, in general, be taught by Teachers who could not secure situations in larger ones. and would fail if they did.

Small Sections, Bad School Houses.—Small Sections will be likely to have bad School Houses.   The expense of building and repairing falls heavily upon ten or a dozen Tax-payers.   And the old School Houses, many of them, unfit even for stalled cattle, will have to serve till that time when we have grown wiser and adopted a new order of things. for there is no hope under the present system that the future will afford relief.   The population, except at business centres, is year by year gradually growing less.   Small Sections are far less likely to furnish those facilities for illustration and reference so necessary to the Teacher.   Indeed, everything which involves an expenditure, is likely to remain undone.   The Trustee feels like being very economical when he reflects that he will be assessed one-tenth of any expenditure; so that Globes, Dictionaries and Maps, Prizes, and all School Apparatus, are excluded from the School.

Competitive Examinations.—Making one Central Board of supervision would render possible Competitive Examinations, which are now practically impossible.   Such Examinations would immediately shut out the most incompetent of our Teachers.   They would discourage mere Girls, scarcely beyond the age which the Law designates as infancy, from seeking places in our Schools as Teachers, when they should be there as Pupils.

Evils of Nepotism.—Fewer Daughters and Nieces, and Wives' Sisters would be employed.   Even when they are thoroughly competent, their employment is often seen to awaken such a spirit of antagonism as will impair the efficiency of the School.   Nepotism is as baneful an evil in the politics of the School Section as in the broader field of the State.

Better Teachers.—Again, a better class of Teachers would be secured in the smaller Sections.   It could not be expected that all the Schools of a Township would be of equal size.   The larger ones, the Village Schools, as now, would secure the Teachers without regard to expense.   The lesser communities, noticing that they were obliged to help to support good Schools and pay large prices to the Teachers of larger Schools would very soon begin to feel that if they were obliged to help to support good Schools for their townsmen, it would be wise to compel their townsmen to sustain good Schools for them.

Permanence of Teachers.—This change of supervision would tend to remove the evil of a constant change of Teachers.   Permanency of supervision would result in permanency of Teachers.   The frequency of change in Teachers is a most alarming evil with us. It breaks up all connection between one Term and another. Each Teacher has his own ways, and it takes some time to get out of the old ways and into the new, and quite a portion of each Term is spent in getting started. It thus often happens that a Term is one-third spent before the work is well begun. It requires a Term of ordinary length for a Teacher to become familiar with the peculiar characteristics of his Pupils. No very efficient work can be done till this is known. He has first to learn their needs and their capacities, before he can adapt his instruction to the necessities of each Pupil. An ordinary Teacher, who has taught a School for one Term, will do more for that School than one of superior endowments and acquirements, who is an entire stranger to the wants of the School. Perpetual change of Teachers and Inspectors of Schools utterly ignores the value of experience. I can conceive of no remedy for these evils which will be likely to prove so efficient as this change of system.

Evils of Change of Teachers.—Ex-Governor Boutwell, afterwards the experienced Secretary to the Massachusetts State Board of Education, thus depicts the evils of a change of Teachers under the School Section plan. He says:—

Practically the School Section System denies the value of experience. Each year sees a new Trustee and each Term a new Teacher. The experience of a year is often rendered valueless by the election of a new Trustee; and the Teacher labours for a single Term, commencing without a knowledge of what the Pupils have previously accomplished, and ending without an interest in their future. Under these circumstances, it is not strange that Section Schools are kept, Term after Term, and year after year, without an appreciable increase of power. "The quality of the School depends upon the character of the Teacher; and the character of the Teacher depends upon accident, or the caprice, prejudices, or convenience of the Trustee. Each Teacher brings into the School his own ideas of teaching, and after two, three, or four months he goes away, and his place is taken by a stranger who introduces new methods, without the judgment of anybody concerning their relative value. The successive Terms of School in the same Section have not, usually, any personal, or educational, connection or comparative success; and it does not even furnish, either in its failure or its success, a basis for future operation.

Equalization of Taxation.—Again, this change would result in an equalization of the burden of supporting Schools. It now costs each Tax-payer in a small Section more to support a poor School than it costs the Tax-payer in the larger Section to support a good School. Statistics show that the expense per Pupil increases in the inverse ratio as the size of the School diminishes. Why should not taxation for the support of Schools be equalised? Equity demands that it should. Every reason which can be urged in favour of good Schools demands that it should.

Division of Labour.—No one, I suppose, at this day, assumes to doubt the wisdom of the application of the principle of division of labour, as applied to the Mechanical pursuits. The Manufacturer who should require each Workman to make all parts of a Watch, would find that he could not compete with his rival who put each Workman upon a single piece; even in the manufacture of Boots and Shoes, where no great mechanical genius is required, it is found to be economy to allow each man to do a distinct part, so that the Boot, or Shoe, is not the work of one hand, but of several. If this be economy in the Mechanical pursuits, how much more apparent is the wisdom of applying this principle to the more delicate and responsible work of developing and training the human mind?

Classified Schools.—Now, this is the principle upon which the graded Schools is based. It is found that the Teacher who teaches a few branches, and concentrates all his time and efforts upon these branches, can give more efficient instruction than the one who attempts to teach all. It is upon this principle, in part, that each College Professor has his distinct department. This, however, is not the most substantial argument in favour of grading Schools. A graded School is simply a classified School. Every one knows, who is at all familiar with Schools, that their success depends very largely upon their classification. It requires just as much time to instruct one individual as to instruct a Class; just as long to instruct a Class of three as a Class of twenty. If your School has as many Classes as individuals, and this often happens in small Schools, the Teachers' time is frittered away to little purpose. No School whose Curriculum comprises all the Studies from the A B C to the highest branches taught in the Public Schools, can be thoroughly classified without having more Classes than the Teacher can well instruct.

Evils of Heterogeneous Classes.—Every Teacher knows how difficult it is to make an impression upon the heterogeneous mass grouped together and called a Class,—made up of Pupils pursuing the same Studies, indeed,—but of diverse age, diverse capacity, and diverse acquirements, is is usual in an ungraded School. The more gifted and accomplished are held back, while those of lesser gifts and acquirements are dragged on beyond their strength. The former grow lazy and indifferent; the latter discouraged and disgusted. The former acquire an overweening confidence in their own abilities; the latter fail to cultivate that healthful self-appreciation essential to success, which is naturally developed by association with one's peers. Thus it happens that all stimulus, both to the bright and the dull, is removed.

Unclassified Classes.—Besides, it is impossible for any Teacher to adapt his instruction to the varied capacities and diverse accomplishments of unclassified Classes. This is difficult enough in a Class which has been selected and grouped with reference to like capacities and similar acquirements. If he adapts his instruction to the more advanced, it will be beyond the comprehension of those less advanced. If, on the other hand, it is adapted to the needs of those less gifted, it becomes tedious and uninstructive to the others. Thus will all the interest be dissipated, while, if well classified, each individual inspirits the other. Mutual labour and mutual sympathy are powerful stimulants, especially to the young. Each spurs and supports the other, and industry and diligence are secured in all.

Specified Work for Each Class.—Again, the graded School furnishes additional inducement to effort in this way:—Each Class has its specified work, and no advancement to a higher grade can be secured until that work is done. Each grade is a position which cannot be reached except by passing step by step over all the intermediate ground. The Pupils in each grade have the perpetual incitement of their more advanced associates. From one grade to another is to them a long stride. It seems a thing worthy to strive for. Now, these stimulants are especially needed by slow and not over-gifted minds, and to this class a majority of children belong. The result is, that progress is far more rapid and thorough in a graded than in an ungraded School.

Systematic Instruction.—Still, again, the graded system secures a systematic course of Education. Each Pupil does not for himself, nor can his Parents for him, elect this Study, or that, as whim, or caprice, may dictate. He must take each in due time and order. That Course of Study is prescribed which will secure the best and most symmetrical mental development, embracing those Studies a knowledge of which is likely to prove of the most practical benefit to the Pupil in the business pursuits of after-life.

Intelligence and Value of Property.—Take another important view of the case. Go into any of our Townships which have been blessed with a good School for thirty, or forty, years, and you will find the aggregate of intelligence to be far greater than in those Townships which have enjoyed less educational facilities. Is the intelligence of its inhabitants nothing to a Township? Is not the expenditure which shall secure this a good investment? True, we cannot estimate it in money, yet it is an investment that will make its return in kind. It is an invariable rule that the percentage of increase of valuation of property in any community is in the direct ratio of the increase of intelligence and virtue. Every citizen of extraordinary intelligence, or extraordinary virtue, enhances the value of all property of the Township in which he lives. By just so much as you add to the virtue and intelligence of the inhabitants of the Township do you add to the value of its acres. It is thus that it is true that "every man's sin is every other man's business." It is just as true that every man's ignorance is every other man's business.

Evils of Want of Classification.—The Honourable Henry Barnard thus sets forth the evils that result from the lack of proper classification of Schools:—

From the number of class and individual recitations, to be attended to during each half-day, these exercises are brief, hurried, and of little practical value. They consist, for the most part, of senseless repetitions of the words of a book. Instead of being the time and place where the real business of teaching is done, where the ploughshare of interrogation is driven down into the acquirements of each Pupil, and his ability to comprehend clearly is cultivated and tested; where the difficult principles of each lesson are developed and illustrated, and additional information imparted, and the mind of the Teacher brought in direct contact with the mind of each Pupil, to arouse, interest, and direct its opening powers; instead of all this and more, the brief period passed in recitation consists, on the part of each Teacher, of hearing each individual and Class, in regular order and quick succession, repeat words from a book, and on the part of the Pupils, of saying their lessons, as the operation is most significantly described by most Teachers, when they summon the Class to the stand. In the meantime, the order of the School must be maintained, and the general business must go forward. Little children, without any authorized employment for their eyes and hands, and ever active curiosity, must be made to sit still, while every muscle is aching from suppressed activity; problems must be solved, excuses for tardiness, or absence, received, questions answered, whisperings allowed, or suppressed, and more, or less, of extempore discipline administered. Were it not a most ruinous waste of precious time,—did it not involve the deadening, crushing, distorting, dwarfing of immortal faculties and noble sensibilities, —were it not an utter perversion of the noble objects for which Schools are instituted,— it would be difficult to conceive of a more diverting farce than an ordinary session of

a large Public School, whose chaotic and discordant elements have not been reduced
to system by proper classification. The Teacher,—at least the conscientious Teacher,—
thinks it anything but a farce to him. Compelled to hurry from one Study to another,
requiring a knowledge of methods altogether distinct; from one recitation to another
equally brief and unsatisfactory, one requiring a liveliness of manner that he does not
feel, and cannot assume, and the other closeness of attention and abstraction of thought,
which he cannot give amid the multiplicity and variety of cares; from one case of
discipline to another pressing on him at the same time,—he goes through the same
circuit, day after day, with a dizzy brain and aching heart, and brings his School to
a close with a feeling that, with all his diligence and fidelity, he has accomplished but
little good.

Amendment to our own School Law relating to Township Boards of Trustees.

One or two difficulties have been experienced in giving effect to our own School
Law on the subject.* These difficulties, and a mode of overcoming them, have been
pointed out by one of our Inspectors, (Mr. D. J. McKinnon, of Peel), as follows:—

I have expressed my belief that under the Township System, Schools might be so
placed that every child in the Townships of Toronto and Chinguacousy would be within
two miles of some School. This might be done by planting Schools ten lots apart one
way, and four Concessions the other, with one in the centre of each, (almost), square,
thus giving two Concessions, (1¾ miles), as the maximum distance to be travelled by any
child.

But here a difficulty meets us at the outset in the shape of several really good
School Houses already,—many of them lately,—built, and which it would be most
unreasonable to close merely because a little out of place. I have found, however, that
by slightly modifying the original scheme these Schools may be all brought in by
leaving only one corner of either Township, (seven lots), more than two miles distant
from some School,—children from the same corner having now to go more than four
miles.. . . . .

We have at present forty-six Sections in Toronto and Chinguacousy, of which nine
are Unions, and supposing the burden of five of these to fall upon these two Townships,
there are still forty-one left. Besides, there was presented to the County Council at
its last Session a petition from certain Farmers in Chinguacousy, showing that some
of their children had from four or five miles to walk to School, and praying for a new
Section. Should the wish of these Ratepayers be granted, there would be forty-two
Schools to support under the present system instead of thirty-seven under the Township
plan. Should Ratepayers in each of the five Sections in Chinguacousy, whose outskirts
lie three miles or more from their respective School Houses take the same course, it
would, by multiplying the number of Schools, very materially increase taxation in that
Township. . . . .

But even reckoning the number of Schools to be kept up under the present system
as only forty-two, there would still be five more than under the Township plan; and
counting the cost of maintaining each School in the future as $500 per annum, the
amount saved on the five Schools would be $2,500, or $60 apiece to each of the thirty-
seven Schools, and $280 over for "contingencies." That is to say, it would cost the
people exactly the same to have a $360 Teacher under the Township System as a $300
man at present; or rating Teachers according to Salaries, the efficiency of the Schools
would be increased by twenty per cent.

But here I anticipate an objection. If the number of the Schools were reduced to
thirty-seven, would not the increased attendance at each make the work too great for
thirty-seven Teachers to overtake? I answer decidedly, no, for the aggregate attendance
of the Townships for the first half year of 1871, was only about 1,400, or less than
thirty-eight apiece for thirty-seven Teachers, while for the second half it was some fifty
less, so that even if the attendance should increase by one-fourth, on account of the
greater facilities afforded to children who are now at too great a distance, it would
still fall below the fifty allowed to each Teacher by Law.

Another great advantage of the Township System would be the equalization of
Taxation. I shall at this time merely say, that the present System is most unjust,
some Sections in the County having double the amount of rateable property that others
have, and consequently requiring to pay each man less than half the Taxes for the same
class of School.

But what about the new and good Houses already built? Will those who have paid
some $40 apiece for School Houses in their own Sections be required to turn round

---

*The same difficulties, in giving effect to the law, are, no doubt, experienced by other Inspectors, so that the
example and illustrations here given, may be taken as a fair specimen of similar difficulties in other parts of the
Province.

16a XXIII.

and pay their (say) $20 additional for similar Buildings in other parts of the Township? This would assuredly be most unfair as men in Sections that have been enterprising enough to put up expensive Houses would have paid some $60 for Schools belonging to the whole Township, while their more canny neighbours, whose present Schools were built some thirty years ago, would get off with $20! But fortunately the remedy is simple. If A and B, two Merchants in the dry goods trade, having stocks valued at $7,000 and $3,000 respectively, agree to go into partnership on even terms, with a capital of $20,000, on the understanding that their present stocks shall be the property of the firm, it would be absurd for B to say,—"We have now $10,000 between us, and the $10,000 more required will be just $5,000 apiece, because, you know, we're equal partners." "No," A would say, "I've $7,000 in now, and you've $3,000, so I shall put in $3,000 and you $7,000, and then we'll be on even footing." And so it may be arranged with existing School property. Let the Township Board, if formed, buy up all the School property of the various Sections at a valuation, so that the value of such property shall be deducted from the building Taxes of those who have paid for it, and thus evenhanded justice done.

But what of the fairly good School Houses,—those not quite coming up to the requirements of the Law, but yet too good to throw away entirely? Make them into Teachers' Residences. A partition, or two, run through, and a kitchen attached, will convert the most of them into very comfortable little Houses, and this would be by no means a useless investment, for fully one-third of the Teachers at present engaged are married men; and I have known of several instances during the past year where a good School has been refused by a good Teacher simply because he could not get a House.

Of course, even if Township Boards were at once established we couldn't expect to see all these changes at once. New Schools would have to be built no sooner than they will if no such change take place, but when built they would be in the most convenient places, and every child could at once be allowed to go to the School nearest him. After all, it would perhaps be hardly worth while to make such a change for the sake of saving a couple of dollars a year to each Farmer, but for the sake of the little ones who now must wait to be ten or twelve years of age before they can walk their three miles or so to School in winter, it is worth while to go to some trouble.

In a Memorandum addressed to the Government last year on some amendments to the School Law, the following Suggestions were made:—

The 14th Section of the School Act of 1871 might be amended so as to provide that School Sections which have erected good School Houses of a certain valuation to be determined, should be exempted from Taxation for new Houses in other parts of the Townships where this had not been done. It might be well to consider whether it would not be better further to amend the Law, so as to authorize two, or three, of the existing School Sections, (according to the size of the Township), to unite and elect one Member to the Township Board, to retain the existing boundaries, (subject to alteration by the Board), for Taxation purposes, but to abolish them so far as they now restrict the right of each Ratepayer to send his child to the School of the Section in which he pays School Rates.

Disadvantages of a School Section, and the Advantages of a Township Board, System.

The following enumeration of some of the prominent obstacles which are in the way of the greater efficiency of our Schools under the School Section System is worthy of attentive studying. They are a summary of what has been stated at length in the preceding pages:—

The evils are:—

1. Total lack of efficient supervision.
2. Constant change in the Schools as supervised.
3. Many badly qualified Teachers.
4. Constant change of Teachers.
5. Lack of interest in Schools on the part of Teachers and Trustees.
6. Employment of relatives, often without any regard to proper qualifications.
7. Too small Schools in many Sections.
8. Too short School time in small Sections.
9. Employment of immature and incompetent Teachers in small Sections.
10. Miserable School Houses in many Sections.
11. Irregular attendance of Pupils.
12. General lack of facilities to aid the Teachers.

13. No Schools in many Sections.

14. Lack of proper qualifications, such as would be required in a uniform Township School System.

15. Total disregard to the Programme, Pupils often studying what they choose and not what they ought.

These twice seven and one evils of our Public School System will be recognized by every one who has had any experience in connection with our Public Schools.

2. *The Advantages of a Township System.*

The following are given as some of the desirable results to be realized by abandoning the Section System, and placing the Schools under the care of a Township Board:—

1. It would secure just as many Schools as the necessities of the community demand, each being an integral part of one central organization, and adapted to the wants of individuals.

2. It would dispense with a large number of School Trustees, Collectors, etcetera.

3. It would establish a uniform rate of Taxation over the entire Township.

4. It would furnish more uniform and equal advantages and privileges to every resident.

5. It would allow the child to attend School where his own interests would be best conserved, with no restraint save what the general interest might require.

6. It would prevent endless difficulties and strife about School Section boundaries.

7. It would diminish the aggregate expenditure for Schools.

8. It would secure a more efficient System of School Inspection and Classification.

9. It would secure a permanency of the advantages of supervision.

10. It would secure greater permanency of Teachers.

11. It would secure a better class of Teachers.

12. It would secure better compensation to competent Teachers, and less employment for incompetent ones.

13. It will secure better School Houses.

14. It will secure greater facilities to Teachers for reference and illustration.

15. It will enable Townships to establish graded Schools.

16. It will secure uniformity of Text Books in the Township.

17. It will result in more uniform methods of teaching.

18. It will secure the establishment of a Course of Study, and will tend to keep Pupils longer in School.

19. It will secure to the Education Department more reliable statistics.

20. It will insure Schools in every Section of the Township, and prevent a bare majority from depriving a respectable minority of School privileges.

21 It will tend to diminish neighbourhood boundary quarrels.

22. It would insure the employment of fewer Nephews and Nieces, Sisters and Sisters-in-law.

23. It would insure a larger aggregate of interest on the part of the community in each School.

24. It would render possible Competitive Examinations.

There is no gainsaying the force of the argument presented by the above points, all of which are susceptible of the clearest proof and demonstration. Nothing but apathy and prejudice can prevent a reasonable person from seeing that they are conclusive in favour of a change. Are Persons who cling to the School Section System aware of the following fact? That of those Townships in Massachusetts and other States, which have abandoned the District System, it is very rare that one, after a fair trial, has any inclination to return to that System. The advantages of the Township System are too apparent and too important to be lost when they have once been attained and enjoyed.

V.—ADDITIONAL NORMAL SCHOOLS FOR THE PROVINCE.

1. It is gratifying to observe that one of the most important results of the operation of the School Law of 1871 has been the almost simultaneous demand all over the Province for additional Normal Schools. I have already referred, in another part of the Report, to the gratifying success of our present Normal School, and will now devote a short space to the illustration of the value of training, and will then refer to what is doing elsewhere in this direction.

Impulse Given by a Uniform Standard of Excellence in Examination.

2. The impulse which the recent Examinations of Public School Teachers throughout the Province has given to the profession, can scarcely be over-estimated. When brought to the test of a uniform standard of excellence, many Teachers throughout the Province felt that they were much below that standard, and a desire sprang up among them that they should avail themselves of the advantages of Normal School Training without delay. Hence the desire for the establishment of additional Normal Schools at various places in the Province. I had suggested to the late Attorney-General Macdonald, that he should take steps for the establishment of these Schools. He concurred in the suggestion, and the intentions of the Government on the subject were intimated in the Speech from the Throne, in December of last year. Various circumstances prevented the carrying out of the suggestion during that year, but I am glad to know that steps will now be taken to give it effect, and to establish two, if not three new Normal Schools, at as many different parts of the Province.

The Value of Normal School Training in Ontario.

3. We have in our own Province abundantly demonstrated the value to the Normal Schools, and to the profession of teaching, of the Toronto Normal School, established in 1847, and so successfully conducted for the last twenty-five years.

There are many among us who remember not only the inferior character of the teaching practised in most of our Schools twenty-five years ago, (although there were many excellent individual Schools), but also the characterless class of very many of the Teachers who were freely employed all over the Province. Men who had failed in other pursuits, men who had no adaptation to the work,—men whose drinking habits were a reproach to the neighbourhood, and men who had scarcely mastered even the merest rudiments of Education, were in numberless Schools set over the youth of the Country, and were without question entrusted with the responsible, and almost sacred duty of training the future men and women of the land. There were in many cases noble exceptions, in which men of sterling character, and unexceptional attainments, were employed; and these Teachers and their labours are remembered with gratitude in many neighbourhoods to this day. From the ranks of these Teachers, and of the intelligent youth in the various Counties, our Normal School was first filled. The effect of the training of the early Normal School Students, under the lamented Mr. T. J. Robertson, the first Head Master, was soon felt. Not only was the character of the teaching in the Schools, where these Students were employed, at once elevated, but soon the felt influence of their improved methods of teaching was extended to other Schools. The demand for the better trained Normal School Students, caused the Salaries of the Teachers generally to be gradually raised; and happily although too slowly, the Salaries of Members of this important profession have since continued to advance.

Necessity and Importance of Normal School Training.

4. I shall now illustrate the necessity and importance of Normal School Training, from two or three sources. The Superintendent of Public Instruction in the State of Minnesota, very properly remarks:—

Something besides technical knowledge is necessary to enable an individual to perform successfully the responsible and difficult work of teaching, and this something must be secured, either by unaided efforts in the practice of teaching, or by preparatory training in a School established for the purpose.

It is not denied that experience will make excellent Teachers; but while it is being gained, who can estimate the damage inflicted upon the children? While it is admitted that many persons make in time excellent Teachers,—industrious, conscientious, ambitious, and skilful, this success is attained at great cost to the people, who pay the expense of the Schools and the children who attend them. The Pupils under such Teachers answer to the raw material practised upon by the unskilled hand of an awkward Apprentice. It should be self-evident that the profession of the Teacher does not stand alone, requiring no preliminary induction into the mysteries of the art.

Necessity of Training for the Profession of Teaching.

5. The Honourable J. P. Wickersham, State Superintendent of Schools, in Pennsylvania, speaking of the great necessity for a supply of properly trained Teachers, uses the following language:—

Few will, at this day, seriously question the truth of the assertion, that Teachers need preparation for their work. They must either learn to teach by experimenting upon their Pupils, or by undergoing a preparatory course of instruction.

Mr. Niles, another writer, in speaking of the necessity of proper training for the profession of teaching, thus forcibly refers to the infliction caused by unskilled Teachers in the Schools:—

To those who know that the lowest grade of Certificate is given to persons of "no particular qualifications," and to such as lack experience in teaching, comment is unnecessary. As the guardians of the Public Schools, can we do less than suggest the means by which the thousand yearly beginners in the work of teaching shall receive some profesional training? As a knowledge of the Art of teaching is essential to success, and as it is the policy of the State to educate her Teachers, we must make such use of existing agencies, and others which may be created, as will render it possible to place, in the near future, a Teacher, qualified in the branches to be taught, and in methods of imparting instruction, in every School.

We should constantly impress upon the mind of every Student who expects to teach, that no Pupil from the Public School, Graded School, College, or University, is fitted to begin teaching in the primary department of the Village School, or even in the poorest Log School House in the backwoods, until he had added to all other natural and acquired qualifications, a knowledge of the great art of teaching.

When we, as the exponents of all that is advanced in Education, we, who are brought in daily contact with inefficiency in the School Rooms; who see the people's money wasted by the unskilful; who see thousands of young children submitted to processes which make our souls sad, come to regard this knowledge as indispensable, there will be more applicants for seats in Normal Schools.

Time Lost in the Normal Schools from want of Literary Qualification on the Part of Students.

6. Owing to the very limited scholarship of those who have applied for admission, the Normal Schools have been obliged to begin their work of Education far down, to consume much time in giving Students a knowledge of the elements of English Grammar, Geography and Arithmetic. It has been found necessary to drill almost every Student in the branches, which the Law requires to be taught, before he could take instruction in methods. So long as the grade of scholarship is so low as to make this course unavoidable, a large number of trained Teachers cannot be expected.

The True Province of the Normal School.

7. The Superintendent of Education of Iowa correctly observes:—

It is the office of Normal training to develop, strengthen, and stimulate whatever latent talent the individual may have in various directions, and not to impart to him faculties which he does not possess.

It is pre-eminently the province of the Normal School to drill in method, and enforce the underlying principles, which commend recent and improved methods to the acceptance of its Pupils. Indeed, as a plan for professional training, the instruction should be exclusively special, at least, as nearly so as circumstances will allow.   The general Education should have been secured by the Applicant before he subjects himself to a Course of Normal School Instruction.   He comes to make search, under the direction of competent Trainers and Instructors, into the experience of the past, and puts himself down to a regimen of practice and criticism in Model Schools and elsewhere, upon such methods of instruction and School Government as shall best meet the wants, capabilities, and unfolding stages of the human mind.

Number of Normal Schools Elsewhere.

8. There are in England and Scotland thirty-eight Normal, or Training, Schools, (almost entirely denominational), and one in Ireland.   These Schools were in 1870-71 attended by upwards of 3,000 Students.   Admission to them was by competitive Examination, open only to those who intend to adopt or follow the profession of teaching, and who have either served the apprenticeship of "Pupil Teachers," or are over eighteen years of age.*

The expenditure for these Schools in 1870-71 was about $560,000.   The original cost of the Buildings for them was $1,540,050.

In the German Empire there are abount 100 Public and 40 Private Training Schools for Teachers.

In Norway and Sweden there are fifteen Normal Schools; in Switzerland four; in Portugal two; and several for females are projected under the new School Law of Turkey.

In the United States there are eighty-seven Normal Schools, and twenty-seven Normal or Training Departments in Colleges, or Universities.   The annual State appropriations for each of these Schools varies from $2,000 to $20,000.   The number of Normal Schools and Normal Departments of the Colleges in the various States are as follows: —

State.	No.	When Established.	State.	No.	When Established.
Illinois.............	10	1857—1869	Virginia...........	2	1867—1868
New York..........	11	1844—1867	California.........	2	1862—1869
Ohio...............	9	1852—1865	Florida............	2	....
Massachusetts.......	7	1839—1872	Maine............	2	1863—1867
Missouri	6	1857—1869	New Jersey..:.....	2	
Pennsylvania.......	8	1848—1869	Maryland	2	1865
Wisconsin..........	5	1862—1867	Mississippi........	2	....
Iowa..............	4	1863—1866	Louisiana.........	2	1858—1869
West Virginia.......	5	1868—1870	North Carolina.....	2	1868
Tennessee	4	1866	Oregon............	2	....
Indiana	3	1867	Other States and Territory	13	1854—1870
Minnesota..........	3	....			
Vermont...........	.3	1867—1868			
Kentucky	3	....		114	

Normal Schools in Pennsylvania.

9. In the Report of the State Superintendent for 1871, he says:—

The State is divided into twelve Normal School Districts.   To nine of these the State has appropriated $15,000 and upwards each, towards the erection of Buildings for Normal School purposes.   The balance of the money for their erection either has been, or must be, raised by local contributions.   The Buildings, when erected, do not belong to the State, but to the Stock-holders, or Contributors, who, however, cannot dispose of them, or use them for any other purpose, without the consent of the State Authorities. The State has appropriated considerable money to the several Schools for the purchase

---

* The experienced Agent of the State Board of Education for Massachusetts (Mr. A. T. Phipps), in speaking of the age at which Students should be admitted to the Normal Schools, remarks:—
   I am decidedly of the opinion that it would be wiser to add a year to the minimum age required for admission to the Normal Schools, at least for the women, and not admit any under seventeen years of age, than to admit them at sixteen as now required, or considerably under sixteen, as occasionally permitted. With a higher standard of scholarship for admission, and with greater maturity, physical and mental, of those admitted, I think we should secure a superior class of Teachers for graduation, and thus elevate the character of our Normal Schools.

of Apparatus. No School can be recognized as a State Normal School until it has been found by the State Authorities to conform to the requirements of Law, and when recognized, its charges, Course of Study and disciplinary Regulations must be approved by the State Superintendent. The State furnishes Diplomas for all Graduates of Normal Schools, and the State Superintendent is Chairman of the Board that conducts the Examination of the graduating Classes. The State pays each Student, who is attending a Normal School for the purpose of becoming a Teacher, fifty cents a week towards his expenses, and gives him a gratuity of fifty dollars at graduation. All apprporiations to State Normal Schools are paid by the State Superintendent.

10. The value of the Normal School Buildings and Grounds in Pennsylvania is estimated at $380,720, and the aggregate Annual Expenditure at $154,320. During the year 1872, the State appropriations in aid of Normal Schools were as follows:—

Name.	Amount.	Name.	Amount.
	$		$
Millersville	50,293	Kulztown	21,999
Mansfield	39,842	West Chester	15,557
Bloomsburg	27,388	Sheppensburg	15,000
California	25,000	Indiana	15,000
Edinboro	22,462	Lock Haven	15,000

or a grand total of $247,541.

11. *Cost of Massachusetts Normal Schools.*

Name	Cost of Land and Bldgs.	Yearly Cost	Name	Cost of Land and Bldgs.	Yearly Cost
	$	$		$	$
Framingham	121,787	10,796	Bridge Water	116,400	12,591
Westfield	102,000	13,048	Salem	116,200	11,394

or a total cost of Land and Buildings $456,387, and of yearly cost $47,829.

The State Legislature has also appropriated $60,000 towards the erection of a new Normal School at Worcester, and the City of Worcester has given Land for a Site, valued $25,000; total $85,000.

12. *Cost of the New York Normal Schools.*

Name	When Established.	Value of Site and Buildings.	Value of Furniture.	Value of Library and Apparatus.	Total Value.	Received from Treasurer.	Yearly Expenditure.
		$	$	$	$	$	$
Albany	1844	75,000	3,000	6,000	84,000	4,823	22,490
Blockfort	1866	115,380	5,800	9,900	131,080	3,902	28,204
Buffalo	1867	125,000	7,500	4,500	13,700		
Cortland	1866	89,500	6,500	5,134	101,134	431	17,927
Freedonia	1866	97,000	4,200	6,430	107,630	1,117	18,857
Genesee	1867	82,000	3,000	5,350	90,350		
Oswego	1863	70,000	5,500	9,000	84,500		17,718
Potsdam	1866	84,000	3,998	5,229	94,045	1,352	21,639
Plattsburg		The Town was authorized in 1869 to erect a Building for a Normal School, to be supported by the State.					
New York City	1871	350,000					

VI.—COUNTY TEACHERS' INSTITUTES AS AIDS TO TEACHERS.

Provision Made for Teachers' Institutes in Ontario in 1850.

1.—In the Upper Canada School Act passed early in the year 1850, an appropriation was made "for the encouragement of Teachers' Institutes," which was intended to assist in defraying the incidental expenses of such Institutes, such as the accommodation, Stationery, Maps, Apparatus, and sometimes special Lectures to Teachers on special subjects. This is the mode in which they have been encouraged by public aid in the neighbouring States, where they have become an institution, and almost a regular branch of the School System.

I never acted upon this provision of the Law but once, namely, in 1850. That year we dispensed with a Summer Session of the Normal School, and I got two principal Masters of the Normal School to conduct Teachers' Institutes in the several Counties of Upper Canada.

But as there has been no proper classification of Teachers, or classified Programme of Studies, such as could be carried into effect, no Local Superintendents competent to conduct such Institutes, or Teachers of sufficient and acknowledged eminence among their fellow Teachers to designate for that purpose, I had thought it would be useless and a waste of time and money to recommend them, and to aid in defraying their expense. But now there are experienced and distinguished Teachers as Inspectors, and others in each County of sufficient qualifications to assist in conducting such Institutes, and, as several informal ones have been held with good results during the past few months, I have thought the time arrived when their agency might be usefully introduced for improvement of Teachers, and especially in teaching those subjects of elementary Science now required to be taught. Under these circumstances I have recommended that the provision of the School Act of 1850 be acted upon to a limited extent during the year 1873.

Object of the Teachers' Institutes.

2. A Teachers' Institute is a meeting of Teachers assembled two, four, or ten days, or two, or four weeks, for the purpose of improvement in their profession. During each evening of such Institute, a Public Lecture is usually delivered on some subject connected with Public School Education. It is suggested that during each day, the Teachers composing the Institute be either formed into Classes, for School Exercises, under able Instructors, or to discuss the modes of teaching the various subjects of Common School Instruction, and School Organization and Discipline.

The subjects which should engage attention during these exercises ought to be, chiefly, the Methods and Principles of Teaching, Reading, Writing, Arithmetic, Orthography, Geography, (with Mapping), Natural and General History, Grammar, and, in some instances, perhaps, higher subjects; also School Government and Discipline. Some of these subjects may occupy much less time and attention than others, according to their relative importance; and as circumstances suggest, collateral subjects may on some special occasions, be introduced; but I propose that the proceedings of such Institutes will be governed by Regulations to be prepared.

Desire and Necessity for Teachers' Institutes in Ontario.

3. Within the last year or two, a great desire has been felt among Teachers in this Province for the establishment of County Teachers' Institutes. This feeling has arisen chiefly from two causes:—1st. The institution of a more extensive, simultaneous and thorough System of Examination in the several Counties has demonstrated to Teachers the necessity of making additional efforts to qualify themselves for passing that Examination; and 2nd. The desire of many Teachers, who have been for many years in the profession, to avail themselves of the advantages of such a valuable and suggestive

help as that of an Institute, rather than attend and submit to the routine of a Normal School, with their younger brethren. As a substitute for a Teachers' Institute, the County Teachers' Associations have, as a general rule, held Meetings, or Conventions throughout the Country, to discuss subjects of study and matters pertaining to their profession. At some of these gatherings Resolutions have been passed, urging the necessity of establishing Teachers' Institutes. In the County of Huron, the following Resolution was passed:—

That, under the present System of Examination, it is essentially necessary to have some connecting link between our Schools and Examining Boards, to provide professional training for such Teachers as do not feel disposed to attend the Normal School. Believing, therefore, that Teachers' Institutes, properly conducted, would remedy the existing state of things, and tend to systematize the whole work of Public Schools throughout the Province, we would strongly recommend the formation of County Institutes, to be held immediately before the Summer Examinations, attendance at such Meetings to be noticed on awarding Certificates. We would recommend that the Chief Superintendent be respectfully requested to take steps to bring the matter under the notice of the Government, so that Institutes may be established as soon as possible.

The County of Durham Teachers' Association also unanimously passed the following Resolution:—

Being fully impressed with the importance of having trained Teachers, we would most respectfully and earnestly impress upon Government the necessity of establishing County Institutes for the training of Teachers.

Provision for Holding Teachers' Institutes in the United States.

A recent number of the *Michigan Teacher* thus explains the provisions for holding Teachers' Institutes in various American States:—

Wisconsin compels the County Superintendents to "organize and conduct at least one Institute for the instruction of Teachers in each year," and authorizes the Board of Regents of Normal Schools to use any sum within $5,000 per annum for Institute expenses. In the expenditure of this allowance, they must give preference to the sections of the State receiving least direct benefit from the Normal Schools. School Boards are authorized to allow Teachers their Salaries for time spent in actual attendance upon Institutes. In Maine, whenever twenty-five Teachers in any County make a written request to that effect, the State Superintendent may hold an Annual Institute in that County, of at least ten days' duration, and may expend $4,000 per year upon such Institutes. California appropriates $100 for each County Institute of three to five days' length, which the Local Superintendent must hold annually in Counties having ten, or more, School Districts. Every Teacher of a Public School must attend, and the School Board "shall not only allow, but shall require the Teachers in their employ to attend every Teachers' Institute held in the County," and their pay is not diminished for such attendance. Any County having a regularly organized Teachers' Association, or Institute, holding Meetings monthly, may be exempted, if a majority of the Teachers in the County vote to sustain monthly Meetings. Pennsylvania appropriates $60 to $200, (according to attendance), for every five days' Institute. Each County Superintendent must hold one yearly. The Teachers may be allowed their time; and "any Teacher who absents himself from the Institute of his County without a good reason, may have his want of professional spirit and zeal indicated by a lower mark on his Certificate, in the practice of teaching, than he would otherwise have received." Two Saturdays in every School month may be used for Institutes in any District, and reported as a part of the School month. Iowa gives subsidy, not exceeding $50, for each Institute of not less than twenty Members and six working days. Any School in the County must be closed while the Institute is in Session, and the Teachers' pay goes on during the time. They, as well as all Candidates for Certificates, are required to attend, or present satisfactory reasons for non-attendance, before receiving License to teach. Similar provisions subsist in Kansas. Indiana allows $50 for an Institute having an average attendance of forty, and $35 for one with an average of twenty-five. The Public Schools must be closed during the Session, but the Teachers are not compelled to attend, nor is their time allowed even although they do attend. A good foundation for an Institute fund is provided in Ohio, where Teachers pay a Fee of fifty cents for Examination, which is set apart for their benefit, in meeting the expenses of County Institutes. The plan contemplates a permanent organization with at least forty Members. In most of these States, and in New York, the County School Officers are required to hold Institutes once a year. In the State last named, the Commissioner must "induce, if possible, all the Teachers in his District to be present and take part in the

Exercises." A Teacher who closes his School to attend an Institute, does not thereby forfeit his contract, and has his time allowed. The necessary expenses are paid by the State. In Vermont, only two days' time is allowed Teachers for attendance upon Institutes, without diminution of wages. Louisiana has a curious provision that Institutes shall be held "where the Teachers will receive the encouragement of hospitality." Illinois makes very indifferent provision for Institutes, but, by a recent Law, provides for the organization of County Normal Schools.

Great Value of Teachers' Institutes in Awakening Interest.

The following testimony as to the great influence of Teachers' Institutes on the Teachers' profession, and in promoting educational zeal, is of interest and value. The Superintendent of one of the neighbouring States says:—

If any one doubts·the utility of County Teachers' Institutes, such an acquaintance with their practical workings and results, as I have enjoyed during the last four years would effectually remove such doubts. In some Counties the first real impulse to the cause of Education dates from the first Institutes held in them. They have done incalculable good. Not only has the enthusiasm of Teachers for their profession been kindled by them, their ideas enlarged, and their knowledge of methods increased, but the interests of Parents and the public generally awakened in behalf of the cause of popular Education. "They have saved many an inexperienced Teacher from despondency and failure. They have placed in many hands the key of success for lack of which they had groped in darkness. They have sent many weary hearts back to their School Rooms, full of the inspirations of hope. They have imparted to each one the collected wisdom and experience of all, and thus reduplicated the teaching power of a whole Country. They have so held the mirror of true excellence, that all could see in what it consisted, and thus enable many a community to judge and act more wisely in the choice of Teachers. They have been the forums where popular errors and fallacies have been discussed and exposed, and great truths in educational philosophy have been vindicated."

The United States Commissioner of Education at Washington, in surveying the educational field in the various States, remarks:—

It is gratifying to observe how widely and uniformly the Teachers' Institutes have been employed through the Country for the improvement of Teachers, and through them of the Schools. Many of the ablest Teachers and Educators have contributed to their success. For many Teachers they are the only source of correct ideas in regard to methods of Instruction, Discipline, and School Management. They scatter the gems of the best thought upon Education, and, by the general attendance of the citizens of the places where they are held, contribute greatly to improve the public mind, and correct and elevate the educational sentiment.

Stimulating Effects of Teachers' Institutes.

The Superintendent of Iowa, thus describes the effect of Teachers' Institutes in his State:—

In some of the Counties, the Institute season has been made the occasion of enthusiastic revivals, so to speak, of energies long languishing; and we have been informed that the effect on the Teachers' profession in those localities, and on the School Officers, and on the condition of the Schools, has been electric. Such results must follow from Institutes when properly conducted. In accordance with their original intent, they are thus demonstrated to be, not only an indispensable link in that admirable System of State Supervision, which keeps the machinery of popular Education running; but also, and chiefly a stimulus to the Teacher, and through him a mighty agency for arousing and shaping all the School elements of the Country. The Framers of the Law have borne testimony to the value they place upon this part of the School work, by providing that a Teacher's attendance upon an Institute, whilst the term of his School is in progress, shall cause no reduction in his stipulated wages; and that it shall even be made binding upon him, as a condition for his securing a Certificate, that he be in attendance, unless unavoidably prevented.

During the past year, seventy-six Counties have had the benefit of $50 each, making an appropriation of $3,800 for the support of these professional gatherings.

I have met two hundred and forty Teachers in convocation in a single County. And it is a grand sight, and a privilege to be envied, to stand before an audience of such labourers in the cause of universal, free Education.

One of the most prominent and judicious State Superintendents in the United States makes the unqualified assertion:— "No other agency has done more to strengthen and vitalise our system of public Education than the meeting of Teachers, School Officers and friends of Common Schools, known as Teachers' Institutes."

Who Should Conduct Teachers' Institutes.

In Iowa, the management of Teachers' Institutes is, by Statute, put into the hands of the County Superintendent, and is, of course, the most difficult and responsible labour he has to perform. If, in other departments of his office, he can succeed well with an ordinary share of scholarship and fair administrative ability; here, he will have occasion for the exercise of the highest attainments and best qualifications of an experienced Educator. It is at this point, and in this trying situation that the ability of the County Superintendent is most effectually tested. The County Superintendent should be a well-known, practical, tried Educator, a man of experience in all departments of Public School work, conversant with the details of School Organization, in Schools that are graded and Schools that are not, with the advantage, if possible, of a thorough Normal training in his profession,—in short, he should be an approved Public School man. If he can bring to his task the implements which the higher ranges of culture will provide him, so much the better. But it is insisted, that he should at least be a man who has devoted himself *durante vita*, to the profession of teaching, and can furnish evidence that his undivided energies are given to the work.

Suggestions as to Mode of Conducting Teachers' Institutes.

The Superintendent of the State of Minnesota makes the following general remarks on the mode of conducting Institutes.

In order that a Teachers' Institute may be profitable to those in attendance, the Teaching Exercises should be by the best and most experienced Teachers that can be procured. The character of the teaching must be confined principally to instruction in Methods and matters strictly professional; and less to the instruction in the branches of Study required to be taught in School.

The plan of conducting the State Teachers' Institutes has been as follows:—

Teachers were required to assemble punctually at nine o'clock on Monday morning, and to be present at all the Exercises, day and evening. The daily instructions were confined to Methods of Teaching the common branches required by Law; special attention being devoted to the oral elements of our Language, Phonetic Spelling, etcetera.

Questions were submitted to the Class during each Exercise, for the purpose of fixing more firmly the principles enunciated. At the close of each day some time was spent in answering questions from the "Question Box." The evenings were devoted to the discussion of School matters by Teachers and others, or to Lectures, as might be previously arranged.

One evening during the Session the State Superintendent gave a practical Lecture upon School Discipline, how to secure good Order, the relation of the Teacher to his Pupils, to their Parents, to the School Officers, the method of securing Punctuality, System in Study, the importance of daily Moral Instruction, and other kindred subjects.

Written Examinations at the Close of the Institute.

The following valuable practical suggestions occur in the last Report of the State Superintendent of Maine:—That of holding Written Examinations for Certificates at the close of the Examination. That plan might be adopted with profit at the close of the Institutes in midsummer. The Superintendent states that in Maine "more than forty County Institutes have been held the past year, with an attendance of nearly four thousand Teachers. These Institutes have been conducted entirely by our County Supervisors.

The Written Examination on the closing day of the Institute has constituted one of the chief features in the Institute work of the past two years. In my humble estimation there can be no doubt about the value of this last day's work, and the accompanying issue of graded Certificates. It serves as a point to reach, a mark to aim at during the preceding days; it stimulates the industrious to increased activity, and drives away the drones; in indicates the weak point in the Teachers' attainments, and intimates the direction for future efforts; especially does such an Examination bring to the surface and to notice the truly meritorious and persistent Teacher,—persistent in a laudable determination and ambition to master his profession. More than fifteen hundred graded Certificates have been thus issued the past year. School Agents and superintending School Committees are now beginning to ask Teachers to exhibit their record at the Institute Examination. This is right, and corresponds to the New York plan of employing as Teachers only those who have attended the Institute.

The amount appropriated for Institutes by the last Legislature was $8,000.

Facilities for Attending Teachers' Institutes.

Another good suggestion is made in the Report of the State of Massachusetts for 1871, as follows:—

In several of the States,—New York, for instance,—where Institutes are annually held in each County, the Common School Teachers are required by Law to attend them, as one of the conditions of receiving a Certificate of Qualification to teach.

I therefore recommend that the Legislature be requested to pass an Act which shall give the School Board of any Township authority to allow the Teachers in their employ to close their Schools and attend upon any Institute held in Term time, and in their Returns to the State Board to make no deductions for the time thus employed.

VII.—SUPERANNUATION OF WORN-OUT TEACHERS.

Having in my last Report entered fully into the question of the "Duty of Teachers to provide for the support of those worn out in the profession," I need only in this Report refer to one or two points. . . . .*

(NOTE. The Chief Superintendent here quotes the remarks on this subject which he made in his Report of last year, but I do not repeat them here.)

Objection by a Certain Class of Teachers in 1871 to Contribute to the Fund.

Notwithstanding the great boon conferred upon Teachers by the establishment of such a Fund for their benefit, a certain class of objectors has sought to create hostility to the Fund, and to the mode of contributing to it. In order to ascertain the number and classes of Teachers who have taken part in the agitation for and against the Fund, I addressed a note to the Inspectors on the subject. In regard to the classes of Teachers opposed to, or in favour of, the Section of the Act of 1871, the Inspectors almost invariably reported the former to be "those who do not intend to continue long in the profession of School teaching." "Young men who intend to teach only until they can secure money sufficient to carry them through College, or into something else,"—"persons who intend to make teaching a stepping-stone to something else." "Those who look more at the Money than to the principle involved." "Those who have received incorrect, or partial, information on the subject,"—those "who are opposed to compulsion in every form," and those "who oppose the scheme on various grounds."† The great mass of the Teachers are, however, either passive in the matter, or, having been for some time in the profession, are strongly in favour of it, and hope some day to derive advantage from it.

Reasonable Objections Met,—Proposed Modifications.

As to the grounds of objection to the distribution of the Fund, (as now authorised by the School Act of 1871), which have been urged by very many earnest and faithful Teachers, I entirely sympathize, and would gladly see the Law modified so as to meet their reasonable wishes. These Teachers object to the present scheme, chiefly on the following grounds:—1st. That Teachers must be "worn out" before they can receive any aid from the Fund. As one Inspector remarks, "many of the best and most devoted Teachers look forward to a time when the work and worry of the School Room will be over, and they hope that their withdrawal from the profession may take place, at all events, a few years before they are incapacitated by infirmity, and unable to teach a School any longer. Like the Merchant, the Mariner, and others, they hope for retirement while health and the capacity for enjoying retirement remain. Many of them would rather die in harness than confess themselves incapable or doing a day's work. The feeling is not unknown to many of the best men in other professions when they begin

---

* The present Bishop of Manchester, in his Report on the Schools of Ontario, after giving the facts, thus speaks of the fund as follows: " The whole plan does credit both to the wisdom and the liberality of its framers."

† We have shown, in this Report, the pernicious influence of such Teachers upon the Schools. They lower the tone and *esprit* of the profession, are a fruitful cause of change in Teachers, give a temporary and fugitive character to teaching, and thus bring discredit both upon the profession and the Schools.

to grow old. 2nd. The second reasonable ground for objection is the uncertainty of the amount of the pension payable for each year's service. For some years, the state of the Fund has been such that I have only been able to apportion from one to two dollars for each year's service; last year the amount was only Two 33/100 dollars a year; but this year, (out of the $12,500 which I took the liberty to recommend being placed in the Estimates for this Service), I shall be able to apportion at the rate of about Four dollars for each year's service. If the Teachers, who become Superannuated, could rely upon the maximum fixed by Law many years ago, (videlicet, Six dollars for each year's service), I think they would be satisfied. It is the continual fluctuation in the amount payable to them which has reasonably caused much discontent. In regard to the first ground of complaint which has been urged, I would recommend a fixed age to be determined at which every Teacher who has subscribed to the Fund should have a right to retire and receive a Pension. A sliding scale of allowance might also be fixed, definite in amount, and not liable, under any circumstances, to fluctuation. The basis to be adopted might be that fixed in the Superannuation Act of the Civil Service, as used by the Parliament of the Dominion. In regard to the objection against compulsory payment to the Fund, I need only remark that it is a principle invariably incorporated into every pension scheme which has been adopted either in the Civil Service in various Countries, or among different Religious Bodies everywhere.

Compulsory Payments to such a Fund Universal.

3. In a recent Report on Popular Education in Victoria, Australia, the principle of compulsory payment to the Superannuation Fund is discussed as follows:—

In the Civil Service of India, retiring Pensions are raised partly by compulsory subscriptions to a Superannuation Fund. Among the parochial Teachers of Scotland. also, a Fund, similarly raised, exists for granting Pensions to.Teachers, and Annuities to their Widows. The Teachers of Baden, (and probably of other German States,) enjoy. I learn, the benefits of an exactly similar plan; and, for the like good object, a Fund is in the same way created among the Clergymen of the Presbyterian and other Churches. Upon this principle, it would be easy to establish, without extra cost to the State, a Teachers' Superannuation Fund, to be raised by compulsory deductions made by the Board of Education from Salaries and results only. As this subject is a very important one, I may be excused for going into details, and will, therefore, jot down my ideas as to the basis on which it should be developed.

The Superannuation Fund should be created by compulsory contributions from all Teachers, Assistant Teachers, Pupil Teachers, and Work Mistresses, directly recognized by the Board of Education. The contributions should consist in a deduction of —— per cent., made by the Board of Education, half-yearly, monthly, or otherwise, from the Salaries and "result" payments to every School in receipt of aid. The rate of Pension, varying according to sex and classification, should be so much for every year of service up to a given maximum. Pensions for Teachers' Widows should be awarded on the same principle. I deem it indispensable that a Fund should be raised by compulsory contributions, and that it should be managed by the Board of Education, who alone have the necessary machinery to make its collection and distribution an easy matter. My own belief, fortified by the opinion of the leading Teachers in my District. is that the distribution of a Superannuation Fund would be comfort to the declining years of aged Teachers, worn out by good service; and it would also offer an inducement to present Teachers to continue in their occupation, and devote the best years of their life to teaching; and, further, it might attract into the Teachers' ranks many more men of the best and and most desirable type.

Provision for Superannuation of Teachers in Other Countries.

Provision has, since 1851, been made in Great Britain and Ireland for the retirement and superannuation of Teachers. In June of this year, however, a Select Committee was appointed by the House of Commons:—"To enquire whether, by a deduction from the Parliamentary Grant in aid of Public Elementary Schools, or by any other means, a provision can be made for granting Annuities to the Certificated Teachers of such Schools upon their retirement, by reason of age and infirmity." Several schemes were laid before the Committee, but no conclusions were arrived at. It is proposed to re-appoint the Committee and fully consider them next Session. The first scheme proposed was that every male Teacher employed for not less than thirty years, and attaining the age of fifty-five years, shall be entitled to a Pension of twenty shillings for each year of service. It also proposed that every female Teacher employed for not less than twenty-five years, shall, on attaining the age of fifty, be entitled to a Pension of 13s. 4d. for each year of service. The Education Department to deduct from the Parliamentary Grant for 1872 one per cent., for 1873 two per cent., for 1874 three per cent., for 1875 four per cent., and for each subsequent year five per cent. for this service.

A second scheme proposed that (1) the Pension Fund should be established by a percentage deduction from the Salaries of all Certificated Teachers; (2) that the Pension should depend upon the length of service and the amount contributed by the Teacher; (3) that a service of forty years should entitle a Teacher to the maximum Pension, (amount not stated); (4) that Teachers permanently disabled should receive an annuity after ten years' service, (or a Gratuity for a less period of service); and (5) that a Teacher should be entitled to a Pension after the age of fifty years.

A third scheme proposed as a minimum scale of Pension one-third of the average Salaries of male and female Teachers; (2) that all Certificated Teachers should pay an annual premium to ensure this minimum scale.

A fourth scheme laid down the principles, (1) that whatever was done by Government should be in the nature of a Grant-in-aid; (2) that every one qualified to be a recipient should be absolutely certain of receiving it; (3) that, within a certain time, the amount and the age at which the Pension becomes payable to be left to the choice of each Teacher; (4) that no Annuity begin before the Annuitant has reached the age of fifty years, and (5) that no Annuity to be of greater value than £1 for each year of service.

In Germany proper, Teachers' Widows receive an Annual Pension of one hundred Florins and Teachers' Orphans of twenty Florins.

In Hesse a new Pension Law has been passed which enables Superannuated Teachers to pass the close of life in comparative ease.

In Sweden and Norway examined Teachers of the Elementary School, who have reached sixty years of age, receive, on retiring, after thirty years of service, three-fourths of their Annual Income as a Pension. Pensions are also granted, in some cases, after twenty-five years of service, but with some deduction in amount.

Necessity for a Teachers' Superannuation Fund in Ontario.

5. As to the necessity for this Fund, we would say, that so long as Teachers devote their lives to a profession so generally underpaid as theirs is, so long will there be a necessity for either friends, (if there be any, but who are often poor themselves), or the Teachers themselves, to provide for the quiet and comfort of the declining years of their Brethren, who, in less prosperous days, and with scanty remuneration, led the van in that calling in which they feel proud to follow. Even now, at the Salary given to Teachers, (considering the increased cost of living), it is almost impossible to lay by a sum which would realize more than a few dollars a year. But by availing themselves of the provisions of the new School Act, Teachers can, on the payment of a small sum of Two dollars each half year, secure an allowance for life, after their retirement from the profession, of Six dollars a year for every year they may have taught School. For instance, if a Teacher has been twenty-five years in the profession, and has complied with the Law and Regulations on the subject, he will, on his retirement, be entitled to an allowance of $150 a year for life, should the Fund permit it,—although, at Four dollars a year, he will have only paid $100 in all into the Fund; if he has been twenty years teaching, he will secure an allowance of $120 a year, although his total subscriptions for the twenty years have only been $80 in all; if for fifteen years, $90, total subscriptions $60 in all; and if for ten years $60 a year, while he has only paid $40 in all into the Fund. In other words, he will receive for his first year's Pension fifty per cent. more than he has paid into the Fund altogether! These facts are irresistible, and

only show what a boon the Teachers are thoughtlessly throwing away in petitioning against their contributing to the Fund, as provided by the new School Law. For it should not be forgotten that, if the Section of the new Law on the subject is repealed, the entire Law on the subject will, no doubt, be swept away, and the $6,500 per annum now generously given to the old Teachers by the Legislature, will be withdrawn. In that case Teachers will be left to provide for their old age as they best can, or rather they will be left with no provision whatever for their retirement from the profession.

The Old Teachers Keep Down the General Scale of Remuneration.

6. There is another reason why, in the interests of the profession, the Superannuated Teachers' Fund should be sustained by them. Among the more than 5,000 Teachers in Ontario, some hundreds are getting advanced in life, and many of them are even old and infirm. Because of their age and infirmity they find it difficult to get employment, and yet, for want of means of support they cannot retire and make way for younger men. The consequence is that they offer their services at a very low rate, and thus find employment, to the exclusion of better Teachers at a higher Salary. Thus, in their need, they help to keep down the rate of remuneration, which would otherwise be paid to more active Teachers, while they keep up a competition from which the other Teachers are made to suffer. Would it not, therefore, be better for all parties concerned, that the younger Teachers should provide for the honourable retirement of a section of their own profession grown grey in the service, and enfeebled by their sedentary life? This feature of the question has been pressed upon the attention of the Department, and we present it in the following extract from the Letter of a highly respected Inspector, who has felt the embarrassment arising from the existence of old Teachers in his County. He says:—

There are a few old Teachers in this County who, perhaps, answered an important purpose in the Teacher's calling twenty-five, or thirty, years ago, but whose stereotyped methods of procedure in the School Room are opposed to every kind of modern improvement in the art of teaching. It has become a serious matter with our Board of Examiners to know what is to be done with such Teachers. They are poor, and have not yet made the necessary payments into the Superanuation Fund. He then asks if they can be placed on the Superannuation list, and desires other information on the subject, etcetera.

7. Now Teachers will see that if, (as has been the case for many years, when the matter was left to their voluntary action), they neglect to sustain the Fund in the manner provided by Law, they can neither expect to superannuate their older, worn-out Brethren nor can they, with any show of justice, or propriety, ask the Legislature even to make the generous Grant which it has done for the past few years, but which, it is well known, is quite inadequate for the maintenance of the Fund. The agitation has raised the question of the very existence of the Fund itself; and, if the younger Teachers refuse to make the small sacrifice in the interests of their profession, of paying Two dollars every half year into the Fund, (from which they themselves will derive a substantial benefit, and in the maintenance of which they are interested), how can they expect the Legislature,—which has recently so greatly raised the standard of their qualification, and incidentally of their emoluments,—to provide for their retirement from the profession and support when they are worn-out? In this view of the case, we think Teachers have not sufficiently weighed the matter in this agitation, but we trust that they will be induced to do so, when they consider the foregoing facts.*

VIII.—THE PRESENT THOROUGH AND SYSTEMATIC INSPECTION OF THE SCHOOLS.

No one can read the extracts from the general remarks of the Public School Inspectors, which are published in the Appendix to this Report, without being impressed with the fact of the competence and efficiency of the present Inspectors of the Public Schools. They have, as a whole, entered upon their work with a heartiness, an intelli-

---

* An Inspector writing on this subject says:—"It cannot be denied that the Fund itself is a most excellent one, and that it has already proved a great boon to many members of the profession."

gence, and a zeal which augurs well for the future welfare of the Schools, and which indicate a reality and thoroughness in the work of supervising the daily work in them.

It has been well said by Doctor Fraser, the present Bishop of Manchester, (who, in 1865, visited this Province, and made his Report to the English Commissioners on our Schools), that "Inspection is the salt of elementary Education." He goes on to insist upon its application to the higher Schools of England, and says:—

The publicity with which "all material facts" relating to each School "are annually made known to the State," through the machinery of the Board of Education, is considered in Massachusetts to be the secret of the immense progress that has taken place in Education in that commonwealth in the last thirty years.

As to the felt necessity for our present system of School Inspection in Ontario, we have the testimony of the Bishop. He remarks:—

Thorough inspection of Schools, such as we are accustomed to in England, is a great desideratum both in the United States and Canada, (page 8). . . . Something like our English mode of inspection of Schools, by a body of perfectly independent and competent gentlemen, would be a great and valuable addition to the School System both of the United States and Canada. . . In fact, the great desideratum of the Common School System, both in Massachusetts and generally in the States, is adequate, thorough, impartial, independent inspection of Schools. In New York and Pennsylvania, a system of supervision by Counties or wide districts has been introduced, and is at work with tolerable success; but even here, the Superintendents, (or Commissioners, as they are called in New York), appear, from their reports, to be more or less hampered by local prejudices and jealousies, and their Salary is in part provided by the District which is the sphere of their labours. They are elected, too, in Pennsylvania, by the "School Directors" of the several Townships; in New York, by the Electors of Assembly Districts, by ballot. A similar organization is strongly recommended by the Ohio State Commission. . . . The agent of the Massachusetts Board of Education, in a lecture, says:—

My observations, on visiting thousands of Schools throughout Massachusetts, and many in twelve other States, have clearly proved to my mind the wisdom of maintaining a Superintendent in all our Cities and large Townships, who shall devote his whole time to the care and improvement of the Schools. (Page 25).

In discussing the defects in the administration of Schools in the United States, Doctor Fraser says:—

The supreme control of the Schools is too absolutely in the hands of local Administrators, with no absolute guarantee of competency. The inspection, even, of County Superintendents and Commissioners is often found to be nugatory and ineffective. Legal requirements are constantly ignored, or evaded, and a properly authenticated and independent Officer, like Her Majesty's Inspector of Schools among ourselves, armed with visitorial powers, and with means provided for giving effect to his recommendations, appears to be the element wanted in the machinery of the system, to give it that balance which the complication of its parts requires. (Pages 61, 62).

Our American neighbours have thoroughly tried the system of both Township and County Superintendents. The State Commissioner of Schools in Ohio says:—

Our system of Township supervision of Schools has proved a lamentable failure. Similar Systems in other States have uniformly failed. Any system of supervision for the country Schools must necessarily fail, that does not make provision for the employment of competent Superintendents whose entire energies are given to the work.

The value of local supervision, through the agency of competent County Superintendents, has been tested in other States. Pennsylvania adopted the system in 1854, New York in 1856, Illinois, Wisconsin, Maryland, West Virginia, California, and several other States subsequently; and the testimony of each of them is, that it has proved a most valuable feature in their School Systems. The Superintendent of Public Instruction in Pennsylvania says:—

County Superintendents were first elected in this State in 1854, and it is not claiming too much for the office to say that it has vitalized the whole System. To it, more than to any other agency, or to all other agencies combined, we owe our educational progress of late years.

I may observe that more than four-fifths of the County School Conventions held in the several Counties of this Province two years since, desired duly qualified County Superintendents in place of Township Superintendents.

The Travelling Agent of the Board of Education for the State of Massachusetts uses the following forcible language in regard to this matter:—

17—XXIII.

It has been said, and with great truthfulness, that "the most important branch of administration, as connected with Education, relates to school inspection." It is asserted by some careful observers, that the Dutch School Masters are decidedly superior to the Prussian, notwithstanding the numerous Normal Schools of Prussia, and the two, or three, only in Holland; and this superiority in attributed entirely to a better system of inspection. This is the basis on which the whole fabric of their popular instruction rests. The absence of such a thorough supervision of Schools as is maintained in Holland with such admirable results, is the weakest part of our system.

What is needed for all our Schools, and what is essential to their highest efficiency, is a constant, thorough, intelligent, impartial and independent supervision. Comparatively few persons possess the varied qualifications so indispensable to success in this delicate and important work. So important was it regarded by the distinguished Author of the Dutch system of inspection, that, after a long life devoted to educational labour, he said, "Take care how you choose your Inspectors; they are men whom you ought to look for 'lantern in hand.' "

"A School," says Everett, "is not a Clock, which you can wind up, and then leave it to go of itself. Nor can other interests be thus neglected. Our Railroads and Factories require some directing, controlling, and constantly supervising mind for their highest efficiency, and do not our Schools need the same? To meet this great want, eleven of the fifteen Cities of our State, and numerous large Towns, have availed themselves of the provision of the Statute, and elected School Superintendents who devote their whole time and energies to this work of supervision. I have visited all, or nearly all, these Towns and Cities, and several of them frequently, and can bear my decided testimony to the great benefit that has resulted to their Schools in consequence."

Spirit in Which Inspection should be Performed.

The Regulations in regard to inspection, which have been adopted by the Council of Public Instruction, are sufficiently explicit as to the general details of inspection, and the mode in which it should be conducted. I will, therefore, only repeat here what I wrote on this subject in 1846 and 1850, when our present System of Education was inaugurated. I said:—

To perform the duty of Inspector with any degree of efficiency, the Inspector should be acquainted with the best modes of teaching every department of an English School, and be able to explain and exemplify them. It is, of course, the Inspector's duty to witness the modes of teaching adopted by the Teacher, but he should do something more. He should, some part of the time, be an actor as well as spectator. To do so he must keep pace with the progress of the Science of Teaching. Every man who has to do with Schools, ought to make himself master of the best modes of conducting them in all the details of arrangement, Instruction, and Discipline. A man commits a wrong against Teachers, against children, and against the interests of School Education, who seeks the office of Inspector without being qualified and able to fulfil all its functions.

Summary of the Benefits of a Thorough System of Inspection.

The State Superintendent of Maine, in his last Report, thus sums up the benefits of an efficient system of inspection for the Public Schools. "It promotes" (he says):—

1st. An increased interest among the people in relation to public Education.

2nd. Systematic efforts to improve the Schools on the part of Educators and School Officers.

3rd. An improvement in the scholarship of Teachers, and in the quality of their instruction.

4th. More intelligent supervision on the part of Trustees.

5th. A quick appreciation and promotion of those who are likely to prove our best Teachers.

6th. Increasing indirectly the average attendance of Scholars.

7th. Raising the compensation of Teachers.

8th. Furnishing the State with a number of competent Institute Instructors.

9th. Elevating and sustaining public sentiment in giving it a higher educational tone, and in general quickening the whole body politic to the mighty necessity of universal intelligence.

IX.—INSPECTION OF HIGH SCHOOLS AND COLLEGIATE INSTITUTES.

The Inspectors, (Messieurs Mackenzie and McLellan), have, in Appendix A to this Report, so fully and so ably discussed the serious defects which still exist in most of

17a—XXIII.

our High Schools, that I find it unnecessary to do more than briefly to refer in general terms to the subject.

Separate Course of Study for the High Schools.

1. One important object of the new School Law was to discriminate, by a clearly defined line in the Course of Study, between Public and High Schools, and to prescribe a separate Programme of Studies for High Schools. In practice it had been found that, in the anxiety of Trustees and Masters of a majority of our High Schools to crowd children into these Schools, in the hope thereby to increase the Grant to their Schools, they had virtually merged the High into the Public School, with the nominal addition in most cases of only a little Latin and Greek. The object of the High School Sections of the new Act is to put an end to this anomalous state of things, and to prescribe for each class of Schools its own legitimate work.

2. In point of fact, the Grammar, (now High), Schools have never occupied the position which they ought to have done in the Country. They were originally designed to be Classical Schools, but they were made the Schools of certain classes, rather than. Classical Schools, wholly doing, or professing to do, Common School work for certain classes, thus being made and viewed as a kind of aristocratic Schools, poaching upon the ground of Common School work, and being regarded as distinct from, and even antagonistic to, the Common Schools, rather than supplementary to them and identical with them in the public interests. It has, therefore, been found extremely difficult to get any considerable support for them from local sources. To get support enough to exist, more than two-thirds of the High School Boards have had to seek amalgamation with the Public School Boards of their localities; but this amalgamation is attended with many inconveniences and does not by any means accomplish the objects proposed. Nevertheless, it has not been deemed expedient to interfere with this amalgamation in any way, but to leave the Boards of Trustees as formerly to unite, or, when united, to dissolve the union at their pleasure. The necessity for the union does not now exist as before, since the Legislature has in effect declared that High Schools shall be provided for by local Rate equally with Public Schools. It should be remembered, however, that the experience of the great Cities in the neighbouring States shows, that consolidating all the Public Schools in Cities and Towns under one Board of Management, and that Board elected chiefly by the Ratepayers, has contributed even more to the efficient support and elevation of the Classical School than to that of the Public Schools.

3. In the Programme of Study for High Schools, prescribed under the new School Act, it is especially provided that they shall be High English Schools as well as Elementary Classical Schools, and for Girls as well as for Boys. When it is provided in the Act that in each High School, "provision shall be made for teaching to both male and female Pupils the higher branches of an English and Commercial Education, including the Natural Sciences, with special reference to Agriculture," it was clearly intended that the lower, or elementary, branches of an English Education should not be taught in the High Schools, but in the Public Schools. It was also intended that all Pupils to be eligible for admission to the High Schools for the study of Classics, as well as for higher English, must first be grounded in the elements of a sound Education in their own native Language, as strongly urged by the latest Royal and Parliamentary Commission on Education in England, but strangely overlooked hitherto, as little Boys six and seven years of age have been put to the study of ancient and foreign languages, and left to grow up to manhood without ever having been formally taught their native tongue, or the essential elements of a practical English Education. This anomaly is provided against by the new School Act in the future education of Canadian youth, at least so far as the Public and High Schools are concerned, and the Council of Public Instruction has prescribed, that "the subjects of examination for admission to the High Schools shall be the same as those prescribed for the first four classes of the Public Schools." It will be seen from the explanatory remarks preceding the Programme, that some subjects of the fourth Class of the Public School Programme are omitted, in regard

to Pupil Candidates for the Classical Course of the High School. The examination for admission to the High School must be on paper, and the Examination Papers with the Answers are to be preserved for the examination of the High School Inspector, that he may not depend wholly on the individual examination of Pupils as to whether the Regulations have been duly observed in the examination and admission of Pupils.

4. The fundamental principle of our System of Public Instruction is that every youth, before proceeding to the subjects of a higher English, or of a Classical Education, shall first be grounded in the elementary subjects of a Public School Education. No Candidates are, therefore, eligible for admission to the High Schools except those who have manifested proficiency in the subjects of the first four Classes of the Public School Programme, by passing a satisfactory examination.

5. It is to be observed also, that although Pupils are eligible for promotion from the Public to the High School, after passing a satisfactory examination in the subjects of the first four Classes of the former, omitting Natural History, Chemistry and Botany, it is quite at the option of the Parents, or Guardians, of Pupils, whether they shall enter the High School, or not, before they complete the whole Programme of Studies in the Public Schools, when the can enter an advanced Class in the High School.

6. The objects and duties of the High Schools are two-fold:—

First, commencing with Pupils who, (whether educated in either a Public, or Private, School), are qualified as above, the High Shcools are intended to complete a good English Education, by educating Pupils not only for Commercial, Manufacturing and Agricultural pursuits, but for fulfilling with efficiency, honour and usefulness, the duties of Municipal Councillors, Legislators, and various public Offices in the service of the Country.

The *Second* object and duty of the High Schools, (commencing also with Pupils qualified as above), is to teach the languages of Greece and Rome, of Germany and France, the Mathematics, etcetera, so far as to prepare youth for certain professions, and especially for the Universities, where will be completed the education of men for the learned professions, and for the Professorships in the Colleges, and Masterships in the Collegiate Institutes and High Schools.

High School Standard in Massachusetts.

It may be interesting in this connection to notice what is, (and has been for many years), the provision in the School Laws of the State of Massachusetts, in regard to High Schools. They contain the following provisions:—

Every Township may, and every Township containing five hundred Families, or householders . . . shall "maintain a School, to be kept by a Master of competent ability and good morals, who . . . shall give instruction in General History, Book-keeping, Surveying, Geometry, Natural Philosophy, Chemistry, Botany, the Civil Polity of this Commonwealth and of the United States, and the Latin language. . . . And in every Township containing four thousand inhabitants, the Teacher, or Teachers of the Schools required by this Section of the Act, shall, in addition to the branches of instruction in the Greek and French languages, teach Astronomy, Geology, Rhetoric, Logic, Intellectual and Moral Science, and Political Economy.'' These Schools "shall be kept for the benefit of all the inhabitants of the Town." "not less than thirty-six weeks, exclusive of Vacations, in each year." Two adjacent Townships, having each less than five hundred families or householders, may form one High School District, for establishing such a School . . . when a majority of the legal Voters of each Township, in Meetings called for that purpose, so determine."

The Report of the Massachusetts Board of Education to the Legislature, in 1870, says:—

High Schools are maintained in 162 Townships. (out of 335), embracing in the aggregate 1,000,000 inhabitants, or 82 per cent. of the population.

An examination of the United States Census of 1870, shows that exactly 162 Townships in Massachusetts had then a population of over 2,000,196 of them having over 4,000. We shall, therefore, be very nearly correct of we consider the above Law practically equivalent to requiring every Township with a population of over 2,000 to maintain a High School.

The Necessity of Well Trained Teachers for the High Schools.

I quite concur in the remarks of the High School Inspectors as to the necessity of some modification in the Law in regard to the qualifications of Masters of High Schools.

In order to secure a class of better educated men for High School Masterships, the present School Law was passed, requiring that each High School Master should be a Graduate, (in Arts), of some University in Her Majesty's Dominions. Experience has proved the necessity of the addition of some training on the part of these gentlemen in the Art of Teaching, before undertaking the new and responsible duties of the Mastership of a High School.

The High, Equally with the Public, Schools, supported by Municipal Rates.

The School Law of 1871 at length embodies a principle for which I had contended for years. In submitting the first draft of Bill in 1854, for the improvement of our Grammar Schools, I sought to get inserted in it a recognition of the principle,—which has at length been conceded,—that it was the duty of the County, or other Municipal, Councils, to provide, by Rate upon property, for the support of the Grammar School equally with the Common School. Experience has shown how utterly impossible it was to maintain a good Grammar School without Municipal aid, in addition to the Legislative Grant. The history of our High Schools since 1854 has, (with some honourable exceptions), been a chronicle of failures, owing chiefly to want of means to employ a sufficient number of Teachers, and to prevent the wholesale thrusting into them of a number of ill-qualified children, in the vain hope of thereby increasing the Government Grant. The obvious fact was overlooked that if one School resorted to this improper means of swelling its average attendance, another would do the same. Thus, in the race for numbers, the quality deteriorated, and the ratio of Apportionment to each School was largely reduced. This was the case, especially as regards the better class of Schools, which did not resort to this questionable means of obtaining, as was hoped, an increased Grant, but which were made to suffer severely by this unjust competition. Happily the motive for a continuance of this unfortunate state of things has been entirely removed, and the Councils are now authorized and required by Law to provide all necessary means for carrying on our High Schools in a state of efficiency. I have no doubt that the High School Sections of the Act will inaugurate a new and auspicious era in the higher English and Commercial, as well as elementary Classical Education of the Country, in regard to both sexes of our youthful population.

X.—THE NEW PRINCIPLE OF "PAYMENT BY RESULTS."

Our School Law of 1871 has introduced a new principle into the mode of payments to High Schools. Formerly the system adopted was, (as in the case of Public Schools), to distribute the High School Fund on the basis of average attendance of the Pupils at the School. This was found to work injuriously to the best class of Schools. For instance, a very inferior School with an average attendance, say, of fifty, would be entitled to receive precisely the same Apportionment as another School with the same attendance, but which might be greatly superior,—if not the very best School in the Province. To remedy this defect and remove this injustice, a new principle of payment was introduced into the Act,—videlicet:—the payment, (as it is technically termed in England), "by Results," or, as in the words of the Act itself, according to "proficiency in the various branches of Study."

The Inspectors, in their Report, [Chapter XV], have fully discussed this new principle, but as considerable misapprehension appears to exist in regard to its introduction into our School Law, I shall explain the successive steps which have been taken on the subject:—

The principle of "Payment by Results," as it is technically termed, has long been applied to the English Elementary Schools, and it has within the last year, or two, been recommended by the Royal Commission Inquiry for introduction into the Schools of the Irish National Board.

In 1865, when the amended Grammar School Act was passed, the Education Department for this Province had the matter under consideration. The subject was discussed at the time, and enquiries made into the working of the System. The want of an additional Inspector for the Grammar Schools was, however, felt to be an obstacle to its introduction at that time, apart from the inferior character of very many of the Grammar Schools which then existed.

An important step was, however, taken at that time; and the principle of payment according to the "average attendance of Pupils" was then first applied to Grammar Schools. This change was thus explained in the Memorandum which was published with the new Act in 1865:—*

The Seventh Section of the new Grammar School Act is intended to remove a gross anomaly in the present system of apportioning the Grammar School Fund,—a relic of the old Law of 1806-8,—which gave to the Senior County Grammar School more than to the Junior Schools, unless the average daily attendance should fall below ten Pupils, —although every one of these Schools may have been vastly superior to the Senior School of the County. This Section of the new Act reduces the system of apportioning the Grammar School Fund to a simple and equitable principle of aiding each School according to its work. The application of this principle to Common Schools in the rural Sections has given them a much greater impulse forward than the old mode of apportionment on the basis of School population, or length of time during which they might have been kept open, whether the work was done or not. It has also induced the Trustees to keep the School open one, or two, months longer in the year than formerly. Then, as to the basis of apportionment itself, the subjects of teaching in a Grammar School were designed to differ from those in a Common School. Grammar Schools are intended to be intermediate between Common Schools and Universities. The Common School Law amply provides for giving the best kind of a superior English education in Central Schools, in the Cities, Towns, and Villages, with primary Ward Schools as feeders, (as in Hamilton); while to allow Grammar Schools to do Common School work is a misapplication of Grammar School Funds for Common Schools purposes; Common Schools are already adequately provided for. By the old Law of 1807, and subsequently, the number of Classical Pupils was fixed at twenty, and afterwards at ten. In our Regulations we take the latter number.

Under these circumstances it was felt to be undesirable at that time to make any further change in the mode of apportioning money to the High Schools. The subject of "Payment by Results" was, however, not lost sight of; but on the visit in that same year, (1865), of Reverend Doctor Fraser, (now Bishop of Manchester),—one of the Royal Commissioners to enquire into the State of Education in the United States and Canada, —the matter was discussed with him. I, also that year referred the question to the then Inspector of Grammar Schools, (Reverend G. P. Young), who thus reported upon it, 'in his Annual Report), for 1869:—

I have come to the conclusion, after having devoted much thought to the subject, that, until educational results are combined with attendance as the basis of apportionment, it will be impossible to devise any scheme of distribution, that shall not be open to grave objections. More than a year ago, you asked me to consider whether "results" might not in some way be reached with sufficient accuracy to be taken into account, to a certain extent, in deciding the Grants to be made to the several Schools. I stated to you my conviction that it could not be done, with the present provision for the inspection of Grammar Schools, etcetera.

At length, the appointment of two Inspectors of High Schools, having been secured a Section of the new Act was submitted to the Legislature for its adoption in 1870-71, and embodied the new principle of "Payment by Results" in the 37th Section. The threefold principle embodied in this Section, upon which High Schools are hereafter to be aided, is declared by the new Law to be as follows:—Each High School conducted according to Law, [and the Regulations], shall be entitled to an Apportionment . . . according,—

First,—To the average attendance of Pupils.

Second,—Their proficiency in the various branches of Study.

Third,—The length of time each such High School is kept open as compared with other High Schools.

As it was clearly impossible to apply the new principle of "Payment by Results" to the High Schools until a classification of them had been made, the Council of Public

Instruction requested the High School Inspectors to make such a classification, and report the result to the Chief Superintendent. This they have done in their Report, [printed in Chapter XV], and have suggested one or two plans for carrying the new system into full effect in 1873.

It is a question, however, whether any system of classification of the High Schools will be entirely satisfactory, or at best anything more than, (probably a just), approximation to the relative standing of the several High Schools. The only really satisfactory method of determining the relative standing and excellence of these Schools, for the purposes of correct classification, would be to subject the whole of the Pupils in them to a uniform test Examination on questions prepared and printed for that purpose. The result of such an Examination would be to determine, with an almost exact certainty, the relative position which every School should occupy in an Official preliminary classification of them. It would also furnish an indisputable starting-point, from which future progress or retrogression could be easily ascertained by the half-yearly examination of the High School Inspectors on their visits to the Schools.

The English System of "Payment by Results."

In England the Parliamentary aid to Elementary Schools is distributed as follows:— The Managers of every School entitled to the aid may claim, annually, the sum of four shillings per Scholar, according to the average number in attendance throughout the year, at the morning and afternoon School, not being less than 400 attendances at their School; and one-half of that sum per Scholar, according to the average number throughout the year at the evening School, not being less than forty attendances at the School; also, for every Scholar who attended more than 200 mornings or afternoons at the School. If more than six years of age, eight shillings, subject to examination. If under six years of age, and present on the day of examination, six shillings and sixpence, subject to a report by the Inspector that such children are suitably instructed. For every Scholar who has attended more than twenty-four evenings at the School, five shillings, subject to examination. Every day Scholar entitled to eight shillings, forfeits two shillings and eightpence for failure to satisfy the Inspector in either Reading, Writing or Arithmetic. Every evening Scholar entitled to five shillings, forfeits one shilling and eightpence for similar failure. The Grant is, moreover, increased at the rate of one shilling and fourpence per pass in Reading, Writing, or Arithmetic, up to any number not exceeding 120; provided, that the passes exceed 200 per cent. of the number of Scholars in attendance over six years of age; that one-fifth of the passes are within the three highest Standards; that one-fifth of the average number of Scholars, over six years of age, have passed a satisfactory examination in one or more specific subjects above the Standard; and the number of Pupil Teachers, or Assistant Teachers, employed, bears a certain proportion of the number of Scholars. Thus, every Manager had a direct pecuniary interest in maintaining regularity of attendance, in the improvement of each individual Scholar, and in providing a sufficient corps of Teachers.

Great Advantage of the Systems of Payment by Results.

The three great excellencies of the System were:—

1st. The employment of Certificated Teachers.

2nd. Provision for training a corps of Teachers under the name of Pupil Teachers

3rd. The individual examination of Scholars upon certain Standards clearly defined for each grade of Schools.

On the new Code, Her Majesty's Education Committee of the Privy Council remark:—

We have carefully maintained the principles of payment by "results;" we have endeavoured to lay down terms of aid which, while increasing the efficiency of the inspected Schools, will materially simplify the administration of the Grants.

In Victoria, (Australia), "payment by results," to the Schools, is the system adopted. In the last Report of the Board of Education for that Country, published this year, the Board says:—

The system of "payment by results," now in use, appears to be working well, and to give general satisfaction. The fact, that at every Examination, each School's force is recorded as having gained a certain percentage of a possible maximum, affords a means of comparison between different Schools which, if not conclusive as to their relative merits, is sufficiently so to cause considerable emulation amongst Teachers. Indeed, the wish to obtain a high percentage, materially increases the stimulus afforded by the "result" payments.

XI.—COLLEGIATE INSTITUTES, OR LOCAL COLLEGES.

The High Schools having of necessity been thrown open to Girls, and provision having been made in them for giving a purely English Education apart from Classics, it was thought desirable to prevent the possible extinction, in our Educational System, of a purely Classical School which should serve as a proper link between the Public School and the University. With this view, a provision was introduced into the High School portion of the Act of 1871, authorizing the establishment of Collegiate Institutes, and fixing the minimum standard to be reached, by any High School, the Trustees of which desired it to be recognized as a Collegiate Institute. This standard is the daily average attendance of at least sixty Boys in Greek, or Latin, and the employment, *bona fide*, of at least four Masters, who shall devote the whole of their time to the work of instruction in the Institute. The standard fixed is not an ideal one, but has already been surpassed by more than one of our existing High Schools,—that of Galt. It is hoped that the establishment, throughout the Country, of local Colleges, of the comparatively high standard which such Institutions must reach and maintain, in order to be recognized as such, will be a great and substantial boon to the Country, and will promote, in the highest degree, the best interests of superior Education throughout the Province.

The Study of Latin Necessary in Collegiate Institutes.

Among the many reasons which justify the provision in the new School Act, requiring an absolute daily average attendance in Collegiate Institutes of at least sixty Boys in Greek and Latin, are the following, which we have quoted, with the recommendations of the English Royal Commissions on the subject. In their Report of 1868, they say:—

All the Masters examined by us appear to be agreed that nothing teaches English Grammar so easily, or so well, as Latin Grammar, and, next to that, they would place the teaching of some other foreign Grammar, such as French. The preference is given to Latin for many reasons. There is something, no doubt, in the beauty of the language itself. But the chief stress is laid on the fulness and precision of its accidence, in which no modern language can rival it. Further, it has entered so largely into English, that the meaning of a very large proportion of our words is first discovered to us on learning Latin. And to a no less degree has it entered into English Literature, so that many of our classical writers are only half intelligible unless some knowledge of Latin precede the reading. Latin, again, is a common gateway to French, Italian and Spanish. Some Teachers even maintain that French can be taught more easily in company with Latin, than by giving all the time to French alone. . . .

Conclusions and Recommendations of the English Commissioners.

The conclusions to which we were brought by a review of the opinions put before us, in regard to the subjects of instruction are strongly confirmed by the experience of those Countries that have been most successful in the management of Education. Everywhere we find the Classics still regarded as the best instrument now to be obtained for the highest Education, and when the Classics are neglected, the Education seems to be lowered in character. But we see also that two important modifications must be made in this general statement.

One is, that the time given to Classics must be so far curtailed, if necessary, as to admit of other important Studies by their side. France curtails the study of Greek for this purpose; Prussia, the practice of Composition; but neither gives up the Classics in her highest Education, nor Latin, even in ranks much below the highest. The Scotch Parents, who can choose at their own discretion, still make Latin the staple of instruction, while they are not content with Latin only. Even Zurich, with a decided leaning to Industrial Education, has a large proportion of Scholars in Classical Schools. But all these Countries appear to stand above us in the teaching of every subject except the Classics, and England is quite alone in requiring no systematic study in the Mother Tongue.

The other modification of the general rule in favour of Classics is that room must be made for Schools of an altogether different type. There are minds fitted to be developed by other Studies than that of the most perfect known languages. There are occupations for which Classical studies do not give the proper preparation. Schools like the Realschulen of Prussia, or the Schools of Industry of Switzerland, have become a positive need of modern times.

Suggestions in Regard to the High Schools and Collegiate Institutes.

From the Report of the Inspectors, and the foregoing remarks, I would strongly urge the following:—

1. That the standard of admission to the High Schools and Collegiate Institutes be uniform throughout the Province.

2. That no Pupils be admitted to the High Schools except on satisfactorily passing a Written Examination, and obtaining a minimum of fifty per cent. of the value of the Papers.

3. That suitable Accommodation be provided, in all cases, for the High Schools.

4. That the Programme of Studies and Limit Table, when finally prepared and authorized, be strictly adhered to, except by permission obtained upon the report and recommendation of the Inspector.

5. That at least two competent Masters be employed in every High School.

6. That before the principle of "payment by results" be applied to High Schools, their status and classification, (as a starting point), be ascertained by a Written Examination of the Pupils in one or more of the Classes,—say the highest and lowest.

7. That, in all cases, the Council of Public Instruction shall have the right, through its Inspectors, to determine whether the Answers given in the Written Examination come up or not to the minimum standard.

8. That an additional High School Inspector be appointed, in order that effect may be given to the new System of Payment by Results; and that the three Inspectors be authorised and required, in places where there are High Schools, or Collegiate Institutes, to inquire into the condition and efficiency of the Public and Separate Schools, which are entitled to prepare and send Pupils to the High Schools, or Collegiate Institutes.

9. That Masters of High Schools should, before appointment, be required to furnish some evidence of a knowledge of the Art of Teaching.

XII.—THE ESTABLISHMENT OF INDUSTRIAL SCHOOLS.

Although the School Law of 1850 authorized Boards of Trustees in Cities, Towns and Villages, to establish "any kind, or description, of Schools" they might see fit, yet it was regarded as doubtful whether it was sufficiently comprehensive to admit the establishment of Industrial Schools. To remove this doubt, and to give effect to the wishes of many interested in the condition of the "Street Arabs" of our Cities, Towns and Villages, the Section of the Act of 1871 authorizing the establishment of these Schools was passed, as follows:—

42. The Public School Board of each City, Town and Village may establish one, or more, Industrial Schools for otherwise neglected children, and to make all needful Regulations and employ the means requisite to secure the attendance of such children, and for the support, management and discipline of such School, or Schools. The third Section of the Act also provides, "that refractory Pupils may be, where practicable, removed to an Industrial School."

With a view to afford information in regard to the manner in which Industrial Schools are managed elsewhere, I add the following sketch of the routine in an "Industrial School for Girls," in Connecticut. The State Superintendent in his Report says:—

The number of Girls now in the School is nearly eighty. In most of them a marked improvement is noticed, both in conduct and study. Many of them came covered with rags and filth, hitherto ignorant, vagrant, friendless and depraved. Sixty per cent. were Orphans. In nine cases out of ten their Parents had been criminals, or intemperate. Their early associations and surroundings were vicious and corrupting. The results prove the necessity of such an Institution. Already a manifest change is noticed in their language and conduct. The habits of order, neatness, obedience, industry and study here formed, are all reformatory in their tendency.

We have unlimited faith in the power of kindness. Not that mawkish sensibility which forbids control, which like Eli says,—"Why do ye such things?" but a love which restrains, even with physical pain, if necessary, always regretting the necessity, and always proving the motives to be only good. It does people good to discipline them. No character is fully developed that has not been restrained by Law. To do just as one is inclined to is not productive of high character. A kindness that is patient, persevering, slow to wrath, but plenteous in mercy, that is willing to perform almost any labour and endure any privation to do one good, will induce reform where there is any possibility of it. If that fails, any other means would fail; the case is comparatively hopeless.

Another principle we have faith in is liberty. It may be necessary to hedge confined criminals around with stone and iron to cause them to enjoy liberty.

License is not liberty. Girls in this Institution are trusted. They are put upon their honour. Perhaps they have no sense of it.

If not, it will not come by locks and bars. After proving themselves unfit for liberty, they are allowed to reflect for a time, deprived of it, and with the first sign of promise of honour are tried again. No Girl is put under lock and key unless she forfeits the right to liberty. The reason for this is evident. She must be trusted some time. To cultivate with all possible rapidity that sense of honour which renders it safe to trust, is the shortest road to reform. When a Girl can be fully and thoroughly trusted in all situations, she is no longer a subject for a Reform School. How shall we know except by trial? Put her on her honour, give her some responsibility, and hold her to a strict account, and the sense of self-control will be developed most rapidly. What is the result here of this mode of treatment? Out of ninety-four Girls, not one eloper is reported. All are accounted for. For more than one year, no attempt was made to escape. Yet, we tell them they can run away at any time, night or day, and they know they can, and that is one reason why they do not go. What one can do at any time is most generally neglected. They feel that forfeiting their honour is a greater disgrace than staying here for years. Of course, we try and make a pleasant home for them, to interest them in the various departments of labour and study. This is our Home, our work, our School, our Chapel, they say. Each Girl is taught that she may honour, or disgrace, not only herself, but the whole School, and every means is used to make them choose to stay and be contented and happy.

A system of marking conduct was put in practice, which has produced good results. Every Officer marks the conduct of every Girl in her department, daily, on a scale of five; if she is punished she gets 0; if reproved, 1, etcetera. We mark thirty days for each month; have three grades and eight badges, denoted by coloured ribbons, worn as a Rosette as follows:—Badge 1, perseverance, Black ribbon; 2, carefulness, Green; 3, sobriety, dark Blue; 4, neatness, Red; 5, kindness, light Blue; 6, industry, Pink; 7, excellence, Orange; 8, honour, White.

The Girls are allotted, one each month, to various departments, as Cooking, Washing, Ironing, Sewing, etcetera. Every one has a task for the morning, and all work is completed by the ring of the first bell at 1.30 p.m., when the Girls prepare for School, where they remain from 2 to 5 p.m.

Besides doing this, our Girls have made over 40,000 Paper Boxes, and several of them have learned the Trade, so as always to be able to get good wages, and hence have no excuse for a vicious life. In summer, the Girls are employed to some extent in the open air. If we had the means to enable us to erect a Hot-house, we would cultivate Flowers and Plants for market, thus adding another link to the chain of love to bind Girls to this home.

XIII.—COMPREHENSIVE VIEW OF THE NEEDS OF AND PROVISION FOR NATIONAL EDUCATION IN THE UNITED STATES.

Having completed my more minute survey of our own System of Public Instruction, I would now devote a page, or two, to a subject of much interest to us as close neighbours of a great and powerful people, who are running a gigantic race with us in educational matters. I do not do so with any expectation that we can either approach, or rival, them in the aggregate of their educational labours, or gifts; but because that, as a Province, and as a Dominion, we cannot, in justice to ourselves, remain uninterested or silent spectators of their wonderful efforts, their amazing progress, and their practical experiments in educational matters.

The information which I have gathered is taken chiefly from the Report of the United States Commissioner of Education at Washington for 1871. It is contained in four tables, videlicet:-

I. Table showing the number of native and foreign illiterates in the various States and Territories of the Union, and which demonstrates to the American people the necessity of making great efforts to counteract the terrible evil of ignorance and its twin companion, crime.

II. Table showing the amount of national Benefactions in the shape of Land Grants to the several States and Territories for the promotion, (1), of Common School Education; (2), of University Education, and (3), of Education in Agriculture and the Mechanic Arts. I have also added in a note a list of personal Benefactions in aid of Education in various States, made during 1870-71, many of them reflecting great honour on the princely donors.

III. Table showing the yearly Receipts and Expenditure for Public Schools in the several States, and the amount of permanent School Fund in each.

IV. Table showing the cost, *per capita*, for Public School Education in each of the States, and also the assessed valuation of property, *per capita*, of the total population.

A Noble Example for our New Dominion to Emulate.

These Tables present great facts in a strong light. That Table especially (Number II), which contains a list of the Land Benefactions of the General Government to the several States, indicates a far-sighted national sagacity for which the American people are noted. These Grants date back to 1793, and were continued in 1803, 1816-20, and down to 1868, when 3,480,081 Acres were set apart in Wyoming Territory for Common Schools! True to their national instincts in favour of Free Education for the masses, nine-tenths of the Grants, or 68,000,000 of Acres out of 78,600,000, are appropriated in aid of these Elementary Schools, and 9,500,000 Acres, (as against 1,120,000 to the Universities, for the promotion of Education in Agriculture and the Mechanic Arts. These latter Grants were made as late as in 1862-66, and were at the rate of 30,000 for each Senator and Representative in Congress from the several States and Territories.

There is no reason why our Dominion Government should not emulate so noble an example as the General Government of the United States has set them, and set apart as sacred, out of the magnificent domain now in its possession in the North West, an endowment in Lands which, in after years, would be a noble heritage to the after possessors of the embryo Provinces which are being formed in the Dominion. If Wyoming Territory should in 1868 receive three millions and a half acres of Land as an Endowment for her Public Schools, there is no reason why Manitoba, Saskatchewan, British Columbia and Vancouver Island should not receive at least 2,000,000 of Acres each for the same great national object, and Ontario at least 1,500,000 Acres, in addition to her share in the 1,000,000 set apart some years ago, (1849), through the exertions of the late Honourable W. Hamilton Merritt.

TABLE I.—SHOWING THE NUMBER OF NATIVE AND FOREIGN ILLITERATE PERSONS TEN YEARS OLD AND OVER, OF ALL RACES, IN THE STATES AND TERRITORIES, ARRANGED IN DIVISIONS FROM THE CENSUS OF 1870.

States and Territories.	Number of Illiterates.		
	Native.	Foreign.	Total.
Grand aggregate, United States..........	4,882,210	777,864	5,660,074
Aggregate, Northern Division...........	690,117	665,985	1,356,102
Maine..	7,986	11,066	19,052
New Hampshire.............................	1,992	7,934	9,926
Vermont.....	3,902	13,804	17,706
Massachusetts	7,912	89,830	97,742
Rhode Island........	4,444	17,477	21,921
Connecticut.................................	5,678	23,938	29,616
New York	72,583	168,569	241,152
New Jersey..................................	29,726	24,961	54,687
Pennsylvania................................	126,803	95,553	222,356
Ohio..	134,102	39,070	173,172
Michigan....................................	22,547	30,580	53,127

TABLE L.—SHEWING THE NUMBER OF NATIVE AND FOREIGN ILLITERATE PERSONS.—*Continued.*

States and Territories.	Number of Illiterates.		
	Native.	Foreign.	Total.
Indiana	113,185	13,939	127,124
Wisconsin	14,113	41,328	55,441
Illinois	90,605	42,979	133,584
Minnesota	5,558	18,855	24,413
Iowa	24,980	20,691	45,672
Nebraska	3,552	1,309	4,861
Kansas	20,449	4,101	24,550
Aggregate, Pacific Division	74,504	39,496	114,000
California	9,520	22,196	31,716
Oregon	3,003	1,424	4,427
Nevada	98	774	872
Arizona Territory	262	2,591	2,753
Washington "	852	503	1,355
Idaho "	138	3,250	3,388
Utah "	3,334	4,029	7,363
Montana "	394	524	918
Dakota "	758	805	1,563
Wyoming "	266	336	602
Colorado "	6,568	255	6,823
New Mexico "	49,311	2,909	52,220
Aggregate, Southern Division	4,117,589	72,383	4,189,972
Delaware	20,631	2,469	23,100
Maryland	126,907	8,592	135,499
District of Columbia	26,501	2,218	28,719
Virginia	444,623	1,270	445,893
West Virginia	78,389	3,101	81,490
Kentucky	324,945	7,231	332,176
North Carolina	397,573	117	397,690
Tennessee	362,955	1,742	364,697
South Carolina	289,726	653	290,379
Georgia	467,503	1,090	468,593
Alabama	382,142	870	383,012
Florida	71,235	568	71,809
Mississippi	312,483	827	313,310
Missouri	206,827	15,584	222,411
Arkansas	133,042	297	133,339
Louisiana	268,773	7,385	276,158
Texas	203,334	18,369	221,703

TABLE II.—SHOWING THE NUMBER OF ACRES OF PUBLIC LANDS GRANTED, OR RESERVED, FOR EDUCATIONAL PURPOSES IN THE UNITED STATES.

STATES.	Acres granted, or reserved, for the support of Common Schools	Acres granted, or reserved, for Universities.	Acres granted for Colleges of Agriculture and the Mechanical Arts.	Total Acres granted, or reserved.
Alabama	902,774	46,080	240,000	1,188,854
Arkansas	886,460	46,080	150,000	1,082,540
California	6,719,324	46,080	150,000	6,915,404
Connecticut			180,000	180,000
Delaware			90,000	90,000
Florida	908,503	96,160	90,000	1,090,663
Georgia			270,000	270,000
Illinois	985,066	46,080	480,000	1,511,146
Indiana	650,317	46,080	390,000	1,086,397
Iowa	905,144	46,080	240,000	1,191,224

TABLE II.—SHOWING THE NUMBER OF ACRES OF PUBLIC LANDS GRANTED.—*Continued.*

STATES.	Acres granted, or reserved, for the support of Common Schools	Acres granted, or reserved, for Universities.	Acres granted for Colleges of Agriculture and the Mechanical Arts.	Total Acres granted or reserved.
Kansas	2,891,306	46,080	90,000	3,027,386
Kentucky			330,000	330,000
Louisiana	786,044	46,080	210,000	1,042,124
Maine			210,000	210,000
Maryland			210,000	210,000
Massachusetts			360,000	360,000
Michigan	1,067,390	46,080	240,000	1,353,477
Minnesota	2,969,990	82,640	120,000	3,172,630
Mississipi	837,584	46,080	210,000	1,093,664
Missouri	1,199,139	46,080	330,000	1,575,219
Nebraska	2,702,044	46,080	90,000	2,838,124
Nevada	3,985,428	46,080	90,000	4,121,508
New Hampshire			150,000	150,000
New Jersey			210,000	210,000
New York			990,000	990,000
North Carolina			270,000	270,000
Ohio	704,488	69,120	630,000	1,403,608
Oregon	3,329,706	46,080	90,000	3,465,786
Pennsylvania			780,000	780,000
Rhode Island			120,000	120,000
South Carolina			180,000	180,000
Tennessee			300,000	300,000
Texas			180,000	180,000
Virginia			300,000	300,000
Vermont			150,000	150,000
West Virginia			150,000	150,000
Wisconsin	958,649	92,160	240,000	1,290,809
Washington Territory	2,488,675	46,080		2,534,755
New Mexico Territory	4,309,368	46,080		4,355,448
Utah Territory	3,003,613	46,080		3,049,693
Dakota Territory	5,366,451			5,366,451
Colorado Territory	3,715,555			3,715,555
Montana Territory	5,112,035			5,112,035
Arizona Territory	4,050,350			4,050,350
Idaho Territory	3,068,231			3,068,231
Wyoming Territory	3,480,281			3,480,281
Total	67,983,922	1,119,440	9,510,000	78,613,362

NOTE. It is believed that the unsolicited Contributions by private citizens of the United States, for the educational interests of the community, are, at the present time, without a parallel in any other Country of the world. Wealth thus recognizes its responsibility and indicates its wisdom;—for the education of her children is at once the duty and the safety of the Commonwealth.

In California, during 1870-71, Gifts of private individuals, to Education, amounted to $2,000,000; in Connecticut, to $845,665, of which Yale College received $319,865; in Georgia, $1,000; in Indiana, $537,025; in Illinois, $391,000; in Iowa, $75,000; in Kansas, $50,000; in Louisiana, 1,090; in Massachusetts, $2,502,000; in Minnesota, $50,500; in Missouri, $205,000, (entirely for Washington University, St. Louis); in Michigan, $15,000; in New Hampshire, $168,000, of which Dartmouth College received $121,000; in New Jersey, $323,500, of which Princeton College received $223,500; in New York, $765,000; in Ohio, $23,250; in Oregon, $5,000; in Pennsylvania, $312,000; in Rhode Island, $24,000; in South Carolina, $13,000; in Tennessee, $4,000; in Virginia, $45,000; in Wisconsin, $80,000, making a total of $8,435,990.

Of these individual donations, two were of $1,000,000 or over; twenty-three were of $100,000 and over; fifteen of $50,000 and over; eleven of $25,000 and over; twenty of $10,000 and over; and thirty-three of $1,000 and over.

TABLE III.—FINANCES OF PUBLIC

STATES.	From Taxation.	Interest on Permanent Fund.	Revenue from other Funds.	Proceeds of Sale of Land.	From other Sources.	Total.
	INCOME.					
	$	$	$	$	$	$
Alabama	82,579 66	115,268 85	51,078 53		341,678 50	590,605 54
Arkansas	221,011 07	3,016 25	334,952 13	66,074 02		625,053 47
California						
Connecticut	1,067,233 59	125,409 00	53,570 96		237,802 80	1,484,016 35
Delaware	81,697 46	32,030 31				113,727 77
Florida						
Georgia	327,083 09				105,199 89	432,282 98
Illinois	5,666,108 61	442,382 07		154,459 76	1,948,741 50	8,057,232 18
Indiana	1,339,472 55	369,798 32			100,794 62	1,810,065 49
Iowa	3,030,193 14	226,110 92				3,256,304 06
Kansas	518,323 85	21,274 50	74,268 09	44,010 30	14,260 19	672,136 93
Kentucky						
Louisiana	590,703 52		24,480 00	5,472 00	320,154 52	915,810 04
Maine	910,555 00	15,440 00	14,639 00			940,638 00
Maryland	1,083,843 80	63,664 02			186,177 48	1,315,685 30
Massachusetts	5,453,276 09	190,000 00	82,049 16		12,540 26	5,737,865 51
Michigan	2,172,690 41	186,485 24			801,365 67	3,160,541 32
Minnesota		173,335 55		89,696 41	4,862 28	267,894 24
Mississippi	700,000 00	50,000 00			190,000 00	940,000 00
Missouri						
Nebraska						337,047 14
Nevada	59,260 24	16,957 59			18,895 02	95,112 85
New Hampshire	306,826 59				101,718 29	408,544 88
New Jersey	2,227,347 18	35,000 00	39,000 00		62,100 90	2,364,441 58
New York	9,011,745 65	325,000 00		22,550 45	1,847,660 12	11,216,956 22
North Carolina	114,624 75			12,991 35	102,374 69	229,990 79
Ohio	6,342,325 97	234,749 86			849,957 67	7,427,053 50
Oregon	113,699 00	40,000 00				153,699 00
Pennsylvania	7,194,356 65					7,694,356 65
Rhode Island	90,000 00				424,040 00	514,040 00
South Carolina	240,000 00				1,000 00	241,000 00
Tennessee						
Texas						
Vermont	326,647 87				101,847 77	428,495 64
Virginia						
West Virginia	528,855 33	13,758 00			43,235 82	585,849 15
Wisconsin	1,705,546 70	158,249 60			714,696 63	2,578,492 93

SCHOOLS IN THE UNITED STATES.

EXPENDITURE							
CURRENT EXPENSES.			INCIDENTAL EXPENSES.			Total Expenditure.	Amount of Permanent School Fund.
Teacher's Wages.	Fuel, etcetera.	Total.	Sites, Buildings, and Repairs.	Libraries and Apparatus.	For other Objects.		
$	$	$	$	$	$	$	$
405,748 37	....	405,748 37	204,974 22	1,000 00	37,942 00	645,664 49	....
785,680 04	101,086 94	886,766 98	550,318 10	8,065 20	176,247 48	1,621,397 78	2,043,375 62
84,157 02	....	84,157 02	....	....	31,250 13	115,407 15	....
....	....	....	....	....	8,308 31	....	350,000 00
3,970,693 04	647,439 50	4,618,132 54	1,371,052 90	39,124 05	853,228 13	6,881,537 62	6,132,086 28
2,035,288 28	....	2,035,288 28	....	....	1,173,155 96	3,208,444 24	8,826,665 03
1,900,893 54	176,317 76	2,077,211 30	914,297 05	21,319 66	256,363 14	3,269,191 15	3,174,578 01
318,596 31	94,644 33	413,240 64	....	....	....	....	560,775 00
654,800 00	43,000 00	697,800 00	45,000 00	....	40,000 00	782,800 00	....
400,000 00	100,000 00	500,000 00	117,364 00	....	300,000 00	917,364 00	303,109 00
808,860 45	79,967 98	888,828 43	219,087 29	....	196,844 98	1,304,760 70	315,370 01
....	....	3,284,875 59	2,058,853 30	....	406,676 88	5,750,405 77	2,211,410 00
1,391,801 61	....	1,391,801 61	852,122 62	50,000 00	....	2,821,160 23	2,700,834 63
432,443 02	....	432,443 02	272,646 38	....	87,853 51	792,852 91	2,476,222 19
200,000 00	....	300,000 00	....	....	....	900,000 00	2,000,000 00
133,274 79	....	133,274 79	....	....	....	330,924 87	....
45,409 49	6,369 64	51,779 13	21,700 10	358 01	....	73,836 64	67,587 38
....	....	....	107,627 00	....	....	....	....
1,677,691 38	61,550 00	1,739,241 38	597,400 20	27,800 00	....	2,364,441 58	550,783 50
6,584,017 54	1,164,142 67	7,748,160 21	1,982,547 29	210,073 98	268,930 61	10209,712 09	2,915,633 04
42,862 40	....	42,862 40	....	....	....	....	....
4,005,800 00	1,165,188 54	5,170,988 54	1,979,577 54	....	....	7,150,566 08	3,912,497 00
....	....	....	70,098 00	....	....	70,098 00	....
3,926,529 88	1,167,124 94	5,093,654 82	3,386,263 51	....	101,000 00	8,580,918 33	....
....	....	312,325 00	148,834 00	....	....	461,159 00	....
....	....	....	....	....	....	....	....
357,885 00	37,086 05	394,971 05	70,162 01	....	15,363 46	480,496 52	....
220,753 84	....	220,753 84	207,237 66	1,864 69	9,404 24	439,260 43	229,300 00
1,302,363 83	....	1,302,363 83	417,775 22	7,771 85	278,909 76	2,006,820 66	2,290,627 51

TABLE IV.—GRADUATED TABLE, SHOWING FOR EACH STATE OF THE UNION THE PUBLIC SCHOOL EXPENDITURE PER CAPITA OF THE SCHOOL POPULATION, AND THE ASSESSED VALUATION OF PROPERTY PER CAPITA OF THE TOTAL POPULATION.

Number.	STATES.	Public School expenditure *per capita* of the school population.	Assessed valuation of property *per capita* of the total population.
		$ cts.	$ cts.
1	Massachusetts	20 66	972 39
2	Nevada	19 17	605 79
3	Connecticut	12 92	600 15
4	Rhode Island	11 89	982 59
5	California	11 44	481 29
6	New Jersey	8 89	689 62
7	Nebraska	8 06	460 06
8	Illinois	7 97	190 13
9	Pennsylvania	7 86	353 04
10	Michigan	7 33	229 92
11	Iowa	7 10	253 91
12	New York	6 89	448 80
13	Ohio	6 86	438 13
14	Kansas	6 45	252 80
15	Vermont	6 09	310 23
16	Indiana	5 15	394 75
17	Wisconsin	4 86	316 16
18	Minnesota	4 85	191 36
19	Maryland	4 73	542 76
20	New Hampshire	4 46	468 31
21	Maine	4 06	357 71
22	Arkansas	3 53	194 38
23	Louisiana	3 17	349 93
24	Mississippi	2 95	214 10
25	West Virginia	2 84	317 97
26	Delaware	2 70	518 23
27	Missouri	2 65	323 08
28	Oregon	2 06	349 73
29	Alabama	1 49	157 24
30	Florida	91	173 00
31	Tennessee	91	202 35
32	Kentucky	60	310 02
33	North Carolina	48	121 69
34	Georgia		191 00
35	South Carolina		260 64
36	Texas		182 92
37	Virginia		298 27
	United States		358 06

NOTE. The Public School expenditure in Ontario *per capita* of the School population (5 and 16) for 1871 was only $4.32.

THE RELIGIOUS ELEMENT IN OUR SCHOOLS.

I had intended discussing in this Report some additional matters relating to the well being of our Public Schools, and on which legislation might be desirable. I had also intended referring to two or three points of gratifying interest in connection with our Schools; but having reached the reasonable limits of an Annual Report, I forbear. One point, to which I had desired to refer, was the patriotic spirit of unanimity which pervades all classes of the people in their cordial support of our Public School System, and the other was the pleasing fact of the satisfactory working of the Regulations in regard to the Religious Exercises and Instruction in our Schools. In regard to this latter point, the testimony of the late venerated Bishop Strachan, and of his courteous and venerable successor, Bishop Bethune, that I have done what I could to invest our School System with a Religious character, is especially gratifying to me now, at so advanced a period of my official connection with that System. In his Address at the recent Synod of the Clergy and Laity of the Church of England in the Diocese of Toronto, the Bishop made some kind references to my efforts in that direction. Subsequently, in reply to a Note of thanks which I addressed to him, he said :—

I have to express my gratification that I had the opportunity to bear my humble testimony to your zealous and righteous efforts to promote the sound Education of the youth of this Province. I believe that, in the endeavours to give this a moral and Religious direction, you have done all that, in the circumstances of the country, it was in your power to accomplish.*

My own views as to the possibility of imparting to the daily teaching of the School a Moral and Religious tone, and of the practicability of the Teacher bringing home to the young hearts of his Pupils the glorious truths of our common Christianity, are so admirably expressed by a prelate of the Episcopal Church in the United States, that I insert them in this place. Bishop Whipple, of Minnesota, in a recent Address at an Educational Convention, uttered the following impressive and eloquent remarks :—

The Common School, the Normal School, and the University, are the endowments of the State. The urgent necessities of the State created them. They are our common heritage. With my whole soul I protest against their perversion to give power into the hands of any sect, or party, in the State. The difficulty is not as real as we think. Our own bitter jealousies have blinded us to a whole world of Christian Truth, which lies behind this chaos of opinion, which has divided us into Sects. The things wherein we differ are our opinions, and the opinions of one class of men can never become the bond of union for all men. I would as soon believe that, because all men had the same features, their faces must be cast in the same mould, as to believe that all opinions about Religious Truth must be alike. I am sure that the things that keep us apart are for the most part things which never have been, and from their nature never can be, of the essentials of the faith. I am sure that whenever we realise this, and long for a regained brotherhood, we shall begin to feel heart beat against heart, and hand be joined unto hand.

There are truths that underlie all obligation. The Teachers of this day owe it to themselves and to their work to strive to get out of this din and conflict of sectarian strife into a higher atmosphere of faith.

It is not sectarian for the Teachers of a Christian State to teach its children that there is a God. It is not sectarian for the Teachers of a Christian State to look to God for help to teach helpless childhood to look to Him for help. It is not sectarian for the Teachers of a Christian State to tell His redeemed children of a Saviour. It is not sectarian for the Teachers of a Christian State to teach childhood's dependence on God's grace, reverence for His Law, and to confess His holy Name.

We are a Christian Land, or we are not. If not, we owe it to ourselves and our Homes to bow our heads and hearts in humble acceptance of these truths. There can be no reason why unbelief shall seal our lips to the Truth of God. If any Church, or Sect, of professed Christian men, object to such simple faith, it is because they fear a Christian Teacher's care will disarm the prejudice which is the corner-stone of their creed. For myself, I ask nothing which I am not willing to concede to every Christian man. I am willing to take my place beside any Christian Labourer in the State, and I pledge him every sympathy of my heart. If I have said one word more earnestly than I ought, I crave your pardon. God knows I would not wound any heart. I know of no civilization which I desire for my Home save that which comes by the Religion of Jesus Christ. So long I to see every nursery of the State a Christian School.

---

* Among his very latest utterances on the Separate School Question in the Synod in 1856, the late lamented Bishop Strachan thus referred to the Head of the Education Department and his labours :—

" One new feature which I consider of great value, and for which, I believe, we are altogether indebted to the able Superintendent of Education, deserves special notice : it is the introduction of Daily Prayers. We find that 454 [3,366 in 1871 !] Schools open and close with Prayer. This is an important step in the right direction, and only requires a reasonable extension to render the system in its interior, as it is already in its exterior, nearly complete. But till it receives this necessary extension, the whole system, in a religious and spiritual view, may be considered almost entirely dead. [The increase from 454 in 1856 to 3,366 in 1871 would have gratified the venerable Prelate had he lived.]

" I do not say that this is the opinion of the Reverend Doctor Ryerson, who no doubt believes his System very nearly perfect ; and as far as he is concerned, I am one of those who appreciate very highly his exertions, his unwearied assiduity, and his administrative capacity. I am also most willing to admit that he has carried out the meagre provisions of the several enactments that have any leaning to Religion, as far as seems consistent with a just interpretation of the School Law."—*Charge of 1856,* pages 15, 16.

18—XXIII.

We are working out one of the greatest problems of this world's history. It is a marvel that a Continent like America should have been for so many thousand years unoccupied by civilization, and more strange procedure of God, that after Spain, France and Holland had taken it under their possession, it should be given from the North to the South, and from the East to the West, to the race that represents Constitutional Government the world over. There are times in the world's history when races of men stand in peculiar relations to all other races. The great characteristic of the Saxon race at this time, is that it never loses its individuality. You may place its children in the Isles of the sea, in Africa, or India, and they are Anglo-Saxon still. In this land they are receiving unto themselves the people of every tongue and clime and kin, and in two generations their children are as one with us, and they have received our traditions, our customs, and our Laws.

In these Valleys of the Mississippi the fusing of nations into one family ought to teach us that there will grow up here a race of men more powerful for good, or terrible for evil, than any other people on the face of the earth.

My fellow Teachers, in such a field God has given us our work,—it is to lay broad and deep the foundations of a Christian State, which will soon have its million of souls. Do all work unto God. Plant your feet in His truth. Be his soldier to hate all shams and cant and cunning lies,—to be sure in thought,—in word,—in deed,—to have that gentleness, which is learning as a child sitting at Christ's feet, and that patient toil which knoweth how to work and wait, believing in God's promise that "He that goeth forth bearing precious seed and weeping, shall doubtless come again rejoicing, and bringing His sheaves with Him."

Concluding Remarks.

I have thus, as stated to Your Excellency last year, again entered somewhat fully into an exposition and justification of the various new features of our System of Public Instruction, which have been embodied in the "School Law Improvement Act of 1871." I have felt it the more necessary to furnish, in this Report, the many friends of our School System with the facts and reasonings illustrative of the necessity for the recent changes in our School Law, which influenced me in endeavouring to embody in our School Law of 1871, certain great principles which underlie and are common to every really comprehensive System of National Education. In fact, no intelligent person can carefully read over the extracts which I have given of the views and proceedings of Educationists in other Countries without coming to the conclusion, that, to have done less than we have done, would be to place this Province in the rear rather than abreast of other Educating Countries. They would have felt that I should have been recreant to my duty had I failed to strongly press upon the Government and Legislature the necessity of giving their highest sanction to the recommendations which I have made with a view to improve the School Law of this Province,—recommendations which were founded, (as I have shown in this Report), upon the knowledge and experience of the most accomplished Educationists of the present day.

After nearly thirty years' service in promoting what I believed to be the best interests of our School System, I am more than ever profoundly impressed with the conviction of the correctness of the views on these subjects which I expressed in my preliminary "Report on a System of Public Instruction for Upper Canada," which I submitted to the Government in 1846. It has been the purpose and aim of my life, since I assumed the direction of the Education Department, to give practical effect to these views, and, with the Divine favour, to secure and perpetuate to my Native Country the inestimable blessings of a free, comprehensive, Christian Education for every child in the land.

Toronto, October, 1872.   Egerton Ryerson.

18a—XXIII.

CHAPTER XVII.

INDUSTRIAL SCHOOLS IN THE CITIES AND CHIEF TOWNS OF ONTARIO.

In Chapters XXXI and XXXII of the preceding Volume of this Documentary History I have recorded the proceedings of a Public Meeting in 1868 at Toronto in regard to Vagrant Children, and the formation of a scheme of Industrial Schools to which such Children could be sent. An appeal was then made to the Board of School Trustees of Toronto to establish such a School, which, for various reasons then assigned, it declined to do. . . The project was again revived in 1871, on the passage of the Comprehensive School Act of 1871, under the authority of the Fortieth Section of that Act Boards of School Trustees in Cities and Towns were authorized to establish these Schools. The question was then brought up in the Toronto City Board of School Trustees and a Committee was appointed to consider the matter. That Committee brought in a Report as follows:—

That this question was considered by the Board in June, 1868, upon a Communication received from Professor Wilson, with accompanying Report, based upon Resolutions adopted at a meeting of influential gentlemen who took a warm interest in the welfare of the juvenile Vagrant population of this City, and the Board of that day, while frankly admitting the evil in question, and entertaining the greatest respect for the philanthropic movement in this direction by those gentlemen, being of opinion that they had, at that time, no legal powers to establish such an Institution, did not recommend Professor Wilson's scheme for the then present action. That the same question was again considered in April, 1869, but the Board being equally divided on this question no action could be taken. That the Legislature of Ontario at its last Session on the School Law Improvement Act of 1871, having by Section Forty-two given the Public School Boards of Cities authority to establish one, or more, Industrial Schools for otherwise neglected children, and to employ the means requisite to secure the attendance of such children, and for the support and management of such School, or Schools, your Committee have carefully considered the question referred to them, and have come to the conclusion that, in the opinion of your Committee, the time has arrived when an Industrial School ought to be established in this City. That having gone through the facts and figures relating to Industrial Schools in successful operation in Great Britain and the United States, your Committee are of opinion, that it is desirable to add to the knowledge thus acquired by means of the information printed and published with regard to these Institutions, a personal knowledge, by actual observation of the practical working of these Schools chiefly in the States of New York and Massachusetts, and, therefore, recommend that a Deputation, to be named by the Board, be empowered to visit certain Cities in the two States named, for the purpose of collecting such information as may enable an Industrial School to be established in this City on the most improved system calculated to realize the end in view.

Mr. W. B. McMurrich said that he considered that the Industrial Schools were the one link that was required to complete the chain of the Educational System in this City, and would remove a complaint that was often made against the Board, that their Public School System did not reach a certain class. The Board was empowered by the new School Act, to compel attendance at School, and, if they forced the vagrant class to attend the Public Schools, the result would be that a great many other children would leave them. In England the Industrial School System had proved very satisfactory.

Doctor Ogden said that the object of the report was only that they might obtain information with regard to the conduct of Industrial Schools in the United States, and, therefore, he hoped there would be no objection offered to it.

The Report was adopted, and the Committee arose and reported. Mr. Lee moved, seconded by Doctor Ogden, "That the Chairman of the Special Committee and Mr. Coatsworth be appointed a Committee to carry out the last clause of the Report." Carried.

The Deputation appointed by the Board having visited the United States and collected a great deal of information on the subject presented the following Report to a Special Committee of the Board of Trustees:—

SPECIAL REPORT OF THE COMMITTEE ON INDUSTRIAL SCHOOLS IN THE CITY OF TORONTO.

Your Committee having received from the Deputation appointed by the Board to visit the States of New York and Massachusetts, a full and comprehensive Report in regard to the form and working of Industrial and Reformatory Schools in those portions of the above States that were visited, have now, in obedience to the Resolution passed by the Board, to submit the following information for its guidance, embracing in the same the information supplied by the Deputation; and in doing so, would remark that they have endeavoured to place the facts at their disposal in as concise a form as possible, dealing primarily with the general principles, or groundwork, of the methods employed, leaving other information, as regards the details, to be embodied as Schedules to the Report.

Authority to Establish such Schools in Ontario.

It will be in the recollection of the Board that the subject of Industrial Schools is not now brought forward for the first time. On the 19th of April, 1868, a very large and influential Meeting of citizens was held in the Rooms of the Canadian Institute, with a view to the establishment of Schools of this class for reclaiming Vagrant children of both sexes, and a series of very important Resolutions were passed by the Meeting, which were afterwards transmitted to the Board of School Trustees with a request for their joint coöperation.

The plan proposed was based on voluntary aid to be given by the citizens, who were to supply the Food and Clothing to the Scholars, the educational part of the system to be under the control of the School Board. The Committee on School Management, in their Report, declining to recommend the adoption of the plan proposed,—owing to the then existing state of the School Law,—expressed their opinion that two things were vitally important to the success of such Schools:—1st. The entire separation, through the night as well as the day, of these juvenile Vagrants, for a period longer, or shorter, according to circumstances, from all association with the corrupt sources by which they are surrounded and, of course, influenced, as experience has fully proved that nothing short of complete isolation can or will meet the question; and 2nd. The securing of the object in view by a Compulsory Attendance.

The matter was again brought before the Board during the ensuing year, on a motion to bring the advisability of establishing such a School under the notice of the Provincial Legislature; but their being an equality of votes, the question was carried in the negative.

At the last Meeting of the Legislature, the School Law was amended by 34 Victoria, Chapter 33, and Section 42 of the amending Act provides that,—

"The Public School Board of each City, Town, and Village, may establish one, or more, Industrial Schools for otherwise neglected children, and make all needful Regulations and employ the means requisite to secure the attendance of such children, and for the support, management, and discipline of such School, or Schools."

The same Act gives the right to all children to attend School and introduces the principle of Compulsory Attendance.

The Board, by the passage of the above Act, being now in a position to deal with the subject legally and effectually, it is but right that Toronto, the Capital of Ontario, should take the lead in providing for her Vagrant population that training and that kind of education which they so greatly require, and from which they are debarred it may be by the extreme poverty, ignorance, vice, greed of gain, or indifference of their Parents, or Guardians; a System of Education and Industrial Training that will convert what would otherwise be the costly inmates of our Gaols and Penitentiaries into industrious citizens, capable of working for the common good, and with honour to themselves and those connected with them.

The Necessity for these Schools.

1st. To reach a class not yet provided for by our City Schools and complete the system of natural education. Although our Schools are Free to all, still experience has shown that the Vagrant class and the children of Parents too poor to provide them with Clothes, or whose employment is thought necessary for the family sustenance, seldom, or ever, find their way into our Schools. In the year 1863 a School Census was taken under the authority of the Board, when it was found that no less than 1,165 Protestant children of School age were not attending any School, or receiving any kind of Education. This number in the year 1868 had risen to 1,600 children, and with our growing population, the number may now be taken to be considerably larger than this. How important, then, to provide at once for these poor children growing up in our midst in ignorance and neglect.

2nd. To enable the Board properly and efficiently to carry out the truant system, or compulsory attendance at our Schools, and thus ensure the education of all at the expense of all.

Were the Board at present to put in force the power given them to enforce attendance at our Schools, the first difficulty to be overcome would be, where to send children of the class referred to? To send them to our Schools in the condition in which they would most likely be found, without the necessary Clothing, dirty, and with all their wild untutored habits, must tend to demoralize our present Schools and impair their efficiency. Proper Accommodation must, therefore, at once be found in the shape of an Industrial School, or allow the School Law to remain a dead letter.

3nd As a matter of self-defence and gain, to add to the wealth of the community by rendering the vagrant and neglected class industrious, teaching them to earn an honest livelihood, and thus lessen the enormous expenditure required to keep them from doing us harm, or punishing them for harming us.

The truth of this proposition is so universally recognized as to require but few remarks. It has been conclusively proved that the more remunerative the employment, the less incentive there is to crime, and the greater the self-respect. In Industrial Schools the inmates are taught different branches of Trade, so that, on leaving the School for active life. they find themselves able at once to command employment at remunerative wages, being educated and skilled Workmen, and the increase of "self-respect" enables the delinquent to look back on his former life with fear and trembling, and to be avoided in future.

Lastly. As a matter of philanthropy, to house the homeless, reclaim the vagrant, elevate the debased, reform the vicious, and prevent pauperism, from which this Province is so happily free.

Industrial Schools in Great Britain.

Your Committee are indebted for the following information to the able Report of Mr. Sidney Turner, the Inspector appointed to visit the certified Reformatory and Industrial Schools of Great Britain, published in 1869.

There are over seventy-seven certified Industrial Schools at present in operation in Great Britain, two being School Ships, where Boys are sent to be educated and trained as Sailors. Four others, Farm Schools, with land attached for Farm, or Garden cultivation; and two free Ragged Industrial Schools supported by voluntary subscription; and these Schools are being each year considerably enlarged, and their number added to.

These Schools are of two classes,—1st. For both sexes, in which a certain number of the children attending are day Scholars, who receive instruction, but are only partially fed; the 2nd, for either Boys, or Girls, exclusively, in which the children are entirely lodged and boarded, and the majority detained under Magistrate's Warrant. Thirty Schools are in operation in Great Britain under the first class, and suit children under twelve years of age, placing children more on the footing of common life, but are not found suited when children over this age are admitted. There were over 5,738 children under instruction in the second class on the 31st of December, 1868, the number admitted for the year being 2,488, the ages of the children varying from seven to fifteen years. Of this number 99 were illegitimate, 322 were orphans, 1,000 had either lost Father, or Mother, 287 had been totally deserted, 95 were children of destitute or criminal parents, and only one-third had both parents living and able to take care of them.

The children so detained are kept during good behaviour, and then apprenticed out or placed in some kind of employment, and the result of the system has been very marked. Of the 3,282 children discharged since the passing of the English Industrial Act, 1857, up to December the 31st, 1868, about two-thirds, videlicet, 2,111, had been placed in employment and doing well, 173 had died, 230 had been committed to Reformatories, 391 had been specially discharged as diseased, imbecile, illegally committed, or incorrigible; 333 had absconded and were not recovered.

A large number of children of the poorest and most neglected class attend the Industrial Schools in large Towns, such as Hull, Leeds, etcetera, voluntarily as day Scholars, with very beneficial results. It is remarked, however, that this class is decreasing, while the proportion of those committed regularly for detention is rapidly advancing.

These Schools are supported mainly by aid from the State and local taxation, also by Subscriptions, Legacies, and profit on Industrial departments; the total Receipts for the year 1868 amounting to £122,682 11s.

In the Industrial departments the following seem to be the principal Trades. or occupations, taught:—Tailoring, Shoemaking, Printing, Gardening, Cabinet-making, Carpentry, Sack-making, etcetera.

The Inspector, in closing his Report for 1868, says:—

The working and results of the Reformatory Schools will stand the test, I think, of the closest investigation, and when another year or two's experience has brought the accounts and operations of the Industrial Schools to the same well-defined and organised condition, I believe they will be equally able to meet and satisfy inquiry as to the good they do, and the method and costs of doing it.

These remarks are now realized to the fullest degree.

Industrial Schools in the United States.

The following Schools visited by Messieurs Coatsworth and McMurrich, in the States of New York and Massachusetts, may be taken as types of the different Systems at present in operation in the United States, for the reclaiming and educating of the Vagrant, neglected, and criminal classes.

1. Western House of Refuge.

Situation.—The Western House of Refuge for Juvenile Delinquents is located about one mile and a quarter's walk from the central part of the City of Rochester, and embraces forty-two Acres of excellent land. Six and a half Acres are surrounded by a stone Wall twenty-two feet in height, within which stand all the Buildings belonging to the Institution, except the Barns. Twenty-six acres are constantly under cultivation, and ten Acres used for pasturage. The Buildings enclose three sides of a quadrangle, and are tasteful, though plain in outward architecture, and built in a very substantial manner; the Board of Managers believing and acting on the principle "that true economy for the State demands that all of its buildings should be of the most durable and substantial kind." A description of the interior arrangements is added in Schedule A to this Report.

Its Objects.—The Refuge was originally built for the reception of both males and females; but by an amending Clause to the Act of Incorporation, only Boys under the age of sixteen years are now admitted. Being purely reformatory in its character, only Boys can legally be committed to the Refuge for Vagrancy, or, on 'conviction of any criminal offence by any Court having authority to make such commitments, the Managers having power to place the children committed to their care, during the minority of such children, at such employments and cause them to be instructed in such branches of useful knowledge as shall be suitable to their years and capacities, with further powers to bind them out as Apprentices or Servants. Although purely reformatory, the Deputation were given to understand that it was probable legislation would soon be asked for, to admit of Boys being received on the voluntary principle by surrender with the consent of their Parents, or Guardians. The object of the Institution is, therefore, as mentioned in one of their Annual Reports, "to receive such Boys and benefit them so far as possible, mentally, morally, and physically; to give them a fair education; to induce them, if possible, to break off their bad habits and to form good habits; and to teach them to be industrious, and to earn their livelihood by honest labour."

The System Employed.—It is the constant endeavour of the Managers to do away with the penal characteristics of the Institution, and cultivate Home influences as much as possible. With this end in view, the Officers are instructed to kindly reprimand violations of the Rules of the Institution by any of the inmates. "To encourage cleanliness of person, habits of neatness, pride in dress, and personal appearance, order and gentlemanly deportment, never to call a Boy by any other name than his real name, and, as far as possible, to break up the practice of their calling one another by nicknames, to answer and treat every Officer, or other Person about the Premises with civility and respect. To watch the language of the Boys, and see that none use vulgar or profane language; that they are kept clean, their Clothing whole, Buttons all on and in use, and that their Clothes are of suitable size. All offences to be reported to the Superintendent, who alone punishes. Boys to be treated kindly; Officers never to show passion, but firmness and evenness of temper, and be dignified and never use profane, or vulgar, language. Such are the general Rules guiding the working of the Institution; the two great elements, however, or guiding Rules, are Education and Employment. The education of the inmates, numbering 362, for 1870, is presided over by two Principals and a staff of seven Teachers whose great aim is to impart a thorough knowledge of the most useful branches of an English Education, and so instruct the Boys in such a manner as will contribute to their future success in life. Reading, Writing, and Arithmetic are the principal subjects taught, and before a Boy can be discharged, he is required to have obtained a certain proficiency in each of these subjects, no matter what his progress in the Industrial department has been. The number of hours employed in study, and in work is given under Schedule A. The Deputation were particularly struck with the pleasant, large, and airy School Rooms of the Institution, furnished throughout with the latest and most approved style of modern School Furniture, the walls particularly, nicely painted and decorated, and ornamented with choice Mottoes rendered the Rooms particularly attractive.

In the Industrial departments, the Boys are employed in Shoemaking and Seating Chairs with Cane and Flag; work being done under contract; while the Tailoring, Shoemaking. Baking, Washing, and other work required for the House are also performed by the Boys. Last year the sum of $17,970.60 was obtained from the labours of the inmates. In this way the Boys are fitted for the practical duties of life "by inculcating habits of neatness, order, promptness, and thoughtful active industry, and instructing them in some useful Trade whereby, on their release, they may be enabled to find remunerative employment, and not be compelled to again resort to crime."

The system of classification is carried out as far as practicable, separating the younger and less hardened of the inmates from the older and more vicious.

Boys are not discharged and indentured as formerly, but are simply placed in the care of some proper Person to remain during good behaviour, and, in case of delinquency to be returned to the House. Two years is the average length of time a Boy is detained.

The Institution is maintained by the State at an annual cost of say $40,000.

2. Rochester "Children's Home."

This Institution is supported principally by Taxation by the City; receiving also a small Appropriation from the State; and was erected for the purpose of receiving Truant, Homeless, Destitute, and Vagrant children, not convicted of crime, and giving them a Secular and Industrial Education.

Children of both sexes are received and detained during good behaviour, being housed, clothed, fed and educated. The Teachers seem to be very faithful in the discharge of their duties. The children are employed in Chair Seating.

3. The House of Refuge, New York.

Is situated on Randall's Island, in the City of New York, and corresponds to the Institution at Rochester, with this difference, that children of both sexes are received. On the 1st of January, 1871, there were 690 inmates. The whole number of children received into the Institution since its opening in 1825, being 13,727.

Its Objects are similar to those of the Rochester House, videlicet, the reforming of those committed to their care, all of whom are committed by Magistrate's Warrant, either for Vagrancy, or petty offences, and in this way these youthful Offenders are saved from the contaminating influence of older and confirmed criminals, to which they would be exposed if committed to the ordinary Jails and Prisons.

The System Employed is also similar to the Institution at Rochester, with this exception, that a further incentive to good conduct is provided by giving to those children beyond the age of sixteen, after proper trial and the acquisition of the requisite skill, a part of the price paid by the contractor for their labour; the Managers reserving merely enough to pay their cost to the House. This has had a wonderful influence on the Inmates, and has the effect of bridging over the period that elapses between the time of their leaving the Institution and getting employment in the Trades which they have been taught. They thus go forth with a good character, skill in workmanship, means in their pockets, and an unwavering trust in the promises made to them, together with the foundations of a good education.

The Educational Department is carried on under the superintendence of a Principal and staff of eleven Teachers, who give the inmates a thorough drilling in Arithmetic, Reading, and Writing, and if possible impart some Geographical knowledge; and no child is eligible to a discharge who has not passed the third class in School, which would insure a knowledge of the ground rules of Arithmetic, and ability to read and write.

The Industrial Departments consist of Shoe-making, Wire-working, Hoop-skirt manufacturing, and the making, mending, and washing of Clothes by the Girls, for the whole Establishment. The amount realized during the year 1870, from the labour of the Inmates, was $39,218.53. The Institution is supported by an annual allowance from the State, of $40,000, and from the City Comptroller and Board of Education, of $30,000.

Both the Institutions at Rochester and New York have resident Chaplains for imparting to the children Religious Instruction.

4. *The New York Catholic Protectory.*

This Institution is situated at West-Chester, and receives children of both sexes on commitment by Magistrate's Warrant, who belong to the Roman Catholic faith, and is supported in the same manner as the House of Refuge on Randall's Island, with similar objects in view. Thirteen Teachers are employed, giving instruction under the superintendence of the Rector, Brother Teliow. There are thirteen Class Rooms in use, each containing about an average number of eighty Pupils. The great majority of the children,—some 900,—get on an average six hours of School exercise per day; and advanced Lads, who have attained their sixteenth year, besides their work during the day, attend night School. The Industrial department is prosecuted on the principle of varying the kind of Trades taught, lest by one Trade being overdone, instead of making the Inmates good and useful members of society, the effect would simply be to propagate a caste of paupers. The Industrial branches consist at present of Tailoring, Printing, Stereotyping, Shoemaking, Music, Gardening, etcetera, and in the female department, Shirtmaking, Washing, instruction in special Sewing, Machine work, Laundry, and Housework. The children, as in the other Institutions, are indentured out, or get situations when leaving the Institution.

5. *The Children's Aid Society of New York.*

This Society and that of the New York Juvenile Asylum are doing a noble work in the City of New York. The oldest of these is the New York Juvenile Asylum, established with a view of taking charge of Truant, Disobedient, and Neglected children between the ages or seven and fourteen years, who might be either committed to its care by Magistrates, or voluntarily surrendered to its custody. Its main object is to give the children a suitable moral and intellectual training, and to fit them by habits of industry for the practical affairs of life. An important department of its business is to bind out, with the consent of relatives and friends, the children as Apprentices to useful occupations. The Children's Aid Society, founded in 1855, is managed upon a wholly different theory, the leading thought being to elevate the character of the degraded and neglected child, and to so reform its habits of life that it shall develop a new character, which will be able to withstand the shock of ordinary temptations and from which will spring new and virtuous habits. The agencies used are free Reading Rooms, Lodging Houses, Industrial Schools, and a system of emigration. It claims to bring 20,000 different poor children under its influence in a single year, and is conducted on the voluntary principle.

The Deputation visited the Newsboys' Lodging House and two of the Industrial Schools, and inquired minutely into the working of the latter.

The policy of "diffusion rather than aggregation," of making use of the natural Home offered in the County Districts for orphan and homeless children, rather than the Asylum, is steadily carried out by the Society, hence the Deputation found that these Industrial Schools were for the most part educational, where the children, however, received Food and Clothing as well, and in some instances were housed. In other words, the Schools were made use of by those children not able, from some reason, to attend regularly the daily City Schools, or those poor and destitute children of the City, unable to attend from poverty, who here receive the comforts of a home and a sound elementary education until transplanted to the west to the home influences of some western Employer, where many are now property holders and respectable Farmers and Mechanics.

There are on the rolls of the Schools 9,429 Pupils, and the costs of keeping up the Schools for these children amounts to $49,880.33.

The Emigration Committee, the peculiar feature of the system, has, since the year 1854, provided western homes for 25,215 children, the number sent last year being 3,386.

6. *Industrial Schools in Massachusetts.*

The Deputation have not thought it necessary to go into details in regard to the Schools at Lancaster and Westboro, and Deer Park in the Harbour of Boston, as their general features are very similar to one or other of the Institutions which have just been touched upon. There is one feature, however, pertaining especially to the two first Schools, mentioned, videlicet, the dividing the children into Homes, each one distinct and complete in itself, and surrounded with all the home influence possible. This system has worked very well, and is worthy of imitation.

Your Committee have thus endeavoured to give the general features of the different Systems, and besides the additional information in the Schedules to this Report, have collected together other facts connected with the details, which will be reported upon as required.

Recommendations of the Committee.

From the above information and facts your Committee would recommend,—

1. That the system of Compulsory Attendance be put into operation in the City of Toronto, and a Truant Officer appointed in the Eastern and Western divisions of the City to see that the same is properly carried out.

2. That the establishment and equipment of an Industrial School is desirable.

3. That the School partake of the Reformatory and Voluntary character, so happily combined in some of the above Institutions in the United States, due provision being made for the classification of the Inmates.

4. That such amendments be asked for to the existing School Law, if necessary, as will give the Board the power of detention in the School of the children committed to their care during minority, or until such time as the Board may consent to their discharge.

5. That a special application be made through the Education Department to the Legislature for a Special Grant from the School Fund towards the establishment of the said School to cover the expenses over and above that which would be incurred, for purely educational purposes.

The Committee, in closing their Report, cannot but convey their thanks to the Managers of the Institutions visited, and particularly to Doctor Charles H. Hoyt, Secretary of the Board of State Charities for the State of New York and other friends, for their very cordial reception of, and attention to the Deputation and the valuable Reports received from them.

TORONTO, 26th December, 1871.   W. BARCLAY McMURRICH, Chairman of Committee.

Schedule A.—1. Interior Arrangements of the Western House of Refuge at Rochester.

The centre Building of the House proper fronts the East, and is eighty-six feet wide, sixty feet deep, and three stories in height above the basement. There are two Wings extending to the North and South, each one hundred and forty-eight feet long, thirty-two feet deep, and two stories in height above the Basement, excepting the square towers at the extremities, which are three stories in height. The whole front of the Buildings, it will be seen, is three hundred and eighty-two feet in length. Two other Wings of similar dimensions, and extending directly Westward, are connected with the front at the extremities. In the Basement of the centre Building are a Kitchen for the Superintendent, Dining Room and Store Rooms, and also similar apartments for the subordinate Officers. On the first floor are the Parlour and Visiting Room of the Superintendent, the Manager's Room, or Office, and a Room for one of the subordinates; on the second floor are Rooms for the subordinate Officers and the Superintendent, and on the third floor, occupying the whole area of the Building, is the Chapel, neatly arranged and furnished, and affording abundant room for five hundred persons.

In the Basement of the North Wing is a Washing Room for Boys, furnished with a plunging Bath twenty feet long, by fifteen wide and three and a quarter feet deep, and with water pipes so arranged that every one can perform his ablutions under running water and free from interruption by others; a Store Room is also in this Wing. On the first floor is a Laundry, Seamstress' Room and Apartments for Officers and Employés. The Northwest Wing has in its Basement a spacious Dining Room, and Cook Room adjoining; also a Tailor Shop and Shoe Shop, where the Clothes and Shoes of the Inmates are made and repaired, and on the first floor a large fine School Room. The Basement and first floors of the South and Southwest Wings have a Wash Room, Dining Room, Cook Room and School Room corresponding to those on the North side.

The Upper floors of all the Wings are arranged into Dormitories for the Inmates, and furnish separate sleeping accommodations for five hundred Boys.

In the Northwest and Southwest corners of the inclosure are two Workshops, built of brick, each forty-five feet by one hundred feet, and three stories in height, affording abundant room for the employment of five hundred Boys.

The Hospital on the South side of the Premises, and connected with the corridor which unites the South and West Wings, is built of brick, thirty-three by forty-one feet, and two stories above the Basement The ceilings are sixteen feet in height, and the whole is ventilated and heated on the most approved plan.

A stone wall eight feet high extends from the centre of the Buildings to the rear inclosure wall, dividing the Building and Grounds into two equal corresponding parts, one for the larger Boys and the other for the smaller Boys, who are thus entirely separated.

2. *Number of Hours for Work, and Study, and Play during the Year.*

	Working honrs.	School hours.	Play hours.
January	6¾	4	1¼
February	7	3¾	1¾
March	7½	3½	2
April	8	3½	2
May	8¼	3½	2¼
June	8¼	3½	2¼
July	8¼	3½	2¼
August	8¼	3½	2¼
September	8	3½	2
October	7½	3½	2
November	7	3½	2
December	6¾	4	1¼

Schedule B.—New York House of Refuge.

1. *General Rules.*

1. Tell no lies.
2. Always do the best you can.

2. *Table Showing the Cost of Support per Capita, Yearly and Daily, in the Different Items of Expense; also the Gross Cost, the Earnings by the Children, and the Net Cost to the State and City.—Average Number of Inmates, 671 36-52.*

Provisions.			Clothing.			Salaries.		
Whole Amount.	Per Capita Annually.	Per Capita Daily.	Whole Amount.	Per Capita Annually.	Per Capita Daily.	Whole Amount.	Per Capita Annually.	Per Capita Daily.
\$ c.	\$ c. m.	\$ c. m.	\$ c.	\$ c. m	\$ c. m	\$ c.	\$ c. m	c. m.
39,885 57	59 35 9½	0 16 2½	7,115 30	10 58 8	0 2 9	27,712 35	41 23 4	11 3

2. *Table Showing the Cost of Support per Capita.*—Continued.

Fuel and Light.			Bedding and Furniture.			Building and Repairs.		
Whole Amount.	Per Capita Annually.	Per Capita Daily.	Whole Amount.	Per Capita Annually.	Per Capita Daily.	Whole Amount.	Per Capita Annually.	Per Capita Daily.
$ c. 4,562 71	$ c. 6 79	c. m. 1 8½	$ c. 2,645 16	$ c. m 3 92 1½	c. m. 1 7	$ c. 1,784 03	$ c. m 2 65 4½	c. m. 0 7.2

Books and Stationery for Schools and Chapels.			Hospital.			All other items of expense not included above.		
Whole Amount.	Per Capita Annually.	Per Capita Daily.	Whole Amount.	Per Capita Annually.	Per Capita Daily.	Whole Amount.	Per Capita Annually.	Per Capita Daily.
$ c. 645 15	$ c. 0 96	c. m. 0 2½	$ c. 159 28	c. m. 23 7	c. m. 0 0.65	$ c. 3,610 62	$ c. m. 5 35 8	c. m. 1 4½

Gross Expense.			Earnings by Children and received from Dock, etcetera.			Net expense.		
Whole Amount.	Per Capita Annually.	Per Capita Daily.	Whole Amount.	Per Capita Annually.	Per Capita Daily.	Whole Amount.	Per Capita Annually.	Per Capita Daily.
$ c. 88,120 37	$ c. 131 13	c. m. 35 9	$ c. 40,458 20	$ c. 60 20	c. m. 16 5	$ c. 47,662 16	c. m. 70 93	c. m. 19 4

3. *Table showing the Work Done in the Female Department during the Year 1870.*

Dresses made	319	Napkins	48
Aprons	228	Crumb Cloths	4
Chemises	126	Rollers	46
Skirts	58	Carpet Balls	144
Shirts	672	Pairs of Pants	1,248
Under-shirts	44	Jackets	782
Sheets	83	Caps	720
Pillow-cases	30	Pairs Suspenders	497
Towels	64	Pairs Mittens	13
Night-gowns	4	Garments repaired	54,726
Drawers	39	Stockings mended	16,851
Bed-ticks	36	Pieces washed	210,183
Table Cloths	7		

Schedule C.—Compulsory Attendance in Boston.

The Truant System has been carried out to perfection in this City, until now it has come to be regarded quite generally as an indispensable feature in the System of Public Education. Ten Officers are employed, who have an Office for Head Quarters in the Court House where they meet every Monday morning, and meet the Superintendent the first Monday in each month for consideration. A weekly Report is sent in of the number of cases investigated and the results. During last year no less than 15,000 cases were investigated. Each Officer has one or more order boxes located in his District, to which the Teachers of his District may send their Truant Cards, containing notices of cases to be investigated. Each School possesses a Truant Book as well. Convicted Truants, Absentees and Vagrants are sent to the Institution on Deer Island.

CHAPTER XVIII.

PROCEEDINGS OF THE LEGISLATIVE ASSEMBLY OF ONTARIO, 1871-72.

December 8th, 1871. His Excellency the Lieutenant-Governor opened the Session by the usual Speech in which he said :—

The liberal measures which the Legislature adopted at its last Session to improve our System of National Education, by making the Public Schools Free by Law, by providing for their more efficient Inspection, by giving stability to and elevating the profession of Teachers, and by rendering practically symmetrical and coherent the Public and High Schools have been brought into operation, and they are likely to fulfil the most sanguine expectations of the friends of thorough and universal Education.

The demand for regularly trained Teachers has augmented from year to year, and the number of young persons desirous of properly qualifying themselves for the profession of teaching by a regular Course of Training is so largely increasing, that it may be worthy of your consideration whether additional facilities should not be provided for that purpose.

Nor less useful do I think will prove the measures of the same Session for providing by a new School of Technology now shortly to be opened for preparatory Education of skilled men as Engineers, Managers, and Operators in the various Manufacturing Establishments, and in the Steamboat and Railway Systems of the Country. When we find these Establishments are springing up and dotting our Country on every side, and a network of Railways is covering its surface, we should be wanting in wisdom and common prudence not to provide, as every progressive People is providing, for the Scientific and Practical Education of classes of men to conduct these vast and important operations, and thus develop the latent and unmeasured resources of our favoured Land. No maxim of civil government is more sound than that each Country should provide, as far as possible, by its own culture and skill, for the supply of its own wants, and the development of its own resources, and it is unquestionable that money expended to educate Men for these purposes is a most profitable public Investment.

I am to inform you that arrangements are in active progress for the establishment of a School of Agriculture. A suitable Site comprising six hundred Acres of Land, of varied soil and easy access to the Public, has been purchased; and no time will be lost in bringing this important scheme into operation; whereby those of our youth who desire to follow agricultural pursuits may obtain the education specially adapted to their wants.

December 11th, 1871. The Order of the Day for taking into consideration the Speech of His Excellency the Lieutenant-Governor having been read, it was proposed to state :—

That we are pleased to hear the statement by His Excellency that the liberal measures which the Legislature adopted at its last Session to improve our System of National Education by making the Public Schools Free by Law, by providing for their more efficient Inspection, by giving stability to and elevating the profession of Teachers, and by rendering practically symmetrical and coherent the Public and High Schools have been brought into operation, and that they are likely to fulfil the most sanguine expectations of the friends of thorough and universal Education.

5. That, recognizing the fact that the demand for regularly trained Teachers has augmented from year to year, and the number of young Persons desirous of properly qualifying themselves for the profession of teaching by a regular Course of Training is so largely increasing, we shall gladly act on the suggestion of His Excellency and consider whether additional facilities should not be provided for that purpose.

That we believe with His Excellency, that not less useful will prove the measure of the same Session for providing, by a new School of Technology now shortly to be opened for preparatory education of skilled men as Engineers, Managers and Operators in the various Mechanical and Manufacturing Establishments, and in the Steamboat and Railway Systems of the Country; that, when we find that these Establishments are springing up and dotting our Country on every side, and a network of Railways is covering its surface, we should be wanting in wisdom and common prudence not to provide, as every progressive People is providing, for the Scientific and Practical Education of the classes of Men to conduct these vast and important operations, and thus develop the latent and unmeasured resources of our favoured Land. We also agree with His Excellency that no maxim of civil Government is more sound than that each Country should provide, as far as possible by its own culture and skill, for the supply of its own wants and the development of its own resources, and that it is unquestionable that money expended to educate Men for these purposes is a most profitable public Investment.

That we receive with satisfaction the information that arrangements are in active progress for the establishment of a School of Agriculture, that a suitable Site, comprising six hundred Acres of Land, of varied soil and easy access to the Public, has been purchased, and no time will be lost in bringing this important scheme into operation, whereby those of our youth who desire to follow Agricultural pursuits may obtain the education specially adapted to their wants.

December 13th, 1871. The following Petition was received and read:—Of Mr. Archibald McKellar and others, of Kent, praying that an Act may pass to incorporate the Wilberforce Educational Institute.

December 14th, 1871. The following Petition was received and read:—Of Mr. John George and others, of New Hamburgh, praying for the repeal of certain clauses of the School Act.

December 15th, 1871. The following Petition was received and read:—Of Mr. John Johnson and others, of Hastings, praying that the School Act be kept intact as to the Superannuation of School Teachers.

December 22nd, 1871. The following Petition was received and read:—Of Mr. W. C. Parkhill and others, of Ontario; also, of Mr. John Dowswell and others, of Ontario, severally praying that the Teachers' Superannuated Sections of the School Act may not be repealed.

The House, according to Order, resolved itself into a Committee, to consider the Motion proposed, 'That a Supply be granted to Her Majesty," for Education, videlicet:—

	$ cts.
Grammar Schools	28,000 00
Separate Schools	4,500 00
Superannuated Teachers	5,000 00
Normal Schools	2,000 00
Educational Depository	11,500 00
Journal of Education	430 00
Museum	500 00
Salaries	4,000 00
Contingencies	800 00
	$56,730 00

January 22nd, 1872. The following Petition was received and read:—Of the Trinity College School of Port Hope, praying that an Act may pass to incorporate the School.

January 24th, 1872. The following Petition was received and read:—Of Mr. James H. Wilson and others, Public School Teachers of Ontario, praying that no alteration be made in the Law respecting the Superannuated Teachers' Fund.

January 25th, 1872. Mr. C. J. Rykert, from the Committee on Standing Orders, presented their Fourth Report which was read as follows:—Your Committee have examined the following Petitions, and find that the notices in each case are correct:—Of Mr. Archibald McKellar and others, praying that an Act may pass to incorporate the Wilberforce Educational Institute; of Trinity College School of Port Hope, praying that an Act may pass to incorporate the School.

The following Bills were introduced and read the first time:—

Bill, (Number 37), intituled:—"An Act to incorporate the Trinity College School." —Mr. A. T. H. Williams, (Durham).

Bill, (Number 52), intituled:—"An Act to incorporate the Wilberforce Educational Institute."—Mr. J. Dawson. Referred to the Committee on Private Bills.

January 26th, 1872. The following Petition was received and read:—Of Mr. John Sutton and other Public School Teachers, praying that no alteration be made in the Law respecting the Superannuated Teachers' Fund.

January 29th, 1872. The following Petition was received and read:—Of Mr. R. E. Canfield and others, Public School Teachers of Ontario, praying that no alteration be made in the Law respecting the Superannuated Teachers' Fund.

On motion of Mr. F. W. Cumberland, seconded by Mr. A. T. H. Williams, (Durham).

Resolved, That an humble Address be presented to His Excellency the Lieutenant-Governor, praying His Excellency to cause to be laid before this House, a Return of the Names and Residences of the Members of the Senate of the University of Toronto during the years 1867, 1868, 1869, 1870 and 1871, respectively, of the numbers of the Meetings of the Senate called and actually held during the said years respectively, and of the number of the said Meetings in each of the years aforenamed at which each of the Members of the said Senate respectively attended.

Mr. James Bethune moved, seconded by Mr. W. Robinson, That an humble Address be presented to His Excellency, the Lieutenant-Governor, praying His Excellency to cause to be laid before this House, copies of all Regulations, issued by the Council of Public Instruction respecting Public Schools, and copies of the Programme of Studies prescribed for Public Schools and High Schools.

Mr. D. Sinclair moved in amendment, seconded by Mr. H. Finlayson, That the Resolution just read be amended by adding after the word "School," and before the word "and" in the last line but one, the following words,—"now in force; a list of the Persons to whom the Council granted Certificates; a Statement of the results in detail of the late Examination for Certificates of Qualification of School Teachers; copies of the Minutes of the Council of Public Instruction for the year 1867, 1868, 1869, 1870 and 1871."

The Amendment having been put, was carried, and it was,—

Resolved, That an humble Address be presented to His Excellency the Lieutenant-Governer, praying His Excellency to cause to be laid before this House, copies of all Regulations issued by the Council of Public Instruction respecting Public Schools, now in force; a list of the Persons to whom the Council granted Certificates; a Statement of the results in detail of the late Examination for Certificates of Qualification of School Teachers; copies of the Minutes of the Council of Public Instruction for the years 1867, 1868, 1869, 1870 and 1871, and copies of the Programme prescribed for Public Schools and High Schools.

January 30th, 1872. The following Petitions were received and read:—Of Brother Aphraates and others, of Toronto, praying that an Act may pass to incorporate the Brothers of the Christian Schools of Ontario; of the Ladies' Colleges of Ottawa, praying that an Act may pass to amend their Act of Incorporation; of Mr. G. W. Sheldon and other Public School Teachers, praying that no alteration be made in the Law relating to the Superannuated Teachers' Fund; of Mr. Joseph Staples and others of Victoria, praying that the Education Department may furnish Books, Maps, etcetera, to Schools.

The following Bill was introduced and read the first time:—Bill, (Number 80), intituled "An Act to amend the Law respecting Public Schools."—Mr. James Bethune.

NOTE. As this Bill did not pass, I insert it as follows:—

BILL.—AN ACT TO AMEND THE LAW RESPECTING PUBLIC SCHOOLS.

Her Majesty, by and with the advice of the Legislative Assembly of the Province of Ontario, enacts as follows:—

34 V., c. 33, s. 2, amended.

1. The Second Section of the Act of the Parliament of Ontario passed in the Thirty-fourth year of the Reign of Her Majesty, chaptered Thirty-three, and intituled:—"An Act to improve the Common and Grammar Schools of the Province of Ontario," is hereby repealed, and the following Section substituted in lieu thereof:—

High School and Public School accommodation.

(2) Every High School Corporation shall provide adequate Accommodation for all children of School age in their School Division and Municipality, and each Public School Corporation shall provide such School Accommodation as the majority of the Trustees shall from time to time deem adequate for all the children of School age in their School Section, or Municipality.

s. 20 amended.

3. The Twentieth Section of the said Act is hereby repealed, and the following Section shall be substituted in lieu thereof:—

Residences for teachers.

(20) The Trustees of any Public School Section, or Municipality, shall after a Resolution to provide a Residence for a Teacher has been passed by the votes of a majority of the Ratepayers present at the Annual Meeting have the same authority to provide such Residence as they now have to provide a School Site in their Section, or Municipality.

Ordered, That the Bill be read the Second time on Friday next.

January 31st, 1872. The following Petitions were received and read:—Of Trinity College of Toronto, praying to be exempt from Municipal Taxation; of Mr. Joseph G. Ward and others, Public School Teachers, praying that no alteration may be made in the Law relating to Superannuated Teachers' Fund; of Mr. George A. McIntyre and others; also of Mr. Robert Fletcher and others; also of Mr. Robert McQueen and others, all Public School Teachers, severally praying that an Act may pass to repeal the Superannuated Section of the School Act of last Session; of Mr. Frederick Burrows and others, of Lennox, praying that the Education Department may be directed to furnish Schools with Maps.

The following Bill was introduced and read the First time:—

Bill, (Number 91), intituled, "An Act to amend the Act passed in the 34th year of Her Majesty's Reign, intituled, 'An Act to improve the Common and Grammar Schools of the Province of Ontario,' "—Mr. Fairbairn.

[NOTE. In regard to this Bill the following Letter was written to the Honourable Edward Blake in regard to it:—

Presuming, as intimated to Mr. Fairbairn, that he had your consent to his introduction of a Special Remedial Bill, to amend the Fortieth Section of the School Act of last Session, I enclose herewith a copy of his Bill, as revised.

If special legislation of public measures be permitted to private Members of the House, the Chief Superintendent approves of this Bill in its present shape, but he has never consented to any private legislation on the School Law, and has, from the beginning, mentioned that it should always be in the hands of the Government, and conducted on their responsibility alone.

Mr. Fairbairn called on this subject and we revised his Bill, as suggested, but submit the matter to you with this explanation.

TORONTO, 31st January, 1872.   J. GEORGE HODGINS, Deputy Superintendent.

[In reply to this Note, Mr. Blake stated that he had no conversation with Mr. Fairbairn on the subject.]

As this Bill did not pass, I insert a copy of it, as follows:—

BILL.—AN ACT TO AMEND THE ACT PASSED IN THE THIRTY-FOURTH YEAR OF HER MAJESTY'S REIGN, INTITULED "AN ACT TO IMPROVE THE COMMON AND GRAMMAR SCHOOLS OF THE PROVINCE OF ONTARIO."

Whereas by an Act passed in the Thirty-fourth year of Her Majesty's *Preamble.* Reign, chaptered Thirty-three, intituled:—"An Act to improve the Common and Grammar Schools of the Province of Ontario," it is provided in the Fortieth Section thereof "that every County Council shall determine the limits of each High School District for each Grammar School now existing within the County, and may form the whole, or part, of one or more Townships, Towns and Villages within its jurisdiction into a High School District;" and whereas, no provision is made in the said Act for the case where a Town has withdrawn from and ceased to be within the jurisdiction of the Council of the County within which the Town is situated;

Therefore Her Majesty, by and with the advice and consent of the Legislative Assembly of the Province of Ontario, enacts as follows:—

Section Forty of the said Act is hereby amended, so as to read as *34 Vic., c 33,* follows:— *s. 40 amended.*

40. Every County Council shall determine the limits of each High School *Formation of* District for each Grammar School now existing within the County, and each *High School districts.* such Council may form one, or more, Townships, Towns and Villages within its jurisdiction, or Towns withdrawn from its jurisdiction for Municipal purposes into a High School District; and the High School Board of such District shall possess all the powers within the said District for the support *Powers of* and management of their High School, and in respect to the County Council *High School Boards.* and the Councils of such Towns as are withdrawn from the jurisdiction of the Council of the County as are possessed under the Grammar School Acts, and this Act by High School Boards in respect to the support and management of the Schools under their care; and such County Council may appoint *Appointment of members of* and determine the continuance and succession in office of six duly qualified *Board and trustees.* Persons as Members of such High School Board, and the appointment of High School Trustees shall, in each case, devolve in equitable proportions, (as determined by the Chief Superintendent), upon and be made by the Municipal Councils, which, by the Thirty-sixth Section of this Act are required to raise moneys for the support of the High Schools concerned; *Proviso.* Provided however that existing Grammar School divisions already established shall be called High School Districts until altered according to Law, and all appointments of High School Trustees made by Municipal Councils shall be confirmed until altered according to the provisions of this Act.

Ordered, That the Bill be read the Second time To-morrow.

February 1st, 1872. The following Petitions were received and read:—Of the Public School Board of Toronto, praying that an Act may pass to extend the powers given to Public School Boards in relation to Industrial Schools; of Mr. Richard Preston and others of Leeds; also of Mr. James Coyle Brown and others of Peterborough; also of Mr. Schuyler Shibley and others, of Frontenac, severally praying that the Department of Education may be directed to furnish Maps, etcetera, to Schools.

Mr. J. C. Rykert, from the Committee on Standing Orders, presented their Seventh Report, which was read as follows:—Your Committee have examined the following Petitions, and find the notices in each case correct:—Of the Ladies' College at Ottawa, praying that an Act may pass to amend their Act of Incorporation; of Brother Aphraates and others, praying that an Act may pass to incorporate the Brothers of the Christian Schools of Ontario.

The Honourable Peter Gow presented to the House, by command of His Excellency the Lieutenant-Governor:—

A Return, in part, (being the official Regulations of the Council of Public Instruction for Ontario, relating to Public and High Schools), to an Address of the Legislative Assembly to His Excellency the Lieutenant-Governor, praying that His Excellency will cause to be laid before the House, copies of all Regulations, issued by the Council of Public Instruction, respecting Public Schools now in force; a list of the Persons to whom the Council granted Certificates; a statement of the results in detail of the late Examinations for Certificates of Qualification of School Teachers; copies of the Minutes of the Council of Public Instruction for the years 1867, 1868, 1869, 1870 and 1871; and copies of the Programme of Studies prescribed for Public Schools and High Schools.

February 2nd, 1872. The following Petition was received and read:—Of Mr. Donald McColl and others, Public School Teachers of the East Riding of Northumberland, praying that no alteration be made in the Law relating to the Superannuated Teachers' Fund.

The following Bill was introduced and read the First time:—

Bill, (Number 116), intituled:—"An Act to amend the Act incorporating the Ottawa Ladies' College."—The Honourable R. W. Scott, (Ottawa).

February 5th, 1872. The following Petition was received and read:—Of Mr. John Jameson and others; also of Mr. E. A. Bowes and others; also of Mr. John Teviotdale and others, all of Victoria, severally praying that the Department of Education be instructed to furnish Maps to Schools.

February 7th, 1872. On motion of the Honourable Archibald Kellar, seconded by the Honourable Edward Blake,—

Resolved, That this House will, on Friday next, resolve itself into a Committee of the Whole House to consider the following Resolution:—

That it shall be lawful for the Lieutenant-Governor-in-Council to direct the payment out of the Consolidated Revenue of the sum of not less than   Dollars to the County Inspector of Schools, for every Mechanics' Institute which he may inspect and report upon to the Commissioner of Agriculture.

February 8th, 1872. The following Petition was received and read:—Of Mr. Samuel McAllister and others, of Toronto; also of Mr. William McIntosh and others, of Hamilton; also of Mr. David J. Johnston and others, of Cobourg; also of Mr. H. Montgomery and others, of Milbrook; also, of Mr. D. W. Malcolm and others, of Townsend; also of Mr. W. Cummings and others, of Goderich; also of Mr. Hector Baxter and others, of Woodville; severally praying for the repeal of the Superannuation Clause of the School Act.

The Order of the Day for the House to resolve itself into a Committee to consider a certain proposed Resolution respecting Grants to Mechanics' Institutes having been read, it was,—

Resolved, That it shall be lawful for the Lieutenant-Governor-in-Council to direct the payment out of the Consolidated Revenue of the sum of not less than five dollars to the County Inspector of Schools, for every Mechanics' Institute which he may inspect and report upon to the Commissioner of Agriculture.

19a—xxiii

February 9th, 1872. Mr. H. S. Macdonald, (Leeds), from the Committee to whom was referred to consider a certain proposed Resolution respecting Grants to Mechanics' Institutes, reported the following Resolution:—

Resolved, That it shall be lawful for the Lieutenant-Governor-in-Council to direct the payment out of the Consolidated Revenue of the sum of not less than five dollars to the County Inspector of Schools, for every Mechanics' Institute which he may inspect, and report upon to the Commissioner of Agriculture.

Ordered, That the foregoing Resolution be referred to the Committee of the Whole House on Bill, (Number 16), To amend the Agriculture and Arts Act.

February 12th, 1872. The following Petition was received and read:—Of Mr. J. F. Partridge and others, of Oro, praying for a repeal of the present School Law.

February 13th, 1872. The following Petition was received and read:—Of the County Council of the United Counties of Northumberland and Durham, praying for certain amendments to the School Act.

Your Committee have examined the following Bills, and report the same:—

Ordered, That the fees, less actual expenses, on Bill, (Number 37), relating to Trinity College School, Port Hope, be remitted.

February 14th, 1872. The Honourable Attorney General Adam Crooks, from the Committee on Private Bills, presented their Eleventh Report which was read as follows:—Your Committee have examined the following Bills, and report the same without amendment:—

Bill, (Number 116), To amend the Act to incorporate the Ottawa Ladies' College.

Ordered, That the Fees on Bill, (Number 116), relating to the Ottawa Ladies' College be remitted.

The Honourable Peter Gow presented to the House, by command of His Excellency the Lieutenant-Governor:—

Return to an Address of the Legislative Assembly to His Excellency the Lieutenant-Governor, praying that he will cause to be laid before the House, a Return of the Names and Residences of the Members of the Senate of the University of Toronto, during the years 1867, 1868, 1869, 1870 and 1871 respectively, of the number of the Meetings of the said Senate called, and actually held, during the said years respectively, and of the number of the said Meetings in each of the years aforenamed, at which each of the Members of the said Senate respectively attended.

The following Bill was read the Second time:—Bill, (Number 37), To incorporate the Trinity College School, Port Hope.

The Order of the Day for the Second reading of Bill, (Number 80), To amend the Law respecting Public Schools, having been read, it was,—

Ordered, That the Order be discharged, and that the Bill be withdrawn.

The Order of the Day for the Second reading of Bill, (Number 91), To amend the Act passed in the 34th year of Her Majesty's Reign, intituled:—"An Act to improve the Common and Grammar Schools of the Province of Ontario," having been read, it was,—

Ordered, That the Order be discharged, and that the Bill be withdrawn.

February 15th, 1872. The following Petition was received and read:—Of Mr. William Brown and others, of Blenheim, praying against the arbitrary powers of the Council of Public Instruction, as regards the management of Schools.

The House resolved into a Committee to consider Bill, (Number 37), To incorporate the Trinity College School, Port Hope; and after some time spent therein, Mr. Speaker resumed the Chair; and Mr. H. S. Macdonald, (Leeds), reported, That the Committee had directed him to report the Bill without any amendment.

Ordered, That the Report be now received.

Ordered, That the Bill be read the Third time To-morrow.

The following Bill was read the Second time:—

Bill, (Number 116), To amend the Act to incorporate the Ottawa Ladies' College. Referred to a Committee of the Whole House, To-morrow.

The House, according to Order, resolved itself into Committee of Supply.

Resolved, That there be granted to Her Majesty, for the service of the year 1872 the sum:—

To defray the expenses of works at the Technological College.
    Revote, unexpended balance $11,490 66
To defray the expenses of work at the Model Schools,
    Toronto, as follows:—

For Furniture, Steam-heating Apparatus, Superintendence, etcetera ...	$2,718 00	
Plastering walls of Model School	600 00	
		3,318 00

To defray the expenses of Public and Separate Schools   200,000 00
To defray the expenses of Poor Schools 6,000 00
To defray the expenses of Agricultural Instruction 3,000 00
To defray the expenses of the Normal and Model Schools,
    as follows:—

Salaries:— $ cts.

	$ cts.
Head Master	2,000 00
Mathematical Master	1,500 00
Natural Science Master	1,500 00
Writing Master	750 00
Drawing Master	400 00
Music Master	400 00
Gymnastic Master	300 00
Master, Boys' School	900 00
First Assistant Master, Boys' School	700 00
Second Assistant Master, Boys' School	550 00
Third Assistant Master, Boys' School	500 00
Mistress, Girls' School	700 00
First Assistant, Girls' School	500 00
Second Assistant, Girls' School	425 00
Third Assistant, Girls' School	400 00
Clerk of the Normal School	600 90
Janitor, salary and cleaning	410 00
Gardener	410 00
First Engineer	410 00
Second Engineer	360 00
Caretaker and Messenger	410 00
Furnaceman and Assistant Gardener	360 00
Second Assistant	360 00

Contingencies:—

Printing and Binding	500 00
Books, Stationery and Apparatus	3,000 00
Expenses of Grounds and Plant House	550 00
Fuel and Light	1,250 00
Water	300 00
Petty furnishings and repairs	500 00
Carpenter's Work	200 00
Tinsmithing and Hardware	100 00

' Contingencies.—*Continued.*

Smith's Work, Heating Apparatus	300 00	
Plumbing and Gasfitting	200 00	
Painting and Glazing	500 00	
Bricklayer's and Carpenter's Work	100 00	
Slater's Work	100 00	
Repairing Roofs	1,200 00	
		23,645 00
To defray the expenses of High School		72,000 00
To defray the expenses of Libraries, Apparatus and Prizes		38,500 00

To defray the expenses of the Depository, as follows:—
Salaries:—

Clerk of Libraries	$1,200 00	
Assistant Clerk	600 00	
Despatch Clerk	425 00	
Assistant Clerk of Sales	300 00	
Assistant in Depository	200 00	
Assistant in Packing Room	150 00	
Junior Assistant	130 00	
Packer and Messenger	365 00	
Labourer and Furnaceman	300 00	

Contingencies:—

Postages	250 00	
Stationery	250 00	
Fuel, Water and Light	450 00	
Printing Forms	350 00	
Printing Forms, new Catalogue	400 00	
Packing Paper, Twine, Nails, etcetera	280 00	
Furnishings and petty repairs	350 00	
		6,000 00
To defray the expenses of Superannuated Teachers		8,000 00
To defray the expenses of Museum, (including Fuel)		3,850 00

To defray the expenses of the *Journal of Education*, as
follows:—

Deputy Superintendent, as Editor	$400 00	
Printing and mailing 6,000 copies at $140 per month	1,680 00	
Postages, Periodicals and Contingencies	300 00	
Engraving Prize Plans of School Houses and other illustrations	150 00	
		2,530 00

To defray the expenses of School Inspection, as follows:—

High School Inspection	$ 4,000 00
Public School Inspection	25,000 00
Examiners of School Teachers	500 00
Printing Examination Papers, Forms and Certificates	800 00
Postages, Stationery and Contingencies	250 00
	$30,550 00
To defray the expenses of Collegiate Institutes	6,000 00

To defray the expenses of Education Office, as follows:—
Salaries:—

Chief Superintendent	$4,000 00
Deputy Superintendent	2,200 00
Senior Clerk, Acountant and Registrar	1,600 00

Salaries.—Continued

Clerk of Statistics	1,500 00	
Clerk of Records	1,100 00	
Clerk of Correspondence	900 00	
Assistant Clerk of Correspondence	550 00	
Assistant Clerk	350 00	
Junior Clerk	350 00	
Messenger	365 00	
Cleaning	48 00	
		12,323 00

Contingencies:—

Postage	$750 00	
Printing Forms, Blanks, and Paper	550 00	
Fuel and Water	400 00	
Stationery and Books	300 00	
Newspapers, Law, and other Reports	175 00	
High School Registers and Forms	275 00	
Printing 5,000 copies of School Law	650 00	
Printing First Part of Annual Report, 4,500 copies	450 00	
Law Appeal Cases	280 00	
Furniture, petty repairs and incidentals	300 00	
		4,130 00

Repairs:—

Repairing Roofs and Gutters	$1,200 00	
Repairs to plank Walks	300 00	
		1,500 00

Total for Education	$417,818 00

To defray expenses of Maintenance of the Technological College, as follows:—

Salaries	$5,000 00	
Gas	600 00	
Fuel	400 00	
Ordinary Repairs and incidentals	200 09	
Housekeeper	600 00	
		$7,000 00

To pay Examiners of Public School Teachers, (arrears)	300 00
Education:—Preparing Examination Papers, Public School Teachers	600 00

February 16th, 1872. The following Petitions were received and read:—Of Mr. James McBride and others, of Ontario, praying that the Department of Education be authorized to furnish Maps to Schools; of Mr. William Millar and others, of Oro, praying for certain amendments to the School Law.

The Honourable Attorney-General Crooks, from the Committee on Private Bills, presented their Thirteenth Report, which was read as follows:—Your Committee have examined the following Bill, and report the same with certain amendments:—

Bill, (Number 52), To incorporate the Wilberforce Educational Institute.

The following Bill was read the Third time and passed:—

Bill, (Number 37), To incorporate the Trinity College School, Port Hope.

The House resolved itself into a Committee to consider Bill, (Number 116), To amend the Act to incorporate the Ottawa Ladies' College; and, after some time spent therein, Mr. Speaker resumed the Chair; and Mr. Thomas Hodgins reported, That the Committee had directed him to report the Bill without any amendment.

Ordered, That the Report be now received.

Ordered, That the Bill be read the Third time forthwith.

The Bill was then read the Third time, and passed.

The House went into Committee of Supply.

Balance to be provided for in 1872, to complete the services
of 1870:—

Normal and Model Schools $1,013 50

February 19th, 1872.   The following Petition was received and read:—Of Mr.
Walter Macfarland and others, of Bruce, praying for certain amendments to the School
Act.

The following Bill was read the Second time:—Bill, (Number 52), To incorporate
the Wilberforce Educational Institute.   Referred to a Committee of the Whole House,
To-morrow.

On motion of Mr. A. W. Lauder, seconded by Mr. W. Fitzsimmons,—

Resolved, That an humble Address be presented to His Excellency the Lieutenant-
Governor, praying that His Excellency will cause to be laid before the House copies of
all Memorials and Communications addressed to the Government or any Member thereof,
or to the Department of Public Instruction, from the German population of the Counties
of Bruce and Grey, relating to the School Law.

(NÒTE. This Return was laid before the House on this Day).

February 20th, 1872.   The following Petition was received and read:—Of Mr. John
Beardsall and others, of East Zorra; also, of Mr. Joseph Pettigrew and others, of
Blandford; severally praying against the arbitrary powers of the Council of Public
Instruction, as regards the management of Schools.

February 21st, 1872.   The following Petitions were received and read:—Of the
County Council of Simcoe; also, of Mr. Ellis Hughes and others, severally praying for
certain amendments to the School Act; of Mr. J. C. Morgan and others, of Simcoe,
praying that the Department of Education may be authorized to furnish Maps to
Schools.

Mr. Galbraith, from the Committee on Printing, presented their Fifth Report,
which was read as follows:—Your Committee recommend that the following Document
be not printed:—Return of Memorials, or Communications, from the German population
of Bruce and Grey, relating to the School Law.

Resolved, That this House doth concur in the Fifth Report of the Committee on
Printing.

The House resolved itself into a Committee to consider Bill, (Number 52), To incorporate the Wilberforce Educational Institute; and, after some time spent therein, Mr.
Speaker resumed the Chair; and Mr. H. M. Deroche reported, That the Committee
had directed him to report the Bill without amendment.

Ordered, That the Report be now received.

Ordered, That the Bill be read the Third time To-morrow.

February 23rd, 1872.   The following Bill was introduced and read a First time:—
Bill, (Number 150), intituled:—"An Act to amend the Act, 16th Victoria, Chapter 89,
relating to the University of Toronto."—Mr. F. W. Cumberland.

(NOTE. As this Bill did not pass, I insert as follows:—

An Act passed to amend the Act passed in the Sixteenth year of the Reign of Her
Majesty, Queen Victoria, and chaptered Eighty-nine, relating to the University of
Toronto.

Whereas it is expedient that a change in the Corporation of the University of
Toronto be made, and in the composition of the Senate of the said University, and in
the number and manner of the appointment of the Members of the said Senate, and

also that a change be made in the manner of the appointment of the Chancellor and of the Vice Chancellor of the said University;

Therefore Her Majesty, by and with the advice and consent of the Legislative Assembly of the Province of Ontario, enacts as follows:

1. The Fourth, Fifth, Sixth, Seventh and Eighth Sections of the Act of the late Province of Canada, passed in the Sixteenth year of the Reign of Her Majesty Queen Victoria, chaptered Eighty-nine, and intituled: "Toronto University Amendment Act," are hereby repealed.

2. Until their Successors shall have been appointed under this Act, the present Chancellor, Vice-chancellor and Members of the Senate shall hold office, and continue with all their respective duties and powers unimpaired, as if the said Fourth, Fifth, Sixth, Seventh and Eighth Sections had not been repealed; and all Statutes, By-laws, Resolutions, Rules and Regulations of the Senate at present existing, or which shall be passed, or adopted, by the present Senate until their said Successors are so appointed as aforesaid, except so far as the same are, or shall be, inconsistent with this Act, shall remain in full force and effect until altered by the Senate, to be appointed as hereinafter provided for.

3. The Corporation of the University of Toronto shall hereafter consist of one Chancellor, one Vice-chancellor, the Members of the Senate for the time being, and all registered Graduates of the University.

4. The Chancellor, Vice-chancellor, and, exclusive of *ex-officio* Members, seventeen other Members of the Senate shall constitute the Senate of the University, and of the said Senate, exclusive of the Chancellor, and of the said *ex-officio* Members, nine shall be appointed by the Lieutenant-Governor of this Province under his hand and Seal at Arms, and nine shall be elected by the Graduates of the University, in manner hereinafter provided.

5. The President of University College for the time being; the Chief Superintendent of Education for this Province for the time being; the Treasurer of the Law Society of Ontario for the time being; the Principal of Upper Canada College for the time being; the Bursar of the University and Colleges at Toronto for the time being; the President, or other Chief Executive Officer, for the time being, of each College in this Province in actual affiliation with the University, shall respectively *ex-officio* be Members of the same.

6. The office of Chancellor of the said University shall be a triennial one,—that is t. say, the term of office of each Chancellor shall expire on the election of his Successor, in the year next but two after that in which he shall have been elected, and the day on which the Chancellor, (except the first Chancellor to be elected under this Act, and for whose election provision is hereinafter made,) shall be elected, shall be appointed by Statute of the University, and the Members of the Corporation entitled to vote shall on that day, of which notice shall be given in such manner as shall be directed by Statute, elect a fit and proper Person to be Chancellor, and thereupon the term of office of the then Chancellor shall expire, and so, from time to time, triennially; or in case of the death, resignation or other vacancy in the office of any such Chancellor, before the expiration of his term of office, then, at a special election to be holden for that purpose, of which election notice shall be given in such manner as shall be provided by Statute, the Members of the Corporation entitled to vote shall elect a Chancellor for the remainder of the term in which such death, resignation or other avoidance, shall happen.

7. The office of Vice-chancellor of the said University shall be a biennial one, that is to say, the term of office of such Vice-chancellor shall expire on the election of his Successor, in the year next but one after that in which he shall have been appointed, and the day on which the Vice-chancellor, (except the first Vice-chancellor to be appointed under this Act, for whose election provision is hereinafter made,) shall be elected, shall be appointed by Statute of the University, and the Members of the Senate shall, at a Meeting then to be held, elect some one of the then Members of the

Senate to be Vice chancellor, when the term of office of the then Vice chancellor shall expire, and so, from time to time, biennially; or, in case of the death, resignation, or other vacancy, in the office of such Vice chancellor, before the expiration of his term of office, the then Members of the Senate shall, at a Meeting to be holden by·them for that purpose, as soon as conveniently may be, of which Meeting notice shall be given in manner aforesaid, elect one of the said Members of the Senate to be Vice-chancellor for the remainder of the term in which such death, resignation or other avoidance, shall happen.

8. The election of the first Chancellor to be appointed under this Act, and of the first nine elective Members of the Senate to be appointed under this Act, shall be held in Toronto, on the eighth day of May, One thousand eight hundred and seventy-two.

9. The first Vice-chancellor to be appointed under this Act shall be elected at the first Meeting of the Senate of the University appointed and elected under this Act, when the Members of the Senate then present shall elect one of the then Members thereof to be Vice-chancellor for the then ensuing two years.

10. For the purpose of any election authorized by this Act, each registered Graduate of the University of the standing of at least one year, may vote for one person to be Chancellor, and for such number of Persons as are then to be elected as Members of the Senate.

11. The votes shall be separately given for the Chancellor, and for the Members of the Senate, by closed voting papers, in the form in Schedules "A" and "B" of this Act, or to the like effect, being delivered to the Registrar of the University at such time and place, prior to the closing of such election, as may be prescribed by Statute, and any voting papers received by the said Registrar by post during the time of such election, or during the preceding week, shall be deemed as delivered to him for the purpose of such election.

12. The Registrar of the University shall, at least one month previous to the time of any election under this Act, make out an alphabetical list, or register, to be called "The Election Register," of the names and known addresses of the Members of the Corporation, being Graduates of the University as aforesaid, who are entitled to vote at such succeeding election, and such Register may be examined by any Member of the Corporation at all reasonable times at the office of the said Registrar, and no person whose name is not inserted in the said list shall be entitled to vote at such election: Provided always that, in case any Member of the Corporation complains to the said Registrar in writing of the improper omission, or insertion, of any name in the said list, it shall be the duty of the said Registrar forthwith to examine into the said complaint and rectify such error, if any there be, and, in case any such Person so complaining is dissatisfied with the decision of such Registrar, he may appeal to the Scrutineers of the election, whose decision shall be final, and the list shall remain, or be altered, in accordance with such decision.

13. It shall be the duty of the Registrar to send to each Graduate of the University whose name is on the Register, or list of persons entitled to vote, one copy of the form, or forms, of voting Papers in Schedules "A" and "B" of this Act, as the same may respectively apply to the election, or elections, then next to be held, and such forms shall be sent in such manner, and at such time before the holding of such election as shall be directed by the Statute of the University.

14. It shall be the duty of the said Registrar to send with the said forms of Voting Papers, to each Graduate of the University whose name is on the list of those Persons entitled to vote, a list of the names of those Persons appointed by the Lieutenant-Governor, next preceding the day of such election to sit as Members of the Senate, together with a list of those other Persons then already Members of the Senate, and of those whose retirement has created the vacancies to be filled at the then ensuing election.

15. The said Voting Papers shall, upon the appointed day of election, and at an hour to be stated by the Statute, be opened by the Registrar of the University in the presence of the Scrutineers to be appointed, as hereinafter mentioned, who shall scrutinise and count the votes, and keep a record thereof in a proper Book to be provided by the Senate.

16. The Person who shall have the highest number of votes for Chancellor by Voting Papers, in the form of Schedule "A," shall be Chancellor of the University for the three years then next ensuing.

17. The nine Persons who shall have the highest number of votes for Members of the Senate by Voting Papers, in the form of Schedule "B," shall be the nine elective Members of the Senate of the said University.

18. Any Person entitled to vote at such election shall be entitled to be present at the opening of the said Voting Papers.

19. In case of an equality of votes between two, or more Persons which leaves the election of the Chancellor, or of one, or more, Members of the Senate undecided, then the said Scrutineers shall forthwith put into a Ballot-box a number of Papers with the names of the Candidates respectively having such equality of votes written thereon one for each such Candidate, and the Registrar of the University shall draw by chance from such Ballot-box in the presence of the said Scrutineers, one of such Papers in the election of Chancellor, and one or more of such Papers, in the case of the election of Members of the Senate, sufficient to make up the required number, and the Persons whose names are upon such Papers so drawn, shall be respectively the Chancellor and such Members of the Senate.

20. Upon the completion of the counting of the votes and of the scrutiny, the Vice-chancellor, or other Person acting as, and for, him, shall forthwith declare the result of the election to the Senate of the University; and shall, as soon as conveniently may be, report the same in writing, signed by himself and by the Scrutineers, to the Senate and to the Secretary of this Province for the time being.

21. The Senate of the University shall, at least two months previous to such election, appoint two Persons who, with the Vice chancellor, shall act as Scrutineers at the next ensuing election; and the said Senate shall also, at the same time, appoint a third Person, who shall act for, and as, the Vice-chancellor, should he be absent from such election.

22. In the event of any Elector placing more than one name on his voting paper for Chancellor, or more than the required number on his Voting Paper for Members of the Senate, the first name only shall be taken for Chancellor, and the first names not exceeding the required number shall only be taken for the Members of the Senate.

23. At the first Meeting of the Senate next after the first election of Members thereto, as provided in this Act, the Chancellor, Vice chancellor, or other presiding Officer, shall put into a Ballot-box nine Papers with the names of the nine persons elected as Members of the Senate, one name upon each Paper; and the Registrar, or other Officer to be appointed to act as, and for, him in his absence, shall draw by chance from such Ballot-box, and in the presence of the Senate, the nine Papers in succession, and the Persons whose names are upon the first three Papers so drawn, shall serve as Members of the Senate for three years from the date of the election, and the Persons whose names shall, in like manner, be drawn by the second series of three shall serve for two years, and the three remaining shall serve for one year from the date of the said election.

24. After the first election of Members of the Senate, as directed by this Act, the vacancies in the Senate, by expiry of term of service, shall be three in each year; the rotation of retirement being first determined by ballot as hereinbefore provided; and on such day in each year thereafter, as shall be appointed by Statute, three Persons shall be elected in manner aforenamed, to fill the vacancies thus arising, and to be Members of the Senate for the three years then next ensuing such election.

25. At all the Meetings of the Corporation in Convocation, the Chancellor, or in his absence, the Vice-chancellor shall preside as Chairman, or in the absence of both a Chairman shall be chosen by the Members present, or a majority of them.

26. The Corporation of the University in Convocation assembled, shall have power to adjourn from time to time by Resolution to discuss all questions relating to the government and working of the University and of the Colleges affiliated therewith, so far as affects the same; and to adopt Memorials to the Visitor, or to the Senate, within such limitations and restrictions as may be provided by Statute; but no discussion, or action, by Convocation, excepting only in relation to the elections authorized by this Act, shall be in order unless at least, twenty-four Members of the Corporation shall be present.

27. The Chancellor, or Vice-chancellor, shall have power to call a Meeting of the Corporation upon the requisition of at least twelve of the Members of the said Corporation, not being Members of the Senate of the University.

28. The Lieutenant-Governor of this Province, may, at least one month before the day appointed for the election of the first nine elective Members, appoint nine Persons to be Members of the Senate of the said University, and thereupon the Secretary of the Province for the time being, shall forthwith communicate the names of the Persons so appointed to the Registrar of the University, to the end that the same may be announced to the Members of the Corporation as directed by Section Fourteen.

29. The nine Persons so appointed by the Lieutenant-Governor shall retire in rotation by seniority, that is to say the first three named by the Lieutenant-Governor shall retire in one year from the date of their appointment, the second three in two years from such date, and the remaining three in three years from such date, and the vacancies in the Senate respectively created by such retirements in each year, shall be filled by appointment by the Lieutenant-Governor, at least one month before the day appointed for the election in that year of the three, or more, elective Members, and so on in each succeeding year, the Members so appointed holding office for three years and retiring by rotation on expiry of the said term.

30. And whenever any such appointment shall be made by the Lieutenant-Governor to fill vacancies, whether on retirement by rotation, or from other cause arising, the Secretary of the Province, for the time being, shall forthwith communicate the names of the Person so appointed to the Registrar of the University.

31. If, at any time, by death, or otherwise, the number of the said appointed Members of the Senate shall be reduced below the number of nine, and shall so remain reduced for three months, then and in such case, and as often as the same shall happen, if the Lieutenant-Governor do not think proper to complete the said number by appointment, the Members of the Senate may, at a Meeting to be holden for that purpose, of which notice shall be given to the Provincial Secretary, and to the Members of the Senate, in such manner as shall be provided by Statute, elect one or more fit and proper Persons to be Members of the Senate in addition to the then remaining appointed Members thereof to the end, that by means of such election the number of nine appointed Members of the Senate may thus be completed, and such Members so elected to vacancies by the Senate shall hold office for the term, or for the remainder of the term, pertaining to each such vacancy respectively.

32. If at any time, by death, or resignation, or otherwise than by retirement by rotation, the number of Members of the Senate elected thereto by the Corporation, shall be reduced below the number of nine, then at the next ensuing annual election to be held, as directed by Section Twenty-one of this Act, such additional Persons shall be elected in manner therein provided, as may be necessary to complete the number of elected Members of the Senate to the number of nine.

33. At all elections to take place under this Act, all retiring Chancellors or Members of the Senate shall be re-eligible for election.

SCHEDULE "A."

ELECTION OF CHANCELLOR OF THE UNIVERSITY OF TORONTO.

I,   M.A., (or other Degree), of the University of Toronto, resident at
          , in the County of   , do hereby declare:—
I. That the signature affixed thereto, is my proper handwriting.
II. That I vote for the following Person as Chancellor of the University of Toronto,
videlicet,   of   in the County of   .
III. That I have signed no other Voting Paper at this election.
IV. That this Voting Paper was executed on the day of the date hereof.
Witness my hand this   day of   , A.D. 187   .

SCHEDULE "B."

ELECTION OF MEMBERS OF SENATE OF THE UNIVERSITY OF TORONTO.

I,   M.A., (or other Degree), of the University of Toronto, resident at
          , County of   ,do hereby declare:
I. That the signature affixed hereto, is my proper handwriting.
II. That I vote for the following Persons as Members of the Senate of the University
of Toronto, videlicet:—

A.B. of   in the County of
C.D. of   in the County of
E.F. of   in the County of

III. That I have signed no other Voting Paper at this election.
IV. That this Voting Paper was executed on the day of the date hereof.

Witness my hand this   day of   187   .

February 24th, 1872. The following Petitions were received and read:—Of Mr.
W. Butler and others, of Wilmot, praying against the powers of the Council of Public
Instruction in the management of Schools; of Mr. Seth Lyons and others, of Ernestown,
praying that the Superannuated Section in the School Act may not be repealed.

The House, according to Order, again resolved itself into a Committee of Supply.
The Message of His Excellency and the Supplementary Estimates having been read.
it was,—

Resolved, That there be granted to Her Majesty for the service of the year 1872
the following sums:—

To defray the expenses of the Education Department for
          additional payments to Superannuated Teachers $4,000 00

February 26th, 1872. The following Petition was received and read:—Of Mr. Robert
Cochrane and others, praying that the Superannuation Section of the School Act may
not be repealed.

February 27th, 1872. The House resolved itself into a Committee to consider Bill,
(Number 146), To make temporary provisions as to the Regulations of the Council of
Public Instruction; and after some time spent therein, Mr. Speaker resumed the Chair;
and Mr. Thomas Hodgins reported, That the Committee had directed him to report the
Bill with certain amendments.

Ordered, That the Report be now received.
The amendments having been read the Second time, were agreed to.

Ordered, That the Bill be read the Third time at the first sitting of the House,
To-morrow.

February 28th, 1872. The following Petitions were received and read:—Of Mr.
James Andrews and others, of Woodhouse; of Mr. Robert Law and others, of the same
place, severally praying for the repeal of the School Law.

The following Bill was read the Third time, and passed:—

Bill, (Number 146), To make temporary provision as to the Regulations of the Council of Public Instruction.

On motion of the Honourable M. C. Cameron, seconded by Mr. C. J. Rykert, and,—

Resolved, That an humble Address be presented to His Excellency the Lieutenant-Governor, praying His Excellency to cause to be laid before this House a Return of all Correspondence which has passed between any Member of the present Government and the Chief Superintendent of Education during the present Session.

The Honourable Peter Gow presented to the House, by command of His Excellency the Lieutenant-Governor:—

Return to an Address to His Excellency the Lieutenant-Governor, praying His Excellency to cause to be laid before the House a Return of all Correspondence which has passed between any Member of the present Government and the Chief Superintendent of Education during the present Session, in so far as such Correspondence relates to any proposed changes in the School Law, and in the management of the Education Office, (not including Correspondence already brought down).

Also the Annual Report of the Senate of the University of Toronto for the Academic year, 1870, 1871.

March 1st, 1872. The following Petitions were received and read:—Of Mr. H. Reazin and others of Victoria, praying that the Department of Education may be authorized to furnish Maps to Schools; of Mr. Peter Fisher and others, of Turnberry, relative to the reduction of prices of School Lands.

The Order of the Day for the Second reading of Bill, (Number 150), To amend the Act, 16 Victoria, Chapter 89, relating to the University of Toronto, having been read, it was,—

Ordered, That the Order be discharged, and that the Bill be withdrawn.

Mr. Galbraith, from the Committee on Printing, presented their Seventh Report, which was read as follows:—Your Committee recommend that the following Documents be printed:—

Return respecting the Agricultural College and Experimental Farm.

Return of Correspondence in relation to the proposed changes in the School Law and management of the Education Office.

Annual Report of the Senate of the University of Toronto for the academic year 1870, 1871.

Return of Names and Residences of the Members of the Senate of the University of Toronto.

Copies of Regulations issued by the Council of Public Instruction respecting Public Schools.

March 2nd, 1872. The Honourable Peter Gow presented to the House, by command of His Excellency the Lieutenant-Governor:—

Further Return to an Adress to His Excellency the Lieutenant-Governor, praying His Excellency to cause to be laid before the House a Return of all Correspondence which has passed between any Member of the present Government and the Chief Superintendent of Education during the present Session.

His Excellency William Pearce Howland, C.B., Lieutenant-Governor of the Province of Ontario, being seated on the Throne, the Clerk of the Crown in Chancery read the titles of the several Bills to be assented to, as follows:—

An Act to amend the Act to incorporate the Ottawa Ladies' College.

An Act to incorporate the Trinity College School, Port Hope.

An Act to make temporary provision as to the Regulations of the Council of Public Insruction.

An Act to incorporate the Wilberforce Educational Institute.

CHAPTER XIX.

EDUCATIONAL ACTS PASSED BY THE HOUSE OF ASSEMBLY, 1872.

35 VICTORIA, CHAPTER XXX.

AN ACT TO MAKE TEMPORARY PROVISION AS TO THE REGULATIONS OF THE COUNCIL OF PUBLIC INSTRUCTION.

Received the Royal Assent on the 2nd of March, 1872.

Her Majesty, by and with the advice and consent of the Legislative Assembly of the Province of Ontario, enacts as follows:—

Powers of Lieutenant-Governor over rules, etcetera of Council of Public Instruction. 1. The Lieutenant-Governor-in-Council shall have power to cause inquiry to be made into the working of any Rules, Regulations, Instructions, or Recommendations which have been made, or may be made, or issued, by the Council of Public Instruction, or by the Chief Superintendent of Education, and to abrogate, suspend, or modify, any such Rules, Regulations, Instructions, or Recommendations.

Duration of this Act. 2. This Act shall remain in force until the end of the next ensuing Session of the Legislative Assembly, and no longer.

35 VICTORIA, CHAPTER CXI.

AN ACT TO INCORPORATE THE TRINITY COLLEGE SCHOOL, PORT HOPE.

Received the Royal Assent on the 2nd of March, 1872.

Preamble. Whereas, the Bishop of the Diocese of Toronto and others, have, by their Petition, represented that the said School has been for the last six years and upwards, and is now in successful operation, and that the usefulness of the said School will be extended, and the purposes for which it was formed will be promoted by an Act of incorporation;

Therefore Her Majesty, by and with the advice and consent of the Legislative Assembly of the Province of Ontario, enacts as follows:—

School incorporated. 1. The Bishop of the Diocese of Toronto, for the time being; the Chancellor of the University of Trinity College, for the time being; the Provost of Trinity College, for the time being; the Professors in Arts of Trinity College, for the time being; the Head Master of Trinity College School, for the time being; the Venerable Arthur Palmer, M.A.; the Reverend John Gamble Geddes, M.A.; the Honourable George W. Allan, Mr. Charles J. Campbell, and Mr. Frederick W. Cumberland, and their successors, shall be and are hereby constituted a body politic and corporate, under the name **Name.** of the Corporation of "The Trinity College School;" and shall have perpetual succession and a common seal, and shall have power to add to their numbers and appoint their Successors, by election, or otherwise, as may by the said Corporation be determined upon.

Power to acquire real property. 2. The said Corporation may from time to time, and at all times, acquire and hold, as purchasers, any interests in Lands and Tenements, and the same alienate, lease, mortgage and dispose of, and purchase others in their stead; Provided always, and it is enacted, that the said Corporation shall at no time acquire, or hold, as purchasers any Lands, or Tenements, or interests therein, exceeding in the whole at any one time the annual value of Five thousand dollars, nor otherwise than for their actual use, or occupation, for the purposes of the said Corporation; And it is further enacted, that the said Corporation may, by the name aforesaid, from time to time, take, or hold, by gift, devise, or bequest, and Lands, or Tenements, or interests therein, if such gift, or devise, or bequest, be made at least six months before the death of the person making the same; but the said Corporation shall, at no time, take and hold by any gift, devise, or bequest, so as that the annual value of any Lands, or Tenements, or interests therein so to be taken, or held, by gift, devise, or bequest, shall at any one time in the whole exceed the annual value of One thousand dollars; and no Lands, or Tenements, or interests therein, acquired by gift, devise, or bequest, shall be held by the said Corporation for a longer period than seven years after the acquisition thereof; and within such period they shall respectively be absolutely disposed of by the said Corporation, so that it no longer retain **And sell.** any interest therein; and the proceeds of such disposition shall be invested in Public Securities, Municipal Debentures, or other approved Securities, not including Mortgages, for the use of the said Corporation; and such Lands, Tenements, or interest therein, or such thereof which may not within the said period have been so disposed of, shall revert to the Person from whom the same was acquired, his Heirs, Executors, Administrators, or Assigns.

3. The Bishop of the Diocese of Toronto, for the time being, shall be **Visitor.** the Visitor of the said School; and the Governing Body of the said School shall consist of the Bishop of the Diocese of Toronto, for the time being, the Chancellor of the University of Trinity College, for the time being, the Provost of Trinity College, for the time being; the Professors in Arts of **Governing** Trinity College, for the time being, the Head Master of the said School, for **body.** the time being, (all of whom shall, *ex officio*, be Members of the said governing body), and such, and so many other Persons, as shall be appointed, from time to time, as occasion may require, in such manner and for such term as may be provided in the By-laws, Rules and Regulations of the Governing Body.

4. The first Governing Body of the said School shall consist of the said **Governing** *ex officio* Members, and the said Venerable Arthur Palmer, the Reverend **body.** John Gamble Geddes, the Honourable George W. Allan, Mr. Charles J. Campbell and Mr. Frederick W. Cumberland, who shall hold office until their successors shall be appointed.

5. The Governing Body of the said School, shall have the control, man- **Powers of** agement and government of the said School, and shall have power to make **governing** By-laws, Rules and Regulations not contrary to Law, or to the provisions of **body.** this Act, for the working and management thereof; and may also determine upon the number of the said Governing Body which shall form a quorum thereof, and may regulate all matters appertaining to Meetings of the said Governing Body.

6. The Governing Body of the said School, may for the purposes of pay- **Corporation** ing for the Real Estate they may purchase under this Act, and for the **may issue** **debentures** erection and completion of the Buildings required for the said School, borrow **for certain** money on Debentures of the said Corporation, at such rates of interest, and **purposes.** upon such terms, as they may think proper; and may, for that purpose, make, or cause to be made, Debentures under the common seal of the Corporation, for sums not less than One hundred dollars, which may be payable at any place, and either to order, or Bearer, and may have interest Coupons attached; Provided that the aggregate amount of such Debentures shall not at any time exceed Ten thousand dollars.

Corporation to make returns when required. 7. The said Corporation shall, whenever required by the Lieutenant-Governor of this Province, make a return of its Property, Real and Personal, and of its Annual Receipts, Expenditure with such details and information as the said Lieutenant-Governor may require.

35 VICTORIA, CHAPTER CXII.

An Act to amend the Act to Incorporate the Ottawa Ladies' College.

Received the Royal Assent on the 2nd of March, 1872.

Preamble. Whereas the Managers of the Ottawa Ladies' College have prayed for an Act to amend their Act;

Therefore Her Majesty, by and with the advice and consent of the Legislative Assembly of the Province of Ontario, enacts as follows:—

34 Victoria, chapter 90, section 7, amended. 1. Section Seven of the Act passed in the Thirty-fourth year of the Reign of Her Majesty Queen Victoria, and chaptered Ninety, shall be and is hereby amended by inserting in the sixth line thereof, between the words "Meetings" and "the," the following words:—"and at each Annual General Meeting thereafter."

Section 16 amended. 2. Section Sixteen of the said Act is hereby repealed, and, in lieu thereof, the following is substituted:—

Vacancies in office of manager, how filled. 16. If any of the Managers resign, or become incompetent, or ineligible to act, or cease to be a Proprietor of the requisite number of Shares, the remaining Managers shall appoint a Shareholder with the necessary qualification to fill the vacancy at a Special Meeting of the Managers to be called by the Secretary for that purpose.

Quorum of managers.

Their powers. 3. That for and notwithstanding anything in the Eighteenth Section of the said Act contained, five of the Managers shall form a quorum for the transaction af all business; provided that such Managers shall not deal with, sell, or dispose of, the Lands, Property, or effects of the said Corporation, or purchase, or acquire Lands for the said Corporation, unless at a Meeting of the Managers at which eight at least of their number shall be present.

35 VICTORIA, CHAPTER CXIII.

An Act to incorporate the Wilberforce Educational Institute.

Received the Royal Assent on the 2nd of March, 1872.

Preamble. Whereas it has been represented to the Legislature of this Province that about the year One thousand eight hundred and forty-one, there was established in the County of Kent an Educational Institute called the British and American Institute; and that by a decree of Her Majesty's Court of Chancery for Upper Canada, bearing date the Twenty-fourth day of March, One thousand eight hundred and sixty-eight, made in a cause then pending in said Court, of Her Majesty's Attorney-General for Upper Canada against Mr. John Scobie and Mr. James C. Brown, the said James C. Brown and Messieurs Archibald McKellar, Morris Potter, Stanton Hunton, Isaac Holden, Hayward Day, Wiliam Chandler and the Reverend Thomas Hughes, all of the said County of Kent, were appointed Trustees for the purpose of carrying out the said trust, and the Trust Estates were, by the said Decree, declared to be vested in them; and whereas the said Mr. James C. Brown is since dead, and the remaining Trustees have petitioned for an Act of Incorporation, and it would tend greatly to advance and extend the usefulness of the Institution that it should be incorporated;

Therefore Her Majesty, by and with the advice and consent of the Legislative Assembly of the Province of Ontario, enacts as follows:—

1. There shall be, and there is hereby constituted and established, in the County of Kent, in the Province of Ontario, a body politic and corporate under the name of "The Wilberforce Educational Institute," which shall be an Institution of learning for the purpose of affording the means of a moral, mental and physical education to the Coloured population of Canada, not excluding white persons and Indians; which Corporation shall consist of the said Messieurs Archibald McKellar, Morris Potter, Stanton Hunton, Isaac Holden, Hayward Day, William Chandler and the Reverend Thomas Hughes, who shall be the Trustees of the Corporation, with power in their descretion to increase their number to nine, in such manner as shall be provided by the Rules and Regulations of the Corporation; and such Trustees shall have the control, management and government of the Corporation, and shall also have power to make Rules and Regulations, not contrary to Law, or the provisions of this Act, for the government, or management, of the said Corporation and the affairs and property thereof, and also for the guidance of themselves, the said Trustees, in the execution of their duties; and, in case of any vacancy, or vacancies, occurring in the number of the said Trustees by death, resignation, or otherwise, such vacancy, or vacancies, shall be filled up in such manner as may be provided for in the Rules and Regulations of the said Corporation, subject to the approval of a Judge of the Court of Chancery in Chambers. *Incorporation. Name. Trustees. Their powers. Vacancies in office of trustee how filled.*

2. Such Corporation shall have perpetual succession, and may have a common seal, with power to change, alter, break and renew the same when, and so often as, they shall think proper; and the said Corporation may, under the same name, contract, and be contracted with, sue and be sued, implead and be impleaded, prosecute and be prosecuted, in all Courts and places whatsoever in this Province, and shall have power to acquire and hold personal or moveable property for the purposes of the Corporation, and to alienate the same at pleasure; and all the acts and doings of a majority of the Members of the Corporation shall be of the same force and effect as if all of them had joined in such acts, or doings; and no individual Member of the Corporation shal be personally liable for the debts, acts, or obligations, of the Corporation. *Powers of corporation.*

3. The said Corporation may, from time to time, and at all times, acquire and hold, as purchasers, any interests in Lands and Tenements, and the same may alienate. lease. mortgage and dispose of and purchase others in their stead; Provided always, and it is enacted, that the said Corporation shall at no time acquire, or hold, as purchasers any Lands, or Tenements, or interest therein, exceeding in the whole at any one time the annual value of Five thousand dollars, nor otherwise than for their actual use, or occupation, for the purposes of the said Corporation; And it is further enacted, that the said Corporation may. by the name aforesaid, from time to time, take, or hold by gift, devise, or bequest, any Lands, or Tenements, or interest therein, if such gift, devise, or bequest be made at least six months before the death of the person making the same; but the said Corporation shall at no time take, or hold, by any gift, devise, or bequest, so as that the annual value of any Lands, or Tenements, or interests therein, so to be taken, or held, by gift, devise, or bequest, shall at any one time in the whole exceed the annual value of One thousand dollars; and no Lands or Tenements, or interests therein, acquired by gift, devise or bequest, shall be held by the said Corporation for a longer period than seven years after *Power to acquire real property.*

20—XXIII.

the acquisition thereof; and within such period, they shall respectively be absolutely disposed of by the said Corporation; so that it no longer retain any interest therein; and the proceeds of such disposition shall be invested in Public Securities, Municipal Debentures, or other approved Securities, not including Mortgages, for the use of the said Corporation; and such Lands, Tenements, or interest therein, or such thereof which may not, within the said period, have been so disposed of, shall revert to the Person from whom the same was acquired, his Heirs, Executors, Administrators, or Assigns.

And sell.

4. All the Real and Personal Estate, Property, Assets and Effects, and all Titles, Securities, Instruments and Evidences, and all rights and claims of, or belonging to, the said British and American Institute, or to the Trustees thereof, as such Trustees, or to any other person, or body politic, or corporate, on behalf of, or in trust for the said British and American Institute, including any moneys at present in the said Court of Chancery in the said cause above referred to, and any Mortgages held by the said Court of Chancery, or by any Officer thereof, to secure payment of the purchase money of any Lands sold in the said cause, are hereby vested in the said Wilberforce Educational Institute, notwithstanding any of the provisions contained in the Third Section of this Act, and shall, for the purpose, and upon the trusts in the preamble to this Act mentioned, be deemed and taken to be the property of the said Corporation; Provided always, that any Lands acquired by the Corporation under this Section, and not required for their actual use and occupation, shall not be held by them for a longer period than seven years, but shall be disposed of by them within that period.

Property of British American Institute vested in the Wilberforce Educational Institute.

Proviso.

5. All moneys of the Corporation, not required for immediate use in maintaining and promoting the objects of the Corporation, may be invested by the Trustees in the Public Securities of the Dominion of Canada, or of this Province, or in the Stocks of any chartered Bank, or Building Society, or in the Bonds, or Debentures of any City, Town, or Municipality, authorized to issue Bonds, or Debentures, or in Mortgages of Real Estate, or other approved Securities for the use of the Corporation, subject to the approval of a Judge of the Court of Chancery in Chambers.

Investment of moneys.

6. The Corporation may convey to such Trustee, or Trustees, as they think proper, for the purpose of a Burying Ground, that Plot of Land containing about six Acres in the Village of Dresden, set apart by the Trustees of the said the British and American Institute for such purpose, and represented in the registered Plan of the said Village as "Cemetery Ground," with power to the Corporation to make such provisions and conditions in the Conveyance of the said Plot for the future management of it, for the purpose aforesaid, as they may see fit; and the Corporation may convey to the Municipality of the Village of Dresden, in the said County of Kent, so soon as said Village is incorporated, for the purpose of a Market Square, that Plot of Land, containing about one Acre and a half of an Acre, in the said Village set apart by the Trustees, and represented on the registered Plan of the said Village, as the "Market Square."

Certain land may be conveyed for a burying-ground.

Certain lands may be conveyed for a market-square.

7. It shall be the duty of the said Corporation at all times, when they may be called upon to do so by the Lieutenant-Governor of this Province, to render an Account in writing of their Property, in which shall be set forth, in particular, the Income by them derived from Property held under this Act, and the source from which the same has been derived; also the number of Members of the said Corporation, the number of Teachers employed in the various branches of instruction, the number of Scholars under instruction, and the Course of Instruction pursued.

Return to be made to the Lieutenant-Governor.

LaVergne, TN USA
08 February 2011
215741LV00006B/5/P